microsoft® office excel®

A Professional Approach

EXCEL 2007

Kathleen Stewart

McGraw-Hill
Higher Education

Boston   Burr Ridge, IL   Dubuque, IA   New York   San Francisco   St. Louis
Bangkok   Bogotá   Caracas   Kuala Lumpur   Lisbon   London   Madrid   Mexico City
Milan   Montreal   New Delhi   Santiago   Seoul   Singapore   Sydney   Taipei   Toronto

MICROSOFT® OFFICE EXCEL® 2007: A PROFESSIONAL APPROACH
Published by McGraw-Hill, a business unit of The McGraw-Hill Companies, Inc., 1221 Avenue
of the Americas, New York, NY, 10020. Copyright © 2008 by The McGraw-Hill Companies, Inc.
All rights reserved. No part of this publication may be reproduced or distributed in any form
or by any means, or stored in a database or retrieval system, without the prior written consent of
The McGraw-Hill Companies, Inc., including, but not limited to, in any network or other
electronic storage or transmission, or broadcast for distance learning.

Some ancillaries, including electronic and print components, may not be available to customers
outside the United States.

This book is printed on acid-free paper.

1 2 3 4 5 6 7 8 9 0 DOW/DOW 0 9 8 7

ISBN   978-0-07-351921-0 (student edition)
MHID   0-07-351921-9 (student edition)
ISBN   978-0-07-329467-4 (annotated instructor's edition)
MHID   0-07-329467-5 (annotated instructor's edition)

Publisher: Linda Schreiber
Associate sponsoring editor: Janna Martin
Developmental editor: Alaina Grayson
Marketing manager: Sarah Wood
Media producer: Marc Mattson
Senior project manager: Rick Hecker
Senior production supervisor: Janean A. Utley
Designer: Marianna Kinigakis
Senior photo research coordinator: Jeremy Cheshareck
Media project manager: Mark A. S. Dierker
Cover design: Asylum Studios
Interior design: JoAnne Schopler, Graphic Visions
Typeface: 10.5/13 New Aster
Compositor: Aptara
Printer: R. R. Donnelley

Library of Congress Cataloging-in-Publication Data

Stewart, Kathleen, 1951-
    Microsoft Office Excel 2007 : a professional approach / Kathleen Stewart.
      p. cm.
    Includes index.
    ISBN-13: 978-0-07-351921-0 (student edition : alk. paper)
    ISBN-10: 0-07-351921-9 (student edition : alk. paper)
    ISBN-13: 978-0-07-329467-4 (annotated instructor's edition : alk. paper)
    ISBN-10: 0-07-329467-5 (annotated instructor's edition : alk. paper)
      1. Microsoft Excel (Computer file) 2. Business—Computer programs.
      3. Electronic spreadsheets. I. Title.
HF5548.4.M523S737 2008
005.54—dc22

                                                                    2007011392

www.mhhe.com

contents

EXCEL

Unit 1 Introduction to Excel

Unit 2 *Working with Formulas and Functions*

Unit 3 *Enhancing Worksheet Appearance*

Unit 4 *Expanding Uses of Workbook Data*

Unit 5 Auditing, Analyzing, and Consolidating Data

Unit 6 *Exploring Data and Table Features*

Unit 7 *Exploring Macros, Templates, and Workgroups*

What Does This Logo Mean?

This courseware has been approved by the Microsoft® Office Certification Program as among the finest available for learning *Microsoft® Office Excel® 2007*. It also means that if you complete and fully understand this courseware, you will be prepared to take an exam certifying your proficiency in this application.

What Is a Microsoft Certified Application Specialist?

A Microsoft Certified Application Specialist is a person who has passed exams that certify his or her skills in one or more of the Microsoft Office desktop applications, such as Microsoft Word, Microsoft Excel, Microsoft PowerPoint, Microsoft Outlook, or Microsoft Access. The Microsoft Certified Application Specialist Program is the only program in the world approved by Microsoft for testing proficiency in Microsoft Office desktop applications. This testing program can be a valuable asset in any job search or career advancement.

More Information:

To learn more about becoming a Microsoft Certified Application Specialist, visit www.microsoft.com/officespecialist.

The availability of Microsoft Office certification exams varies by application, application version, and language. Visit the site listed above for exam availability.

preface

Microsoft® Office Excel® 2007: A Professional Approach is written to help you master Microsoft Excel. The text takes you step-by-step through the Excel features that you are likely to use in both your personal and business life.

Case Study

Learning about the features of Excel is one thing, but applying what you learn is another. That's why a case study runs throughout the text. The case study offers the opportunity to learn Excel in a realistic business context. Take the time to read the case study about Klassy Kow Ice Cream, Inc., a fictional business located in San Francisco. All the documents for this course involve Klassy Kow Ice Cream, Inc.

Organization of the Text

The text includes seven units. Each unit is divided into smaller lessons. There are 23 lessons, each self-contained but that build on previously learned procedures. This building block approach, together with the case study and the features listed next, enables you to maximize your learning process.

Features of the Text

- Objectives are listed for each lesson.
- Required skills for the Microsoft Certification Exam are listed for each lesson.
- The estimated time required to complete each lesson up to the Skills Review section is stated.
- Within a lesson, each heading corresponds to an objective.
- Easy-to-follow exercises emphasize "learning by doing."
- Key terms are italicized and defined as they are encountered.
- Extensive graphics display screen contents.
- Command tab buttons and keyboard keys are shown in the text when used.
- Large Command tab buttons in the margins provide easy-to-see references.
- Lessons contain important Notes, useful Tips, and helpful Reviews.
- A Lesson Summary reviews the important concepts taught in each lesson.
- A Command Summary lists the commands taught in each lesson.
- The Concepts Review includes true/false, short answer, and critical thinking questions that focus on lesson content.
- The Skills Review provides skill reinforcements for each lesson.
- Lesson Applications ask you to apply your skills in a more challenging way.
- On Your Own exercises let you apply your skills creatively.
- Unit Applications give you the opportunity to use the skills you learn throughout a unit.
- The text includes an Appendix of Microsoft's Certification standards, a Glossary, and an Index.

Microsoft Office Certification Program

The Microsoft Office certification program offers certification for each application and an overall "Office Specialist" option once you have passed enough exams. This certification can be a valuable asset in any job search. For more information about this Microsoft program, go to www.microsoft.com/officespecialist. For a complete listing of the skills for the Excel 2007 certification exam and a correlation to the lessons in the text, see Appendix: Microsoft Office Certification.

Professional Approach Web Site

Visit the Professional Approach Web site at www.mhhe.com/pas07 to access a wealth of additional materials.

Conventions Used in the Text

This text uses a number of conventions to help you learn the program and save your work.

- Text to be keyed appears either in **red** or as a separate figure.
- Filenames appear in **boldface**.
- Sub-filenames, such as sheets in a workbook, appear in **blue**.
- Options that you choose from tabs and dialog boxes but that are not buttons appear in green; for example, "Choose **Print** from the Office menu."
- You are asked to save each document with your initials followed by the exercise name. For example, an exercise might end with this instruction: "Save the document as *[your initials]*5-12." Documents are saved in folders for each lesson.

If You Are Unfamiliar with Windows

If you are unfamiliar with Windows, review the "Windows Tutorial" available on the Professional Approach Web site at www.mhhe.com/pas07 before beginning Lesson 1. This tutorial provides a basic overview of Microsoft's operating systems and shows you how to use the mouse. You might also want to review "File Management" on the Professional Approach Web site to get more comfortable with files and folders.

Screen Differences

As you practice each concept, illustrations of the screens help you follow the instructions. Don't worry if your screen is different from the illustration. These differences are due to variations in system and computer configurations.

installation requirements

You will need Microsoft Excel 2007 to work through this textbook. Excel 2007 needs to be installed on the computer's hard drive or a network. Use the following checklists to evaluate installation requirements.

Hardware

- Computer with 500MHz or higher processor and at least 256MB of RAM.
- CD-ROM drive and other external media (3.5-inch high-density floppy, ZIP, etc.).
- 1.5GB or more of hard disk space for a "Student" Office installation.
- 1024 × 768 or higher-resolution video monitor.
- Printer (laser or ink-jet recommended).
- Mouse.
- Modem or other Internet connection.

Software

- Excel 2007 (from Microsoft Office System 2007).
- Windows XP with Service Pack 2 or later, or Windows Vista or later operating system.
- Browser and Internet access.

Installing New Features

FEATURE	USE	HOW TO INSTALL/USE
Template data files	Build a new document based on a template.	Copy template files to C:\Users\UserName\AppData\Roaming\Microsoft\Templates for files to appear on the My Templates tab of the New dialog box.
Images	Use images related to the case.	Copy image files to any usable folder.
Installed Templates (Spreadsheet Solutions)	Build a new document based on a template.	Part of typical installation; files are in C:\Program Files\Microsoft Office 11\Templates\1033.
Comments	Add an annotation or comment to a worksheet cell.	Microsoft Office Button, Excel Options, Advanced. Verify that comment indicator displays, with the comment displaying on hover.
Internet functionality	Use online help, use online Template Gallery, use additional research tools, view Web pages.	Specific to classroom.

FEATURE	USE	HOW TO INSTALL/USE
Language tools	Use thesaurus and translation tools in the Research task pane.	Part of a typical installation for Office 2007 Professional. Install if/when prompted at first use. May require installation CD.
Visual Basic Editor	View, edit, and save macros.	Part of a typical installation for Office 2007 Professional. Install if/when prompted. May require installation CD.
Digital Signature	Create a digital signature.	Part of a typical installation for Office 2007 Professional. Listed under Microsoft Office Button, Prepare. Create a digital ID on first use.
Goal Seek	Perform what-if analysis.	Part of a typical installation for Office 2007 Professional.
Solver	Perform what-if analysis.	Choose Microsoft Office Button, Excel Options, Add-Ins. Choose Analysis ToolPak and then Solver Add-in. Click OK.
Microsoft Query	Import a database file.	Part of a typical installation for Office 2007 Professional. Install if/when prompted. May require installation CD.
Notepad or WordPad	Open text files.	Part of typical Vista installation.
XPS/PDF Add-in	Save files in XPS or PDF format.	Available on the installed CD or at Microsoft Office Online.
Compatibility Checker	Save files in XLS format.	Part of a typical installation for Office 2007 Professional.

If you are not familiar with Windows, review this "Windows Tutorial" carefully. You will learn how to

- Use a mouse.
- Start Windows.
- Use the taskbar, menus, Ribbon, dialog boxes, and other important aspects of Windows.

NOTE

All examples in this tutorial refer specifically to Windows Vista. If you are using any other version of Windows, your screen might differ slightly from the images shown in this tutorial. However, because most basic features are common to all versions of Windows, this tutorial should be helpful to you no matter which version of Windows you use.

If you are familiar with Windows but need help navigating Windows files and folders, refer to the section "File Management." There you will find information on how Windows stores information and how to use Windows Explorer, a tool for managing files and folders.

Computers differ in the ways they can be set up. In most cases, when you turn on your computer, Windows loads automatically and the Windows log-on screen appears. When you see the Windows log-on screen, you need to log on and key a password. In order to log on, you need to know how to use the mouse, a device attached to your computer.

Using the Mouse

A *mouse* is a pointing device that is typically attached to your computer. Optical versions, which are not attached, are also available. The mouse is your access to the computer screen, allowing you to accomplish specific tasks. It operates through a pointer, a screen object you use to point to objects on the computer screen. The normal shape for the mouse cursor is an arrow. To move the pointer arrow on the screen, you roll the mouse on any flat object, or on a mouse pad, which has a smooth surface designed for easy mouse rolling. Although you can use the keyboard with Windows, you will probably find yourself using the mouse most of the time.

To use the mouse to position the pointer to an object on the computer screen:

1. Turn on the computer (if it is not on already). Windows loads, and the log-on screen appears. The screen includes a log-on name and picture assigned to you by your instructor.

To log on, you need to move the mouse pointer to the log-on name that was assigned. The pointer on the computer screen mirrors the actions made by the mouse when you roll it. Place your hand over the mouse and roll it to the left. The pointer on the screen moves to the left.

2. Roll the mouse to the right, and watch the pointer on the screen move to the right.
3. Practice rolling the mouse in all directions.
4. Roll your mouse to the edge of the pad, and then lift it up and place it back in the middle of the pad. Try it now to see how it works. When you feel that you can control the mouse position on the screen, roll the mouse to the name you have been assigned.

To log on, you will need to click the name to select it. Mouse clicks are covered in the next section; instructions for logging onto Windows Vista are covered in succeeding sections.

Clicks and Double-Clicks

A mouse typically has two buttons at the front (the edge of the mouse where the cord attaches)—one on the left (primary) and one on the right (secondary). A mouse might also have a center button or a wheel.

Single-click actions with the mouse are used to position the pointer at a specific screen location. To perform a single click:

1. Roll the mouse around on the mouse pad until the pointer on the screen is over an object on the screen. Remember that the direction in which you move the mouse on the pad represents the pointer's movement on the screen.

2. Press and release the left mouse button once. Pressing and releasing the mouse button is referred to as a *click*. The computer tells you that the action has been performed when the object you click is *highlighted* (typically, the color of the selected object changes) to indicate to you that it has been *selected*. In Windows, you often need to select an object before you can perform an action. For example, you usually need to select an object before you can copy it.

Pressing and releasing the mouse button twice is referred to as a *double-click*. When you double-click an object on the screen, it is selected—the object is highlighted—and an action is performed. For example:

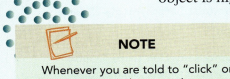

> **NOTE**
>
> Whenever you are told to "click" or "double-click" an object on the computer screen, use the left mouse button.

- When you double-click a folder, it is highlighted and opens to a window showing the items the folder contains.
- When you double-click a word in a text file, it is selected for a future action. In a text file, the pointer becomes an I-beam for selecting text in the document.

Selecting and Dragging

You can also select a larger object such as a picture or a block of text by using the mouse.

1. Position the pointer on one side of the object, and hold down the left mouse button.
2. Roll the mouse until the pointer reaches the other side of the object.
3. Release the mouse button. The selected object is highlighted.

Drag and Drop—Moving an Object Using the Mouse

You can use the mouse to move an object on the screen to another screen location. In this operation, you select an object and drag the mouse to move the selected object, such as an icon. The operation is known as *drag and drop*.

1. Using the mouse, move the pointer over the object you want to drag.
2. Perform a single-click action by pressing the left mouse button but keep it pressed down. The selected object will be highlighted.
3. With the left mouse button still depressed, roll the mouse until the pointer and selected object are placed at the desired new location.
4. Release the mouse button to drop the object. The object is now positioned at the new location.

Using the Right Mouse Button

Pressing and quickly releasing the right mouse button is referred to as a *right-click*. Although the right mouse button is used less frequently, using it can be a real time-saver. When you right-click an icon, a *shortcut menu* appears with a list of commands. The list of commands displayed varies for each icon or object.

As you progress in this tutorial, you will become familiar with the terms in Table 1, describing the actions you can take with a mouse.

TABLE 1 Mouse Terms

TERM	DESCRIPTION
Point	Roll the mouse until the tip of the pointer is touching the desired object on the computer screen.
Click	Quickly press and release the left mouse button. Single-clicking selects objects.
Double-click	Quickly press and release the left mouse button twice. Double-clicking selects an object and performs an action such as opening a folder.
Drag	Point to an object on screen, hold down the left mouse button, and roll the mouse until the pointer is in position. Then release the mouse button (drag and drop).
Right-click	Quickly press and release the right mouse button. A shortcut menu appears.
Select	When working in Windows, you must first select an object in order to work with it. Many objects are selected with a single click. However, depending on the size and type of object to be selected, you may need to roll the mouse to include an entire area: Holding down the left mouse button, roll the mouse so that the pointer moves from one side of an object to another. Then release the mouse button.

Pointer Shapes

As you perform actions on screen using the mouse, the mouse pointer changes its shape, depending on where it is located and what operation you are performing. Table 2 shows the most common types of mouse pointers.

TABLE 2 Frequently Used Mouse Pointers

SHAPE	NAME	DESCRIPTION
	Pointer	Used to point to objects.
	I-Beam	Used in typing, inserting, and selecting text. When the I-beam is moved to a selected location, it turns into a blinking bar.
	Two-pointed arrow	Used to change the size of objects or windows.
	Four-pointed arrow	Used to move objects.
	Busy Working in background	Indicates the computer is processing a command. While the busy or working in background pointer is displayed, it is best to wait rather than try to continue working. Note: Some of the working in background actions will not allow you to perform other procedures until processing is completed.
	Hand	Used to select a *link* in Windows' Help or other programs.

Starting Windows: The Log-on Screen

The Windows Vista log-on screen allows several people to use the same computer at different times. Each person is assigned a user account that determines which files and folders you can access and your personal preferences, such as your desktop background. Each person's files are hidden from the others using the computer. However, users may share selected files using the Public folder. The log-on screen lists each user allocated to the computer by name.

If the administrator has added your name to a given computer, the log-on screen will include your name. If the computers are not assigned to specific individuals, you may find a box for Guest or for a generic user. If your computer is on a network, your instructor might need to provide you with special start-up instructions.

After you have logged on to Windows Vista, the desktop is the first screen you will see. It is your on-screen work area. All the elements you need to start working with Windows appear on the desktop.

1. If you have not already turned on the computer, do so now to begin the Windows Vista loading process. The Windows log-on screen appears.

NOTE

On some computers, the log-on screen does not appear automatically. You might have to press the following keys, all at once, and then quickly release them: Ctrl + Alt + Delete.

2. Click your name to select it. The Password box appears with an I-beam in position ready for you to type your password.

3. Type your password.

4. Click the arrow icon to the right of the box. If you have entered the password correctly, the Windows desktop appears. If you made an error, the Password box returns for you to type the correct password.

The Windows Desktop

The Desktop includes the Start button, taskbar, and sidebar. You may also see icons on the desktop that represent folders, programs, or other objects. You can add and delete icons from the desktop as well as change the desktop background. The Start button is your entry into Vista functions.

Figure 1
Windows Vista
Desktop

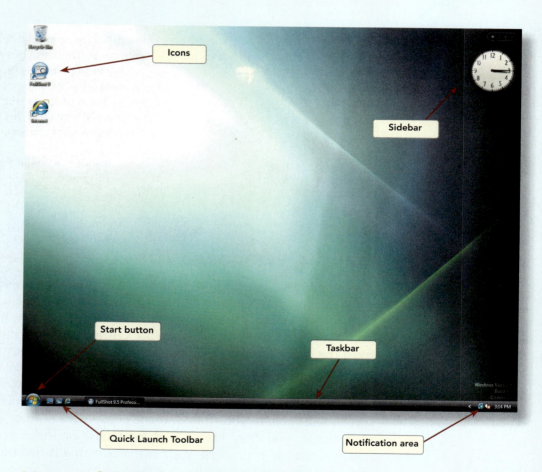

Using the Start Menu

Click the taskbar Start button to open the Start menu. You can also press the Windows logo key on the keyboard to open the Start menu. Use the Start menu to launch programs, adjust computer settings, search for files and folders, and turn off the computer. If this is a computer assigned to you for log-on, your Start menu may contain items that differ from those of another user assigned to the same computer. To open and learn about the Start menu, first click the Start button on the Windows taskbar. The Start menu appears.

Figure 2
Start menu

The left pane consists of three sections divided by separator lines. The top section, called the *pin area*, lists programs that are always available for you to click. These can include your Internet browser, e-mail program, your word processor, and so forth. You can remove programs you do not want listed, rearrange them, and add those you prefer.

Below the separator line are shortcuts to programs you use most often, placed there automatically by Windows. You can remove programs you do not want listed, rearrange them, but not add any manually.

All Programs displays a list of programs on your computer and is used to launch programs not listed on the Start menu.

Below the left pane is the *Search box* which is used to locate programs and files on your computer.

The right pane is also divided into three sections. It is used to select folders, files, and commands and to change settings. Use the icons at the bottom of the right pane to save your session, lock the computer, restart, switch users, and shut down.

Table 3 describes the typical components of the Start menu.

TABLE 3 Typical Components of the Start Menu

COMMAND	USE
Left Pane	
Pin area	Lists programs that are always available. You can add and delete items to the pin area.
Internet	Connects to the default browser.
E-mail	Connects to the chosen e-mail service.
Below the First Separator Line	
Programs	Lists programs that you use most often. You can add to and rearrange the programs listed.
Below the Second Separator Line	
All Programs	Click to display a list of programs in alphabetical order and a list of folders. Click to open a program.
Start Search	Use to search programs and folders. Key text and results appear.
Right Pane	
Personal folder	Opens the User folder.
Documents	Opens the Documents folder.
Pictures	Opens the Pictures folder.
Music	Opens the Music folder.
Games	Opens the Games folder.
Search	Opens the Search Results window. Advanced Search options are available.
Recent Items	Opens a list of the most recent documents you have opened and saved.
Computer	Opens a window where you can access disk drives and other hardware devices.
Network	Opens the Network window where you can access computers and other devices on your network.
Connect To	Opens a window where you can connect to a different network.
Control Panel	Opens the Control Panel.
Default Programs	Opens the Default Programs window where you can define default programs and settings.
Help and Support	Opens the Windows Help and Support window. Help offers instructions on how to perform tasks in the Windows environment.
Power button	Turns off the computer.
Lock button	Locks the computer, or click the arrow beside the Lock button to display a menu for switching users, logging off, restarting, or shutting down the computer.

Using the All Programs Command

Most programs on your computer can be started from the All Programs command on the Start menu. This is the easiest way to open a program not listed directly on the Start menu.

1. To open the All Programs menu, click the Start button. The Start menu appears.

2. Click **All Programs** or the triangle to the left near the bottom of the left pane. The All Programs menu appears, listing the programs installed on your computer. Every computer has a different list of programs. Notice that some menu entries have an icon to the left of the name and others display a folder. Click a folder, and a list of programs stored in that folder appears. Click a program to open it. Point to a program to see a short description of the program.

Figure 3
All Programs window

3. Click **Microsoft Office** to open a list of programs in the Microsoft Office folder. Click **Microsoft Office Word 2007**. (See Figure 3.) In a few seconds, the program you selected loads and the Word window appears. Notice that a button for the program appears on the taskbar. Leave Word open for the present.

Customizing the Start Menu

Both the Start menu and the desktop can be customized. You can add shortcuts to the desktop if you prefer, and you can add and delete items from the Start menu. However, if your computer is used by others, the administrator may limit some customization functions.

To add a program to the pin area of the Start menu:

1. Select the program you want to add to the pin list from the All Programs menu, and right-click it. A shortcut menu appears.
2. Click **Pin To Start Menu** on the shortcut menu. The program will be added to the pin list in the left pane above the first separator line.

To remove a program from the pin area of the Start menu:

1. Select the program you want to remove from the pin list, and right-click. A shortcut menu appears.
2. Click **Unpin From Start Menu**. The program will be removed from the pin list.

To change the order in which programs are listed in the pin area:

1. Point to the program icon.
2. Drag the icon to the desired position.

Using the Taskbar

The taskbar at the bottom of your screen is one of the most important features in Windows Vista. The taskbar is divided into several segments, each dedicated to a different use. It shows programs that are running, and you can use the taskbar to switch between open programs and between open documents within a program. If your computer has the Aero interface, a thumbnail preview appears when you move the mouse over a button on the taskbar.

Figure 4
The Desktop with the taskbar and the Word window

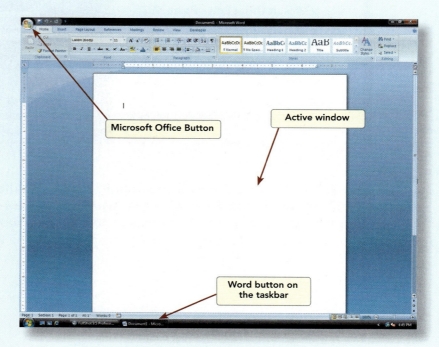

Microsoft Office Button

Active window

Word button on the taskbar

Windows displays a button on the taskbar for each opened program and document. Notice that there is a button for Word, showing the Word icon and the name of the program. Point to the Word button to view a thumbnail of the document window. Since the taskbar can become crowded, Windows combines access to documents or programs under single buttons. The button shows the name of the program (Microsoft Office Word) and the number of items in the group (9). The shape of the arrow varies, depending on what the button contains. Clicking the button opens the menu of available items.

Figure 5
Button contents for
Word documents

List of open documents in Word

Taskbar button to open Word program

Taskbar Notification Area

The *notification area* is on the right side of the taskbar, where the current time is usually displayed. Along with displaying the time, tiny icons notify you as to the status of your browser connection, virus protection, and so forth. It is also known as the *system tray*. In the interests of removing clutter, the notification area hides most of the icons. Clicking the Show Hidden Icons button ◄ "hides" or "unhides" the icons in the notification area. Click the left-pointing arrow next to the icons to expand the notification area. Click the right-pointing arrow to hide the notification area.

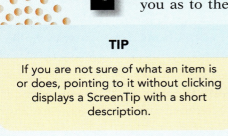

TIP

If you are not sure of what an item is or does, pointing to it without clicking displays a ScreenTip with a short description.

The Active Window

The window in which you are working is called the *active window*. The title bar for the active window is highlighted, and its taskbar button is also highlighted. The program window for Microsoft Word that you opened earlier should still be open. To examine additional features of the taskbar, open a second program, Microsoft Excel, a spreadsheet program in Microsoft Office.

1. If Word is not open, click the **Start** button and then click **All Programs**, **Microsoft Office**, **Microsoft Office Word 2007** from the Start menu. The Word window displays.

2. Click the **Start** button and then click **All Programs**, **Microsoft Office**, **Microsoft Office Excel 2007** from the Start menu. The Excel window displays. Notice how the Excel window covers the Word window, indicating that the window containing Excel is now active. Notice, too, that a new button for Excel has been added to the taskbar.

Figure 6
Excel (the active window) covering the Word window

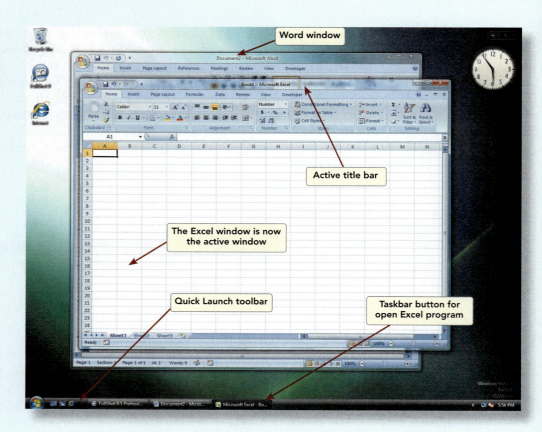

3. Click the button on the taskbar for Word, the first program you opened. Word reappears in front of Excel. Notice the change in the appearance of the title bar for each program.

4. Click the button on the taskbar for Excel. Notice that you switch back to Excel.

5. Click the button on the taskbar to return to Word.

6. Locate the Quick Launch toolbar to the right of the Start button, and point to the Switch between windows button .

7. Click the Switch between windows button, and notice the desktop view.

8. Click the Excel window.

Changing the Size of the Taskbar

You can change the size of the taskbar using your mouse if your toolbar is crowded. It is usually not necessary, because of the multiple document style buttons and other hide/unhide arrows on the taskbar. Before you can change the size of the taskbar, it may be necessary for you to unlock it. To unlock the taskbar, right-click an open area of the taskbar and click **Lock the Taskbar** to remove the checkmark. A checkmark is a toggle command. Click to turn it off, and click a second time to turn it on.

1. Move the pointer to the top edge of the taskbar until it changes from a pointer to a two-pointed arrow . Using the two-pointed arrow, you can change the size of the taskbar.

2. With the pointer displayed as a two-pointed arrow, hold down the left mouse button and move the arrow up until the taskbar enlarges upward.

3. Move the pointer to the top edge of the taskbar once again until the two-pointed arrow displays. Hold down the left mouse button, and move the arrow down to the bottom of the screen. The taskbar is restored to its original size.

Using Menus

Windows uses a system of menus that contain a choice of options for working with programs and documents. Most Windows programs use a similar menu structure. These operations are either mouse or keyboard driven. They are called commands because they "command" the computer to perform functions needed to complete the task you, the user, initiate at the menu level.

Executing a Command from a Menu

In Windows, a program may display a *menu bar*, a row of descriptive menu names at the top, just below the title bar. You open a menu by clicking the menu name listed in the menu bar. When a menu is opened, a list of command options appears. To execute a particular command from an open menu, press the left mouse button and then drag down and release the chosen option (click and drag). You can also click the command once the menu is open.

Keyboard Menu Commands

For people who prefer to use the keyboard to a mouse, Windows has provided keyboard commands for many menu items. You can use the keyboard to open menus and choose menu options.

Some menu items include not only the name of the command but a combination of keyboard keys. For example, under the File menu in WordPad, the Save command contains the notation Ctrl+S to its right. This means that you can also execute the command by pressing the Ctrl key together with the S key to save a document.

Figure 7
Title and menu bars with the File menu Open

Command name

Command with three dots opens a dialog box.

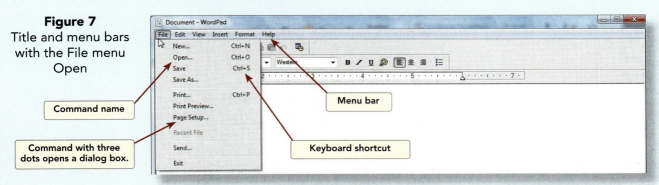

Menu bar

Keyboard shortcut

Other Menu Symbols

Three dots following a menu option indicate that a dialog box is displayed when that menu option is chosen. (Dialog boxes, discussed later, are small windows requesting and receiving input from a user.) Some commands also display a check box. Click an empty check box to select the option. A checkmark will appear in the square and indicates the option is selected. To turn off the option, click the check box to remove the checkmark. Commands that appear gray or dimmed are currently not available.

Perform the following steps for keyboard command practice:

1. Open the **Start menu**, click **All Programs**, and click the **Accessories** folder. Click **WordPad**. The WordPad program opens, and a button appears on the Windows taskbar.

2. Click **File** in the menu bar. The File menu displays. Click **File** to close the menu.

3. Press [Alt], and notice that the items in the menu bar display underlined letters (File, Edit). The underlined letters are a shortcut to open a menu. Press the letter "f" to open the File menu. Release [Alt], and click outside the menu in a blank area to close the menu.

4. Press [Alt]+[V], the keyboard shortcut for the View menu. The View menu displays.

5. Notice the four check boxes. All are selected. Click the **Options** command. The Options dialog box opens.

6. Click **Cancel** to close the dialog box.

7. Click **File** in the menu bar. Click **Exit**. Click **Don't Save** if prompted to save the document.

Displaying a Shortcut Menu

When the mouse pointer is on an object or an area of the Windows desktop and you right-click, a shortcut menu appears. A shortcut menu typically contains commands that are useful in working with the object or area of the desktop to which you are currently pointing.

1. Position the mouse pointer on a blank area of the desktop, and right-click. A shortcut menu appears with commands that relate to the desktop, including view and sort options.

2. Click outside the shortcut menu to close it.

3. Right-click the time in the bottom right corner of the taskbar. A shortcut menu appears.

4. Click Adjust Date/Time on the shortcut menu. The Date/Time Properties dialog box appears. You can use this dialog box to adjust your computer's date and time.

Figure 8
The time shortcut menu

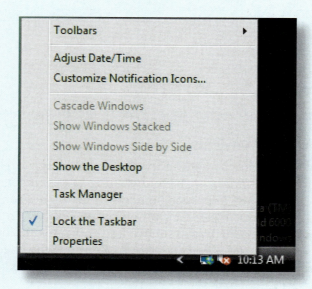

5. Click **Cancel**.

6. Right-click an icon on the desktop to display its shortcut menu, and then close the shortcut menu.

Using the Ribbon

Microsoft Office 2007 applications include a Microsoft Office Button, a Quick Access Toolbar, and a Ribbon. The *Microsoft Office Button* displays the File menu which lists the commands to create, open, save, and print a document. The *Quick Access Toolbar* contains frequently used commands and is positioned to the right of the Microsoft Office Button. The *Ribbon* consists of seven tabs by default, and each tab contains a group of related commands. The number of commands for each tab varies. A command can be one of several formats. The most popular formats include buttons and drop-down lists.

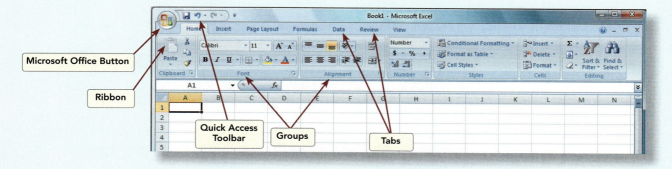

1. Activate the Excel program.

2. Point to and click the **Microsoft Office Button**. Notice the commands and icons in the menu.

3. Click a blank area of the window to close the menu.

4. Locate the Quick Access Toolbar beside the Microsoft Office Button. Point to each button in the Quick Access Toolbar to identify it. Notice that a keyboard shortcut displays beside each button.

5. Click the **Page Layout** tab. Notice the change in the groups and commands.

6. Click the **Home** tab.

Using Dialog Boxes

Windows programs make frequent use of dialog boxes. A *dialog box* is a window that requests input from you related to a command you have chosen. All Windows programs use a common dialog box structure.

1. Click the Excel program button on the taskbar to make Excel the active window if necessary.

2. Click the **Microsoft Office Button**. The File menu displays.

3. Click **Print** to display the Print dialog box.

4. The Print dialog box contains several types of dialog box options.

NOTE

A keyboard shortcut is available for the print dialog box: Press Ctrl + P to open the Print dialog box.

Figure 10
Print dialog box in Excel

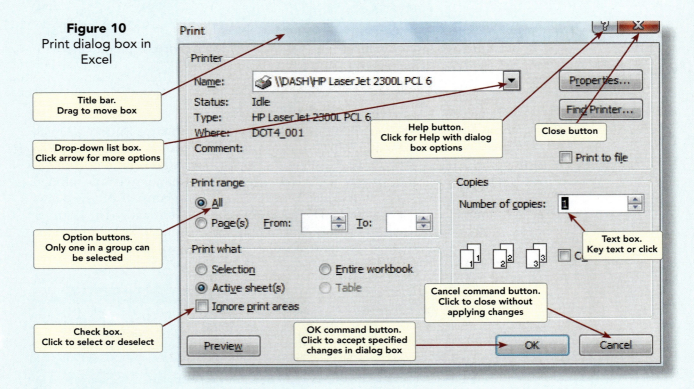

Title bar.
Drag to move box

Drop-down list box.
Click arrow for more options

Option buttons.
Only one in a group can
be selected

Check box.
Click to select or deselect

Help button.
Click for Help with dialog
box options

Close button

Text box.
Key text or click

Cancel command button.
Click to close without
applying changes

OK command button.
Click to accept specified
changes in dialog box

5. To close the Print dialog box, click **Cancel**, located in the lower right corner of the dialog box. The Print dialog box closes without applying any changes.

Another type of dialog box uses tabs to display related options. Only one tab can display at a time. The Word Font dialog box offers many options for choosing character formatting.

1. Make Word the active window.
2. Click the **Home** tab, and click the small arrow that appears on the right of the Font group ▭. The Font dialog box displays.

Figure 11
Font dialog box

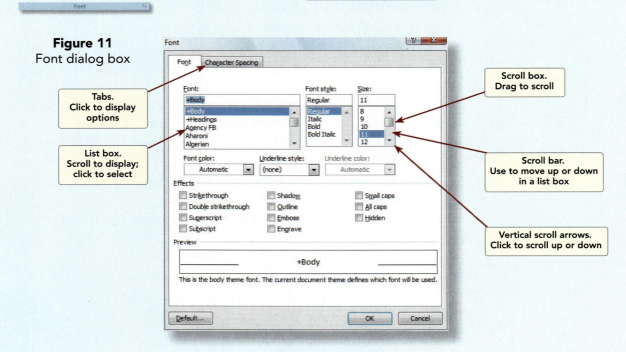

Tabs.
Click to display
options

List box.
Scroll to display;
click to select

Scroll box.
Drag to scroll

Scroll bar.
Use to move up or down
in a list box

Vertical scroll arrows.
Click to scroll up or down

The scroll boxes are used to specify a font by name, its style, and its size. When you select a paragraph in a Word document, you can select its typographic features using this dialog box. The Font list box at the top left displays a list of all the typefaces installed on your computer. By clicking the name of the font, you select it for your paragraph.

The vertical scroll bar on the right side of a list box or a window indicates that there is more content to view. To view the hidden content, click the downward-pointing arrow or the upward-pointing vertical scroll arrow. You can also drag the scroll box on the scroll bar up or down to view all the content. The Character Spacing tab at the top of the Font dialog box displays additional character formatting options. Click the Character Spacing tab to view its contents, and then return to the Font tab.

Use the Font dialog box to style a paragraph as follows:

1. Type a very short paragraph in your Word document.
2. Position the I-beam at the beginning of the text, and hold down the left mouse button.
3. Drag the mouse to the end of the paragraph. The paragraph will change color, showing that it has been selected.
4. Open the Font dialog box by pressing Ctrl+D.
5. In the Font list box, click **Verdana**. You may need to scroll down to locate it.
6. In the Font style box, click **Bold**.
7. In the Size box, click **12**.
8. If you wish to change the color of your paragraph, move your pointer to the Font color drop-down list box and click the down-facing arrow. A color pallet appears. Point to the color you wish to use, and click.
9. When you have completed your selections, click **OK** at the bottom of the Font dialog box and look at the paragraph you have styled. If you wish, you can try other font formats, while your paragraph is selected.

Changing the Size of a Window

You can change the size of any window using either the mouse or the sizing buttons. Sizing buttons are the small buttons on the right side of the title bar that allow you to minimize or maximize the window (see Figure 12). This can be especially useful when you would like to display several open windows on your desktop and see them simultaneously.

NOTE

Notice that the window occupies the entire desktop, and the Maximize button has changed to a Restore Down button. This type of function is known as a toggle: When a button representing one state (Maximize) is clicked, an action is performed, the button toggles to the alternate state, and the other button (Restore Down) appears. A number of actions in Windows operate this way.

1. Make Excel the active window, if it is not already. Click the Maximize button on the Excel title bar if the Excel window does not fill the entire desktop.

Figure 12
Sizing buttons

Close

Minimize   Maximize

Table 4 describes these buttons. To practice changing the size of a window, follow these steps:

TABLE 4 Sizing Buttons

BUTTON	USE
Minimize	Reduces the window to a button on the taskbar.
Maximize	Enlarges the window to fill the entire desktop (appears only when a window is reduced).
Restore Down	Returns the window to its previous size and desktop position (appears only when a window is maximized).

NOTE

You can double-click a window title bar to maximize or restore the window or right-click the program button on the taskbar and choose minimize, maximize, restore, or close.

2. Click the **Restore Down** button on the Excel title bar. The Excel window reduces in size, and the Word window appears behind it. The Restore Down button has now changed to a Maximize button. Notice that the highlighted title bar of the Excel window indicates it is the active window.

3. Click the **Minimize** button. The Excel window disappears, and its button appears on the taskbar.

How to Display Two Program Windows Simultaneously

1. Open the **Start** menu, and click **All Programs** to open Excel and Word if they are not already open from an earlier section of the tutorial.

2. Click the **Excel** button on the taskbar to move its window to the front of the screen.

3. Click the **Restore Down** button if the Excel window is maximized.

TIP

Sometimes the borders of a window can move off the computer screen. If you are having trouble with one border of a window, try another border or drag the entire window onto the screen by using the title bar.

4. Move the pointer to the right border of the Excel window. The pointer changes to a horizontal two-pointed arrow.

5. With the two-pointed arrow displayed , drag the border to the left to make the window narrower.

Figure 13
Sizing a window

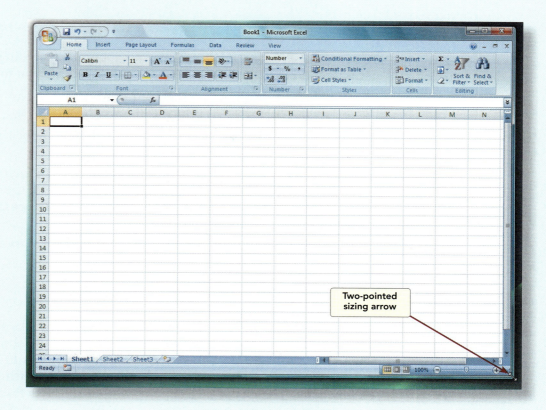

Two-pointed
sizing arrow

NOTE

You can place the pointer on any part of the window border to change its size. To change both the height and width of the window, move the pointer to the bottom right corner of the window. The double-pointed arrow changes its orientation to a 45-degree angle (see Figure 13). Dragging this arrow resizes a window vertically and horizontally.

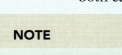

NOTE

The taskbar contains options to Show Windows Stacked, Cascade Windows, and Show the Desktop.

6. Click the title bar or any part of the Word window behind the Excel window. The Word window becomes the active window. The Excel window is still open, but it is now behind the Word window.

7. Click the **Maximize** button if the Word window does not fill the entire desktop.

8. Click the **Minimize** button on the title bar of the Word window. The Excel window becomes the active window.

9. Make the Word window the active window by clicking the **Word** button on the taskbar.

10. Click the **Restore Down** button on the Word window. The Word window reduces in size. The Excel window might be partially visible behind the Word window. You can drag the two reduced windows so that parts of both can be seen simultaneously.

11. Right-click the taskbar, and click **Show Windows Side by Side**. The windows display vertically.

12. Press the [Alt] key, and hold it down while pressing [Tab]. You can switch to the previous window by pressing this shortcut, or you can continue to press [Tab] to switch to an open window on the desktop.

13. Click the **Show Desktop** button [icon] located on the Quick Launch toolbar to see the desktop. The Word and Excel programs are minimized.

14. Click the **Show Desktop** button again to restore the programs.

15. Click the **Close** buttons on the title bars of each of the two program windows to close them and to show the desktop.

Using the Documents Command

Windows lets you open a recently used document by using the Recent Items command on the Start menu. This command allows you to open one of up to fifteen documents previously saved on your computer.

1. Click the **Start** button on the taskbar to display the Start menu.
2. Click **Recent Items**. The Recent Items submenu appears, showing you up to the last fifteen documents that were saved.
3. Click a document. The program in which the document was created opens, and the document displays. For example, if the document you chose is a Word document, Word opens and the document appears in a Word program window.
4. Click the program window's **Close** button. The program window closes, and the desktop is clear once again.

Changing the Desktop

The Control Panel lets you change the way Windows looks and works. Because your computer in school is used by other students, you should be very careful when changing settings. Others might expect Windows to look and work the standard way. (Table 5 describes how to access other settings.)

To change the appearance of your computer, follow these steps:

1. Click the **Start** button on the taskbar.
2. Click **Control Panel** on the right pane. The Control Panel window displays.
3. Click the **Appearance and Personalization** link. The Appearance and Personalization window displays.
4. Click **Personalization** and click **Window Color and Appearance**.
5. Click **Default** and click **OK**.
6. Close the Appearance and Personalization window.

TABLE 5 Setting Options

OPTION	USE
Control Panel	Displays the Control Panel window, which lets you change background color, add or remove programs, change the date and time, and change other settings for your hardware and software. The items listed below are accessed from the Control Panel.
Network and Internet	Includes options to view the network status, connect to a network, set up file sharing, change Internet options, and so on.
Hardware and Sound	Includes options to add a printer, change default settings for AutoPlay, sound, mouse settings, keyboard, and so on.
Appearance and Personalization	Includes options to change the desktop background, adjust screen resolution, customize the Start menu and icons on the taskbar, and change sidebar properties.

Using the Search Command

If you do not know where a file or folder is located, you can use the Search command on the Start menu to help you find and open it.

1. Click the **Start** button on the taskbar. Notice the blinking insertion point in the Start Search box. You can start typing the name of a program, folder, or file immediately.

2. Click **Search** in the right pane of the Start menu. The Search Results dialog box appears.

3. Click **Document** in the Show Only section.

Figure 14
Search Results
dialog box

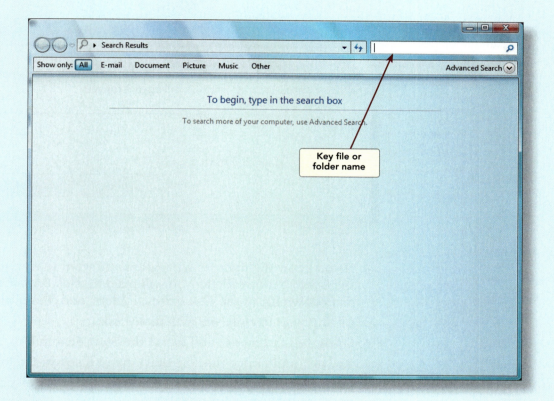

4. Type the name of the file or folder you want to find in the Search box. View the search results.

To search for files by date, size, type, or other attributes, click **Advanced Search**.

1. Click the arrow to the left of the Search Results text box to specify where you want Windows to search. The default location is the C drive.

2. Click **Search** to start the search. Any matches for the file are shown in the right pane of the dialog box.

3. Double-click any found item to open the program and view the file or folder Windows has located.

4. When you are finished with your search, close all open windows and clear your desktop.

Using the Run Command

Windows allows you to start a program by using the Run command and typing the program name. This command is often employed to run a "setup" or "install" program that installs a new program on your computer. It is best to use this command after you have become more familiar with Windows Vista.

1. Click the **Start** button on the taskbar.
2. Click All Programs, and click the Accessories folder.
3. Click **Run**.

Figure 15
Run dialog box

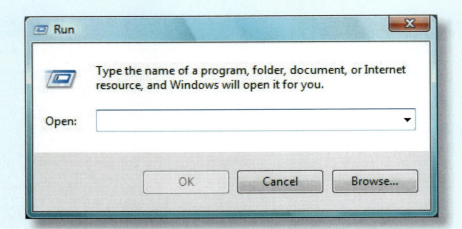

4. If you know the name of a program you want to run, type the name in the Open text box. Often you will need to click **Browse** to open a drop-down list of the disk drives, folders, and files available to you.
5. Click **Cancel** to close the Run dialog box.
6. Open the **Start** menu, and locate the Start Search box.
7. Key **run**, and notice that the Start menu displays the Run program.
8. Click the program name, and the Run dialog box displays.
9. Close the Run dialog box.

Deleting Files Using the Recycle Bin

The *Recycle Bin* is the trash can icon on your desktop. To delete a file:

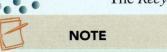

NOTE

As a protection against deleting a file unintentionally, any file you have placed in the Recycle Bin can be undeleted and used again.

1. Click its icon, and drag it to the Recycle Bin.
2. Double-click the **Recycle Bin** icon. A window opens listing files you have deleted.
3. To undelete a file, merely drag it out of the Recycle Bin window and place it on the desktop or right-click the file and click Restore.
4. To empty the Recycle Bin and permanently delete files, click Empty Recycle Bin in the Recycle Bin dialog box, or right-click the Recycle Bin icon. The shortcut menu appears.
5. Click **Empty Recycle Bin**.

Exiting Windows

You should always exit any open programs and Windows before turning off the computer. This is the best way to be sure your work is saved. Windows also performs other "housekeeping" routines that ensure everything is ready for you when you next turn on your computer. Failure to shut down properly will often force Windows to perform time-consuming system checks the next time it is loaded. You can either log off the computer to make it available for another user, or shut it down entirely.

To Log Off

1. Click the **Start** button on the taskbar.
2. Click the arrow to the right of the Lock this computer button , and click **Log Off**.

To Shut Down

To exit Windows, use the Lock this computer command on the Start menu. This command has several shut-down options.

- *Restart:* Restarts the computer without shutting off the power. This is sometimes necessary when you add new software.
- *Shut down:* Closes all open programs and makes it safe to turn off the computer. Some computers will turn off the power automatically.
- *Sleep:* Puts the computer in a low-activity state. It appears to be turned off but will restart when the mouse is moved. Press the computer power button to resume work.

1. Click the **Start** button on the taskbar.
2. Click the arrow beside the Lock this computer button.
3. Click the **Shut Down** option.
4. Windows prompts you to save changes in any open documents. It then prepares the computer to be shut down.

case study

There's more to learning a spreadsheet program like Microsoft Office Excel than simply keying data. You need to know how to use Excel in real-world situations. That's why all the lessons in this book relate to everyday business tasks.

As you work through the lessons, imagine yourself working as an intern for Klassy Kow Ice Cream, Inc., a fictional San Francisco business that manufactures and sells ice cream.

Klassy Kow Ice Cream, Inc.

Klassy Kow Ice Cream, Inc., was formed in 1985 by Conrad Steele, shortly after the death of his father. Since 1967, Conrad's father and mother had been dairy farmers in Klamath Falls, Oregon. As an addition to their farm, Archibald and Henrietta Steele opened a small ice cream shop. They made their own ice cream from fresh cream, eggs, and butter—starting simply with vanilla, chocolate, and strawberry flavors. They also sold cones, sundaes, shakes, and malts.

As word spread about their delicious ice cream, Archie and Henrietta's business blossomed from a seasonal shop to a year-round store. Eventually, the Steeles expanded the number of flavors and started to offer hand-packed ice cream pies and cakes. They also started to sell to small supermarkets in southern Oregon under the "Klassy Kow" name, allowing their many local customers to buy half-gallons at their favorite supermarkets.

The business continued to expand and soon reached into supermarkets in the Pacific Northwest. Archibald and Henrietta opened new ice cream shops in Medford, Oregon, and Eureka and Red Bluff, California.

After Archibald Steele died, Conrad and his mother sold the dairy farm but kept the ice cream shops. They continue to buy ice cream from the new owners (the Klamath Farm) and have expanded the ice cream business to include 33 franchised ice cream shops in the western United States.

In 1998, with Klassy Kow continuing to grow steadily, Conrad decided to move the corporate headquarters to San Francisco, California. His mother, Henrietta, is retired and still lives in Klamath Falls, where she continues to help create and test new flavors for the Klamath Farm.

The company now has more than 200 employees, but the number of employees in the San Francisco office is surprisingly small. Most employees work in the ice cream shops scattered across Washington, Idaho, Oregon, Nevada, and northern California.

Conrad Steele, who is now president and chief executive officer of Klassy Kow, is responsible for the general operations of the company. He says, "I love to see a big smile on a customer's face after the first lick. It makes it all worth it."

Conrad visits many of the ice cream shops and likes to keep in touch with customers. He visits Klamath Farms at least four times a year to keep in contact with his major supplier.

All the worksheets, data, and graphics you will use in this course relate to Klassy Kow Ice Cream, Inc. As you work with the worksheets in the text, take the time to notice the following:

- The types of worksheets needed in a small business to carry on day-to-day business.
- The formatting of worksheets. Real businesses don't always pay attention to formatting internal worksheets. However, they do focus on formatting worksheets that customers will see.
- The types of business activities required by a company such as Klassy Kow. For example, it must deal with employees, internal accounting, and suppliers.

As you use this text and become more experienced with Microsoft Office Excel, you will also gain expertise in creating, editing, and formatting the sort of worksheets generated in a real-life business environment.

Klassy Kow Klassics

Sugar Cones	Waffle Cones
Ice Cream	Frozen Yogurt
Shakes	Malteds
Ice Cream Sodas	Ice Cream Sundaes
Ice Cream Cakes	Ice Cream Pies
Ice Cream Sandwiches	Soda
Coffee	

Kowabunga
(An ice cream beverage available in several flavors)

KowOwow
(A cow-shaped ice cream bar)

unit 1

INTRODUCTION TO EXCEL

EXL1.1

Getting Started with Excel

OBJECTIVE

MCAS OBJECTIVES

In this lesson:
XL07 1.3
XL07 1.4.1
XL07 1.4.3
XL07 5.4
XL07 5.4.2
XL07 5.5

After completing this lesson, you will be able to:

1. Start Excel.

2. Navigate in a workbook.

3. Open an existing workbook.

4. Edit a worksheet.

5. Manage files.

6. Print Excel files.

Estimated Time: 1 hour

Microsoft Excel is *electronic spreadsheet software.* You can use Excel to create professional reports that perform business or personal calculations, display financial or scientific calculations, complete table management tasks, and show charts. Excel is powerful but easy to use. You'll become a productive Excel user as soon as you learn the basics.

Starting Excel

NOTE

The command tabs in the Ribbon are similar to panes or tabs in a dialog box.

Excel opens showing a blank workbook, the Microsoft Office Button, the Quick Access toolbar, and the Ribbon (see Figure 1-1). New workbooks are named Book1, Book2, and so on during each work session.

The *Ribbon* is a set of command tabs. Each command tab has buttons, galleries, or other controls related to a specific task group or object. Some command tabs

Figure 1-1
Excel screen

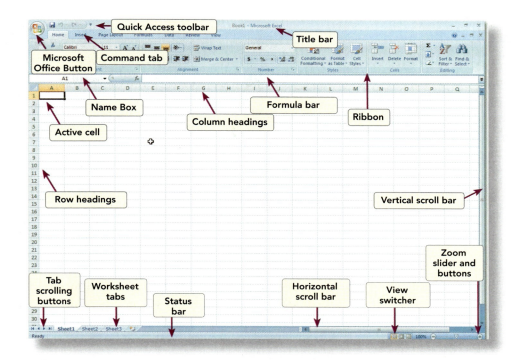

TABLE 1-1 Parts of the Excel Screen

Part of Screen	Purpose
Active cell	The cell outlined in a heavy black border. It is ready to accept new data, a formula, or your edits.
Column headings	Alphabetic characters across the top of the worksheet that identify columns.
Command tabs	A Ribbon tab control with command buttons, galleries, and other controls for creating, managing, editing, and formatting data.
Formula bar	Displays the contents of the active cell. You can also enter text, numbers, or formulas in the formula bar. It can be expanded and collapsed as needed.
Microsoft Office Button	Opens a menu with basic commands for working with the document.
Name Box	A drop-down combo box that shows the address of the active cell. You can also use it to move the pointer to a specific location.
Quick Access toolbar	Toolbar with shortcut command buttons for common tasks.
Ribbon	Organizes and displays command tabs.
Row headings	Numbers down the left side of the worksheet that identify rows.
Scroll bars	Used to move different parts of the screen into view.
Status bar	Displays information about the current task and mode of operation as well as View choices and the Zoom control.
Tab scrolling buttons	Navigation buttons to scroll through worksheet tabs.
Title bar	Contains the program name and the name of the workbook.
View switcher	Buttons to change the view of the current sheet among Normal, Page Layout, and Page Break Preview.
Worksheet tabs	Indicators at the bottom of the worksheet to identify sheets in the workbook.
Zoom controls	Buttons and slider to change the view magnification.

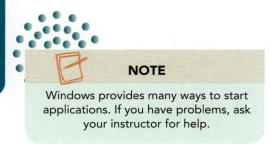

NOTE

Windows provides many ways to start applications. If you have problems, ask your instructor for help.

are context-sensitive and appear only when needed to accommodate what you are doing. The *Quick Access toolbar* provides one-click access to frequently used commands. You can add command buttons to this toolbar, and you can reposition it below the Ribbon. The *Microsoft Office Button* replaces the File menu in previous versions of Office, but it still lists commands such as Save and Print.

Exercise 1-1   WORK WITH THE EXCEL INTERFACE

There are several ways to start Excel, depending on how your software is installed. You can use the Start button on the Windows taskbar to choose Excel from the list of available programs. There may be an Excel icon on the desktop that you can double-click to start Excel.

Your screen size and resolution affects how the command buttons look and how much you see at once. Do not be concerned if your screen looks slightly different from illustrations in this text.

When the instructions tell you to "click" a tab, a command button, or a menu option, use the left mouse button. Use the left mouse button to carry out commands unless you are told explicitly to use the right mouse button.

1. Start Excel. A blank workbook opens.

2. Click the **Home** tab in the Ribbon. Commands on this tab are organized into seven groups: Clipboard, Font, Alignment, Number, Styles, Cells, and Editing.

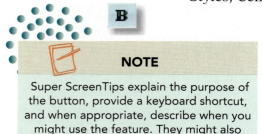

NOTE

Super ScreenTips explain the purpose of the button, provide a keyboard shortcut, and when appropriate, describe when you might use the feature. They might also include a thumbnail image of a dialog box to be opened.

3. In the **Font** group, rest the mouse pointer on the Bold button 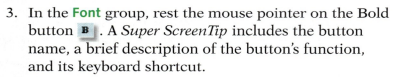. A *Super ScreenTip* includes the button name, a brief description of the button's function, and its keyboard shortcut.

4. In the **Font** group, rest the mouse pointer on the Dialog Box Launcher. A Super ScreenTip describes and previews the dialog box that will be opened when you click this button. Many command groups have a Dialog Box Launcher.

Figure 1-2
Dialog Box Launcher
for the Font group

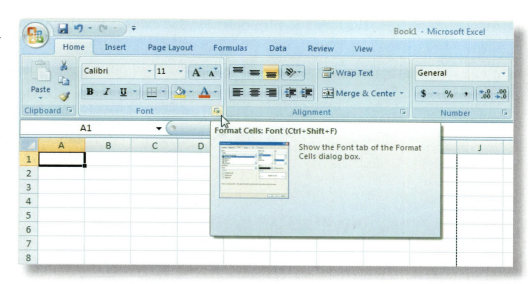

5. Click the Dialog Box Launcher for the **Font** group. The Format Cells dialog box opens with the **Font** tab visible.

6. Click **Cancel** to close the dialog box.

7. Click the **View** tab in the Ribbon. Commands on this tab are organized into five groups: Workbook Views, Show/Hide, Zoom, Window, and Macros.

8. In the **Workbook Views** group, move the mouse pointer to Full Screen and click. A Full Screen view shows only worksheet cells with row and column headings.

NOTE

The Esc key is at the top left of most keyboards.

9. Press Esc on the keyboard to return to normal view.

10. Click the Page Layout View button . This view is an interactive preview of how the page will print and shows margins, the ruler, and header/footer areas. The grid does not print.

11. Click the Normal button .

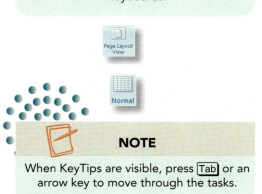

12. Press and release the Alt key. *KeyTips* appear over a command name when you press the Alt key. They show keyboard shortcuts.

13. Key **h** to activate the **Home** tab.

NOTE

When KeyTips are visible, press Tab or an arrow key to move through the tasks.

14. Press Tab four times. The active task cycles through the commands in the Clipboard group, and the KeyTips are no longer visible. The Clipboard group is now active.

15. Press Esc.

16. Press F10 and key **h**. This is another keyboard shortcut to display KeyTips. Each task now shows a key.

17. Key **1** to turn on bold. You can see that bold is applied by the button color.

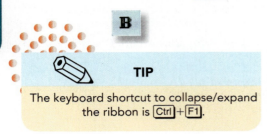

TIP

The keyboard shortcut to collapse/expand the ribbon is Ctrl + F1.

18. Click the Bold button B. Bold is toggled off.

19. Double-click the **Home** tab. The ribbon collapses and more working space is available.

20. Right-click the **Home** tab. Click to deselect **Minimize the Ribbon**. You can right-click any tab to expand or collapse the ribbon.

Navigating in a Workbook

A *workbook* is the file Excel creates to store your data. When you look at the screen, you are viewing a worksheet. A *worksheet* is an individual page or sheet tab. A new workbook opens with three blank worksheets. You can insert or delete worksheets in the workbook. A workbook must have at least 1 worksheet and can have as many as your computer's memory allows.

TABLE 1-2 Navigation Commands in a Workbook

Press	To Do This
Ctrl + Home	Move to the beginning of the worksheet.
Ctrl + End	Move to the last used cell on the worksheet.
Home	Move to the beginning of the current row.
PageUp	Move up one screen.
PageDown	Move down one screen.
Alt + PageUp	Move one screen to the left.
Alt + PageDown	Move one screen to the right.
↑, ↓, ←, →	Move one cell up, down, left, or right.
Ctrl + arrow key	Move to the edge of a group of cells with data.
Ctrl + G or F5	Open the Go To dialog box.
Click	Move to the cell that is clicked.
Tab	Move to the next cell in a left-to-right sequence.
Shift + Tab	Move to the previous cell in a right-to-left sequence.
Ctrl + Backspace	Move to the active cell when it has scrolled out of view.
Ctrl + PageUp	Move to the previous worksheet.
Ctrl + PageDown	Move to the next worksheet.

A worksheet is divided into *rows* and *columns*. The rows are numbered and reach row 1,048,576. There are 16,384 columns, lettered from A to Z, then AA to AZ, BA to BZ, AAA to AAZ, ABA to ABZ, and so on, up to column XFD.

The intersection of a row and a column forms a rectangle known as a *cell*. You enter data (text, a number, or a formula) in a cell. Cells have *cell addresses* or *cell references*, which identify where the cell is located on the worksheet. Cell B2, for example, is the cell in column B, row 2.

The *active cell* is the cell that appears outlined with a thick border. It is ready to accept data or a formula, or if it already contains data or a formula, it is ready to be modified. It is the cell in which you are currently working. When you open a new workbook, the active cell is cell A1, the top-left cell in the worksheet. Cell A1 is referred to as "Home."

The mouse pointer displays as a thick white cross when you move it across cells in the worksheet. When you point at a Ribbon or worksheet tab, a command button, or a menu item, the pointer turns into a white arrow.

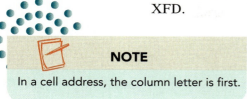

NOTE

In a cell address, the column letter is first.

NOTE

Pointing and resting the mouse pointer on a button is known as "hovering."

Exercise 1-2 MOVE BETWEEN WORKSHEETS

A new workbook has three worksheets named **Sheet1**, **Sheet2**, and **Sheet3**. **Sheet1** is displayed when a new workbook is opened.

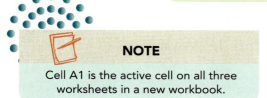

NOTE

Cell A1 is the active cell on all three worksheets in a new workbook.

NOTE

When keyboard combinations (such as Ctrl + PageUp) are shown in this text, hold down the first key without releasing it and press the second key. Release the second key and then release the first key.

1. Click the **Sheet2** worksheet tab. You can tell which sheet is active because its tab appears more white and the tab name is bold.

2. Click the **Sheet3** worksheet tab. All three sheets are empty.

3. Press Ctrl + PageUp. This shortcut moves to the previous worksheet, **Sheet2**, in this case.

4. Press Ctrl + PageDown. This command moves to the next worksheet, **Sheet3**.

5. Click the **Sheet1** tab to return to **Sheet1**.

Exercise 1-3 GO TO A SPECIFIC CELL

When you move the mouse pointer to a cell and click, the cell you clicked becomes the active cell. It is outlined with a black border, and you can see the cell address in the *Name Box*. The Name Box is a drop-down combo box at the left edge of the formula bar. You can also determine the cell address by the orange-shaded column and row headings.

1. Move the mouse pointer to cell D4 and click. Cell D4 is the active cell, and its address appears in the Name Box. The column D and row 4 headings are shaded.

Figure 1-3
Active cell showing a thick border

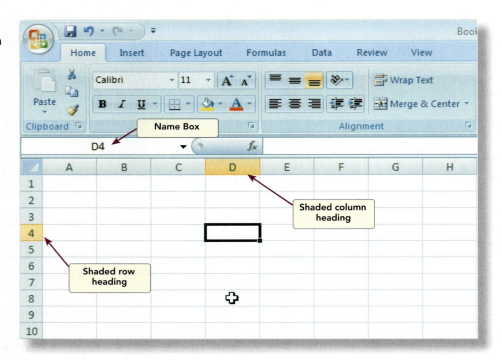

2. Press Ctrl+Home. This shortcut makes cell A1 the active cell.

3. Press Ctrl+G to open the Go To dialog box.

4. Key **b19** in the **Reference** box and press Enter. Cell B19 becomes the active cell, and its address is shown in the Name Box.

TIP

As an alternative, open the Go To dialog box by clicking the Find & Select button in the Editing group on the Home tab and choosing **Go To**.

Figure 1-4
Go To dialog box

5. Press Ctrl+G. Recently used cell addresses are listed in the **Go to** list in the Go To dialog box.

6. Key **c2** and click **OK**.

7. Click in the **Name Box**. The current cell address is highlighted.

8. Key **a8** in the Name Box and press Enter.

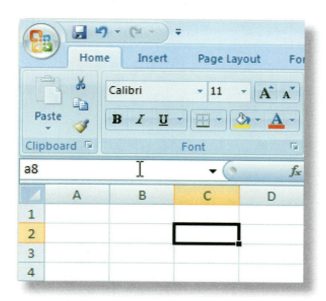

9. Press Ctrl+Home to return to cell A1.

Exercise 1-4 SCROLL THROUGH A WORKSHEET

When you scroll through a worksheet, the location of the active cell does not change. Instead, the worksheet moves on the screen so that you can see different columns or rows. The number of rows and columns you see at once depends on screen resolution and the Zoom size in Excel.

1. On the vertical scroll bar, click below the scroll box. The worksheet has been repositioned so that you see the next group of about 20 to 30 rows.

2. Click above the vertical scroll box. The worksheet has scrolled up to show the top rows.

3. Click the right scroll arrow on the horizontal scroll bar once. The worksheet scrolls one column to the right.

4. Click the left scroll arrow once to bring the column back into view.

NOTE

You cannot see the active cell (cell A1) during your scrolling.

5. Click the down scroll arrow on the vertical scroll bar twice.

6. Drag the vertical scroll box to the top of the vertical scroll bar. As you drag, a ScreenTip displays the row number at the top of the window. During all this scrolling, the active cell is still cell A1.

Figure 1-6
Using scroll bars

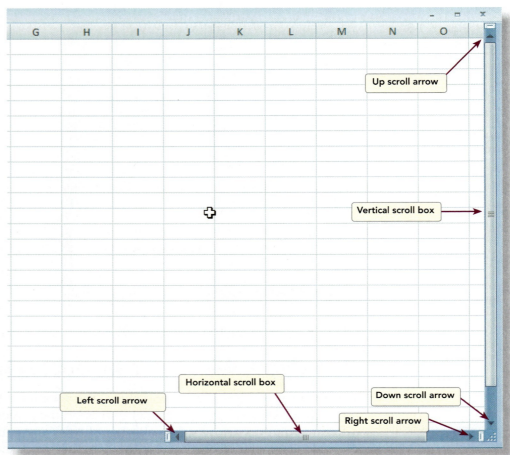

TABLE 1-3 Scrolling Through a Worksheet

To Move the View	Do This
One row up	Click the up scroll arrow.
One row down	Click the down scroll arrow.
Up one screen	Click the scroll bar above the scroll box.
Down one screen	Click the scroll bar below the scroll box.
To any relative position	Drag the scroll bar up or down.
One column to the right	Click the right scroll arrow.
One column to the left	Click the left scroll arrow.

Exercise 1-5   CHANGE THE ZOOM SIZE

The *Zoom size* controls how much of the worksheet you see on the screen. You can set the size to see more or less on screen and reduce the need to scroll. The **100%** size shows the data close to print size. A Zoom slider and two buttons are at the right edge of the status bar.

1. Click the Zoom In button on the status bar. The worksheet is resized to 110% and you see fewer columns and rows.

Figure 1-7
Changing the Zoom size

2. Click the Zoom Out button . The worksheet is reduced to 100% magnification.

3. Click the Zoom Out button again. Each click changes the magnification by 10%.

4. Point at the Zoom slider button , hold down the mouse button, and drag the slider slowly in either direction. You can set any magnification size.

5. Click the **View** tab in the Ribbon. There is a Zoom button on this tab.

6. Click the Zoom button . The Zoom dialog box opens.

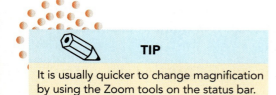

7. Choose **200%**. Click **OK**.

8. Click **200%** in the status bar. The dialog box opens.

9. Choose **100%** and click **OK**.

TIP

It is usually quicker to change magnification by using the Zoom tools on the status bar.

Exercise 1-6   CLOSE A WORKBOOK

After you finish working with a workbook, you should save your work and close the workbook. You can close a workbook in several ways.

- Click the Microsoft Office Button 🔘 and choose **Close**.
- Click the Close Window button ⊠ at the right end of the Ribbon tabs.
- Use keyboard shortcuts, Ctrl+W or Ctrl+F4.

1. Click the Microsoft Office Button 🔘.
2. Choose **Close**. (If you have made a change to the workbook, a dialog box asks if you want to save the changes. Click **No** if this message box opens.) The workbook closes, and a blank blue screen appears.

Opening an Existing Workbook

There are several ways to open an existing workbook.

- Click the Microsoft Office Button 🔘 and choose **Open**.
- Use the keyboard shortcut Ctrl+O or Ctrl+F12.
- Navigate through folders in Windows Explorer or Computer to find and double-click the filename.

Exercise 1-7   OPEN A WORKBOOK

1. Click the Microsoft Office Button 🔘 and choose **Open**. The navigation line shows the most recently used folder.
2. Choose the drive/folder according to your instructor's directions.

> **NOTE**
>
> Your instructor will advise you on the drive/folder to use for this course.

3. Click the arrow next to the Organize button  and hover over **Layout**.
4. Click to select **Details Pane**. The Details pane is at the lower part of the dialog box. (Navigation Pane should also be selected. If it is not, repeat these steps to select it.)

5. Click the arrow next to the Views button 🔲 and choose **Small Icons**.

Figure 1-8
Open dialog box

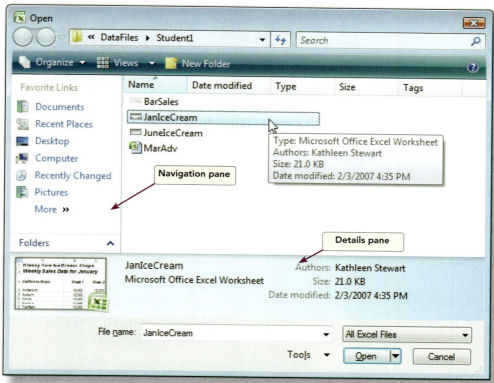

NOTE

The workbooks in this course relate to the Case Study about Klassy Kow Ice Cream, Inc., a fictional manufacturer of ice cream (see the Case Study in the frontmatter).

6. Find and click **JanIceCream**. The Details pane shows a thumbnail of the document.

7. Double-click **JanIceCream**. The workbook opens.

Editing a Worksheet

The **JanIceCream** workbook has three worksheets. The worksheets have been renamed WeeklySales, Owners, and Chart to better indicate what is on the sheet. For instance, the WeeklySales sheet shows sales for each city in each of the four weeks in January.

Worksheet cells contain text, numbers, or formulas. A formula calculates an arithmetic result. By simply viewing the worksheet, you might not know if the cell contains a number or a formula. However, you can determine a cell's contents by checking the formula bar. You can also use the formula bar to change the contents of cells.

Exercise 1-8   VIEW WORKSHEETS AND CELL CONTENTS

1. Click the **Owners** worksheet tab. The **Owners** worksheet shows the city and the name of the shop owner.

2. Click the **Chart** tab. This bar chart illustrates January sales for each city.

3. Press Ctrl + PageUp. This moves to the **Owners** worksheet.

4. Press Ctrl + PageDown. Now, the active tab is the **Chart** sheet.

5. Click the **WeeklySales** tab.

6. Press F5 to open the Go To dialog box.

7. Key **a5** and press Enter. The active cell is changed to cell A5. This cell contains the name of a city (Auburn), which you can see in the formula bar and on the worksheet.

REVIEW

If you cannot see column F or row 19, adjust the Zoom size.

Figure 1-9
Cell contents and the formula bar
JanIceCream.xlsx
WeeklySales sheet

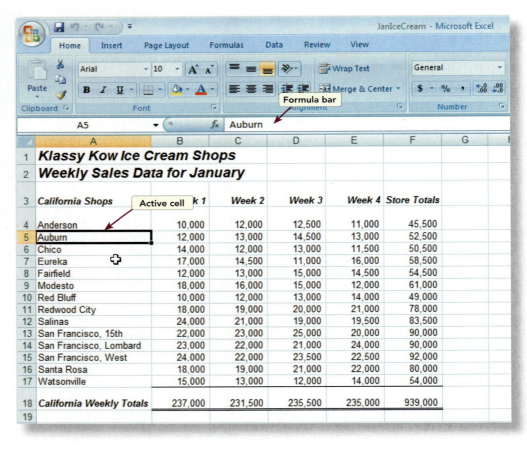

8. Press F5, key **c10**, and press Enter. Cell C10 contains a number. In the formula bar, the number does not show the comma.

9. Press F5, key **f17**, and press Enter. Cell F17 contains a formula, which you can see in the formula bar. Formulas calculate a result.

Exercise 1-9 REPLACE CELL CONTENTS

When the workbook is in Ready mode, you can key, edit, or replace the contents of a cell. To replace a cell's contents, make it the active cell, key the new data, and press Enter. You can also click the Enter button ✓ in the formula bar or press any arrow key on the keyboard to complete the replacement.

If you replace a number used in a formula, the result of the formula automatically recalculates when you complete your change.

1. Click cell B5 to make it the active cell.

2. Key **20000** without a comma. As you key the number, it appears in the cell and in the formula bar. The status bar shows **Enter** to indicate that you are in Enter mode.

Figure 1-10
Replacing cell contents
JanIceCream.xlsx
WeeklySales sheet

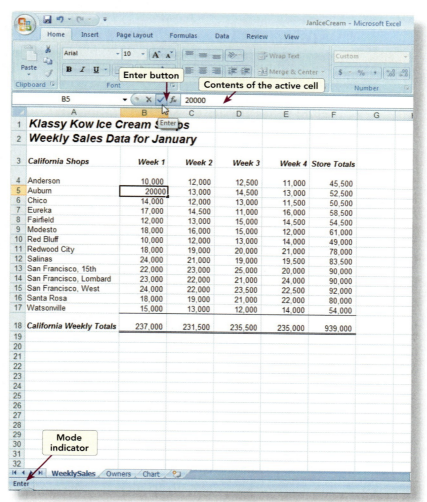

3. Press Enter. Excel inserts a comma, and the next cell in column B is active. The "Store Total" (cell F5, 60,500) and the "California Weekly Totals" amounts (in cells B18 and F18, 245,000 and 947,000) are recalculated. The worksheet returns to Ready mode.

4. Press ↑ to move to cell B5. Key **10000** without a comma. Click the Enter button ✓ in the formula bar. Notice that when you use the Enter button ✓, the pointer stays in cell B5.

5. Click the **Chart** tab. Notice the length of the Auburn bar, showing sales near $50,000.

6. Click the **WeeklySales** tab.

7. In cell B5, key **0**, and press Ctrl+Enter. A zero appears as a short dash in this worksheet.

8. Click the **Chart** tab. The chart on this worksheet is based on the data in the **WeeklySales** worksheet. Now that you have reduced sales, the Auburn bar is shorter.

9. Click the **WeeklySales** tab and key **10000** in cell B5. Press →.

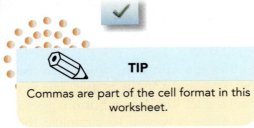

TIP

Commas are part of the cell format in this worksheet.

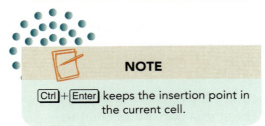

NOTE

Ctrl+Enter keeps the insertion point in the current cell.

Exercise 1-10   EDIT CELL CONTENTS

If a cell contains a long or complicated entry, you can edit it rather than rekeying the entire entry. Edit mode starts when you:

- Double-click the cell.
- Click the cell and press F2.
- Click the cell and then click anywhere in the formula bar.

TABLE 1-4 Keyboard Shortcuts in Edit Mode

Key	To Do This
Enter	Complete the edit, return to Ready mode, and move the insertion point to the next cell.
Alt+Enter	Move the insertion point to a new line within the cell, a line break.
Esc	Cancel the edit and restore the existing data.
Home	Move the insertion point to the beginning of the data.
End	Move the insertion point to the end of the data.
Delete	Delete one character to the right of the insertion point.
Ctrl+Delete	Delete everything from the insertion point to the end of the line.
Backspace	Delete one character to the left of the insertion point.
← or →	Move the insertion point one character left or right.
Ctrl+←	Move the insertion point one word left.
Ctrl+→	Move the insertion point one word right.

TIP

In Edit mode, double-clicking highlights or selects a word.

1. Click cell A2. The text in cell A2 is long, and its display overlaps into columns B and C.

2. Press F2. **Edit** mode is shown in the status bar. An insertion point appears in the cell at the end of the text.

3. Double-click "Data" in the cell. A Mini toolbar appears with buttons for font editing.

4. Point at the Mini toolbar. Its appearance brightens for easy viewing.

Figure 1-11
Using Edit mode
JanIceCream.xlsx
WeeklySales sheet

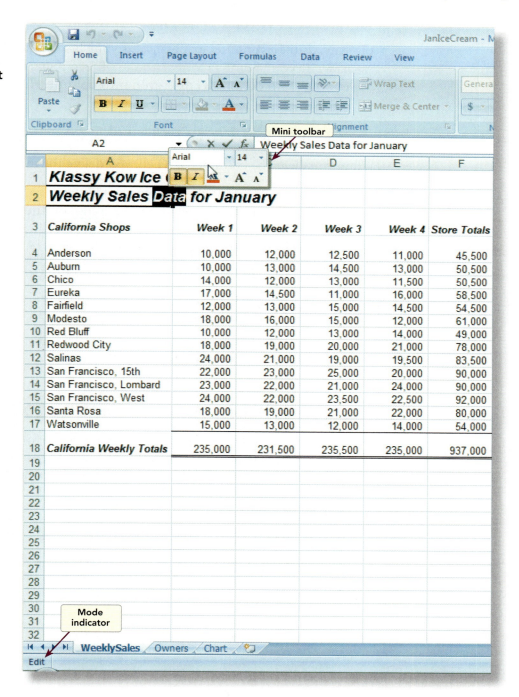

5. Key **Information**. It replaces the word "Data." The Mini toolbar has disappeared.

6. Press Enter to complete the edit. Pressing Enter does not start a new line in the cell when the worksheet is in Edit mode.

7. Double-click cell A3. This starts Edit mode, and an insertion point appears in the cell.

8. In the cell, click to the left of the first "S" in "Shops."

9. Key **Retail** and press Spacebar. Press Enter.

10. Click cell F1. There is nothing in this cell.

11. Key your first name, a space, and your last name in the cell. Press Enter. If your name is longer than column F, part of its display might overlap into column G and even into column H.

Exercise 1-11   CLEAR CELL CONTENTS

When you clear the contents of a cell, you delete the text, number, or formula in that cell.

NOTE

A green triangle may appear in the corners of cells F5 and B18 to indicate that a formula error has occurred. Ignore the triangles for now.

1. Click cell B5. Press Delete on the keyboard. The number is deleted, and Excel recalculates the formula results in cells F5, B18, and F18.

2. Press → to move the pointer to cell C5.

3. On the **Home** tab in the **Editing** group, click the Clear button .

4. Choose **Clear Contents**. The number is deleted, and formulas are recalculated.

Exercise 1-12   USE UNDO AND REDO

The Undo command reverses the last action you performed in the worksheet. For example, if you delete the contents of a cell, the Undo command restores what you deleted. The Redo command reverses the action of the Undo command. It "undoes" your Undo.

To use the Undo command, you can:

• Click the Undo button on the Quick Access toolbar.

• Press Ctrl+Z or Alt+Backspace.

To use the Redo command, you can:

- Click the Redo button on the Quick Access toolbar.

- Press Ctrl+Y or F4.

Excel keeps a history or list of your editing commands, and you can undo several at once.

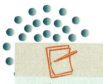

NOTE

The ScreenTip for the Undo button includes the most recent task, such as Undo Clear.

1. Click the Undo button . The number in cell C5 is restored.

2. Click the Redo button . The number is cleared again.

3. Click cell A8 and key **Gotham**. Press Enter.

4. In cell A9 key **Los Angeles** and press Enter.

5. Click the arrow next to the Undo button to display the history list.

NOTE

Depending on the actions that have been undone and redone on your computer, your list might be different from the one shown in Figure 1-12.

6. Move the mouse to highlight the top two actions and click. The last two changes are undone, and the original city names are restored.

Figure 1-12
Undoing multiple edits
JanIceCream.xlsx
WeeklySales sheet

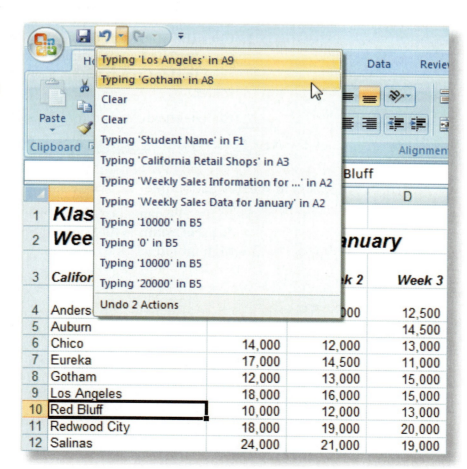

7. Click the Redo button 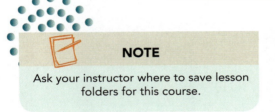. The first action is restored.

8. Click the Redo button again.

9. Press Ctrl+Home to place the pointer in cell A1.

Managing Files

Workbook files are usually stored in folders. A *folder* is a location on a disk, network, or other drive. Folders are organized in a structure like a family tree. The top level of the tree is a letter such as C, F, or G to represent the disk or other storage device. Under each letter, you can create folders to help you organize and manage your work.

For your work in this text, you will save your files in a folder you create for each lesson.

Exercise 1-13   CREATE A NEW FOLDER AND USE SAVE AS

1. Click the Microsoft Office Button  and choose **Save As**. The Save As dialog box opens. You will save **JanIceCream** with a new filename in a lesson folder.

2. Choose the drive and folder location for your work.

3. Click the New Folder button. A New Folder icon opens.

4. Key *[your initials]***Lesson1**. Press Enter. Your new folder's name now appears in the navigation line.

5. In the **File name** box, make sure the filename **JanIceCream** is highlighted or selected. If it is not highlighted, click to select it.

6. Key *[your initials]***1-13** and click **Save**. Your new filename now appears in the title bar.

Figure 1-13
Save As dialog box

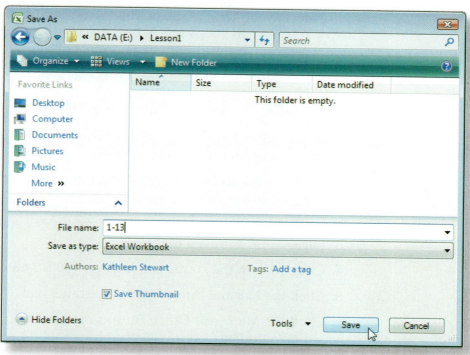

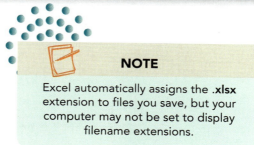

NOTE

Excel automatically assigns the **.xlsx** extension to files you save, but your computer may not be set to display filename extensions.

Printing Excel Files

You can use any of these methods to print a worksheet:

- Press Ctrl + P.

- Click the Microsoft Office Button 🔵 and choose **Print** and then **Quick Print**.

- Click the Print button 🖨 while in Print Preview.

- Click the Quick Print button 🖨 on the Quick Access toolbar.

Some methods open the Print dialog box, in which you can change printing options. The Quick Print button 🖨, if it is on the Quick Access toolbar, and choosing Quick Print from the menu send the worksheet to the printer with default print settings.

Page Layout View displays your sheet with margin and header/footer areas. You can edit your work in Page Layout View. Print Preview also shows your worksheet as it will print in a normal or reduced view. You cannot make any changes in Print Preview.

Exercise 1-14   PREVIEW AND PRINT A WORKSHEET

1. In the status bar, click the Page Layout View button 🔲. The page shows margin areas and the rulers.

2. Click the Zoom Out button ⊖ in the status bar. The worksheet is reduced to 90% magnification.

3. Click the Zoom Out button ⊖ to reach 50% magnification. Unused pages appear grayed out.

4. Click **50%** in the status bar. Choose **100%** and click **OK**.

5. Click the Normal button ⊞ in the status bar.

6. Click the Microsoft Office Button 🔘 and hover over **Print**. A submenu opens.

7. Choose **Print Preview**. The worksheet is shown in a reduced size so that you can see the entire page.

Figure 1-14
Worksheet in Print Preview
1-13.xlsx WeeklySales sheet

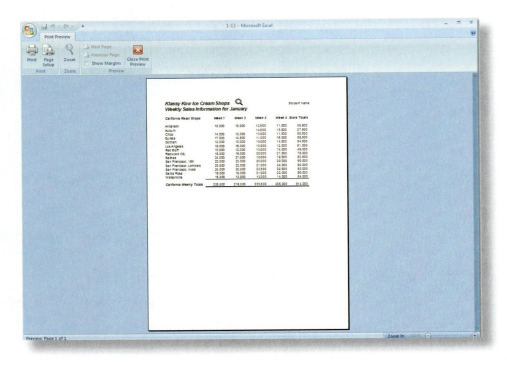

8. Move the mouse pointer near the main headings. The pointer appears as a small magnifying glass icon.

9. Click while pointing at the headings. The worksheet changes to a larger size, close to the actual print size.

10. Click anywhere to return to a reduced size. The mouse pointer appears as a white solid arrow when it will zoom out.

11. Zoom in on the "California Weekly Totals" row. Click anywhere to zoom out.

12. Click the Print button 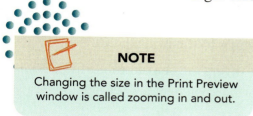. The Print dialog box opens.

13. Press **Enter**. A printer icon appears on the taskbar as the worksheet is sent to the printer. Only the **WeeklySales** worksheet is printed.

NOTE

Changing the size in the Print Preview window is called zooming in and out.

Exercise 1-15   PRINT A WORKBOOK

You can print all sheets in a workbook with one command from the Print dialog box.

1. Press **Ctrl**+**P**. The Print dialog box opens with your default settings.

Figure 1-15
Print dialog box

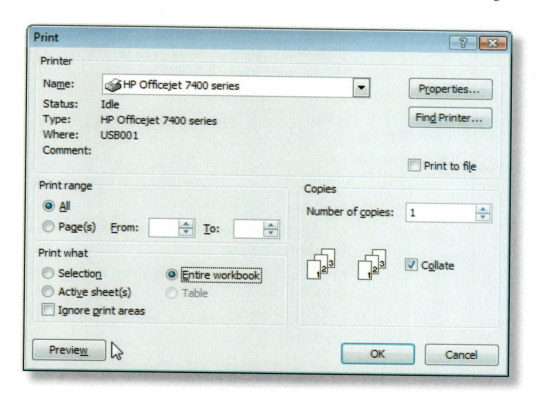

2. In the **Print what** section, choose **Entire workbook**.

3. Click **Preview**. The reduced size shows the first page, the **WeeklySales** sheet. The status bar shows that this is page 1 of 3.

4. Press PageDown. This is the second sheet, the **Owners** worksheet.

5. Press PageDown. This is the **Chart** sheet. It is set to print in landscape orientation.

6. Click **Previous Page** two times to return to the first sheet.

7. Click the Print button . All three sheets are sent to the printer and Print Preview closes.

Exercise 1-16   SAVE AN XPS FILE

XPS is *XML Paper Specification (XPS)*, a file type that maintains document formatting so that you or others can view or print the worksheet exactly as it was designed, with or without Excel. You need a viewer to open an XPS document, available in Windows Vista or free from Microsoft's Web site. To save a file as an XPS (or PDF) document, you must have installed this add-in at your computer.

1. Click the Microsoft Office Button and choose **Save As**. The Save As dialog box opens. If you have opened the Publish as PDF or XPS dialog box, close it and try again.

2. Choose *[your initials]* **Lesson1** as the location.

3. In the **File name** box, make sure the file name *[your initials]***1-13** is highlighted or selected. If it is not highlighted, select it.

4. Key *[your initials]***1-16**.

TIP

You can also save a document as an Adobe PDF file so that others can view it without Excel.

5. Click the **Save as type** arrow. A list of file types opens.

6. Find and choose **XPS Document**. The same document name is assumed, but it will have a different extension.

7. Choose **Standard** as the **Optimize for** option. Click to deselect **Open file after publishing**.

8. Click **Options** and choose **Entire workbook** in the **Publish what** group. Click **OK** (see Figure 1-16).

9. Click **Save**. Your workbook is still open, and the XPS file is saved separately.

Figure 1-16
Saving an XPS
document

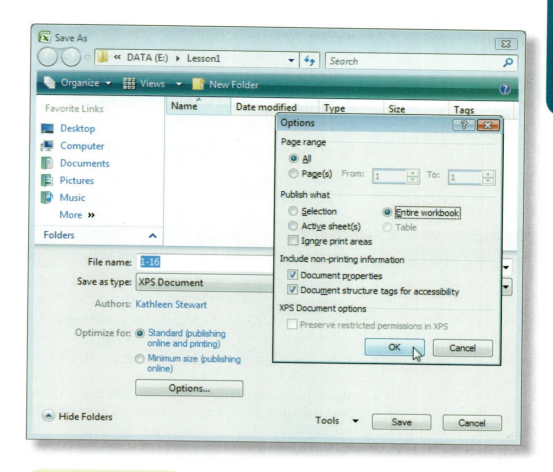

Exercise 1-17   EXIT EXCEL

You can exit Excel and close the workbook at the same time. If you give the command to exit Excel, you will see a reminder to save the workbook if you have not yet done so.

There are several ways to close a workbook and exit Excel:

- Click the Microsoft Office Button 🪟 and choose **Exit Excel**.

- Use the Close button ⓧ to first close the workbook and then to close Excel.

- Use the keyboard shortcut Alt + F4 to exit Excel.

1. Click the Microsoft Office Button 🪟.

2. Choose **Exit Excel**. Do not save changes if asked.

Using Online Help

Online Help is available at your computer and on the Microsoft Office Web site. An easy way to use Help is to key a short request in the search text box at the top of the opening screen.

GET ACQUAINTED WITH USING HELP

1. Start Excel and click the Microsoft Office Excel Help button 🔵 .

2. In the search box, key **get help** and press ⌴Enter⌴.

3. From the list of topics, find a topic that will explain how to use help and click it. Click **Show All**.

4. Read the information and close the Help window.

Lesson 1 Summary

- Excel opens with a blank workbook and the Ribbon. The active command tab on the Ribbon changes depending on what you are doing.

- A new workbook opens with three worksheets. A worksheet is an individual page or tab in the workbook.

- Press ⌴Ctrl⌴+⌴PageUp⌴ and ⌴Ctrl⌴+⌴PageDown⌴ to move between worksheets in a workbook.

- Worksheets are divided into cells, which are the intersections of rows and columns. The location of the cell is its address (also called its cell reference).

- Move the pointer to a specific cell with the Go To command or by clicking the cell.

- The active cell is outlined with a black border. It is ready to accept new data or a formula or to be edited.

- The Name Box shows the address of the active cell. You can also use it to change the active cell.

- If you use the scroll box or arrows to reposition the worksheet on the screen, the active cell does not change.

- The Zoom size controls how much of the worksheet you can see at once.

- Replace any entry in a cell by clicking the cell and keying new data. Edit long or complicated cell data rather than rekeying it.

- The Undo button 🔵 and the Redo button 🔵 both have history arrows so that you can undo or redo multiple commands at once.

- Preview your worksheet or the entire workbook before printing it. To preview and print all the worksheets in a workbook, click the Microsoft Office Button and choose Print. Then choose **Entire workbook**.

LESSON 1		Command Summary	
Feature	**Button**	**Task Path**	**Keyboard**
Collapse ribbon			Ctrl + F1
Clear cell contents		Home, Editing, Clear, Clear Contents	Delete
Close workbook	X	Microsoft Office, Close	Ctrl + W or Ctrl + F4
Exit Excel	X	Microsoft Office, Exit Excel	Ctrl + F4
Full Screen	Full Screen	View, Workbook Views, Full Screen	
Go To	Find & Select ▾	Home, Editing, Find & Select, Go To	Ctrl + G or F5
KeyTips			Alt or F10
Normal View	Normal	View, Workbook Views, Normal	
Open workbook		Microsoft Office, Open	Ctrl + O
Page Layout View	Page Layout View	View, Workbook Views, Page Layout View	
Print		Microsoft Office, Print	Ctrl + P
Print Preview	Print	Microsoft Office, Print, Print Preview	
Redo	↻ ▾		Ctrl + Y or F4
Save As		Microsoft Office, Save As	F12 or Alt + F2
Undo	↺ ▾		F2 + Z or Alt + Backspace
Zoom In	⊕		
Zoom Out	⊖		
Zoom Size	Zoom	View, Zoom	

Concepts Review

True/False Questions

Each of the following statements is either true or false. Indicate your choice by circling T or F.

T F   1. A worksheet contains at least one workbook.

T F   2. The Name Box shows the address of the active cell.

T F   3. The Zoom size for a particular worksheet is permanent.

T F   4. You can use the scroll bars to move the pointer to a specific cell.

T F   5. You can replace a cell's contents by clicking the cell and keying new data.

T F   6. You must use Windows Explorer to create a new folder.

T F   7. Edit mode starts when you press F2.

T F   8. If you click the Print button 🖨 while viewing a sheet in print preview, all worksheets in a workbook are printed.

Short Answer Questions

Write the correct answer in the space provided.

1. What is the name for the cell with a heavy black border that is ready to accept new data or a formula?

_____

2. Give an example of a cell address in the first column of a worksheet.

_____

3. What is the screen element that contains command tabs?

_____

4. What command enables you to use a different filename for a workbook as it is saved?

_____

5. What is the keyboard shortcut to move the pointer to cell A1?

_____

6. Which part of the Excel screen shows the contents of the active cell?

_____

7. How do you print all three sheets in a workbook with one command?

_____

8. What do you use to reposition the worksheet on the screen without changing the location of the active cell?

_____

Critical Thinking

Answer these questions on a separate page. There are no right or wrong answers. Support your answers with examples from your own experience, if possible.

1. You can replace or edit cell contents. Discuss when you might use each procedure.

2. Why should you use folders for organizing your files? Give examples of folder names that might be used in an auto dealership's office.

Skills Review

Exercise 1-18

Start Excel and navigate in a workbook.

NOTE

Prepare your answers to questions in the Skills Review exercises as instructed for submission to your instructor. Include your name, the exercise number, and the question number.

NOTE

If Excel is already running, press Ctrl + N to start a new workbook.

1. Start Excel and navigate in a workbook by following these steps:

   a. Turn on the computer and start Excel.

   b. Press Ctrl + PageDown two times. Which sheet is active?

   c. Drag the scroll box on the vertical scroll bar to the bottom of the scroll bar. What is the last row shown on the worksheet?

   d. Press Ctrl + PageUp two times. Which sheet is active?

   e. Press Ctrl + G and key a35. Press Enter. What appears in the Name Box?

   f. Press Tab. What is the active cell?

   g. Press Shift + Tab. What is the active cell?

NOTE

When there is no data on a worksheet, Ctrl+End goes to cell A1.

NOTE

This worksheet has an icon set, a conditional format. Values equal to or greater than 50 have a green circle; others have a yellow circle.

NOTE

Prepare your answers to questions in the Skills Review exercises as instructed for submission to your instructor. Include your name, the exercise number, and the question number.

h. Press Ctrl+Home. What is the active cell?

i. Press Ctrl+G, key **d15**, and press Enter. Press Ctrl+End. What is the active cell?

j. Press Alt. What is the KeyTip for the Formulas tab? Press Esc.

k. Press Ctrl+F1. What has happened?

l. Press Ctrl+F1 again.

m. Click the Close button ✕. Do not save the workbook if a message box appears.

Exercise 1-19

Open a workbook. Edit a worksheet.

1. Open a workbook by following these steps:
   a. Click the Microsoft Office Button and choose **Open**.
   b. Choose the drive and folder according to your instructor's directions.
   c. Find **MarAdv** and double-click it.

2. Edit a worksheet by following these steps:
   a. Press Ctrl+G, key **b5**, and press Enter.
   b. Key **2000** and press Enter. What is the new total for the Bremerton store?
   c. Click cell D10 and press Delete. What is the total for this week?
   d. Click the arrow next to the Undo button. What are the first two tasks listed?
   e. Press Esc.
   f. Click the Close Window button ✕. Choose **No** to discard your changes.

Exercise 1-20

Edit a worksheet. Manage files.

1. Open **MarAdv**.

2. Edit a workbook by following these steps:
   a. Click cell A2 and press F2. What is the current mode for your worksheet?

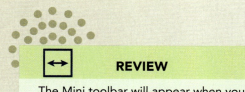

REVIEW

The Mini toolbar will appear when you select text for editing.

b. Double-click "March" and key **April**. Press ⌨Enter⌨. What is the active cell?

c. Double-click cell A11. How can you select or highlight the word "California"?

d. Delete "California." Delete the space before "W."

e. What key will finish your editing in cell A11?

3. Manage files by following these steps:

a. Click the Microsoft Office Button 🔘 and choose **Save As**. What folder appears in the navigation line?

b. Set the folder to **[your initials]Lesson1.** Where is this folder located?

c. In the **File name** box, make sure the original name is highlighted. If it is not, select the filename.

d. Key **[your initials]1-20** and press ⌨Enter⌨.

TIP

Click or double-click to select a filename with no spaces.

e. What filename appears in the title bar?

4. Click the Close Window button ⌨x⌨.

Exercise 1-21

Edit cells. Print a worksheet.

1. Open **MarAdv.**

2. Press ⌨F12⌨. Set the **Save in** folder to **[your initials]Lesson1.**

TIP

⌨F12⌨ is the keyboard shortcut for File, Save As.

3. In the **File name** box, select the filename. Key **[your initials]1-21** and press ⌨Enter⌨.

4. Edit cells by following these steps:

a. Click cell A2 and press ⌨F2⌨.

b. Double-click "March" and key **May**. Press ⌨Enter⌨.

c. Double-click cell A11. Double-click "California."

d. Key **Washington** and press ⌨Enter⌨.

e. Click cell F1. Key your first and your last name and press ⌨Enter⌨.

5. Print a worksheet by following these steps:

a. Click the Microsoft Office Button 🔘 and hover over **Print**.

b. Choose **Print Preview**.

c. Point near the main heading and click. Point anywhere and click again.

d. Click the Print button 🖨. Click **OK** in the dialog box.

6. Click the Close Window button ⌨x⌨.

7. Choose **Yes** to save changes.

Lesson Applications

REVIEW

Set the Zoom size so that you can see as much of the data as possible.

TIP

You do not need to key commas in this worksheet. They are part of the formatting.

NOTE

Numbers align at the right edge of a cell; text aligns at the left edge. You may see green triangles in cells C11 and D11 to mark formula errors.

NOTE

This sheet uses separator rows and columns with borders.

Exercise 1-22

Open a workbook. Edit and print a worksheet.

1. Open **JanIceCream**.

2. Edit cell A2 to show the current month.

3. Change the first week total for Modesto to **15500**.

4. Key your first and your last name in cell A20. Press `Ctrl`+`Home`.

5. Save the workbook as *[your initials]*1-22 in your Lesson 1 folder.

6. Prepare and submit your work. Close the workbook.

Exercise 1-23

Open a workbook. Edit a worksheet. Print a worksheet.

1. Open **BarSales**.

2. Without changing the en dash (–), edit cell B4 to show **2006–2008**.

3. Change the fourth quarter amount for 2007 to **55000**.

4. Key your first and your last name in cell A14. Press `Ctrl`+`Home`.

5. Save the workbook as *[your initials]*1-23 in your Lesson 1 folder.

6. Prepare and submit your work. Close the workbook.

TIP

It is good practice to position the pointer at cell A1 before saving so the worksheet opens with that cell as the active cell.

NOTE

The chart shows shades of gray for the bars on a non-color printer.

TIP

Start in cell B4 and press Enter to key the values down a column.

Exercise 1-24

Open and edit a workbook. Print a workbook.

1. Open **JuneIceCream**. This worksheet has data bars, another type of conditional format.

2. In cell F1 on the **WeeklySales** sheet, key your first and last name. Press Ctrl + Home.

3. In cell B18 on the **Owners** sheet, key your first and last name. Press Ctrl + Home.

4. Press Ctrl + P and select the option to print the entire workbook. Preview the workbook before printing it.

5. Save the workbook as *[your initials]*1-24 in your Lesson 1 folder.

6. Prepare and submit your work. Close the workbook.

Exercise 1-25 ◆ Challenge Yourself

Open a workbook. Edit worksheets. Print a workbook.

1. Open **JanIceCream**.

2. On the **WeeklySales** sheet, change the values for the first week as shown here.

3. In cell E1, key **Prepared by** *[your first and last name]*. Press Ctrl + Home. Preview and print the sheet.

4. On the **Owners** sheet, key your first and last name in cell C1. Press Ctrl + Home. Preview and print the sheet.

5. Save the workbook as *[your initials]*1-25 in your Lesson 1 folder.

6. Prepare and submit your work. Close the workbook.

Figure 1-17

	A	B
4	Anderson	12000
5	Auburn	14000
6	Chico	12000
7	Eureka	18000
8	Fairfield	15000
9	Modesto	16000
10	Red Bluff	11000
11	Redwood City	16000
12	Salinas	26000
13	San Francisco, 15th	24000
14	San Francisco, Lombard	24000
15	San Francisco, West	[Do not change]
16	Santa Rosa	19000
17	Watsonville	16000

On Your Own

In these exercises you work on your own, as you would in a real-life work environment. Use the skills you've learned to accomplish the task—and be creative.

Exercise 1-26

Open **JuneIceCream.** On the WeeklySales sheet, practice each of the navigation shortcuts shown in Table 1-2. On the Owners sheet, change each owner's name to someone you know. Include your own name as one of the owners. Print this worksheet. Save the workbook as *[your initials]*1-26 in your Lesson 1 folder. Prepare and submit your work. Close the workbook.

Exercise 1-27

Open **MarAdv.** Change the month to this month. Using the Internet or a map, change each city to a different city in your state. Change other labels to specify your state, too. Key your first and last name in cell A14. Save the workbook as *[your initials]*1-27 in your Lesson 1 folder. Prepare and submit your work.

Exercise 1-28

In the Open dialog box, experiment changing the views. Select and highlight the filename of each of the workbooks you used in this lesson (BarSales, JanIceCream, JuneIceCream, and MarAdv). Which of these files does not have a thumbnail preview? In the Excel Help system, look up document properties. Then open the Lesson 1 file(s) without a thumbnail and resave them with that property in your folder.

Lesson 2

Creating a Workbook

OBJECTIVES

After completing this lesson, you will be able to:

1. Enter labels.
2. Change the document theme.
3. Select cell ranges.
4. Modify column width and row height.
5. Enter values and dates.
6. Save a workbook.
7. Enter basic formulas.

MCAS OBJECTIVES

In this lesson:
XL07 1.3
XL07 1.5.3
XL07 2.1.1
XL07 2.1.3
XL07 2.2.2
XL07 2.2.4
XL07 2.3.2
XL07 2.3.4
XL07 3.1.1
XL07 3.2.1
XL07 5.4

Estimated Time: 1$\frac{1}{2}$ hours

A new workbook opens with three blank worksheets. You can key text, numbers, or formulas in any cell in any of the worksheets. Excel uses a default document theme in a new workbook, but you can change the theme or any formatting elements used in the worksheet. You can also adjust the width and height of columns, edit colors, and more.

Entering Labels

When you key data that begins with a letter, Excel recognizes it as a *label*. Labels are aligned at the left edge of the cell and are not used in calculations.

As you key data, it appears in the active cell and in the formula bar. If you make an error, press Esc to start over. You can also press Backspace to edit the entry.

There are several ways you can complete an entry.

TABLE 2-1 Ways to Complete a Cell Entry

Key or Button	Result
Press Enter	Completes entry and moves the pointer to the cell below.
Press Ctrl + Enter	Completes entry and leaves the pointer in the current cell.
Press Tab	Completes entry and moves the pointer to the cell to the right.
Press Shift + Tab	Completes entry and moves the pointer to the cell to the left.
Press an arrow key	Completes entry and moves the pointer one cell in the direction of the arrow.
Click another cell	Completes entry and moves the pointer to the clicked cell.
Click the Enter button ✓	Completes entry and leaves the pointer in the current cell.

Exercise 2-1   ENTER LABELS IN A WORKSHEET

1. Start Excel with a blank workbook. Cell A1 on **Sheet1** is active.

2. In cell A1, key **Klassy Kow Sa** to start a label. The worksheet is in Enter mode, shown in the status bar. The label appears in the formula bar and in the cell.

3. Press Backspace to delete **Sa**.

4. Key **Promotions**. Notice that an Enter button ✓ and a Cancel button ✗ appear in the formula bar when you are in Enter mode.

NOTE

The first new workbook in a work session is named **Book1** until you save it with another name. The next new workbook is **Book2**, and so on.

Figure 2-1
Label appearing in the formula bar and the cell

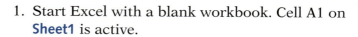
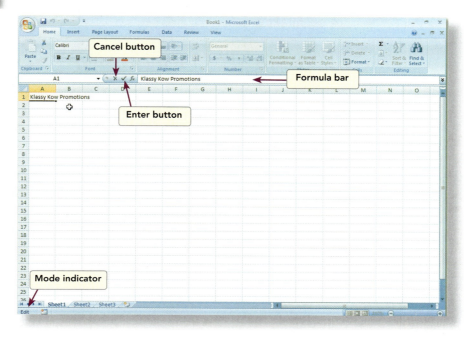

5. Press [Enter]. The label is completed in cell A1, and the pointer moves to cell A2. The label is longer than column A, so it appears to spill into columns B and C.

6. In cell A2, key **Market** to start a label. Press [Esc] to delete your entry. You can use [Esc] to delete an entry if you haven't yet pressed [Enter] or moved away from the cell.

7. Key **Company Plan** and click the Enter button 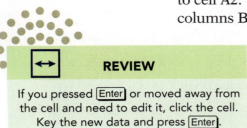 in the formula bar. The label appears to spill into cell B2.

8. Click cell A3 to make it active.

9. Key **Name** and press [→]. The pointer is now in cell B3.

10. Key **Starting Date** and press [Tab]. The label is too long for column B and spills into column C.

11. Key **Ending Date** in cell C3 and press [→]. This label cuts off the label from column B and spills into cell D3. You will fix these problems soon.

12. Key **Price** and press [Tab]. Key **Special Price** in cell E3 and press [Enter]. This label is not cut off, because there is nothing in the cell to the right.

13. Key the following labels in column A, starting in cell A4. Press [Enter] after each.

Berry Kowabunga
Easter Bunny Pie
Triple-Scoop Cone
24 oz. Shake

Changing the Document Theme

A *document theme* is a set of 2 fonts, 12 colors, and effects for shapes and charts. Each new workbook uses the Office document theme. The default body text font for this theme is 11-point Calibri. There is also a font for headings, Cambria.

Document themes have been developed by designers to use fonts, colors, and effects that are coordinated and balanced. You can use any of the themes, or you can choose any available font, color, or effect.

REVIEW

If you pressed [Enter] or moved away from the cell and need to edit it, click the cell. Key the new data and press [Enter].

NOTE

Text display can spill into adjacent cells only if they are empty.

NOTE

Although a theme includes 12 colors, 2 are for hyperlinks and do not appear in color palettes.

Exercise 2-2   CHANGE THE THEME

If you have used theme fonts in your worksheet, you can change the document theme and immediately see font changes applied from the new theme. The *Live Preview* feature allows you to see the changes before they are applied.

NOTE

Your font list probably does not match the one in the text illustration.

1. Click cell A1. Click the **Home** tab. Hover over the **Font** box in the **Font** group to see the ScreenTip.

2. Click the arrow next to the **Font** box. The theme fonts are at the top of the list, Cambria for headings and Calibri for body data. Other fonts on your computer are listed below these two.

Figure 2-2
Choosing a theme
font

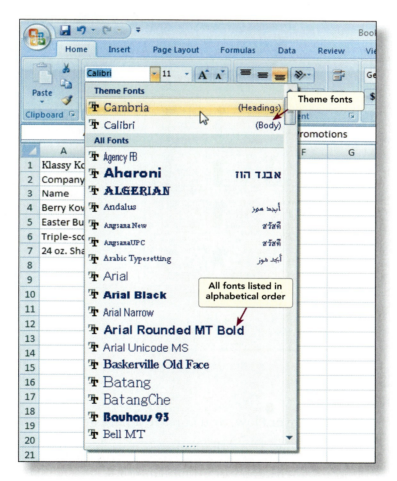

3. Choose **Cambria**. The label in cell A1 is changed.

4. Choose the Cambria font for the label in cell A2. Your data now uses Cambria for these two labels and Calibri for the remaining data. These are both theme fonts.

TIP

Calibri is a sans serif font; Cambria is a serif font. Serifs are tiny strokes at the end of a character.

5. Click the Zoom In button on the status bar four times. It will be easier to watch the changes in a larger view.

6. Click the **Page Layout** tab in the Ribbon. The first group is **Themes**.

7. Hover over the Themes button . The ScreenTip includes the current theme name.

8. Click the Themes button to open its gallery of built-in themes.

Figure 2-3
The Document
Theme gallery

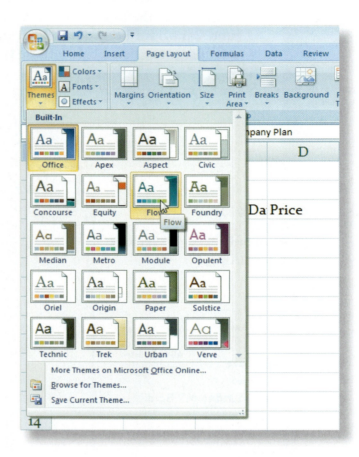

9. Hover over **Flow**. You can see a part of your data with the change.

10. Click **Flow**. The gallery closes, and the data uses new theme fonts.

11. Click the **Home** tab in the Ribbon.

12. Click the arrow next to the **Font** box. The theme fonts are Calibri for headings and Constantia for body text.

Exercise 2-3 CHANGE THE FONT, FONT SIZE, AND STYLE

You are not limited to the fonts in the document theme. You can use any font, font style, or size from the Font group on the Home tab or from the Format Cells dialog box. When you choose a larger font size, the height of the row is automatically made taller to fit the font. Font style includes bold, italic, and underline.

1. Click cell A1.

2. Click the arrow next to the **Font** box. A drop-down list box appears, showing font names for your computer.

3. Key **t** to move to the font names starting with "T." Live Preview shows the data in the new font as you scroll the list.

NOTE

You can also scroll in the Font list to a new font.

4. Find and choose **Times New Roman**.

5. Click the arrow next to the **Font Size** box. Choose **16**. Notice that row 1 is made taller to accommodate the larger font size.

Figure 2-4
Choosing a font size

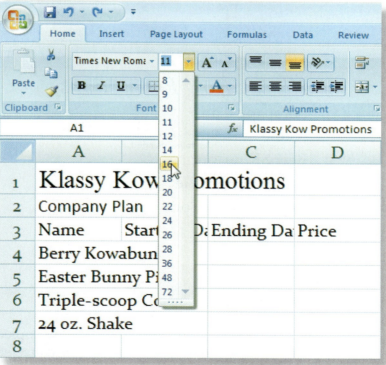

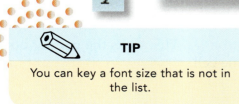

6. Click the Italic button.

TIP

You can key a font size that is not in the list.

Exercise 2-4   USE THE FORMAT PAINTER

With the Format Painter, you can copy cell formats from one cell to another. This is often faster than applying formats individually.

To use the Format Painter, make the cell with formatting the active cell. Then click the Format Painter button in the Clipboard group on the Home tab. While the pointer is a white cross with a small paintbrush, click the cell to be formatted.

1. Make sure cell A1 is the active cell. Click the **Home** tab if necessary.

2. Hover over the Format Painter button and read the ScreenTip.

3. Click the Format Painter button. Cell A1 shows a moving marquee, and the pointer is a thick white cross with a paintbrush.

Figure 2-5
Using the Format
Painter

4. Click cell A2. The font, size, and style are copied, and row 2 is made taller. The Format Painter command is canceled.

5. Make sure cell A2 is now the active cell.

6. Double-click the Format Painter button. This locks the painter on so that you can format more than one cell.

7. Click cell A3 to copy the format. Then click cell B3.

8. Click the Format Painter button to cancel the command.

9. Click the arrow next to the Undo button . Excel shows Format Painter as **Paste Special** in the Undo history list.

10. Undo two **Paste Special** commands. The labels in row 3 return to the theme font (11-point Constantia).

11. Press Esc to cancel the marquee.

12. Click the Zoom Out button to return to a 100% size.

Selecting Cell Ranges

A *range* is a group of cells that forms a rectangle on the screen. In many cases, you work with a range of cells. For example, you might need to format all the cells in rows 3 through 7 in the same style.

When a range is active, it is highlighted or shaded on the screen. Like an individual cell, a range has an address. A *range address* consists of the upper-left cell address and the lower-right cell address, separated by a colon.

TABLE 2-2 Examples of Range Addresses

Range Address	Cells in the Range
A1:B3	6 cells on 3 rows and in 2 columns
B1:B100	100 cells, all in column B
C3:C13	11 cells, starting at cell C3, all in column C
D4:F12	27 cells on 9 rows and in 3 columns
A1:XFD1	16,384 cells or the entire row 1

Exercise 2-5 SELECT RANGES WITH THE MOUSE

The *selection pointer* within the worksheet grid is a thick white cross shape. When you point at a row or column heading, the selection pointer appears as a solid black arrow. There are several ways to select a range of cells by using the mouse:

- Drag across adjacent cells to select the range.

- Click the first cell in the range. Hold down Shift and click the last cell in the range.

- Click a column heading letter to select a column or click a row heading number to select a row.

- Drag across adjacent column heading letters or row heading numbers to select multiple columns or rows.

- Click the Select All button 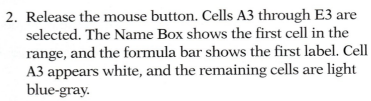 (see Figure 2-6) to select every cell on the worksheet.

1. With the thick white cross-shaped pointer, click cell A3 and drag to the right to cell E3.

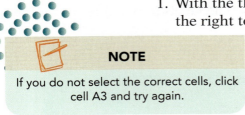

NOTE

If you do not select the correct cells, click cell A3 and try again.

2. Release the mouse button. Cells A3 through E3 are selected. The Name Box shows the first cell in the range, and the formula bar shows the first label. Cell A3 appears white, and the remaining cells are light blue-gray.

Figure 2-6
Selecting a range of cells

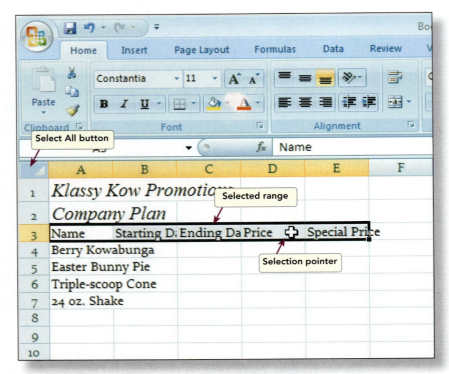

3. Click the Bold button **B**. The labels in the cells in the selected range are bold. Bold data is often slightly larger than data in the Regular style of the same font.

TIP

You can apply bold by using the keystroke combination Ctrl + B. You can apply italic by using Ctrl + I.

4. Click cell A1. This makes cell A1 active and deselects the range.

5. Click cell A1 and drag to cell F1. Do not release the mouse button.

6. Drag down to cell F3 and then release the mouse button. The selected range is A1:F3.

7. Click cell A1 to deselect the range and make cell A1 active again.

8. Point to the row 1 heading. The pointer changes shape and is a solid black arrow.

9. Click the row 1 heading to select the row.

10. Click cell B2. You can click any cell to deselect a range.

11. Point to the row 1 heading. Click and drag down through the row headings from row 1 to row 5.

12. Release the mouse button. Five rows are selected.

13. Click any cell to deselect the rows.

14. Click the column A heading. This selects the column.

15. Click any cell to deselect the column.

16. Click the column B heading and drag to the column G heading. This selects a range that includes all the cells in columns B through G.

17. Click cell B5. Hold down [Shift] and click cell E18. This is another way to select a range. This range is B5:E18.

Exercise 2-6   SELECT RANGES WITH KEYBOARD SHORTCUTS

You can select a range of cells by using keyboard shortcuts. These shortcuts work for selecting data in many Windows programs.

TABLE 2-3 Keyboard Shortcuts to Select Cell Ranges

Keystroke	To Do This
[Shift]+arrow key	Select from the active cell, moving in the direction of the arrow.
[Shift]+[Spacebar]	Select the current row.
[Shift]+[PageDown]	Extend selection from active cell down one screen in the same column.
[Shift]+[PageUp]	Extend selection from active cell up one screen in the same column.
[Ctrl]+[A]	Select the entire range with data or the entire worksheet.
[Ctrl]+[Spacebar]	Select the current column.
[Ctrl]+[Shift]+[Home]	Extend selection from active cell to beginning of data.
[Ctrl]+[Shift]+[End]	Extend selection from active cell to end of data.
[F8]	Start Extend Selection mode.
[F8]+arrow key	Extend selection from active cell in the direction of the arrow.
[Esc]	End Extend Selection mode.

1. Click cell A3. Hold down [Shift] and press [→] four times. The range is A3:E3.

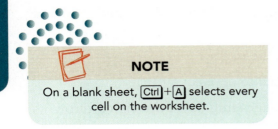

NOTE

On a blank sheet, Ctrl+A selects every cell on the worksheet.

2. Click the arrow next to the Font box. Key **c** and choose **Calibri** (or scroll to the font).

3. Click the arrow next to the Font Size box. Choose **14**.

4. Click the Bold button **B** to remove bold.

5. Click cell A1. Hold down Shift and press ↓ once. Choose **Calibri** for the font.

6. Click cell A3 and press F8. This starts Extend Selection mode. Notice that **Extend Selection** appears in the status bar.

7. Press → four times. Press ↓ to reach row 15. The range A3:E15 is selected.

8. Press Esc to cancel Extend Selection mode.

9. Click cell A3. Hold down Shift and click cell E15. This is another way to select the range.

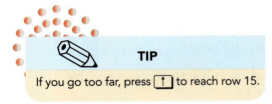

TIP

If you go too far, press ↑ to reach row 15.

10. Hold down Ctrl. Click cell A17 and drag across to cell E17.

11. Release the Ctrl key. Two different-sized ranges that are not next to each other are selected at the same time.

Figure 2-7
Selecting two ranges

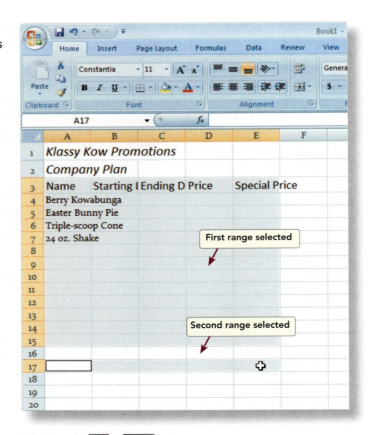

12. Press Ctrl+Home.

Modifying Column Width and Row Height

In a new workbook with the Office document theme, columns are 8.43 spaces (64 pixels) wide. If the column on the right is empty, a label larger than 8.43 spaces spills into it so that you can see the entire label on screen.

If the column on the right is not empty, you can widen the column so that the label is not cut off.

Rows in a new workbook are 15.00 points (20 pixels) high to fit the default 11-point Calibri font. A *point* is 1/72 inch. Generally Excel resizes the row height as needed, but you can size it manually, too.

Here are the ways you can resize column widths and row heights:

NOTE

If you change the document theme before keying any data, column width and row heights are set for the new theme.

- Drag a column or row border to a different size.

- Double-click a column's right border to AutoFit the column. *AutoFit* means the column is widened to fit the longest entry in the column.

- Double-click a row's bottom border to AutoFit the row height. A row is AutoFitted to fit the largest font size currently used in the row.

- On the Home tab in the Cells group, click the Format button ⊞ Format ▾ and then choose Row Height or Column Width.

When you use the mouse to change the row height or column width, you will see the size in a ScreenTip. For rows, the height is shown in points (as it is for fonts) as well as in pixels. For columns, the width is shown in character spaces and in pixels. A *pixel* is a screen dot, a single point of color on the screen. A *character space* is the average width of a numeric character in the standard font used in the worksheet.

If you use Ribbon commands to change the column width or row height, you must key the entry by using points for row height or character spaces for column width.

Exercise 2-7   MODIFY COLUMN WIDTH

1. Place the pointer on the vertical border between the column headings for columns A and B. The pointer changes to a two-pointed arrow with a wide vertical bar.

2. Drag the sizing pointer to the right until the ScreenTip shows **15.63 (130 pixels)** and release the mouse button. At this width, the column should be wide enough for the longest promotion item.

Figure 2-8
Resizing columns

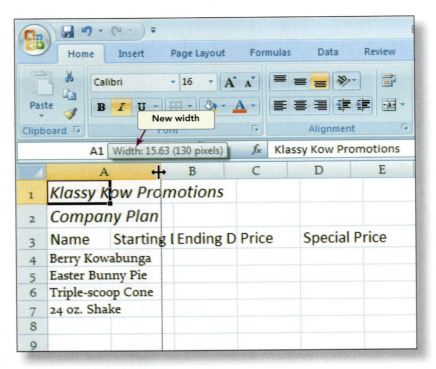

TIP

Be careful about AutoFitting columns that include titles in rows 1 or 2. Excel will AutoFit a column to accommodate long labels.

Format ▾

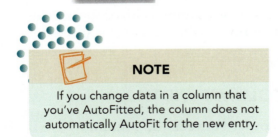

NOTE

If you change data in a column that you've AutoFitted, the column does not automatically AutoFit for the new entry.

3. Place the pointer between the column headings for columns B and C. Double-click. Excel AutoFits column B to fit the label.

4. Double-click the border between the column headings for columns C and D. Excel AutoFits column C.

5. Click anywhere in column D.

6. In the **Cells** group, click the Format button Format ▾ and then choose **Column Width**. The Column Width dialog box opens.

7. Key **10** and press Enter. The column width is changed to 10 spaces.

8. Double-click the border between the column headings for columns E and F to AutoFit column E.

Exercise 2-8   **MODIFY ROW HEIGHT**

1. Place the pointer on the horizontal border between the headings for rows 3 and 4. The pointer turns into a two-pointed arrow.

2. Drag down until the ScreenTip shows **22.50 (30 pixels)** and release the mouse button.

Figure 2-9
Resizing rows

3. Click anywhere in row 4.

4. In the **Cells** group, click the Format button ![Format] and then **Row Height**. The Row Height dialog box opens.

5. Key **22.5** and press Enter. The row is 22.5 points (30 pixels) high.

Entering Values and Dates

When you key an entry that starts with a number or an arithmetic symbol, Excel assumes it is a *value*. A value is right-aligned in the cell and is included in calculations. Arithmetic symbols include =, −, and +.

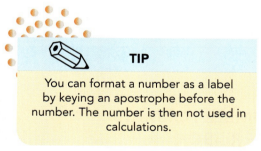

TIP

You can format a number as a label by keying an apostrophe before the number. The number is then not used in calculations.

Exercise 2-9   **ENTER DATES AND VALUES**

Excel recognizes dates if you key them in a typical date style. For example, if you key "1/1/08," Excel formats it as a date. Dates have special formats and can be used in date arithmetic.

Excel 2007

1. Click cell B4.

2. Key **12/1/08** and press ⌷Enter⌷. Excel recognizes the numbers as a date and shows four digits for the year. If SmartTags are enabled, you will see an indicator in the lower-right corner of the cell. Ignore the indicator for now.

3. Continue keying the following dates in column B. Press ⌷Enter⌷ after each one:
   3/15/08
   8/1/08
   10/15/08

4. Key these dates in cells C4:C7:
   12/31/08
   4/15/08
   8/31/08
   11/15/08

5. Click cell D4. Drag to select cells D4:E7. With the range selected, you can press ⌷Enter⌷ to move from cell to cell, going top to bottom and then left to right.

6. Key the prices shown in the "Price" and "Special Price" columns in Figure 2-10.

Figure 2-10
Worksheet data
entry completed

	A	B	C	D	E	F
1	*Klassy Kow Promotions*					
2	*Company Plan*					
3	Name	Starting Date	Ending Date	Price	Special Price	
4	Berry Kowabunga	12/1/2008	12/31/2008	3.19	2.99	
5	Easter Bunny Pie	3/15/2008	4/15/2008	24.99	20.99	
6	Triple-scoop Cone	8/1/2008	8/31/2008	3.29	2.99	
7	24 oz. Shake	10/15/2008	11/15/2008	3.29	2.99	
8						

Exercise 2-10   APPLY NUMBER FORMATS FROM THE RIBBON

If you key only a value, it is formatted in a General style. This style shows only digits, no commas. If the value has a decimal point, it is shown with as many places after the decimal point as you key.

To increase the readability of your worksheet, you can apply common formats from the Ribbon. You first select the range of cells to be formatted and then click a task button in the Ribbon.

1. Click cell D4. Drag to select cells D4:E7.

2. In the **Number** group, click the Accounting Number Format button. The cells in the range are formatted to show a dollar sign and two decimal places. The dollar signs are aligned at the left edge of the cell.

Exercise 2-11   APPLY DATE FORMATS FROM THE DIALOG BOX

Excel includes many date formats in the Format Cells dialog box. You can open the Format Cells dialog box for the active cell or range by:

- Pressing Ctrl+1.

- Right-clicking the cell or range and choosing Format Cells from the shortcut menu.

- On the Home tab in the Cells group, clicking the Format button and then choosing Format Cells.

1. Click cell B4. Click and drag to select cells B4:C7.

2. Point at any of the selected cells and right-click. A shortcut menu opens with the Mini toolbar.

3. Choose **Format Cells**. The Format Cells dialog box opens; it should show the appropriate tab and category.

4. Click the **Number** tab if necessary.

5. Click **Date** in the **Category** list on the left if necessary. Many preset date formats are displayed in the **Type** box on the right.

6. Click a type in the list that shows the date first, a hyphen, an abbreviation for the month, another hyphen, and a two-digit year (example "14-Mar-01") and click **OK**. (See Figure 2-11 on the next page.) All of the dates are reformatted.

Figure 2-11
Choosing a date
format

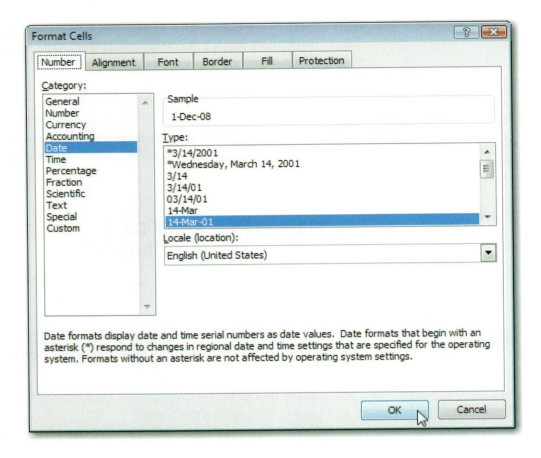

NOTE

Two-digit years between 00 and 29 are assumed to be the twenty-first century (2000, 2001, 2015). Two-digit years between 30 and 99 are assumed to be the twentieth century (1930, 1950, and 1999).

NOTE

Two theme colors are for hyperlinks. These colors do not appear in the palettes. The color swatches in the palette have ScreenTips indicating the color's purpose, intensity, or name.

Exercise 2-12   CHANGE THE FONT COLOR

In addition to changing the font, size, and style, you can set a new font color. The document theme includes 12 colors and various intensities (or saturations) of that color. You can also choose from standard colors, too. You can change the font color for a selected cell or range by:

- On the Home tab in the Font group, clicking the Font Color button.

- Opening the Format Cells dialog box and choosing the Font tab.

1. Select cells E4:E7 (the special prices).

2. Click the Font Color button. The color shown on the button is applied to the selected range, probably red.

3. Click the arrow next to the Font Color button. A color palette opens with 10 theme colors in the top row. The first 4 are text/background colors; the remaining 6 are accent colors. Standard colors are near the bottom of the palette.

4. Hover over several colors anywhere in the palette and watch the live preview in the worksheet.

5. Click **Dark Teal, Text 2** in the fourth column, first row. This is one of the theme colors. The palette closes, and the color is applied to the selected range.

6. Select cells A1:A2.

7. Press Ctrl + 1 and click the **Font** tab.

8. Click the arrow for **Color**. The same theme colors are listed as well as the standard colors.

9. Choose **Dark Teal, Text 2** and click **OK**.

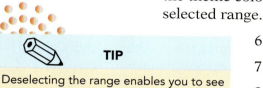

TIP

Deselecting the range enables you to see the color more clearly.

Figure 2-12
Changing the color from the Format Cells dialog box

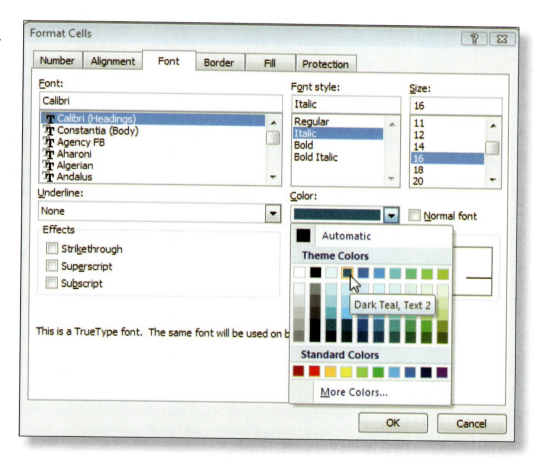

Exercise 2-13   RENAME A WORKSHEET AND CHANGE THE TAB COLOR

You can rename a worksheet tab with a more descriptive name to help you and others remember the worksheet's purpose. Worksheet names can be up to 31 characters. You can use spaces in the name of a worksheet tab.

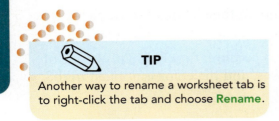

TIP

Another way to rename a worksheet tab is to right-click the tab and choose **Rename**.

1. Double-click the worksheet tab for **Sheet1**. The tab name is selected.

2. Key **Promos** and press ⎕Enter.

3. Double-click **Sheet2** and name it **Plans**. The **Plans** sheet is empty.

4. Right-click the **Promos** tab and choose **Tab Color**. The Theme Colors dialog box opens with the palette of colors.

5. Choose **Dark Teal, Text 2** as the tab color.

Figure 2-13
Changing the tab color

6. Click the **Plans** tab. Now you can see the color of the **Promos** tab better.

7. Click the **Promos** tab to make it the active sheet.

Saving a Workbook

When you create a new workbook or make changes to an existing one, you must save the workbook to keep your changes. Until you save your changes, your work can be lost if there is a power failure or computer problem.

To save a workbook, you must first give it a filename. A *filename* is the file identifier you see in the Open dialog box, Computer, or Windows Explorer. When you name a file in Windows, you can use up to 255 characters. Included in those 255 characters are the drive and folder names, so the actual filename is really limited to fewer than 255 characters. Generally, it is a good idea to keep filenames as short as possible.

You can use uppercase or lowercase letters, or a combination of both, for filenames. Windows is case-aware, which means it does recognize uppercase and lowercase that you key. However, it is not case-sensitive, so it does not distinguish between "BOOK1" and "book1." You can use spaces in a filename, but you cannot use the following characters: \ ?: * " <> |

Filenames are followed by a period and a three- or four-letter extension, supplied automatically by the software. Excel 2007 workbooks have the extension ".xlsx." Extensions identify the type of file.

For a new workbook, you can use either the Save or the Save As command to save and name the workbook. When you make changes to an existing workbook and want to save it with the same filename, use Save. If you want to save a workbook with a different filename, use Save As.

Excel saves workbooks in the current drive or folder unless you specify a different location. You can easily navigate to the appropriate location in the Save dialog box.

Throughout the exercises in this book, filenames consist of two parts:

NOTE

You may not see filename extensions if your Folder Options (Organize button in the Explorer dialog box) are set to hide them.

- *[your initials]*, which might be your initials or an identifier your instructor asks you to use, such as **kms**

- The number of the exercise, such as **2-14**

TIP

Wherever the pointer is when you save a workbook is where it appears the next time you open the workbook.

Exercise 2-14   SAVE A WORKBOOK

Depending on how difficult it would be to redo the work, you should save your file every 15 to 30 minutes.

1. Click cell A1.

2. Click the Save button 🖫 on the Quick Access toolbar.

3. Choose the appropriate drive and folder location.

4. Click the New Folder button .

5. Key *[your initials]***Lesson2** and press Enter. The location is updated to your folder.

NOTE

Your instructor will tell you what drive/folder to use to save your workbooks.

6. In the **File name** box, double-click **Book1** and key *[your initials]***2-14**.

7. Click **Save**. The title bar shows the new filename.

Entering Basic Formulas

A *formula* is an equation that performs a calculation on values in your worksheet and displays an answer. You key a formula in a cell. After you press a completion key, the formula results appear in the cell. The formula itself is visible in the formula bar.

Formulas are one of the main reasons for using Excel, because a formula performs calculations for you. If you later change any of the numbers used for the calculations, Excel quickly recalculates the formula to show a revised answer.

Formulas begin with an = sign as an identifier. After the = sign, you enter the address of the cells you want to add, subtract, multiply, or divide. Then you use *arithmetic operators* in the 10-key pad or at the top of the keyboard to complete the calculation. You probably recognize all of the arithmetic operators shown in Table 2-4, with the possible exception of exponentiation. The *exponentiation* operator raises a number to a power. For example, 2^3 represents 2 to the third power, or 2^3, which means $2 \times 2 \times 2$ or 8.

> **NOTE**
>
> Arithmetic operations are calculated in a specific order: first, exponentiation; second, multiplication and division; and finally, addition and subtraction.

TABLE 2-4 Arithmetic Operators

Key or Symbol	Operation
^	Exponentiation
*	Multiplication
/	Division
+	Addition
–	Subtraction

Exercise 2-15   KEY A BASIC FORMULA

In your workbook, you can calculate the difference between the regular price and the promotion price. This is a simple subtraction formula. You will be working in column F. If you cannot see column F, set your Zoom size to a smaller size so you can see it.

1. Click cell F3. Key **Difference** and press [Enter]. The label is formatted with the same style as other labels in the row.

2. Double-click the border between the column headings for columns F and G to AutoFit column F.

3. Key **=d** in cell F4 to start the formula. *Formula AutoComplete* shows a list of built-in formulas that begin with the letter "d." You can continue keying your own formula for now.

>
> **NOTE**
>
> Excel applies the same format to a cell in which you are entering data as the three or more cells to the immediate left or top of the cell.

Figure 2-14
Formula
AutoComplete list
2-14.xlsx
Promos sheet

	A	B	C	D	E	F	G
	Klassy Kow Promotions						
	Company Plan						
	Name	Starting Date	Ending Date	Price		Special Price	Difference
	Berry Kowabunga	1-Dec-08	31-Dec-08	$ 3.19	$ 2.99	=d	
	Easter Bunn	Returns the number that represents the date in Microsoft Office Excel date-time code				_fx_ DATE	
	Triple-scoop Cone	1-Aug-08	31-Aug-08	$ 3.29	$ 2.99	_fx_ DATEVALUE	
	24 oz. Shake	15-Oct-08	15-Nov-08	$ 3.29	$ 2.99	_fx_ DAVERAGE	

_fx_ DAY
_fx_ DAYS360
_fx_ DB
_fx_ DCOUNT
_fx_ DCOUNTA
_fx_ DDB
_fx_ DEC2BIN
_fx_ DEC2HEX
_fx_ DEC2OCT

4. Key **4-e4** in cell F4. You'll see another Formula AutoComplete list when you key **e**. Your formula should be **=d4-e4** and it appears in the cell and in the formula bar. The cells used in the formula are outlined in colors that match the colors of the formula in the cell.

Figure 2-15
Keying a formula
2-14.xlsx
Promos sheet

_fx_ =d4-e4

B	C	D	E	F
motions				
Starting Date	Ending Date	Price	Special Price	Difference
1-Dec-08	31-Dec-08	$ 3.19	$ 2.99	=d4-e4
15-Mar-08	15-Apr-08	$ 24.99	$ 20.99	
1-Aug-08	31-Aug-08	$ 3.29	$ 2.99	
15-Oct-08	15-Nov-08	$ 3.29	$ 2.99	

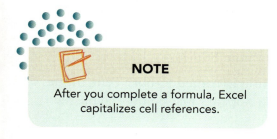

NOTE

After you complete a formula, Excel capitalizes cell references.

5. Press Enter. The difference in price is 20 cents. It is shown in the same number format as the cells used in the formula.

6. Press ↑ to return to cell F4. Notice that the formula bar shows the formula, but the cell displays the result of the formula.

Exercise 2-16 ENTER A FORMULA BY POINTING

You can use the mouse to point to cells used in a formula. This increases accuracy, because you don't have to worry about keying the wrong cell address.

1. Click cell F5. Key **=** to start the formula.

2. Click cell D5. The address appears in cell F5 and in the formula bar. Cell D5 has a moving marquee.

3. Key **–** to subtract the next cell.

4. Click cell E5. It is placed in the formula after the minus sign and now has the moving marquee.

Figure 2-16
Entering a formula
by pointing
2-14.xlsx
Promos sheet

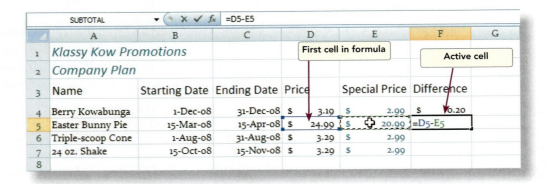

5. Click the Enter button ✓ in the formula bar. The difference of $4 is calculated.

Exercise 2-17 COPY A FORMULA BY USING THE COPY AND PASTE BUTTONS

The formula in cell F5 is the same as the one in cell F4 except for the row references. The formula is relative to its location on the worksheet. When you copy a formula with row or cell references, Excel makes this adjustment automatically.

1. Click cell F5. Click the Copy button 📋. The cell now has a moving marquee. The status bar tells you to select the destination for the copy.

2. Click cell F6 and drag to select the range F6:F7.

3. Click the Paste button 📋. The formula is copied to both cells in the range. The Paste Options button 📋 appears just below the pasted data.

4. Hover over the Paste Options button 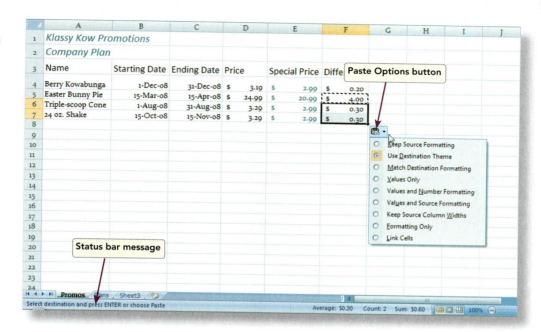. A down arrow appears next to the button. Click the down arrow; options for copying the data are listed. You need not change the option.

Figure 2-17
Copying a formula
2-14.xlsx
Promos sheet

5. Press [Esc] twice to cancel the moving marquee and finish the Paste command.

6. Click cell F6 and review the formula. Notice that Excel has adjusted the formula to take into account the relative position of the cell.

7. Click cell F7. Review the formula. Excel has adjusted it as well.

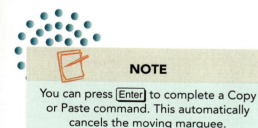

NOTE

You can press [Enter] to complete a Copy or Paste command. This automatically cancels the moving marquee.

NOTE

The screen resolution at your computer affects how a button looks. It may include an icon and text, and the text may be below or next to the button. Check the ScreenTip when in doubt.

Exercise 2-18　USE AUTOSUM, AVERAGE, AND MAX

Some calculations are so common in business and personal use that Excel includes them as functions. A *function* is a built-in formula in Excel. An example of a function is "SUM," in which Excel automatically totals a column or row. A function starts with =, just like a formula. Excel has several "auto" functions available on the Formulas tab and the Home tab.

TABLE 2-5 Function Library Group

Button	Action
Insert Function	Opens the Insert Function dialog box
AutoSum	Displays the sum, average, count, maximum, or minimum of selected cells
Recently Used	Lists the most recently used functions
Financial	Displays a list of financial functions
Logical	Displays a list of logical functions
Text	Displays a list of text functions
Date & Time	Displays a list of date and time functions
Lookup & Reference	Displays a list of lookup and reference functions
Math & Trig	Displays a list of mathematical and trigonometry functions
More Functions	Displays a list of statistical, engineering, cube, and information functions

TIP

Click the AutoSum button, not its arrow.

1. Click the **Formulas** tab in the Ribbon. The Function Library group includes buttons for each major function category.

2. Click cell F8. Click the AutoSum button ⟨Σ AutoSum ▾⟩ in the Function Library group. A formula is placed in the cell followed by the range that will be summed. A moving marquee surrounds cells that will be summed. A ScreenTip for the function appears.

Figure 2-18
Using AutoSum
2-14.xlsx
Promos sheet

3. Press Enter. The formula is completed.

4. Click cell F8. Notice that the formula includes the function name SUM and an assumed range in parentheses.

5. Click cell D8.

6. Click the arrow with the AutoSum button Σ AutoSum ▾ .

7. Choose **Average**. The AVERAGE function appears in the formula bar and in the active cell. A moving marquee surrounds the cells in the assumed range.

8. Press Ctrl + Enter to complete the function. Notice that now the formula includes the function name AVERAGE and the range of cells that is averaged.

9. Click cell D9. Click the arrow with the AutoSum button Σ AutoSum ▾ .

10. Choose **Max**. A moving marquee surrounds the cells that will be used by the MAX function. The MAX function is used to determine the largest value in a range.

11. Click cell D4 and drag to select the range D4:D7. Don't include cell D8 in this function, because it is the average you just calculated.

12. Press Ctrl + Enter. The result of the formula shows the highest price in the column.

TIP

There is a Sum button in the Editing group on the Home tab. Both buttons are called AutoSum in this text.

NOTE

The SUM function adds the values in the cells. The AVERAGE function adds the values in the range and then divides by the number of cells in the range.

NOTE

Functions ignore titles in a column/row because they are not values; they are labels, which are not used in calculations.

Exercise 2-19   CHECK RESULTS WITH AUTOCALCULATE

The *AutoCalculate* feature displays formula results for a selected range in the status bar. AutoCalculate can display sums, averages, counts, maximums, or minimums. You set AutoCalculate choices by right-clicking the status bar.

1. Right-click the status bar. Verify that there are check marks for **Average**, **Count**, and **Sum**. Press Esc.

2. Select the range F4:F7. AutoCalculate shows the average, a count, and the sum for the selected range in the status bar.

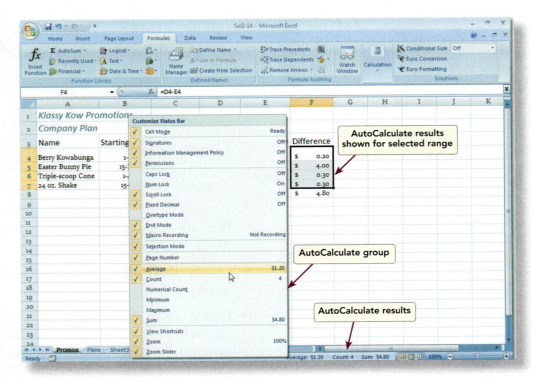

3. Right-click the status bar and click to select **Minimum** and **Maximum**. Press [Esc].

4. Select the range D4:D7. AutoCalculate shows more information about these cells.

5. Select cells A4:A7. These are labels, so AutoCalculate only shows a count.

6. Right-click the status bar and click to deselect **Minimum** and **Maximum**. Press [Esc].

7. Key your first and last name in cell A10.

8. Press [F12] and save the workbook as *[your initials]2-19* in your Lesson 2 folder.

9. Prepare and submit your workbook.

10. Close the workbook.

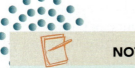

NOTE

Your instructor will tell you how to submit your work for each lesson. Lesson 1 includes exercises with steps detailing how to print your work or save it as an XPS file.

Using Online Help

Building basic formulas is an important skill. You will use it as the basis for becoming a proficient Excel user.

LOOK UP FORMULAS

1. Start Excel and click the Microsoft Office Excel Help button 🔘.

2. Click in the Search box, key **create formula**, and press Enter.

3. In the list of topics, find and click a topic related to creating a formula.

4. Click **Show All** at the top of a Help window to expand all explanations.

5. When you finish investigating formulas, close the Help window.

Lesson 2 Summary

- In a blank workbook, you can key values, labels, dates, or formulas. Excel recognizes data by the first character you key in the cell.

- Labels are aligned at the left edge of a cell. If they are longer than the column width, they spill into the next column if it is empty. Otherwise, they appear cut off on the screen.

- To complete a cell entry, press Enter, Tab, or any arrow key or click another cell. You can also click the Enter button ✓ in the formula bar.

- New workbooks use the Office document theme. The default font for data is 11-point Calibri. You can change the font, the font size, the color, and the style.

- Use the Format Painter to copy formats from one cell to other cells.

- Many commands require that you first select a range of cells. You select a range of cells by using the mouse or keyboard shortcuts.

- The default row height matches the default font size in the document theme. The row height adjusts if you choose a larger font.

- Common formats, such as Accounting, can be applied to cells from the Number group on the Home tab. Many other formats are available in the Format Cells dialog box.

- It's usually a good idea to change the default worksheet tab name to a more descriptive name. You can also change the worksheet tab color for visual cues.

- You must save a new workbook to keep your work. For a new workbook, you can use the Save or the Save As command.

- To create a formula in a cell, you can key it or you can construct it by pointing to the cells used in the formula. All formulas begin with the = symbol.

- When you copy a formula, Excel adjusts it to match the row or column where the copy is located.
- Excel has functions for common calculations such as Sum, Average, Maximum, Minimum, and Count.
- You can see results for common functions without keying a formula if you use AutoCalculate.

LESSON 2		Command Summary	
Feature	**Button**	**Task Path**	**Keyboard**
Accounting Number	$ ▾	Home, Number	
AutoSum	Σ AutoSum ▾	Formulas, Function Library	
Column Width	Format ▾	Home, Cells, Format, Column Width	
Copy		Home, Clipboard	Ctrl + C
Font		Home, Font	Ctrl + 1
Font Color	A ▾	Home, Font	Ctrl + 1
Font Size		Home, Font	Ctrl + 1
Format Painter		Home, Clipboard	
Paste	Paste	Home, Clipboard	Ctrl + V
Rename sheet	Format ▾	Home, Cells, Format, Rename Sheet	
Row Height	Format ▾	Home, Cells, Format, Row Height	
Save		Microsoft Office, Save	
Tab color	Format ▾	Home, Cells, Format, Tab Color	
Themes	Themes	Page Layout, Themes	

Concepts Review

True/False Questions

Each of the following statements is either true or false. Indicate your choice by circling T or F.

T   F   1. If you key **ABC Company** in a cell, Excel will recognize it as a label.

T   F   2. When text is too long for a row, it spills to the next row.

T   F   3. A range is a rectangular group of cells.

T   F   4. Formulas must be keyed in the formula bar.

T   F   5. Common number formats are shown as buttons on the Page Layout tab.

T   F   6. The AutoSum button includes options for other common functions.

T   F   7. AutoCalculate and AutoSum both display results in a cell.

T   F   8. If you copy a formula from one cell to another, Excel changes it to match the new row and column.

Short Answer Questions

Write the correct answer in the space provided.

1. What symbol is used to start a formula?

   _____

2. Describe how to rename a worksheet tab.

   _____

3. What is included in a document theme?

   _____

4. If the pointer is in cell B3 as you key a label and you want to key a label in cell C3, what key can you press to go directly to cell C3?

   _____

5. Give an example of a range address.

   _____

6. What function key starts Extend Selection mode?

   _____

7. How can you AutoFit a column to the longest text in it?

_____

8. List three arithmetic operators that might be used in a formula.

_____

Critical Thinking

Answer these questions on a separate page. There are no right or wrong answers. Support your answers with examples from your own experience, if possible.

1. A new workbook opens with three worksheets. Give examples of how you might use different sheets in the same workbook if you worked in the office for a movie theater.

2. Why does Excel have different data types such as values, labels, and dates? What are some of the differences among these types?

Skills Review

Exercise 2-20

Enter labels. Change the font and the document theme.

1. Create a workbook and enter labels by following these steps:

   a. Press Ctrl+N. This opens a new workbook.

   b. Double-click the **Home** tab to collapse the Ribbon.

   c. Key the labels shown in Figure 2-20.

REVIEW

Press Backspace to correct errors in a cell, or press Esc to start over. Remember that labels in some cells might spill over to other cells.

Figure 2-20

	A	B	C	D	E
1	Klassy Kow Ice Cream				
2	Ice Cream Pie Sales for September				
3		1st Qtr	2nd Qtr	3rd Qtr	4th Qtr
4	Chocolate				
5	Vanilla				
6	Strawberry				
7	Turtle				

2. Change the font by following these steps.

    a. Click cell A1. Click the **Home** tab.

    b. Click the down arrow next to the Font box. Key **c** and choose **Cambria**.

    c. Click the down arrow next to the Font Size box. Choose **18**.

    d. Click cell A2 and change it to 14-point Cambria.

3. Key your first and last name in cell A9. Press [Ctrl]+[Home].

4. Save the workbook as *[your initials]2-20a* in your Lesson 2 folder.

5. Change the document theme by following these steps.

    a. Click the **Page Layout** tab in the Ribbon.

    b. Click the Themes button.

    c. Choose **Concourse**.

    d. Click the Microsoft Office Button. Point at the **Print** arrow and choose **Print Preview**. Close the preview.

6. Save the workbook as *[your initials]2-20b* in your Lesson 2 folder.

7. Prepare and submit your work. Close the workbook.

NOTE

Follow your class procedures for submitting work.

Exercise 2-21

Select cell ranges. Change the font and the document theme.

1. Open **CakeSales** and click the **CakeSales** worksheet tab.

2. Press [F12] and save the workbook as *[your initials]2-21* in your Lesson 2 folder.

3. Select cell ranges and change the font by following these steps:

    a. Click cell A1 and drag to select cells A1:A2. Change the size to 16.

    b. Click cell B3 and press [F8] to start Extend Selection mode.

    c. Press [End].

    d. Click the Bold button. Change the font size to 12 points.

    e. Click cell A4 and press [F8]. Press [Ctrl]+[↓]. Then press [Ctrl]+[→].

    f. Change the font size to 10 points.

4. Key your first and last name in cell A9. Press [Ctrl]+[Home].

5. Click the Microsoft Office Button. Choose **Print** and then **Quick Print**. This worksheet prints with row and column headings.

6. Change the document theme by following these steps.

    a. Click the **Page Layout** tab. Click the Themes button. Choose the **Urban** theme.

    b. Click cell B3 and press [F8] and then [End].

    c. Change the font to the headings font for this document theme.

d. Click cell A4 and press [F8]. Press [Ctrl]+[→]. Then press [Ctrl]+[↓]. Change the font size to 11 points.

e. Click the Microsoft Office Button ⬤. Point at the **Print** arrow and choose **Print Preview**. Close the preview.

f. Click the Save button 🖫. This resaves the workbook with the same name.

7. Prepare and submit your work. Close the workbook.

Exercise 2-22

Set column width and row height. Enter and format values and dates.

1. Open **PromoPlans**. Press [F12] and save the workbook as *[your initials]*2-22 in your Lesson 2 folder.

2. Set column width and row height by following these steps:

NOTE

This worksheet uses the Oriel document theme.

a. Place the pointer on the border between the column headings for columns A and B.

b. Drag the pointer to the right to **17.86 (130 pixels)**.

c. Click the column B heading and drag to select columns B through F.

d. Double-click the border between the column headings for columns F and G to AutoFit the selected columns.

e. Click the row heading for row 3. Drag to select rows 3 through 7.

f. Drag the bottom border for row 7 to **22.50 (30 pixels)**.

3. Enter the values and dates shown in Figure 2-21. Ignore SmartTag Options buttons that may appear.

Figure 2-21

	B	C	D	E	F
4	3/3/08	4/15/08	3.29	2500	2500
5	9/1/08	9/30/08	20.99	950	1800
6	1/15/09	1/31/09	3.19	4000	4700
7	5/1/08	5/31/08	2.99	3500	3900

4. Format values and set font colors by following these steps:

a. Select the range E4:F7. Press [Ctrl]+[1].

b. Click the **Number** tab. Choose **Number** in the **Category** list.

c. Click the down spinner arrow for **Decimal places** to reach **0**.

d. Click to select the **Use 1000 Separator** (,) box and click **OK**.

e. Select the range D4:D7.

f. Click the Accounting Number Format button on the Home tab.

g. Select the range B4:C7. In the **Number** group, click the Dialog Box Launcher. Click the **Number** tab. Choose **Date** in the **Category** list.

h. Choose the format in the **Type** list that spells out the month, shows a comma after the date, and four digits for the year. Click **OK**.

5. Key your first and last name in cell A9 and press Ctrl + Home.

6. Double-click the **Sheet1** tab and key **PricePromos**. Press Enter.

> **NOTE**
>
> Currency format from the Format Cells dialog box uses a floating currency symbol; the symbols are to the immediate left of the first digit.

7. Click the Save button .

8. Prepare and submit your work. Close the workbook.

Exercise 2-23

Save a workbook. Enter labels and values. Enter and copy formulas.

1. Save a workbook by following these steps:

   a. Press Ctrl + N to create a new workbook.

   b. Double-click the **Sheet1** tab. Key **MediaPlans** and press Enter.

   c. Right-click the **MediaPlans** tab and choose **Tab Color**. Choose **Accent 2** from the top row.

   d. Click the Save button . Find and choose your Lesson 2 folder.

   e. Key *[your initials]*2-23 in the **File name** box. Click **Save**.

2. Enter labels and values by following these steps:

   a. In cell A1, set the font for 16-point Cambria.

   b. Key **Klassy Kow Media Schedule** and press Enter.

   c. Select the range A2:D2 and set the font to 12-point Calibri bold italic.

   d. In cell A2, key **Media** and press Enter.

   e. In cell B2, key **Frequency**. In cell C2, key **Cost per Ad**. In cell D2, key **Total** and press Enter.

   f. Click the column B heading and drag to select columns B through D.

   g. Double-click the border between the column headings for columns D and E to AutoFit the selected columns.

   h. Place the pointer on the border between the column headings for columns A and B. Drag the pointer to the right to **15.00 (110 pixels)**.

> **NOTE**
>
> You can click the Microsoft Office Button, choose New, and then choose Blank Workbook to create a new workbook. New workbooks use the Office theme.

> **TIP**
>
> You can set the font for selected cells before keying data.

> **REVIEW**
>
> If you AutoFit column A, the column will be sized to accommodate the label in cell A1.

i. Key the labels and values shown in Figure 2-22.

Figure 2-22

	A	B	C
3	WOW Radio	15	150
4	Channel 3 Cable	10	125
5	Star Newspaper	4	105
6	Clipper Mailer	1	200

   j. Click the row heading for row 1. Drag to select rows 1 through 6. Drag the bottom border for row 6 to **22.50 (30 pixels)**.

3. Enter and copy a formula by following these steps:
   a. Click cell D3. Key **=** to start the formula.
   b. Click cell B3.
   c. Key ⬚ to multiply the next cell.
   d. Click cell C3. Press Enter.
   e. Click cell D3 and click the Copy button 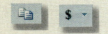 in the Clipboard group.
      f. Click cell D4 and drag to select cells D4:D6. Press Enter to complete the copy.

4. Select cells C3:D6. Click the Accounting Number Format button ⬚.

5. Key your first and last name in cell A9. Press Ctrl + Home.

6. Click the Save button ⬚.

7. Prepare and submit your work. Close the workbook.

REVIEW

Accounting format aligns the dollar signs at the left edge of the cell and adds two decimal places.

Lesson Applications

Exercise 2-24

Enter and format labels and values. Enter and copy a formula.

1. Open **WeeklySales**. Save it as *[your initials]*2-24 in your Lesson 2 folder.

2. Key these labels in the specified cells:
   - **A1** **Klassy Kow Ice Cream**
   - **A2** **Specialty Pie Sales**
   - **A3** **March 31, *<and the current year>***

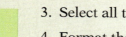

REVIEW

Press [Ctrl]+[1] to format the date.

3. Select all three cells and make them 16-point Cambria.

4. Format the date to show the month spelled out, the date, a comma, and four digits for the year.

5. Make column A **20.71 (150 pixels)** wide.

6. Select cells B5:E8. Key the values shown in Figure 2-23, pressing [Enter] to move in a top-down, left-right direction.

Figure 2-23

4		Week 1	Week 2	Week 3	Week 4	Total
5	Turtle Candy	10	30	50	80	
6	Rainbow	20	40	60	20	
7	Neapolitan	20	10	30	10	
8	Cookie Crunch	30	50	20	30	

7. Make the labels in row 4 bold. Change the height of rows 4 through 8 to **22.50 (30 pixels)**.

8. Click cell F5 and use AutoSum. Copy the formula in cell F5 to cells F6:F8.

9. Key your first and last name in cell A10. Return the pointer to cell A1.

10. Change the tab name to **SpecialtyPies** and choose a tab color.

11. Prepare and submit your work. Save and close the workbook.

Exercise 2-25

Enter labels and format data. Use a formula. Save a workbook.

1. Open **PieSales**.

2. Select cells B9:E9 and click the AutoSum Σ AutoSum ⏷ button.

3. Key an appropriate label in cell A9 and make it bold.

4. Set the font size for this row to match the other data rows.

5. In cell F4, key **Year Totals**. Copy the format from another label and widen the column.

6. Select cells F5:F9 and use AutoSum. Set the font size to match.

7. Select all the values and use the Format Cells dialog box to set **Number** format with no decimals and the thousands separator.

8. Make the totals in row 9 and in column F bold.

9. Rename the worksheet **Pies**. Choose a color for the tab.

10. Change to the **Metro** theme.

11. Key your first and last name in cell A12. Preview the worksheet.

12. Make cell A1 the active cell, and save the workbook as *[your initials]*2-25 in your Lesson 2 folder.

13. Prepare and submit your work. Close the workbook.

> **NOTE**
>
> When you select multiple cells for AutoSum, there is no moving marquee and you do not need to press Enter. You can use the AutoSum button on the Formulas or the Home tab.

Exercise 2-26

Enter and copy a formula. Save a workbook.

1. Open **MediaPlans**. Save it in your Lesson 2 folder as *[your initials]*2-26.

2. In cell E4, use a formula to multiply "# of Times Run" by "Individual Cost." Copy the formula to appropriate cells.

3. Use AutoSum in cell E10. Set the values in column E to match the color used in the main label and borders.

4. Match the row height for rows 5 through 10 to that of row 3. Check for other problems that you should fix.

5. Rename the sheet **MediaPlans**. Choose the tab color to match the font and borders.

6. Key your first and last name in cell A13.

7. Preview the worksheet. Return the pointer to cell A1.

8. Prepare and submit your work. Save and close the workbook.

> **NOTE**
>
> This sheet uses narrow columns and short rows as separators for adding borders.

Exercise 2-27 ◆ Challenge Yourself

Create a workbook. Enter and format labels and values. Enter formulas.

1. In a new workbook, name **Sheet1** as **DailySales**.

2. Choose a document theme and then choose a tab color. Save the workbook as *[your initials]*2-27 in your Lesson 2 folder.

3. Key the following labels in the specified cells with the Headings font for your theme:
   A1   Klassy Kow Ice Cream Shops
   A2   Daily Double Scoop Sales in *<your home city>*
   B3   Friday
   C3   Saturday
   D3   Sunday

NOTE

If you type a flavor name that begins with a *k*, *d*, or the same letter as one of your other flavors, you might see an AutoComplete ScreenTip. Ignore it and continue typing.

4. In cells A4 through A8, key the names of five flavors of ice cream, one in each cell.

5. Decide how to format these labels.

6. Key values to show how many double-scoop cones were sold on each day. Format the values with no decimals and with a thousands separator.

7. Key **Number of Flavors** in cell A9 and then use **Count Numbers** from the AutoSum options in cell B9.

8. Key your first and last name in cell A12. Return the pointer to cell A1. Preview the worksheet. Prepare and submit your work.

9. Save the workbook and close it.

On Your Own

In these exercises you work on your own, as you would in a real-life work environment. Use the skills you've learned to accomplish the task—and be creative.

Exercise 2-28

Open **MediaPlans**. Change the names in column A to the names of radio stations, TV stations, newspapers, or magazines in your city. Key a new cost for a weekday ad for each medium. Change to the Verve theme. Add your name and the exercise number to the worksheet. Make sure all data is visible and save the workbook as *[your initials]*2-28 in your Lesson 2 folder. Prepare and submit your work and close the workbook.

Exercise 2-29

Sketch on paper a worksheet with the names of five people in your class or with whom you work. List each person's city, phone number (with area code in parentheses), and birthday. Determine a main title and titles for the columns.

Create a workbook based on your sketch. Format it attractively. Add your name and the exercise number to the worksheet. Save it as *[your initials]*2-29 in your Lesson 2 folder. Prepare and submit your work and close the workbook.

Exercise 2-30

Look through a print or Internet catalog and list five products to purchase. In a new workbook, list the product name, the store or Web site, and the price for each product. Add a quantity column to show how many of each item you would purchase. Create a formula to show what it would cost to buy your items (do not include sales tax or shipping charges). Decide how to format your sheet. Add your name and the exercise number to the worksheet. Save it as *[your initials]*2-30 in your Lesson 2 folder. Prepare and submit your work.

Using Editing and Style tools

After completing this lesson, you will be able to:

1. Use AutoCorrect and Error Checking.

2. Check spelling.

3. Use Find and Replace.

4. Use series and AutoFill.

5. Apply table and cell styles.

6. Prepare headers and footers.

Estimated Time: 1¹/₂ hours

MCAS OBJECTIVES

In this lesson:
XL07 1.1.1
XL07 1.1.2
XL07 1.3
XL07 2.1.2
XL07 2.3
XL07 2.4.1
XL07 5.5.1
XL07 5.5.3
XL07 5.5.4

Excel has many tools to increase your accuracy. Excel finds and flags common types of formula errors. It has electronic dictionaries that correct spelling errors as you type. Other tools enable you to quickly find and replace data or formats and to fill in data automatically.

Using AutoCorrect and Error Checking

AutoCorrect makes spelling corrections as you type. It recognizes common errors such as "teh," and changes it to "the." It capitalizes the days of the week and the months and corrects capitalization errors, such as THis. You can also set it to enter routine data automatically.

AutoCorrect makes its change when you press the spacebar, the Enter key, or a punctuation mark.

Exercise 3-1   USE AUTOCORRECT TO CORRECT ERRORS

The **KowaSales** workbook measures sales of the Kowabunga ice cream novelty over a three-year period. For the years 2008 and 2009, a percentage increase is estimated.

NOTE

As you key the labels for this exercise, be sure to key the errors that are shown.

1. Open **KowaSales**. The Kowabunga worksheet has a two-color scale applied to columns F and G.

2. Double-click the Home tab to collapse the ribbon. This provides more working space.

Figure 3-1
Keying a deliberate error
KowaSales.xlsx
Kowabunga sheet

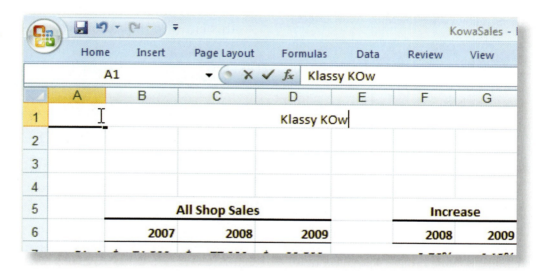

3. In cell A1, key **KLassy KOw** and press Spacebar. The two incorrect uppercase letters are corrected. Notice that horizontal centering is preset for cell A1.

4. Key **Ice Cream Shops** to complete the label. Press Enter.

5. Key **saturday and sunday Sales** and press Enter. As you can see, AutoCorrect capitalizes the days of the week.

6. Double-click the Home tab. Select cells A1:A2 and set them to Cambria 18 point.

NOTE

This workbook uses the Office document theme. Cambria is the headings font; Calibri is for body text.

7. In cell A3, change the font to 9-point Calibri.

8. Key **these aer sales fro all Kowagunga flavors**. Press Enter. Not all errors are found by AutoCorrect. "Aer" and "fro" have not been corrected, and neither has "Kowagunga." Leave these errors for now.

Exercise 3-2   SET AUTOCORRECT OPTIONS

If you key "acn," AutoCorrect changes your typing to "can." If "ACN" were the initials of an employee or a company, you would want to delete this correction from AutoCorrect. You can also add new corrections to AutoCorrect.

1. Click the Microsoft Office Button 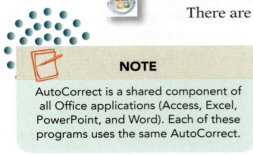 and choose **Excel Options**. There are nine panes with features that can be customized.

2. Choose **Proofing**. Click **AutoCorrect Options**. The errors and corrections in AutoCorrect are listed in alphabetical order.

3. In the **Replace** box, key **kk**. Press Tab.

4. In the **With** box, key **Klassy Kow**. Click **Add** to add this entry to the AutoCorrect list. Click **OK**.

> **NOTE**
>
> AutoCorrect is a shared component of all Office applications (Access, Excel, PowerPoint, and Word). Each of these programs uses the same AutoCorrect.

Figure 3-2
AutoCorrect dialog box

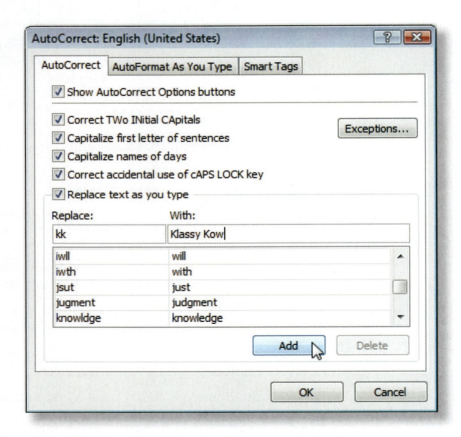

5. Click **OK** to close the Excel Options dialog box.

6. Click cell B25, key **kk**, and press Spacebar. The initials are changed to "Klassy Kow."

7. Key **Marketing Department** to finish the label. Press Enter.

8. Click the Microsoft Office Button 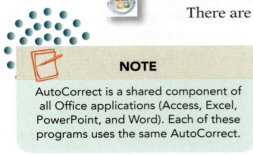 and choose **Excel Options**. Choose **Proofing**. Click **AutoCorrect Options**.

9. In the **Replace** box, key **kk** to move to the "Klassy Kow" entry.

10. Click **Delete** to remove the entry. Click **OK**.

> **NOTE**
>
> You have been instructed to delete the "Klassy Kow" AutoCorrect entry so that students in other classes can use the computer without having this entry listed among the AutoCorrect entries.

11. Click **OK** to close the Excel Options dialog box.

12. Click cell G25, key **kk**, and press [Enter]. The initials are not changed, because the entry has been deleted from AutoCorrect.

13. Delete the contents of cells B25 and G25.

14. Press [Ctrl]+[Home].

Exercise 3-3   REVIEW ERROR CHECKING

Excel automatically alerts you to problems with formulas by showing an error indicator and an Error Checking Options button. The error indicator is a small green triangle in the top-left corner of the cell. The Error Checking Options button is a small exclamation point within a diamond. It appears when you click the cell with the error indicator. When an error indicator warns of a potential error, you can review the type of error, fix it, or ignore the error.

> **NOTE**
>
> If you do not see error indicators, click the Microsoft Office Button and choose Excel Options. In the Formulas pane, select Enable background error checking.

1. Click cell B11. The Error Checking Options button appears to the left of the cell.

2. Position the mouse pointer on the Error Checking Options button to see a ScreenTip.

3. Click the arrow next to the button. Its shortcut menu opens. The first menu item explains the error, that the formula omits adjacent cells. Excel assumes that a SUM formula in cell B11 would sum the cells directly above, cells B6:B10. However, the formula is correct because the year in cell B6 should not be included in the formula.

Figure 3-3
Error Checking options
KowaSales.xlsx
Kowabunga sheet

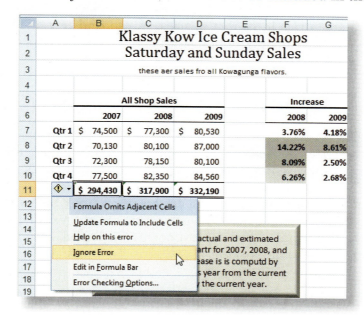

4. Choose **Ignore Error**. The small triangle is removed.

5. Click the **Formulas** command tab. There are four command groups on this tab.

6. In the Formula Auditing group, click the Error Checking button . The Error Checking dialog box opens with the next error noted, cell C11. This formula is correct.

Figure 3-4
Error Checking
dialog box
**KowaSales.xlsx
Kowabunga sheet**

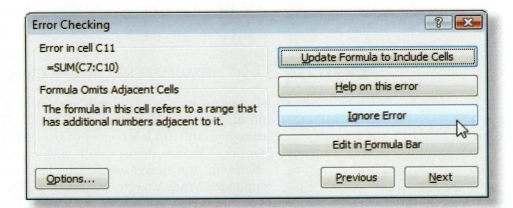

7. Click **Ignore Error** in the dialog box. The error triangle in cell C11 is removed. Cell D11 is flagged.

8. Click **Ignore Error**. A message box notes that error checking is complete.

9. Click **OK**. Press Ctrl + Home.

Checking Spelling

Excel's Spelling feature scans the worksheet and finds words that do not match entries in its dictionaries. It also finds repeated words. The Spelling dialog box provides options for handling errors. These options are described in Table 3-1.

Exercise 3-4　SPELL-CHECK A WORKSHEET

Excel starts spell-checking at the active cell and checks to the end of the worksheet. When the spell-checker reaches the end of the worksheet, a dialog box opens, asking if you want to continue spell-checking from the beginning of the worksheet.

　The **Kowabunga** worksheet has a text box below the data with several spelling errors. A text box is used for special text displays and notations. If you accidentally click the text box in this lesson, click any cell away from the box to continue working.

TABLE 3-1 Spelling Dialog Box Options

Command	Action
Ignore Once	Do not change the spelling of this occurrence of the word. If it is a repeated word, do not delete one of the words.
Ignore All	Do not change the spelling of any occurrences of the word. If it is a repeated word, do not delete the double word.
Add to Dictionary	Add this word to the dictionary so that Excel will not regard it as misspelled.
Change	Replace the current spelling with the highlighted alternative in the **Suggestions** box.
Delete	Appears only for repeated words. Click to delete one occurrence of the word.
Change All	Replace the current spelling with the highlighted alternative every time this mis-spelling occurs.
AutoCorrect	Add the misspelled word with its correction to the AutoCorrect list.
Undo Last	Reverse/undo the last spelling correction.
Options	Offers choices for changing the dictionary language, ignoring uppercase and words with numbers, and ignoring Internet addresses.

TIP

You can select a range of cells and then click the Spelling button to spell-check only that range.

1. Click the **Review** command tab. Three command groups on this tab are used to examine and annotate your worksheet.

2. Click the Spelling button. Excel finds "worksht" in the text box. It offers a suggestion for the correct spelling.

Figure 3-5
Spelling dialog box
KowaSales.xlsx
Kowabunga sheet

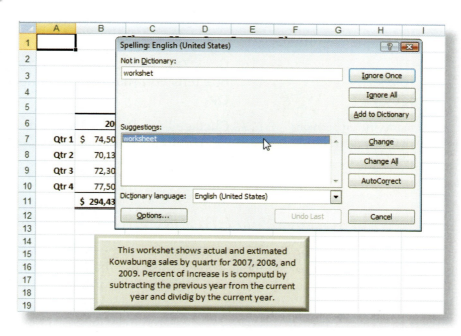

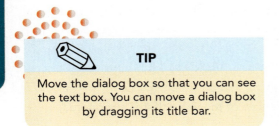

3. Double-click **worksheet** in the **Suggestions** list. A double-click is the same as clicking the word and then clicking **Change**. The correction is made, but you will not see it until you close the Spelling dialog box.

4. The next error is "extimated." Double-click **estimated** in the **Suggestions** list. "Kowabunga" in the text box is next. This word is correct.

5. Click **Ignore Once**. The word "quartr" appears next in the text box.

6. Double-click **quarter** in the **Suggestions** list. The next error is a **Repeated Word**, two occurrences of the word "is."

7. Click **Delete** to remove one occurrence of the word.

8. Correct "computd" and "dividng."

9. Excel shows "Klassy" in the **Not in Dictionary** box and offers one suggestion for the correct spelling. Since this is how the company spells its name, you can ignore all occurrences of this spelling.

10. Click **Ignore All**. Excel will ignore any more occurrences of "Klassy" in this worksheet. The word "Kow" is the next error. This is the same issue.

11. Click **Ignore All**. The word "aer" appears next with a list of possible corrections.

12. Click **are** in the **Suggestions** list and click **Change**. The next error is "Kowagunga."

13. Click in the **Not in Dictionary** box. There are no suggestions, but you can key the correction.

14. Edit the spelling to **Kowabunga** in the **Not in Dictionary** box.

15. Click **Change**. A message box notes that this word is not in the dictionary.

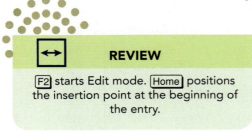

16. Click **Yes**. When Spelling is complete, a message box tells you that the spell check is complete. Click **OK**.

17. Click cell A3. Press F2 and press Home. Spelling has not found all errors in this sheet.

18. Capitalize **These** and change "fro" to **for**. Press Enter.

Using Find and Replace

You use the Find command to locate a *character string,* a sequence of letters, numbers, or symbols. You can also use the Find command to locate formats, such as everything in the worksheet that is bold.

You can use wildcards in a Find command when you are not sure about spelling or want to find a group of data. A *wildcard* is a character that represents one or more numbers or letters. Excel recognizes two common wildcard characters:

- * Represents any number of characters

- ? Represents any single character

TIP

If you want to find a word or value that includes an asterisk or a question mark, precede the wildcard with a tilde (~). For example, "25~*" would find **25***.

The character string "ce*" would find everything in the worksheet that includes the characters "ce" followed by any number of letters or values. This might include "central," "nice," and "ocean." The character string "s?t" would locate entries that have an "s" followed by any character and a "t." Examples are "sit," "reset," and "S4T."

There are two ways to start the Find command:

- Click the Find & Select button 📖 in the Editing group on the Home tab and choose **Find**.

- Press Ctrl+F or Shift+F5.

The Replace command locates occurrences of a character string and substitutes a replacement string. A *replacement string* is a sequence of characters that is exchanged for existing data. The Replace command can also search for a format, replacing it with another format.

There are two ways to start the Replace command:

- Click the Find & Select button 📖 in the Editing group on the Home tab and choose **Replace**.

- Press Ctrl+H or Shift+F5.

Find and Replace share a dialog box, so you can actually use any of these four methods to start either command.

Exercise 3-5 FIND DATA

In the Find and Replace dialog box, you can choose whether to search the worksheet or the workbook. You can search by column or row. If you know that the name you are looking for is in column A or B, it is faster to search by column. You can also choose to search formulas or the value results. Other options let you match capitalization or the entire cell contents. The Find command searches cells. It does not search *objects* in a worksheet such as the text box in **KowaSales**.

In Find and Replace character strings, do not key format symbols such as the dollar sign or a comma.

NOTE

An object is a separate, clickable element or part of a worksheet.

1. Press Ctrl+Home.

2. Press Ctrl+F. The Find and Replace dialog box opens. Notice that each command has a separate tab.

3. Key **2008** in the **Find what** box.

4. Click **Find All**. The dialog box expands to list information about two cells that include this string of numbers. The first occurrence is outlined in the worksheet and highlighted in the list.

Figure 3-6
Find and Replace
dialog box, Find tab

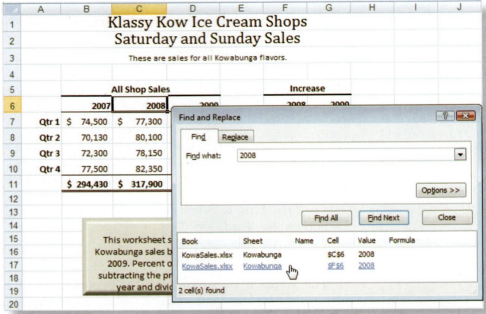

TIP

You can size the Find dialog box by dragging one of its corners.

5. Click the second cell identifier in the dialog box. The pointer moves to that cell in the worksheet.

6. Double-click **2008** in the **Find what** box and key **qtr**. Character strings you key in the **Find what** box are not case-sensitive unless you turn on the **Match case** option.

7. Click **Options >>**. The dialog box expands with additional settings.

8. Click the arrow next to the **Within** box. You can find data within the active sheet or the entire workbook.

NOTE

If the dialog box shows Options <<, it is expanded.

9. Choose **Sheet**.

10. Click the arrow next to the **Search** box. For many worksheets, you might not see much difference in speed if you search by columns or by rows.

11. Choose **By Rows**.

12. Click the arrow next to the **Look in** box. Excel searches the underlying formula or the values. A *comment* is a text message attached to a cell.

13. Choose **Formulas**.

14. Click **Find All**. Four cells include the "qtr" character string.

15. Drag the sizing handle at the lower-right corner of the dialog box to see the list.

Exercise 3-6   USE WILDCARDS

1. Double-click **qtr** in the **Find what** box and key ***500**. This character string is used to find all cells with an entry that ends in "500."

2. Click **Find All**. Two values in the worksheet match this character string.

3. Double-click ***500** in the **Find what** box and key **u*** (lowercase letter "U" and an asterisk). This character string is used to find all cells with an entry that includes the letter "u" followed by any number of other characters.

4. Click **Find All**. There are several cells with such entries. Some appear to be values.

5. Click the cell identifier for cell B11 in the dialog box. The value of **$294,430** is calculated from a SUM formula. That's the "u."

6. Click the arrow next to the **Look in** box. Choose **Values**.

7. Click **Find All**. The Values option checks the actual contents of the cells.

8. Double-click **u*** and key **t?e** in the **Find what** box.

9. Click **Find All**. There is one cell that includes this three-letter string.

10. Select **Match entire cell contents**. Click **Find All**. There are no cells that contain only this string. The message box says that Excel cannot find data to match.

11. Click **OK** to close the message box. Click **Close** to close the Find and Replace dialog box.

NOTE

Cell addresses in the Find and Replace dialog box are shown with dollar signs ($) to indicate an absolute reference. Absolute references are covered in another lesson.

Exercise 3-7   REPLACE DATA

You can replace a character string one occurrence at a time or all at once. Sometimes replacing them all at once can be a problem, because you might locate some character strings you didn't anticipate.

1. Press Ctrl+Home to make cell A1 active.

2. Press Ctrl+H. The same Find and Replace dialog box opens, this time with the **Replace** tab active. Excel remembers your most recent Find character string.

3. Double-click **t?e** in the **Find what** box and key **2009**.

4. Click in the **Replace with** box and key **2010**. This will change occurrences of "2009" to "2010."

5. Click to deselect **Match entire cell contents**.

6. Click **Find Next** to locate the first occurrence of "2009."

Figure 3-7
Find and Replace
dialog box,
Replace tab

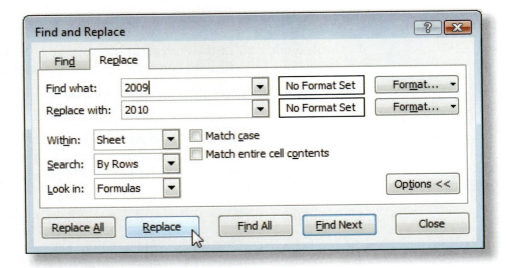

7. Click **Replace** to change "2009" to "2010." Excel locates the next occurrence.

8. Click **Replace**. The replacement is made.

9. Click **Replace**. There are no more occurrences of "2009."

10. Click **OK** in the message box.

Exercise 3-8   REPLACE A FUNCTION IN A FORMULA

1. Double-click **2009** in the **Find what** box and key **sum**.

2. Click **Find All**. Excel locates three cells with the SUM function.

3. Double-click **2010** in the **Replace with** box and key **avg**. This is not the correct spelling for the AVERAGE function.

4. Click **Replace**. The first occurrence is replaced. The cell shows **#NAME?**, a type of error.

5. Click **Replace All**. Two more replacements are made.

6. Click **OK**. You have replaced all instances of "sum" with a misspelled function name.

7. Click **Close** to close the Find and Replace dialog box. You will correct the errors in the next exercise.

Exercise 3-9   CORRECT ERRORS WITH REPLACE

1. Click cell B11. Position the pointer on the Error Checking Options button ⬥.

2. Click the arrow next to the button. This is an **Invalid Name Error**. The name of the function is "average," not "avg."

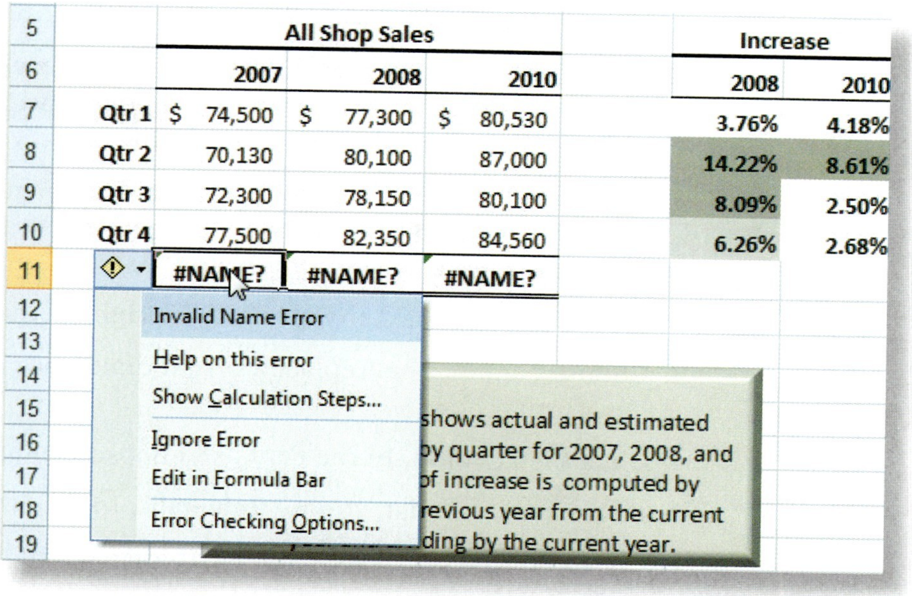

Figure 3-8
Error messages
KowaSales.xlsx
Kowabunga sheet

5		All Shop Sales			Increase	
6		2007	2008	2010	2008	2010
7	Qtr 1	$ 74,500	$ 77,300	$ 80,530	3.76%	4.18%
8	Qtr 2	70,130	80,100	87,000	14.22%	8.61%
9	Qtr 3	72,300	78,150	80,100	8.09%	2.50%
10	Qtr 4	77,500	82,350	84,560	6.26%	2.68%
11	◇ ▾	#NAME?	#NAME?	#NAME?		

Invalid Name Error

<u>H</u>elp on this error

Show <u>C</u>alculation Steps...

Ignore Error

Edit in <u>F</u>ormula Bar

Error Checking <u>O</u>ptions...

...shows actual and estimated
...by quarter for 2007, 2008, and
...of increase is computed by
...revious year from the current
...ding by the current year.

3. Click cell B11 to close the shortcut menu.

4. Press Ctrl + H. Double-click in the **Find what** box and key **avg**.

5. Press Tab. In the **Replace with** box, key **average**, the correct spelling.

6. Click **Find All**. All the cells with the misspelled function are listed.

7. Click **Replace All**. The replacements are made, and the function is now correct.

8. Click **OK** and then click **Close**. Another Error Checking Options button ◈ has appeared.

9. Click cell B11 and display the Error Checking Options menu. The AVERAGE function assumes that all cells immediately above the cell with the function should be included in the range, cells B6:B10. Cell B6 is the year and should not be included.

10. Drag to select the range B11:D11. Position the mouse pointer on the Error Checking Options button ◈. Click the arrow and choose **Ignore Error**.

Exercise 3-10   FIND AND REPLACE FORMATS

In addition to finding or replacing characters, you can find and replace formats. For example, you can find labels and values that are 11-point bold Calibri and change them to bold italic. When you replace formats, you should not show any text or numbers in the Find what or Replace with boxes.

1. Press Ctrl + Home. Press Ctrl + H.

2. Double-click in the **Find what** box and press Delete. The box is empty.

3. Double-click in the **Replace with** box and press Delete.

Excel 2007

4. Click the arrow next to **Format** to the right of the **Find what** box.

5. Click **Choose Format From Cell**. The dialog box closes, and the pointer shows the selection pointer with an eyedropper. This pointer will copy the format of the cell to the dialog box.

6. Click cell A7. The dialog box expands. The format from cell A7 (11-point bold Calibri) is shown in the **Preview** area for **Find what**. These cells are also right-aligned.

7. Click the arrow next to **Format** to the right of the **Replace with** box.

8. Choose **Format**. The Replace Format dialog box opens. You can set a new format here.

9. Click the **Font** tab. In the **Font** list, choose **Cambria (Headings)**.

10. In the **Font style** list, choose **Bold Italic**. In the **Size** list, choose **11**.

11. Click **OK**. The previews show what format will be found and how it will be replaced.

12. Click **Find All**. Four cells are listed.

Figure 3-9
Replacing formats

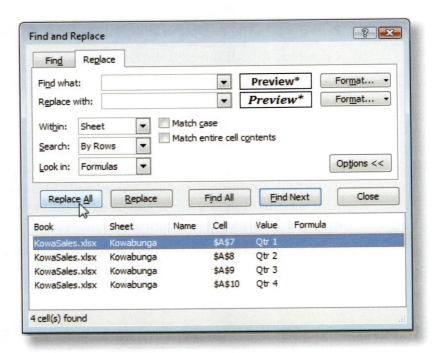

13. Click **Replace All**. The replacements are made.

14. Click **OK** and then click **Close**. The labels in row 5 include a centering command, so they were not matched. Values in row 6 include top and bottom borders, and the other values include some type of number formatting.

NOTE

You can click the Close button ✕ to close the Find and Replace dialog box.

Exercise 3-11 RESET FIND AND REPLACE FORMATS

After replacing formats, you should reset the dialog box. If you don't, the formats will be in effect the next time you use Find and Replace and could affect your results.

1. Press Ctrl+H.

2. Click the arrow next to **Format** for the **Find what** box.

3. Click **Clear Find Format**. The area shows **No Format Set**.

4. Click the arrow next to **Format** for the **Replace with** box.

5. Click **Clear Replace Format**. Click **Close**.

Using Series and AutoFill

A *series* is a list of labels, numbers, dates, or times that follows a pattern. The days of the week are a series that repeats every seven days. Months repeat their pattern every 12 months. These are common series that Excel recognizes if you key a label in the series.

You can create your own series by keying two values or labels to set an interval or pattern. The *interval* is the number of steps between numbers or labels. For example, the series "1, 3, 5, 7" uses an interval of two because each number is increased by 2 to determine the next number. The series "Qtr 1, Qtr 2, Qtr 3" uses an interval of one.

Exercise 3-12 CREATE MONTH AND WEEK SERIES

The easiest way to create a series is by using the *AutoFill command,* which copies and extends data from a cell or range of cells to adjacent cells. The AutoFill command uses the *Fill handle,* a small rectangle at the lower-right corner of a cell or range.

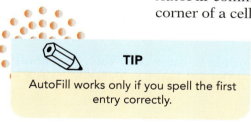

TIP

AutoFill works only if you spell the first entry correctly.

1. Press Ctrl+G. The Go To dialog box opens.

2. Key **a26** and press Enter. The insertion point is in cell A26.

3. Key **January** and press Enter.

4. Click cell A26. Scroll the worksheet until you can see rows 26 through 37.

5. Place the pointer on the Fill handle for cell A26. The pointer changes to a solid black cross.

6. Drag down to cell A37. As you drag, a ScreenTip shows each month as it is filled in.

Excel 2007

Figure 3-10
Creating a month
series
KowaSales.xlsx
Kowabunga sheet

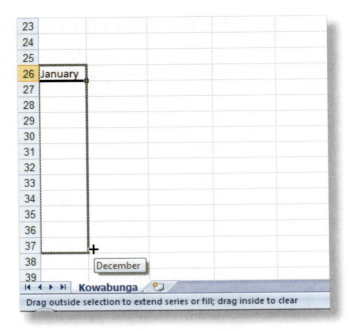

Drag outside selection to extend series or fill; drag inside to clear

7. Release the mouse button. The series is filled. The AutoFill Options button ▥ appears below your filled selection. It includes options for filling data.

8. Hover over the AutoFill Options button ▥ and click its arrow.

9. Choose **Fill Series** for a regular AutoFill task.

10. In cell B25, key **Week 1** and press Ctrl + Enter.

11. Place the mouse pointer on the Fill handle for cell B25.

12. Drag right to cell E25. Release the mouse button. The series is filled.

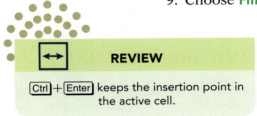

REVIEW

Ctrl + Enter keeps the insertion point in the active cell.

Exercise 3-13   CREATE A NUMBER SERIES

To establish a value series, first key two values in the series. Then select both cells and drag the Fill handle. If you drag the Fill handle too far, just drag it back to where you wanted to finish.

1. Click cell B26. Key **5** and press Enter.

2. Key **10** in cell B27. This sets a pattern with an interval of 5, increasing each value by 5.

3. Click cell B26 and drag to select cell B27. There is one Fill handle for the range.

4. Place the pointer on the Fill handle for cell B27.

5. Drag down to cell B37 and release the mouse button. The series is filled in, and the range is selected.

6. Hover over the AutoFill Options button and click its arrow.

7. Choose **Copy Cells**. The series is adjusted to be a copy.

8. Click the arrow with the AutoFill Options button . Choose **Fill Series**.

Exercise 3-14　COPY DATA WITH THE FILL HANDLE

When there is no apparent pattern in the range, the Fill handle copies data rather than creating a series.

1. The series you just filled in should still be selected. The Fill handle for the range is located in cell B37. Place the mouse pointer on the Fill handle.

2. Drag right to column E and release the mouse button. The range is copied, because no pattern was set for going from one column to the next.

Figure 3-11
Using the Fill pointer
to copy
KowaSales.xlsx
Kowabunga sheet

		Weel 1	Weel 2	Weel 3	Weel 4
23					
24					
25					
26	January	5			
27	February	10			
28	March	15			
29	April	20			
30	May	25			
31	June	30			
32	July	35			
33	August	40			
34	Septemb	45			
35	October	50			
36	Novemb	55			
37	Decembe	60			
38					+
39				5	

3. Make column A **10.00 (75 pixels)** wide.

Exercise 3-15　COPY A FORMULA WITH THE FILL HANDLE

1. Click cell F26. Click the **Home** tab.

2. In the **Editing** group, click the AutoSum button Σ ▾. The SUM function shows the range to be summed as B26:E26.

3. Press Ctrl + Enter. The formula is completed.

4. Look at the formula bar. You can copy this formula to the rest of the rows by using the Fill handle.

5. Place the pointer on the Fill handle for cell F26.

6. Drag down to cell F37 and release the mouse. Excel copies the formula, and the AutoFill Options button ⊞ appears.

7. Display the AutoFill Options menu. You do not need to make a change.

8. Click cell F27. The copied formula is relative to where it is on the worksheet, just as when you use Copy and Paste.

Applying Table and Cell Styles

A *table* is an arrangement of data in which each row represents one item or element. In your worksheet, each item is a month. Tables usually have a *header row* for each column to define the column's data. In this lesson, you will learn how to create a table from your data using built-in table styles.

Excel also has many cell styles for formatting labels and values based on the current document theme. These styles can include font and border settings, number formats, alignment settings, background colors, and more.

Exercise 3-16   CREATE A TABLE

1. In cell F25, key **Total** and press Enter. In cell A25, key **Month** and press Enter. Each column now has a header.

2. On the **Home** tab in the **Styles** group, click the Format as Table button ⊞. The Table Styles gallery opens with previews of many table styles. The styles are categorized as Light, Medium, or Dark based on the color scheme.

Figure 3-12
Table Styles gallery

3. Hover the mouse pointer over several thumbnails to find **Table Style Light 8** and click the icon. The gallery closes, your data is marqueed, and the Format As Table dialog box opens with a suggested range for your table.

Figure 3-13
Format As Table
dialog box
KowaSales.xlsx
Kowabunga sheet

4. Make sure there is a check mark for **My table has headers**. Click **OK**. Excel applies the style, adds Filter buttons to the header labels, and displays the **Table Tools Design** command tab.

NOTE

Filter buttons are used to sort and filter the rows. The buttons do not print.

5. Click cell G23. **Table Tools Design** is a context-sensitive tab that only appears when the insertion point is within a table.

6. Click cell D27. The **Table Tools Design** tab appears.

Figure 3-14
New Table
KowaSales.xlsx
Kowabunga sheet

	Month	Weel 1	Weel 2	Weel 3	Weel 4	Total	
24							
25	Month	Weel 1	Weel 2	Weel 3	Weel 4	Total	
26	January	5	5	5	5	20	
27	February	10	10	10	10	40	
28	March	15	15	15	15	60	
29	April	20	20	20	20	80	
30	May	25	25	25	25	100	
31	June	30	30	30	30	120	
32	July	35	35	35	35	140	
33	August	40	40	40	40	160	
34	September	45	45	45	45	180	
35	October	50	50	50	50	200	
36	November	55	55	55	55	220	
37	December	60	60	60	60	240	
38							

Exercise 3-17   CHANGE THE TABLE STYLE

You can easily change the style of a table and adjust several other design elements.

1. Click the **Table Tools Design** tab.

2. Click the More button ⬚ in the **Table Styles** group to open the gallery.

3. Hover over several different styles. Live Preview shows the table as it would appear with each style as you hover.

4. Find **Table Style Medium 8** and click the icon. The gallery closes, and the table is restyled.

5. In the **Table Style Options** group, click to deselect **Header Row**. The header row is no longer visible.

6. In the **Table Style Options** group, click to select **Total Row**. A grand total is shown for the last column.

7. Click to deselect **Total Row**.

8. In the **Table Style Options** group, click to select **First Column**. The first column is styled differently for emphasis.

9. Click to deselect **First Column**.

10. Click to select **Header Row** to show the header row again.

Exercise 3-18   APPLY A CELL STYLE

1. In cell A23, key **Monthly Estimates** and press ⏎.

2. Click cell A23. In the **Styles** group on the Home tab, click the Cell Styles button. The Cell Styles gallery opens. The styles are divided into five groups. You can use any style for any worksheet cell; the categories are just guidelines.

Figure 3-15
Cell Styles gallery
KowaSales.xlsx
Kowabunga sheet

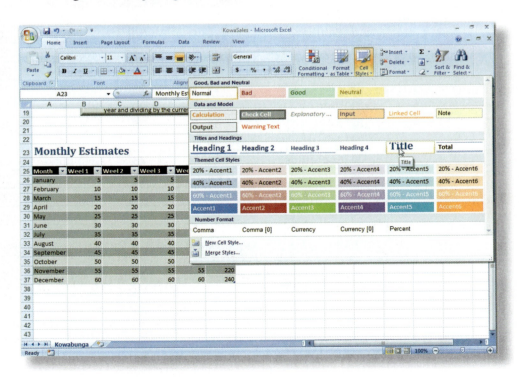

3. Hover the mouse pointer over different thumbnails and watch cell A23. Live Preview shows how the label will appear with the style.

4. Find and click the **Title** style (under Titles and Headings). The label is reformatted as Cambria 18 point in a theme color.

5. In the **Font** group, click the Font Color button . The color on the button is applied (probably red). You can apply your own formatting after choosing a cell style.

Exercise 3-19 **PRINT A SELECTION**

In the current worksheet, you might want to print only the table. To print a portion of a worksheet, select the range of cells you want to print. Open the Print dialog box and choose **Selection**.

1. Go to cell A38 and key your first and last name. Excel assumes your name is another row in the table and formats it to match.

> **NOTE**
>
> A table has a sizing handle at the bottom right corner.

2. Rest the mouse pointer on the table-sizing handle in cell F38. The pointer changes to a two-pointed arrow.

3. Drag the handle up to row 37. Your name is no longer part of the table.

4. Click cell F38 and press Delete. The formula was copied, too.

5. Click cell A23 and press F8. Extend Selection mode starts.

6. Press → five times to reach column F.

7. Press Ctrl+↓ three times. Each press of this key combination highlights up to the current range of your data.

8. Press Ctrl+P. The Print dialog box opens.

9. Choose **Selection** in the **Print what** area.

10. Click **Preview**. The Print Preview shows the range that will be printed.

11. Click the Print button. Only the range that you specified is printed.

12. Save the workbook as *[your initials]*3-19 in a folder for Lesson 3.

Preparing Headers and Footers

Headers and footers can be used to display a company name, a department, the date, or a company logo. A *header* prints at the top of each page in a worksheet. A *footer* prints at the bottom of each page. Excel has preset headers and footers, and you can create your own.

A header or footer can have up to three sections. The left section prints at the left margin. The center section prints at the horizontal center of the page. The right section aligns at the right margin.

You can create headers and footers by:

Header & Footer

- Clicking the Header & Footer button in the Text group on the Insert tab.

- Clicking the Page Layout View button on the status bar.

- Clicking the Page Layout View button in the Workbook View group on the View tab.

- Clicking the Dialog Box Launcher in the Page Setup group on the Page Layout tab.

Page Setup

- Clicking the Page Setup button in Print Preview.

Exercise 3-20   SET HEADERS AND FOOTERS

1. With *[your initials]*3-19 open, press Ctrl + Home.

2. Click the **Insert** tab in the Ribbon.

3. In the **Text** group, click the Header & Footer button. The Header/ Footer Tools Design tab is a context-sensitive tab that opens when the insertion point is within a header or footer section. The worksheet is in Page Layout View.

Header

> **NOTE**
>
> The same preset layouts are available for footers and headers.

4. Click the Header button to display a gallery of header arrangements. Header sections are separated by commas. If you choose a single item, it prints in the center section. Two items print in the center and at the right margin. Three items print at the left margin, in the center, and at the right margin.

Figure 3-16
Choosing a preset header
3-19.xlsx
Kowabunga sheet

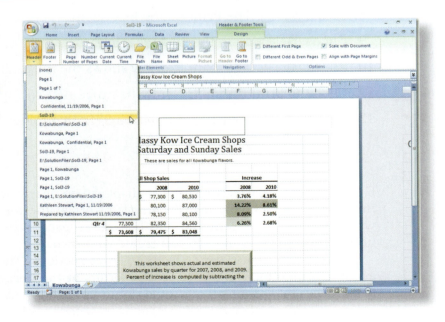

5. Find and click the first occurrence of your filename. You can see the header in the center section.

6. Point at the filename in the header and click. The code for displaying the filename is **&[File]**.

Go to Footer

7. In the **Navigation** group, click the Go to Footer button . The insertion point is in the center section.

8. Point at the left section and click. The insertion point moves there.

9. Key your first and last name in the left section and press Tab. The insertion point moves to the center section.

Page Number

Number of Pages

10. In the **Header and Footer Elements** group, click the Page Number button.

11. Press Spacebar, key **of**, and press Spacebar again.

12. In the **Header and Footer Elements** group, click the Number of Pages button.

13. Press Tab. The insertion point moves to the right section.

NOTE

You can use the buttons in the Ribbon or key the codes in the header/footer areas.

Current Date

14. Click the Current Date button. The code for displaying the current date is **&[Date]**.

Figure 3-17
Creating a custom footer
3-19.xlsx
Kowabunga sheet

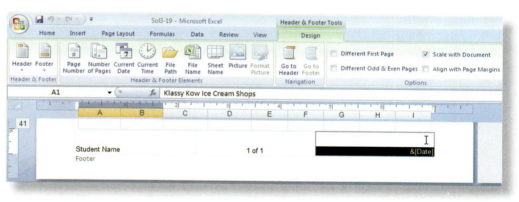

15. Click a cell above the footer area. This completes the footer and returns the focus to your worksheet.

16. Press Ctrl + Home. The worksheet is in Page Layout View while you work with headers and footers.

Exercise 3-21 PRINT GRIDLINES AND ROW AND COLUMN HEADINGS

Gridlines and row and column headings are visible while you work on a worksheet. They do not print as a default, but you can set them to print. Printing a worksheet with the gridlines and row and column headings makes it easy to locate data or to re-create a worksheet, if needed.

1. With *[your initials]*3-19 in Page Layout view, click the **Page Layout** tab in the Ribbon.

2. In the **Sheet Options** group, click to select the **Print** box below **Gridlines**.

3. Click to select **Print** below **Headings**.

Exercise 3-22   CHANGE MARGINS AND COLUMN WIDTHS IN PAGE LAYOUT VIEW

Excel sets 0.75 inch for left and right margins in a new workbook. The top and bottom margins are both set at 0.7 inch. The header and footer are preset to print 0.3 inch from the top and bottom of the page, within the top and bottom margin areas.

You can change the margins and the column widths in Page Layout View by dragging a margin marker or a column heading border. As you drag, the margin setting or column width is shown in inches or character spaces.

1. Hover over the left margin marker. The pointer changes to a two-pointed arrow.

2. Click and drag right to set a left margin of about **1.00**. Watch the ScreenTip for the setting as you drag. Your margin setting does not need to be exact.

Figure 3-18
Changing page margins in Page Layout View
3-19.xlsx
Kowabunga sheet

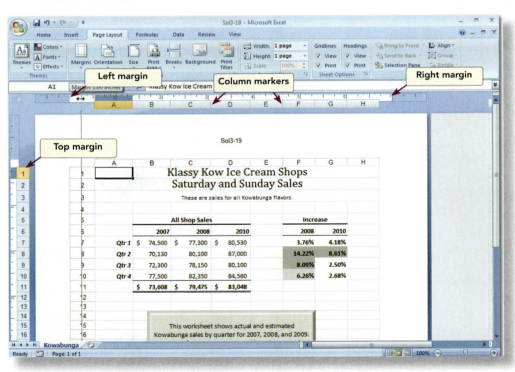

3. Hover the pointer over the right margin marker. Click and drag left to reach about **1.00**.

NOTE

The column headings for adjusting the width are just below the ruler.

4. Place the pointer on the column marker between columns A and B. The pointer changes to a two-pointed arrow. Drag right to make column A wider at **1.00 inches (101 pixels)**.

5. Make column E slightly less wide.

6. Press F12 and save the workbook as *[your initials]3-22* in your Lesson 3 folder.

7. Prepare and submit your work. Close the workbook.

Using Online Help

Series and AutoFill are time-saving features of Excel. They enable you to work more quickly and more accurately. Read more about series and the AutoFill command.

LOOK UP AUTOFILL AND SERIES

1. In a new workbook, press F1.

2. In the Search text box, key **autofill** and press Enter.

3. Find topics about filling in data in cells. Read the help information.

4. Close the Help window.

Lesson 3 Summary

- AutoCorrect corrects common typing errors as you work. You can add your own entries or delete existing ones.

- The Spelling command spell-checks a worksheet by comparing labels to dictionary entries. Options let you decide if and how to make the correction.

- The Find command locates and lists all occurrences of data that match your Find what character string. You can use wildcards in the character string.

- The Replace command locates and substitutes new data for existing data. You can complete the changes one at a time or all at once.

- Excel displays options buttons for some commands and formula errors. You can look at the message for the button, make a change, or ignore it.

- All cells have a Fill handle that can be used for filling in a series or for copying data.

- Excel recognizes common series for the days of the week, the months, and patterns such as "Week 1," "Week 2," and so on.

- You can create your own series with any interval by keying at least two cells that define the pattern.
- A table is a consistent pattern of data rows with a header row. Tables can be formatted with a style from the gallery.
- Cell styles apply colors, fonts, and other formatting options to a cell or range.
- Headers and footers print at the top or bottom of every page. There are preset headers and footers, or you can create your own.
- You can view and print a worksheet with or without the gridlines and row and column headings.
- You can change margins and column widths in Page Layout View and immediately see the results.

LESSON 3		Command Summary	
Feature	**Button**	**Task Path**	**Keyboard**
Error checking		Formulas, Formula Auditing	
Error checking options		Formulas, Formula Auditing	
Fill series		Home, Editing	
Find		Home, Editing, Find	Ctrl + F
Gridlines, print/view		Page Layout, Sheet Options	
Header/Footer		Insert, Text	
Header, preset		Header & Footer Tools Design, Header & Footer	
Headings, print/view		Page Layout, Sheet Options	
Print selection		Microsoft Office, Print	Ctrl + P
Replace		Home, Editing	Ctrl + H
Spelling		Review, Proofing	F7
Style, cell		Home, Styles	
Table, create		Home, Styles	
Table, style		Table Tools Design, Table Styles	

Concepts Review

True/False Questions

Each of the following statements is either true or false. Indicate your choice by circling T or F.

T F   1. If you key **THe** as part of a label, AutoCorrect will automatically fix the error.

T F   2. Options buttons are screen messages that tell you what command to choose next.

T F   3. The Replace command can be used to locate and change the font size.

T F   4. The Spelling command completes columns of month or day names.

T F   5. You can format data as a table if it has a header row followed by data rows.

T F   6. The Fill handle displays a small hollow circle.

T F   7. A series is a list with a recognizable pattern.

T F   8. The option to print a selected range is in the Page Layout dialog box.

Short Answer Questions

Write the correct answer in the space provided.

1. How can you collapse the Ribbon?

   _____

2. Name the feature that enables you to automatically complete a list of 12 months after you key one month.

   _____

3. What keyboard shortcut opens the Replace dialog box?

   _____

4. How are table styles categorized or grouped in the gallery?

   _____

5. Name two context-sensitive command tabs.

   _____

6. How can you print row and column headings?

_____

7. How can you change the margins in Page Layout View?

_____

8. What does Excel display when you release the mouse button after using the Fill handle?

_____

Critical Thinking

Answer these questions on a separate page. There are no right or wrong answers. Support your answers with examples from your own experience, if possible.

1. Find and Replace are powerful time-saving commands. Think of times/ situations when they might create problems in your work.

2. You can copy a formula with the Copy and Paste buttons (as you did in Lesson 2) or with the Fill handle. Which do you prefer and why? When wouldn't it be a good idea to use the Fill handle to copy a formula?

Skills Review

Exercise 3-23

Use AutoCorrect. Use Error Checking. Check spelling.

1. Open **ExpWA**. Press [F12] and save the workbook as *[your initials]*3-23 in your Lesson 3 folder. This worksheet has a two-color scale to differentiate high and low values.

2. Use AutoCorrect by following these steps:

   a. Click cell A2.

   b. Key (with the error) **Expenses Already Sceduled** and press [Spacebar].

   c. Click cell A14.

   d. Key (with errors) **Thsi workshet was prepared by STudent [your last name] on monday.** Press [Enter].

NOTE

Row 4 is a separator row with a bottom border as part of the worksheet design.

3. Change the height of rows 5 and 12 to **22.50 (30 pixels)**. Select rows 6:11 and make them **16.50 (22 pixels)** tall. Make row 4 **6.00 (8 pixels)** tall.

4. Select cells A1:A2 and change to the Headings font for the theme.

5. Click the Save button 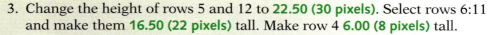.

6. Use Error Checking by following these steps:

   a. Click the **Formulas** tab.

   b. In the **Formula Auditing** group, click the Error Checking button .

   c. Look at the formula for cell F7. It is not the same as others in the column; it does not include cell E7.

   d. Click **Copy Formula from Above**.

   e. Look at the formula for cell B12. This formula is missing cell B11.

   f. Choose **Update Formula to Include Cells**.

   g. Click **OK** in the message box.

7. Check spelling by following these steps.

   a. Press Ctrl + Home.

   b. Click the **Review** tab. Click the Spelling button .

   c. What is the first misspelled word? What will you do about it?

   d. Take the action you described in the previous step.

   e. List each error and how you correct it.

   f. There is one more error on this sheet. Find it and correct it.

8. Press Ctrl + Home.

9. Click the Microsoft Office Button 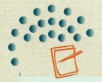 and hover over the arrow next to **Print**. Choose **Print Preview**. Preview your worksheet in a reduced and in a normal size.

10. Prepare and submit your work. Save and close the workbook.

Exercise 3-24

Use Find. Use Replace.

1. Open **MayPromo**. Save it as *[your initials]*3-24 in your Lesson 3 folder.

2. Use Find by following these steps:

   a. Press Ctrl + F.

   b. Key **ee** in the **Find what** box.

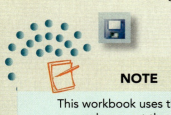

NOTE

This workbook uses the Zenith document theme.

TIP

Drag the dialog box so that you can see the cells with formulas.

NOTE

Prepare your answers to questions in the Skills Review exercises as instructed for submission to your instructor. Include your name, the date, the exercise number, and the question number.

NOTE

Follow your usual class procedures for submitting work.

c. Click **Find All**. How many cells include this character string?

d. Double-click **ee** in the **Find what** box and key **a?** in its place.

e. Click **Find All**. How many cells include an **a** followed by any character?

f. Double-click **a?** and key **r*** and click **Find All**. How many cells include an "**r**" followed by any character?

g. Double-click **r*** and key **P** in the **Find what** box.

h. Click **Options** to expand the dialog box and click to select **Match case**. Click **Find All**. How many cells include an uppercase "**P**"?

i. Turn off **Match case** and hide the options.

3. Use Replace by following these steps:

a. Click the **Replace** tab.

b. Double-click **P** and key **20** in the **Find what** box.

REVIEW

Move the dialog box if you cannot see the affected cells.

c. In the **Replace with** box, key **50**. Click **Find All**. There are four cells with this value.

d. Click **Replace** to change the first occurrence.

e. Click **Replace** to change the second occurrence.

f. Click **Find Next** to skip the next occurrence.

g. Double-click **20** and key **25** in the **Find what** box.

h. Press ⌧Tab to reach the **Replace with** box and press ⌧Delete. Click **Find All**. There are five cells with a value of 25.

REVIEW

You can determine the document's theme from the Page Layout Tab. Just hover over the Themes button ⃞.

i. Click **Replace All** to make these cells blank. Click **OK** in the message box.

j. Close the dialog box.

4. Key your first and last name in cell A13. Change the tab name to **MayExp** and choose a tab color from the theme colors.

5. Press ⌧Ctrl+⌧Home. Prepare and submit your work.

6. Save and close the workbook.

Exercise 3-25

Create series. Use AutoFill to copy values.

1. Create a new workbook. Save it as *[your initials]*3-25 in your Lesson 3 folder.

2. Change the document theme to **Flow**.

3. Key **Klassy Kow Ice Cream Shops** in cell A1. Format it as 18-point Calibri.

4. Use 12-point Calibri in cell A2 and key **Summary prepared by *[your first and last name]***.

REVIEW

AutoCorrect capitalizes the names of the days of the week.

5. Create a series by following these steps:

a. Click cell B3 and key **monday**. Press →.

b. Key **wednesday** in cell C3 and press ←.

TIP

Make the first label bold and then use AutoFill.

REVIEW

If you use the Home tab, Cells group, Format, and Row Height, use points (not pixels) to change the row height.

c. Select cells B3:C3. Make these labels bold.

d. Place the pointer on the Fill handle.

e. Drag right far enough to build a series ending with Sunday.

f. Key **Week 1** in cell A4 and make it bold.

g. Place the pointer on the Fill handle for cell A4 and drag down to build a series ending with Week 4.

6. Set the height of rows 2, 3, and 8 to **22.50 (30 pixels)**. Then choose a height slightly less than that for the other rows.

7. Use AutoFill to copy values by following these steps:

a. Click cell B4 and key **10**. Press ⟶.

b. In cells C4:E4, key **20**, **40**, and **30**.

c. Select cells B4:E4. Place the mouse pointer on the Fill handle for the range. Drag down to reach row 7.

8. Select cells B8:E8. Click the AutoSum button Σ⋅ on the **Home** tab. Make these values bold.

9. Adjust column widths using your judgment.

10. Press Ctrl+Home. Click the Save button 💾.

11. Prepare and submit your work. Then close the workbook.

Exercise 3-26

Create a table. Use cell styles. Prepare headers/footers.

1. Open **MayCakes**.

2. Save the workbook as *[your initials]*3-26 in your Lesson 3 folder.

3. Create a table by following these steps:

a. Click cell B3.

b. In the **Styles** group on the **Home** tab, click the Format as Table button.

c. Scroll to find **Table Style Medium 10** and click the icon.

d. In the Format As Table dialog box, change the range to **=$A$3:$E$7**.

e. Click to select **My table has headers**. Click OK.

4. Use cell styles by following these steps:

a. Select cells A1:A2.

b. In the **Styles** group on the **Home** tab, click the Cell Styles button.

c. Click **Accent2** in the gallery.

d. Set 14-point Cambria as the font for cells A1:A2. Make both cells bold.

  e. Autofit column A. Make rows 3:7 each **30.00 (40 pixels)** tall.

  f. Click cell A3 and key **Flavor**. Press `Ctrl`+`Home`.

5. Prepare a footer by following these steps:

  a. Click the **Insert** tab.

  b. In the **Text** group, click the Header & Footer button.

  c. Click the Go to Footer button in the **Navigation** group.

  d. Click in the left section and key your first and last name.

  e. Press `Tab` to move to the center section.

  f. Click the File Name button in the **Header & Footer Elements** group. Press `Tab`.

  g. Click the Current Date button.

  h. Click a cell in the worksheet and press `Ctrl`+`Home`.

  i. Click the **Page Layout** tab.

  j. In the **Sheet Options** group, click to deselect both **Print** boxes.

  k. Hover over the left margin marker. Drag left to set a left margin of about **.50** inches.

  l. Hover the pointer over the right margin marker. Click and drag right to reach about **.50**.

  m. Click the Normal button in the status bar.

6. Prepare and submit your work. Save and close the workbook.

Lesson Applications

Exercise 3-27

Use Find and Replace. Create a footer. Change the left margin.

1. Open **MayPromo**. Save it as *[your initials]*3-27 in your Lesson 3 folder.

2. Replace all occurrences of **california** with **Washington**.

3. Replace all occurrences of **75** with **0** (zero).

4. Find and correct formula errors.

5. Change the tab name to **MayExpense** and choose a tab theme color.

6. Create a footer that shows your name in the left section. In the center section, click the Sheet Name button . Add the date to the right section.

7. Change the left margin to about 1.25 inches.

8. Preview the worksheet and prepare and submit your work. Save and close the workbook.

NOTE

You do not need to key uppercase characters in a Find character string, but you should key them in the Replace character string.

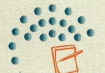

NOTE

A zero (0) in this worksheet will display as a hyphen. Zero is treated differently from empty/blank in calculations.

Exercise 3-28

Create a series. Create a table and use cell styles. Prepare a header.

1. Create a new workbook and choose the **Paper** document theme. Save the workbook as *[your initials]*3-28 in your Lesson 3 folder.

2. Using the Headings font, key **Klassy Kow Specials** in cell A1. In cell A2, key **Price Promotions** with the same font.

3. In cell B3, key **Regular Price**. In cell C3, key **Special Price**. In cell D3, key **Savings**. AutoFit each column to show the label.

4. In cell A5, key **Ice Cream Cakes**.

5. In cell A6, key **January 1, 200x** (using next year in place of the "x"). Key **February 1, 200x** in cell A7, with the same year. Select both cells and format the date to spell out the month and show the date, a comma, and a four-digit year.

6. Select cells A6:A7 and use the Fill handle to extend the dates to May 1.

7. Format cells B6:D10 as Accounting format.

REVIEW

Press Ctrl + 1 to format the date.

NOTE

Ignore Smart Tag Actions buttons.

8. Key **24.5** in cell B6. Copy this value to cells B7:B10.

9. Key the following special prices:

January	**20.5**
February	**21.5**
March	**20.5**
April	**19.99**
May	**22.5**

10. Use a formula in cell D6 to compute the difference between the regular price and the special price. Copy the formula to cells D7:D10.

11. Press Ctrl + Home. Rename the tab as **Cakes** and choose a tab theme color.

12. Select cells A5:D10 and format them using a medium style table. Your table does not have a header row. In the Table Style Options group on the Table Tools Design tab, deselect **Header Row**.

13. Make row 4 very small. Then choose font sizes, styles, and colors for the labels and set row heights and column widths to build an attractive report.

14. Add a header to show your name at the left, the sheet name in the center, and the filename at the right. Change the left margin to make the sheet appear centered on the page.

15. Prepare and submit your work. Save and close the workbook.

NOTE

Blank cells in the Quantity column are formatted to appear red. This is a conditional format. The color changes when you enter a value.

Exercise 3-29

Spell-check a worksheet.

1. Open **OrderSheet**. Find and correct misspelled words.

2. In cell C5, key today's date in this format: mm/dd/yy.

3. In cell C6, key *[your last name]*'s **Supermarket**.

4. Key the following quantities for the ice cream flavors shown. No quantity appears for flavors that are not being ordered.

Vanilla	**25**
Chocolate	**25**
Strawberry	**20**
Butter Pecan	**10**
French Vanilla	**10**
Chocolate Chip	**10**
Chocolate Mint Melody	**10**
Peppermint Candy	**10**
Raspberry Swirl	**15**
Purple Kow	**12**

The flavors in Rows 17-24 are not being ordered.

Apple Pie	**5**
Rum Raisin	**5**
Blueberry	**5**
New York Cherry	**5**

5. Select the cells with dollar values and use the Format Cells dialog box to change to the Currency format (floating dollar sign). Paint this format to cell F34.

6. Press Ctrl + Home . Save the workbook as *[your initials]3-29* in your Lesson 3 folder.

7. Prepare and submit your work. Close the workbook.

Exercise 3-30 ◆ Challenge Yourself
Create a series. Create a table and use cell styles. Prepare a footer.

1. Create a new workbook. Rename Sheet1 as ShakeSales. Save the workbook as *[your initials]3-30* in your Lesson 3 folder.

NOTE

New workbooks use the Office document theme.

2. Key Klassy Kow Ice Cream Shops in cell A1. Key Daily Shake Sales in *[your home city]* in cell A2.

3. In cell B3, key Chocolate. In cell C3, key Vanilla.

4. In cell A4, key monday. Fill in the days of the week up to and including Sunday in column A. Key Day in cell A3.

5. In cell B4, key 4. In cell B5, key 8. Extend this series down column B to fill in values up to Sunday. Copy the entire range of values to the Vanilla column.

6. Create a table for rows 3:11 using any style. Set your own row heights.

7. Use the cell style gallery to format the labels in cells A1:A2 to coordinate with your table, or apply your own formatting.

8. Select the Total Row from the Table Tools Design tab. Show totals for both columns.

9. Add a footer with your name at the left, the filename in the center, and the sheet name at the right.

10. Prepare and submit your work. Close the workbook.

On Your Own

In these exercises you work on your own, as you would in a real-life work environment. Use the skills you've learned to accomplish the task—and be creative.

Exercise 3-31

Open **SepPies**. Change the labels to the Headings font and the values to the Body font. Change the date to today's date. Use AutoFill to complete the labels in row 3. Key the names of four ice cream pies in cells A5:A8. Create a table for the data rows and use cell styles for the main labels. Make your own changes, too, for an attractive layout. Add a footer with your name, the filename, and the date. Save the worksheet as *[your initials]*3-31. Prepare and submit your work. Save and close the workbook.

Exercise 3-32

Create a new workbook and save it as *[your initials]*3-32. In cell A1, key **Using AutoFill and Series**. Create a 15-month series in column A, using a 3-month interval (January, April; fill 15 rows; start with any month). Build a 15-day series in column B, using an every-other-day interval (Monday, Wednesday; 15 rows; start with any day). In row 20, build a 10-year series, using a 4-year interval (2000, 2004; start with any year). In row 22, build a 10-value series starting at 2 and using an interval of 2 (2, 4). In cell A24, key today's date. In cell A25, key the date one week from today. Build a 12-date series in column A from these two dates. Apply a different cell style to each series and the main label, too.

Add a header with appropriate information. On the Page Layout tab, find and use the command to print the worksheet in landscape orientation. Prepare and submit your work. Save and close the workbook.

Exercise 3-33

Use the Internet or printed maps to determine the mileage between your city and five major cities in your part of the country. Calculate a driving time to each city from your city. Create a workbook that shows this information in an easy-to-read layout. Include a main label and column titles. Spell-check it and use a table or cell styles. Add an appropriate header. Save the workbook as *[your initials]*3-33. Prepare and submit your work. Close the workbook.

Exploring Home tab Commands

OBJECTIVES

After completing this lesson, you will be able to:

1. Insert and delete sheets and cells.

2. Use AutoComplete and Pick From Drop-Down List.

3. Copy, cut, and paste cell contents.

4. Work with columns and rows.

5. Work with alignment.

6. Apply borders and fill.

7. Use data bars.

MCAS OBJECTIVES

In this lesson:
XL07 1.2
XL07 1.3.1
XL07 1.4.2
XL07 1.5.1
XL07 1.5.5
XL07 2.2.1
XL07 2.2.3
XL07 2.3.2
XL07 2.3.3
XL07 2.3.4
XL07 2.3.6
XL07 2.3.7
XL07 4.3.1
XL07 4.3.3

Estimated Time: 1¹/₄ hours

The Home tab includes commonly used tasks and commands. The groups on this tab are Clipboard, Font, Alignment, Number, Styles, Cells, and Editing. The Home tab is the active tab when you open a new workbook.

Inserting and Deleting Sheets and Cells

A new workbook opens with three blank sheets. You can insert and delete sheets as needed. You insert a new worksheet when you:

• Click the **Insert Worksheet** tab.

• Press Shift + F11.

- In the Cells group, click the arrow with the Insert Cells button and choose **Insert Sheet**.

- Right-click a worksheet tab and choose **Insert**. Then choose **Worksheet** in the dialog box.

You delete a worksheet when you:

- Right-click the worksheet tab and choose **Delete**.

- In the Cells group, click the arrow next to the Delete Cells button  and choose **Delete Sheet**.

TIP

You can change the default number of sheets in a new workbook in the Popular pane in the Excel Options dialog box.

Exercise 4-1   INSERT WORKSHEETS

Excel names new sheets starting with the next number in sequence. For example, if the workbook already has **Sheet1**, **Sheet2**, and **Sheet3**, a new sheet would be named **Sheet4**.

1. Open **AcctRec**. This workbook has one worksheet named **AR2007** for Accounts Receivable in 2007. Notice that there is no **Sheet1**.

2. Click the **Insert Worksheet** tab.

3. Double-click the **Sheet1** worksheet tab.

4. Key **SalesReps** and press Enter. The worksheet tab is renamed.

5. Right-click the **SalesReps** tab. Choose a color different from the color of the **AR2007** sheet.

6. Press Shift + F11. A new worksheet named **Sheet2** is placed in front of the **SalesReps** sheet.

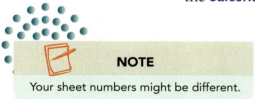

NOTE

Your sheet numbers might be different.

7. Right-click the **AR2007** tab and choose **Insert**. The Insert dialog box opens.

8. Click the **General** tab. This tab shows the types of objects you can insert in your workbook. You likely have objects different from the text figure.

Figure 4-1
Insert Worksheet
dialog box

9. Click **Worksheet** and click **OK**. **Sheet3** is placed before the **AR2007** worksheet.

Exercise 4-2   MOVE AND DELETE WORKSHEETS

You can rearrange worksheet tabs in any order. Additionally, if you don't need all the sheets in a workbook, you can delete blank ones to conserve file space. You cannot delete the only sheet in a workbook.

1. Click the **AR2007** tab to make it active.

2. Point at the tab to display a white arrow pointer.

3. Click and drag the tab to the left of **Sheet3**. As you drag, you see a small sheet icon and a triangle that marks the new position of the sheet.

4. Release the mouse button. The **AR2007** sheet is now the leftmost tab.

5. Right-click the **Sheet3** tab. The sheet becomes the active sheet and a shortcut menu opens.

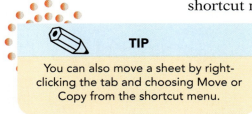

TIP

You can also move a sheet by right-clicking the tab and choosing Move or Copy from the shortcut menu.

6. Choose **Delete**. The sheet is deleted, and **Sheet2** is active.

7. In the **Cells** group, click the arrow with the Delete Cells button . Choose **Delete Sheet**. The sheet is deleted, and the **SalesReps** worksheet is active.

Exercise 4-3   INSERT CELLS

When you insert or delete cells, you affect the entire worksheet, not just the column or row where you are working. You can accidentally rearrange data if you don't watch the entire sheet. When you insert or delete cells, you decide if existing cells should move up, down, left, or right.

NOTE

If you use a laptop computer that does not have a numeric keypad, press Ctrl+Shift+[+], using the [+] in the top row of keys.

1. Click the **AR2007** tab. Set the Zoom size so that you can see columns A through H.

2. Click cell B8.

3. Press Ctrl+[+] in the numeric keypad. (The *numeric keypad* is the set of number and symbol keys at the right side of the keyboard.) An Insert dialog box opens with choices about what happens after the cell is inserted.

Figure 4-2
Insert dialog box
AcctRec.xlsx
AR2007 sheet

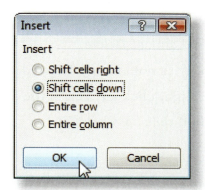

4. Choose **Shift cells down** if it's not already selected and click **OK**. A blank cell is inserted. The cells originally in cells B8:B15 have moved down to cells B9:B16. The data in the other columns did not shift.

5. Click cell C12. The reference number and related paid date are in the wrong columns.

6. Right-click cell C12 and choose **Insert**.

7. Choose **Shift cells right** and click **OK**. All the cells in the worksheet shift to the right, including those in column H and beyond.

NOTE

You will see the Mini toolbar when you right-click a cell; just ignore it for now.

Figure 4-3
One cell inserted, with other cells shifted right
AcctRec.xlsx
AR2007 sheet

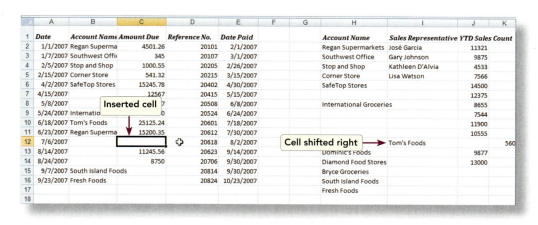

Excel 2007

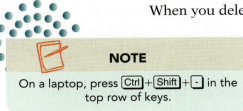

Exercise 4-4   DELETE CELLS

When you delete cells, watch the entire worksheet for changes.

1. Scroll the worksheet so that you can see columns D through I.

2. Click cell H7.

3. Press Ctrl + - in the numeric keypad. The Delete dialog box opens.

4. Choose **Shift cells up** and click **OK**. Now there is no room to return "Tom's Foods" to column H.

5. Click the Undo button in the Quick Access toolbar.

6. Click cell H12. Press Ctrl + - on the numeric keypad.

7. Choose **Shift cells left** and click **OK**. Only the cells in columns H and beyond are shifted to the left.

8. Right-click cell H7 and choose **Delete**.

9. Choose **Shift cells up,** if it's not already selected, and click **OK**.

10. Select cells H8:H10. Right-click any cell in the range.

11. Choose **Delete** and **Shift cells up**. Click OK.

12. Press Ctrl + Home.

Using AutoComplete and Pick from Drop-Down List

Excel has two features that make it easy to enter labels in a column. Both features use text already in the column.

- *AutoComplete* displays a suggested label after you key the first character(s) in a cell. AutoComplete works for text and labels that are a combination of text and numbers.

- *Pick From Drop-Down List* displays a list of labels already in the column for your selection. This method is helpful when it is important that you use exactly the same data as already entered. It's a way to validate data as it is entered.

Exercise 4-5 USE AUTOCOMPLETE

When you key the first few characters of a label, Excel scans the column for the same characters. If it finds a match, it displays a proposed entry. If the suggestion is correct, press [Enter]. If the suggested label is not what you want, ignore it and continue to key the new label. You may need to key more than one character before Excel proposes a label.

> **TIP**
>
> You can key lower- or uppercase letters to see a proposed label.

1. Click cell B7.

2. Key **r** to see an AutoComplete suggestion. In this case, Excel's suggestion is accurate.

Figure 4-4
An AutoComplete suggestion
AcctRec.xlsx
AR2007 sheet

	A	B	C	D
1	*Date*	*Account Name*	*Amount Due*	*Reference No.*
2	1/1/2007	Regan Superma	4501.26	20101
3	1/7/2007	Southwest Offi	345	20107
4	2/5/2007	Stop and Shop	1000.55	20205
5	2/15/2007	Corner Store	541.32	20215
6	4/2/2007	SafeTop Stores	15245.78	20402
7	4/15/2007	regan Supermarkets		20415
8	5/8/2007		3677.87	20508
9	5/24/2007	International Gr	5590	20524
10	6/18/2007	Tom's Foods	25125.24	20601

3. Press [Enter]. The label is entered with the same capitalization as the existing label in the column.

4. Key **s** in cell B8. No suggestion is made, because several labels in the column start with "s." Excel needs more information.

5. Key **t** to see a suggestion for "Stop and Shop."

6. Press [Enter].

7. Click cell B12 and key **south**. Excel has not found a match.

8. Press [Spacebar]. Excel suggests "South Island Foods," because the space distinguishes it from "Southwest."

9. Press [Enter].

10. Key **PDQ Shop** in cell B13 and press Enter. No suggestion was made, because no existing label starts with "p."

11. Click cell C15 and key **87**. Excel does not make AutoComplete suggestions for values.

12. Press Esc.

Exercise 4-6   USE PICK FROM DROP-DOWN LIST

The Pick From Drop-Down List option appears on the shortcut menu when you right-click a cell.

1. Right-click cell I6.

2. Choose **Pick From Drop-Down List.** Excel displays a list of labels already in column I.

3. Click **José Garcia**.

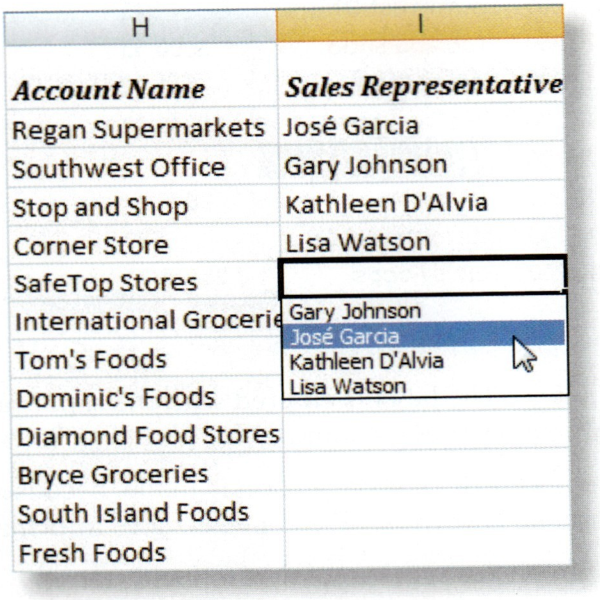

Figure 4-5
Using Pick From
Drop-Down List
**AcctRec.xlsx
AR2007 sheet**

4. Right-click cell I7. Choose **Pick From Drop-Down List**.

5. Click **Lisa Watson**.

6. Right-click cell B14. Choose **Pick From Drop-Down List**. The list is longer and includes a scroll bar.

7. Find and click **Tom's Foods**.

8. Right-click cell C12. Choose **Pick From Drop-Down List**. Excel does not display a list for values.

9. Press Esc.

Copying, Cutting, and Pasting Cell Contents

You can copy, cut (move), and paste cell contents in a worksheet. When you copy or cut a cell or range of cells, a duplicate of the data is placed on the *Windows Clipboard*. This is a temporary memory area used to keep data you have copied or cut.

Data that is cut can be pasted once. Data that is copied can be pasted many times and in many locations. Copied data stays on the Windows Clipboard until you copy or cut another cell or range. Then that data replaces the data on the Clipboard.

The Cut and Paste commands are used to move labels and values from one cell to another. To use Cut and Paste, first select the cells you want to cut, and then you can:

- Click the Cut button ✄ in the Clipboard group. Position the pointer at the new location and click the Paste button 📋 or press Enter.

- Press Ctrl+X. Position the pointer at the new location and press Ctrl+V or press Enter.

- Right-click the selected cells. Choose **Cut** from the shortcut menu. Right-click the new cell location and choose **Paste** from the shortcut menu.

- Select the cell or range. Drag it to a new location.

The Copy and Paste commands make a duplicate of the data in another location. To use copy and paste, select the cells you want to copy, and then you can:

- Click the Copy button 📑 in the Clipboard group. Position the pointer at the new location and click the Paste button 📋 or press Enter.

- Press Ctrl+C. Position the pointer at the new location and press Ctrl+V or press Enter.

- Right-click the selected cells. Choose **Copy** from the shortcut menu. Right-click the new cell location and choose **Paste**.

- Select the cell or range. While holding down the Ctrl key, drag it to a new location.

Exercise 4-7   CUT AND PASTE CELL CONTENTS

When you paste cells that have been cut, the cut data replaces existing data unless you tell Excel to insert the cut data.

1. Click cell C14. Click the Cut button ✄. A moving marquee surrounds the cell.

2. Click cell C12 and then click the Paste button 📋. The data is removed from cell C14 and pasted in C12. The marquee is canceled.

3. Select cells B15:B16. Press Ctrl+X. The range displays the moving marquee.

4. Click cell B17 and press Enter. The pasted range is selected.

Figure 4-6
Cutting cell contents
AcctRec.xlsx
AR2007 sheet

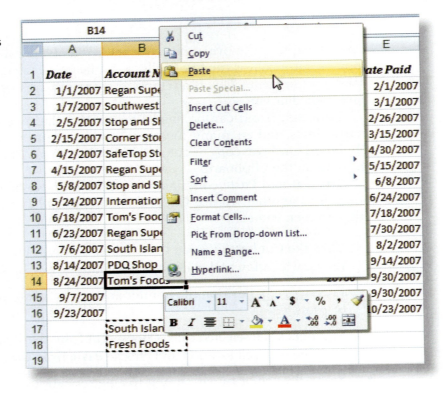

5. Click the Cut button ✄. The range displays the moving marquee.

6. Right-click cell B14. Choose **Paste**. A regular Paste command replaces existing data. "Tom's Foods" is gone from cell B14.

7. Select cells B5:B6. Press Ctrl+X.

8. Right-click cell B4 and choose **Insert Cut Cells**. The data from cells B5:B6 is inserted before Stop and Shop, which has shifted down.

Exercise 4-8   COPY AND PASTE CELL CONTENTS

The Paste Options button 📋 appears below a pasted selection. When you click it, you see a list of options that establish how the selection can be pasted.

1. Click cell B1 and click the Copy button 📋. The cell is surrounded by the moving marquee.

2. Click cell B13 and click the Paste button 📋. The label is pasted, the original data is removed, and the Paste Options button 📋 appears.

3. Rest the mouse pointer on the Paste Options button 📋. Click its arrow.

NOTE

Close the Clipboard pane if it opens.

4. Choose **Formatting Only**. This option copies only the formatting; it does not copy the actual label.

Figure 4-7
Using Paste Options
AcctRec.xlsx
AR2007 sheet

	A	B	C	D	E
1	*Date*	*Account Name*	*Amount Due*	*Reference No.*	*Date Paid*
2	1/1/2007	Regan Superma	4501.26	20101	2/1/2007
3	1/7/2007	Southwest Offi	345	20107	3/1/2007
4	2/5/2007	Corner Store	1000.55	20205	2/26/2007
5	2/15/2007	SafeTop Stores	541.32	20215	3/15/2007
6	4/2/2007	Stop and Shop	15245.78	20402	4/30/2007
7	4/15/2007	Regan Superma	12567	20415	5/15/2007
8	5/8/2007	Stop and Shop	3677.87	20508	6/8/2007
9	5/24/2007	International Gi	5590	20524	6/24/2007
10	6/18/2007	Tom's Foods	25125.24	20601	7/18/2007
11	6/23/2007	Regan Superma	15200.35	20612	7/30/2007
12	7/6/2007	South Island Fo	8750	20618	8/2/2007
13	8/14/2007	*Account Name*	11245.56	20623	9/14/2007
14	8/24/2007	South Island Foc		20706	9/30/2007
15	9/7/2007	Fresh Foods			9/30/2007
16	9/23/2007				9/23/2007
17					
18					
19					
20					
21					
22					
23					

Paste Options menu:
- ○ Keep Source Formatting
- ◉ Use **D**estination Theme
- ○ **M**atch Destination Formatting
- ○ Values and **N**umber Formatting
- ○ Keep Source Column **W**idths
- ○ **F**ormatting Only
- ○ **L**ink Cells

TIP

The marquee is not automatically canceled after you click the Paste button. This enables you to paste the data again in a different location.

5. Click the Undo button. Press [Esc].

6. Click cell I2 and drag to select the range I2:I7.

7. Press [Ctrl]+[C]. Excel displays a marquee around the range.

8. Click cell I8. You only need to click in the first cell for the copy as long as the destination range is empty.

9. Press [Ctrl]+[V]. The range of names is duplicated. The marquee is shown as well as the Paste Options button.

10. Click cell I14. Press [Ctrl]+[V] to paste the data again.

REVIEW

Copied cells replace existing data unless you choose the option to insert them.

11. Press [Esc] to cancel the marquee.

12. Select the range C8:C10 and press [Ctrl]+[C] to copy the range.

13. Right-click cell C11.

14. Choose **Insert Copied Cells**. The Insert Paste dialog box opens.

15. Choose **Shift cells down**. Click **OK**. The copied cells are inserted, and the existing cells are shifted down in the column.

16. Press Esc to cancel the marquee.

Exercise 4-9   USE DRAG AND DROP

Use the drag-and-drop method to cut or copy data when you can see the original and the destination cell on screen. The *drag-and-drop pointer* is a four-pointed arrow.

1. Select cell C16. Place the pointer at the top or bottom edge/border of the cell. The drag-and-drop pointer appears.

2. Hold down the mouse button and drag to cell C17. A ScreenTip identifies the destination cell. You can also see a ghost highlight that shows where the data will be placed.

Figure 4-8
Using drag and drop to cut and paste
AcctRec.xlsx
AR2007 sheet

10	6/18/2007	Tom's Foods	25125.24	20601
11	6/23/2007	Regan Superma	3677.87	20612
12	7/6/2007	South Island Fo	5590	20618
13	8/14/2007	PDQ Shop	25125.24	20623
14	8/24/2007	South Island Fo	15200.35	20706
15	9/7/2007	Fresh Foods	8750	20814
16	9/23/2007		11245.56	20824
17				
18			C17	
19				

3. Release the mouse button. You have used the drag-and-drop method to perform a cut and paste.

4. Place the pointer at the top or bottom edge/border of cell C17 to display the drag-and-drop pointer.

5. Hold down Ctrl. You will see a tiny plus sign (+) with a solid white arrow to signify this will be a copy and paste. Do not release Ctrl.

6. Click and drag to cell C16. Release the mouse button first and then release Ctrl. This is drag and drop to perform a copy and paste.

7. Select cells B6:B7. Place the pointer at the top or bottom edge of the range to display the drag-and-drop pointer.

NOTE

Drag and drop works in most Windows applications.

8. Hold down the [Ctrl] key to display the plus sign (+) and the white arrow pointer. Do not release the [Ctrl] key.

9. Click and drag down to cells B16:B17. Release the mouse button and then [Ctrl]. Both labels are copied.

Exercise 4-10 USE THE OFFICE CLIPBOARD

The *Office Clipboard* is a temporary memory area that can hold up to 24 copied items. It is separate from the Windows Clipboard. The Office Clipboard is available when any Office application (Excel, Access, Word, or PowerPoint) is running. It is shared among these programs, so something you copy in Excel can be pasted in Word. The options for the Office Clipboard allow you to set it to open automatically when you first copy an object and to show a screen message after copying.

1. Click the Dialog Box Launcher in the Clipboard group. The Clipboard task pane opens. You may see values and labels from your last copy task.

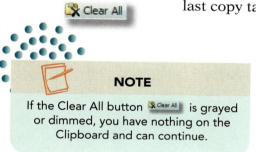

> **NOTE**
>
> If the Clear All button ![Clear All] is grayed or dimmed, you have nothing on the Clipboard and can continue.

2. Click the Clear All button ![Clear All] in the task pane.

3. Select the range A4:E4 and click the Copy button ![icon]. An Excel icon and the data appear in the task pane. There is an icon in the lower-right corner of the Windows taskbar.

4. Select the range A6:A7 and click the Copy button ![icon]. Another icon and data appear in the pane, above the first set.

5. Select the range A8:E8 and click the Copy button ![icon]. Three items have been copied and are on the Office Clipboard.

6. Press [Esc]. The marquee is removed.

7. Click cell A17. Click the date object in the task pane to paste two dates (see Figure 4-9 on the next page).

Figure 4-9
Using the Clipboard
task pane
AcctRec.xlsx
AR2007 sheet

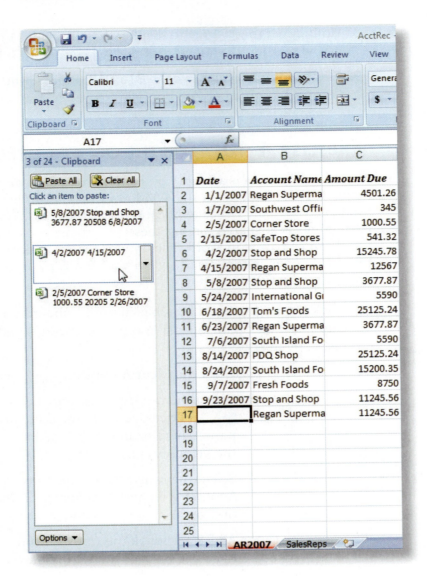

8. Click cell A19. Click the **Stop and Shop** object in the task pane to paste it.

9. Repeat these steps to paste the **Corner Store** object in cell A20.

10. Click the Clear All button in the task pane and then close the task pane.

Working with Columns and Rows

Inserted or deleted rows and columns extend across the entire worksheet. If you have used different parts of the worksheet, you could interrupt data elsewhere on the sheet after adding or deleting rows or columns.

When you insert a column or row, check formulas that might be affected. Excel updates formulas to include an inserted row or column if it falls within the original range used in the formula.

Exercise 4-11 INSERT ROWS

When you insert a row, it extends from column A to column XFD.

1. Click the Microsoft Office Button and choose **Excel Options**. Click **Formulas**.

2. Verify that all **Error checking rules** including **Formulas referring to empty cells** are active. Click **OK**.

3. In cell B18, key **p** and press Tab to insert **PDQ Shop**.

4. Key **345.7** in cell C18.

5. Click cell C21, click the AutoSum button Σ ▾ , and press Enter.

6. Click cell C21 and view the formula. The SUM function sums the range C2:C20.

7. Click cell J21 and click the AutoSum button Σ ▾ . Press Enter.

8. Click cell J21. Position the mouse pointer on the Error Checking Options button and click its arrow. The formula refers to empty cells.

9. Press Esc.

10. Click cell A12. Press Ctrl+ + in the numeric keypad. The Insert dialog box opens.

11. Choose **Entire row** and click **OK**. A new row is inserted, and the existing rows shift down. Notice that the new row spans the worksheet.

12. Click cell C22. The formula has been updated to include rows 2 through 21 and now refers to empty cells (see Figure 4-10 on the next page).

Figure 4-10
Row inserted
AcctRec.xlsx
AR2007 sheet

	A	B	C	D	E	F
1	*Date*	*Account Name*	*Amount Due*	*Reference No.*	*Date Paid*	
2	1/1/2007	Regan Superma	4501.26	20101	2/1/2007	
3	1/7/2007	Southwest Offic	345	20107	3/1/2007	
4	2/5/2007	Corner Store	1000.55	20205	2/26/2007	
5	2/15/2007	SafeTop Stores	541.32	20215	3/15/2007	
6	4/2/2007	Stop and Shop	15245.78	20402	4/30/2007	
7	4/15/2007	Regan Superma	12567	20415	5/15/2007	
8	5/8/2007	Stop and Shop	3677.87	20508	6/8/2007	
9	5/24/2007	International Gi	5590	20524	6/24/2007	
10	6/18/2007	Tom's Foods	25125.24	20601	7/18/2007	
11	6/23/2007	Regan Superma	3677.87	20612	7/30/2007	
12						
13	7/6/2007	South Island Fo	5590	20618	8/2/2007	
14	8/14/2007	PDQ Shop	25125.24	20623	9/14/2007	
15	8/24/2007	South Isla		706	9/30/2007	
16	9/7/2007	Fresh Foo		814	9/30/2007	
17	9/23/2007	Stop and S		824	10/23/2007	
18	4/2/2007	Regan Sup				
19	4/15/2007	PDQ Shop				
20	5/8/2007	Stop and S		508	6/8/2007	
21	2/5/2007	Corner Sto		205	2/26/2007	
22			154452.72			
23						

Shortcut menu (over rows 13–22):
Formula Refers to Empty Cells
Trace Empty Cell
Help on this error
Ignore Error
Edit in Formula Bar
Error Checking Options...

13. Click the row heading for row 15.

14. With the black right-arrow pointer, drag to select the row headings for rows 15 through 17. Three rows are selected or highlighted.

15. Right-click any of the selected row headings. The shortcut menu opens.

16. Choose **Insert**. Three rows are inserted, because you selected three rows before giving the Insert command.

Figure 4-11
Inserting three rows
at once
AcctRec.xlsx
AR2007 sheet

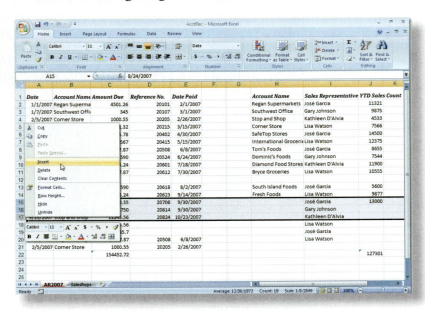

Exercise 4-12   DELETE ROWS

1. Click cell A12 and press Ctrl+−. The Delete dialog box opens.

2. Choose **Entire row** and click **OK**. The row is deleted.

3. Select the range A6:E7.

> **NOTE**
>
> You can use the − in the numeric keypad or in the top row of keys to delete cells.

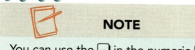

4. Drag the range to the new range A14:E15 and drop it.

5. Click the row heading for row 6. Drag to select the row headings for rows 6 and 7.

6. Right-click one of the selected row headings. Choose **Delete**. Two rows are deleted. Data is now missing from columns H, I, and J.

7. Click anywhere in row 14. In the **Cells** group, click the arrow with the Delete Cells button  and choose **Delete Sheet Rows**. One row is deleted.

8. Click cell C21. The formula has been updated to sum the correct rows.

Exercise 4-13   INSERT AND DELETE COLUMNS

When you insert a column, it extends to row 1,048,576.

1. Right-click the column D heading. The column is selected and the shortcut menu opens.

2. Choose **Insert**. One column is inserted, and existing columns move right.

> **NOTE**
>
> When you choose **Insert** or **Delete** from the shortcut menu, the dialog box does not open.

3. Key **Discount** in cell D1 and press Enter. Excel copies the format from the three columns that precede the new column.

4. Click anywhere in column G. Press Ctrl+−.

5. Choose **Entire column** and click **OK**. Column G is deleted, and the other columns move left to fill the space.

Exercise 4-14   HIDE AND UNHIDE COLUMNS AND ROWS

Since you have not filled in discount amounts, you can temporarily hide the column. In that way, your worksheet does not print with an empty column taking up space. You can hide columns or rows with data that need not be viewed or printed. Even though a row or column is hidden, its values are used in calculations.

You can determine when columns or rows are hidden, because their column or row headings are hidden. There is also a slightly thicker border between the column/row headings.

1. Right-click the column heading for column D to select the column.

2. Choose **Hide** from the shortcut menu. Column D is hidden.

3. Drag across the row headings for rows 12 through 14.

4. In the **Cells** group, click the Format button 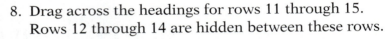. Hover over **Hide & Unhide**. Choose **Hide Rows**.

5. Click cell C21. Notice that the formula sums all the rows, even though three are hidden from view.

6. Drag across the column headings for columns C through E. Column D is hidden between these two columns.

7. Point at the column heading for either column and right-click. Choose **Unhide** from the shortcut menu.

8. Drag across the headings for rows 11 through 15. Rows 12 through 14 are hidden between these rows.

9. In the **Cells** group, click the Format button. Hover over **Hide & Unhide**. Choose **Unhide Rows**.

10. Press Ctrl + Home.

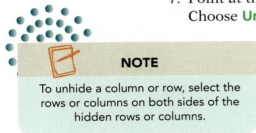

NOTE

To unhide a column or row, select the rows or columns on both sides of the hidden rows or columns.

Exercise 4-15   FREEZE AND SPLIT THE WINDOW

In large worksheets, seeing related columns or rows on-screen at the same time can be difficult if they are not close to each other. You can keep data in view by freezing one of the columns or rows. You can also split the window and show different parts of the same sheet in separate panes.

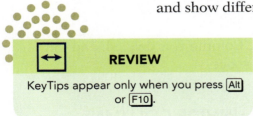

REVIEW

KeyTips appear only when you press Alt or F10.

1. Click the Zoom In button in the status bar to reach **130%**. This enlarges the display so that you cannot see all the rows. (Use a higher Zoom setting if you still see all the rows.)

2. Click cell A2. Press Alt and key **w** to open the **View** tab.

3. In the **Window** group, click the Freeze Panes button.

4. Choose **Freeze Top Row**. A solid horizontal line identifies where the row(s) are locked in position, between rows 1 and 2. This line does not print.

5. Press the ↓ arrow to reach row 30. The labels in row 1 do not scroll out of view.

6. Press Ctrl+Home. The pointer returns to the first unfrozen cell (cell A2).

7. In the **Window** group, click the Freeze Panes button 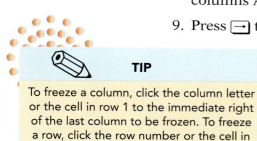. Choose **Unfreeze Panes**.

8. Click cell C1. In the **Window** group, click the Freeze Panes button . Choose **Freeze Panes**. The solid line is vertical to show that columns A and B are frozen.

9. Press → to reach column K. Columns A and B do not scroll.

10. Press Ctrl+Home. The pointer returns to the first unfrozen cell.

11. In the **Window** group, click the Freeze Panes button . Choose **Unfreeze Panes**.

12. In the **Window** group, click the Split button . The window splits at column C.

13. Rest the mouse on the vertical split bar. The pointer displays a two-pointed arrow.

14. Drag the split bar to be between columns C and D.

15. Click in the pane on the right and press Tab or → to position the sales reps' names as the first visible column on the left.

TIP

To freeze a column, click the column letter or the cell in row 1 to the immediate right of the last column to be frozen. To freeze a row, click the row number or the cell in column A immediately below the last row to be frozen.

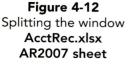

Figure 4-12
Splitting the window
AcctRec.xlsx
AR2007 sheet

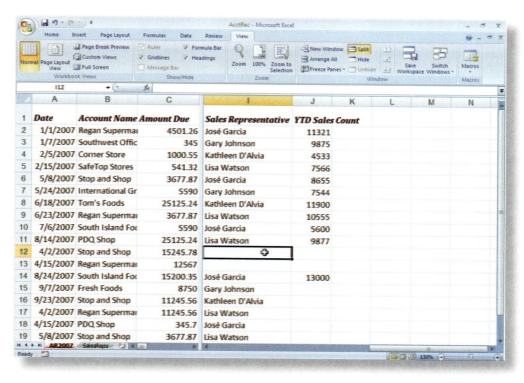

16. Click the Split button ⟨ 🗗 Split ⟩ to remove the split.

17. Set the Zoom size to **100%**.

18. Press ⟨Ctrl⟩+⟨Home⟩. Save the workbook as *[your initials]***4-15** in a new folder for Lesson 4.

Working with Cell Alignment

Cell alignment establishes how the contents of a cell are positioned in the cell. Cell contents can be aligned horizontally and vertically.

TABLE 4-1 Horizontal Alignment Options

Setting	Result
General	Aligns numbers and dates on the right, text on the left, and center-aligns error and logical values.
Left (Indent)	Aligns cell contents on the left of the cell indented by the number of spaces entered in the Indent box.
Center	Aligns contents in the middle of the cell.
Right (Indent)	Aligns cell contents on the right side of the cell indented by the number of spaces entered in the Indent box.
Fill	Repeats the cell contents until the cell's width is filled.
Justify	Spreads text to the left and right edges of the cell. This works only for wrapped text that is more than one line.
Center across selection	Places text in the middle of a selected range of columns.
Distributed (Indent)	Positions text an equal distance from the left and right edges including the number of spaces entered in the Indent box.

If a label is too wide for a cell, it generally spills into the cell to the right if that cell is empty and if the label is left-aligned. If the adjacent cell is not empty, the label is partially visible in the cell but completely visible in the formula bar.

TABLE 4-2 Vertical Alignment Options

Setting	Result
Top	Aligns cell contents at the top of the cell.
Center	Aligns cell contents in the vertical middle of the cell.
Bottom	Aligns cell contents at the bottom of the cell.
Justify	Spreads text to fill to the top and bottom edges of the cell. This works only for wrapped text that is more than one line.
Distributed	Positions text an equal distance from the top and bottom edges.

Exercise 4-16   CHANGE THE HORIZONTAL ALIGNMENT

The Alignment group on the Home tab contains three horizontal alignment buttons: the Align Text Left button, the Center button, and the Align Text Right button.

1. Press Alt and key **h** to open the **Home** tab.

2. Click cell A1. This label is left-aligned, but the dates in the column are right-aligned.

3. Click the Align Text Right button . The label is aligned at the right edge of the cell and balances the dates better.

4. Double-click the border between the column headings for columns B and C. The column title and the entries are left-aligned labels.

5. Click cell B1 and click the Center button ☰. Column titles are often centered over labels.

6. Click cell C1. Click the Align Text Right button ☰. Now the label better aligns with the values in the column.

Exercise 4-17   USE CENTER ACROSS SELECTION

The Center Across Selection command allows you to horizontally center multiple rows of labels across a part of the worksheet.

1. Point at the row 1 heading and drag to select rows 1 and 2.

2. Right-click either row heading and choose **Insert**. Two rows are inserted.

3. In cell A1, key **Klassy Kow Accounts Receivable** and press Enter.

4. In cell A2, key **Commercial Accounts**.

5. Select cells A1:A2 and right-click either cell. The Mini toolbar appears above the shortcut menu. Choose **Cambria** from the Font list (see Figure 4-13 on the next page).

NOTE

The Mini toolbar does not display ScreenTips. It fades from view as soon as you start another command.

6. Click the Increase Font Size button A˙ in the Mini toolbar three times to reach 16 point. Watch the Font size box in the Font group to check the size.

Figure 4-13
Using the Mini
toolbar
4-15.xlsx
AR2007 sheet

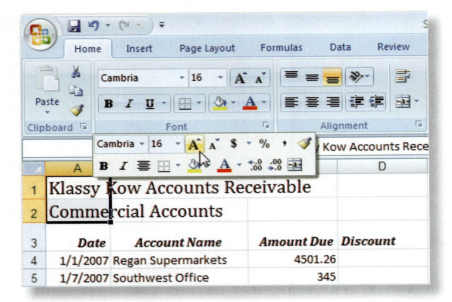

7. Click cell A2. In the **Font** group on the **Home** tab, click the Decrease Font Size button Ⓐ to reach 14 point.

8. Select cells A1:F2. This includes the labels and the range over which they will be centered.

9. Right-click any cell in the range and choose **Format Cells**.

10. Click the **Alignment** tab.

11. Click the arrow for the **Horizontal** box to display the options.

Figure 4-14
Alignment tab in the
Format Cells dialog
box

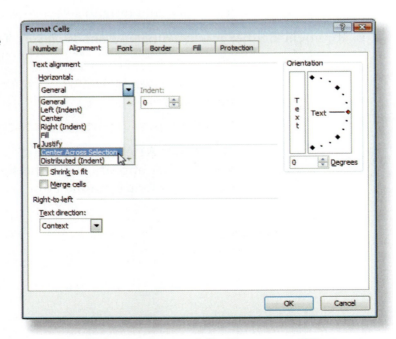

12. Choose **Center Across Selection**. Click **OK**. The labels are centered over the columns you selected.

Exercise 4-18   CHANGE THE VERTICAL ALIGNMENT

The Alignment group contains three vertical alignment buttons: Top Align ≡ , Middle Align ≡ , and Bottom Align ≡ . You can also set any alignment choice from the Format Cells dialog box.

1. Change row 1 to **37.50 (50 pixels)** high. You can see that the label is aligned at the bottom of the cell.

2. Click cell A1. Press Ctrl+1 to open the Format Cells dialog box.

3. On the **Alignment** tab, click the arrow for the **Vertical** box.

4. Choose **Center** and then click **OK**. The label is centered in the row.

Exercise 4-19   WRAP TEXT AND CHANGE INDENTS

Multiple-word labels can be split into multiple lines in a cell using the **Wrap Text** setting. With this choice, a narrow column can accommodate a wider label. The label will, of course, occupy more vertical space.

You can improve the readability of adjacent labels and values by adding an indent to one or the other. This moves the data away from the edge of the cell but maintains the alignment.

NOTE

Your screen size and resolution setting affect how buttons look in the Ribbon. They may or may not include both an icon and text. The arrow may be next to or below the icon, too.

TIP

While keying a label, press Alt+Enter to force a line break between words. Then adjust column width and row height as needed.

1. Change column E to **10.71 (80 pixels)** wide. Notice that this is wide enough for the data, but not wide enough for the label.

2. Click cell E3 and click the Wrap Text button ≡ in the **Alignment** group. The label splits into two lines, but now the row isn't high enough.

3. Change row 3 to **30.00 (40 pixels)** high.

4. Click cell E3 and click the Center button ≡ . The wrapped label looks better centered.

5. Click cell B3. Press F8 to start Extend Selection mode.

6. Press Ctrl+Down. This shortcut selects contiguous cells with data in the column.

7. Press Ctrl+1. On the **Alignment** tab, click the arrow for the **Horizontal** box.

8. Choose **Left (Indent)**. Click the up arrow for **Indent** to change it to **1**.

9. Click **OK**. The labels are indented one space from the left edge of the cell, leaving some space between them and the right-aligned dates in column A.

10. Double-click the border between the column headings for columns B and C.

Exercise 4-20   USE MERGE AND CENTER

The Merge and Center command combines a selected range of cells into one cell that occupies the same amount of space and centers the contents. You can merge any number of columns and rows to create special effects and alignment settings. The range of cells to merge should be empty except for the top-left cell.

1. Select the range H1:J23 and click the Cut button ✂.

2. Click the **SalesReps** worksheet tab and press Enter. The data is moved.

3. AutoFit each column.

4. Select the range B16:C23 and press Delete.

5. In cell A1, key **Supermarket Sales Associates**. Press Ctrl + Enter.

6. Select the range A1:C1.

7. In the **Alignment** group, click the Merge and Center button. Cells A1:C1 are now one cell (A1), and the label is centered.

8. Right-click the row 2 heading and choose **Delete**.

9. Click cell C2 and point at an edge to show the drag-and-drop pointer.

10. Click and drag the cell to cell D3.

11. Select cells D3:D12.

> **NOTE**
>
> You can unmerge cells by clicking the Merge and Center button to turn off the command.

12. Click the Merge and Center button. Cells D3:D12 are now one cell (D3) that occupies the same amount of space, and the label is horizontally centered at the bottom.

Exercise 4-21   CHANGE CELL ORIENTATION

The label in the merged cell D3 is horizontal like the rest of your data. Because the cells were merged vertically, you should change the data's rotation to match.

1. Right-click cell D3 and choose **Format Cells**.

2. On the **Alignment** tab, click the red diamond in the **Orientation** box.

3. Drag the red diamond down to show −90 degrees (that's "minus 90 degrees"). Click **OK**. The text is rotated −90 degrees. Now you should change the vertical centering as well.

Figure 4-15
Rotating text
−90 degrees

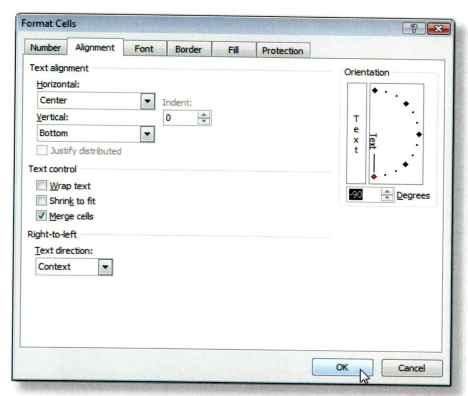

4. Press [Ctrl]+[1]. On the **Alignment** tab, click the arrow next to the **Vertical** box. Choose **Center** and click **OK**.

5. Change column C to **11.43 (85 pixels)** wide.

6. Make cell A1 14-point Cambria.

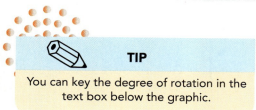

TIP

You can key the degree of rotation in the text box below the graphic.

Applying Borders and Fill

A *border* is a line around a cell or a range of cells. You can use borders to draw attention to a part of a worksheet, to show totals, or to group information in your worksheet.

Shading or *fill* is a background pattern or color for a cell or a range of cells. You can use fill in much the same way as a border—to group data or to add emphasis.

Exercise 4-22   **APPLY BORDERS USING THE BORDERS BUTTON**

Cells share borders, so adding a border to the bottom of cell A1 has the same effect as adding a border to the top of cell A2.

Excel provides two methods to apply a border to a cell or a range of cells:

- Use the Borders button ⊞▾ in the Font group.
- Use the Format Cells dialog box.

1. Click cell C12.

2. Click the arrow with the Borders button ⊞▾. A gallery of border styles opens.

Figure 4-16
Borders gallery
4-15.xlsx
SalesReps sheet

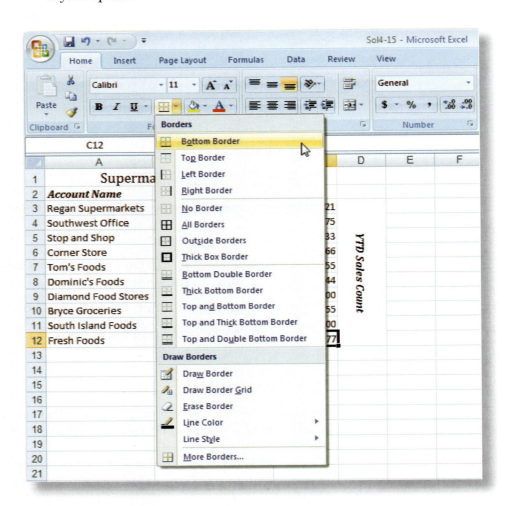

3. Choose **Bottom Border**. A thin solid bottom border is applied to the cell.

4. Click cell C14 to better see the border. Notice that the border fills the width of the cell.

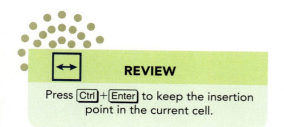

REVIEW

Press Ctrl+Enter to keep the insertion point in the current cell.

5. Select cell C13 and click the AutoSum button . Press Ctrl+Enter.

6. Click the arrow next to the Borders button. Click **Bottom Double Border**.

7. Click cell B13 to see the border. Notice that the Borders button shows the last-used style.

TIP

Totals in accounting and financial reports are often shown with a single border above and a double border below. There is a border style called Top and Double Bottom.

Exercise 4-23   APPLY BORDERS USING THE DIALOG BOX

The Format Cells dialog box provides more choices for designing borders.

1. Click the **AR2007** worksheet tab and press Ctrl+Home.

2. Press F5. Key **c23** and press Enter.

TIP

Inside borders are applied to multiple cells, not to a single cell.

3. Press Ctrl+1. Click the **Border** tab. There are presets for **None**, **Outline**, or **Inside**.

4. Click **Outline**. The Border buttons around the preview show the top, bottom, and left and right side borders active in an outline border.

5. Click **None** to remove the border in the preview.

6. Click the arrow for the **Color** box. Choose **Accent 2** in the first row, sixth column.

NOTE

Choose the **Color** and **Style** of line before setting the location of borders in the Format Cells dialog box.

7. In the **Style** box, choose a single line (first column, last line).

8. In the **Text** preview area, click where the top border will be located. A preview of the red/brown single-line border is shown (see Figure 4-17 on the next page).

Figure 4-17
Border tab in the
Format Cells dialog
box
4-15.xlsx
AR2007 sheet

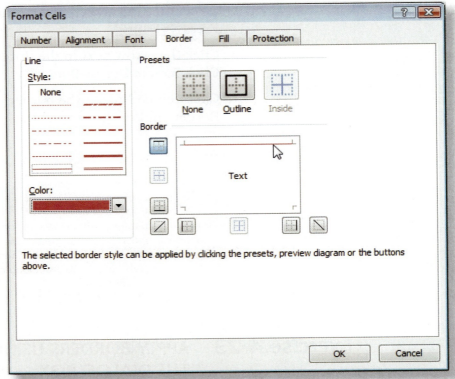

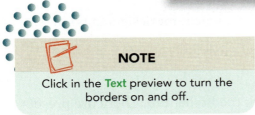

NOTE

Click in the **Text** preview to turn the borders on and off.

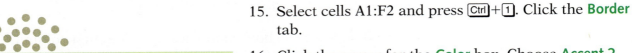

REVIEW

Borders appear in a shade of gray if your default printer is a non-color printer.

9. In the **Style** box, choose a double line (second column, last line). The color is still red/brown.

10. In the **Text** preview area, click where the bottom border will be located.

11. Click **OK**.

12. Deselect the cell to see the borders.

13. Click the Page Layout View button ▣ in the status bar.

14. Set the Zoom size to **70%**. It will be easier to preview your work in this size and view.

15. Select cells A1:F2 and press Ctrl+1. Click the **Border** tab.

16. Click the arrow for the **Color** box. Choose **Accent 2**.

17. In the **Style** box, choose a single line (first column, last line).

18. Click **Outline**. Click **OK**.

Exercise 4-24 ADD SOLID FILL

The background of a cell or a range of cells can be shaded with a solid color or a pattern. Excel provides two methods for applying fill to a cell or a range of cells:

- Use the Fill Color button in the Font group.
- Use the Format Cells dialog box.

1. Click the **SalesReps** worksheet tab. This worksheet is in Normal view.

2. Select the range A3:C3. In the **Font** group, click the Fill Color button . Excel applies the color shown beneath the paint bucket icon.

3. Click in row 5 to see the shading.

4. Click the Undo button . The fill is removed, and the range is still selected.

5. Click the arrow next to the Fill Color button . The color palette opens.

6. Choose **Background 1, Darker 25%** in the first column.

7. Select the range A5:C5. Press Ctrl+1 and click the **Fill** tab.

8. For the **Background Color**, choose the first color in the third row below the theme colors. Click **OK**.

9. Double-click the Format Painter button . This locks the painter on, and a marquee appears around the selected range.

10. Select the range A7:C7 to paint the format. Then select cells A9:C9 and A11:C11.

11. Click the Format Painter button to turn it off.

Exercise 4-25 USE PATTERN FILL

A pattern might be dots or crisscrossed lines. Patterns are acceptable for cells that do not contain data or for cells with minimal data.

1. Click cell D3 and press Ctrl+1.

2. Click the **Fill** tab.

> **TIP**
>
> Many patterns can make it difficult to read data in the cell.

3. Click the arrow for the **Pattern Style** box. Patterns include dots, stripes, and crosshatches.

4. Choose **12.5% Gray** in the first row of patterns, second from the right. This is a dotted pattern (see Figure 4-18 on the next page).

Figure 4-18
Changing the
pattern
4-15.xlsx
Sales Reps sheet

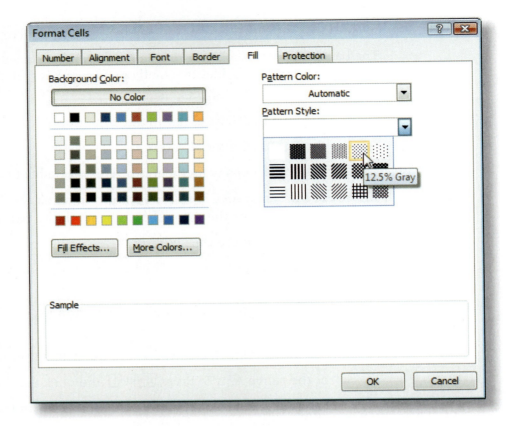

5. Click **OK**.

6. Right-click the column A heading and choose **Insert**. Right-click the row 1 heading and choose **Insert**.

7. Make both columns A and F **5.00 (40 pixels)** wide. Set the height of rows 1 and 15 at **15.00 (20 pixels)**.

8. Select cells A1:F15 and press Ctrl+1. Click the **Border** tab.

9. Choose a double-line style and an outline. Click **OK**.

10. Click the Page Layout View button 🔲 in the status bar. Click cell A1.

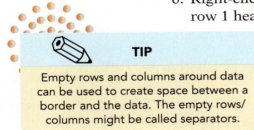

TIP

Empty rows and columns around data can be used to create space between a border and the data. The empty rows/columns might be called separators.

Exercise 4-26   COMPLETE THE NUMBER FORMATTING

The Comma Style button 🔳 inserts commas and two decimal places in a value. If you want fewer decimal places, you can use the Decrease Decimal button 🔳 to remove positions one at a time.

You can build your own number formats from the Format Cells dialog box. For example, you can create a format that shows a *leading zero*, which is a zero (0) as the first digit in a number, typically a decimal number (example "0.59"). Normally, Excel does not show a leading zero because it has no value.

1. Select the range D4:D14. On the **Home** tab in the **Number** group, click the Comma Style button . Commas and two decimal places are added to the values.

2. In the **Number** group, click the Decrease Decimal button . One decimal position is removed.

3. Click the Decrease Decimal button again. The values still have the commas, but no decimals.

4. Click the **AR2007** worksheet tab.

5. Click cell C4. Hold down Ctrl and click cell C23.

6. Press Ctrl+1. Click the **Number** tab.

7. Choose **Accounting** in the **Category** list. A sample is displayed in the dialog box.

8. Click **OK**. This is the same format applied by the Accounting Number Format button .

9. Select the range C5:C22. Click the Comma Style button .

10. Select the range E4:E22. Press Ctrl+1 and click the **Number** tab.

11. Choose **Custom** in the **Category** list. Click **0** in the **Type** list. The zero appears in the entry box under **Type**.

12. Click after the **0** in the box and key **00000** to show six zeros. Zero (0) means that a digit is required. This format requires that the entry be six digits. If the value uses only five digits, Excel inserts a zero in the first position.

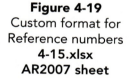

Figure 4-19
Custom format for Reference numbers
4-15.xlsx
AR2007 sheet

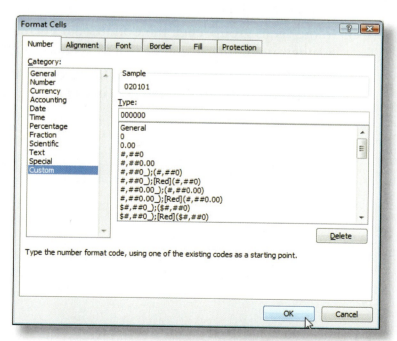

13. Click **OK**.

Using Data Bars

The Styles group on the Home tab includes Conditional Formatting tasks. These commands enable you to set formatting for a range of cells based on cell contents. For example, if a value is over 100, you can format it to appear in a particular color or with a fill. As part of the conditional formatting features, you can apply a data visualization. A *visualization* is a format element that displays bars, colors, or icons with the values. The formatting identifies trends and exceptions or compares values. It is a quick way to analyze data across many rows.

Excel has three types of visualizations.

- *Data bars* fill each cell with varying lengths of a color based on the highest and lowest values.

- A *color scale* shades each cell with varying colors based on the values. There are two- and three-color scales.

- An *icon set* displays an icon at the left of each cell based on the values. There are sets of three, four, and five icons.

Exercise 4-27   USE DATA BARS

With data bars, you can determine the value of a cell relative to the other cells in the range. The highest value displays the longest bar, and the lowest value displays the shortest bar.

1. Return to Normal view.

2. Select cells C4:C22.

3. In the **Styles** group, click the Conditional Formatting button . A subgroup of formatting rules and visualizations opens.

4. Hover over **Data Bars**. Choose the first icon for **Blue Data Bar**. You can see the visualization immediately on screen.

Figure 4-20
Choosing a data bar
format
4-15.xlsx
AR2007 sheet

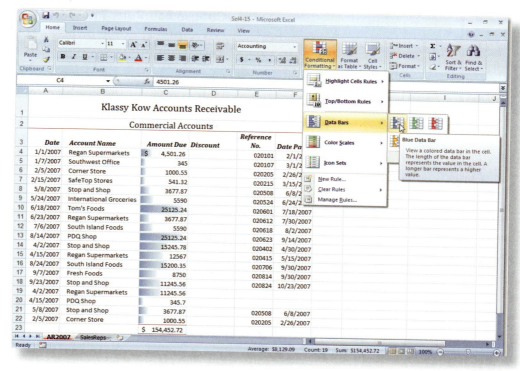

5. Click in column D. You can better see the bars.

Exercise 4-28 EDIT THE DATA BAR RULE

You can edit the rules used to build data bars by choosing colors, setting a value, a percent, a percentile, or by building a formula.

1. Select cells C4:C22.

2. In the **Styles** group, click the Conditional Formatting button 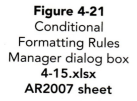.

3. Choose **Manage Rules**. The Conditional Formatting Rules Manager dialog box opens. Your current selection uses a data bar.

Figure 4-21
Conditional
Formatting Rules
Manager dialog box
4-15.xlsx
AR2007 sheet

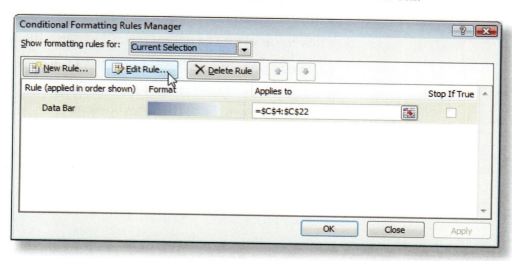

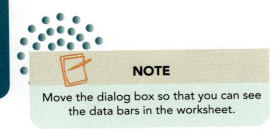

NOTE

Move the dialog box so that you can see the data bars in the worksheet.

4. Choose **Edit Rule**. The Edit Formatting Rule dialog box shows that the cells are formatted based on the lowest and highest value with a blue bar.

5. Click the arrow for **Bar Color**. Choose **Accent 2, Lighter 40%** in the sixth column.

6. Click to select **Show Bar Only**. Click **OK**. Click **OK** again. This option hides the values.

Figure 4-22
Edit Formatting Rule dialog box
4-15.xlsx
AR2007 sheet

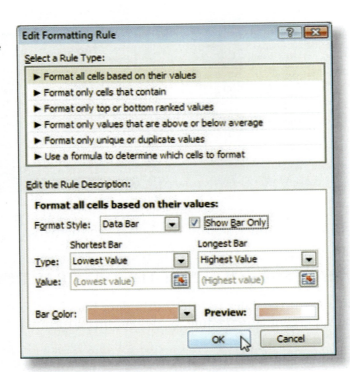

7. Click the Conditional Formatting button. Choose **Manage Rules** and then **Edit Rule**.

8. Click to deselect **Show Bar Only**. Click **OK**. Click **OK** again.

9. Key your first and last name in cell A24. Key your first and last name in cell B17 on the **SalesReps** worksheet.

10. Press Ctrl + Home. Save the workbook as *[your initials]***4-28** in your Lesson 4 folder.

11. Prepare and submit your work. Then close the workbook.

Using Online Help

In addition to data bars, color scales and icon sets are quick ways to add conditional formatting to your data.

EXPLORE CONDITIONAL FORMATTING

1. In a new workbook, press F1.

2. In the Search box, key **conditional formatting** and press Enter.

3. Find and review topics to learn more about data bars, color scales, icon sets, and other rules. Read the help information.

4. Close the Help window.

Lesson 4 Summary

- You can insert, delete, move, and rename worksheets in a workbook.

- Insert or delete cells when you need space for missing data or have blank rows or columns in a worksheet.

- The AutoComplete feature makes suggestions when you key a label that begins with the same characters as labels already in the column.

- The Pick From Drop-Down List displays a list of all labels already in the current column.

- When you cut or copy data, it is placed on the Windows Clipboard and the Office Clipboard. Copied data can be pasted more than once.

- The Office Clipboard stores up to 24 copied elements. It is shared among Word, Excel, Access, and PowerPoint.

- When you delete or insert a row or column, it is inserted across the entire worksheet. Be careful about data that is on the sheet but out of view.

- Change the cell alignment to make data easier to read and more professional-looking. There are several horizontal and vertical alignment choices.

- You can use the Mini toolbar to apply cell formats.

- Text can be wrapped, indented, or rotated.

- The Merge and Center command combines a range of cells into one cell.

- Borders outline a cell or range of cells with a variety of line styles and colors.

- Shading is the background pattern or color for a cell or range of cells.

- Data bars are data visualization that applies conditional formatting based on the cell's value.

- You can edit the color of a data bar and the way in which it is applied.

LESSON 4   Command Summary

Feature	Button	Task Path	Keyboard
Bottom Align	≡	Home, Cells, Format, Format Cells	Ctrl + 1
Align Text Left	≡	Home, Cells, Format, Format Cells	Ctrl + 1
Middle Align	≡	Home, Cells, Format, Format Cells	Ctrl + 1
Align Text Right	≡	Home, Cells, Format, Format Cells	Ctrl + 1
Top Align	≡	Home, Cells, Format, Format Cells	Ctrl + 1
Borders	⊞ ▾	Home, Alignment	Ctrl + 1
Center	≡	Home, Alignment	Ctrl + 1
Center across selection	Format ▾	Home, Cells, Format, Format Cells	Ctrl + 1
Comma Style	,	Home, Number	Ctrl + 1
Copy	📋	Home, Clipboard	Ctrl + C
Cut	✂	Home, Clipboard	Ctrl + X
Data bars	Conditional Formatting	Home, Styles, Conditional Formatting	
Data bars, edit	Conditional Formatting	Home, Styles, Conditional Formatting, Manage Rules	
Decrease Decimal	.00 →.0	Home, Number	Ctrl + 1
Decrease Font Size	A▾	Home, Font	Ctrl + 1
Delete cell, row, column	Delete ▾	Home, Cells, Delete	Ctrl + −
Fill color	🎨 ▾	Home, Font	Ctrl + 1
Freeze rows/columns	Freeze Panes ▾	View, Window	
Hide/unhide row/column	Format ▾	Home, Cells, Format	
Increase Font Size	A▴	Home Font	Ctrl + 1
Indent text	≣	Home, Cells, Format	Ctrl + 1
Insert cell, row, column	Insert ▾	Home, Cells, Insert	Ctrl + +
Merge and Center	▦ ▾	Home, Alignment	
Paste	Paste	Home, Clipboard	Ctrl + V
Split window	⬚ Split	View, Window	
Text orientation	⬗ ▾	Home, Cells, Format, Format Cells	V + 1
Unfreeze rows/columns	Freeze Panes ▾	View, Window	
Wrap text	≣	Home, Alignment	V + 1

Concepts Review

True/False Questions

Each of the following statements is either true or false. Indicate your choice by circling T or F.

T F   1. Inserted cells do not affect the position of existing cells.

T F   2. A column is hidden when it is frozen.

T F   3. Freezing rows and columns locks them in position on the screen.

T F   4. AutoComplete fills in formulas and cell addresses.

T F   5. Data bars are relative to the cell's value.

T F   6. Fill creates a shadow effect around cell borders.

T F   7. The Merge and Center command works for multiple rows or columns.

T F   8. The Windows Clipboard and the Office Clipboard both store 12 items of cut or copied data.

Short Answer Questions

Write the correct answer in the space provided.

1. What two commands help you enter labels in columns that already have many labels?

_____

2. If you want to repeat a lengthy label several times throughout a worksheet, would you cut it or copy it?

_____

3. What does the term "drag and drop" mean?

_____

4. What is the default alignment for values and dates in a cell?

_____

5. What command will lock rows or columns in position on the screen?

_____

6. What command combines several cells into one cell occupying the same screen space?

_____

7. How can you format a number to show leading zeros?

_____

8. What alignment option allows a label to split within a cell?

_____

Critical Thinking

Answer these questions on a separate page. There are no right or wrong answers. Support your answers with examples from your own experience, if possible.

1. When you delete a row or a column, it is deleted across the entire worksheet. What problems could result from this?

2. What are the advantages of AutoComplete and Pick From Drop-Down List? What are the disadvantages of each?

Skills Review

Exercise 4-29

Insert/delete sheets. Insert/delete cells. Use AutoComplete and Pick From Drop-Down List.

1. Open **Personnel**. Save it as *[your initials]*4-29 in your Lesson 4 folder.
2. Rename **Sheet1** as **Employees**. Choose a tab color from the document theme colors.
3. Insert and delete worksheets by following these steps:
   a. Right-click **Sheet2** and choose **Delete**.
   b. Repeat these steps to delete **Sheet3**.
   c. Point at the **Insert Worksheet** tab and click.
   d. Name the new sheet **Interviews** and choose a theme color.

NOTE

If you click an e-mail address, Excel launches your e-mail service and adds the address to the recipient list.

4. Insert and delete cells by following these steps:
    a. On the **Employees** sheet, right-click cell E13 and choose **Insert**.
    b. Choose **Shift cells down** and click **OK**.
    c. Key **5/29/78** in cell E13.
    d. Select cells F13:F14. Press ⌨Ctrl+⌨−.
    e. Choose **Shift cells up** and click **OK**.

5. Add data with AutoComplete by following these steps:
    a. Click cell A16 and key **Biesterfield**. Press ⌨Tab.
    b. Key **ka** and press ⌨→ or ⌨Tab.

6. Key **kbiesterfield@kkic.net** and press ⌨Tab or ⌨→.

7. Key today's date in cell D16.

8. Add data with **Pick From Drop-Down List** by following these steps:
    a. Right-click cell F16 and choose **Pick From Drop-Down List**.
    b. Choose **Human Resources**.
    c. Right-click cell G16 and choose **Pick From Drop-Down List**.
    d. Choose **Klamath Falls**.
    e. Insert **Finance** in cell F14 and **Marketing** in cell F15.

9. AutoFit column C. Change columns A and B to **10.71 (80 pixels)**.

10. Press ⌨Ctrl+⌨Home.

  11. Click the **Insert** tab. Click the Header & Footer button 🔳. Click the Go to Footer button 🔳. Key your first and last name in the left section. Insert the filename in the center and the current date at the right.

12. Click the **Page Layout** tab. Drag the left margin marker to **.50** inches or slightly less. Do the same for the right margin marker. Adjust column widths, if needed, to fit the worksheet on one page.

13. Prepare and submit your worksheet. Save and close the workbook.

Exercise 4-30

Copy and paste cell contents. Insert and delete columns and rows.

1. Open **Personnel**. Save the workbook as *[your initials]*4-30 in your Lesson 4 folder.

2. Click cell A16 and key **McTavish**. Ignore the AutoComplete suggestion. Press ⌨Tab.

3. Key **Diane** and press ⌨Tab. Key **dmctavish@kkic.net** and press ⌨Tab.

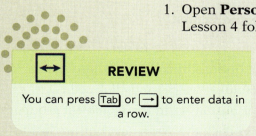

REVIEW

You can press ⌨Tab or ⌨→ to enter data in a row.

4. Copy and paste cell contents by following these steps:

    a. Press [Alt] and key **h**.

    b. Click cell D8 and click the Copy button 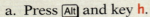.

    c. Click cell D16 and press [Enter].

    d. Click cell E15 and display the drag-and-drop pointer.

    e. Hold down [Ctrl] and drag a copy to cell E16.

       f. Click cell F7 and press [Ctrl]+[C].

       g. Click cell F16 and press [Ctrl]+[V]. Press [Esc].

       h. Copy any city from a cell in column G to cell G16.

5. Insert columns by following these steps:

    a. Right-click anywhere in column A. Choose **Insert**.

    b. Choose **Entire column** and click **OK**.

6. Key **Emp #** in cell A2. Copy the format from cell B2 to cell A2.

7. In cell A3, key **1** and press [Enter]. In cell A4, key **2** and press [Enter]. Select cells A3:A4 and use the Fill handle to fill in values down to cell A16.

8. Drag the label in cell B1 and drop it in cell A1.

9. Delete columns and insert rows by following these steps:

    a. Right-click the column D heading and choose **Delete**.

    b. Right-click the row 2 heading and choose **Insert**.

10. In cell A2, key **January 200X** using the current year. Press [Ctrl]+[Home].

11. From the Insert tab, create a header with your first and last name at the left, the filename in the center, and the date at the right.

12. From the Page Layout tab, set the left and right margins to **.50** inches.

13. Prepare and submit your work. Save and close the workbook.

NOTE

If you paste copied cells where there is existing data, the copy replaces the existing data.

REVIEW

Use the Format Painter to copy the font, size, and style.

NOTE

The date is formatted in a default style for your computer.

Exercise 4-31

Use cell alignment options. Use Merge and Center.

1. Open **EmpNo**. Save it as *[your initials]***4-31** in your folder.

2. Use cell alignment options by following these steps:

    a. Click cell D2. Hold down [Ctrl] and click cell G2.

    b. Click the Center button 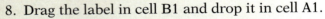 in the **Alignment** group.

    c. Click cell A2 and click the Wrap Text button 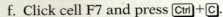.

    d. Click the Center button 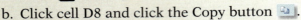.

3. Change column A to **10.71 (80 pixels)** wide. Change row 2 to **30.00 (40.00 pixels)** high.

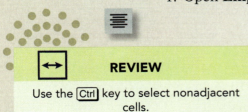

REVIEW

Use the [Ctrl] key to select nonadjacent cells.

4. Rotate text by following these steps:
   a. Edit the label in cell A2 to show # instead of **Number**.
   b. Select the range A2:G2 and press Ctrl+1.
   c. Click the **Alignment** tab.
   d. Drag the red diamond in the **Orientation** box to reach **30** degrees. Click **OK**.

5. Change row 2 to **60.00 (80 pixels)** high.

6. Use Merge and Center by following these steps:
   a. Select the range A1:G1.

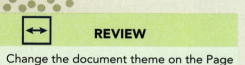

   b. Click the Merge and Center button.

7. Delete **Sheet2** and **Sheet3**. Rename **Sheet1** as **Personnel** and choose a tab color.

8. Create a footer with your first and last name in the left section, the sheet name in the center section, and the date in the right section.

9. In Page Layout View, change the left and right margins to fit the worksheet on the page.

10. Prepare and submit your work. Save and close the workbook.

Exercise 4-32

Use cell alignment. Apply borders. Use data bars.

⟷ REVIEW

Change the document theme on the Page Layout tab.

1. Create a new workbook and save it as *[your initials]*4-32 in your folder.

2. Key **Klassy Kow Ice Cream, Inc.** in cell A1 and make it 16-point. Key **Planned Interviews** in cell A2 and format it as 12-point bold. Change to the **Solstice** document theme.

3. Key the labels, dates, and times shown in Figure 4-23. Use default date and time formats for your computer.

Figure 4-23

	A	B	C	D
3	Name	Date	Time	Experience
4	Jonathan Aria	May 24	9 am	2
5	Christophe Kryztish	June 5	11 am	5
6	Melinda Dapoulas	June 5	2 pm	3
7	Pamela Dryzski	June 8	10 am	5
8	Yoshima Sato	June 9	10 am	2

NOTE

Character space and pixel measurements depend on the default font.

4. Make the labels in row 3 bold. Change column A to **16.88 (140 pixels)** wide. Change columns B:D to **10.00 (85 pixels)** wide.

5. Use cell alignment by following these steps:

    a. Select the range A1:D2.

    b. In the **Alignment** group, click the Dialog Box Launcher.

    c. Click the **Horizontal** arrow and choose **Center Across Selection**. Click **OK**.

    d. Select the labels in row 3 and click the Center button .

    e. Select cells D6:D10 and click the Dialog Box Launcher in the **Alignment** group.

    f. Click the **Horizontal** arrow and choose **Right (Indent)**. In the **Indent** box, choose or key **2**. Click **OK**.

6. Apply borders by following these steps:

    a. Click the row 4 heading and drag to select row 5. Right-click and choose **Insert**.

    b. Select the range A3:D3.

    c. In the **Font** group, click the arrow next to the Borders button. Choose **Top and Bottom Border.**

    d. Select the range A4:D4. Click the Dialog Box Launcher in the **Font** group. Click the **Border** tab.

    e. In the **Style** list, choose the dot-dot-dash line (first line, second column). Click the bottom border area in the preview box. Close the dialog box.

    f. Set row 4 to a height of **4.50 (6 pixels)**. Set the height of row 5 to **15.00 (20 pixels)**.

    g. Select the range A12:D12. Click the down arrow next to the Borders button. Choose **Bottom Border**.

    h. Select the range A11:D11. Press Ctrl+1. Click the **Border** tab.

    i. In the **Style** list, choose the dot-dot-dash line. Click the bottom border area in the preview box. Close the dialog box.

    j. Set the height of row 11 to **15.00 (20 pixels)** and row 12 to **4.50 (6 pixels)**. Make row 3 the same height as row 2.

7. Use data bars by following these steps:

    a. Select cells D6:D10. Click the Conditional Formatting button in the **Styles** group.

    b. Choose **Data Bars** and then **Green Data Bar.**

    c. Click the Conditional Formatting button. Choose **Manage Rules**.

    d. Choose **Edit Rule**. Set the **Bar Color** to a shade of gray. Click **OK** to return to the worksheet.

8. Press Ctrl+Home. Delete **Sheet2** and **Sheet3**. Rename **Sheet1** as **Interviews** and choose a tab color to coordinate with the data bar.

9. In Page Layout View, change the left and right margin to **2.25** inches.

10. Create a header with your first and last name at the left, the sheet name in the center, and the date at the right.

11. Prepare and submit your work. Save and close the workbook.

TIP

Use the view switcher buttons on the status bar to quickly change views while working.

Lesson Applications

Exercise 4-33

Cut, copy, and paste data. Use borders and cell alignment. Add data bars.

1. Open **KowOwow** and save it as *[your initials]***4-33** in your folder.

2. On the **Oregon** sheet, cut the "Ashland" row and insert it before the "Eugene" row. Cut the "Medford" row and insert it before the "Roseburg" row.

3. Copy the range A7:A11 to cells A15:A20.

4. Key the following values for 2007:

Figure 2-24

		Chocolate	Vanilla
2007			
Ashland		22000	21000
Eugene		27000	28000
Klamath Falls		20000	18000
Medford		18000	16000
Roseburg		17000	15000

5. Shows sums in the range D7:D11 and in the range B12:D12. Apply the Comma style with no decimals to cells B7:D12.

6. Center the labels in rows 1:2 over the data. Align the labels in row 3 to balance the data in each column.

7. Set the row height for rows 14:19 to match the 2007 data. Create borders in rows 20:21 to mirror those in rows 4:5.

8. Use orange data bars for cells D7:D11.

9. Add a footer. Set the left margin so that the sheet appears centered on the page.

NOTE

Use the Borders dialog box to design special borders.

10. On the **California** sheet, copy cells A5:A19 to cells A22:A36. Show totals for 2007.

11. Format values to show commas and no decimals. Center the labels in rows 1:2 over the data. Adjust the alignment of the labels in row 3 for better balance.

12. Select cells A5:D18. Apply dotted-line middle and bottom horizontal borders. Do the same for the lower half of the sheet.

13. Add a custom header to the sheet. Set the left margin so that the sheet appears centered.

14. Prepare and submit your work. Save and close the workbook.

Exercise 4-34

Insert and move worksheets. Align labels; use borders and fill. Copy data and formats.

1. Open **EstKowO** and save it as *[your initials]*4-34 in your folder.

2. Insert two new worksheets and name them **Nevada** and **Washington**.

3. Arrange the worksheets so that they are in alphabetical order, left to right. Use a different accent color for each tab.

4. On the **Oregon** sheet, center the labels in rows 1:2 over the data and apply a lighter shade of the tab color as fill. Right-align the labels in row 3.

5. Use the tab color for a double top border for row 1. Apply a double bottom border to row 2 using the same color. Make each of these rows slightly taller. Then set the vertical alignment of cell A2 to **Center** so that the amount of space above the labels appears to be equal to the space below.

6. Select cells A3:D18. Use the **Border** tab to apply single inside borders and single left, right, and bottom borders (same color as the tab). Apply single side borders to rows 1:2 to complete the design.

7. Copy and paste cells A1:D4 on the **Oregon** sheet to the same range on the **Nevada** sheet. Click the Paste Options button and choose **Keep Source Column Widths**. Paste with the same options to the **Washington** sheet.

NOTE

Do not press [Enter] to complete a paste command if you want to use the Paste Options.

8. Copy cells B5:D11 from the **Oregon** sheet to the **Nevada** sheet. From the Paste Options, choose **Formatting Only**. Paste with the same options to the **Washington** sheet.

9. Change the fill and border colors on the **Nevada** sheet to match its tab color. Add a footer. Do the same for the **Washington** sheet.

10. Add a header to the **Oregon** sheet. Prepare and submit your work.

11. Save and close the workbook.

Exercise 4-35

Insert columns. Cut cells. Use cell alignment and borders. Add data bars.

1. Open **EstKowO** and save it as *[your initials]*4-35 in your folder.

2. On the **California** sheet, insert a column at column C. Move the label in cell A4 to cell B4. Move the label in cell A21 to cell C4.

TIP

If you prefer to use drag and drop, reduce the Zoom size to see more on screen.

TIP

A column filled with # symbols means the column is not wide enough.

3. Move cells B22:B36 to cells C5:C19.

4. Insert a column at column E. Copy the labels in cells B4:C4 to cells D4:E4. Move cells D22:D36 to cells E5:E19.

5. Fix the formula in cell F5 and copy it to the appropriate cells.

6. Center-align the labels in row 4 and cell F3. Merge and center cells B3:C3; do the same for Vanilla. Center the labels in rows 1:2 over the data. Delete all data below row 21.

7. Apply Accounting Number Format for rows 5 and 19 but remove the decimal places.

8. Insert a column at column D and make it 2.14 (20 pixels) wide. Then set single left and right borders for cells D3:D19. Apply a single-line top border to cells A3:G3.

9. Set gray data bars for cells G5:G18.

10. Add a header and prepare and submit your work.

11. Save and close the workbook.

Exercise 4-36 ◆ Challenge Yourself

Cut and paste rows. Change cell alignment and data bars.

1. Open **JulyCakes** and save it as *[your initials]*4-36.

2. Arrange the flavors in alphabetical order. Show quarterly sums.

3. Change the labels in rows 1:3 to the headings font. Then choose a larger size for the labels in rows 1:2 and center them across the data.

4. Format the values with Comma style but no decimals.

5. Change to the Concourse document theme. Make other adjustments and/or format enhancements that you think are necessary.

6. Delete the data bars.

7. Add a header. Turn off printing and viewing for gridlines and row and column headings.

8. Prepare and submit your work. Save and close the workbook.

On Your Own

In these exercises you work on your own, as you would in a real-life work environment. Use the skills you've learned to accomplish the task—and be creative.

Exercise 4-37

Create a new workbook and save it as *[your initials]*4-37 in your Lesson 4 folder. Key the names of eight people in your class, relatives, or coworkers. List each person's city, state, favorite color, and preferred season, using AutoComplete or Pick From Drop-Down List when possible. Include a main label and labels for the columns. Apply fill and borders to enhance the readability. Add a header and save the workbook. Prepare and submit your work.

Exercise 4-38

Create a new workbook and save it as *[your initials]*4-38 in your folder. In cell A1, key **Restaurants and Fast Food Shops**. Enter column labels for the names of restaurants, phone numbers, cuisine ("Italian," "Seafood,"), and average price. Key data for 15 establishments. Set data bars for the price cells. Format your work attractively. Add a footer and save the workbook. Prepare and submit your work.

Exercise 4-39

Create a new workbook that lists the day of the week and the actual date for every day last month in two columns. In a third column, key the outdoor temperature. Experiment with alignment and borders. Add data bars to the temperature data. Add a header and save the workbook as *[your initials]*4-39. Prepare and submit your work.

Unit 1 Applications

Unit Application 1-1

Rename and delete sheets. Use Find and Replace and Spelling. Key formulas. Format data.

Klassy Kow Ice Cream maintains a statement of assets that includes cash, equipment, and supplies. You will be editing the worksheet.

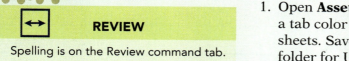

REVIEW

Spelling is on the Review command tab.

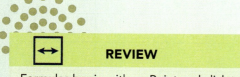

REVIEW

Formulas begin with =. Point and click to enter a cell address in a formula.

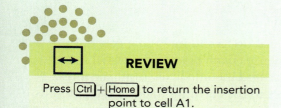

REVIEW

Press Ctrl + Home to return the insertion point to cell A1.

1. Open **Assets**. Rename **Sheet1** as **Assets** and choose a tab color from the theme colors. Delete the other sheets. Save the workbook as *[your initials]*u1-1 in a folder for Unit 1.

2. Format the headings in rows 1:2 with the Headings font for the document theme. Adjust column widths as needed. Use Comma style with no decimals for cells C4:C13.

3. Replace all occurrences of **valuables** with **assets**. Check spelling and look for inconsistent capitalization.

4. Sum the value of current assets in cell C8. In cell C12, subtract depreciation from the property, plant, and equipment amount. Add the current and fixed assets in cell C13. Add a dollar sign to the first value in each section and to the total.

5. Use borders, fill, or other methods to better design the worksheet.

6. Add a header and place the insertion point in cell A1.

7. Prepare and submit your work. Save and close the workbook.

Unit Application 1-2

Enter and format values and labels. Key formulas. Insert rows. Format data.

An income statement shows revenues (money from sales), expenses, and net income (sales minus expenses). You are to prepare and format this month's statement.

1. Create a new workbook with one sheet named **IncStatement** and save the workbook as *[your initials]*u1-2 in your Unit 1 folder.

2. Key the data as shown in Figure Unit 1-1.

Figure Unit 1-1

	A	B
1	Revenue	1500000
2	Cost of goods sold	975000
3	Sales expenses	57000
4	Administrative expense	50000
5	Depreciation	8000
6	Other expenses	2500
7	Total operating expenses	
8	Earnings before interest and taxes	
9	Interest expense	10000
10	Income taxes	150000
11	Net income	

3. Move the contents of cell B1 to cell C1.

4. In cell B7, sum the values in column B up to and including row 6. In cell C8, subtract total operating expenses from revenues. For net income (C11), subtract both interest expense and income taxes from earnings. Apply **Top and Double Bottom Borders** to the earnings and net income cells.

5. Insert two rows at the top of the data. As the first label, key **Klassy Kow Ice Cream, Inc.** In cell A2, key *[This Month]* **Income Statement**.

6. Format all values to show a comma with no decimals and the values in column C to include a dollar sign.

7. Use cell alignment, borders, fill, font styles and colors, and other tools to format the sheet.

8. Add a footer and use margins that place the data attractively on the page.

9. Prepare and submit your work. Save and close the workbook.

NOTE

You can insert rows and columns to be used as separators in designing borders and shading effects.

TIP

Position the pointer in cell A1 before you save a workbook.

Unit Application 1-3

Use AutoComplete or Pick From Drop-Down List. Find and correct errors. Use AutoCalculate.

The corporate office offers training for employees on various topics in various locations. You are to edit the worksheet that tracks this data.

1. Open **HRClasses** and choose a more descriptive name for the sheet. Save the workbook as *[your initials]*u1-3 in your Unit 1 folder.

2. Key the missing e-mail addresses using the same pattern as the other e-mail addresses.

3. Use AutoComplete or Pick From Drop-Down List to choose a department, location, and class for the missing entries. You may make your own selections.

4. Check the data carefully for errors and correct them.

5. In cell B27, key the value that results from AutoCalculate **Numerical Count** for the last names. Show the appropriate result in cell E27. Format these two values to use the same font and size as the related label.

6. Adjust the height of rows 2 and 3 so that there is a bit more fill below the labels.

7. Add a header and use margins that make the sheet appear centered on the landscape page.

8. Prepare and submit your work. Save and close the workbook.

REVIEW

Right-click the status bar to change AutoCalculate options.

NOTE

This worksheet is set for landscape printing.

Unit Application 1-4 ◆ Using the Internet

Search online booksellers for book and video titles about Excel. Make a list of 10 titles, including author(s), publisher(s), number of pages, price, and type of media.

Prepare a worksheet for your data with additional columns for shipping charges and a total cost. Format the data as a table or develop your own design. Use a header or a footer with appropriate information. Save your workbook as *[your initials]*u1-4 in your Unit 1 folder. Prepare and submit your work. Close the workbook.

unit 2

WORKING WITH FORMULAS AND FUNCTIONS

EXL2.5

Exploring Formula Basics

OBJECTIVES

After completing this lesson, you will be able to:

1. Use a template to create a workbook.
2. Build addition and subtraction formulas.
3. Build multiplication and division formulas.
4. Use order of precedence in a formula.
5. Use relative, absolute, and mixed references.
6. Work with the Page Layout tab.

Estimated Time: 1½ hours

NOTE

The workbooks you create and use in this course relate to the Case Study (see the Case Study in the frontmatter of the book) about Klassy Kow Ice Cream, Inc., a fictional ice cream company.

Formulas use common arithmetic operations (addition, subtraction, multiplication, and division). When building formulas, you should keep in mind mathematical order of precedence, which determines how Excel completes a series of calculations.

Excel usually updates a reference in a formula relative to its position when the formula is copied. It also has other types of references for copying formulas.

Using a Template to Create a Workbook

A *template* is a model workbook that can include labels, values, formulas, themes, styles, alignment settings, borders, and more. A template is used as the starting point for routine workbooks.

You can use a template as the model for a workbook by:

- Choosing My Templates in the Templates group of the New Workbook dialog box.

- Choosing Installed Templates in the Templates group of the New Workbook dialog box.

- Choosing the template name from the Blank and Recent pane in the New Workbook dialog box.

NOTE

Copy the templates to the folder Users\ UserName\AppData\Roaming\Microsoft\ Templates. Check with your instructor if you need help locating the templates used in this lesson.

Templates are saved with an **.xltx** filename extension in a Templates folder for your computer. Templates must be in this Templates folder to be listed in the New Workbook dialog box.

Exercise 5-1   CREATE A WORKBOOK FROM A TEMPLATE

When you create a new workbook from a template, a copy of the template opens as the new workbook. It has the same name as the template, followed by a number.

1. Click the Microsoft Office Button 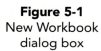 and choose **New**. The New Workbook dialog box opens.

Figure 5-1
New Workbook
dialog box

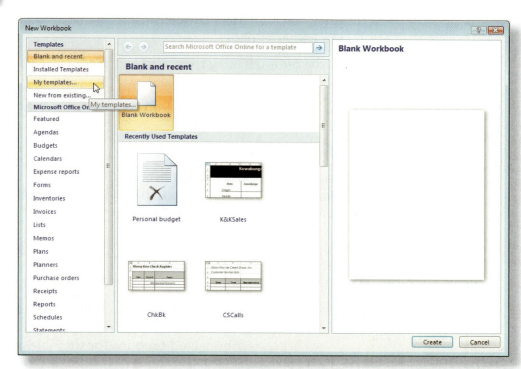

TIP

Excel includes several professionally designed templates, and you can download more from the Microsoft Office Web site.

2. Click **My templates**. The New dialog box opens.

3. Find the template **KlassyKow**.

4. Click **KlassyKow** and click **OK**. A new workbook opens with labels, values, and images. The title bar shows the template name with a number, probably 1.

Building Addition and Subtraction Formulas

Addition formulas total or sum cell values using the plus sign (+). Subtraction formulas compute the difference between cell values using the minus sign (−).

TIP

When cells are next to each other in a row or a column, it is usually faster to use AutoSum than to key a formula for addition.

Exercise 5-2   CREATE AND COPY ADDITION FORMULAS

This worksheet tracks monthly expenses of sales representatives. The budgeted amounts are part of the template, but expenses are keyed.

1. Click the Microsoft Office Button and choose **Excel Options**. Open the **Formulas** pane.

2. In the **Error checking rules**, verify that all rules show a check mark. Click **OK**.

3. Set the Zoom size so that you can see rows 1 through 30. Then click cell B27.

4. Press **=** to start a formula.

5. Click cell B8, the budget amount for the first week for Kim Tomasaki. A marquee appears around the cell, and it is outlined in a color.

TIP

You can use [+] on the numeric keypad or at the top of the keyboard to key the plus symbol in a formula.

6. Key **+** and click cell B13, the second week budget amount.

7. Key **+** and click cell B18, the third week.

8. Key **+** and click cell B23, the fourth week. This addition formula determines the monthly total budgeted amount for this salesperson.

Figure 5-2
Entering an addition
formula
KlassyKow.xltx
Expenses sheet

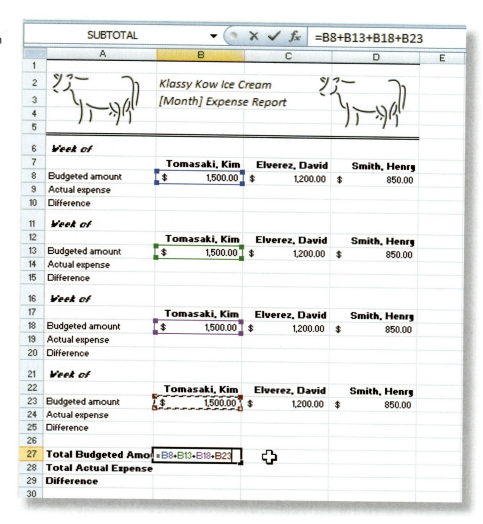

9. Press Enter. The result is $6,000.

10. In cell B28, key = to start the formula.

11. Click cell B9, the cell where the first week's actual amount will be keyed.

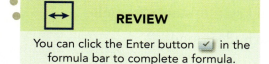

12. Key + and click cell B14, the second week.

13. Key + and click cell B19, and then key + and click cell B24.

14. Key + again to make a deliberate error.

15. Press Enter. A message box opens. The last plus sign is not necessary, and Excel proposes a correction, eliminating it.

Figure 5-3
Error message box
about incorrect
formula

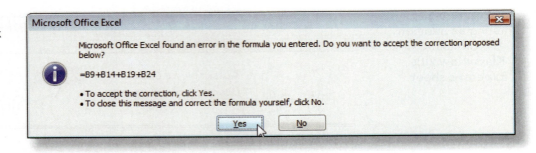

16. Choose **Yes**. This worksheet displays a single dash to indicate zero, and the cell shows a small green triangle indicating an error.

17. Click cell B28 and position the mouse pointer on the Error Checking Options button ◈.

18. Click the arrow next to the button to see that the formula refers to empty cells.

19. Choose **Ignore Error**.

20. Select cells B27:B28. Position the mouse pointer on the Fill handle.

21. Drag the Fill handle to cell D28 to copy the formulas. The AutoFill Options button ⊞ appears below the filled range. Results appear in row 27, and green triangles mark errors in cells C28:D28.

22. Select cells C28:D28 and ignore the errors.

Exercise 5-3   **CREATE AND COPY SUBTRACTION FORMULAS**

The difference between budgeted and actual expenditures is computed by subtracting the actual amount from the budgeted amount. You can use ⊟ on the numeric keypad or at the top of the keyboard.

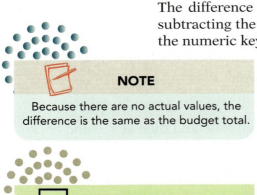

NOTE

Because there are no actual values, the difference is the same as the budget total.

REVIEW

Ctrl + Enter leaves the insertion point in the cell.

1. Click cell B29 and key **=** to start a formula.

2. Click cell B27, the budget total.

3. Key **−** and click cell B28, the actual total. Press Enter.

4. Copy the formula in cell B29 to cells C29:D29.

5. Click cell B10. Key **=** and click cell B8, the budgeted amount for the week.

6. Key **−** and click cell B9, the actual amount. Press Ctrl + Enter.

7. Copy cell B10 to cells C10:D10. The AutoFill Options button 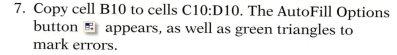 appears, as well as green triangles to mark errors.

8. While cells B10:D10 are selected, click the Copy button .

9. Click cell B15 and click the Paste button .

10. Click cell B20 and click the Paste button . Paste again in cell B25.

> **NOTE**
>
> Error triangles do not print and have no effect on your worksheet, so you can ignore them when you know that nothing is wrong.

11. Press Esc to cancel the marquee. The differences are the same as the budget amounts, because no actual expenses are shown yet.

Building Multiplication and Division Formulas

A multiplication formula can calculate an employee's weekly wages by multiplying hours worked by the rate of pay. Multiplication formulas use an asterisk (*).

Division formulas can be used to determine percentages, averages, individual prices, and more. A division formula uses a forward slash (/).

The result of a multiplication or division formula is formatted with decimals if the result is not a whole number. A *whole number* is a value without a fraction or decimal.

> **TIP**
>
> You can use * and / on the numeric keypad or * at the top of the keyboard and / at the bottom.

Exercise 5-4   CREATE MULTIPLICATION FORMULAS

You can multiply the current total amounts by 10 percent to determine next year's amounts, assuming a 10 percent increase. When you multiply by a percent, you can key the value with the percent sign (%) in the formula. If you do not key the percent sign, you must key the decimal equivalent of the value.

> **TIP**
>
> Convert a percent to its decimal equivalent by dividing the percent amount by 100. For example, 89% is 89/100 or 0.89.

1. Select cell A27. Display the drag-and-drop pointer, hold down Ctrl, and drag a copy of the cell to cell A31.

2. Click cell A31 and press F2. Press Home and key **Increased**.

3. Delete **Total** and press Enter.

4. Widen column A to fit the label.

> **REVIEW**
>
> Display the drag-and-drop pointer by pointing at the top or bottom edge of a selection.

5. Click cell B31 and key **=**.

6. Click cell B27, key *****, and then key **10%**. Press Ctrl+Enter. This amount is the increase in dollars, but not the new total.

Exercise 5-5 **EDIT A FORMULA IN THE FORMULA BAR**

To determine the new total amount, multiply by 110%, because 110% is the current amount (100%) plus the increase (10%).

1. With cell B31 active, click in the formula bar. A text insertion point appears, and the cell in the worksheet is outlined in the same color as the cell address in the formula bar.

2. Click between the **1** and the **0** in the formula bar.

3. Key **1** to change the percent to **110%**.

Figure 5-4
Editing a formula in the formula bar
KlassyKow.xltx
Expenses sheet

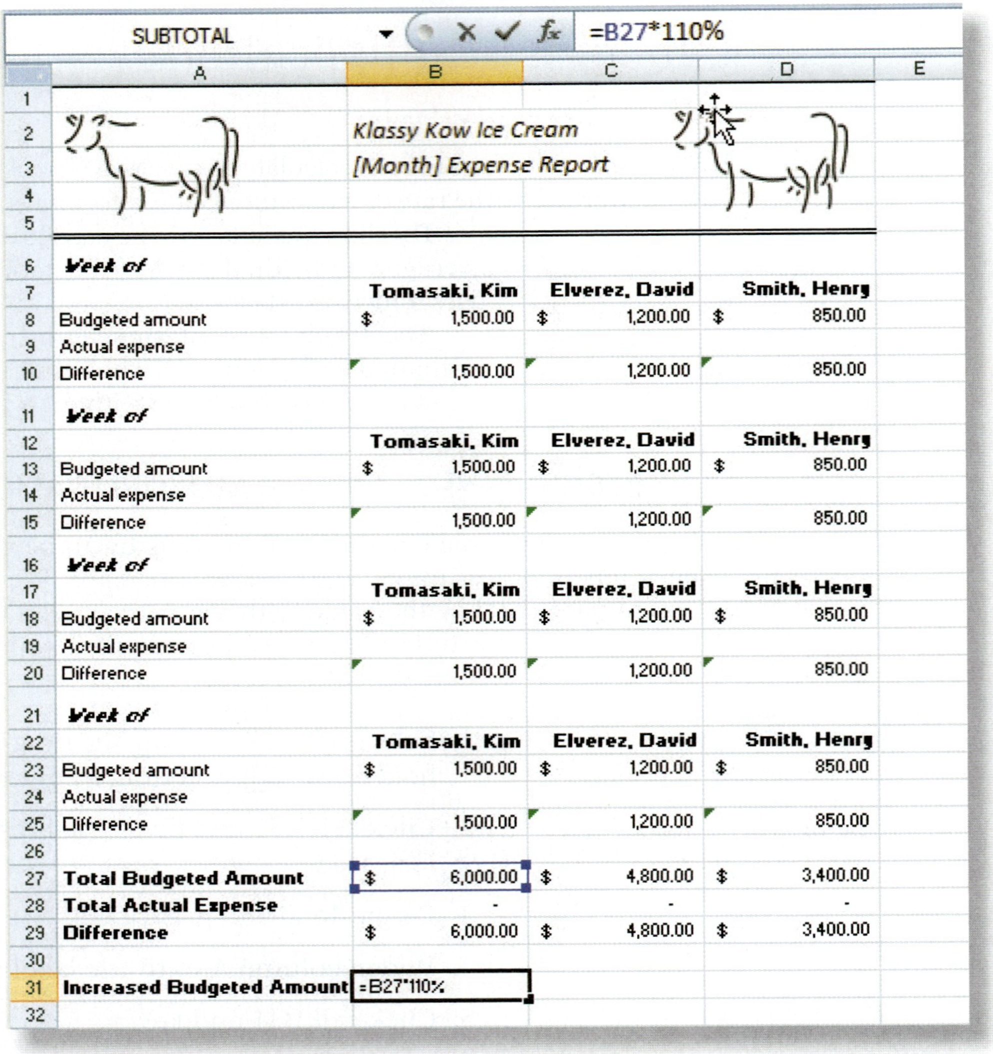

4. Press Ctrl + Enter. The new total ($6,600) is calculated.

5. Copy cell B31 to cells C31:D31.

Exercise 5-6　CREATE DIVISION FORMULAS

If you select a range before keying data, you can press [Enter] to move from one cell to the next in top-to-bottom, left-to-right order.

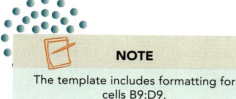

NOTE

The template includes formatting for cells B9:D9.

1. Select cells B9:D9.
2. Key **1000** and press [Enter].
3. Key **950** and press [Enter].
4. Key **725** and press [Enter]. As you fill in the amounts, the difference is calculated.
5. Select cells B14:D14 and key these values:

   　1300　　　　　**1250**　　　　　**925**

6. Key these values in cells B19:D19 and cells B24:C24. The totals are calculated in rows 28 and 29 as you key the values:

   　900　　　　　**850**　　　　　**625**
   　1000　　　　**750**　　　　　**575**

7. Click cell B30 and key **=** to start a formula.
8. Click cell B28 and key **/** for division. Dividing the actual amount (cell B28) by the budget amount (cell B27) determines the percent actual expenses are of the budget amount.
9. Click cell B27 and press [Enter]. The result is formatted as a decimal.

Exercise 5-7　APPLY THE PERCENT STYLE AND INCREASE DECIMAL POSITIONS

Excel converts a decimal to a percent when you apply the Percent Style. It multiplies the decimal value by 100. For example, 0.7 is 0.7*100 or 70%.

1. Click cell B30. In the **Number** group on the **Home** tab, click the Percent Style button [%]. The percent symbol is added, and the value is converted.

2. Click the Increase Decimal button [.00] two times. A decimal position is added with each click.
3. Copy the formula in cell B30 to cells C30:D30.
4. In cell A30, key **Actual as % of Budget** and press [Enter]. Because three rows precede this row, the format of those rows is applied.
5. Press [Ctrl]+[Home]. Press [F12] and save the workbook as *[your initials]5-7* in a new folder for Lesson 5.
6. Close the workbook.

Using Order of Precedence in a Formula

Excel follows mathematical rules as it calculates a formula. These rules include an *order of precedence,* sometimes called *order of operation* or *math hierarchy.* The order of precedence determines what part of a formula is calculated first. Generally, a formula is calculated from left to right, but some arithmetic operators take priority over others. For example, if you key a formula with both a multiplication symbol (*) and an addition symbol (+), Excel calculates the multiplication first even if it is the second symbol as you move from left to right. You can override the order of precedence by enclosing parts of the formula within parentheses.

When two operators have the same order of precedence—for example, multiplication and division—the operations are performed from left to right (see Table 5-1).

Figure 5-5 shows three formulas with the same values and the same operators. The results differ depending on the placement of the parentheses.

Figure 5-5
Parentheses change the order of operations

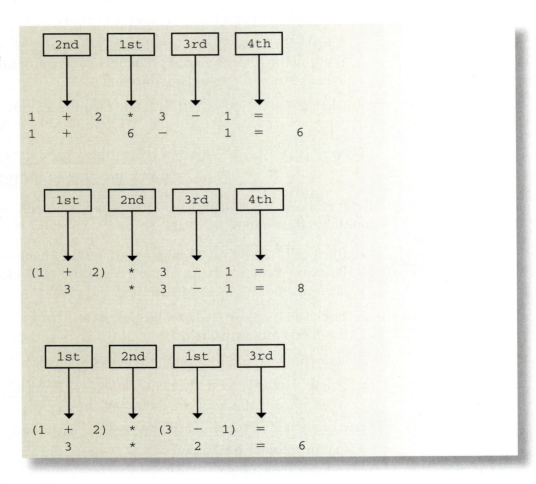

TABLE 5-1 Operator Precedence in Excel

Operator		Precedence Description
∧	1st	Exponentiation
*	2nd	Multiplication
/	2nd	Division
+	3rd	Addition
−	3rd	Subtraction
&	4th	Concatenation (symbol used to join text strings)
=	5th	Equal to
<	5th	Less than
>	5th	Greater than

Exercise 5-8 USE MULTIPLICATION AND ADDITION IN A FORMULA

In this exercise, you use a formula that seems logical to determine a dollar amount of sales. You will see, however, that it results in an incorrect total.

TIP

You can memorize the order of precedence for parentheses and the first five operators: "Please excuse my dear Aunt Sally" (parentheses, exponentiation, multiplication, division, addition, subtraction).

1. Open **DrinkSize**. Click cell E15. You need to total the items for each state and multiply by the price.

2. Key **=** and click cell C6, the price for a 16-ounce soda.

3. Key ***** to multiply the price by the number sold.

4. Select cell D6 and key **+**.

5. Click cell E6, key **+**, click cell F6, key **+**, and click cell G6. This part of the formula adds state unit totals.

6. Press Enter. The result looks reasonable, but it is wrong.

7. Click cell E15. The formula includes a multiplication symbol, so cell C6 is first multiplied by cell D6. Then the other cells are added to the result of C6*D6.

REVIEW

AutoCalculate results are visible in the status bar.

8. Right-click the AutoCalculate area and verify that **Sum** is selected.

9. Select cells D6:G6. Check AutoCalculate for the sum of 30,000.

10. Click cell J6 and key **=** to start a formula. You are temporarily using this empty cell to calculate the correct amount.

11. Click cell C6, key ***30000**, and press ⌷Enter⌷. This is the correct amount—the total number sold (30,000) multiplied by the price.

12. Delete the contents of cell J6.

Exercise 5-9   SET ORDER OF PRECEDENCE

1. Double-click cell E15 to start Edit mode. The formula is in the cell and in the formula bar. The referenced cells are outlined in color.

2. In the worksheet cell, click in front or to the left of **D6**.

3. Key a left parenthesis **(** in front of **D6**.

4. Press ⌷End⌷. The insertion point moves to the end of the formula.

5. Key a right parenthesis **)**.

6. Press ⌷Enter⌷. These parentheses force the additions to be calculated first. That result is multiplied by the value in cell C6.

Figure 5-6
Changing the order
of precedence
DrinkSize.xlsx
DrinkSales sheet

	A	B	C	D	E	F	G	H
1								
2			*Klassy Kow Ice Cream Shops*					
3			*Comparison of Drink Sizes Sold*					
4			*Count of Items for June*					
5			Price	California	Washington	Oregon	Nevada	
6		16 oz. Soda	$0.89	8,000	6,000	5,000	11,000	
7		32 oz. Soda	$1.59	12,000	7,500	4,000	15,000	
8		12 oz. Coffee	$1.29	7,500	8,000	5,000	11,500	
9		20 oz. Coffee	$1.59	5,400	8,500	5,500	16,000	
10		Tea	$1.29	2,500	2,000	2,300	4,000	
11								
12								
13								
14				Total Dollar Values Sold				
15				16 oz. Soda	=C6*(D6+E6+F6+G6)			
16				32 oz. Soda				
17				12 oz. Coffee				
18				20 oz. Coffee				
19				Tea				
20								
21								

7. Apply Accounting format to cell E15 but show no decimals.

8. Copy the formula in cell E15 to cells E16:E19.

9. Click cell E16. Notice that the formula multiplies the price in cell C7 by the values in row 7 for a 32-ounce soda. This is correct.

10. Widen columns as needed. Press ⌈Ctrl⌉+⌈Home⌉.

11. Save the workbook as *[your initials]5-9* in your Lesson 5 folder.

12. Close the workbook.

Using Relative, Absolute, and Mixed References

When you copy a formula, Excel adjusts the formula relative to the row or column where the copy is located. This is known as a *relative reference*.

There are situations, however, when you want Excel to copy the formula exactly. A formula with an *absolute reference* does not change when it is copied into another cell. An absolute reference uses two dollar signs ($) in its address, one in front of the column reference and one in front of the row reference. $B$5 is an absolute reference to cell B5.

Excel can also use a *mixed reference,* in which a dollar sign is placed in front of the reference for either the row or the column. In a mixed reference, part of the cell reference is adjusted when a formula is copied; the other is not. $B5 is a mixed reference with an absolute reference to column B but a relative reference to row 5.

Dollar signs used in a cell address do not signify currency. They are a reserved symbol used to mark the type of cell reference.

TABLE 5-2 Cell References

Address	Type of Reference	
B1	Relative	
$B$1	Absolute	
$B1	Mixed	Column letter is absolute; row number is relative.
B$1	Mixed	Row number is absolute; column letter is relative.

Exercise 5-10 USE A LINE BREAK

You can place labels on two lines in a cell by pressing ⌈Alt⌉+⌈Enter⌉ at the point where you want the second line to start. This is known as a *line break* in a cell. You often need to adjust the row height or the column width if you use line breaks.

1. Open **ShopDownTime**.

2. In cell G5, key **Cost per** and press ⌈Alt⌉+⌈Enter⌉.

3. Key **Down Hour** and press ⏎.

4. Adjust the column width so that the label splits only between "per" and "Down."

5. Click cell G5 and look at the formula bar. It is not tall enough to show the complete label.

6. Rest the mouse pointer on the splitter bar above the column headings.

Figure 5-7
Sizing the formula bar
ShopDownTime.xlsx AllStates sheet

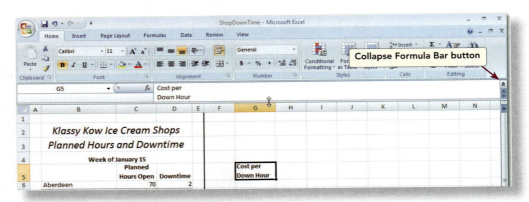

7. Drag down until you see the label in the formula bar. The formula bar occupies more space and your data rows occupy less.

8. In cell G6, key **25** and format it as Accounting with two decimals.

Exercise 5-11   COPY A FORMULA WITH A RELATIVE REFERENCE

1. Insert a column at column E. In cell E5, key **Cost**. Its formatting matches the preceding columns.

2. Click cell E6. Key **=** to start the formula.

3. Click cell D6, key *****, and then click cell H6. This formula uses relative references.

4. Press ⏎. The result is $50.

5. Drag the Fill handle for cell E6 to copy the formula to cell E25. The copied formulas show a dash for zero and an error triangle. The cells that should show a total cost do not.

6. Click each copied cell in column E and look in the formula bar. Each time the formula went down a row, the row reference adjusted. That works for column D, but not for column H.

7. Click the Undo button .

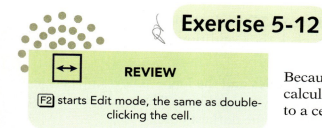

Exercise 5-12   CREATE A FORMULA WITH AN ABSOLUTE REFERENCE

REVIEW

F2 starts Edit mode, the same as double-clicking the cell.

Because absolute references are common to many calculations, Excel has a quick way of adding dollar signs to a cell reference. It's the F4 key.

1. Click cell E6 and press F2.

2. Click between **H** and **6** in the worksheet cell.

3. Press F4. Two dollar signs are inserted, one before **H** and one before **6**.

Figure 5-8
Making a cell reference absolute
ShopDownTime.xlsx
AllStates sheet

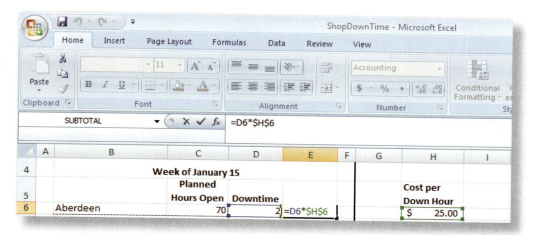

4. Press F. The dollar sign appears only with **6**.

5. Press F again. The dollar sign appears only with **H**.

6. Press F again. The dollar signs are removed.

7. Press F once more. The absolute reference appears again.

8. Press Ctrl+Enter. Look in the formula bar.

9. Use the Fill handle for cell E6 to copy the formula into cells E7:E37.

10. Click each copied cell and look in the formula bar. Cell H6 did not change in any of the copies.

11. Select cells E6:E37 and apply a dashed middle and bottom horizontal border.

Exercise 5-13   USE A COLOR SCALE

In addition to data bars, the Conditional Formatting command includes color scales. This command applies fill to the range based on the values. You can use two- or three-color arrangements.

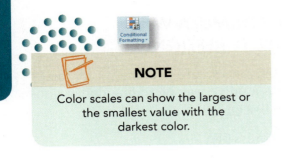

NOTE

Color scales can show the largest or the smallest value with the darkest color.

1. Select cells E6:E37. In the **Styles** group on the **Home** tab, click the Conditional Formatting button.

2. Choose **Color Scales** and the **Red – Yellow Color Scale** in the second row, second icon. This scale shows the highest values in the darkest color.

Figure 5-9
Choosing a color scale
ShopDownTime.xlsx
AllStates sheet

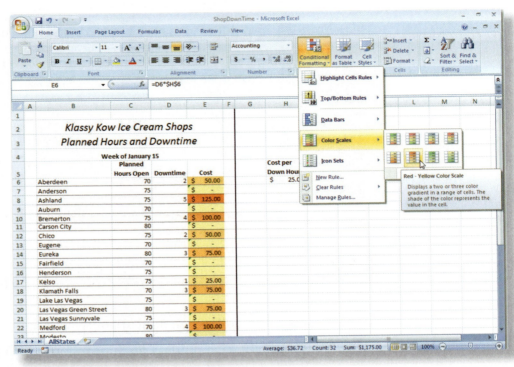

3. Click in column H to better see the color scale.

4. Select cells E6:E37 and click the Conditional Formatting button.

5. Choose **Manage Rules**. The Conditional Formatting Rules Manager dialog box opens.

6. Click **Edit rule**. The Edit Formatting Rule dialog box is the same as the one for data bars.

7. Choose a different light and dark color from the same hue.

8. Click **OK** twice to see your changes.

9. Press Ctrl+Home. Save the workbook as *[your initials]*5-13 in your folder.

10. Close the workbook.

11. At the right end of the formula bar, click the Collapse Formula Bar button. The formula bar collapses to its default height.

Exercise 5-14 USE MIXED REFERENCES

A multiplication table will be printed as a promotional item and posted on the company's Web site. This multiplication table uses mixed references.

1. Open **MultTable**.

2. Set the Zoom percent to a size that lets you see the entire worksheet.

3. Click cell B3. You want to show the result of multiplying 1 by 1 in cell B3.

4. Key **=** and click cell A3. This will be a mixed reference.

5. Press F4 three times to show **$A3**. This part of the formula will always use column A, but the row will change.

6. Press ***** and click cell B2.

7. Press F4 two times to show **B$2**. This part of the formula will always use row 2, but the column will change.

Figure 5-10
Mixed reference formula
MultTable.xlsx
Sheet1 sheet

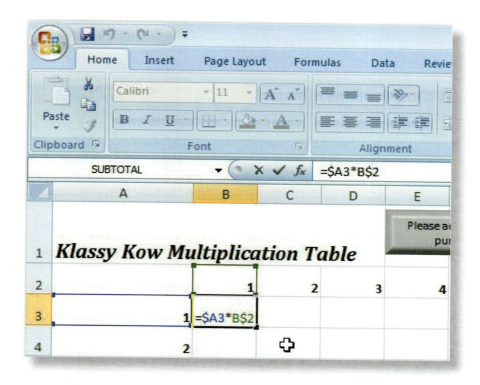

8. Press Ctrl + Enter.

9. Use the Fill handle to copy cell B3 to cell K3.

10. Use the Fill handle to copy cells B3:K3 down to row 12.

Exercise 5-15 ADD BORDERS AND FILL FOR PRINTING

Borders and fill will make it easier to follow numbers across a wide layout.

1. Select cells A2:K12 and press Ctrl+1.

2. Click the **Border** tab.

3. In the **Border** preset group, click the Top Border button.

4. Click the Middle Horizontal Border and then the Bottom Border buttons. Click the Left Border and the Right Border buttons. Click **OK**.

Figure 5-11
Setting top, middle, bottom, left, and right borders

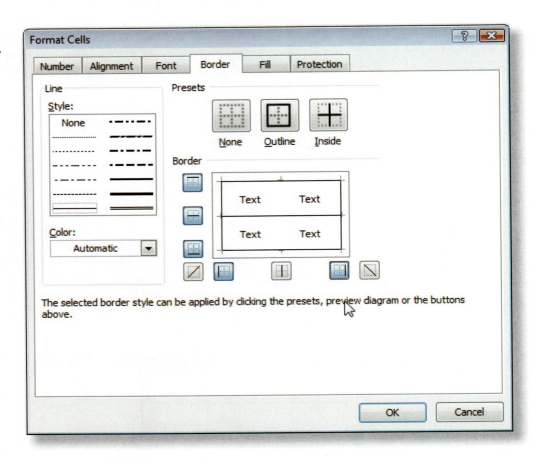

5. Select cells A2:K2 and cells A3:A12.

6. Click the arrow next to the Fill Color button 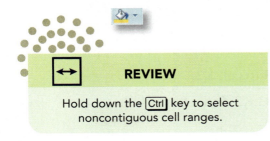.

7. Choose **White, Background 1, Darker 25%** in the first column.

8. Press Ctrl+Home.

REVIEW

Hold down the Ctrl key to select noncontiguous cell ranges.

Working with the Page Layout Tab

There are many options for how to print a worksheet as well as several ways to change these options. From the Page Layout tab, you can:

- Change margins.

- Change the page orientation.

- Choose a paper size.

- Set a print area or print titles.

- Scale the worksheet to fit the page or print larger than the page.

- Change page breaks.

- Add a background image.

Page orientation determines if the worksheet prints landscape or portrait. The default is *portrait* orientation, one that is taller than it is wide.

Scaling commands enable you to set a size percentage for the printed page. This size can be smaller or larger.

Exercise 5-16   CHANGE PAGE ORIENTATION

Many worksheets are too wide to fit portrait orientation on 8½ by 11 inch paper. A *landscape* orientation is horizontal—the page is wider than it is tall.

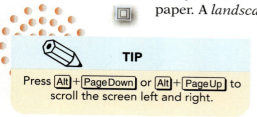

TIP

Press Alt+PageDown or Alt+PageUp to scroll the screen left and right.

1. Click the Page Layout View button in the status bar. The worksheet does not fit on a single page in portrait orientation. You can see in the status bar (at the left) that the worksheet requires more than one page.

2. Click the Zoom Out button to reach **80%**. Excel splits the worksheet between columns.

3. Click the **Page Layout** command tab.

4. In the **Page Setup** group, click the Page Orientation button. Choose **Landscape**. The worksheet fits on a single page in landscape orientation.

Exercise 5-17   CHANGE SCALING AND PAGE MARGINS

You can set a worksheet to print at 50 percent of its size or 150 percent of its size. You might need to do this if you want to print the worksheet on a 5- by 7-inch card or if you want to enlarge it for a special display. When you enlarge a worksheet, the output device will split the pages between columns so that you can tape the parts together.

You change margins by dragging the margin markers in Page Layout View. If you need to set a precise margin, you can use the Margins tab in the Page Setup dialog box to key a specific setting.

1. In the **Scale to Fit** group, double-click **100** and key **75**. Click any cell or press Enter. The worksheet is reduced to 75 percent of its normal size. This is only an output adjustment and does not change any format settings.

Figure 5-12
Scaling the worksheet
MultTable.xlsx
Sheet1 sheet

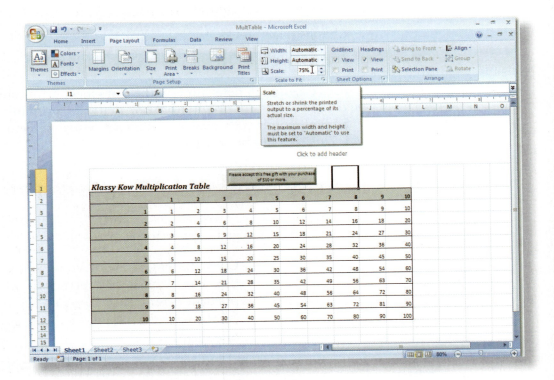

2. In the **Page Setup** group, click the Margins button . Choose **Custom Margins**. The Page Setup dialog box opens with the **Margins** tab active.

3. Double-click in the **Left** box and key **2.25**.

4. Double-click in the **Right** box and key **1**. Click **OK**.

5. Zoom out to **70%**.

6. In the **Sheet Options** group, click to deselect **Gridlines: View** and **Headings: View**. This represents how the worksheet will print.

7. Save the workbook as *[your initials]5-17* in your folder.

Exercise 5-18 COPY A WORKSHEET AND DISPLAY FORMULAS

You can easily review and troubleshoot formulas by displaying them all at once on screen. A copy of the worksheet with formulas visible also provides clear documentation for your work.

In order to keep the original version of your worksheet, you'll make a copy and show formulas on the copy.

1. Rename **Sheet1** as **PrintTable**.

2. Right-click the **PrintTable** tab and choose **Move or Copy**.

3. In the Move or Copy dialog box, click to select **Create a copy**. Click **OK**. The copy is named **PrintTable (2)** and is inserted in front of the original.

4. Press Ctrl+~. The formulas in each cell are visible.

5. In the **Sheet Options** group on the **Page Layout** tab, click to select **Gridlines: View**, **Gridlines: Print**, **Headings: View**, and **Headings: Print**.

6. Click the column A heading. Scroll right and hold down Shift while clicking the column K heading. All the columns are selected.

NOTE

The tilde (~) is located at the top left of the keyboard. You can display formulas by clicking the Microsoft Office Button 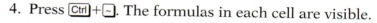 and choosing **Excel Options**, **Advanced** pane (Display Options for this Worksheet).

7. Double-click the border between columns K and L. Excel AutoFits each column to its longest entry.

8. In the **Scale to Fit** group, double-click **75**, key **100**, and click any cell. The worksheet occupies two pages, because formulas require more space than values.

NOTE

Column headings are above the header area.

9. Click the Margins button . Choose **Custom Margins**. Double-click in the **Left** box and key **.5**. Press Tab and key **.5** in the **Right** box.

10. Click the **Page** tab. In the **Scaling** section, click to select **Fit to**.

11. Choose **1 page(s) wide** by **1 tall**.

TIP

You can set your own scaling percentage or choose the **Fit to** option.

12. Click **OK**. Excel fits the worksheet to a single landscape page with 0.5-inch left and right margins (see Figure 5-13 on the next page).

Excel 2007

Figure 5-13
Formulas visible
5-17.xlsx
PrintTable (2) sheet

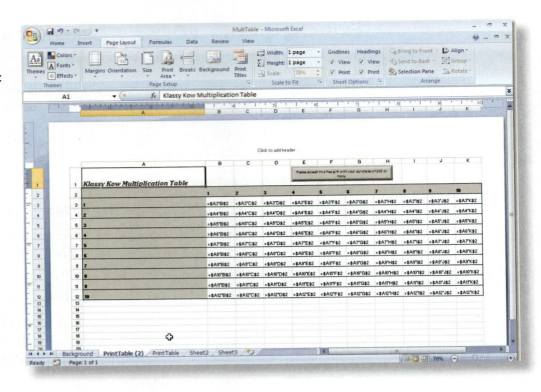

13. Press Ctrl+Home. Save the workbook as *[your initials]*5-18 in your folder.

Exercise 5-19 ADD A BACKGROUND

A *background* is an image that appears on screen and on the Web. It fills or spans the entire worksheet. It does not print.

1. Right-click the **PrintTable** tab and choose **Move or Copy**.

2. In the Move or Copy dialog box, click to select **Create a copy**. Click **OK**. The copy is named **PrintTable (3)**.

3. Rename **PrintTable (3)** as **Background**.

4. Click the Normal button ⊞ on the status bar.

5. On the **Page Layout** tab, click to select **Gridlines: View** and **Headings: View**.

6. Click the Background button 🖼 in the **Page Setup** group. The Sheet Background dialog box opens.

7. Navigate to the folder with the **KKBack** file. Click to select the file.

Figure 5-14
Using a sheet
background
5-18.xlsx
Background sheet

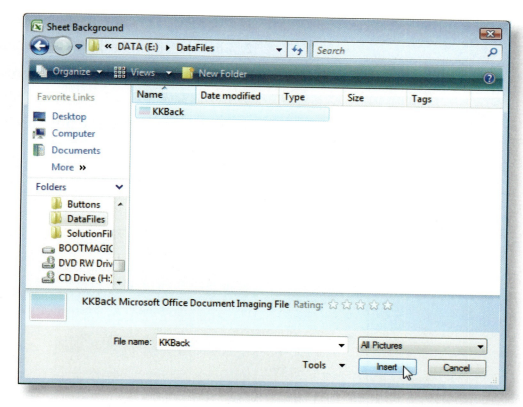

8. Click **Insert**. The background is a blend of colors and fills the worksheet.

9. Select cells A2:K2 and cells A3:A12.

10. Click the **Home** tab. Click the arrow with the Fill Color button and choose **No Fill**. You don't need a fill color with the background.

11. Press Ctrl + Home.

12. Press Ctrl + P. The Print dialog box opens.

13. Press Alt + W to open Print Preview. Backgrounds do not print; they are visible on screen and on a Web site.

14. Close Print Preview.

Exercise 5-20   SAVE A WORKBOOK AS A WEB PAGE

You can save an Excel workbook as an HTML file so that it can be viewed on the World Wide Web. An *HTML* file uses *Hypertext Markup Language,* a widely used and recognized format for Web pages. Web pages are saved with an **.htm** extension. You can save the entire workbook or an individual worksheet as a Web page. When you save the entire workbook, the Web page shows the worksheet tabs.

NOTE

Do not use Single File Web Page to save a Web page unless you are familiar with HTML and can edit it on your own.

1. Press F12. The Save As dialog box opens.

2. Click the arrow for **Save as type** and choose **Web Page**.

3. Set the **Save in** folder to your Lesson 5 folder.

4. In the **Save** area, choose **Entire Workbook**.

5. Click **Change Title**. The title appears in the title bar of the browser.

6. Key **Klassy Kow Multiplication Table** and click **OK**.

Figure 5-15
Saving a Web page

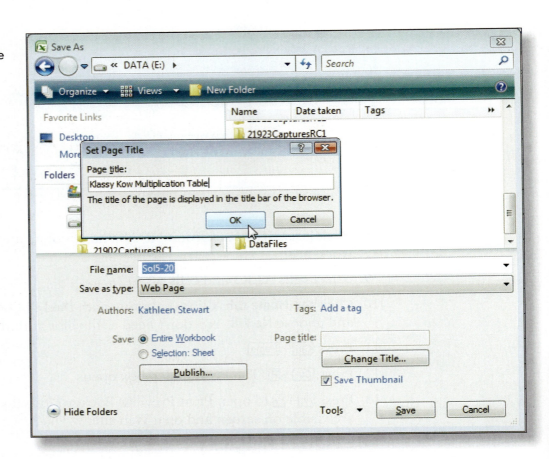

7. Name the file *[your initials]5-20*. Click **Save**. If a message box opens about incompatible features, choose **Yes**.

8. Close the workbook.

9. Start your Web browser and maximize the window.

10. Press Ctrl+O. Click **Browse** and navigate to your folder. Find and click *[your initials]5-20* and click **Open**. Click **OK**.

11. Look for the title and at each of the tabs in the browser.

 12. Click the Close button to close the browser.

Using Online Help

USE HELP TO VIEW ADDITIONAL INFORMATION ABOUT FORMULAS

1. In a new workbook, press F1.

2. In the Search box, key **create formula** and press Enter.

3. Find and review topics to learn more about building formulas. Read the help information.

4. Close the Help window.

Lesson 5 Summary

- Use a template to create workbooks that use the same labels and other basic information on a routine basis.

- Templates can include labels, values, formatting, formulas, and pictures.

- You can edit a formula in the formula bar and within the cell in Edit mode.

- The Percent Style converts a decimal value to its percent equivalent.

- In calculating formulas, Excel follows mathematical order of precedence.

- You can establish a different order of precedence in a formula by keying parentheses around the calculations that you want performed first.

- Excel has relative, absolute, and mixed references. These references determine what happens when a formula is copied.

- A color scale is a conditional formatting rule that fills a range of cells with various intensities of a color based on the values.

- A portrait orientation prints a vertical page. A landscape page prints a horizontal page.

- The Scale to Fit group on the Page Layout tab enables you to print the worksheet in a reduced or enlarged size. You can also choose to have Excel fit the worksheet on a page.

- To set a precise margin, use the Margins tab in the Page Setup dialog box.
- You can print a worksheet with formulas displayed for documentation or help in locating problems.
- You can add an image as a sheet background for display on a Web page.
- You can save a workbook as a Web page for viewing in most browsers.

LESSON 5		Command Summary	
Feature	**Button**	**Task Path**	**Keyboard**
Absolute reference			F4
Background	Background	Page Layout, Page Setup	
Collapse formula bar	⌃		Ctrl + Shift + U
Color scale	Conditional Formatting	Home, Styles, Conditional Formatting	
Copy sheet		Home, Cells, Format, Move or Copy Sheet	
Show/hide formulas	Show Formulas	Formulas, Formula Auditing	Ctrl + ~
Edit mode			F2
Fit to page	Height: Automatic / Width: Automatic	Page Layout, Scale to Fit	
Increase Decimal	.0 .00	Home, Number	Ctrl + 1
Margins	Margins	Page Layout, Page Setup	
New, from template		Microsoft Office, New	
Page Orientation	Orientation	Page Layout, Page Setup	
Percent Style	%	Home, Number	Ctrl + 1
Scaling		Page Layout, Scale to Fit	
Web page		Microsoft Office, Save As	F12

Concepts Review

True/False Questions

Each of the following statements is either true or false. Indicate your choice by circling T or F.

T F 1. A template opens as a new workbook with the template name and a letter.

T F 2. You can apply one-, two-, and three-color scales to a range.

T F 3. The multiplication symbol in a formula is /.

T F 4. To multiply by a percent, you must key the decimal equivalent of the percent.

T F 5. You can control the order of precedence in a formula with parentheses.

T F 6. Division is calculated before addition in a formula without parentheses.

T F 7. Column widths adjust automatically when you display formulas.

T F 8. An absolute reference does not adjust when the formula is copied to another cell.

Short Answer Questions

Write the correct answer in the space provided.

1. What is the keyboard shortcut to display or hide formulas?

_____

2. Which page orientation is taller than it is wide?

_____

3. How would the cell reference **$F$3** be described?

_____

4. What are the four arithmetic symbols that can be used in a formula?

_____

5. What type of operation is being performed in the formula = A4*B4?

_____

6. What command option allows you to print a worksheet on a smaller piece of paper?

_____

7. What term describes a model workbook used as the basis for other workbooks?

_____

8. How can you start Edit mode to edit a formula?

_____

Critical Thinking

Answer these questions on a separate page. There are no right or wrong answers. Support your answers with examples from your own experience, if possible.

1. Why is it helpful to adjust the Zoom percentage while working? How is this different from scaling the worksheet?

2. Why is it necessary to have an absolute cell reference in some formulas? Why can't all formulas use relative references?

Skills Review

Exercise 5-21

Use a template to create a new workbook. Build addition and subtraction formulas.

1. Create a workbook from a template by following these steps:
    a. Click the Microsoft Office Button 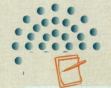 and choose **New**.
    b. Click **My templates**.
    c. Choose **ChkBk** and click **OK**.

2. In cell A4, key today's date in mm/dd/yy format. Key tomorrow's date in cell A5 in the same format. Adjust the column width if necessary.

3. Press F12 and save the workbook as *[your initials]*5-21 in your Lesson 5 folder.

NOTE

Copy the **ChkBk** template file into the appropriate folder for your computer before starting this exercise.

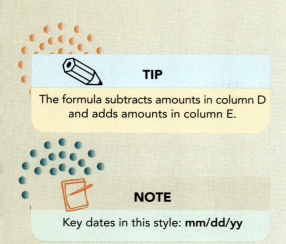

TIP

The formula subtracts amounts in column D and adds amounts in column E.

NOTE

Key dates in this style: **mm/dd/yy**

4. Build addition and subtraction formulas by following these steps:

   a. Click cell F5. Key **=** to start a formula.

   b. Click cell F4 and key **−** for subtraction.

   c. Click cell D5 and key **+** for addition.

   d. Click cell E5. Press Enter and ignore any error triangles.

5. Copy the formula in cell F5 to cells F6:F15. The results are all the same at this point.

6. Key the following information, starting in cell A6.

Figure 5-16

	Date	Check #	Payee	Credit Amount	Deposit
6	[2 days from today]	1002	Helpful Hand Computers	1250	
7	[3 days from today]				2500
8	[4 days from today]	1003	Greenberg and Whitefield	575	
9	[5 days from today]	1004	[your school name]	435	
10	[6 days from today]				1200

7. Hide rows 11 through 15.

8. Add a footer with your name at the left and the filename at the right.

9. In Page Layout View, adjust the margins if necessary to fit the worksheet on a single portrait page.

10. Press Ctrl+Home. Prepare and submit your work. Save and close the workbook.

Exercise 5-22

Build multiplication and division formulas. Set the order of precedence.

1. Open **TasteTest**. Save the workbook as *[your initials]*5-22 in your Lesson 5 folder.

2. Build a multiplication formula by following these steps:

   a. Click cell F4 and key **=**. Click cell D4. This is a taste-tester's regular hourly pay rate.

   b. Key **+**. Click cell E4. The tester receives a holiday rate increase, added to the regular pay rate.

   c. Key *****. Click cell C4. The hourly rate is multiplied by the number of hours worked to determine pay.

   d. Press Enter.

NOTE

This pay formula is not correct. You will correct it later.

3. Copy the formula in cell F4 to cells F5:F8.

4. Build a division formula by following these steps:

   a. Click cell H4 and key =. Click cell F4. The pay is divided by the number of items tested.

   b. Key /. Click cell G4. Press [Enter].

   c. Copy the formula to cells H5:H8.

5. Set the order of precedence by following these steps:

   a. Click cell F4. This formula should first add cells D4 and E4 and then multiply that sum by cell C4.

   b. Press [F2]. Click between = and **D**.

   c. Key (and click before *. Key) and press [Enter].

   d. Recopy the formula in cell F4 to cells F5:F8. Column H is recalculated.

6. Apply the Accounting format to cells D4:F8 and cells H4:H8.

7. Apply bold to cells A3:H3 and use Wrap Text. Center-align these labels. Make row 3 **45.00 (60 pixels)** tall.

8. Make column A **13.57 (100 pixels)** wide. AutoFit the other columns.

9. Center the labels in rows 1:2 over the worksheet data. Apply a medium tint of one of the accent colors to these cells and **Outside Borders**.

10. Select cells A9:H9 and apply a **Bottom Border**. Make this row **7.50 (10 pixels)** tall. Apply a **Bottom Border** to the labels in row 3 and set row 4 to a height of **20.25 (27 pixels)**.

11. Add a header with your name at the left, the filename in the center, and the date at the right. Use a left margin that allows the sheet to fit on one portrait page and makes the data appear to be horizontally centered.

12. Press [Ctrl]+[Home]. Prepare and submit your work. Save and close the workbook.

Exercise 5-23

Build formulas. Use an absolute reference.

1. Open **InsClaims.** Save it as *[your initials]*5-23 in your Lesson 5 folder.

2. Right-click the row 21 heading and choose **Insert**. Click the Insert Options button ✎ and choose **Format Same as Below**. A row without fill is inserted.

3. Insert two more rows without fill so that there are four empty rows above the row with solid black fill.

4. In cell B22, key **Total Number of Claims** and make it bold. If Excel copies the fill used in the rows, set the cell to use **No Fill**.

5. Build formulas by following these steps:

   a. Click cell C22. Key = to start the formula.

   b. Click cell C7 and click + to build an addition formula.

   c. Click C10 and click **+** to continue.

   d. Continue by adding each cell in column C with a value. When all cells are listed, press Enter.

6. Create similar formulas in cells D22 and E22. Center-align the results.

7. In cell B23, key **Total Processing Cost**. In cell B24, key **Single Claim Processing**. Make these labels bold.

8. In cell C24, key **15.45** and format it as Accounting.

9. Use an absolute reference in a formula by following these steps:

   a. Click cell C23. Key **=** to start the formula.

   b. Click C24 and press F4 to make it absolute.

   c. Key ***** and click cell C22. Press Ctrl + Enter.

10. Copy this formula to cells D23:E23.

11. Select all cells with currency values and apply **Currency** format from the Format Cells dialog box to show the dollar sign ($) next to the first digit.

12. Add a footer with your name at the left, the sheet name and the filename in the center, and the date at the right. Adjust the margins to fit the sheet to a single page.

13. Press Ctrl + Home. Prepare and submit your work. Save and close the workbook.

Exercise 5-24

Use relative, absolute, and mixed references. Change page orientation and margins. Display formulas. Save a Web page.

1. Open **Henderson** and save it as *[your initials]*5-24 in your Lesson 5 folder. Change to the **Opulent** document theme.

2. Click cell G3 and click after the **m** in **Cream** in the formula. Press Alt + Enter and then press Enter. Adjust the column width to show **Ice Cream** on one line and **Cost** on the second.

3. Center the labels in row 3.

4. Key the values shown below.

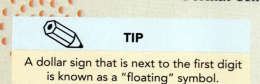

		Friday	Saturday	Sunday
4	One scoop	100	150	125
5	Two scoops	155	175	135
6	Three scoops	70	85	55

5. Use relative references by following these steps:

   a. Click cell B7 and click the AutoSum button Σ ▾.

   b. Copy the formula to cells B7:G7.

   c. Click cell E4 and click the AutoSum button Σ ▾.

   d. Copy the formula to cell E5:E6.

6. Use absolute references by following these steps:

    a. Click cell F4 and key **=** to start a formula.

    b. Click cell E4 and key ***** to multiply.

    c. Click cell B10 and press `F4`. Press `Ctrl`+`Enter`.

    d. Copy this formula to cells F5:F6.

7. Use mixed references by following these steps:

    a. Click cell G4 and key **=** to start.

    b. Click cell E4 and key ***** to multiply.

    c. Click cell B11 and press `F4` three times to show **$B11**. Press `Ctrl`+`Enter`.

    d. Copy this formula to cells G5:G6.

8. In cell E9, key **Grand Total** and make it bold. In cell G9, create a formula to add the total cone and ice cream costs. Copy formatting as needed.

9. Change the page orientation and margins by following these steps:

    a. Click the **Page Layout** tab.

    b. In the **Page Setup** group, click the Page Orientation button 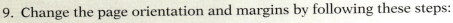. Choose **Landscape**.

    c. In the **Page Setup** group, click the Margins button. Choose **Custom Margins**.

    d. Double-click in the **Left** box and key **2.5**. Double-click in the **Top** box and key **2**. Click **Print Preview**.

    e. Close Print Preview.

10. Add a footer.

11. Display formulas by following these steps:

    a. Right-click the **Sheet1** tab and choose **Move or Copy**.

    b. Click to select **Create a copy**. Click **OK**.

    c. Rename the copied sheet **Formulas**. Press `Ctrl`+`~`.

    d. Click the column A heading. Scroll the worksheet, hold down `Shift`, and click the column G heading. Double-click the border between the column headings for columns G and H.

    e. Click the **Page Layout** tab.

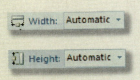

    f. In the **Scale to Fit** group, click the arrow for the Width button. Choose **1 page**.

    g. In the **Scale to Fit** group, click the arrow for the Height button. Choose **1 page**.

12. Add a background by following these steps:

    a. Right-click the **Sheet1** tab and choose **Move or Copy**. In the **Before sheet** list, choose **Formulas**. Click to select **Create a copy**. Click **OK**.

    b. Rename the copied sheet **Background**.

    c. Click the **Page Layout** tab. In the **Page Setup** group, click the Background button.

    d. Navigate to the folder with the **KKBack** file. Click to select the file and click **Insert**.

e. Press Ctrl+Home. Delete **Sheet2** and **Sheet3**.

f. Click the Save button to resave your workbook.

13. Save the workbook as a Web page by following these steps:

    a. Press F12. Click the arrow for **Save as type** and choose **Web Page**.

    b. Set the **Save in** folder to your Lesson 5 folder.

    c. In the **Save** area, choose **Entire Workbook**.

    d. Click **Change Title**. Key **Henderson Costs** and click **OK**.

    e. Name the file *[your initials]5-24*. Click **Save**. Choose **Yes** in the message box about incompatible formats.

    f. Close the workbook.

    g. Start your Web browser and maximize the window.

    h. Press Ctrl+O. Click **Browse** and navigate to your folder. Find and click *[your initials]5-24* and click **Open**. Click **OK**.

    i. Look for the title and at each of the sheets in the browser.

    j. Click the Close button to close the browser.

14. Prepare and submit your work.

TIP

You can use the same filename for the workbook and the Web page because they use different extensions.

Lesson Applications

Exercise 5-25

Create a workbook from a template. Build addition and subtraction formulas.

TIP

Check the Recently Used Templates list in the New Workbook dialog box. Double-click the filename if it is listed.

REVIEW

Select cells in a row, key data, and press Enter to move left to right from cell to cell.

NOTE

Negative numbers are shown in parentheses in this workbook. A negative number means the sales rep spent more money than budgeted.

Σ ▾

NOTE

Unless your instructor tells you otherwise, include your name, the sheet name, the filename, and the date in a header/footer.

1. Use the **KlassyKow** template as the basis for a workbook. Save the new workbook as *[your initials]5-25*.

2. Edit the label in cell B3 to show the current month.

3. Edit cells A6, A11, A16, and A21 to show the date of each Friday in the current month. If the month has a fifth Friday, do not include it.

4. In cells B9:D9, key the following expenses:

1300	1000	895

5. Key actual expenses for the weeks as follows:

Second week	1600	900	750
Third week	1000	1300	850
Fourth week	1200	2000	500

6. In cell B10, subtract the actual expense from the budgeted amount. Copy the formula to cells C10:D10 and then to the appropriate cells in rows 15, 20, and 25.

7. In cell B27, add the budget amounts for Kim Tomasaki. Copy the formula for the other salespeople.

8. In row 28, copy or create formulas to add the actual expense amounts for the salespeople. In row 29, calculate the differences.

9. Select cells E27:E29 and click the AutoSum button Σ ▾. Widen the column to show the data.

10. Add a footer. Prepare and submit your work. Save and close the workbook.

Exercise 5-26

Use a mixed reference. Change page orientation and scaling.

1. Open **DrinkSize** and save it as *[your initials]5-26* in your folder.

2. Copy/paste cells A1:H11 to cells A23:H33. Compare and fix row heights. Delete the unit values for the states in rows 28:32.

3. In cell D28, multiply the item count for California by the price of a 16-ounce soda, using a mixed reference so that you can copy this formula for the other states and then for the other rows.

4. Format these results as Currency with two decimals and a dollar sign (from the Format Cells dialog box). Adjust column widths. Change the label to **Dollar Sales for June**.

5. In cells E15:E19, use a formula to calculate the total dollar sales for each beverage. Use the same currency format as other values on the sheet.

6. Use a two-color scale for cells E15:E20 that shows a darker shade for the largest values. Edit the rule to show a color that coordinates with the existing sheet.

7. Change the page orientation to landscape. Set the scaling to print the worksheet at **90%** of normal size.

8. Add a header.

9. Make a copy of the worksheet and name the tab **Formulas**. Choose a blue color for the tab to match the font.

10. Display the formulas and fit the columns. Scale the worksheet to **75%**.

11. Prepare and submit your work. Save and close the workbook.

Exercise 5-27

Use order of precedence. Change page layout options. Print formulas.

1. Open **ICOrder** and save it as *[your initials]*5-27 in your folder.

2. Center the two main labels across columns A:C.

3. Insert a row at row 1 and make it **7.50 (10 pixels)** tall. Apply a dash-dot-dash-dot top border to this row up to column C.

4. Apply the same border to the bottom of row 3. Apply a solid vertical border to the right edge of cells A5:A12 and cells B5:B12.

5. Apply **White, Background 1, Darker 25%** fill to cell C16 with a single top and double bottom solid border.

6. In cell C14, create a formula to calculate a subtotal by multiplying the quantity by the price for each item. In cell C15, create a formula to calculate the sales tax. Finally, in cell C16, create the formula to calculate the total amount due.

7. Select cells A1:C16 and press Ctrl+C to copy. Click cell E1 and press Ctrl+V to paste. Right-click the Paste Options button and choose **Keep Source Column Widths**.

TIP

You can use any combination of pointing, clicking, or keying to complete a formula.

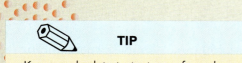

TIP

Key sample data to test your formulas.

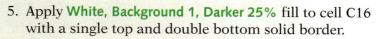

NOTE

The Footer margin is on the Margins tab of the Page Setup dialog box.

NOTE

Choose a print range in the Print dialog box.

8. Copy and paste cells A1:G16 to start in cell A18 so that there are four copies of the order form on your worksheet. Check for discrepancies in row height and make adjustments.

9. Change the page orientation to landscape. Scale the worksheet to 95% and set the top and bottom margins at .5 inches and the left margin at 1 inch. Change the footer margin to .35 inches.

10. Add a footer.

11. Make a copy of the worksheet and name it **Formulas**. Display the formulas. Size the columns to show the complete formulas. Set 75% scaling and print only the first page.

12. Prepare and submit your work. Save and close the workbook.

Exercise 5-28 ◆ Challenge Yourself

Use order of precedence. Print formulas.

TIP

A 4.5% tax rate makes the final cost 104.5% of the pre-tax total. Correct the first occurrence of the formula and copy it to the other locations.

1. Open **OrderForm**. Save it as *[your initials]*5-28 in your folder.

2. The **Amount Due** formula calculates the total amount due by multiplying quantity by price, summing these results, and multiplying by 104.5%, the tax rate. Review and correct the formula.

3. Add a header.

4. Make a copy of the worksheet and name it **Formulas**. Hide all columns except those with formulas.

5. Prepare and submit your work. Save and close the workbook.

On Your Own

In these exercises you work on your own, as you would in a real-life work environment. Use the skills you've learned to accomplish the task—and be creative.

Exercise 5-29

Open **MultTable** and edit it to build a division table. Apply borders and/or fill to make the worksheet easy to read. Add a header or footer. Save the workbook as *[your initials]*5-29 in your Lesson 5 folder. Set the page for landscape orientation on one page. Make a copy of the sheet with formulas. Prepare and submit your work. Save and close the workbook.

Exercise 5-30

Create a new workbook and save it as *[your initials]*5-30 in your folder. In cell A1, key **Tip Calculator**. In cell B2, key **10%**; in cell C2, **15%**; in cell D2, **18%**; and in cell E2, **20%**. Starting in cell A3, create a series with a $5 interval that goes from $10 to $100. Using mixed references, create and copy formulas to determine the tip based on the sales amount and a tip percentage. Show two decimal places for the results. Apply formatting, borders, and fill for an attractive appearance. Prepare a formulas sheet. Prepare and submit your work. Save the workbook and close it.

Exercise 5-31

Develop a worksheet that tracks the number of e-mail and instant messages you receive per day. Build a date series in column A for a four-week period. In column B, key a value to show the number of messages with some variety of numbers. Make all data bold. Apply a three-color scale that uses a dark color for the smallest value. Add a header or footer. Save your workbook as *[your initials]*5-31. Prepare and submit your work. Save and close the workbook.

Working with Functions

OBJECTIVES

After completing this lesson, you will be able to:

1. Use math and trig functions.

2. Use statistical functions.

3. Use icon sets.

4. Group worksheets.

5. Use date and time functions.

Estimated Time: 1½ hours

MCAS OBJECTIVES

In this lesson:
XL07 1.3.1
XL07 1.5.1
XL07 1.5.2
XL07 1.5.5
XL07 2.3.1
XL07 2.3.2
XL07 3.2
XL07 3.2.1
XL07 3.4.1
XL07 4.3.1
XL07 4.3.3
XL07 5.5

Excel has several categories of functions that perform common mathematical, statistical, financial, and other calculations. A *function* is a built-in formula.

Many functions do things automatically that would be difficult or time-consuming for you to do manually. For example, in a list of accounts with each customer's amount due, Excel can quickly calculate a total, find the largest amount due, or calculate an average amount due.

Using Math and Trig Functions

All functions have a *syntax*, which defines the necessary parts of the formula and the order of those parts. The syntax consists of an equal sign and the name of the function, followed by parentheses. Inside the parentheses, you place arguments.

An *argument* is the information the function needs to complete its calculation, usually one or more values or cell ranges. A few functions do not have arguments, but most have at least one argument. If a function has more than one argument, the arguments are separated by commas. A function's arguments can consist of:

- Cell references (individual cells or ranges)

- Constants (a number keyed in the formula)

- Another function (known as a nested function)

- Range names

Figure 6-1
Syntax for the SUM
function

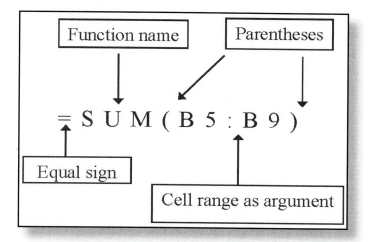

Exercise 6-1 USE SUM AND THE FORMULA BAR

The SUM function in the Math & Trig category adds columns or rows of values. The SUM function ignores cells with:

NOTE

Excel inserts the SUM function when you use the AutoSum button Σ AutoSum ▾ .

- Text

- Error values such as #NAME?

TABLE 6-1 Examples of the SUM Function

Function(argument/s)	Cell Data	Result
=SUM(A1:A3)	A1=10, A2=20, A3=30	60
=SUM(50,60)	None	110
=SUM(A1,250)	A1=25	275
=SUM(A1,B2,C1:C2)	A1=10, B2=20, C1=10, C2=30	70
=SUM(A1,B2)	A1=25, B2="Ice Cream"	25
=SUM(A1,B2)	A1=25, B2=#NAME?	25

1. Open **DownTime**.

2. Click cell E17.

3. Key **=su**. *Formula AutoComplete* displays a list of functions that match what you have keyed so far. There is also a descriptive ScreenTip for the highlighted function.

Figure 6-2
Formula
AutoComplete
DownTime.xlsx
Jan15Plan sheet

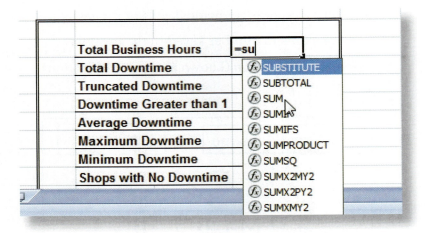

TIP

You can click the function name to highlight it in the Formula AutoComplete list and then press [Tab] to insert it.

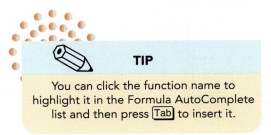

4. Double-click **SUM** in the list. The opening parenthesis is inserted with the function name. An Argument ScreenTip illustrates the syntax for the function with the first argument shown in bold.

5. Click cell C7 and drag to select cells C7:C14. As you drag, the ScreenTip shows the number of rows and columns. The function will sum the range C7:C14.

Figure 6-3
SUM function with its
Argument ScreenTip
DownTime.xlsx
Jan15Plan sheet

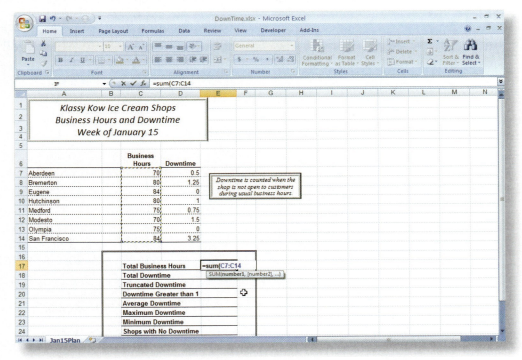

6. Press [Ctrl]+[Enter]. The result is 618.

7. Look in the formula bar. For the SUM function, Excel adds a closing parenthesis for you. This formula is the same as keying **=c7+c8+ c9+c10+c11+c12+c13+c14**.

Exercise 6-2 USE INSERT FUNCTION

The Insert Function dialog box enables you to choose a function from all available. After you choose a function, the Function Arguments dialog box opens and guides you in building the formula. An Insert Function button appears at the left of the formula bar. There is also an Insert Function button on the Formulas tab.

1. Click cell E18. This will be a sum of the values from column D.

2. Click the Insert Function button in the formula bar. The Insert Function dialog box opens.

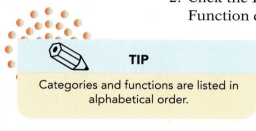

TIP

Categories and functions are listed in alphabetical order.

3. Click the arrow next to the **Or select a category** list. Choose **Math & Trig**.

4. In the **Select a function** list, scroll to find **SUM**.

5. Click **SUM** to see its syntax and a description in the dialog box.

Figure 6-4
Insert Function dialog box

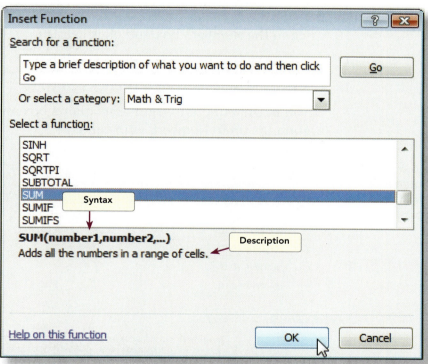

REVIEW

Drag a dialog box by pointing at its title bar.

6. Click **OK**. The Function Arguments dialog box opens. In the **Number1** box, Excel assumes that you want to sum the range above cell E18.

7. Move the dialog box so that you see columns C and D (see Figure 6-5).

Figure 6-5
Function Arguments
dialog box
DownTime.xlsx
Jan15Plan sheet

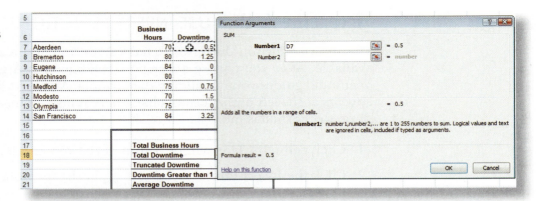

NOTE

If you click in the wrong cell or number box, reposition the pointer and click again in the correct location.

8. Click cell D7. A marquee appears around the cell, and its address is entered in the **Number1** box in the Function Arguments dialog box.

9. Click in the **Number2** box and click cell D8. Notice that the formula appears in both the formula bar and the cell. When cells are listed one by one, they are separated by commas in the function.

10. Click in the **Number3** box and click cell D9.

11. Click in the **Number4** box and click cell D10.

12. Click in the **Number5** box and click cell D11.

13. Scroll in the Function Arguments dialog box and complete the arguments up to **Number8** with cell D14.

Figure 6-6
Function Arguments
dialog box with cells
entered separately

Number4	D10	= 1
Number5	D11	= 0.75
Number6	D12	= 1.5
Number7	D13	= 0
Number8	D14	= 3.25

= 8.25

Adds all the numbers in a range of cells.

Number8: number1,number2,... are 1 to 255 numbers to sum. Logical values and text are ignored in cells, included if typed as arguments.

Formula result = 8.25

Help on this function   OK   Cancel

14. Press Enter. The dialog box closes; the result (8.25) is displayed in the cell.

Exercise 6-3 USE TRUNC

The TRUNC function removes the decimal part of a number or shows a certain number of decimal positions without adjusting the value.

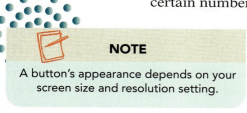

> **NOTE**
>
> A button's appearance depends on your screen size and resolution setting.

Math & Trig ▾

1. Click cell E19. You are going to truncate the results in cell E18 to show no decimals.

2. Click the **Formulas** tab in the Ribbon.

3. In the **Function Library** group, click the Math & Trig button Math & Trig ▾ . The list of functions opens.

Figure 6-7
Choosing TRUNC

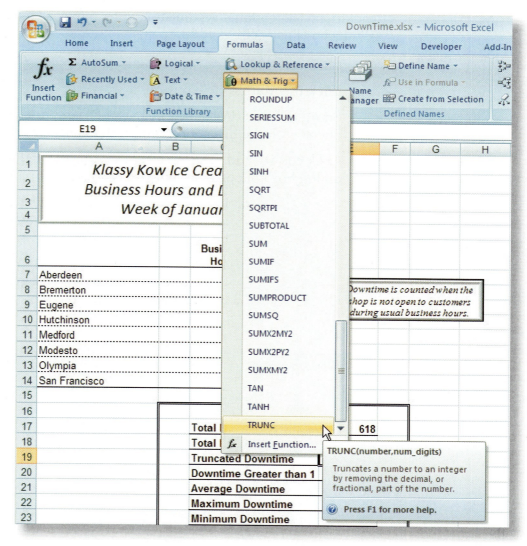

4. Scroll to find **TRUNC** and click. The TRUNC Function Arguments dialog box opens. The insertion point is in the **Number** box.

5. Click cell E18. Its address appears in the **Number** box.

6. Click in the **Num_digits** box. Key **0** to truncate the value to show no decimal positions.

7. Click **OK**. The truncated value of cell E18 is 8.

Exercise 6-4   USE SUMIF

The SUMIF function adds cell values only if they meet a condition. In this case, you will determine the total number of down hours for shops with downtime greater than one hour. The SUMIF function has two required arguments, Range and Criteria. The range is the group of cells to be added. The criteria is a condition that must be met for the cell to be included in the addition. The optional argument is Sum_range, which allows for additional limits on which cells to add.

1. Click cell E20. Click the **Formulas** tab.

2. Click the Math & Trig button 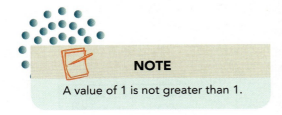 .

3. Scroll to find **SUMIF** and click. The Function Arguments dialog box opens with the insertion point in the **Range** entry box.

4. Click cell D7 and drag to select the range D7:D14. As you drag, the dialog box collapses so that you can see your work better.

5. Release the mouse button. The dialog box expands, and the range you selected is entered in the **Range** box.

NOTE

A value of 1 is not greater than 1.

6. Click in the **Criteria** box. Key **>1** to set a rule that the value in the range D7:D14 be greater than 1 to be included in the sum.

Figure 6-8
SUMIF function in the Function Arguments dialog box

Function Arguments			? ✕
SUMIF			
Range	D7:D14	= {0.5;1.25;0;1;0.75;1.5;0;3.25}
Criteria	>1	=
Sum_range		= reference
		=

Adds the cells specified by a given condition or criteria.

Criteria is the condition or criteria in the form of a number, expression, or text that defines which cells will be added.

Formula result =

Help on this function   OK   Cancel

7. Click **OK**. The result is 6 because only the values in cells D8, D12, and D14 are totaled. You can verify this result with AutoCalculate.

8. Click cell D8. Hold down [Ctrl] and click cells D12 and then D14. These are values greater than 1. The sum appears in the status bar.

9. Click cell E20 and view the formula in the formula bar. The criteria has been inserted with quotation marks. Note that the values in cells E19 and E20 are not aligned.

10. Copy the format from cell E19 to cell E20 to adjust the alignment.

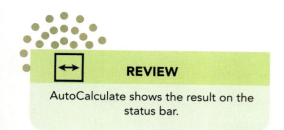

REVIEW

AutoCalculate shows the result on the status bar.

Using Statistical Functions

Another category of Excel functions is the Statistical group. Some of these functions are useful even if you are not a statistician.

Exercise 6-5   USE THE AVERAGE FUNCTION

The AVERAGE function calculates the arithmetic mean of a range of cells. The *arithmetic mean* adds the values in the cells and then divides by the number of values. The AVERAGE function ignores:

NOTE

A logical value is "True," "False," "Yes," or "No."

- Text

- Blank or empty cells (but not zeros)

- Error values such as #NAME?

- Logical values

TABLE 6-2 Examples of the AVERAGE Function

Function(argument/s)	Cell Data	Result
=AVERAGE(A1:A3)	A1=10, A2=20, A3=30	20
=AVERAGE(50,60)	None	55
=AVERAGE(A1,250)	A1=25	137.5
=AVERAGE(A1,B2,C1:C2)	A1=10, B2=20, C1=10, C2=30	17.5
=AVERAGE(A1, B2)	A1=25, B2="Ice Cream"	25
=AVERAGE(A1, B2)	A1=25, B2=#NAME?	25
=AVERAGE(A1:A3)	A1=20, A2=0, A3=TRUE	10
=AVERAGE(A1:A3)	A1=20, A2=Empty, A3=40	30

1. Right-click the row 21 row heading and choose **Insert**. A row is inserted.

2. Key **Average Business Hours** in cell C21.

3. Click cell E21. This cell should average the values from column C.

4. Click the **Formulas** tab. Click the Insert Function button *fx*.

5. Choose **Statistical** in the **Or select a category** list. In the **Select a function** list, locate **AVERAGE**.

6. Click **AVERAGE** to see its syntax and description. Click **OK**.

7. Move the dialog box until you can see column C. The **Number1** box shows the range directly above cell E21.

8. Click cell C7 and drag to select cells C7:C14 to reset the range.

9. Release the mouse button. The dialog box expands, and the range you selected is entered in the **Number1** box.

10. Click **OK**. The result is 77.25.

Exercise 6-6   USE AVERAGEIF

The AVERAGEIF function averages cell values only if they meet a condition. Like SUMIF, AVERAGEIF has two required arguments, Range and Criteria.

1. Click cell E22. Click the Insert Function button *fx*.

2. Choose **Statistical**. In the **Select a function** list, find **AVERAGEIF**.

3. Click **AVERAGEIF** and click **OK**. The Function Arguments dialog box opens with the insertion point in the **Range** entry box.

4. Click cell D7 and drag to select the range D7:D14.

5. Click in the **Criteria** box. Key **>0** to set a rule that the value in the range D7:D14 must be greater than 0 to be included in the average.

6. Click **OK**. The result is 1, formatted without any decimals.

7. Click the **Home** tab. Click the Increase Decimal button three times. The values are not properly aligned.

8. Press Ctrl+1 and click the **Number** tab. Click **General** and click **OK**.

Exercise 6-7   USE THE MIN AND MAX FUNCTIONS

MIN and MAX are statistical functions that show the minimum (smallest) value or the maximum (largest) value in a range. The MIN and MAX functions ignore:

- Text

- Blank or empty cells (but not zeros)

- Error values such as #NAME?

- Logical values

TABLE 6-3 Examples of the MIN and MAX Functions

Function(argument/s)	Cell Data	Result
=MAX(A1:A3)	A1=10, A2=20, A3=30	30
=MAX(50,60)	None	60
=MIN(A1,250)	A1=25	25
=MIN(A1,B2,C1:C2)	A1=10, B2=20, C1=10, C2=30	10
=MAX(A1, B2)	A1=25, B2="Ice Cream"	25
=MAX(A1, B2)	A1=25, B2=#NAME?	25
=MIN(A1:A3)	A1=20, A2=10, A3=FALSE	10
=MIN(A1:A3)	A1=20, A2=Empty, A3=40	20

1. Click cell E23.

2. Press [Shift]+[F3]. This shortcut opens the Insert Function dialog box.

3. Choose **Statistical** and **MAX**. In the Function Arguments dialog box, the **Number1** box shows the range directly above cell E23.

4. Select cells D7:D14 to determine the largest value from column D. The range is shown as **Number1**. Click **OK**. The maximum value is 3.25.

5. Click cell E24 and key **=min** to start the MIN function. Formula AutoComplete shows the function and its ScreenTip.

Figure 6-9
Formula
AutoComplete
and descriptive
ScreenTip
DownTime.xlsx
Jan15Plan sheet

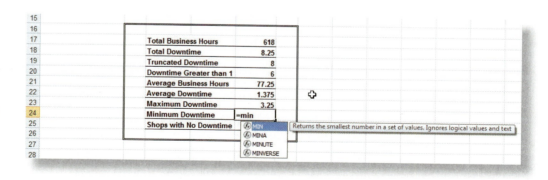

6. Press [Tab]. The opening parenthesis is inserted.

7. Select cells D7:D14 and press [Enter]. The function does not ignore zeros, so the minimum value is zero.

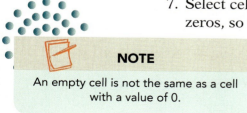

NOTE

An empty cell is not the same as a cell with a value of 0.

8. Delete the contents of cells D9 and D13. The results in cell E24 are recalculated and some cells show error triangles because the formulas now refer to empty cells.

Exercise 6-8 USE COUNT AND COUNTBLANK

The COUNTBLANK function counts empty cells in a range. The COUNT function tallies the number of values in a range. The COUNT function ignores:

- Text

- Blank or empty cells (but not zeros)

- Error values such as #NAME?

- Logical values

TABLE 6-4 Examples of the COUNT Function

Function(argument/s)	Cell Data	Result
=COUNT(A1:A3)	A1=Empty, A2=20, A3=30	2
=COUNT(A1:A3)	A1=30, A2=Empty, A3=#NAME?	1
=COUNT(A1:A3)	A1=25, A2="Ice Cream," A3=3	2
=COUNT(13, 21, 111)	None	3
=COUNT(A1, B2, C1:C2)	A1=25, B2=0, C1="Hello," C2=4	3

1. Key **0** (zero) in cells D9 and D13. The results in cell E24 change.

2. Click cell E25 and click the **Home** tab. Click the Insert Function button ⨍ in the formula bar.

3. Choose **Statistical** and **COUNT**. Click **OK**.

4. Select cells D7:D14. The range appears in the **Value1** box.

5. Click **OK**. The cells with zero (0) are included in the count.

6. Delete the contents of cells D9 and D13. The count tallies the cells with downtime. Blank cells are not included.

7. Edit the label in cell C25 to delete **No**.

8. Right-click the row heading for row 25 and insert a row.

9. Click cell E25 and click the Insert Function button ⨍ .

10. Choose **Statistical** and **COUNTBLANK**. Click **OK**. Select cells D7:D14. Click **OK**.

11. Key **Shops with No Downtime** in cell C25.

12. Insert a row at row 27. Key **Number of Shops** in cell C27.

13. Click cell E27, key **=count**, and press Tab.

14. Drag to select cells A7:A14. The range is **value1** in the ScreenTip.

Figure 6-10
Keying the COUNT
function
DownTime.xlsx
Jan15Plan sheet

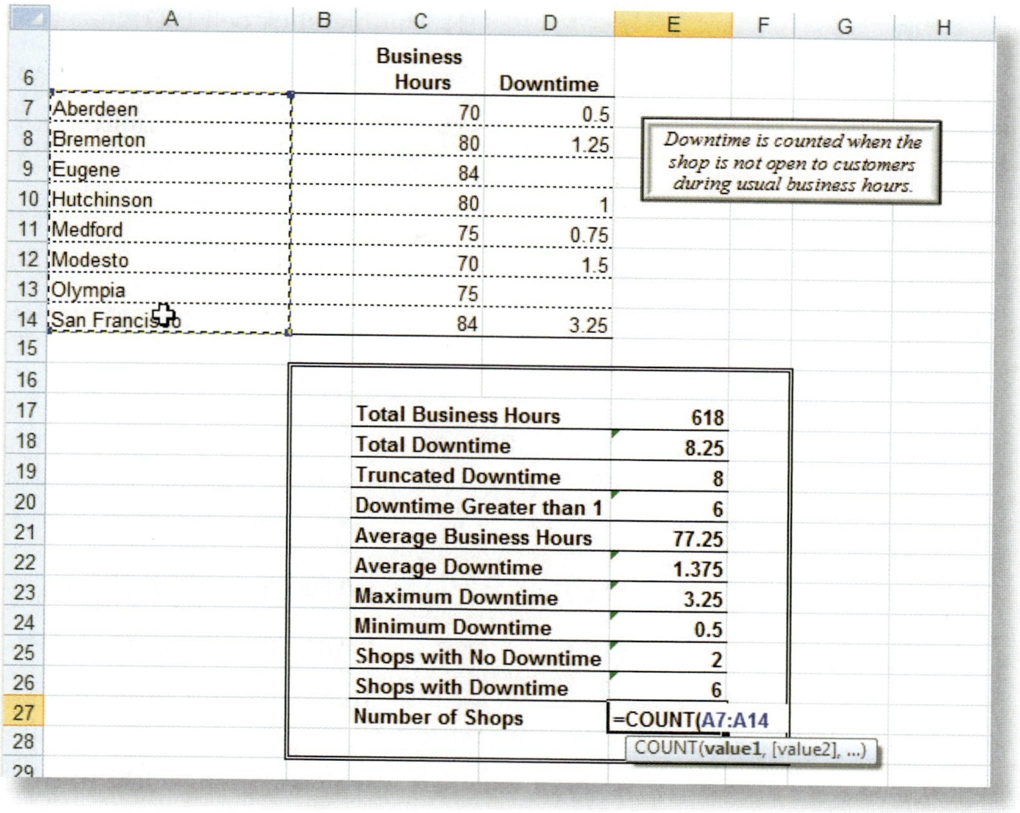

15. Press Enter. The result is 0, because the COUNT function ignores text.

Exercise 6-9   USE THE COUNTA FUNCTION

The COUNTA function tallies values and labels. The COUNTA function ignores:

- Blank or empty cells (but not zeros)

- Error values such as #NAME?

- Logical values

TABLE 6-5 Examples of the COUNTA Function

Function(argument/s)	Cell Data	Result
=COUNTA(A1:A3)	A1=Empty, A2=20, A3=30	2
=COUNTA(A1:A3)	A1=30, A2=Empty, A3=#NAME?	1
=COUNTA(A1:A3)	A1=25, A2="Ice Cream," A3=3	3
=COUNTA(13, 21, 111)	None	3
=COUNTA(A1, B2, C1:C2)	A1=25, B2=0, C1="Hello," C2=TRUE	3

NOTE

The Count option in AutoCalculate shows the same results as the COUNTA function. AutoCalculate's Numerical Count option shows the same results as the COUNT function.

1. Double-click cell E27.

2. Position the insertion point and key **a** after **COUNT**.

3. Press ⌷Enter⌷. The new function COUNTA includes labels; there are eight shops in the list.

4. Add a bottom border to the data in row 27.

5. Save the workbook as *[your initials]*6-9 in a folder for Lesson 6.

Using Icon Sets

Data visualizations are simple conditional formatting rules. They use data bars, color scales, and icon sets. An icon set consists of three to five icons that appear in a range of cells based on the value in the cell.

Exercise 6-10   APPLY ICON SETS

1. With *[your initials]*6-9 open, click the **Home** tab.

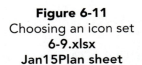

2. Select cells D7:D14. In the **Styles** group, click the Conditional Formatting button 🔳.

3. Hover at **Icon Sets**. A gallery opens with the available styles.

4. Hover at several sets to see the results. Live Preview displays the icon sets before you apply them.

Figure 6-11
Choosing an icon set
6-9.xlsx
Jan15Plan sheet

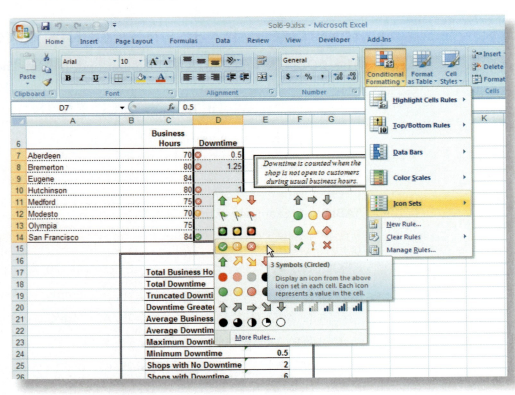

5. Choose **3 Symbols (Circled)** in the first column. The icons appear at the left edge of the cell. The highest value has the green check mark.

Exercise 6-11   EDIT THE ICON FORMATTING RULE

1. Select cells D7:D14 and click the Conditional Formatting button 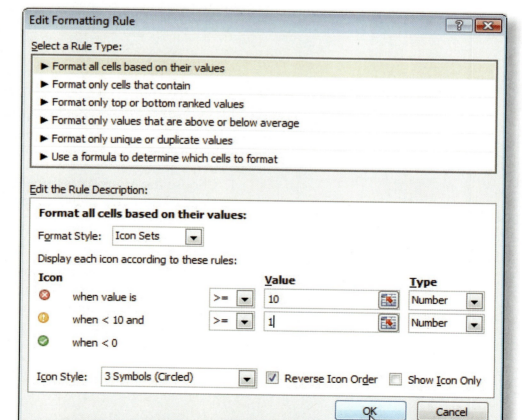.

2. Choose **Manage Rules**. The icon set is listed in the Conditional Formatting Rules Manager dialog box.

3. Click **Edit Rule**. The Edit Formatting Rule dialog box includes options that you can edit for this rule.

4. Click the arrow with **Percent** for the first icon. Choose **Number**. This will set the rule to use a specific value rather than a percent.

5. Change the **Type** for the second icon to **Number**.

6. Click to select **Reverse Icon Order**. This will set the rule to show the green check mark for the lowest value.

7. Key **10** in the **Value** box for the first icon (red X). There are no values greater than or equal to 10 in your list, so this icon won't be shown at all.

8. Key **1** in the **Value** box for the second icon (yellow exclamation point).

Figure 6-12
Editing the icon set rule
6-9.xlsx
Jan15Plan sheet

9. Click **OK**. Click **OK** again. Empty cells are not formatted; they have no value.

10. Key **0** in cells D9 and D13. The icons are inserted.

11. Press Ctrl + Home. Save the workbook as *[your initials]*6-11 in your folder. Close the workbook.

Grouping Worksheets

An Excel workbook can have as many worksheets as your machine's memory allows. Multiple sheets enable you to separate related data when necessary but have it available for managing information. When you work with multiple sheets, you can group the sheets to edit or format them as a group.

TIP

Some tasks do not work on grouped sheets. For example, you cannot add data visualizations (data bars, color scales, icon sets) to grouped sheets.

Exercise 6-12   **GROUP AND DELETE WORKSHEETS**

When worksheets are grouped, editing and formatting commands affect all sheets in the group. This is an efficient way to make changes to several worksheets at once, as long as the sheets are identical.

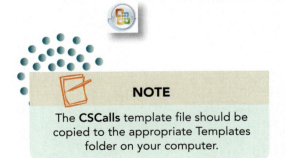

NOTE

The **CSCalls** template file should be copied to the appropriate Templates folder on your computer.

1. Choose the Microsoft Office Button and choose **New**. Choose **My templates** in the New Workbook dialog box.

2. Choose **CSCalls** and click **OK**.

3. Click the **Sheet2** tab, hold down Ctrl, and click the **Sheet3** tab. Both worksheets are selected or active. The word **[Group]** appears in the title bar. The tabs appear more white.

Figure 6-13
Grouped worksheets
CSCalls.xltx

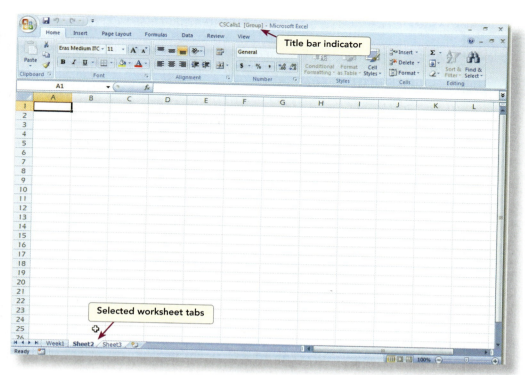

Title bar indicator

Selected worksheet tabs

TIP

You can ungroup sheets by clicking a sheet that is not in the group or by right-clicking a sheet in the group and choosing Ungroup Sheets.

4. Click the **Week1** tab. Selecting a tab outside the group ungroups the sheets.

5. Click **Sheet2**, hold down Ctrl, and click **Sheet3** again.

6. Right-click either tab in the group and choose **Delete**. Both sheets are deleted.

Exercise 6-13   MANAGE WORKSHEETS

When you copy a worksheet with the Move or Copy dialog box, formatting and data are included.

1. Right-click the **Week1** tab. Choose **Move or Copy**. The **To book** list includes the names of open workbooks as well as a new book. The **Before sheet** list allows you to move or copy the sheet to a specific location in the tabs.

NOTE

If you do not select **Create a copy**, the worksheet is moved.

2. Select **(move to end)** in the **Before sheet** list.

3. Click to select **Create a copy**.

4. Click **OK**. The new worksheet named **Week1 (2)** is an exact duplicate of the **Week1** sheet.

REVIEW

You can double-click or right-click a sheet tab to rename it.

REVIEW

You can insert a sheet by right-clicking a worksheet tab and choosing Insert or by clicking the Insert Worksheet tab.

5. Rename **Week1 (2)** tab as **Week2**.

6. Make two more copies of the **Week1** sheet and name them **Week3** and **Week4**.

7. Click the **Week1** tab and press Shift+F11. A blank worksheet is inserted in front of (to the left of) the **Week1** sheet. New sheet numbers start at the next available number in the workbook.

8. Rename the new sheet as **FirstQuarter**.

9. Right-click the **FirstQuarter** tab and choose **Move or Copy**. Choose **(move to end)** and click **OK**. This moves the sheet without making a copy.

10. Choose a different accent color for each tab.

11. Save the workbook as *[your initials]*6-13 in your Lesson 6 folder.

Using Date and Time Functions

Date and time functions can be used to display the current date and time, determine ages, and calculate hours worked, days passed, and future dates.

With dates and times, Excel uses a *serial number* system. A serial number is a date shown as a value. Excel's date system numbers January 1, 1900, as 1 and January 2, 1900, as 2; it assigns a number to every date up to December 31, 9999.

Exercise 6-14 USE THE TODAY() FUNCTION

The TODAY() function displays the current date, using the computer's clock. This function has no arguments, and Excel formats the results in a standard date style. The TODAY() function is *volatile,* which means that the formula results depend on the computer on which the workbook is opened.

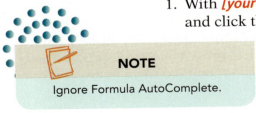

NOTE

Ignore Formula AutoComplete.

1. With *[your initials]*6-13 open, click the **Week1** tab. Hold down Shift and click the **Week4** tab. Four worksheets are grouped.

2. Click cell A3. Key **=today()** and press Enter. The current date is inserted. The ##### symbols indicate that the column is not wide enough to show the date in the current font size.

3. Click cell A3 and look in the formula bar. Excel capitalizes function names after you complete the cell.

4. Press Ctrl+1 and click the **Number** tab. In the **Category** list, choose **General**. The sample box shows the serial number for today.

5. Click **OK**. The serial number that represents today's date is shown.

6. Click the Undo button . The format change is reversed.

7. Press Ctrl + 1 and click the **Alignment** tab.

8. In the **Text control** group, click to select **Shrink to fit**.

9. Click **OK**. The display date is sized to fit the column width, but the font size still shows the original size.

Exercise 6-15   KEY AND FORMAT DATES

When you key a date, Excel assigns the closest matching date format to the date you key. The resulting format may not match what you key. You can, however, use one of many built-in date formats or create your own format.

TABLE 6-6 Sample Keyed Dates and Initial Screen Display

Keyed Characters	Screen Display
1-1-08	1/1/2008
1/1/08	1/1/2008
1-jan-08	1-Jan-08
january 1, 2008	1-Jan-08
jan 1, 2008	1-Jan-08

NOTE

Remember that four worksheets are grouped.

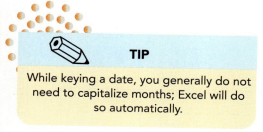

TIP

While keying a date, you generally do not need to capitalize months; Excel will do so automatically.

1. In cell A5, key **01/01/08** and press Enter. The date is formatted without leading zeros and shows the year with four digits.

2. In cell A6, key **1-jan-08** and press Enter. The format matches what you keyed.

3. In cell A7, key **january 1, 2008** and press Enter.

4. In cell A8, key **1-1-08** and press Enter.

5. Select cells A5:A8. Press Ctrl + 1.

6. Click the **Number** tab and choose **Date** in the **Category** list.

7. Choose **March 14, 2001** in the **Type** list.

8. Click **OK**. Widen column A. All the dates are formatted in the same style.

9. Click cell A3.

10. Right-click the **Week4** tab. The **Week4** sheet becomes the active sheet.

11. Choose **Ungroup Sheets**. The **Week4** worksheet shows the dates.

12. Click the **Week1** tab, then the **Week2** tab, then the **Week3** tab. All sheets have the same formatting and data.

Exercise 6-16   USE FILL ACROSS WORKSHEETS

Another way to copy selected data from one worksheet to another is the Fill Across Worksheets command. To use this command, you first select the worksheet with the data and the one(s) where the data should be copied.

1. Click the **FirstQuarter** tab. This is the blank sheet you inserted.

2. Click the **Week4** tab.

3. Hold down the Ctrl key and click the **FirstQuarter** worksheet tab. The title bar shows **[Group]**.

4. On the **Week4** sheet, select cells A1:D8. These are the cells that will be copied to the **FirstQuarter** sheet.

5. On the **Home** tab, click the Fill button in the **Editing** group. Its submenu opens.

6. Choose **Across Worksheets**. The Fill Across Worksheets dialog box has options to copy everything, only the data, or only the formatting.

Figure 6-14
Using Fill Across Worksheets
6-13.xlsx
Week4 sheet

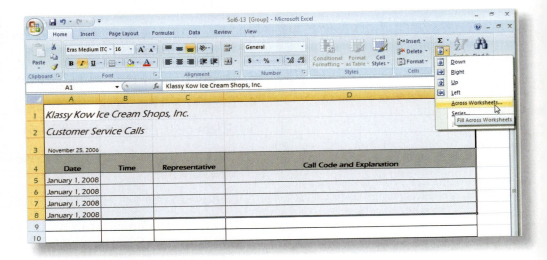

7. Choose **All** and click **OK**.

8. Right-click the **Week4** worksheet tab. Choose **Ungroup Sheets**.

9. Click the **FirstQuarter** worksheet tab. The data and some formatting have been copied. Column widths and row heights are not copied.

10. Make columns A:C **12.56 (120 pixels)** wide. Make column D **57.56 (525 pixels)** wide.

11. Make row 4 **30.00 (30 pixels)** tall. Make rows 5:8 **18.75 (25 pixels)** tall.

Exercise 6-17   CREATE A CUSTOM DATE FORMAT

To create your own date format, you key formatting codes in the Custom category. You can see formatting codes and samples in the Format Cells dialog box.

1. Select cells A5:A8 and press Ctrl + 1.

2. Click the **Number** tab and choose **Date** in the **Category** list.

3. Scroll through the **Type** list. There is no preset format to show the date, the month spelled out, and a two-digit year (14 March 01).

4. Click **Custom** in the **Category** list. The **Type** list shows the codes for a variety of formats, not just dates. You can choose one as a starting point to build your own format.

5. Scroll the **Type** list to find **d-mmm**.

6. Click the code to select it. The **Sample** box shows the date with that format.

7. Click in the **Type** box above the **Type** list.

8. Delete the hyphen and press Spacebar.

9. Edit the code to show **dd mmmm y**. Two **dd**'s show the date with a leading zero. Four **mmmm**'s spell out the month. A single **y** shows a two-digit year.

10. Look at the **Sample** box.

Figure 6-15
Creating a custom
date format

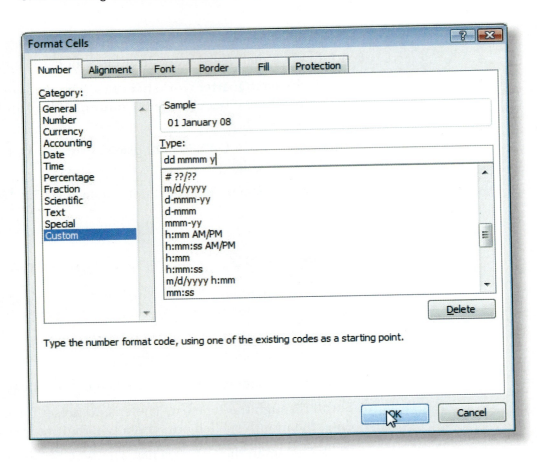

11. Click **OK**. The dates are reformatted. Widen the column if necessary.

Exercise 6-18   KEY AND FORMAT TIMES

1. Click the **Week1** tab. Hold down Shift and click the **Week4** tab. Four worksheets are grouped.

2. Click cell B5 and key **11 am**.

3. Press Ctrl+Enter. The time is shown and AM is capitalized.

> **TIP**
>
> It does not matter which worksheet is on top when you edit data in grouped worksheets.

4. Look in the formula bar to see minutes and seconds.

5. Click cell B6 and key **4:30** and press Ctrl+Enter.

6. Look at the time in the formula bar. If you do not key **am** or **pm**, Excel assumes morning.

7. In cell B7 key **4:30 pm** and press Enter.

8. In cell B8 key **13:30** and press Enter. Excel shows the time using the 24-hour clock.

9. In cell B9 key **2:45 pm**, and in cell B10 key **14:30**.

10. Select cells B5:B10.

11. Press Ctrl+1. Click the **Number** tab and choose **Time** in the **Category** list.

12. Scroll the **Type** list. Then choose **1:30 PM** and click **OK**.

Exercise 6-19 USE THE NOW() FUNCTION

The NOW() function is similar to the TODAY() function. It uses the computer's clock to show the current date and time.

1. Click cell A11. Key **=now(** and press Enter. Excel supplies the closing parenthesis.

2. Widen the column as needed. The default format may not include the time.

3. Click cell A11 and press Ctrl+1.

4. Click the **Number** tab and choose **Time** in the **Category** list.

5. Scroll through the **Type** list. Then choose **3/14/01 1:30 PM** and click **OK**. The function shows the current date and time.

Exercise 6-20 CREATE A CUSTOM TIME FORMAT

1. Click cell A11 and press Ctrl+1.

2. Click **Custom** in the **Category** list.

3. Scroll the **Type** list to find **m/d/yyyy h:mm**.

4. Click the code to select it. The **Sample** box shows the date and time with that format.

5. Click in the **Type** box before the first **m**.

6. Edit the code to show **mmm d, yyyy- -h:mm AM/PM**. Be sure to insert the spaces, the comma, and the hyphens. Check the **Sample** box to verify your format as you build it.

Figure 6-16
Creating a custom
time format

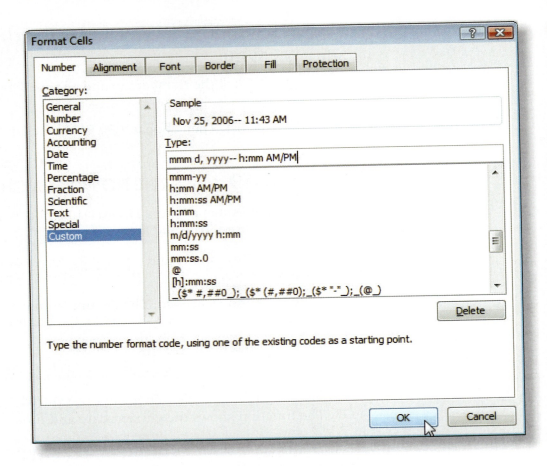

7. Click the **Alignment** tab. In the **Text control** group, click to select **Shrink to fit**.

8. Click **OK**. The time is reformatted and shrunk.

9. Right-click any sheet and choose **Ungroup Sheets**.

Exercise 6-21   ADD A HEADER TO GROUPED SHEETS

You can add the same header or footer to all sheets in a group through the Page Setup dialog box. You can also center the sheets at the same time.

1. Click the **Week1** tab. Hold down ⇧Shift and click the **FirstQuarter** tab.

2. Click the **Page Layout** tab. Click the Dialog Box Launcher for the **Page Setup** group. The Page Setup dialog box opens.

3. Click the **Header/Footer** tab. Click **Custom Header**. The Header dialog box includes the usual three sections.

4. Key your name in the left section.

5. Click in the center and click the Insert Sheet Name button . Click in the right section and click the Insert Date button .

Figure 6-17
Adding a header in
the Header dialog
box

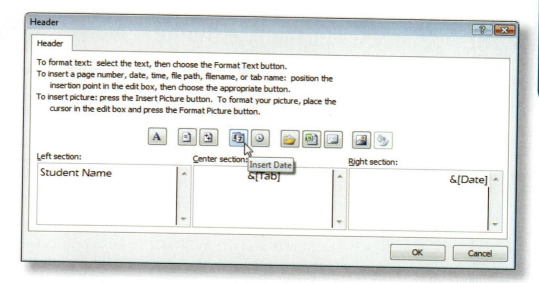

6. Click **OK**. The Page Setup dialog box includes a preview of your header.

7. Click the **Margins** tab. In the **Center on page** group, click to select **Horizontally**.

8. Click **Print Preview** in the **Page Setup** dialog box. This is the first page of five.

9. Press PageDown to see the next sheet. Press PageUp to return to previous pages.

10. Click **Close Print Preview**.

11. Save the workbook as *[your initials]*6-21 in your folder.

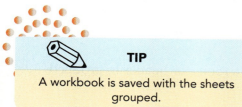

TIP

A workbook is saved with the sheets grouped.

12. Click the Microsoft Office Button. Choose **Print** and then **Quick Print** while the worksheets are grouped. All five sheets print with the same header.

13. Close the workbook.

Using Online Help

USE HELP TO VIEW ADDITIONAL INFORMATION ABOUT FORMAT CODES

1. In a new workbook, press F1.

2. In the Search box, key **format codes** and press Enter.

3. Find and review topics to learn more about format codes. Read the help information.

4. Close the Help window.

Lesson 6 Summary

- Excel has several categories of date, time, mathematical, and statistical functions. You can key them or use the Insert Function dialog box.

- When you key a function name, Formula AutoComplete displays a list of functions that match your keystrokes.

- Functions have a syntax that must be followed. The syntax includes an equal sign, the name of the function, and arguments inside parentheses.

- The SUM function adds the values of the cells indicated in its argument.

- The TRUNC function removes the decimal part of a number.

- The AVERAGE function calculates the arithmetic mean.

- The SUMIF and the AVERAGEIF functions add and average values only if they meet the criteria specified in the argument.

- The MIN function displays the smallest value in a range. The MAX function displays the largest value in a range.

- The COUNT function counts the number of values in a range. The COUNTA function does the same and includes labels. COUNTBLANK counts empty cells in a range.

- The TODAY and NOW functions show the current date and time. Both functions can be formatted using preset or custom formats.

- An icon set is a data visualization that displays an icon at the left edge of the cell based on the value.

- Icon sets can use three, four, or five icons to represent the values.

- Copy selected data from one worksheet to another using the Fill Across Worksheets command.

- You can group multiple worksheets to edit, format, or print several sheets at once.

- Use the Page Setup dialog box to add a footer or header to grouped sheets.

LESSON 6		Command Summary	
Feature	**Button**	**Task Path**	**Keyboard**
Custom format	Format ▾	Home, Cells, Format, Format Cells	Ctrl + 1
Custom header/footer		Page Layout, Page Setup, Dialog Box Launcher	
Fill across worksheets		Home, Editing, Fill	
Icon set		Home, Styles, Conditional Formatting	
Insert Function	fx		Shift + F3
Insert Function	fx Insert Function	Formulas, Function Library	Shift + F3

Concepts Review

True/False Questions

Each of the following statements is either true or false. Indicate your choice by circling T or F.

T F   1. To complete a function, you must include its arguments.

T F   2. Icon sets display an image in the range based on the value.

T F   3. The SUM function calculates a text value as 1.

T F   4. The first character for all functions is a left parenthesis.

T F   5. The TODAY function does not have arguments.

T F   6. Custom formats include **?** and ***** to show days and months.

T F   7. Most statistical functions ignore text in their calculations.

T F   8. You can copy data from one worksheet to another with the Fill handle.

Short Answer Questions

Write the correct answer in the space provided.

1. Name the three types of data visualizations.

_____

2. How can you select more than one worksheet tab?

_____

3. Name the function that adds cell values only if they meet your criteria.

_____

4. What function displays the arithmetic mean of a range of cells?

_____

5. What does Excel do if a function is volatile?

_____

6. What term is used to describe the information between parentheses in a function?

_____

7. What feature helps you complete a function after you key = and its first character in the cell?

_____

8. What function would display the highest sales amount in a column?

_____

Critical Thinking

Answer these questions on a separate page. There are no right or wrong answers. Support your answers with examples from your own experience, if possible.

1. What are some math and trig functions that you did not use in this lesson? How might they be helpful in school work or on the job?

2. What type of businesses might use calculations that would use the date and time functions? Give examples of how they would use the functions.

Skills Review

Exercise 6-22

Use Math & Trig functions. Use Statistical functions.

1. Open **HolidayPay**. Save it as *[your initials]6-22* in your Lesson 6 folder.

2. Click the Select All button ◢. Then click the Bold button **B**. All cells are set for bold.

3. Move the data in cells C13:H16 to start in cell C9.

4. In cell C15, key **Number of Employees**.

5. Use math and trig functions by following these steps:

   a. Click cell H13.

   b. Key **=sum(** to start the function.

   c. Click cell H6 and drag to select cells H6:H12. Press Enter.

   d. In cell E15, key **=counta(** to start the function.

   e. Click cell C6 and drag to select cells C6:C12. Press Enter.

6. In cell I6, key a formula to multiply the hours worked by the holiday rate. Widen the column slightly and copy the formula through row 12.

7. Use math and trig and statistical functions by following these steps:

   a. Click cell I13. Click the **Formulas** tab.

   b. Click the Math & Trig button .

NOTE

If the assumed range is not correct, click and drag to select the correct range.

NOTE

The COUNTIF function is similar to the SUMIF function, but it is in the Statistical category.

c. Scroll and click **SUM**.

d. Check that the range to be summed is I6:I12. Click **OK**.

e. Widen column I as needed.

f. Click cell E16. Click the Insert Function button .

g. In the **Or select a category** list, choose **All**. Quickly key **coun** and find **COUNTIF**. Select it and click **OK**.

h. For the **Range** box, select cells I6:I12.

i. In the **Criteria** box, key **>250** to count employees who earned more than $250. Click **OK**.

8. Key **Over $250** in cell C16.

9. Add **Top and Double Bottom** borders to cells H13:I13.

10. Press ⌃Ctrl+⌂Home. Add a footer and adjust the left and/or right margin to fit the sheet to a portrait page.

11. Make a copy of the worksheet and name it **Formulas**.

12. Press ⌃Ctrl+⌐. AutoFit the columns.

13. Click the **Page Layout** tab. Click the Page Orientation button 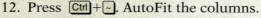 and choose **Landscape**.

14. In the **Scale to Fit** group, click the arrow with the Width button 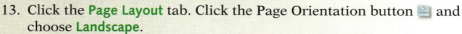. Choose **1 page**. Use the same choice for **Height**.

15. Prepare and submit your work. Save and close the workbook.

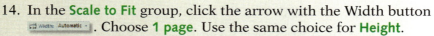

Exercise 6-23

Use Math & Trig and Statistical functions. Use an icon set.

1. Open **Insurance**. Save it as *[your initials]*6-23 in your Lesson 6 folder.

2. Key math and trig and statistical functions by following these steps:

   a. Click cell D17. Key **=coun** and press ⌨Tab.

   b. Click cell C4 and drag to select cells C4:C14. Press ⌨Enter.

   c. In cell D18, key **=sum** and press ⌨Tab. Select cells C4:C14 and press ⌨Enter.

3. Use Insert Function by following these steps:

   a. Click the **Formulas** tab.

   b. Click cell D19. Click the Insert Function button . Choose **Statistical** and **COUNTA**. Click **OK**.

   c. Select cells D4:D14. Click **OK**.

   d. Click cell D20 and press ⇧Shift+⌨F3.

   e. In the **Or select a category** list, choose **Most Recently Used** and **COUNTA**. Click **OK**.

   f. Select cells A4:A14. Click **OK**.

REVIEW

For many functions, you need not key the entire name for AutoComplete to find it.

NOTE

The **Most Recently Used** list shows the functions you have used during the work session.

4. Remove the decimals from the values in column D. Center the labels in rows 1:2 across the data. Change the document theme to **Paper**.

5. Use icon sets by following these steps:

    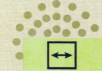

    a. Select cells E4:E14 and click the Conditional Formatting button 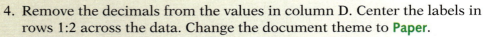.

    b. Choose **Icon Sets** and **Red to Black** in the first column.

    c. Select cells E4:E14 and click the Conditional Formatting button.

    d. Choose **Manage Rules**. Click **Edit Rule**.

    e. Click the arrow with **Percent** for the first icon. Choose **Number**.

    f. Change the **Type** for the second and third icons to **Number**.

    g. Click to select **Reverse Icon Order**.

    h. Key **2000** in the **Value** box for the first icon (black).

    i. Key **1000** in the **Value** box for the second icon (gray).

    j. Key **500** in the **Value** box for the third icon (light red).

    k. Click **OK**. Click **OK** again.

6. Press `Ctrl`+`Home`. Add a header and change the left margin to 1.50 inches.

7. Prepare and submit your work. Save and close the workbook.

Exercise 6-24

Group worksheets. Use Date & Time functions. Use Math & Trig and Statistical functions.

1. Use the **ChkBk** template to create a new workbook. Save it as *[your initials]*6-24 in your Lesson 6 folder.

2. Group worksheets by following these steps:

    ⟷ REVIEW

    Copy the template to the appropriate folder for your computer. Then choose **My Templates** in the **New Workbook** dialog box.

    a. Right-click the **Sheet1** tab. Choose **Move or Copy**. Select **Sheet2** in the **Before sheet** list. Click to select **Create a copy**. Click **OK**.

    b. Make another copy and place it before **Sheet2**.

    c. Click the **Sheet2** tab. Hold down `Ctrl` and click the **Sheet3** tab.

    d. Right-click either tab and choose **Delete**.

    e. Rename the sheets as **Week1**, **Week2**, and **Week3**. Assign an accent color to each tab.

    f. Click the **Week1** tab. Hold down `Shift` and click the **Week3** tab.

3. Use a date function by following these steps:

    a. Click cell A4, key **=to**, and press `Tab`. Press `Ctrl`+`Enter`.

    b. Click cell A5 and key **=** to start a formula.

    c. Click cell A4 and key **+5** to add five days to today's date.

    d. Press `Ctrl`+`Enter`.

e. Copy the formula in cell A5 to cells A6:A15.

f. Key your name in cell A20 while the sheets are grouped.

4. Ungroup worksheets by following these steps:

   a. Right-click any sheet tab in the group. Choose **Ungroup Sheets**.

   b. Click the **Week1** tab.

5. Key the data for columns B:D as shown here.

Figure 6-18

	Check #	Payee	Credit Amount	Deposit
6	1002	[your first and last name]	1250	
7	1003	Sutter, Howe, & Jones	2500	
8	1004	Holberg Markets	575	
9	1005	[your school name]	435	
10	1006	Hacienda Martinez	575	
11	1007	Smithfield Stores	435	
12	1008	Grocerytown Enterprises	1200	

6. Use math and trig and statistical functions by following these steps:

   a. Click cell D16.

   b. Key **=sum** and press Tab.

   c. Click cell D5 and drag to select cells D5:D12. Press Enter.

   d. In cell B16, key **=count(** and ignore Formula AutoComplete.

   e. Click cell B5 and drag to select cells B5:B12. Press Enter.

   f. Press Ctrl + Home.

7. Group the worksheets and click the **Page Layout** tab. In the **Scale to Fit** group, click the arrow with the Height button 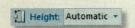. Choose **1 page**. Use the same choice for the **Width**.

8. Prepare and submit your work. Save and close the workbook.

Exercise 6-25

Use Date & Time functions. Format times and dates.

1. Create a new workbook and save it as *[your initials]6-25* in your Lesson 6 folder.

2. Click the Select All button . Set the font to Calibri 12 point bold.

3. In cell A1, key **Klassy Kow Ice Cream Shops**. In cell A2, key **Olympia Shop**. Choose a larger font size for these labels.

4. Key **Date** in cell A3, **Open Time** in cell B3, and **Close Time** in cell C3. Center-align these labels. Make all three columns **12.14 (90 pixels)** wide.

5. Use date functions by following these steps:
    a. In cell A4, key **=today(** and press Enter.
    b. Click cell A5 and key **=** to start the formula.
    c. Click cell A4 and key **+1** to add one day. Press Enter.
    d. Copy the formula in cell A5 to cells A6:A10.
6. Format dates by following these steps:
    a. Select cells A4:A10. Press Ctrl + 1.
    b. Click the **Number** tab and choose **Date** in the **Category** list.
    c. Choose **March 14, 2001** in the **Type** list. Click **OK**.
    d. Widen column A to show the dates if necessary.
7. Key the times as shown in the figure below.

Figure 6-19

	Open Time	Close Time
4	9 am	10 pm
5	10 am	11 pm
6	10 am	12 am
7	11 am	12 am
8	11 am	9 pm
9	11 am	11 pm
10	11 am	11 pm

8. Format times by following these steps:
    a. Select cells B4:C10. Press Ctrl + 1.
    b. Click the **Number** tab and choose **Custom** in the **Category** list.
    c. Choose **h:mm** in the **Type** list.
    d. Edit the code in the **Type** box to show **h AM/PM**. Click **OK**.
9. Center the labels in rows 1:2 across the data. Make all rows **26.25 (35 pixels)** tall.
10. Insert a row at row 1. Insert a column at column A. Select cells A1:E12. Press Ctrl + 1 and choose a double border as an outline.
11. Select cells A1:E3 and change the font color to white. Then apply black fill.
12. Add a header and change the left margin to about 1.75 inches.

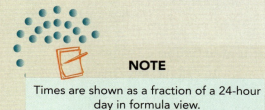

NOTE

Times are shown as a fraction of a 24-hour day in formula view.

13. Make a copy of the worksheet and change the tab name to **Formulas**. Display the formulas and adjust the column widths; columns A and E can be very narrow. Change the left margin to .75 inches. Fit the sheet to a portrait page.
14. Prepare and submit your work. Save and close the workbook.

Lesson Applications

Exercise 6-26

Use Date functions. Group worksheets.

1. Create a new workbook using the **CSCalls** template. Save the workbook as *[your initials]*6-26.

2. Use the TODAY function in cell A3 and format the cell as white so that it is not visible. Key a formula in cell A5 that adds one day to cell A3. Shrink the data to fit if needed.

3. Key a formula in cell A6 that adds one day to the date in cell A5. Copy the formula in cell A6 down to row 25.

4. Format cells B5:B25 to show the time using the **1:30 PM** preset format.

5. Key the times and representative names as shown. Use AutoComplete where appropriate.

REVIEW

Set the Zoom size if you prefer to see the entire worksheet at once.

Figure 6-20

5	9:30 am	Anderson
6	10:25 am	Olmstead
7	12:30 pm	Rogers
8	1:30 pm	Devantes
9	10:45 am	LaPluie
10	2:30 pm	Anderson
11	11:30 am	Anderson
12	8:45 am	Olmstead
13	4:30 pm	LaPluie
14	10 am	Devantes
15	8 am	Devantes
16	3:30 pm	Rogers
17	9:45 am	LaPluie
18	10:15 am	Olmstead
19	12 pm	Devantes
20	12:15 pm	Olmstead
21	11:15 am	LaPluie
22	11:45 am	Olmstead
23	2:25 pm	Devantes
24	9 am	Anderson
25	10:25 am	Olmstead

6. Select cells A1:D25. Then hold down Ctrl and click the **Sheet2** tab. Fill all across the worksheets.

7. Name **Sheet2** as **Week2**. Make the column widths and row heights the same as the **Week1** sheet.

8. On the **Week2** sheet, edit the formula in cell A5 to add seven days to the function.

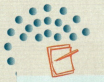

NOTE

Use the Page Setup dialog box to apply settings to grouped sheets.

9. Group the two sheets and open the Page Setup dialog box. From this dialog box, add a footer. Then set landscape orientation and change the top and bottom margins to .5 inch. Delete **Sheet3**.

10. Prepare and submit your work. Save and close the workbook.

Exercise 6-27

Group worksheets. Use Statistical functions.

1. Open **ShopPart** and save it as *[your initials]*6-27 in your folder.

2. Group all four sheets.

3. In cell A22, key **Number of Shops**. Make it 11-point Calibri bold italic.

NOTE

The worksheets should remain grouped throughout this exercise.

4. In cell B22, use **COUNTIF** to count the shops that participated in the Tip Calculator promotion. Copy the formula to cells C22:D22.

5. Center-align the contents in cells B22:D22. Use 11-point Calibri bold italic.

6. Insert a column at column A and make it **3.57 (30 pixels)** wide. Apply a double outline border around cells A5:E23.

TIP

Use the Insert Function dialog box to build the COUNTIF function.

7. From the Page Setup dialog box, add a footer and change the page orientation to landscape.

8. Prepare and submit your work. Save and close the workbook.

Exercise 6-28

Use Math & Trig functions.

1. Open **ORSundaes** and save it as *[your initials]*6-28 in your folder.

2. In cell H3, use **AVERAGE** with cells C4:C8 as **Number1**. Ignore the error.

3. Compute the average sales for medium and large sundaes in cells H4 and H5. Adjust column F to show the labels, and make column G very narrow.

4. In cell H6, calculate the revenue by summing the appropriate sales and multiplying by the related price. Use a similar formula to determine revenue for medium and large sundaes.

5. In cell H13, add the three revenues to find a total.

6. Delete row 14. Add a double top border to the data cells to match the other price listings.

7. Format all non-money values as Comma style with no decimal places.

8. Apply a double outline border around cells E1:I10. Move this entire range so that it starts in row 5.

9. Add a header.

10. Make a copy of the worksheet and change the tab name to **SundaesFormulas**. Display the formulas. Delete columns with no data and AutoFit the other columns. Fit the formula sheet to one landscape page.

11. Prepare and submit your work. Save and close the workbook.

Exercise 6-29 ◆ Challenge Yourself

Use date arithmetic.

1. Open **CoPay**. Save it as *[your initials]*6-29 in your folder.

2. Insert a column before column D. Key **Date Eligible** on two lines as the label for this column.

3. In cell D5, key a formula to determine the date eligible for a reduced copay. The formula should add the appropriate number of days to the enrollment date to determine when the employee is eligible.

4. Copy the formula for the other employees. Make adjustments as needed.

5. Increase the indent once for the department names to create space between the dates in column D and the labels in column E. Then widen column E to show more space between its labels and those in column F.

6. Add a footer and fit the worksheet to one portrait page.

REVIEW

Press Alt + Enter to insert a line break within a label.

NOTE

Many financial and date calculations use 365.25 as the number of days in a year.

TIP

There are buttons to increase or decrease the indent in the Alignment group on the Home tab.

REVIEW

Horizontal centering for the page is on the Margins tab in the Page Setup dialog box.

7. Create a formula sheet. Turn off horizontal centering and fit the formulas to one landscape page.

8. Prepare and submit your work. Save and close the workbook.

On Your Own

In these exercises you work on your own, as you would in a real-life work environment. Use the skills you've learned to accomplish the task—and be creative.

Exercise 6-30

Create a new workbook and save it as *[your initials]*6-30. Key **My Age in Days and Years** as a label. In column A, key the TODAY() function. In the cell below the date, key a formula to add 365.25 days to today. Copy this formula to reach 10 years from now. Key your birthdate in column F. In column B, use the **DAYS360** function to calculate your age in days for each date in column A. In column C, divide the number of days by 360. Format your work attractively. Add a footer. Prepare and submit your work.

Exercise 6-31

In a new workbook, key the first names of 10 people you know in a column. In the column to the right, key each person's eye color. In the next column, key each person's hair color. Add labels and format your work with borders and/or fill so that it looks professional. In a row below your data, key **Number of Persons with Blonde Hair and Blue Eyes**. In a cell next to or below this label, use **COUNTIFS** to determine the answer. If there are no such persons in your list, change your label to another color combination or change some of the colors in your list to test the function. Save the workbook as *[your initials]*6-31. Add a header and prepare and submit your work.

Exercise 6-32

Open **HolidayPay**. Delete column G and then column H. Move rows so that there is no blank space in the middle of the data. Key new labels below row 12 so that you can show these calculations: average regular rate, average rate increase, and average hours worked. Save the worksheet as *[your initials]*6-32. Add a header or footer. Create a formula sheet. Prepare and submit your work.

Using Logical and Financial Functions

OBJECTIVES

After completing this lesson, you will be able to:

1. Use the IF function.

2. Use the AND, OR, and NOT functions.

3. Work with cell styles.

4. Work with page breaks.

5. Use the PMT and FV functions.

6. Use the Depreciation functions.

MCAS OBJECTIVES

In this lesson:
XL07 2.3.1
XL07 2.3.3
XL07 3.1
XL07 3.6.1
XL07 5.5
XL07 5.5.2
XL07 5.5.4

Estimated Time: 1½ hours

A *logical function* is a formula that calculates if an expression is true. There are seven logical functions: AND, FALSE, IF, IFERROR, NOT, OR, and TRUE. Except for the IF and IFERROR functions, a logical function shows the word "TRUE" or "FALSE" as a result.

A *financial function* performs a business calculation that involves money. These include how to figure loan payments and how to determine depreciation.

Using the IF Function

The IF function is a simple analysis and decision-making tool. When working with accounts receivable, for example, you can determine if a late fee should be assessed.

The IF function has three arguments. It follows the form "If X, then Y; otherwise Z." X, Y, and Z represent the arguments.

The syntax for the IF function is:

=IF(logical_test, value_if_true, value_if_false)
Example: =IF(C5>50,C5*2, "None")

- Logical_test is the first argument, the condition. It's a statement or expression that is either true or false. In the example, the expression C5>50 is either true or false, depending on the value in cell C5.

- Value_if_true, the second argument, is what the formula shows if the logical_test is true. In the example, if C5 is greater than 50, the value in cell C5 is multiplied by 2. The value_if_true can be a formula, a value, text, or a cell reference.

- Value_if_false, the third argument, is what the formula shows if the logical_test is not true. The value_if_false can be a formula, a value, text, or a cell reference. In the example, if the value in cell C5 is 50 or less, the result is the word "None."

Exercise 7-1   USE IF TO SHOW TEXT

You can create an IF function to display text. When you use the Function Arguments dialog box, Excel inserts quotation marks around text in an IF function. When you key an IF function, you must key quotation marks.

IF functions can use relational or comparison operators as well as the arithmetic operators.

TABLE 7-1 Relational (Comparison) Operators

Operator	Description
=	Equal to
<>	Not equal to
>	Greater than
<	Less than
>=	Greater than or equal to
<=	Less than or equal to

1. Open **BonusPay** and click cell C4. If a salesperson sells more than $60,000 in goods, this cell should display "Yes."

2. Click the **Formulas** tab.

3. Click the Logical button 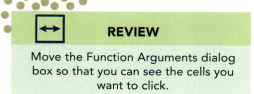.

4. Choose **IF** in the list. The insertion point is in the **Logical_test** box.

5. Click cell B4. The address appears in the **Logical_test** box.

↔ **REVIEW**

Move the Function Arguments dialog box so that you can see the cells you want to click.

6. Key **>60000** in the **Logical_test** box after **B4**. This logical test will determine if the value in cell B4 is greater than 60000.

7. Click in the **Value_if_true** box.

8. Key **Yes**. If the value in cell B4 is greater than 60000, cell C4 will display the word "Yes."

9. Click in the **Value_if_false** box. Note the quotation marks for "Yes."

10. Key **No**. If the value in cell B4 is not greater than 60000, cell C4 will display the word "No."

Figure 7-1
Function Arguments
dialog box for IF
BonusPay.xlsx
Bonus sheet

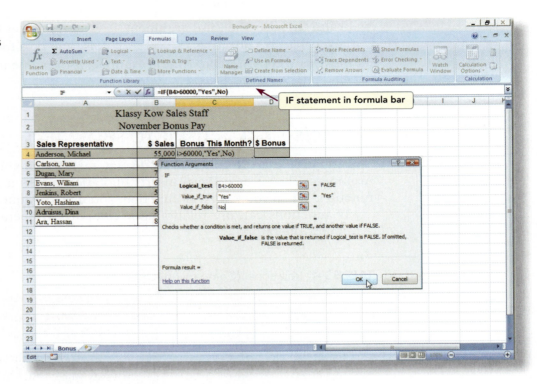

11. Click **OK**. The result of this IF formula for cell C4 is **No**.

12. Look at the formula in the formula bar. You can see the quotation marks for **No** now.

13. Click the **Home** tab and then the Center button ≡. Copy the formula to cells C5:C11. Formatting is copied with the formula.

14. Click the Undo button ↺. Press Esc if you see a marquee.

15. Click cell C4 and press Ctrl + C.

16. Select cells C5:C11 and right-click one of the selected cells.

17. Choose **Paste Special**. Choose **Formulas** and click **OK**.

18. Click the Center button ≡ for the selected range.

Exercise 7-2 USE IF TO CALCULATE A VALUE

Excel can calculate the bonus if a salesperson is eligible. In this case, the bonus will be 2.5% of the sales value.

1. Click cell D4. Key **=if** to see the Formula AutoComplete list.

2. Press Tab. The ScreenTip displays the syntax for the function, and the argument to be keyed next is bold.

3. Click cell C4. A marquee appears around the cell, and the address appears after the left parenthesis. This starts the **Logical_test**.

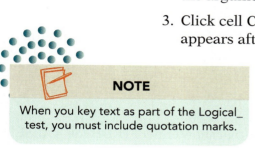

NOTE

When you key text as part of the Logical_ test, you must include quotation marks.

4. Key **="yes"** after **C4**. This logical test will determine if cell C4 shows "Yes." Text in a logical test is not case-sensitive.

5. Key a comma after **"yes"** to separate the logical test from the value_if_true. **Value_if_true** in the ScreenTip is bold.

6. Click cell B4. A marquee appears around the cell, and the address appears after the comma.

7. Key ***2.5%** after **B4**. The formula multiplies the value in cell B4 by 2.5% if cell C4 shows "Yes." This is what the function will do if the test is true (C4 does show "yes").

8. Key a comma after **2.5%** to separate the value_if_true from the value_if_false. Value_if_false in the ScreenTip is bold.

9. Key **""** (two quotation marks with nothing between them). This represents no text, or nothing. If cell C4 does not show "Yes," cell D4 will show nothing. It will be blank.

Figure 7-2
Keying an IF statement
BonusPay.xlsx
Bonus sheet

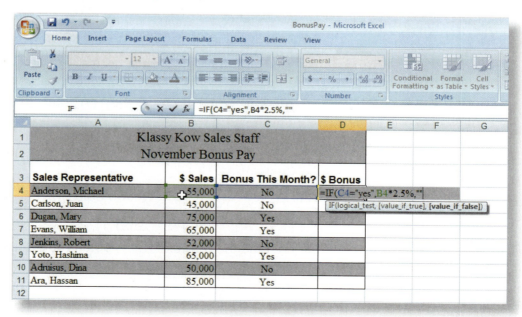

10. Press Enter. Excel added the closing right parenthesis for you. Cell D4 shows nothing, because this sales rep does not receive a bonus.

11. Click cell D4 and press Ctrl+C.

12. Select cells D5:D11 and right-click. Choose **Paste Special**. Choose **Formulas** and click **OK**. Press Esc to remove the marquee.

13. Select cells D4:D11 and click the Comma Style button ,

14. Click the Decrease Decimal button .00→.0 two times.

15. Add a footer and save the workbook *[your initials]*7-2 in a folder for Lesson 7. Close the workbook.

Using AND, OR, and NOT Functions

AND, OR, and NOT are logical functions that show either "TRUE" or "FALSE" as a result. These functions ignore labels and empty cells, so you use them only with values (numbers).

Exercise 7-3　USE THE AND FUNCTION

In an AND function, you can use multiple logical tests. All tests or expressions must be true for the result cell to show TRUE. Otherwise, it shows FALSE.

TABLE 7-2 Examples of the AND Function

Expression	Result
AND(C4>10, D4>10)	TRUE if both C4 and D4 are greater than 10; FALSE if either C4 or D4 is 10 or less.
AND(C4>10, C4<100)	TRUE if C4 is greater than 10 but less than 100; FALSE if C4 is 10 or less than 10 or 100 or greater than 100.
AND(C4>10, D4<10)	TRUE if C4 is greater than 10 and D4 is less than 10; FALSE if C4 is equal to or less than 10 or if D4 is equal to or greater than 10.
AND(C4=10, D4<100)	TRUE if C4 is equal to 10 and D4 is less than 100; FALSE if C4 is equal to any value except 10.

1. Open **CustCount**.

2. In cell J3, key **All Over 150 on** and hold down Alt and press Enter.

3. Key **on Weekend?** and press Enter.

4. Make the label bold. Make row 3 **30.00 (40 pixels)** tall. AutoFit the column.

5. Click cell J4. Click the **Formulas** tab.

6. Click the Logical button 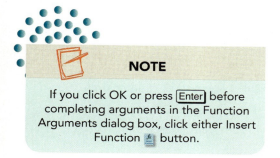. Choose **AND** in the list. The insertion point is in the **Logical1** box.

7. Click cell G4. The address appears in the **Logical1** box.

8. Key **>** in the **Logical1** box after **G4**.

9. Key **150** but don't press Enter. This test will determine if the value in cell G4 is greater than 150.

10. Click in the **Logical2** box. Click cell H4 and key **>150**. The second condition is that the value in cell H4 be greater than 150.

11. Click in the **Logical3** box. Click cell I4 and key **>150**. The third condition is that the value in cell I4 be greater than 150.

NOTE

If you click OK or press Enter before completing arguments in the Function Arguments dialog box, click either Insert Function button.

Figure 7-3
Function Arguments dialog box for AND
CustCount.xlsx
CustCount sheet

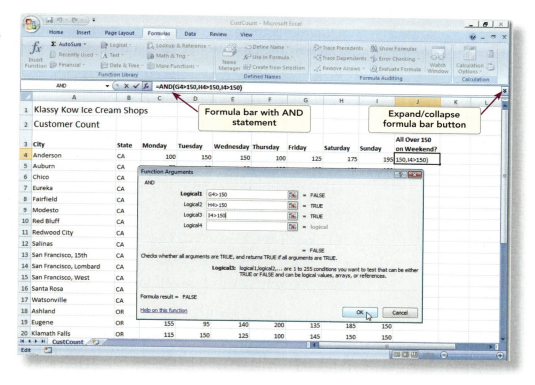

12. Click **OK**. The customer count must be greater than 150 each weekend day to show TRUE; it's not. Look at the formula in the formula bar.

13. Copy the formula to cells J5:J35. Only weekends in which all three days had greater than 150 customers show TRUE (Las Vegas Green Street, Reno, and Olympia). A day's count equal to 150 is not greater than 150.

TIP

Change the Zoom size to see more on screen at once.

Exercise 7-4   USE THE OR FUNCTION

In an OR function, any one of your logical tests can be true for the result cell to show TRUE. If they are all false, the result is FALSE.

TABLE 7-3 Examples of the OR Function

Expression	Result
OR(C4>10, D4>10)	TRUE if either C4 or D4 is greater than 10; FALSE only if both C4 and D4 are less than or equal to 10.
OR(C4>10, D4<100)	TRUE if C4 is greater than 10 or if D4 is less than 100; FALSE only if C4 is equal to or less than 10 and if D4 is equal to or greater than 100.
OR(C4>10, D4=10)	TRUE if C4 is greater than 10 or if D4 is equal to 10; FALSE if C4 is equal to or less than 10 and if D4 is any value other than 10.

1. Copy the label in cell J3 to cell K3.

2. Click the Expand Formula Bar button. Click in the formula bar and edit the label to **Any Over 150 on Weekend?**

3. Press Enter and AutoFit the column.

4. In cell K4, key **=or** and press Tab.

5. Click cell G4. A marquee appears around the cell, and the address appears in the formula.

6. Key **>150** after **G4**. This logical test will determine if the value in cell G4 is greater than 150.

7. Key a comma after **150**.

8. Click cell H4. Key **>150**. The second condition will test if the value in cell H4 is greater than 150.

9. Key a comma and click cell I4. Key **>150** as the third logical test.

Figure 7-4
Keying an OR
function
CustCount.xlsx
CustCount sheet

	F	G	H	I	J	K	L
					All Over 150 on Weekend?	Any Over 150 on Weekend?	
	Thursday	Friday	Saturday	Sunday			
	100	125	175	195	FALSE	=or(G4>150,H4>150,	
	100	135	150	100	FALSE	I4>150	
	225	135	175	1	OR(logical1, [logical2], [logical3], [logical4], ...)		
	100	125	135	150	FALSE		
	100	135	150	100	FALSE		

10. Press Enter. If the customer count is greater than 150 people on any one of the weekend days, the result is TRUE.

11. Copy the formula into cells K5:K35.

12. Click the Collapse Formula Bar button ⌃.

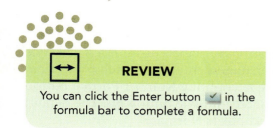

REVIEW

You can click the Enter button ✓ in the formula bar to complete a formula.

Exercise 7-5   USE THE NOT FUNCTION

In a NOT function, the reverse or opposite of your logical_test must be true for the result cell to show TRUE. The NOT function has one argument.

TABLE 7-4 Examples of the NOT Function

Expression	Result
NOT(C4>10)	TRUE if C4 is 10 or less than 10; FALSE if C4 is 11 or greater.
NOT(C4=10)	TRUE if C4 contains any value other than 10; FALSE if C4 is 10.

1. Click cell L3. Key **Sunday>150?**

2. Click cell L4. Key **=not(** and click cell I4.

3. Key **<150**. The formula tests if the value in cell I4 is less than 150. If the value is 150 or a value greater than 150, cell L4 will show TRUE.

Figure 7-5
Keying a NOT function
CustCount.xlsx
CustCount sheet

Saturday	Sunday	All Over 150 on Weekend?	Any Over 150 on Weekend?	Sunday>150?	
175	195	FALSE	TRUE	=NOT(I4<150	
150	100	FALSE	FALSE	NOT(logical)	
175	150	FALSE	TRUE		
135	150	FALSE	FALSE		
150	100	FALSE	FALSE		

4. Press Enter.

5. Copy the formula to cells L5:L35. Look at the results for counts of 150 or more on Sunday.

Working with Cell Styles

A *cell style* is a set of formatting specifications for labels or values. A cell style can contain number format, font, border, alignment, fill, and cell protection. You used cell styles when you clicked the Accounting Number Format button $ ·, the Comma Style button , or the Percent Style button % . The default cell style for all new data keyed in a workbook is Normal.

Exercise 7-6 USE CELL STYLES

1. Click the **Home** tab.

2. Select cells C36:I36 and click the AutoSum button Σ · .

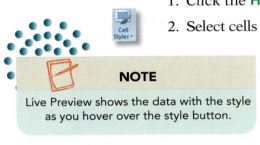

3. While the cells are selected, click the Cell Styles button in the **Styles** group. The Cell Styles gallery opens.

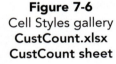

NOTE

Live Preview shows the data with the style as you hover over the style button.

4. Hover over several cell styles to see the change in row 36.

Figure 7-6
Cell Styles gallery
CustCount.xlsx
CustCount sheet

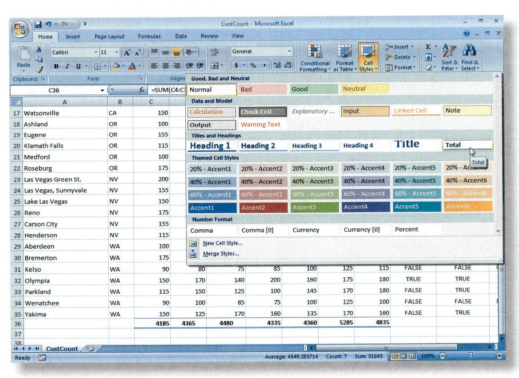

5. Find **Total** in the **Titles and Headings** category. Click to select it. The gallery closes and the style is applied.

6. Click a cell away from the range to see the style. The values are bold and have a top and double bottom blue border.

7. Select cells C36:I36 again. Click the Cell Styles button 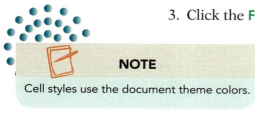 again. Number styles are near the bottom of the gallery.

8. Choose **Comma [0]**. This is the comma style with no decimal places. It overwrites the previous style. Notice that these cells are not right-aligned with other values in the columns. Other values use a different style.

Exercise 7-7 CLEAR AND REAPPLY CELL STYLES

You can remove a cell style or your own formatting from a cell or a range of cells. The cells then return to the default Normal style.

1. While cells C36:I36 are selected, click the Clear button ⌄ in the **Editing** group. Choose **Clear Formats**. The cells are returned to the Normal style.

2. Click cell C4 and press F8 to start Extend Selection mode.

3. Press → six times to select up to column I.

4. Hold down Ctrl and press ↓. This shortcut selects to the last row of data.

5. Click the Cell Styles button.

6. Choose **Comma [0]**. The style is applied, and all values are aligned.

7. Select cells C36:I36 and apply the **Total** cell style.

8. Select cells A1:A2 and apply the **Title** cell style.

9. Press Ctrl + Home.

Exercise 7-8 CREATE A STYLE

You can create your own styles. Styles that you create are listed in the **Custom** category and saved with the workbook.

1. Click the Cell Styles button. Click **New Cell Style**.

2. In the **Style name** box, key **Mine** and click **Format**. The Format Cells dialog box opens.

3. Click the **Font** tab. Choose 11-point regular Calibri. Do not click **OK** yet.

NOTE

Cell styles use the document theme colors.

4. Click the **Border** tab. Set a single bottom black border. Do not click **OK** yet.

5. Click the **Fill** tab. Choose a light shaded accent color to match the blue in cells A1:A2. Click **OK**. This style will apply fill and a bottom border.

6. Click **OK** again.

7. Select cells A4:L4. Hold down Ctrl and select cells A6:L6. Repeat these steps to cells A8:L8 to the selection.

8. Click the Cell Styles button 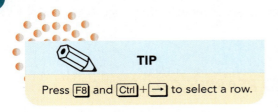. Choose **Mine** at the top of the gallery. Notice that the alignment of values is not correct. The number format in your style does not match the **Comma [0]** style. You'll fix this in the next exercise.

9. Select cells A10:L10. Press Ctrl+Y. This is the keyboard shortcut to repeat the most recent command.

10. Repeat these steps to apply the style to every other row in the sheet, up to and including row 34.

11. Make row 36 the same height as the other rows.

TIP

Press F8 and Ctrl+→ to select a row.

Exercise 7-9   EDIT A STYLE

If you edit a style, all cells with the style are reformatted.

1. Click cell C5 and press Ctrl+1. Click the **Number** tab. The **Number** format (from **Comma [0]**) uses the Accounting option with no decimals and no symbol. Close the dialog box.

2. Click cell C4. This is your style.

3. Click the Cell Styles button . Right-click **Mine** and choose **Modify**.

4. Click **Format**. The Format Cells dialog box opens.

5. Click the **Number** tab. Choose **Accounting**, **0** decimals. In the **Symbol** box, choose **None**. Do not click **OK**.

6. Click the **Fill** tab. Choose a different color if your first choice was too dark. Click **OK**.

7. Click **OK** again. All the cells with the Mine style are restyled. The values are properly aligned, but the number alignment is affecting the labels in columns A:B (cities and states).

8. Select cells A4:B35 and press Ctrl+1. On the **Number** tab, choose **General** and click **OK**. You can override an individual setting of any style.

9. Click the **Page Layout** tab. Click the Margins button. Choose **Custom Margins**.

10. Set the left and right margins at 1 inch; set the top and bottom margins at 1.25 inches. Click **OK**.

Working with Page Breaks

A *page break* is a code that tells the printer to start a new page. When a worksheet is too wide or too tall to fit on the paper, Excel inserts an automatic page break. This page break appears as a dashed line on the screen. You can accept Excel's location for page breaks, you can move the break to a new location, or you can insert your own.

Exercise 7-10   PREVIEW AND CHANGE PAGE BREAKS

1. Click the Microsoft Office Button 🔘. Hover over the **Print** arrow and choose **Print Preview**.

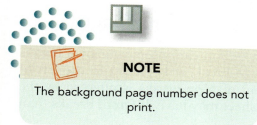

> **NOTE**
>
> In Print Preview, [PageDown] moves to the next page if your screen is showing a reduced view.

2. Point at the page and click anywhere to zoom in/out. The worksheet is too large to print on a single page in portrait orientation.

3. Click to set a reduced view and press [PageDown]. Rows(s) that do not fit on the first page are on page 2.

4. Press [PageDown] again. Columns that do not fit on the first two pages are on page 3. Look at page 4, too.

5. Close Print Preview.

6. Click the Page Break Preview button 🔳 in the status bar. A message box explains how you can adjust page breaks.

> **NOTE**
>
> The background page number does not print.

7. Click **OK**. Pages are arranged in top-to-bottom, left-to-right order with a background page number. Page breaks are blue dashed lines.

Figure 7-7
Page Break Preview
CustCount.xlsx
CustCount sheet

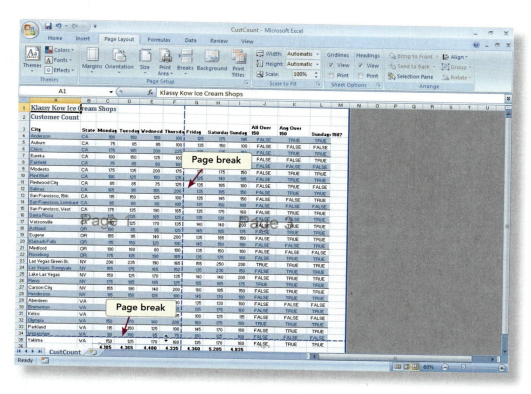

8. Place the pointer on the horizontal blue dashed line below row 35 to display a two-pointed arrow. Your dashed line might be anywhere between rows 33 and 36.

9. Click and drag the dashed blue line up so that it is between rows 22 and 23. The line becomes solid blue if you manually set or adjust it.

10. Click and drag the vertical blue dashed line between columns F and G to the left so that it is between columns E and F.

11. Widen any column in which the label in row 3 is not visible.

12. Click the Normal button ▦ in the status bar. You can see dashed lines for page breaks in Normal view.

TIP

You can AutoFit columns and rows while in Page Break Preview.

Exercise 7-11   REMOVE AND INSERT PAGE BREAKS

You can delete page breaks if necessary, or you can insert your own breaks where you want. When you insert a page break, it is placed to the left of the active cell or column. The placement of page breaks is affected by the currently installed printer, so your worksheet may have different breaks than those shown in this lesson.

1. Click the Page Break Preview button ▦. Click **OK** in the message box.

2. Click and drag the page break below row 22 down and below row 36. You should now have only two pages.

3. Click cell J1. If you insert a page break here, it will be between columns I and J.

4. Click the **Page Layout** tab. In the **Page Setup** group, click the Breaks button ▤.

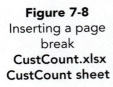

Figure 7-8
Inserting a page break
CustCount.xlsx
CustCount sheet

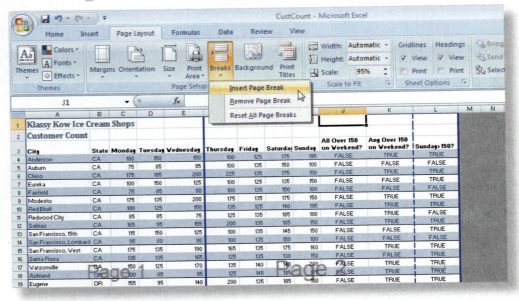

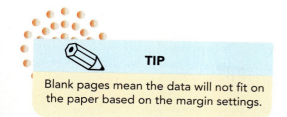

TIP

Blank pages mean the data will not fit on the paper based on the margin settings.

5. Choose **Insert Page Break**. The page break is solid blue because you inserted it manually. Your worksheet should now occupy three pages. If your worksheet is longer, you probably have some blank pages.

6. Click the Microsoft Office Button . Hover over the **Print** arrow and choose **Print Preview**. Press [Page Down] to view the pages.

7. In Print Preview, click to select **Show Margins**. The page shows markers for all margins, including the header and footer. The top margin is the lower of the two horizontal lines; the marker is the tiny rectangle at either edge.

8. Click the top margin marker and drag it up to reach about **.75**. The setting is shown in the status bar as you drag.

Figure 7-9
Changing margins in Print Preview
CustCount.xlsx
CustCount sheet

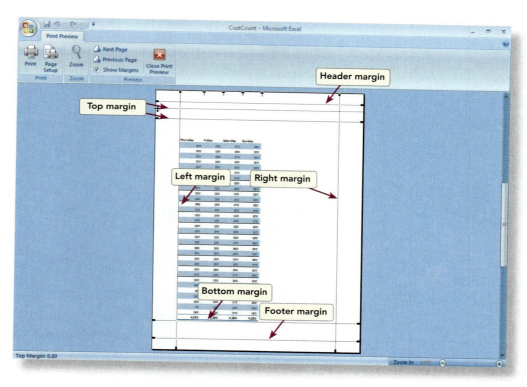

9. Do the same for the bottom margin. Less margin space eliminates any blank pages. Now the worksheet fits on three pages.

10. Close Print Preview.

Exercise 7-12   SET PRINT TITLES

You can repeat the labels in column A on each printed page to make this three-page worksheet easier to read. You will see the city name on each page so that it is easy to determine which values belong with each city.

1. Click the Print Titles button 🖼 on the **Page Layout** tab. The Page Setup dialog box opens with the **Sheet** tab active.

2. Click in the **Columns to repeat at left** text box.

3. Click anywhere in column A. The dialog box shows **$A:$A** as the range for print titles.

Figure 7-10
Setting print titles
CustCount.xlsx
CustCount sheet

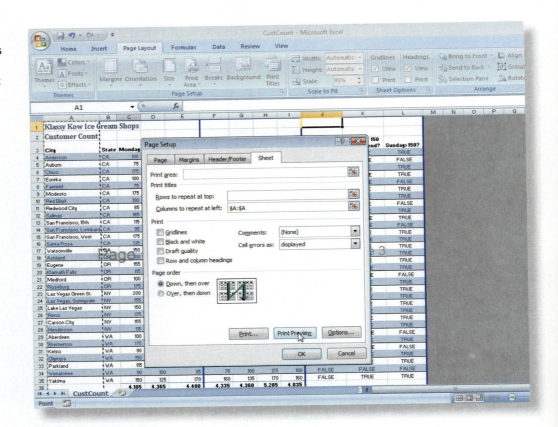

4. Click **Print Preview** in the dialog box.

5. Press PageDown and PageUp to view the pages. Notice that the label in cell A1 is cut off on pages 2 and 3.

6. Close Print Preview. AutoFit column A. Hide column B. Excel probably inserted a new automatic page break, because column A is wider now.

Exercise 7-13   CENTER A PAGE

Although you can change the left and right margins to make a page appear centered, Excel can center a worksheet horizontally or vertically on the printed page. Centering occurs between the margins.

1. On the **Page Layout** tab, click the Margins button . Choose **Custom Margins**.

2. In the **Center on page** section, click to select **Horizontally**.

3. Click to select **Vertically**.

4. Change the left and right margins to **.50**. Change the top and bottom margins to **.75**.

5. Click **Print Preview** in the dialog box. All pages are horizontally centered, and the smaller margins better fit the first page.

6. Close Print Preview.

7. Click the Normal button 🌐 in the status bar.

Exercise 7-14   CHANGE THE FOOTER FONT AND PRINT PAGE NUMBERS

The default font for data in headers and footers is 11-point Calibri for the default Office theme. You can change the formatting for any section in the footer to any font and size available on your computer.

1. Click the **Insert** tab and then click the Header & Footer button 📄.

2. Click the Go To Footer button 📄 in the **Navigation** group. Click in the left section.

3. Click the **Home** tab. Click the Font Size arrow and choose **8**.

4. Key *[your first and last name]*. The font size is applied as you type.

5. Click in the center section. Click the **Header & Footer Tools Design** tab.

6. Click the Page Number button 📄. The code is **&[Page]**, and it is 11-point Calibri.

7. Press ⌨Spacebar⌨ to insert a space after **&[Page]**.

8. Key **of** and press ⌨Spacebar⌨.

9. Click the Number of Pages button 📄. The code is **&[Pages]**. This footer will display **Page 1 of 3** on the first page.

10. Drag across **&[Page] of &[Pages]** to select all of it. The Mini toolbar appears.

11. Click the Decrease Font Size button 🔺 three times. Each click reduces the size by 1 point.

Figure 7-11
Printing page
numbers
CustCount.xlsx
CustCount sheet

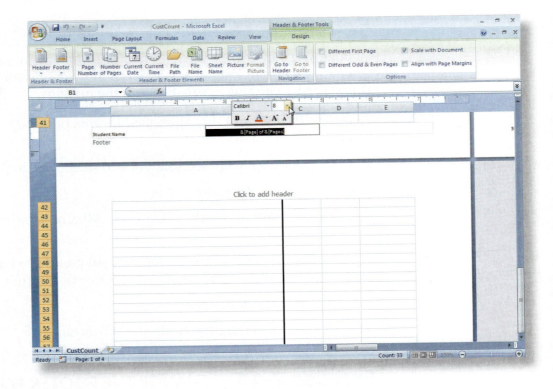

12. Insert the filename in the right section with the same font. Click a worksheet cell.

13. Click the Normal button ▦ in the status bar.

14. Save the workbook as *[your initials]7-14* in your Lesson 7 folder.

Exercise 7-15   REMOVE A PAGE BREAK

You can remove a manual page break and let Excel resume automatic page breaks.

1. Click the Page Break Preview button ▦. Click **OK** in the message box.

2. Click cell J1. The page break is to the left of this column.

3. Click the **Page Layout** tab. Click the Breaks button ▤ and choose **Remove Page Break**. An automatic page break is inserted, probably after column J.

4. Click the Normal button ▦ in the status bar.

5. Save and close the workbook.

Using the PMT and FV Functions

Financial functions analyze money transactions such as loans and savings or investment plans. Many financial functions, including PMT and FV, use the concept of an annuity. An *annuity* is a series of equal payments made at regular intervals for a specified period of time.

Many of Excel's financial functions use these arguments:

- *Rate* is the interest for the period. If you make monthly payments, you must divide the rate by 12 to find the monthly interest rate.

- *Nper* is the total number of periods during which a payment is made. It represents the total number of payments. A five-year loan with monthly payments would have an Nper of 60 (12 months a year * 5 years).

- *PV* is present value or the amount of the loan. It is the current cash value of the money transaction.

- *FV* is future value or the cash balance at the end of the time period. For an investment, FV is how much you will have at the end of your savings or investment time. For a loan, the FV is 0 because you must pay back every penny.

- *Type* specifies whether payments are made at the beginning or the end of the period.

Exercise 7-16   USE THE PMT FUNCTION

The PMT (Payment) function can be used to determine monthly payments if you borrow money to buy a computer, a car, or a house.

1. Open **CU**.

2. In cell C7, key **4** to plan a four-year loan.

3. In cell C8, key **=** to use a formula to compute the number of payments.

TIP

By using a formula in cell C8 to determine the number of payments, you only need to change the number of years to test different loan lengths.

4. Click cell C7 and key ***12**. Press ⌷Enter⌷. You will make a total of 48 payments (4 years * 12 months in a year).

5. In cell C9, key **20000**, the amount of money borrowed.

6. In cell C10, key **4.9%** as the interest rate.

7. Click cell C12. Click the **Formulas** tab.

8. Click the Financial button . Scroll and click **PMT**. The PMT Function Arguments dialog box opens with the insertion point in the **Rate** box, the first argument.

9. Click cell C10, the interest rate. The cell address appears in the **Rate** box.

10. Key **/12** in the **Rate** box after **C10**. An annual interest rate must be divided by 12 to figure a monthly payment.

11. Click in the **Nper** box. This argument is the total number of payments.

12. Click cell C8 for the number of payments.

13. Click in the **Pv** box and click cell C9. The present value is cash you receive now.

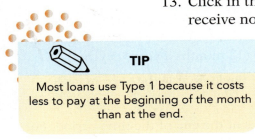

TIP

Most loans use Type 1 because it costs less to pay at the beginning of the month than at the end.

14. Click in the **Fv** box. Future value for a loan is what you will owe at the end of the loan, 0. You do not need to enter anything in this box.

15. Click in the **Type** box and key **1** for a payment at the beginning of the month.

Figure 7-12
Function Arguments
dialog box for PMT
CU.xlsx
CreditUnion sheet

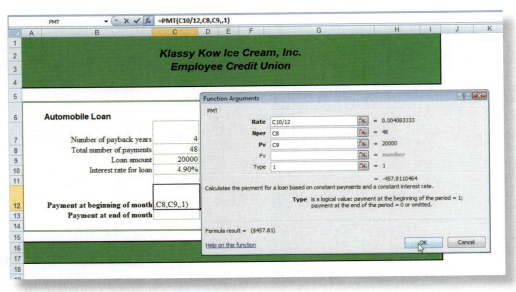

16. Click **OK**. The result ($457.81) is a negative number, because it is money that you have to pay. It is money out of your pocket. Negative formula results are shown in red with parentheses in this worksheet.

Exercise 7-17   **KEY A PMT FUNCTION**

Key a PMT function from scratch in this exercise to determine the payment if made at the end of the month.

1. Click cell C13.

2. Key **=pm** to display the Formula AutoComplete list and press Tab. The ScreenTip reminds you that the first argument is the **Rate**.

3. Click cell C10 for the rate.

4. Key **/12** to divide the rate by 12.

5. Key a comma to separate the arguments. The second argument, **Nper**, is bold in the ScreenTip.

6. Click cell C8 for the number of payments.

7. Key a comma. The ScreenTip shows the next argument as bold, which is the present value or the amount of the loan.

8. Click cell C9. The square brackets with **[fv]** and **[type]** in the ScreenTip mean that these two arguments are optional. If you do not key a future value, Excel assumes the FV is 0. If you do not key a type, it is assumed to be a 0 type.

9. Press Enter. Notice that payment at the end of the month is slightly more than at the beginning of the month.

Figure 7-13
Keying a PMT
function
CU.xlsx
CreditUnion sheet

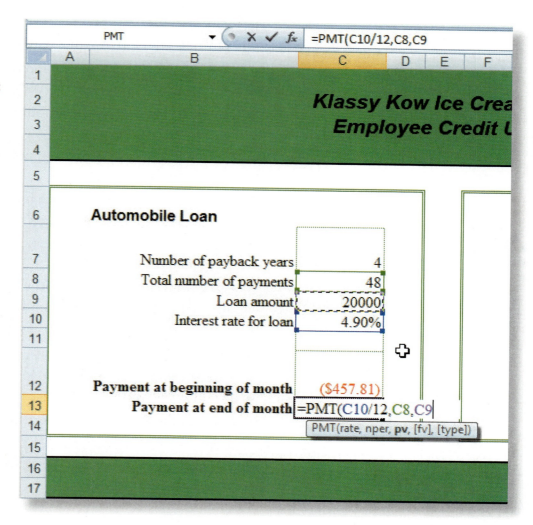

10. Click cell C7. Key **5** and press Enter for a five-year loan. Both functions are recalculated as well as the total number of payments.

11. In cell C10, key **3.9%** and press Enter. Payments with a lower interest rate are lower.

12. Click cell C9 and press F2 to edit the value.

13. Press Home to position the insertion point and key **−** to make this a negative number.

14. Press Enter. The payments now are positive numbers.

Exercise 7-18   USE THE FV FUNCTION

The FV (Future Value) function can be used to determine such things as how much you will have in your savings account at some point in the future if you make regular deposits. You can include money already in the account when you start your savings program.

1. Click cell H7 and key **5** to plan a five-year savings plan.

2. In cell H8, key **=** and click cell H7. Key ***12** and press Enter. You would make 60 total deposits if you save monthly for five years.

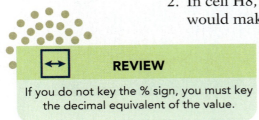

REVIEW

If you do not key the % sign, you must key the decimal equivalent of the value.

3. In cell H9, key **50** as the amount saved each month.

4. In cell H10, key **1000** as the amount of money already in the account.

5. In cell H11, key **5.25%** as the interest rate.

6. In cell H12, click the Financial button . Scroll and click **FV**. The insertion point is in the **Rate** box for the first argument.

NOTE

The Function Arguments dialog box shows the syntax and a description of each argument when you click its box.

7. Click cell H11 for the **Rate**. Key **/12** in the **Rate** box after **H11** to divide the rate by 12.

8. Click in the **Nper** box and then click cell H8.

9. Click in the **Pmt** box and click cell H9. The payment is the amount you plan to deposit into your savings account each month.

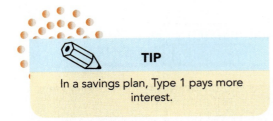

TIP

In a savings plan, Type 1 pays more interest.

10. Click in the **Pv** box and click cell H10. The present value is the amount in the account to start.

11. Click in the **Type** box and key **1** for a deposit at the beginning of the month.

Figure 7-14
Function Arguments
dialog box for FV
CU.xlsx
CreditUnion sheet

Function Arguments | ? X

FV

Rate | H11/12 | = 0.004375
Nper | H8 | = 60
Pmt | H9 | = 50
Pv | H10 | = 1000
Type | 1| | = 1

= -4736.486919
Returns the future value of an investment based on periodic, constant payments and a constant interest rate.

Type is a value representing the timing of payment: payment at the beginning of the period = 1; payment at the end of the period = 0 or omitted.

Formula result = -4736.486919

Help on this function

OK | Cancel

12. Click **OK**. The result is shown as a negative number, because the FV function assumes the bank's or lender's point of view. This is money that they would have to pay to you.

Exercise 7-19 FORMAT NEGATIVE NUMBERS

Many business reports show negative numbers in red. Excel's number formats can show negative numbers in red or black, with or without parentheses, or with a leading minus sign.

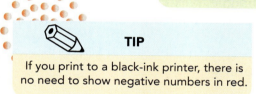

TIP

If you print to a black-ink printer, there is no need to show negative numbers in red.

1. Select cells C9, C12:C13, H9:H10, and H12.

2. Press Ctrl+1. Click the **Number** tab and choose **Currency**. Verify that there will be two decimals and a dollar sign.

3. In the **Negative numbers** list, choose the non-red **($1,234.10)**. Click **OK**.

4. Make cells C12 and H12 bold.

5. Press Ctrl+Home. Add a header.

6. Save the workbook as *[your initials]***7-19** in your Lesson 7 folder. Close the workbook.

Using Depreciation Functions

Depreciation is the decline in value of an asset. Your car depreciates. You pay an amount for the car, but it is not worth that amount in three years because it has been used. In a business, depreciation is an expense that can reduce income taxes. There are widely accepted methods of determining depreciation, and Excel has several functions to calculate the amounts.

Excel's depreciation functions use these basic arguments:

- *Cost* is the original price of the item.

- *Salvage* is the value of the item after it has been depreciated. It is what the item is worth at the end of its life.

- *Life* is the number of periods over which the item will be depreciated. This is usually expressed in years for expensive assets.

- *Period* is the time for which depreciation is calculated. It uses the same units as Life. If an asset has a 10-year life, you would usually figure depreciation for a single year (the period).

Exercise 7-20   USE THE DB FUNCTION

The DB (Declining Balance) function calculates depreciation at a fixed rate and assumes that the value declines each year. You calculate depreciation for each year separately.

1. Open **Depreciation**.

2. Select cells B11:B12. Use the Fill handle to extend the labels down column A to "10th Year." Extend the values in column C to match.

3. Click the **Formulas** tab.

4. In cell D11, click the Financial button **Financial ▾** .

5. Hover over **DB** and read the ScreenTip.

6. Click **DB**. The insertion point is in the **Cost** box for the first argument.

7. Click cell D7 for the **Cost**.

8. Click in the **Salvage** box and then click cell D8. This is the value of the tanks after 10 years.

9. Click in the **Life** box and click cell D9. The life is how long the tanks are expected to last.

10. Click in the **Period** box and click cell C11 to calculate depreciation for the first year.

11. Click in the **Month** box. This allows you to start depreciating an asset in the middle of a year. The label "Month" is not bold, which means this argument is optional. Leave it empty.

Figure 7-15
Function Arguments
dialog box for DB
**Depreciation.xlsx
Sheet1 sheet**

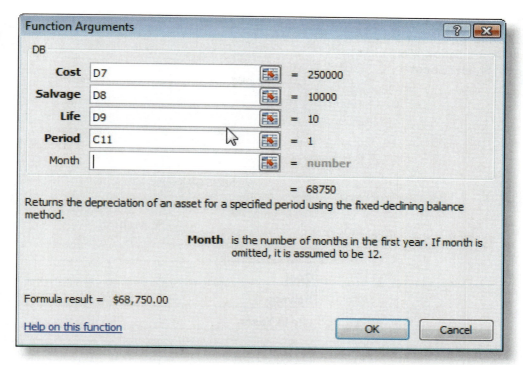

Returns the depreciation of an asset for a specified period using the fixed-declining balance method.

Month is the number of months in the first year. If month is omitted, it is assumed to be 12.

Formula result = $68,750.00

Help on this function

12. Click **OK**. The depreciation for the first year is $68,750.

13. Click cell D12 and key **=db(** to start the function. The ScreenTip shows that the first argument is the **cost**.

14. Click cell D7.

15. Key a comma to separate the arguments. The second argument, **salvage**, is bold in the ScreenTip.

16. Click cell D8 for the salvage value.

17. Key another comma. The ScreenTip reminds you that the next argument is the **life** of the asset.

18. Click cell D9 and key a comma. The **period** argument is next.

19. Click cell C12 for the second year. The next argument in square brackets is **[month]** in the ScreenTip. Do not enter anything here.

Figure 7-16
Keying a DB function
Depreciation.xlsx
Sheet1 sheet

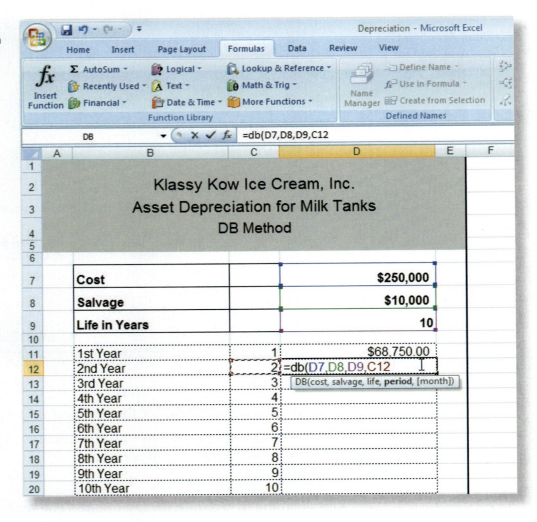

20. Press [Enter]. The depreciation for the second year is less because the asset was worth less at the beginning of the second year.

Exercise 7-21   EDIT AND COPY THE DB FUNCTION

With absolute references to the first three cells, you can copy the formula.

1. Click cell D12.

2. Press [F2]. The references to cells D7, D8, and D9 should be absolute.

3. Click between the **D** and the **7** and press [F4]. The reference is absolute.

4. Do the same for D8 and D9 in the formula and press [Enter].

5. Hide coloumn C.

6. Press [Ctrl]+[Home]. Edit the footer to show your name and save the workbook as *[your initials]7-21* in your folder.

7. Close the workbook.

Using Online Help

Excel has many financial functions that calculate common business arithmetic, including several methods for determining depreciation.

USE HELP TO VIEW ADDITIONAL INFORMATION ABOUT DEPRECIATION

1. In a new workbook, click the Microsoft Office Excel Help button.
2. In the Search box, key **depreciation** and press Enter.
3. Find and review topics about the SLN, SYD, and VDB functions.
4. Close the Help window.

Lesson 7 Summary

- The IF function enables you to create formulas that test whether a condition is true. If it is true, you specify what should be shown or done. You also set what appears or is done if the condition is false.

- The IF function can show text in its result, it can calculate a value, or it can show a cell reference.

- AND, OR, and NOT are logical functions that show either TRUE or FALSE as a result.

- Logical functions use relational or comparison operators.

- A style is a set of formatting attributes for labels and values.

- Cell styles appear in a gallery with Live Preview. They are coordinated with the document theme.

- You can remove all formatting from a cell and return to the default Normal style.

- You can create your own style and save it with the worksheet.

- Page breaks determine where a new page starts. Excel inserts page breaks based on the paper size and the margins.

- You can insert and delete your own page breaks.

- Page Break Preview shows the page breaks as solid or dashed blue lines.

- If a worksheet requires more than one page, you can repeat column or row headings from page to page to make it easier to read the worksheet.

- The Margins tab in the Page Setup dialog box includes options to center a page horizontally or vertically.

- You can print each page number as well as the total number of pages in a worksheet as a header or a footer.

- Financial functions include PMT and FV and other common business calculations such as depreciation.

- The PMT function calculates a regular payment for a loan, using an interest rate.
- The FV function calculates how much an amount will be worth in the future at a given interest rate.
- The DB function calculates how much of its value an asset loses each year during its life.
- Negative numbers can be shown in red, within parentheses, or with a leading minus (−) sign.

LESSON 7		Command Summary	
Feature	**Button**	**Task Path**	**Keyboard**
Apply cell style		Home, Styles, Cell Styles	
Center page		Page Layout, Page Setup, Margins, Custom Margins	Ctrl + 1
Collapse formula bar			
Create cell style		Home, Styles, Cell Styles, New Cell Style	
Delete page break		Page Layout, Page Setup, Breaks, Remove Page Break	
Edit cell style		Home, Styles, Cell Styles	
Expand formula bar			
Insert page break		Page Layout, Page Setup, Breaks, Insert Page Break	
Page break preview			
Print titles		Page Layout, Page Setup	
Repeat command			Ctrl + Y

Concepts Review

True/False Questions

Each of the following statements is either true or false. Indicate your choice by circling T or F.

T F 1. You can repeat the most recent command by pressing Ctrl+R.

T F 2. You must key quotation marks around text that you key in a Function Arguments dialog box.

T F 3. The AND and OR functions usually show the same results.

T F 4. All financial functions include a rate argument.

T F 5. Arguments in a function are separated by commas.

T F 6. The Cell Styles gallery includes styles for values as well as labels.

T F 7. The PMT function determines how much your money will grow over a period of time.

T F 8. The Print Titles option can repeat rows or columns on each page of a worksheet.

Short Answer Questions

Write the correct answer in the space provided.

1. What dialog box helps you complete built-in functions with entry boxes for each argument?

   _____

2. Which argument in a financial function refers to the total number of periods (also the total number of payments or deposits)?

   _____

3. Which logical function shows the opposite of the condition?

   _____

4. What Excel feature lets you see the results of a cell style before applying it?

   _____

5. Which command tab includes choices for page breaks and print titles?

   _____

6. How can you distinguish between an automatic page break and one that you placed?

   _____

7. Which financial function would help you determine how much money will be in your account at the end of a year if you make regular deposits?

_____

8. What is the purpose of the Type argument in financial functions?

_____

Critical Thinking

Answer these questions on a separate page. There are no right or wrong answers. Support your answers with examples from your own experience, if possible.

1. Why are there separate logical operators for greater than (>) and greater than or equal to (>=)?

2. Which financial functions do you recognize or can you figure out from the Financial category? Explain how two financial functions that you did not use in this lesson might work in a business setting.

Skills Review

NOTE

If you see small triangles in the lower-right corners of cells with dates, SmartTags are enabled. You can ignore SmartTags for now.

NOTE

You cannot key a date as the logical test in an IF function, but you can refer to a cell with a date.

REVIEW

Use an absolute reference when the cell address should not change as the formula is copied.

Exercise 7-22

Use the IF function.

1. Open **CustBirth** and save it as *[your initials]*7-22 in your Lesson 7 folder.

2. Right-click the column D heading and insert a column. In cell D3, key **Born after 2000?**

3. In cell A21, key **12/31/00**. This is the last date in 2000, and you will refer to this cell in the IF function.

4. Use the IF function by following these steps:

   a. Click cell D4 and click the **Formulas** tab.

   b. Click the Logical button [Logical ▾] and choose **IF**.

   c. Click cell C4 and key >.

   d. Click cell A21 and press F4 to make the reference absolute. The logical test determines if the date in cell C4 is greater than the date in cell A21 (that is, it is after that date).

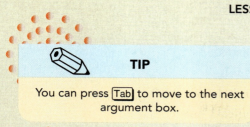

TIP

You can press Tab to move to the next argument box.

TIP

Set the alignment before copying the formula. The copied format does not include a bottom border.

REVIEW

Hidden rows/columns are used in formulas.

NOTE

Ask your instructor for help if you cannot find the template.

   e. Click in the **Value_if_true** box. Key **Yes**.

   f. Click in the **Value_if_false** box. Key **No** and click **OK**.

5. Center the results. Copy the formula to cells D5:D20.

6. Right-click the row 21 heading and hide the row. Add the missing border. Press Ctrl + Home .

7. Add a header. On the Page Layout tab in the Scale to Fit group, set both the Width and Height commands to **1 page**.

8. Make a copy of the worksheet and name it **CustBirthdaysFormulas**. Display the formulas, fit the columns, and fit the sheet to one landscape page.

9. Prepare and submit your work. Save and close the workbook.

Exercise 7-23

Use AND, OR, and NOT functions.

1. Open the New Workbook dialog box. Click **My templates** and double-click **KlassyBirth**.

2. Save the workbook as *[your initials]*7-23 in your folder.

3. Key the following information, starting in cell A8.

Figure 7-17

Name	Shop	Age	Male/Female
[your first and last name]	Wenatchee	[your age]	[your gender]
Carole Greenfield	Olympia	10	F
Michael Westberg	Yakima	5	M
Hashima Yeng	Kelso	6	M
Krystal Chavez	Bremerton	8	F
Pedro Juarez	Yakima	7	M
David Hutchinson	Wenatchee	5	M
Melinda Brown	Kelso	4	F

4. Use an AND function by following these steps:

a. Click cell E8 and click the **Formulas** tab.

b. Click the Logical button and choose **AND**.

c. Click cell C8 and key **>=6** in the **Logical1** box.

d. Click in the **Logical2** box. Click cell C8 and key **>=8**. Click **OK**.

e. Copy the formula in cell E8 to cells E9:E15.

5. Key an OR function by following these steps:

a. Click cell F8 and key **=or(** to start the formula.

b. Click cell C8 and key **<=5**.

c. Key a comma to separate the arguments.

d. Click cell D8, key **="f"** and press Enter.

e. Copy the formula in cell F8 to cells F9:F15.

> **NOTE**
>
> Text in an AND/OR function must be enclosed in quotation marks.

6. Use a NOT function by following these steps:

a. In cell G8, key **=not** and press Tab.

b. Click cell D8 and key **="f"** and press Enter.

c. Copy the formula.

7. Add your footer. Fit the sheet to one landscape page.

8. Make a copy of the sheet and name it **CustBirthdaysFormulas**. Display the formulas and fit this sheet to one landscape page.

9. Prepare and submit your work. Save and close the workbook.

Exercise 7-24

Work with styles. Work with page breaks. Set print titles.

1. Open **PerfRating**. Save the workbook as *[your initials]7-24*.

2. Apply styles by following these steps:

a. Press F8 and then press Ctrl + End.

b. On the **Home** tab, click the Clear button 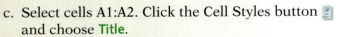 in the **Editing** group. Choose **Clear Formats**.

c. Select cells A1:A2. Click the Cell Styles button and choose **Title**.

> **NOTE**
>
> Column E uses a nested IF formula.

d. Select cells A3:F3 and apply the **Heading 2** style.

e. Make columns A:C each **15.00 (110 pixels)** wide.

3. Create and apply styles by following these steps:

a. Click the Cell Styles button and choose **New Cell Style**.

> **NOTE**
>
> Your style starts as a copy of the Normal style.

b. Key **Amounts** in the **Style name** box and click **Format**.

c. Click the **Number** tab. Set **Currency** with 0 decimal places and a dollar sign, and click **OK**. Click **OK** again.

d. Click the Cell Styles button ⊞ and choose **New Cell Style**. Key **Increase** in the **Style name** box and click **Format**.

e. Click the **Number** tab. Set **Currency** with 0 decimal places and a dollar sign.

f. Click the **Font** tab. Set 11-point Calibri bold. Choose a dark blue theme color from the **Color** list. Click **OK**. Click **OK** again.

g. Create a style named **Ratings**. Click the **Font** tab. Set 11-point Calibri bold. On the **Alignment** tab, choose **Center** for the **Horizontal** setting. Click **OK**. Click **OK** again.

h. Select cells C4:C16 and F4:F16. Apply the **Amounts** style.

i. Apply the **Increase** style to cells E4:E16 and the **Ratings** style to cell D4:D16 and to cells D18:D20.

j. Apply the **Percent** style to cells E18:E20.

4. Click cell D3 and press F2. Click after the final "e" in "Performance" and press Alt+Enter. Then press Enter.

5. Make columns D:E each **15.00 (110 pixels)** wide. Center the label in cell D3.

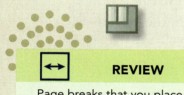

REVIEW

Page breaks that you place appear as solid lines.

6. Work with page breaks by following these steps:

a. Click the Page Break Preview button ⊞. Click **OK** in the message box.

b. Rest the mouse pointer on the blue dashed line to display a two-pointed arrow.

c. Drag the dashed-line page break so that it is between columns C and D.

7. Set print titles by following these steps:

NOTE

Your worksheet will expand to three printed pages when you AutoFit column A.

a. Click the **Page Layout** tab. Click the Print Titles button ⊞.

b. In the **Print titles** section, click in the **Rows to repeat at top** box.

c. Select cells A1:A2. Excel inserts an absolute reference for rows 1:2.

d. Click in the **Columns to repeat at left** box. Click anywhere in column A.

e. Click **Print Preview**. Check the labels in column A on both pages.

f. Close Print Preview.

g. Click the Normal button ⊞. AutoFit column A.

8. Add a header, but change the font to 8 points for each section.

TIP

Enter the header data, select it, and use the Mini toolbar to change the font size.

9. Prepare and submit your work. Save and close the workbook.

Exercise 7-25

Use PMT and FV functions. Use a depreciation function.

1. Open **Comparison** and save it as *[your initials]7-25*.

2. In cells B3:B5, key data for a $15,000 loan at 5.9% for three years. In cell B6, key **=** and click cell B5. Key ***12** and press (Enter).

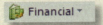

3. In cells E3:E5, key data for a $15,000 loan at 6.5% for four years. Use the formula in cell E6 to determine the number of payments.

4. Use the PMT function by following these steps:

   a. Click the **Formulas** tab.

   b. In cell B7, click the Financial button 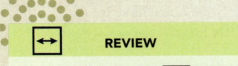. Choose **PMT**.

   c. Click cell B4 and key **/12** in the **Rate** box.

   d. Click in the **Nper** box and then click cell B6.

   e. Click in the **Pv** box and then click cell B3.

   f. Click in the **Type** box and key **1**. Click **OK**.

   g. Copy the formula in cell B7 to cell E7.

5. Copy cells A1:A2 to **Sheet2**. Edit the label in cell A2 to say **Savings Comparison**. In cells A3:A6, key the following labels:
   Savings Amount
   Rate
   Years for Savings
   Total # of Deposits

6. Widen column A for the longest label and format row 3 as **27.00 (36 pixels)** high. Copy cells A3:A6 to cells D3:D6. Make column D the same width as column A.

7. In column B, key data for saving $50 a month at 6.25% for three years. Use a formula to determine the number of deposits.

8. In column E, key data for saving $100 a month at 6.5% for four years.

9. Use the FV function by following these steps:

   a. In cell B7, click the **Formulas** tab and the Financial button . Choose FV.

   b. Click cell B4 and key **/12** in the **Rate** box.

   c. Click in the **Nper** box and then click cell B6. Click in the **Pmt** box and then click cell B3.

d. Click in the **Type** box and key **1**. Click **OK**.

e. Copy the formula in cell B7 to cell E7. Widen columns as needed.

10. Rename **Sheet2** as **Savings**. Group these two sheets and insert a column at column A and a row at row 1.

11. Apply a double outline border to cells A1:G9. Apply dotted middle horizontal and bottom borders to cells B4:C7 and cells E4:E7. Center the two main labels across the data. Ungroup the sheets.

12. Rename **Sheet3 Depreciation**. Set cells A1:A2 for 16-point Calibri. In cell A1, key **Klassy Kow Ice Cream, Inc.** In cell A2, key **Asset Depreciation for Storage Tanks**.

13. Use 14-point Calibri for cell A3 and key **DDB Method**. Make columns A and C each **27.86 (200 pixels)** wide.

14. Set Calibri bold for cells A4:C15. Key the following labels and values:

	A	B	C
4	Cost		$300,000
5	Salvage		$15,000
6	Life in Years		8

15. In cell A8, key **1st Year** and in cell A9, key **2nd Year**. Select these two cells and use the Fill handle to fill down column A to **8th Year**. In cell B8, key **1** and in cell B9, key **2**. Fill this series down to **8**.

16. Use a depreciation function by following these steps:

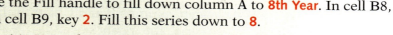

a. In cell C8, click the Insert Function button .

b. Choose **Financial** and **DDB**. Click **OK**.

NOTE

The DDB depreciation function is double-declining balance.

c. Click cell C4 for the **Cost** and press F4 to make the reference absolute.

d. Click in the **Salvage** box, click cell C5, and press F4.

e. Click in the **Life** box, click cell C6, and make it absolute.

NOTE

By showing the years as simple values, you can copy the formula.

f. Click in the **Period** box, click cell B8, and leave it a relative reference.

g. Leave the **Factor** box empty. Click **OK**.

h. Copy the formula down to row 15.

17. Hide column B. Center the labels in rows 1:3 across the data.

18. Group all three worksheets and click the **Page Layout** tab. Click the Dialog Box Launcher for the **Page Setup** group. Horizontally center the sheets. Add a footer to the grouped sheets from this dialog box.

19. Prepare and submit your work. Save and close the workbook.

Lesson Applications

Exercise 7-26

Use the IF function.

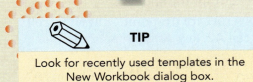

> **TIP**
>
> Look for recently used templates in the New Workbook dialog box.

1. Use the **KlassyBirth** template to create a workbook. Save it as *[your initials]7-26*.

2. Click the Expand Formula Bar button ⌄ and edit the label in cell B3 to show **Favorite Flavor** on the second line. Change **Age** in cell C7 to **Flavor**. Collapse the formula bar.

3. In cells A8:D13, key the following information:

Figure 7-18

	Name	Shop	Favorite Flavor	M/F
4	Marian Most	Las Vegas, Green	Chocolate	F
5	Tommy Dunne	Lake Las Vegas	Bubble Gum Goo	M
6	Luella Orr	Carson City	Chocolate	F
7	Patrick Adams	Reno	Vanilla	M
8	Asata Akai	Henderson	Strawberry	F
9	Efren Aldo	Las Vegas, Sunnyvale	Chocolate	M

4. Widen columns B and C slightly. Left-align the flavors in column C and increase the indent once.

5. Key **Chocolate?** as the label in cell E7 and adjust the column width.

6. Use the IF function in cell E8 with **C8="chocolate"** as the **Logical_test**. Show **Yes** if the customer's favorite flavor is chocolate. Show **Other** if chocolate is not the favorite. Copy the formula for the rest of the names and center the results.

7. Delete columns F and G. One of the images may be deleted with the columns. Center the sheet horizontally. Add a header.

8. Make a copy of the worksheet and name it **CustBirthdaysFormulas**. Display the formulas and adjust column widths. Don't size the picture. Fit the sheet to one landscape page.

9. Prepare and submit your work. Save and close the workbook.

Exercise 7-27

Work with page breaks.

The financial staff keeps track of retirement accounts for Klassy Kow employees. The worksheet should be printed with each year on a separate page. Each year details five funds.

TIP

Set the Zoom percentage to see more on the screen.

REVIEW

The Repeat command is Ctrl + Y.

1. Open **RetireAcct** and save it as *[your initials]*7-27.

2. Increase the left indent 2 spaces for cell A10. Change the page orientation to landscape.

3. Center cell B3 across cells B3:G3. Repeat these steps for all years.

4. Set page breaks so that each year's data is on a separate page. Set rows 1:2 and column A as print titles. Use the Scale to Fit group to fit the sheet to three pages wide, one page tall.

5. Add a header with your name at the left. In the center section, show the filename and the sheet name on one line. Press Enter and on the second line in the center, show **&Page of &Pages**. Include the date in the right section.

6. Prepare and submit your work. Save and close the workbook.

Exercise 7-28

Use AND and OR functions.

1. Open **SerAwards**. Save it as *[your initials]*7-28 in your folder.

2. In cell E4, use an AND function to show TRUE if the employee has greater than two years of service and a performance rating equal to 4. Copy the formula to cells E5:E16.

3. In cell F4, use an OR function to show TRUE if the employee has greater than four years of service or a performance rating equal to 4. Copy the formula.

4. Add an icon set using **3 Symbols (Circled)** for column D. Edit the rule to show a green check mark for any rating equal to or greater than 3. Show an exclamation point for any other number. The red X should not appear at all.

5. Set the page to be horizontally centered. Add a footer using a 9-point font for all sections.

6. Make a formula sheet and fit it to one landscape page.

7. Prepare and submit your work. Save and close the workbook.

Exercise 7-29 ◆ Challenge Yourself

Use the PMT function to calculate mortgage payments at different interest rates.

Klassy Kow Ice Cream, Inc., must choose a construction loan to finance expansion at the headquarters building. This worksheet analyzes information from four lenders. The loan will be for $500,000, 10 years, payments made at the beginning of each month.

1. Open **LoanComp** and save it as *[your initials]7-29*.

2. Review the formulas. There are two errors in formulas that result in incorrect values on this worksheet.

NOTE

A total cost is calculated by multiplying the monthly payment by the total number of payments.

3. Correct the errors and make format adjustments as needed.

4. Add a header and fit the sheet to a single portrait page.

5. Prepare a formula sheet. On this sheet, add different fill to the cells that you edited. Fit the formula sheet to a portrait page.

6. Prepare and submit your work. Save and close the workbook.

On Your Own

In these exercises you work on your own, as you would in a real-life work environment. Use the skills you've learned to accomplish the task—and be creative.

Exercise 7-30

Assume you are a bank professional who expects a 6% return on money you lend. Create a new workbook to determine how much you can lend to a customer who can afford to pay $200 a month for five years. Use Help to learn about the PV function and use it in your workbook. Assume payments will be made at the beginning of the month. Decide how to format your data, and add a header or footer. Save the workbook as *[your initials]7-30*. Prepare and submit your work.

Exercise 7-31

Open **CustCount**. Select the rows for a state and apply a cell style from the Themed Cell Styles group. Use a different style for each state. Set landscape orientation and insert page breaks so that each state is on its own page. Add a footer that includes page numbers. Save the workbook as *[your initials]7-31*. Prepare and submit your work.

Exercise 7-32

Open **AR** and save it as *[your initials]*7-32. Copy cells A2:E16 to cell A17 and again to cells A32 and A47. Add your usual footer and include the page number in the center. Look at the worksheet in Print Preview and in Page Break Preview. Excel prints the pages down and then over. On the **Sheet** tab of the Page Setup dialog box, change this setting to print over and then down. Prepare and submit your work.

Rounding and Nesting Functions

OBJECTIVES

After completing this lesson, you will be able to:

1. Use the INT function.

2. Use the ROUND function.

3. Use date and time arithmetic.

4. Create nested functions.

5. Create a hyperlink.

MCAS OBJECTIVES

In this lesson:
XL07 1.5.4
XL07 2.3.7
XL07 2.3.8
XL07 3.1.1
XL07 4.3.3
XL07 5.4.1
XL07 5.5.4

Estimated Time: 1½ hours

The INT and ROUND functions can be used with formulas or functions to convert a value with decimals. You will learn about these two functions as well as how to nest one function inside another to solve complex problems.

Using the INT Function

Excel stores the full number of decimals that are keyed or calculated in a cell, even if the cell is formatted to show fewer decimal places. For example, if you key 1.2345 and format the cell for two decimal places, Excel displays 1.23 in the cell. In a calculation, however, Excel uses the full value, 1.2345, which you see in the formula bar.

If you want Excel to use the value shown in the cell (not the one in the formula bar), you can use the INT or ROUND functions.

INT stands for "Integer." An *integer* is a whole number, a number with no decimal or fractional parts. The INT function (in the Math & Trig category) shows only the nondecimal portion of a number. To do this, it truncates or cuts off all digits after the decimal point. The INT function has one argument, the value or cell to be adjusted.

TABLE 8-1 Examples of the INT Function

Expression	Cell Data	Result
INT(C4)	C4=9.7	9
INT(9.792)	None	9
INT(A1)	A1=−9.7	−9

Exercise 8-1 USE INT WITH A CELL REFERENCE

1. Open **Recipes.**

2. On the **Recipes** sheet in cell C7, key **=int** to see the Formula AutoComplete list and the ScreenTip.

3. Press Tab to select the INT function. The argument is the value.

4. Click cell B7.

Figure 8-1
Keying an INT function
Recipes.xlsx
Recipes sheet

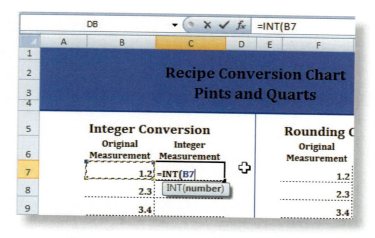

5. Press Enter. The integer value of 1.2 is 1.

6. Copy the formula in cell C7 to cells C8:C12.

Exercise 8-2 COMPARE VALUES WITH INT

1. Key **=** in cell B14 and click cell B7.

2. Key ***2** and press Enter. This is a multiplication formula, doubling the value in cell B7.

3. Use the Fill handle to copy the formula to cells B15:B19.

4. Key **=** in cell C14 and click cell C7.

5. Key ***2** and press Enter. This doubles the integer value in cell C7.

6. Copy the formula to cells C15:C19. Compare the values in columns A and B. There are some noticeable differences between doubling the original value and doubling the integer value.

7. Delete the contents of cells C14:C19.

8. In cell C14, key **=int(** and click cell B14. Press ⬚Enter⬚. This is the integer value of 2.4.

9. Copy the formula to cells C15:C19.

Using the ROUND Function

The ROUND function "rounds" a value to a specified digit to the left or right of the decimal point. *Rounding* a number means that it is made larger or smaller, a greater or lesser value. The ROUND function uses two arguments: the value to be rounded and the number of digits used for rounding. If the second argument is zero or a negative number, the rounding occurs to the left of the decimal point.

TABLE 8-2 Examples of the ROUND Function

Expression	Cell Data	Result
ROUND(C4, 1)	C4=9.736	9.7
ROUND(C4, 2)	C4=9.736	9.74
ROUND(C4, 0)	C4=9.736	10
ROUND(C4, −1)	C4=9.736	10

TIP

Rounding can be used in financial calculations to round to the nearest dollar.

Exercise 8-3   USE ROUND

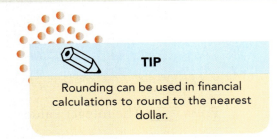

1. Click the **Formulas** tab and click cell G7.

2. Click the Math & Trig button . Hover over **ROUND** to read the ScreenTip.

3. Choose **ROUND**.

4. In the **Number** box, click cell F7.

5. In the **Num_digits** box, key **0**. The value in cell F7 will be rounded to show no decimal positions.

Figure 8-2
Using ROUND in the
dialog box
Recipes.xlsx
Recipes sheet

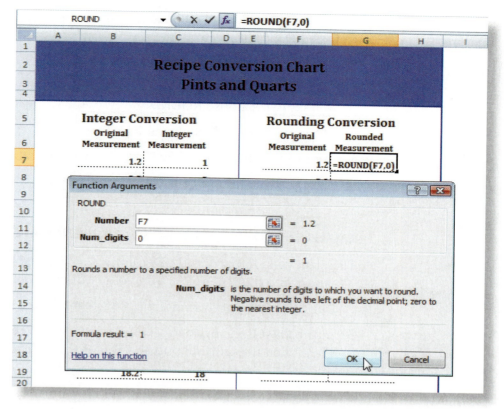

6. Click **OK**. The value 1.2 is rounded to 1. It rounds down because the value after the decimal point is less than 5.

7. Copy the formula down to cell G12.

8. Edit cells F8:F11 to show the following values. As you do, notice how the values in column G are rounded up or down.
   1.6
   3.2
   5.5
   7.2

9. Click the arrow next to the Undo button ↺ and undo the last four edits.

Exercise 8-4   COMPARE ROUNDED VALUES

Note the difference between doubling the rounded values and rounding the doubled values in this exercise.

1. Key **=** in cell F14 and click cell F7. Key ***2** and press Enter.

2. Copy the formula to cells F15:F19.

3. Key **=** in cell G14 and click cell G7. Key ***2** and press Enter. This doubles the rounded value in cell G7.

4. Copy the formula to cells G15:G19. Compare the values in columns C and D.

5. Delete the contents of cells G14:G19.

6. Click the **Formulas** tab. In cell G14, click the Math & Trig button . Choose **ROUND**.

7. In the **Number** box, click cell F14.

8. In the **Num_digits** box, key **0**. Click **OK**. The value **2.4** is rounded to **2**.

9. Copy the formula to cells G15:G19.

Exercise 8-5   CHANGE COLORS AND BORDERS

1. Select cells A1:H21 and press Ctrl+1. Click the **Border** tab. You can determine that there is a thick blue outline border.

2. Click the **Color** arrow and choose **Accent 1** for a softer blue.

3. In the **Presets** group, click None button to remove all borders. Then click the Outline button. Click **OK**. The same border thickness is used.

4. Click the **Home** tab. Select cells A1:H4 and click the arrow next to the Fill Color button.

5. Choose **Blue, Accent 1**.

6. Select cells D5:D21. There should be a vertical border for these cells. Since columns D and E share borders, you can edit this border from either column.

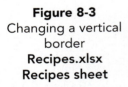

Figure 8-3
Changing a vertical border
Recipes.xlsx
Recipes sheet

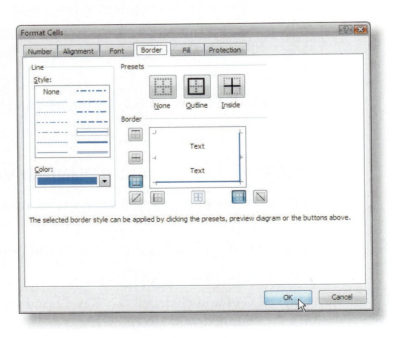

7. Press [Ctrl]+[1]. Click the **Border** tab.

 8. Click the right vertical border preview area or the Right Vertical button to remove the border.

9. Click the **Color** arrow and choose **Blue, Accent 1**. Then click the right vertical border area or its button. Click **OK**.

10. Change the sheet tab color to **Blue, Accent 1**.

11. Save the workbook as *[your initials]*8-5 in a new folder for Lesson 8.

Using Date and Time Arithmetic

TIP

Macintosh systems start counting at January 1, 1904.

Because of its serial number system, Excel's Date & Time functions can calculate ages, hours worked, or days passed. The serial number system treats dates as values. January 1, 1900, is 1; January 2, 1900, is 2; and so on.

Exercise 8-6 **DETERMINE AGES AND DATES**

To determine a product's age, subtract the manufacture date from today. The result is a serial number that can be converted to an age in years.

1. In *[your initials]*8-5, click the **ExpireDate** tab. Replace all occurrences of the year in column A with last year.

2. In cell C4, key **=today()-** to start the formula.

3. Click cell A4. The formula subtracts the manufacture date from today.

REVIEW

A series of #### symbols in a cell means that the value is too wide to be displayed in the currently selected font size.

4. Press [Enter]. The age is formatted as a date and is probably too wide to display.

5. Click cell C4 and press [Ctrl]+[1]. On the **Number** tab, choose **Number** with two decimal places and click **OK**. This is the age in days.

6. Press [F2]. Press [Home] and [→] to position the insertion point after the equal sign.

REVIEW

Excel calculates division before subtraction.

7. Key a left parenthesis **(** after the equal sign.

8. Press [End] and key a right parenthesis **)** after **A4** in the formula.

Figure 8-4
Converting the age
formula to years
8-5.xlsx
ExpireDate sheet

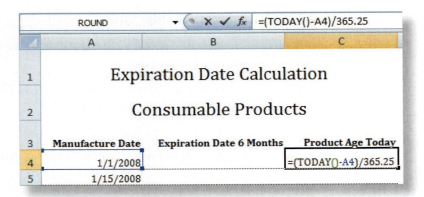

9. Key **/365.25** to divide by the number of days in a year. Press [Enter].

10. Copy the formula in cell C4 to row 19.

11. Click cell B4 and key **=** to start a formula.

12. Click cell A4 and key **+** to add days to the manufacture date.

NOTE

Dividing by 365.25 includes a leap year once every four years.

13. Key **6** and press [Enter]. This adds six days to the date.

14. Click cell B4, press [F2], and edit the formula to add 180 days.

15. Copy the formula to row 19.

Exercise 8-7   DETERMINE TIME PASSED

Calculating time passed is similar to determining an age. You subtract the beginning time from the ending time. Excel usually shows time results as a fraction of a 24-hour day. To convert to hours, multiply the results by 24.

1. Click the **FreezerTime** tab.

2. In cell C6, key **8:30 am** and press [→]. Excel capitalizes the AM/PM reference.

3. In cell D6, key **4:30 pm**. Excel shows times as you key them, using a 12-hour AM/PM clock.

4. Key the following times in columns C and D.

	C	D
7	9 am	5 pm
8	10:30 am	6:15 pm
9	12 pm	8:30 pm
10	6 am	4 pm
11	1 pm	11 pm

5. In cell E6, key **=** and click cell D6, the ending time.

6. Key a minus sign (**–**) and click cell C6, the starting time. Press Enter.

7. Click cell E6 and press Ctrl+1. Click the **Number** tab.

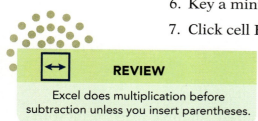

REVIEW

Excel does multiplication before subtraction unless you insert parentheses.

8. Choose **Number** with **3** decimal places. Click **OK**. The result is **.333**, representing one-third of a day.

9. Press F2 and press Home.

10. Press → and key a left parenthesis **(** after the equal sign.

11. Press End and key a right parenthesis **)**.

Figure 8-5
Converting time
to hours
8-5.xlsx
FreezerTime sheet

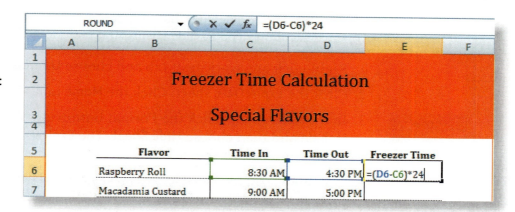

12. Key *****24** to multiply by the number of hours in a day. Press Enter.

13. Copy the formula to row 11.

Exercise 8-8   GROUP SHEETS TO ADD FOOTERS

1. Save the workbook as *[your initials]***8-8** in your Lesson 8 folder.

2. While the **FreezerTime** sheet is active, hold down Shift and click the **Recipes** tab.

3. Click the **Page Layout** tab. Click the Dialog Box Launcher for the **Page Setup** group.

4. Click the **Header/Footer** tab. Click **Custom Footer**.

5. Click the Format Text button and choose 9-point regular Calibri. Key your name in the left section.

6. In the center section, click the Format Text button and choose 9-point regular Calibri. Click the Insert Sheet Name button.

7. Insert the date using the same font in the right section. Click **OK**.

8. In the **Page Setup** dialog box, click the **Margins** tab. In the **Center on page** section, click to select **Horizontally**.

9. Click **Print Preview** in the **Page Setup** dialog box. This is the first page of three.

10. Press `PageDown` to see the other worksheets. Press `PageUp` to return to previous pages.

11. Click **Close Print Preview**.

12. Print while the worksheets are grouped. All three sheets print with the same footer.

Exercise 8-9   HIDE AND UNHIDE A WORKSHEET

You can hide a worksheet so that you do not see its tab while the workbook is open. This allows you to hide sheets that include sensitive information.

1. Right-click any worksheet tab and choose **Ungroup Sheets**.

2. Click the **ExpireDate** sheet. Click the **Home** tab.

3. In the **Cells** group, click the Format button . Choose **Hide & Unhide** and then choose **Hide Sheet**. The **ExpireDate** sheet no longer appears in the workbook.

4. Save and close the workbook. If you save and close a workbook with hidden sheets, the workbook will reopen just like that.

5. Open *[your initials]*8-8. There is no **ExpireDate** sheet visible.

6. In the **Cells** group, click the Format button . Choose **Hide & Unhide** and then choose **Unhide Sheet**. The Unhide dialog box lists the names of hidden sheets.

7. Choose **ExpireDate** in the list and click **OK**. The sheet is visible.

8. Save and close the workbook.

Creating Nested Functions

A *nested* function is a function inside another function. The argument for the main function is another function. The IF function is a function that is often used in nested functions as well as the ROUND function.

Exercise 8-10   NEST SUM AND ROUND

1. Open **CookieCrunch**.

2. Click cell C6 and notice the formula. Click cell D6 and check its formula. This worksheet uses a formula to compute a 5 percent sales increase from one month to the next and results in decimal values for most of the months.

NOTE

A 5 percent increase multiplies the previous month's sales by 105 percent.

3. Click cell H11. Click the Insert Function button  in the formula bar.

4. In the **Select a category** box, choose **Math & Trig**. Key **r** to move to the functions that begin with "r." Scroll and choose **Round**. Click **OK**.

5. Move the Function Arguments dialog box to see column headings and column H.

6. In the **Number** argument box, you will nest the SUM function. With the insertion point in the **Number** box, click the arrow for the **Name Box**.

7. Choose **SUM**. The Function Arguments dialog box now shows the SUM function, but it is nested in the ROUND function in the formula bar. The SUM function is bold in the formula bar, and the suggested range for the argument is highlighted and is correct (H6:H10).

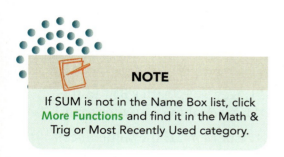

TIP

You must choose the function category and immediately key the first letter of the function name to scroll the function list.

NOTE

If SUM is not in the Name Box list, click **More Functions** and find it in the Math & Trig or Most Recently Used category.

Figure 8-6
Nesting SUM in a ROUND function
CookieCrunch.xlsx
PieSales sheet

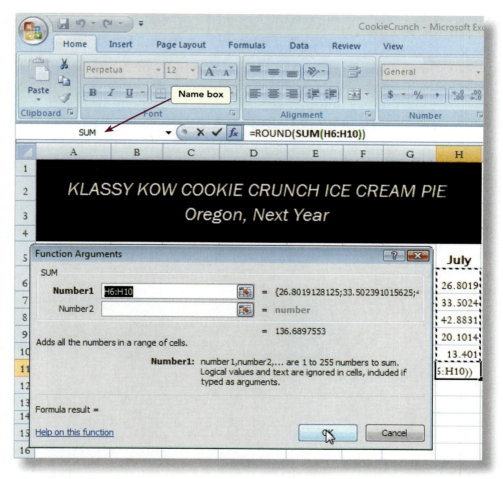

8. Click anywhere in the word **ROUND** in the formula bar. The Function Arguments dialog box returns to the ROUND function and displays **SUM(H6:H10)** as the **Number** argument.

9. Click in the **Num_digits** argument box and key **0**. Click **OK**.

10. Display the Fill handle for cell H11 and drag left to copy the formula to cells G11:B11. All results are rounded to show no decimal places.

Exercise 8-11   CREATE A NESTED IF FUNCTION

A nested IF function tests for more than one logical test. In your worksheet, you will first check to see if the monthly total is greater than 110, and then you'll test if it is greater than 120.

1. Click cell B12 and click the **Formulas** tab. Click the Logical 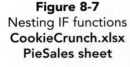. Choose **IF**.

2. In the **Logical_test** box, click cell B11. Key **>=120** after **B11** in the box. This tests if the value in cell B11 is equal to or greater than 120.

3. Click in the **Value_if_true** box. Key **120 or More**. If the value in cell B11 is greater than 120, the text "120 or More" will be shown.

4. Click in the **Value_if_false** box. If the value is not over 120, you will check if it is equal to or over 110. This is another IF function.

5. While the insertion point is in the **Value_if_false** box, click **IF** in the Name Box. The Function Arguments dialog box updates to show another IF statement. The second IF function is bold in the formula bar to show that it is the one you are now building.

6. In the **Logical_test** box, click cell B11. Key **>=110** after **B11**. Now you are determining if the value in cell B11 is equal to or greater than 110.

7. Click in the **Value_if_true** box. Key **110 or More** as the result text.

8. Click in the **Value_if_false** box. Key **Less than 110** and click **OK**.

Figure 8-7
Nesting IF functions
CookieCrunch.xlsx
PieSales sheet

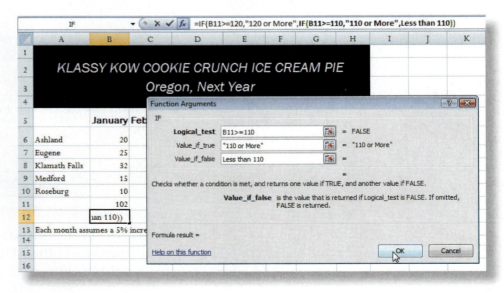

9. Copy the formula to cells C12:H12 and AutoFit columns B:H.

10. Set the height of row 13 to **67.50 (90 pixels)**.

11. Click the **Home** tab. Select cells A13:H13. In the **Alignment** group, click the Merge & Center button . Click the Middle Align button .

12. Right-align the data in row 12.

13. Set the page to landscape orientation and use horizontal centering.

Exercise 8-12   SET TOP/BOTTOM CONDITIONAL FORMATTING

In addition to data visualizations, you can use conditional formatting to display cells with a particular format based on common numerical rankings. The Top/Bottom Rules command has options to format the top or bottom number of items or a percentage. It can also distinguish values above or below average.

1. Select cells B6:H10. On the Home tab in the Styles group, click the Conditional Formatting button .

2. Choose **Top/Bottom Rules** and then **Top 10 Items**. The Top 10 Items dialog box allows you to set how many and which format.

Figure 8-8
Setting top/
bottom conditional
formatting
**CookieCrunch.xlsx
PieSales sheet**

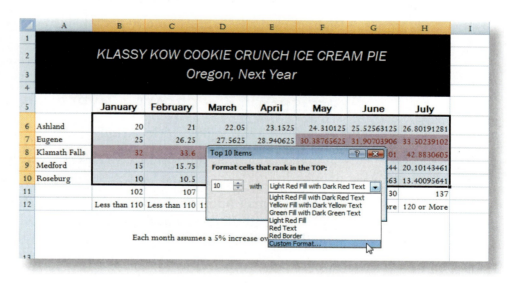

3. Click the arrow next to the **With** box and choose **Custom Format**. The Format Cells dialog box opens. You cannot change the font, but you can change the style, color, fill, and borders.

4. Choose **Bold Italic** on the **Font** tab.

5. Click the **Fill** tab. Choose a medium gray color and click **OK**.

6. Click **OK**. Click a cell away from the values to better see the formatting.

7. Select cells B6:H10. Click the Conditional Formatting button and choose **Manage Rules**.

8. Click **Edit Rule**. The Edit Formatting Rule dialog box opens.

9. Click **Format**. Set the font to be bold, but not italic. Click **OK** to return to your worksheet.

10. Save the workbook as *[your initials]*8-12 in your Lesson 8 folder.

Creating a Hyperlink

A *hyperlink* is a clickable object or text that, when clicked, displays another file, opens another program, shows a Web page, or displays an e-mail address. A hyperlink is a shortcut to files on your computer, your network, or the World Wide Web. As you insert hyperlinks in your work, Excel keeps a list of the addresses in the Insert Hyperlink dialog box. You can key a new entry or choose an existing link from the list.

A text hyperlink is shown in color and is underlined. There are several ways to add a hyperlink to your worksheet:

- Click the Hyperlink button on the **Insert** tab.

- Right-click the cell and choose **Hyperlink** from the shortcut menu.

- Press Ctrl + K.

Exercise 8-13   CREATE A HYPERLINK

1. Click cell A16 and click the **Insert** tab.

2. Click the Hyperlink button . The Insert Hyperlink dialog box opens.

3. Click the **E-mail Address** button in the **Link to** bar. Key **YourE-MailAddress** in the **E-mail address** text box. Excel adds **mailto:** for e-mail addresses and shadows your address in the **Text to display** box.

4. Drag to select the address in the **Text to display** box.

5. Key **Click here to contact our office.**

6. Click the **ScreenTip** button. Key **Oregon Shops Only**. Click **OK**.

Figure 8-9
Insert Hyperlink
dialog box
8-12.xlsx
PieSales sheet

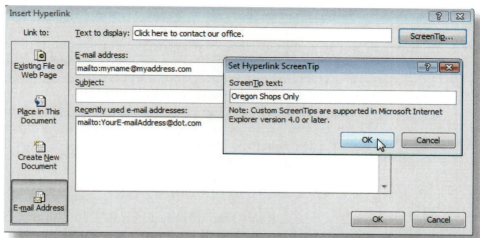

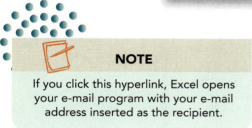

7. Click **OK** again. Hyperlink text appears in color and is underlined. Hyperlink text is styled by the document theme, but its font and color are not shown in any galleries.

8. Position the mouse pointer on cell A16 to see the ScreenTip.

Figure 8-10
Hyperlink and
ScreenTip
8-12.xlsx
PieSales sheet

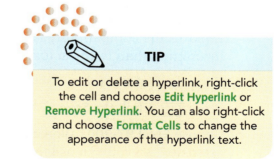

9. Press Ctrl+Home. Save the workbook as *[your initials]*8-13 in your folder.

Exercise 8-14   RUN THE COMPATIBILITY CHECKER

If you work with people who use previous versions of Excel, you can save your work in an appropriate format for them. Two formats that are fairly common are *XLS* (earlier Excel version) and CSV (comma-separated values).

Before saving a workbook as an XLS file, you can determine if any of its elements won't be effective or visible in the previous version.

CSV files are simple text files with commas to separate the columns. CSV files generally do not include any type of formatting. Many software applications, including Word, can open a CSV file.

1. Click the Microsoft Office Button 🪟 and hover over **Prepare**.

2. Choose **Run Compatibility Checker**. The dialog box opens and shows which features will not be functional in the earlier Excel file. Although earlier versions of Excel do have conditional formatting, they do not include all the subtleties of this version.

Figure 8-11
Compatibility
Checker dialog box
8-13.xlsx
PieSales sheet

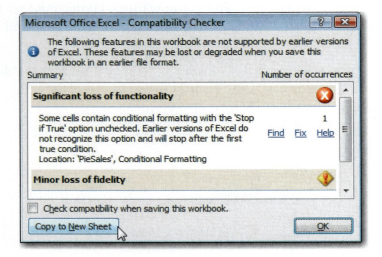

3. Click **Copy to New Sheet**. This creates a documentation sheet that explains the compatibility issues. These issues are more related to formatting than to the actual data.

4. Click the **PieSales** tab.

5. Press F12. Click the **Save as type** arrow.

6. Choose **Excel 97-2003 Workbook**. This workbook will have the **xls** extension, so you can use the same name.

7. Click **Save**. The Compatibility Checker runs automatically when you choose this file type.

8. Click **Continue**. The file has been saved. To really see the difference, you need to open the **.xls** file in an earlier version of Excel.

9. Press F12. Click the **Save as type** arrow.

10. Choose **CSV(Comma delimited)** for a different format. The filename is the same, but the workbook will have the **csv** filename extension.

11. Click **Save**. A message box alerts you that the second sheet will not be included.

12. Click **OK**. There are more problems in converting the file to this format.

Figure 8-12
Message box about converting file
8-13.xlsx
PieSales sheet

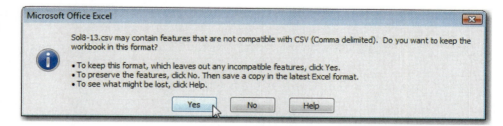

13. Click **Yes**. The file is saved.

14. Close the workbook without saving.

Using Online Help

Excel is a *mail-enabled* program, which means you can e-mail a workbook to a coworker from within Excel.

USE HELP TO LEARN ABOUT EXCEL'S E-MAIL CAPABILITIES

1. In a new workbook, click the Microsoft Office Excel Help button.

2. In the Search box, key **e-mail** and press Enter. Find and review topics about sending a workbook in e-mail.

3. Close the Help window when you are finished reading about e-mail.

Lesson 8 Summary

- Use the INT function to display a value with no decimal positions.
- The ROUND function adjusts a value up or down, depending on how many digits you use for rounding. It can round to the left or right of the decimal point.
- Excel uses a serial number system for dates and times. This allows it to make date and time calculations.

- In most date and time calculations, you need to convert the results to the proper format. This may require additional arithmetic to change days to years or fractional days to hours.

- You can hide a worksheet so that its tab is not visible.

- A nested function is a function used as an argument for another function.

- The Conditional Formatting command includes a Top/Bottom Rules setting that formats the highest or lowest values or percentages in a range.

- Hyperlinks enable you to jump to other files, e-mail addresses, or Web sites.

- Workbooks can be saved in a variety of file formats for exchanging data with others. These include CSV text files and earlier versions of Excel.

- The Compatibility Checker scans a workbook before it is saved as an earlier Excel file. It notes features and commands that will not work in the earlier version.

LESSON 8		Command Summary	
Feature	**Button**	**Task Path**	**Keyboard**
Compatibility Checker		Microsoft Office, Prepare	
CSV file		Microsoft Office, Save As	F12
Hide sheet	Format ▾	Home, Cells, Format, Hide & Unhide	
Insert hyperlink	Hyperlink	Insert, Links	Ctrl + K
Top/Bottom Rule	Conditional Formatting ▾	Home, Cells, Conditional Formatting	
Unhide sheet	Format ▾	Home, Cells, Format, Hide & Unhide	
XLS file		Microsoft Office, Save As	F12

Concepts Review

True/False Questions

Each of the following statements is either true or false. Indicate your choice by circling T or F.

T   F   1. The INT and ROUND functions use the same arguments.

T   F   2. An integer is a whole number, a nondecimal number.

T   F   3. Excel uses a serial number system for dates.

T   F   4. A nested function is placed in the cell below the first formula.

T   F   5. You can hide a worksheet in a workbook.

T   F   6. A hyperlink is a blinking cell with a formula.

T   F   7. An XLS file has all the same features and functions as an XLSX file.

T   F   8. To convert a fraction of a day to hours, multiply by 365.25.

Short Answer Questions

Write the correct answer in the space provided.

1. What is the term used to describe a function inside a function?

_____

2. What would this function display in the cell =INT(3.5643)?

_____

3. What button, when clicked, reveals the Top/Bottom Rules command?

_____

4. What does a hyperlink do?

_____

5. Which function inserts the current date?

_____

6. How can you convert days into years?

_____

7. How would Excel display this value =ROUND(1.567,2) in the cell?

_____

8. Name two functions that are often used in nested formulas.

_____

Critical Thinking

Answer these questions on a separate page. There are no right or wrong answers. Support your answers with examples from your own experience, if possible.

1. How would you determine the number of days until Christmas?

2. Which function do you think has more value in business use: INT or ROUND? Why?

Skills Review

Exercise 8-15

Use the INT and ROUND functions.

1. Open **Miles&Bulk** and save it in your Lesson 8 folder as *[your initials]***8-15**.

2. On the **DeliveryMiles** sheet, format cell A1 as 18-point Calibri. Make the labels in row 3 bold. Then make all three columns **27.86 (200 pixels)** wide.

REVIEW

Drag across three column headings to select them and then set the width.

3. Use the INT function by following these steps:

   a. Key **=int** in cell C4 and press Tab.

   b. Click cell B4 and press Enter.

   c. Copy the formula in cell C4 to cells C5:C8.

4. Format rows 3:8 each **22.50 (30 pixels)** high.

5. Insert a column at column A. Apply a double-line **Outline** border to cells A2:E9. Right-align cells B3 and C3. Apply a dotted middle horizontal and bottom border to cells B3:D8.

6. Move the label in cell B1 to cell A1 and center it across the appropriate selection of cells. Set landscape orientation and horizontal centering. Add a footer.

7. On the **BulkCosts** sheet, click cell C6. Key = and click cell B6. Press F4 three times to make the column reference absolute. Key * and click cell C5. Press F4 two times to make the row reference absolute. Press Enter.

8. Copy the formula in cell C6 to cells C7:E14.

9. Use the ROUND function by following these steps:

   a. Copy cells A6:B14 to cells A19:A27. Copy cells C5:E5 to cells C18:E18.

   b. Click cell C19 and click the **Formulas** tab.

   c. Click the Math & Trig button  and choose **ROUND**.

   d. Click cell C6 for the **Number** box. Click in the **Num_digits** box and key **0**. Click **OK**.

   e. Copy the formula in cell C19 to cells C20:E27.

10. Format cells C6:E14 and cells C19:E27 as **Accounting**. Apply **Tan, Background 2** fill to every other row, starting at rows 6 and 19.

11. Center the main labels across the data and center the page horizontally.

12. Add a header using a 9-point font for each section.

13. Prepare and submit your work. Save and close the workbook.

NOTE

The formula multiplies the cost per unit by a quantity of 10500 units.

Exercise 8-16

Use date and time arithmetic.

1. Open **PTWorkers** and save it as *[your initials]*8-16 in your Lesson 8 folder.

2. On the **Status** sheet, key **=today()** in cell A20. Edit cell A5 to show your first and last name.

3. Use date arithmetic by following these steps:

   a. Click cell C4 and key **=** to start the formula.

   b. Click cell A20 and press F4.

   c. Key **–** and click cell B4. Press Enter.

   d. Click cell C4 and press Ctrl+1. Choose **Number** as the **Category** and use 2 decimal places. Click **OK**.

   e. Copy the formula in cell C4 to cells C5:C8.

   f. Click cell D4, key **=(**, and click cell A20. Press F4.

   g. Key **–** and click cell B4. Key **)/365.25** and press Enter.

   h. Format cell D4 as **Number** with 2 decimal places.

   i. Copy the formula in cell D4 to cells D5:D8.

NOTE

Subtract the hire date from today to determine how long an employee has worked at the shop.

REVIEW

The subtraction is enclosed in parentheses, so it is calculated first.

4. Format cells D4:D8 as 12-point Calibri.

5. Insert a column at column A and a row at row 1. Set an **Outline** border for cells A1:F10. Set dashed middle horizontal and bottom borders for cells B5:E9.

6. Select cells B2:E3 and use **Center Across Selection**. Right-align the labels in row 4.

7. Click the Microsoft Office Button and hover at **Print**. Choose **Print Preview**. Click to select **Show Margins**. Drag the left margin marker to set a 1-inch margin.

8. On the **PartTimeHours** sheet, replace Tom Santana's name (C6 and C12) with your first and last name.

9. Use time arithmetic by following these steps:

    a. Click cell D5, key **=(**, and click cell C5.

    b. Key **–** and click cell B5.

    c. Key **)*24** and press Enter.

    d. Copy the formula in cell D5 to cells D6:D15.

> **NOTE**
>
> Subtract the start time from the finish time to determine hours worked.

10. Center the labels in cells A1:A2 across the data.

11. Click the Microsoft Office Button and choose **Excel Options**. On the Advanced pane, click to deselect **Show a zero in cells that have zero value** in the **Display options for this worksheet** group. Click **OK**.

> **TIP**
>
> You can set a worksheet to show or hide zeros.

12. Press Ctrl+P and then press Alt+W. Click to select **Show Margins**. Drag the left margin marker to set a 1.50-inch margin.

13. Prepare and submit your work. Save and close the workbook.

Exercise 8-17

Use ROUND. Create nested functions.

1. Open **CASupplies**. Save it in your Lesson 8 folder as *[your initials]*8-17. Change to the **Flow** document theme.

2. Use ROUND and create a nested function by following these steps:

    a. Click cell B18. Click the **Formulas** tab. Click the Math & Trig button 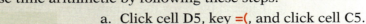 and choose **ROUND**.

    b. In the **Number** argument box, click the arrow with the **Name Box** and choose **AVERAGE** again. The suggested range is B4:B17 for **Number1**.

    c. Click cell B4 and drag to select cells B4:D17 as the **Number1**.

    d. In the formula bar, click anywhere in **ROUND**.

    e. Click in the **Num_digits** box and key **0**. Click **OK**.

> **NOTE**
>
> If AVERAGE is not in the Name Box list, click **More Functions** and find it in the Statistical or Most Recently Used category.

3. Use ROUND and key a nested function by following these steps:

    a. Click cell B19. Key **=rou** and press Tab.

    b. Key **aver** and press Tab to start the nested function.

    c. Select cells E4:E17 and key a comma to separate the arguments.

    d. Select cells F4:F17 and key **)** to close the **AVERAGE** function.

    e. Key **,** to start the **Num_digits** argument.

    f. Key **0)** to complete the **ROUND** function. Press Enter.

4. Use either method to determine the average number of sundae cups ordered (columns G:I).

5. Format cells A1:A2 as 18-point Calibri. Format the labels in row 3 as Constantia 10-point. Apply **Comma Style** with 0 decimal places to all values.

6. Select the cells for cones ordered and apply conditional formatting that shows the top five values in bold text with gray fill.

7. Click the **Page Layout** tab and the Dialog Box Launcher in the **Page Setup** group. On the **Page** tab, choose **Landscape** and **Fit to** 1 page wide by 1 page tall. On the **Header/Footer** tab, click **Custom Footer**. Prepare a footer.

8. Prepare and submit your work. Save and close the workbook.

Exercise 8-18

Insert a hyperlink.

1. Open **CACount** and save it as *[your initials]8-18* in your Lesson 8 folder.

2. Insert a hyperlink by following these steps:

   a. Right-click cell G1 and choose **Hyperlink**.

   b. Click in the **Text to display** box and key **Show Supplies Sheet**.

   c. Click the **Existing File or Web Page** in the **Link to** list.

   d. Find **CASupplies**, click the filename, and click **OK**.

3. On the Home tab, click the Format button . Choose **Hide & Unhide** and then **Unhide Sheet**. Click **CustCount (2)** in the list and click **OK**. Repeat these steps to unhide **CustCount (3)**.

4. Add the same hyperlink to each of these sheets.

5. Group the sheets, right-click the column B heading, and hide it.

NOTE

This hyperlink will open a file. You cannot insert a hyperlink on grouped sheets.

6. Click the **Page Layout** tab and open the **Page Setup** dialog box. Set landscape orientation. Add a header from this dialog box.

7. Prepare and submit your work. Save and close the workbook.

Lesson Applications

Exercise 8-19

Use date arithmetic. Create a nested function.

1. Open **PastDue** and save it as *[your initials]*8-19.

2. Select cells C4:C15. Replace all occurrences of "2005" with the current year. If, after replacing, some dates are in the future, change those cells to the same date but last year.

TIP

You can limit a Find and Replace task to selected cells.

NOTE

Some customers might be very late, and some might show a negative number of days, meaning bills are not yet due.

NOTE

Headings and Gridlines are options on the Page Layout tab as well as on the Sheet tab in the Page Setup dialog box.

3. In cell D4, key a formula to compute the due date 30 days after the invoice date. Copy the formula.

4. In cell E4, use a formula to subtract cell D4 from today. Format the result with no decimal places and negative numbers in red with no parentheses and no minus sign. You may not have negative numbers at this point. Copy the formula.

5. In cell F4, create an IF formula. The first logical test is that cell E4 be greater than 120 days. If this is so, the **Value_if_true** is **Over 120**. As the **Value_if_false**, nest another IF function. The logical test for the second IF function is that cell E4 be greater than 60. The **Value_if_true** for this IF statement is **Over 60**. The **Value_if_false** entry for the second IF statement is **Acceptable**. Right-align the results, and copy the formula.

6. Add a footer. Set a left margin to place the sheet more centered on the page.

7. Make a copy of the sheet. Hide columns A:C and display the formulas. Set this sheet to print **Headings**.

8. Prepare and submit your work. Save and close the workbook.

Exercise 8-20

Use time arithmetic.

1. Create a new workbook and save it as *[your initials]*8-20.

2. Choose the **Urban** document theme. In cell A1, key **Klassy Kow Parkland Shop**. Key **Part-Time Hours** in cell A2.

NOTE

When the time is on the hour, you do not need to key the colon or the zeros. Excel inserts them and capitalizes AM and PM.

3. In cell B3:D3, key the following labels.

   Starting Time   **Ending Time**   **Hours Worked**

4. In cell A4, key **Monday**.

5. Key the data shown in the figure below.

Figure 8-13

	A	B	C
5	Keiko Yang	11 am	8:30 pm
6	Eugene Sanchez	12 pm	10 pm
7	Millie Hanes	9:30 am	4 pm
8	Michael Bianciotto	10 am	5:30 pm
9	Aneta Monroe	2 pm	10 pm

REVIEW

Convert a fraction of a day to hours by multiplying by 24.

6. In cell D5, key a formula to determine hours worked. Format the result as a **Number** with two decimal places. Copy the formula.

7. Format the sheet in an attractive, easy-to-read style. Add a header.

8. Prepare and submit your work. Save and close the workbook.

Exercise 8-21

Use date arithmetic. Use the INT function.

1. Create a new workbook and save it as *[your initials]*8-21. Set the **Metro** document theme.

2. Key **Klassy Kow New Employees** in cell A1. Key **Birthday and Age** in cell A2.

3. Key these labels in cells A3:C3.

   Name   **Birthday**   **Age**

4. In cells A4:A10, key the first and last names of six persons. Use classmates' or family members' names, or create new names.

5. Key birth dates in column B for each of your employees. Format the birthdays in a date format of your choice.

6. Key a formula that determines the person's age as an integer.

7. Format your worksheet in a professional manner. Add a header or footer.

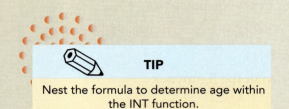

TIP

Nest the formula to determine age within the INT function.

8. Copy the worksheet to prepare a formula sheet.

9. Prepare and submit your work. Save and close the workbook.

Exercise 8-22 ◆ Challenge Yourself

Create a nested function.

A nested IF statement in this worksheet determines the state with the maximum value for each product.

1. Open **JulyDrinks**. Save it as *[your initials]*8-22.

2. In cell G5, start an IF function. Click cell B5 for the **Logical_test**, key **=** after **B5**, and nest the **MAX** function after the equal sign. Select cells B5:E5 as **Number1** for the MAX function.

NOTE

Do not include the Totals column as you check for the highest sales.

3. Click anywhere in the word **IF** in the formula bar. Key **California** in the **Value_if_true** box. Your function states that "California" will be displayed in cell G5 if the value in cell B5 is the maximum value in the range B5:E5.

4. In the **Value_if_false** box, nest a second **IF** function. For the **Logical_test**, click cell C5, key **=** after **C5**, and nest the **MAX** function with cells B5:E5 as **Number1**. If California is not the maximum value, the function will test if cell C5 (Washington) is the maximum.

5. Click in the second occurrence of **IF** in the formula bar. In the **Value_if_true** box, key **Washington**. "Washington" will be shown in cell G5 if the value in cell C5 is the maximum value in the range B5:E5.

NOTE

The structure of the nested IF function does not require a logical test for the Nevada value.

6. In the **Value_if_false** box, nest a third **IF** function. The **Logical_test** is **D5 =MAX(B5:E5)**. Click in the third occurrence of **IF**, and key **Oregon** in the **Value_if_true** box.

7. In the **Value_if_false** box, key **Nevada**. If the value in cell B5, C5, or D5 is not the maximum value, then Nevada is. Click **OK**.

8. Center the results and copy the formula to row 9. Add a **Top and Double Bottom** border to cells B10:F10.

9. Select cells B5:E5 and set a conditional formatting top/bottom rule to show the largest value in bold. Repeat this for each item.

10. Set the page to be horizontally centered. Add a footer.

11. Copy the worksheet and display the formulas. Hide rows 1:3 and fit the columns to the visible data. Remove the horizontal centering, and fit this sheet to one landscape page.

12. Prepare and submit your work. Save and close the workbook.

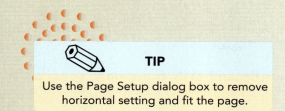

TIP

Use the Page Setup dialog box to remove horizontal setting and fit the page.

On Your Own

In these exercises you work on your own, as you would in a real-life work environment. Use the skills you've learned to accomplish the task—and be creative.

Exercise 8-23

In a new workbook, key your name and the names of three family members in a column. In the next column, key birth dates for this year for each person. In the third column, calculate the number of days until the person's next birthday. Select a document theme and use your own format choices to make the worksheet attractive. Add a footer. Save the workbook as *[your initials]*8-23. Prepare and submit your work.

Exercise 8-24

Open **PerfRating** and review the nested IF function in column E to determine how an increase is calculated. Make a copy of the sheet and delete the contents of column E and re-create the nested IF function. Format the sheet in a professional way. Add a footer and save the workbook as *[your initials]*8-24. Prepare and submit your work.

Exercise 8-25

Create a new workbook with a list of 10 persons' first names in column A. In column B, key each person's height in inches, showing heights in inches. In column C, use an IF formula to show "Tall" if the person is 72 inches or more, "Average" if the person is between 63 and 71 inches, and "Short" if the person is less than 62 inches tall. Add labels and format the sheet with your own design. Add a header. Save the workbook as *[your initials]*8-25. Prepare and submit your work.

Unit 2 Applications

Unit Application 2-1

Use an absolute reference. Use the ABS and MIN functions. Apply a border.

Klassy Kow Ice Cream has a contest in which customers guess how many gumballs are in a large jar. You keep track of customers and their guesses to determine who has won. The correct count is shown in cell B4.

1. Open **Gumballs**. Save the workbook as *[your initials]*u2-1 in a folder for Unit 2.

NOTE

The ABS function calculates the absolute value of a negative number. The formula should use an absolute reference for cell B4.

2. In cell C5, key **Difference**. In cell D5, key **Lowest Difference**. Copy the format from cell D5 to the other labels in row 5.

3. In cell C6, key **=abs** to start the ABS function from the Math & Trig category. As the **Number** argument, subtract the value of cell B6 from the absolute value of cell B4. Copy the formula.

4. In cell D6, use the MIN function to determine which difference in column C is the smallest.

5. Format all values as 11-point regular Calibri with commas and no decimals.

6. Apply a double top and double bottom border to highlight the winner's name and numbers.

7. Add a footer.

8. Prepare and submit your work. Save and close the workbook.

Unit Application 2-2

Use order of precedence. Determine ages. Nest AND and IF functions.

On the customer birthday list, you need to indicate whether a customer is between 1 and 4 years old, between 5 and 10 years old, or over 10. The formula uses AND functions nested in IF functions.

1. Open **CustAge** and save the workbook as *[your initials]*u2-2.

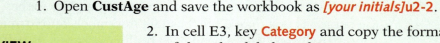

REVIEW

The IF function is in the **Logical** category.

2. In cell E3, key **Category** and copy the format from one of the other labels in this row.

3. Determine the customer's age in column D. Format the results as **Number** with two decimals.

4. In cell E4, start an IF function. For the **Logical_test**, nest **AND**. In the **Logical1** box, click cell D4 and key **>=5**. For the **Logical2** entry, set **D4<=10**. This AND function tests if a customer is between 5 and 10 years old.

5. Return to the **IF** function. For **Value_if_true**, key **Between 5 and 10**. If the results of the AND function are true, this statement will be shown.

6. For **Value_if_false**, nest another **IF** function. For the **Logical_test**, nest **AND**. For **Logical1**, use **D4>=1**. For **Logical2**, use **D4<5**. This tests if the customer is between 1 and 4 years old.

7. Return to the second **IF** function and key **Between 1 and 4** as the **Value_if_true**. For the **Value_if_false**, key **Over 10**. Click **OK**.

8. Format the results to match other labels in the row, and copy the formula. Set a horizontal left indent of 1 for the results.

TIP

Use the Mini toolbar to change the header font.

9. Center the labels in rows 1:2 across the data. Use borders, fill, row height, and column width to enhance the readability of your worksheet.

10. Change the birthday for Maureen Weinberg to one that will make her over 10 years old.

11. Add a header using a 9-point font in all sections. Make sure the sheet will fit on a portrait page.

12. Make a copy of the worksheet and name it **CustBirthdaysFormulas**. Hide column C and display the formulas. Fit this sheet to one landscape page.

13. Prepare and submit your work. Save and close the workbook.

Unit Application 2-3

Use mixed references.

TIP

Group sheets and delete them at once.

Each ice cream shop buys supplies from the San Francisco headquarters. A shop receives a discount based on the quantity ordered. You need to determine the total cost based on the quantity and the discount.

1. Open **SupplyDisc**. Rename **Sheet1** as **Discounts**. Delete **Sheet2** and **Sheet3**. Save the workbook as *[your initials]*u2-3.

2. In cell C6, multiply the quantity by the price using mixed references. Then multiply that result by 1 minus the discount (another mixed reference). You should be able to copy the formula to the rows in column C and then to the other columns.

3. Center cells C4:F4 across the data.

4. Choose a different document theme. Format all values in rows 6:14 with a floating dollar sign and two decimals. Show commas, no decimals, for the values in row 3.

5. Add a header or footer.

6. Make a formula sheet named **DiscountsFormulas**. Fit all the columns to the data and to one landscape page.

7. Prepare and submit your work. Save and close the workbook.

Unit Application 2-4 ◆ Using the Internet

Search online travel sites to determine travel times for trips from cities in the United States to cities in Canada, Mexico, China, France, and Italy (5 rows of data). For each trip, choose a departure city and a destination city (Chicago to Vancouver, Omaha to Paris). Develop your data so that at least one trip is by train and one is by car.

Prepare a worksheet that lists the departure and arrival cities and travel time. Include type of transportation. Show the current date somewhere on the sheet as well as an average travel time for your trips. Choose a document theme and use cell styles to design your work.

Add appropriate labels and a footer. Save your workbook as *[your initials]*u2-4. Prepare and submit your work.

unit 3

ENHANCING WORKSHEET APPEARANCE

Building Charts

OBJECTIVES

After completing this lesson, you will be able to:

1. View and print charts.

2. Work with chart elements.

3. Create charts.

4. Edit chart data.

5. Use images, gradients, and textures for a data series.

6. Create a combination chart.

Estimated Time: 2 hours

MCAS OBJECTIVES

In this lesson:
XL07 4.1
XL07 4.1.1
XL07 4.1.2
XL07 4.1.3
XL07 4.2
XL07 4.2.1
XL07 4.2.2
XL07 4.2.3

A *chart* is a visual representation of information in a worksheet. Charts can help you make comparisons, identify patterns, and recognize trends.

You can create a chart on the same sheet as its data or on its own sheet in the workbook. In either case, a chart is linked to the data used to create it and is updated when you edit the data.

NOTE

The workbooks you create and use in this course relate to the Case Study (see the frontmatter of the book) about Klassy Kow Ice Cream, Inc., a fictional ice cream company.

Viewing and Printing a Chart

A chart that appears on the same sheet as the data is a graphic object and can be selected, sized, moved, and edited. An object is a separate, clickable element or part of a worksheet or chart. When a workbook has objects, you can use the Selection pane to select, view, and rearrange them.

Exercise 9-1   VIEW A CHART OBJECT

When you select a chart, the Chart Tools are activated. These tools include three command tabs: the Design tab, the Layout tab, and the Format tab.

1. Open **SeptChart**. The Zoom size is set to 75% so that you can see more of the worksheet and the chart without scrolling.

2. Click in the white chart background area to select the chart. The Chart Tools command tabs are now visible. The chart is surrounded by a light frame.

3. Press [Alt] to see the KeyTips. Key **jo** to select the Chart Tools Format tab. The Current Selection group shows that the chart area is the active chart element.

4. In the **Arrange** group, click the Selection Pane button [Selection Pane]. This worksheet has a chart and a text box. The Eye button toggles the object's visibility on/off.

Figure 9-1
Chart selected in the worksheet
SeptChart.xlsx
WeeklySales sheet

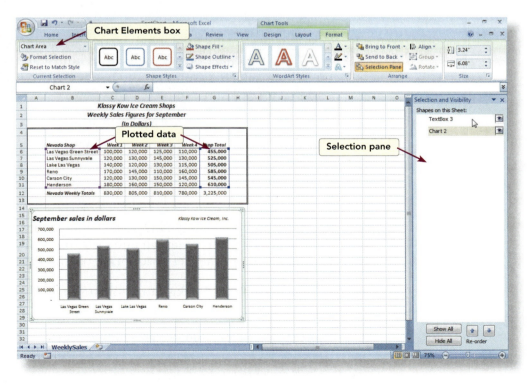

5. Click the Eye button 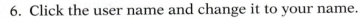 for **TextBox 3**. The text box is the company name in the top-right corner of the chart. It's hidden now.

6. Click the Eye button for **TextBox 3** again to display it.

7. Toggle the visibility of **Chart 2** on/off.

> **NOTE**
>
> In this worksheet, the text box is on top of the chart; otherwise it would be hidden by the chart's white background.

Exercise 9-2   PRINT A CHART OBJECT

1. Click cell A1 to deselect the chart. The background frame is removed from the chart.

2. Press Alt and key **n**. The Insert tab is active.

3. Key **h** to choose **Header & Footer**.

4. Click the Header button . A list of header arrangements opens.

5. Choose the second option from the bottom of the list—the user name, the page number, and the date.

6. Click the user name and change it to your name.

> **NOTE**
>
> The user name in a classroom setting is set by the class or network administrator.

7. Click cell A1 and print the sheet. The worksheet and the chart print on a single page.

8. Click in the white background chart area to select the chart.

9. Press Ctrl+P. In the **Print what** group, **Selected Chart** is chosen. Click **OK**. The chart prints by itself in landscape orientation. When you print a selected element, the header is not included, because a header is a page setting.

10. Click cell A1. Click the Normal button in the status bar.

11. Click the Close button in the **Selection & Visibility** pane.

Working with Chart Elements

A chart is composed of many clickable elements or objects. These elements are formatted by the current layout and style, but you can change each object on its own, too. Here is a brief description of Excel chart elements:

- The *chart area* is the background for the chart. It can be filled with a color or pattern.

- An *axis* is the horizontal or vertical line that encloses the data.

- The *horizontal (category) axis* is created from row or column headings in the data. A category describes what is shown in the chart.

- The *vertical (value) axis* shows the numbers on the chart. Excel creates a range of values (the *scale*) based on the data.

- An *axis title* is an optional title for the categories or values.

- The *plot area* is the rectangular area bounded by the horizontal and vertical axes.

- The *chart title* is an optional title or name for the chart.

- A *data series* is a collection of related values from the worksheet. These values are in the same column or row and translate into the columns, lines, pie slices, and so on.

- A *data point* is a single value or piece of data from the data series.

- A *data marker* is the object that represents individual values. The marker can be a bar, a column, a point on a line, or an image.

- A *legend* is an element that explains the symbols, textures, or colors used to differentiate series in the chart.

- A *gridline* is a horizontal or vertical line that extends across the plot area to make it easier to read and follow the values.

- A *tick mark* is a small line or marker on the horizontal (category) and vertical (value) axes to help in reading the values.

Figure 9-2
Excel chart elements

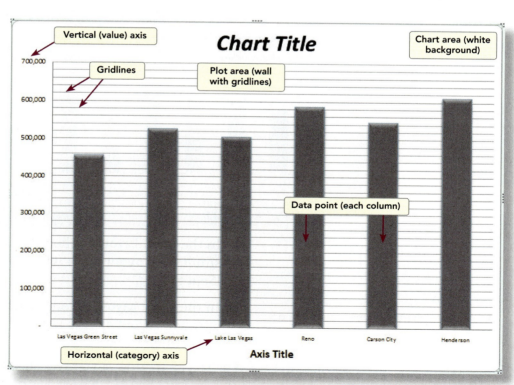

Exercise 9-3   CHANGE THE CHART LAYOUT

The Chart Tools command tabs include layout and style choices to help you build a professional-looking chart. The Chart Layouts gallery offers various arrangements of chart elements for each chart type.

1. Click the chart background. Click the **Chart Tools Design** tab.

2. In the **Chart Layouts** group, click the More button ▾. The Chart Layout gallery opens.

3. Click **Layout 2**. The chart is redesigned to show values above the columns with no values along the vertical axis.

Figure 9-3
The Chart Layouts gallery
SeptChart.xlsx
WeeklySales sheet

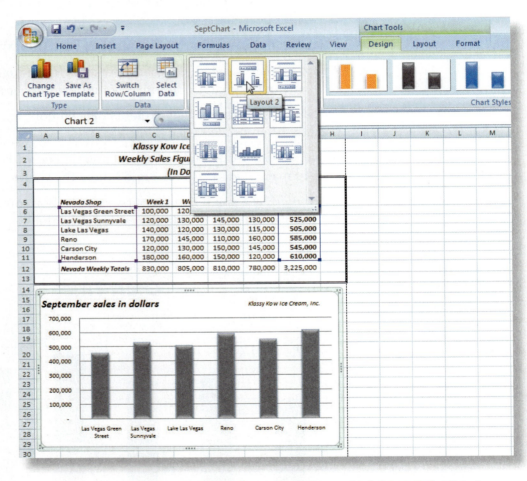

4. In the **Chart Layouts** gallery, click **Layout 3**. This is similar to Layout 1 but with a legend at the bottom (**Series 1**).

5. In the **Chart Layouts** group, click the More button ▾. Click **Layout 4**. This layout does not include a chart title.

6. Choose **Layout 3**. The chart title object is a placeholder and will need to be rekeyed (later in the lesson). There is a legend at the bottom.

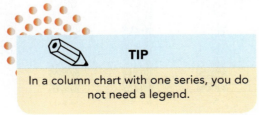

TIP

In a column chart with one series, you do not need a legend.

Exercise 9-4 CHANGE THE CHART STYLE

The Chart Styles gallery provides variations in colors and effects for chart elements using the document theme. There are many predefined styles that combine theme colors and effects.

1. In the **Chart Styles** group, click the More button. The Chart Styles gallery opens. Your chart uses Style 19, but the column colors were modified.

2. Click **Style 34**. The columns show a flat effect in a new color.

Figure 9-4
The Chart Styles gallery
SeptChart.xlsx
WeeklySales sheet

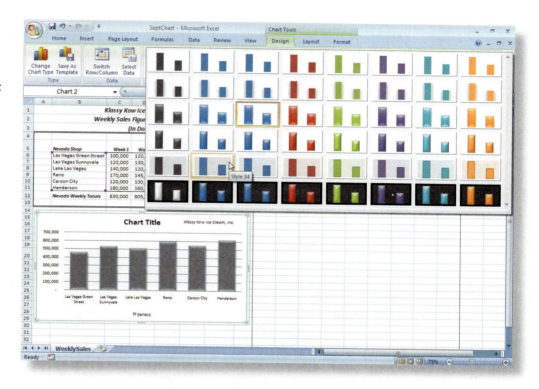

3. In the **Chart Styles** group, click the More button. Click **Style 44**. This style changes the background color, too.

4. Choose **Style 20**. The columns again have a beveled effect.

Exercise 9-5 EDIT AND FORMAT THE CHART TITLE

Chart elements show a ScreenTip when you hover over them. To edit an element, select it by pointing and clicking. When an element is selected, it shows a bounding frame and selection handles, and its name appears in the Chart Elements box on the Chart Tools Format tab. *Selection handles* are small circles, rectangles, or dots at the corners and along each border of the bounding frame. They can be used to size the element.

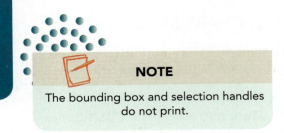

NOTE

The bounding box and selection handles do not print.

1. Click the **Chart Tools Format** tab.

2. Point at the placeholder text **Chart Title** on the chart and click. The object is selected and shows a bounding border with four selection handles. Its name appears in the Chart Elements box in the Current Selection group.

3. Point at an edge of the object to display a four-pointed arrow. This is the move pointer.

4. Drag the object left to align with the values on the vertical axis.

5. Triple-click **Chart Title**. This is placeholder text.

6. Key **Nevada sales for September**. The placeholder text is replaced.

7. Triple-click **Nevada sales for September** to select it. Point at the Mini toolbar.

8. Click the Italic button . Change the font size to 16.

Figure 9-5
Editing the chart title
SeptChart.xlsx
WeeklySales sheet

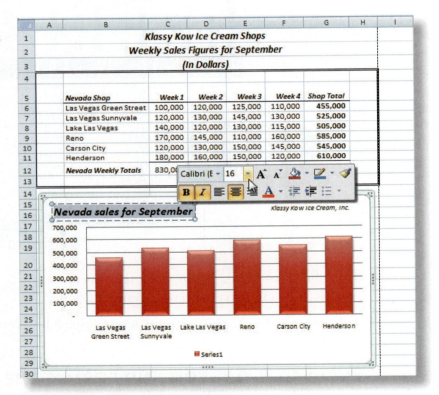

NOTE

If you accidentally select the text box with "Klassy Kow Ice Cream, Inc.," the Drawing Tools Format command tab is activated. Click away from that area in the chart background.

9. Click the white background area of the chart to deselect the title.

Exercise 9-6 SET SHAPE FILL AND EFFECTS

TIP

Many chart experts refer to the value axis as the y-axis and the category (horizontal) axis as the x-axis.

The data series in this chart are the values from column G. Each value is represented by the height of its column. The values are plotted against the value (vertical) axis, the column of numbers at the left. The category for this chart is the city name, shown along the horizontal axis.

1. Make sure the chart is selected.

2. Rest the mouse pointer on the Reno column to see its ScreenTip. It is one data point from the series.

3. Click the Reno column. The entire data series is selected, and the Chart Elements box shows **Series 1**. This is the first (and only) series in this chart.

4. In the **Shape Styles** group on the **Chart Tools Format** tab, click the More button for the **Shape Styles**. The styles include some with an outline and no fill, some with both outline and fill, and beveled and shadow styles.

Figure 9-6
Changing the shape's style
SeptChart.xlsx
WeeklySales sheet

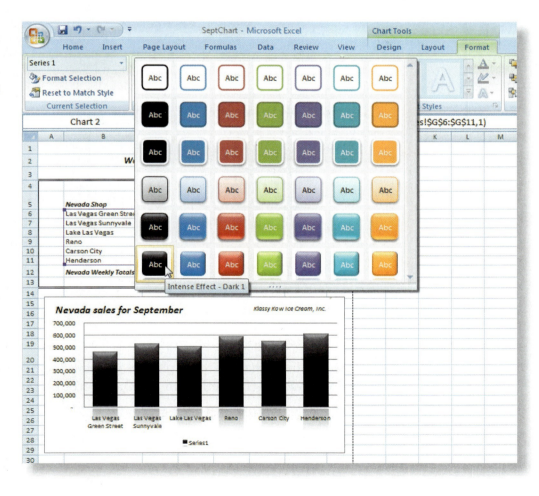

Shape Fill ▾

Shape Effects ▾

5. Choose **Intense Effect, Dark 1**. Each column now has a reflection, too.

6. In the **Shape Styles** group, click the Shape Fill button.

7. Choose **White, Background 1, Darker 35%** in the first column.

8. In the **Shape Styles** group, click the Shape Effects button. Most effects are available for this shape.

Figure 9-7
Changing the
shape's effect
**SeptChart.xlsx
WeeklySales sheet**

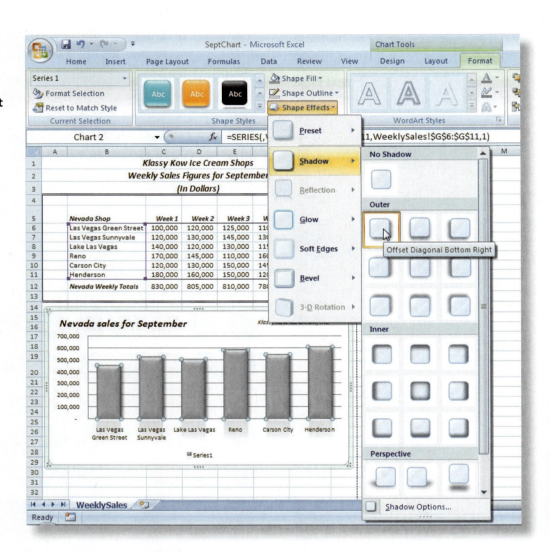

9. Hover over **Shadow** to display its gallery. Then choose **Offset Diagonal Bottom Right** (first effect in the Outer group).

10. Click the white chart background.

Exercise 9-7 SET AND FORMAT DATA LABELS

A *data label* is an optional title shown for each value. It is the value from column G in this case. The Chart Tools Layout tab provides options for setting and positioning individual chart elements.

1. Click the **Chart Tools Layout** tab.

2. Hover over the Data Labels button and read its ScreenTip. Click one of the labels.

3. Click the Data Labels button and choose **Outside End**. The value of each data point appears above its column.

4. Rest the mouse pointer on one of the data labels to see the ScreenTip.

5. Click the **Chart Tools Format** tab. Click the arrow next to the **Chart Elements** box and choose **Series 1 Data Labels**. The data labels are selected and show bounding boxes and selection handles.

6. Click the **Home** tab and change the font size to 9 points.

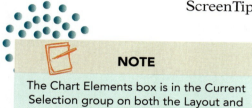

NOTE

The Chart Elements box is in the Current Selection group on both the Layout and Format command tabs.

Exercise 9-8 FORMAT THE AXES

The Horizontal (Category) Axis is the x-axis in this chart, the city names.

1. Position the mouse pointer on a city name to see its ScreenTip.

2. Click the **Chart Tools Format** tab. Click the **Chart Elements** arrow and choose **Horizontal (Category) Axis**. The city names are selected and show a bounding box and selection handles.

3. On the **Home** tab, change the font size to 8 points.

4. Click one of the values along the Vertical (Value) Axis, the y-axis, the sales in dollars.

5. Click the **Chart Tools Layout** tab. Click the Axes button. Choose **Primary Vertical Axis** and **None**. With the data labels displayed, you don't need the axis values.

6. Right-click one of the data labels (above the columns). Choose **Format Data Labels**.

7. Click **Number**. Choose **Currency** with **0** decimals and **$** as the **Symbol**. Click **Close**.

Figure 9-8
Formatted data
labels
SeptChart.xlsx
WeeklySales sheet

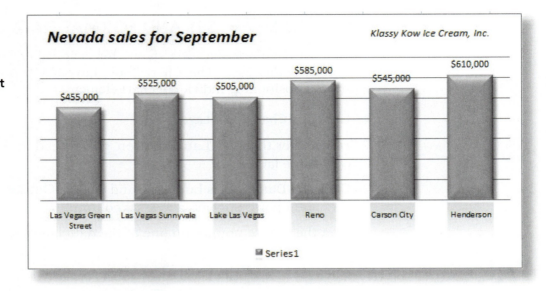

8. Click a cell in column I to better see the chart.

Exercise 9-9 FORMAT THE PLOT AND CHART AREAS

1. Click **Series 1** at the bottom of the chart. This is the legend. There is one series in this chart, the amount shown by each column.

2. Press Delete.

3. Click the **Chart Tools Format** tab. Click the **Chart Elements** arrow and choose **Plot Area**. The plot area is the background grid for the columns, currently white. It is selected.

4. In the **Current Selection** group, click the Format Selection button .

5. On the **Fill** pane, choose **No fill**. Click **Close**. The color (white) is removed but is not noticeable yet.

6. Click the **Chart Elements** arrow and choose **Chart Area**. The chart's background is selected; it is white, too.

TIP

Choosing no background color means your chart will print faster than with a white background color and look the same on white paper.

7. Click the Format Selection button.

8. On the **Fill** pane, choose **No fill**. Click **Close**. You can now see that there is no fill color.

9. Click cell A1.

10. Save the workbook as *[your initials]*9-9 in a folder for Lesson 9.

11. Close the workbook.

Creating Charts

Before you build your own chart, you must consider two questions. First, what data should you use for the chart? And, second, what type of chart is best for that data? With practice and experience, you can develop a good sense of how to identify data and choose chart types.

You can create basic chart types such as column charts, bar charts, pie charts, and line charts. You can also create specialized charts such as doughnut and radar charts. Table 9-1 describes the chart types available.

TABLE 9-1 Chart Types in Excel

Type		Definition
	Column	A column chart is the most popular chart type. Column charts show how values change over a period of time or make comparisons among items. They can be prepared with 3-D effects or stacked columns. Categories are on the horizontal axis (x), and values are on the vertical axis (y). The shape can also be a cone, a cylinder, or a pyramid.
	Line	Line charts show trends in data over a period of time. They emphasize the rate of change. 3-D effects are available. Lines can be stacked and can show markers, a symbol that indicates a single value.
	Pie	Pie charts show one data series and compare the sizes of each part of a whole. Pie charts should have fewer than six data points to be easy to interpret. A pie chart can use 3-D effects and can show exploded slices.
	Bar	Bar charts illustrate comparisons among items or show individual figures at a specific time. Bar charts can use 3-D effects and stacked bars. Categories are on the vertical axis (y). Values are on the horizontal axis (x). The shape can also be a cone, a cylinder, or a pyramid.
	Area	Area charts look like colored-in line charts. They show the rate of change and emphasize the magnitude of the change. 3-D effects are available.
	Scatter	Scatter charts are used to show relationships between two values, such as comparing additional advertising to increased sales. Scatter charts do not have a category; both axes show numbers/values.
	Stock	Stock charts are often called "high-low-close charts." They use three series of data in high, low, close order. They can also use volume as a fourth series.
	Surface	Surface charts illustrate optimum combinations of two sets of data. They show two or more series on a surface. Surface charts can use 3-D effects.
	Doughnut	Doughnut charts compare the sizes of parts. A doughnut chart has a hole in the middle. A doughnut chart shows the relative proportion of the whole. A doughnut chart can show more than one data series, with each concentric ring representing a series.
	Bubble	Bubble charts compare sets of three values. They are like scatter charts with the third value displayed as the size of the bubble. Bubble charts can be 3-D.
	Radar	Radar charts show the frequency of data relative to a center point and to other data points. There is a separate axis for each category, and each axis extends from the center. Lines connect the values in a series.

Exercise 9-10   CREATE AND EDIT A CHART SHEET

After you select values and labels, press F11 to create a chart sheet with the default chart type. It is inserted on a new sheet, and you can edit it like any chart.

1. Open **MayChart**. There is no chart yet.

2. Select cells B6:C11. This range includes the province/country category and the values.

3. Press F11. A column chart is inserted on its own sheet.

4. On the **Chart Tools Design** tab in the **Chart Layouts** group, click the More button ⬇.

5. Choose **Layout 3**. This layout includes a chart title and a legend (at the bottom).

6. Click the chart title object. Its bounding box and selection handles are visible.

7. Triple-click the placeholder text. Key **Number of Kowabungas Sold**.

8. Click any column and notice that the entire series is selected.

9. While all columns are selected, click the "British Columbia" column. It is selected alone.

10. Click the **Chart Tools Format** tab. In the **Shape Styles** group, click the Shape Fill button .

11. Choose **Red, Accent 2** in the sixth column. Only the selected column is changed.

Figure 9-9
Changing an individual column
MayChart.xlsx
Chart1 sheet

12. Click the legend at the bottom of the sheet and press Delete.

Exercise 9-11   CREATE A CHART OBJECT

A *chart object* appears on the same sheet as the data; it may also be called an *embedded chart*. You create it by choosing the chart type from the Insert command tab.

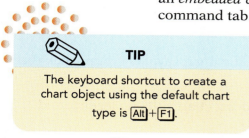

TIP

The keyboard shortcut to create a chart object using the default chart type is Alt + F1.

1. Click the **KowabungaSales** tab. Cells B6:C11 are still selected.

2. Click the **Insert** tab. The Charts group includes buttons for the most commonly used chart types.

3. Click the Pie button. You can create two- or three-dimensional charts. A ScreenTip describes each type when you hover over the icon.

Figure 9-10
Creating a pie chart
MayChart.xlsx
KowabungaSales
sheet

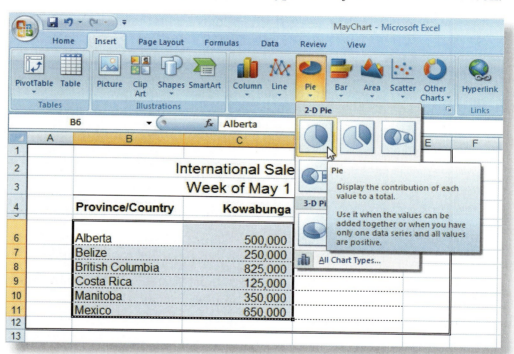

4. In the **2-D** list, choose **Pie**. The chart is on the worksheet with its data.

Exercise 9-12   MOVE AND SIZE A CHART OBJECT

The selection handles for the chart object are three dots arranged in a triangle shape on the corners. The handles are four dots arranged in a row in the middle of each edge. The move pointer is a four-pointed arrow; the sizing pointer is two-pointed.

1. Point at the top edge of the chart object to display a four-pointed arrow. Drag the chart so that its top-left corner aligns at cell A14.

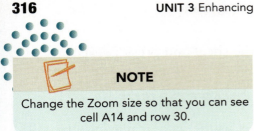

NOTE

Change the Zoom size so that you can see cell A14 and row 30.

2. Point at the bottom-right selection handle. A two-pointed sizing pointer appears.

3. Click and drag the bottom-right selection handle to cover cell E32. As you drag, the chart is made larger.

Exercise 9-13   CHANGE THE LAYOUT AND STYLES

1. Click the **Chart Tools Design** tab. In the **Chart Layouts** group, click the More button.

2. Choose **Layout 5**. This layout includes a chart title, no legend, and data labels inside the pie slices.

3. In the **Chart Styles** group, click the More button.

4. Choose **Style 17**. The slices are shown in shades of gray.

5. Click the **Chart Tools Format** tab. Make sure that the chart area is the current selection.

6. For **Shape Styles**, click the More button.

7. Hover over several different styles. Since the chart area is selected, the entire object is affected.

8. Press Esc to close the gallery without making a change.

9. Point at any pie slice, but away from the label and click.

10. For **Shape Styles**, click the More button.

11. Hover over several styles. Now the slices would be affected, not the background.

12. Press Esc to close the gallery without making a change.

13. While the slices are selected, click only the Alberta slice. You should see selection handles for just this slice.

Figure 9-11
Pie chart with a single slice selected
MayChart.xlsx
KowabungaSales
sheet

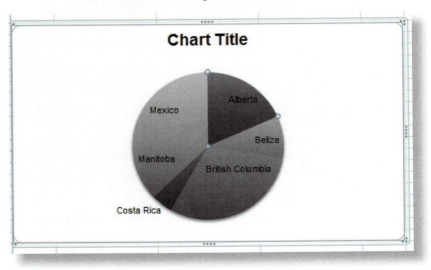

14. Click the More button 🔻 for **Shape Styles**.

15. Hover over several styles. Now just one slice would be affected.

16. Press Esc.

17. Click the chart title object.

18. Triple-click the placeholder text and key **Kowabunga Sales**.

19. Right-click the pie and choose **Format Data Labels**.

20. On the **Label Options** pane, click to select **Percentage**.

21. Click **Close**. The slices now show the name and the percentage.

Exercise 9-14   CREATE A BAR CHART SHEET

You can create a chart object and later move it to its own sheet. It is still linked to the data in the worksheet.

1. Select cells **B6:C11** and click the **Insert** tab.

2. In the **Charts** group, click the Bar button 📊.

3. In the **3-D** group, choose **Clustered Bar in 3-D**, the first icon. The chart object appears on your worksheet.

4. In the **Location** group, click the Move Chart button 📊. The Move Chart dialog box allows you to move the chart to its own sheet or to another worksheet in the workbook.

Figure 9-12
Move Chart dialog box
MayChart.xlsx
KowabungaSales
sheet

5. Choose **New sheet** and click **OK**. The chart is placed on a new sheet.

6. Click **Series 1** and press Delete. That was the legend.

7. Click the **Chart Tools Layout** tab. In the **Labels** group, click the Chart Title button 📊.

8. Choose **Above Chart**. A placeholder object is inserted.

9. Triple-click **Chart Title** and key **Comparison of Weekly Sales**.

10. Click anywhere in the side panel to deselect the chart.

Exercise 9-15   ADD GRIDLINES AND A DATA TABLE

A data table lists the values and names displayed in the chart. It is separate from the chart and appears below the horizontal axis. Gridlines appear on the plot area to make it easy to relate values to the bars or columns. Only major vertical gridlines are shown in this chart.

1. Click the white chart background to select the chart.

2. On the **Chart Tools Layout** tab, click the Gridlines button.

3. Choose **Primary Vertical Gridlines** and then choose **Major and Minor Gridlines**.

4. Click the Data Table button.

5. Choose **Show Data Table**. It appears below the chart and shows "Series 1" as the name.

6. Right-click anywhere in the data table and choose **Select Data**. The source worksheet data is active and the Select Data Source dialog box opens.

7. Click **Series 1** in the Legend Entries list and then click **Edit**. There is no series name at this point.

8. Key **$ Sales** and click **OK**. Click **OK** again. The data table shows the new series name.

Figure 9-13
Editing the series name
MayChart.xlsx
KowabungaSales
sheet

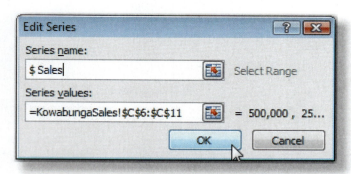

REVIEW

You can right-click a tab to rename it.

9. Name the sheet **BarChart**.

10. Save the workbook as *[your initials]9-15* in your folder.

Editing Chart Data

Because a chart is linked to its data, changes that you make in the worksheet are reflected in the chart. You can add categories or value series to your data and then to its chart.

Exercise 9-16   EDIT CHART DATA

1. Click the **KowabungaSales** tab in *[your initials]***9-15**. Notice the pie-slice size for Manitoba and its corresponding value in the worksheet.

2. Click the **BarChart** tab. Note the length of the bar for Manitoba.

3. Click the **Chart1** tab. Note the height of the Manitoba column.

4. Click the **KowabungaSales** tab.

5. Click cell C10, key **900000**, and press Enter. Notice the larger pie slice for Manitoba.

6. Click the **Chart1** tab. The height of the Manitoba column is increased.

7. Click the **BarChart** tab. Note the length of the Manitoba bar.

Exercise 9-17   ADD A DATA POINT

If you add another country and its total to the worksheet, you add a data point to the data series. If you insert the new data within the chart's current data range, it appears automatically in all charts linked to the data. If you add data below or above the chart's original source data range, you need to reset the data range for each chart.

1. On the **KowabungaSales** sheet, insert a row at row 12.

2. Key **Ontario** in cell B12. Key **1000000** in cell C12. This data is not within the existing data range for the charts.

3. Right-click the white background area for the pie chart. Choose **Select Data**. The Select Data Source dialog box opens, and a moving marquee encloses the current data range.

4. Click **Cancel**. The data range shows sizing handles at each corner.

5. Position the pointer on the bottom-right handle for cell C11. A two-pointed sizing arrow appears.

6. Drag the sizing arrow to include the Ontario information. The chart is updated when you release the mouse button.

Figure 9-14
Adding a data point
9-15.xlsx
KowabungaSales
sheet

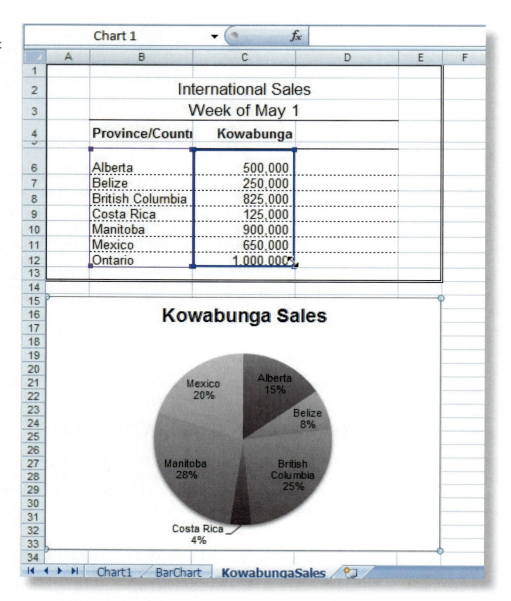

7. Click the **Chart1** tab.

8. Right-click the white chart background. Choose **Select Data**. The Select Data Source dialog box opens on top of the **KowabungaSales** tab with the current data range selected.

9. In the **Chart data range** entry box, edit the address to show **$C$12** instead of $C$11. Click **OK**. The column chart is updated to include Ontario.

Figure 9-15
Edit Data Source
dialog box
9-15.xlsx
KowabungaSales
sheet

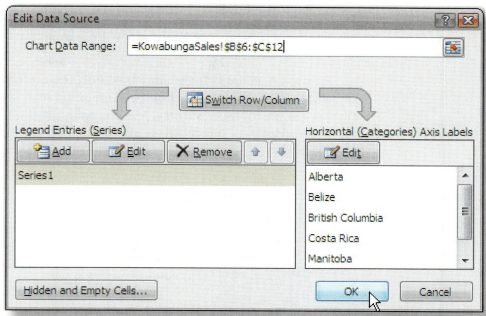

REVIEW

The dialog box collapses as you drag. It expands when you release the mouse button.

10. Click the **BarChart** tab. Right-click the white chart background.

11. Choose **Select Data**. Move the dialog box so that you can see the range.

12. Click cell B6 and drag to select cells B6:C12. Click **OK**. There is now an Ontario bar.

13. Insert a row at row 10 on the **KowabungaSales** sheet.

14. Key **Great Britain** in cell B10 and **250000** in cell C10. This data point is within the existing data range for the charts.

15. Click each sheet tab to see the Great Britain data.

Exercise 9-18 ADD AND RENAME DATA SERIES

NOTE

A pie chart has only one series.

If you add a second product to the data, you can then create a second series for the column and bar charts.

1. On the **KowabungaSales** sheet, key **KowOwow** in cell D4.

2. Key the following values in cells D6:D13:

D6	60000
D7	120000
D8	45000
D9	150000
D10	300000
D11	250000
D12	100000
D13	750000

3. Format the label and values to match the rest of the worksheet.

4. Click the **Chart1** tab. Right-click the white chart background and choose **Select Data**.

5. In the **Chart data range** entry box, edit the address to show **$B$6:d13**. Click **OK**. The column chart now shows two columns for each province/country, one for each product. The British Columbia data has a different color scheme due to your earlier change. Your colors may be different from the text figures.

Figure 9-16
Adding a data series
9-15.xlsx
KowabungaSales
sheet

REVIEW

Hover over a column to determine which one represents "Series 1."

6. Right-click any column for **Series 1** (Kowabunga). Choose **Select Data**.

7. Click **Series 1** in the Legend Entries list and click **Edit**.

8. Key **Kowabunga** and click **OK**.

9. Click **Series 2** in the list and click **Edit**. Key **KowOwow** and click **OK**.

10. Click **OK** again. Hover over several columns to view the series' names.

11. Right-click the **Kowabunga** column for British Columbia. Choose **Reset to Match Style**.

12. Click the white background.

13. On the **Chart Tools Design** tab, choose **Style 6**.

Exercise 9-19   DELETE DATA POINTS AND A DATA SERIES

1. Click the **KowabungaSales** tab.

2. Delete rows 8 and 9. The pie chart is updated.

3. Click the **BarChart** tab. Click the **Chart1** tab. The British Columbia and Costa Rica data is removed from all charts.

4. Click the **KowabungaSales** tab.

5. Delete cells D6:D11. This is an entire data series.

6. Click the **Chart1** tab. The second column (KowOwows) is gone, but the category labels appear out of alignment with the columns.

7. Right-click any column and choose **Select Data**. KowOwow is still listed as a series.

8. Click **KowOwow** in the Legend Entries list and click **Remove**.

9. Click **OK**.

NOTE

You can delete any chart object or the entire chart by selecting it and pressing ⎄Delete⎄.

Using Images, Gradients, and Textures for a Data Series

You can change from a solid color to a gradient or an image for columns, bars, pie slices, and other chart objects. Gradients and textures can be used to better distinguish bars, columns, or slices on a black-and-white printer. Images allow you to show a picture to represent the data.

You can insert an image, a gradient, or a texture by selecting the chart object and:

- Clicking the Shape Fill button [Shape Fill ▾] on the Chart Tools Format tab.

- Clicking the Format Selection button [Selection Pane] on the Chart Tools Format tab or the Chart Tools Layout tab.

- Right-clicking the object and choosing Format Data Series or Format Data Point.

Exercise 9-20   USE AN IMAGE FOR A DATA SERIES

If you want to use an image in a bar or column chart, it looks best if you use a two-dimensional chart rather than 3-D.

1. Click the **BarChart** tab. Select the chart and then click the **Chart Tools Design** tab.

2. Click the Change Chart Type button 📊. The Change Chart Type dialog box lists all the available types.

3. In the **Bar** group, choose **Clustered Bar** (first icon, first row) to change the chart to a two-dimensional chart. Click **OK**.

4. Click any bar in the chart. All the bars show selection handles.

5. Click the **Chart Tools Format** tab. Click the Format Selection button ⚙️ Format Selection. The Format Data Series dialog box opens.

6. On the **Fill** pane, choose **Picture or texture fill**.

7. In the **Insert from** group, click **File**.

8. Navigate to the folder with **Kowabunga** to find the image.

9. Choose **Kowabunga** and click **Insert**. The picture is inserted in the bars and stretched to fit the length of the bar. Move the dialog box to see.

10. In the dialog box, click to select **Stack**. The image is scaled to fit and repeat across the bars.

Figure 9-17
Inserting a picture
9-15.xlsx
BarChart sheet

11. Click **Close**.

Exercise 9-21   USE A GRADIENT FOR A DATA SERIES

A *gradient* is a blend of colors. A gradient can give a special effect to bars, columns, or pie slices in a chart. In Excel, you can build blends that use one, two, or more colors, or you can choose from preset gradients.

1. Click the **Chart1** tab.

2. Right-click any column and choose **Format Data Series**.

3. On the **Fill** pane, choose **Gradient fill**. The dialog box updates to show the related options.

4. Click the arrow for **Preset colors**. A gallery of preset color blends opens.

5. Find and click **Moss** (first tile, third row). Click **Close**.

6. Right-click any column again and choose **Format Data Series**. Click **Fill**.

7. In the **Gradient stops** group, verify that **Stop 1** is current. A *stop* is a color in a gradient and refers to a position on a color scale.

8. Click the arrow for **Color** and choose **White, Background 1**.

9. Click the arrow next to **Stop 1** and choose **Stop 2**. This will be your second color.

10. Click the arrow for **Color** and choose **Black, Text 1**.

11. Click the arrow next to **Stop 2** and choose **Stop 3**. This is a third color from the **Moss** gradient.

Figure 9-18
Building a gradient fill
9-15.xlsx
BarChart sheet

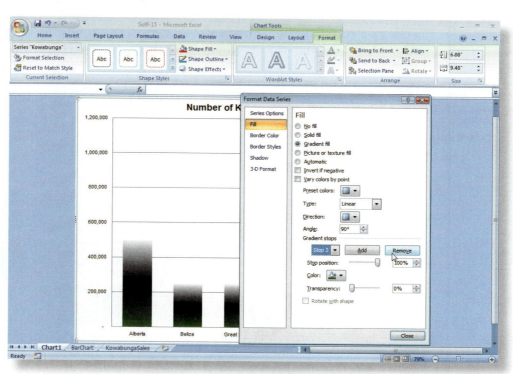

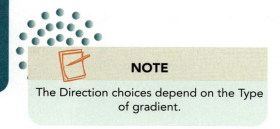

NOTE

The Direction choices depend on the Type of gradient.

12. Click **Remove** to use only two colors (two stops).

13. Click the arrow for **Direction**. Several variations of the way in which the colors blend are shown in a gallery.

14. Find and choose **Linear Up**.

15. Click **Close**.

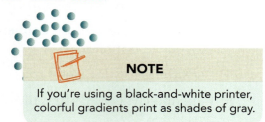

NOTE

If you're using a black-and-white printer, colorful gradients print as shades of gray.

Exercise 9-22   USE A TEXTURE FOR A DATA POINT

A *texture* is a background that appears as a grainy, nonsmooth surface.

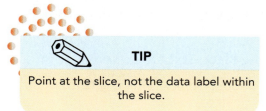

TIP

Point at the slice, not the data label within the slice.

1. Click the **KowabungaSales** tab.

2. Click the pie to select it. Click the Manitoba slice to select that slice only.

3. Right-click the slice and choose **Format Data Point**.

4. On the **Fill** pane, choose **Picture or texture fill**.

5. Click the arrow with **Texture**. A gallery of available textures opens. Notice that textures look similar to marble, wood, or canvas.

Figure 9-19
Using a texture as fill
9-15.xlsx
KowabungaSales
sheet

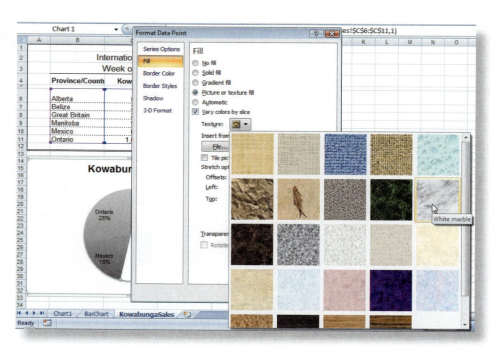

6. Hover over several texture tiles. A description appears with the name.

7. Choose **White marble**. Click **Close**.

8. Select only the Ontario slice. Click the **Chart Tools Format** tab and then click the Format Selection button .

9. On the **Fill** pane, choose **Picture or texture fill**.

10. Click the arrow with **Texture** and choose a different texture. Click **Close**.

11. Click a cell in the worksheet. Save your workbook as *[your initials]9-22* in your folder.

12. Close the workbook.

Creating a Combination Chart

A *combination chart* is a single chart that uses more than one chart type or different number scales. A combination chart has at least two series or sets of values. Some combination charts use the same chart type for each series, but a secondary number scale. A *secondary axis* is a set of axis values that is different from the first (primary) set.

Exercise 9-23 CREATE A CHART WITH TWO CHART TYPES

1. Open **ComboChart**.

2. Select cells A4:C9 and press [F11]. A new chart sheet is inserted and plots two products.

> **NOTE**
>
> The formulas in columns D and E multiply the price by the number sold.

3. On the **Chart Tools Design** tab, click the Select Data button .

4. Choose **Series 1** in the Legend Entries list and click **Edit**.

5. Key **Kowabunga** and click **OK**.

6. Edit **Series 2** to display **KowOwow** and click **OK**.

7. Click **OK** again. The legend is updated.

8. Right-click any Kowabunga bar and choose **Change Series Chart Type**.

9. In the **Line** category, choose **Line with Markers**. Click **OK**. The Kowabunga series is now a line chart.

Figure 9-20
Changing the chart type for a data series
ComboChart.xlsx
Chart1 sheet

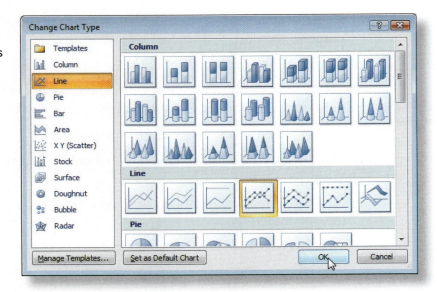

10. Right-click the line and choose **Format Data Series**.

11. On the **Line Style** pane, set the **Width** to **2 pt**.

12. On the **Line Color** pane, choose **Black Text 1** as the **Color**.

13. On the **Marker Options** pane, choose **Built-in**. Set the **Size** to **10**. Click **Close**.

14. Click the white chart background. The markers should be the same color as the line.

15. Right-click the line and choose **Format Data Series**. On the **Marker Fill** pane, choose **Solid fill**. Then set the color to match the line color.

16. On the **Marker Line Color** pane, choose **Solid fill** and the same color. Click **Close**.

17. Save the workbook as *[your initials]***9-23**.

Exercise 9-24 BUILD A CHART WITH TWO SERIES

You can show the dollar sales and the number of items sold on the same chart. These values will be two different series on the chart.

1. Click the **KowabungaSales** tab.

> **NOTE**
>
> Ranges for a chart need not be contiguous. Use Ctrl to select noncontiguous ranges.

2. Select cells A4:A9, C4:C9, and E4:E9. This represents the number of KowOwows sold and the sales dollars.

3. Click the **Insert** tab. Choose a **Clustered Column** 2-D chart.

4. Click the Move Chart button  and place the chart on its own sheet. There are two series, one for the product and one for the dollars. Both series use the same value axis, so the dollar column is disproportionately taller.

5. Right-click the legend and choose **Select Data**.

6. Change **Series 1** to display **Number Sold**.

7. Change **Series 2** to **Dollar Sales** and click **OK**. Click **OK** again.

8. On the **Chart Tools Layout** tab, click the Chart Title button . Choose **Above Chart**.

9. Edit the placeholder to show **Units and Dollars**.

Exercise 9-25   ADD A SECONDARY AXIS

Because the values are very different, you should use two axes on the chart, one for the number of items and one for the dollar amounts. To use a secondary axis, use different chart types for each data series.

1. Right-click any Dollar Sales column and choose **Change Series Chart Type**.

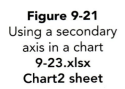

NOTE

Some chart types cannot be combined. Excel displays a message if you choose charts that cannot be combined.

2. In the **Area** category, choose **Area**. Click **OK**.

3. Right-click somewhere in the area and choose **Format Data Series**.

4. On the **Fill** pane, choose **Gradient fill**. Click the arrow with **Preset colors** and choose **Moss**. Click **Close**.

5. Right-click a Number Sold column and choose **Format Data Series**.

6. On the **Series Options** pane, choose **Secondary axis**. The selected series will be plotted on a separate value axis. Click **Close**.

Figure 9-21
Using a secondary axis in a chart
9-23.xlsx
Chart2 sheet

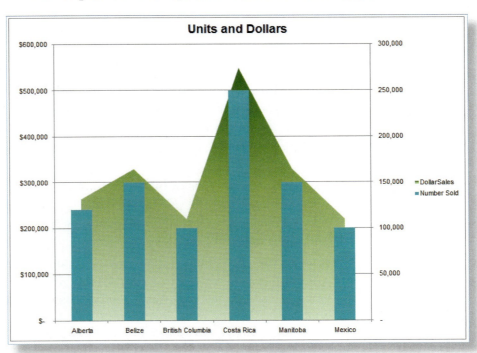

7. Right-click the legend and choose **Format Legend**.

8. On the **Legend Options** pane, choose **Bottom** and click **Close**.

9. Save the workbook as *[your initials]9-25*. Close the workbook.

Using Online Help

In addition to charts, you can use many types of images and graphics in a worksheet. Unlike charts, SmartArt graphics and shapes are usually not based on worksheet data.

USE HELP TO LEARN ABOUT GRAPHICS

1. In a new workbook, press F1.

2. Find and review topics about using SmartArt Graphics in a worksheet. Then find topics about shapes.

3. Close the Help window when you are finished reading about graphics and shapes.

Lesson 9 Summary

- Charts can be objects in a worksheet, or they can be separate chart sheets.
- A chart is linked to the data that it is plotting. If the data is edited, the chart reflects the changes.
- A chart includes many individual elements that can be formatted and edited.
- Right-click a chart element to see its shortcut menu.
- Charts show data series, which are the chart's values. A pie chart can have only one series, but other types of charts can show multiple data series.
- You can make many chart changes directly on the chart.
- If you select data and press F11, Excel creates an automatic column chart sheet.
- Excel's standard types of business charts include bar, column, line, and pie charts.
- Move a chart by selecting it and dragging it. Size a chart by dragging one of its selection handles.
- After a chart is created, you can add a data point or an entire series to it.
- Although charts typically use solid color for columns, slices, and bars, you can use images, textures, or gradients to add visual appeal to your charts.

- You can apply effects to the shapes used in a chart to include shadows, glows, bevels, and more.
- A combination chart has at least two series and uses different chart types for each series.
- Some combination charts use a single chart type but a secondary axis because the series values are disproportionate.

LESSON 9		Command Summary	
Feature	**Button**	**Task Path**	**Keyboard**
Axis, add	Axes	Chart Tools Layout, Axes	
Axis, format	Format Selection	Chart Tools Format, Current Selection	Ctrl + 1
Axis titles, add	Axis Titles	Chart Tools Format, Labels	
Chart object, create		Insert, Charts	Alt + F1
Chart sheet, create		Insert, Charts	F11
Chart title, add	Chart Title	Chart Tools Layout, Labels	
Chart type	Change Chart Type	Chart Tools Design, Type	
Data labels, add	Data Labels	Chart Tools Layout, Labels	
Data labels, format	Format Selection	Chart Tools Format, Current Selection	Ctrl + 1
Data series, edit	Select Data	Chart Tools Design, Data	
Data series, format	Format Selection	Chart Tools Format, Current Selection	Ctrl + 1
Data table, add	Data Table	Chart Tools Layout, Labels	
Legend, add	Legend	Chart Tools Layout, Labels	
Legend, format	Format Selection	Chart Tools Format, Current Selection	Ctrl + 1
Move chart	Move Chart	Chart Tools Design, Location	
Selection pane	Selection Pane	Chart Tools Format, Arrange	

Concepts Review

True/False Questions

Each of the following statements is either true or false. Indicate your choice by circling T or F.

T F 1. A chart sheet includes the related worksheet data.

T F 2. A selected chart element displays selection handles and a bounding frame.

T F 3. The markers for a line chart can be formatted separately from the line.

T F 4. Excel determines the best type of chart for your data after you select it.

T F 5. Some chart layouts do not include a chart title.

T F 6. If you insert a new item in the range used in a chart, you add a data point.

T F 7. Each slice in a pie chart represents a data series.

T F 8. The chart style includes colors for the plot area as well as other chart elements.

Short Answer Questions

Write the correct answer in the space provided.

1. What name describes a chart that appears on the worksheet with the data?

_____

2. What command tab includes the chart layout and style choices?

_____

3. What is the keyboard shortcut to create a chart sheet?

_____

4. If you have one data series with five data points, what type of chart might be best?

_____

5. What term describes a blend of colors for filling a bar or column?

_____

6. What can you use when two data series have drastically different values?

_____

7. What happens if you delete a data series used in a column chart from the worksheet?

_____

8. What is a data table?

_____

Critical Thinking

Answer these questions on a separate page. There are no right or wrong answers. Support your answers with examples from your own experience, if possible.

1. Discuss and determine what data and related charts might be developed for your school.

2. What are some advantages of using charts over tabular data? What are some pitfalls of charts?

Skills Review

Exercise 9-26

View and print a chart.

1. Open **DecChart** and save it as *[your initials]*9-26.

2. View a chart by following these steps:

    a. Click the **Page Layout** tab.

    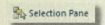

    b. Click the Selection Pane button . There are two objects on this sheet, a chart and a text box.

    c. Click **Chart 4** in the **Selection & Visibility** pane.

    REVIEW

    The chart and text box numbers are not important.

    d. Click **Text Box 2**. The bounding box and selection handles are visible; the box is beneath the chart.

    e. At the bottom of the **Selection & Visibility** pane, click the Bring Forward button. The text box must be on top of the chart to be visible over the white background.

    f. Click cell A1. The chart is deselected.

3. Print a chart object by following these steps:

   a. Close the **Selection & Visibility** pane.

   b. Insert a header that includes the user name, but change it to your name.

   c. Press Ctrl + P and click **OK**. The worksheet and chart print on the same page.

4. Prepare and submit your work. Save and close the workbook.

Exercise 9-27

Change the chart layout and style. Edit the chart title. Format axes. Add data labels.

1. Open **NovReceipts** and save it as *[your initials]*9-27. Change the Zoom size to **80%** and adjust column widths if necessary.

2. Change the chart layout and style by following these steps:

   a. Click the chart background to select the chart.

   b. Click the **Chart Tools Design** tab and change to **Layout 1**.

   c. Change to **Style 45**.

3. Edit the chart title by following these steps:

   a. Click the chart title to select it.

   b. Double-click **November** and key **December** in its place.

   c. Point at the chart title to display a four-pointed arrow. Drag the title left to align with the state names.

   d. Triple-click the title and point at the Mini toolbar. Click the Italic button 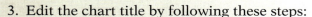 .

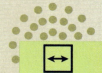

REVIEW

In editing mode, a double-click selects a word.

4. Format an axis and delete the legend by following these steps:

   a. Right-click any value on the horizontal axis. Choose **Format Axis**.

   b. On the **Axis Options** pane, click the arrow for **Display units**. Choose **Thousands** and click **Close**. Excel automatically scales the values.

   c. Click **Series 1** (the legend). Press Delete .

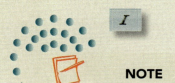

NOTE

The category axis (the state names) is vertical in this chart. The value axis is horizontal.

5. Add data labels by following these steps:

   a. Right-click any bar and choose **Add data labels**.

   b. Right-click one of the data labels. Choose **Format Data Labels**.

   c. Click **Number**. Choose **Currency** with **0** decimals and **$ English (United States)** as the **Symbol**. Click **Close**.

6. Prepare and submit your worksheet. Save and close the workbook.

Exercise 9-28

Create a chart object. Edit chart data and objects. Edit the data source.

1. Create a new workbook and save it as *[your initials]*9-28.

2. In cell A1, key **Sales of Waffle Cones**. Make it 18-point Cambria.

3. In cell A2, key **May 1**. Fill dates to reach **May 15** in cell A16.

4. Key the following values in column B:

NOTE

Excel will assume the current year in the date.

Figure 9-22

01-May	1000
02-May	1200
03-May	1000
04-May	1500
05-May	1400
06-May	1000
07-May	1200
08-May	1000
09-May	1500
10-May	1400
11-May	1400
12-May	1500
13-May	1200
14-May	1000
15-May	800

5. Create a chart object by following these steps:
   a. Select cells A2:B16 and click the **Insert** tab. Click the Line button .
   b. Choose **Line with markers** in the second row.
   c. On the **Chart Tools Design** tab, choose **Layout 3** from the Chart Layouts gallery.
   d. Point at the top edge of the chart to display a four-pointed arrow. Drag the chart so that its top-left corner aligns at cell A18.
   e. Point at the bottom-right selection handle to display a two-pointed arrow. Drag the bottom-right selection handle to cell L32.
   f. Click the **Page Layout** tab. Set landscape orientation.

6. Edit data and objects by following these steps:
   a. Edit cell B5 to show **600** and cell B12 to show **800**.
   b. Right-click the line and choose **Format Data Series**.
   c. On the **Line Style** pane in the **Width** box, set **3 pt**.

d. Click **Marker Options**. In the **Marker type** group, choose **Built-in**. Set the marker **Size** to **10**.

e. On the **Marker Fill** pane, choose **Solid fill**. Set the color to match the line.

f. On the **Marker Line Color** pane, use the same color as the line.

g. Click **Shadow**. Click the arrow for **Presets** and choose **Offset Bottom** in the **Outer** group. Click **Close**.

h. Triple-click **Chart Title** and key **Waffle Cone Sales**.

i. Click the "Series1" legend and press Delete.

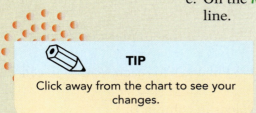

TIP

Click away from the chart to see your changes.

7. Format the axes by following these steps:

a. Click the **Chart Tools Layout** tab. Click the Axis Titles button . Choose **Primary Horizontal Axis Title** and then **Title Below Axis**.

b. Triple-click **Axis Title** and key **May 1 through May 15**.

c. Click the Axes button . Choose **Primary Horizontal Axis** and then **Show Left to Right Axis**.

d. Click the Gridlines button . Choose **Primary Vertical Gridlines** and then **Major Gridlines**.

e. Click the chart background.

f. Click the **Chart Tools Format** tab. Verify that the chart area is the selected element.

g. In the **Shape Styles** group, click the More button .

h. Choose **Subtle Effect – Dark 1**.

8. Edit the data source by following these steps:

a. Select the chart and press Ctrl+C. Click the **Sheet2** tab and press Ctrl+V.

b. On **Sheet1**, insert a row at row 17. Key **May 16** in cell A17 and **2000** in cell B17.

c. Right-click the chart on **Sheet2** and choose **Select Data**.

d. Click cell A2 and drag to select cells A2:B17. Click **OK**.

e. Triple-click the horizontal axis title and change it to **...through May 16**.

f. Click one of the dates to select them. On the **Home** tab, change the font to 9 point.

9. Prepare and submit your work. Save and close the workbook.

Exercise 9-29

Create a combination chart. Use a gradient for a data series. Format a data series. Size a chart.

1. Open **ConeSales** and save it as *[your initials]*9-29.

2. Create a combination chart by following these steps:

   a. Click the **Insert** tab.

   b. Select cells A3:C18 and click the Line button .

   c. Choose **Stacked line with markers** (second icon, second row).

   d. Click the Move Chart button 📊. Choose **New sheet** and click **OK**.

   e. Right-click the waffle cone line and choose **Change Series Chart Type**. Choose **Area** in the **Area** group and click **OK**.

   f. Click the **Chart Tools Layout** tab. Click the Chart Title button 📊. Choose **Centered Overlay Title**.

   g. Triple-click **Chart Title** and key **Waffle and Sugar Cone Sales**.

   h. Click the Gridlines button . Choose **Primary Horizontal Gridlines** and then **Major and Minor Gridlines**.

3. Use a gradient for a series by following these steps:

   a. Right-click in the area for the waffle cone series. Choose **Format Data Series**.

   b. Click **Fill** and then **Gradient fill**. Click the arrow for **Preset colors** and choose **Wheat**.

   c. Click the arrow for **Direction** and choose **Linear Up**.

   d. Click **Close**.

REVIEW

Preset gradients are preselected color blends.

4. Format a data series by following these steps:

   a. Right-click the sugar cone line and choose **Format Data Series**.

   b. Choose **Line Color** and **Solid line**. For the color, choose **Black, Text 1**.

   c. Choose **Line Style**. Set the **Width** to **3 pt**.

   d. Choose **Marker Options**. Choose **Built-in** and set the size to **10**.

   e. Choose **Marker Fill** and use the same color as the line.

   f. Choose **Marker Line Color** and set the same color. Click **Close**.

5. Size a chart by following these steps:

   a. Click the white chart background and click the **Chart Tools Format** tab.

   b. In the **Size** group, click in the **Shape Height** box and key **5.75**.

   c. Set the shape width to **8.5**.

   d. Point at an edge of the chart to display a four-pointed arrow. Drag the chart so that it appears centered on the page.

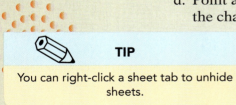

TIP

You can right-click a sheet tab to unhide sheets.

6. Right-click **Sheet1** and choose **Hide**. The data is hidden but is still used for the chart.

7. Prepare and submit your work. Save and close the workbook.

Lesson Applications

Exercise 9-30

Create a scatter chart. Edit chart objects.

A scatter chart (a "scattergram") does not have a category axis. Both axes show values. In the chart for this exercise, you show the relationship between a price decrease and increased sales.

NOTE

The worksheet uses the Aspect document theme.

1. Open **Scatter** and save it as *[your initials]*9-30.
2. Select cells B6:C11 and create a scatter chart with straight lines and markers. Move the chart to its own sheet.
3. Apply **Chart Layout 5** and **Chart Style 38**.
4. Choose a thickness for the line and a size/style for the markers. The line and markers should use **Red Accent 2** as the color.
5. Format the data labels so that there is no Y value included. Delete the legend.
6. Edit the chart title placeholder to **Percentage Price Decrease and Increased Sales**.
7. Edit the vertical axis title to **Additional Sundaes Sold** and make it 9-point Verdana. Edit the horizontal axis title to **Promotional Price Decrease** and make it 9-point.
8. Use 9-point for the numbers along each axis.
9. Prepare and submit your work.

Exercise 9-31

Create an exploded pie chart. Edit chart objects.

An exploded pie chart shows one or more of the slices detached from the rest of the pie to emphasize the slice(s). The Excel chart types show all the slices detached, but you can create your own chart with a single exploded slice.

1. Open **ExPie** and save it as *[your initials]*9-31.

2. Create a 2-D pie chart below the data. Make the chart area as wide as the worksheet data borders. Align the top-left corner near cell A12 and the lower-right corner at about cell D35.

3. Use **Chart Layout 5** and **Chart Style 1**. Key **Shake Flavor Comparison** as the chart title.

4. Format the data labels to use 9-point Calibri and place the labels in the center.

5. Format the data series to set the angle of the first slice to **90**.

6. Select the pie and then the **Butterscotch** slice. Drag the **Butterscotch** slice away from the pie, but not too far.

7. Select the pie and format the data series with a solid black border.

8. Format the **Vanilla** slice as solid white. Format each of the other slices with a color, gradient, or texture that represents the flavor.

9. Prepare and submit your work.

REVIEW

The four-pointed arrow is the move pointer; a two-pointed arrow is a sizing pointer.

Exercise 9-32

Create and format a bubble chart.

The Klassy Kow Credit Union provides savings account records for employees who contribute regularly. You are to prepare a bubble chart to demonstrate why it is best to start saving as soon as possible. A bubble chart is similar to a scatter chart with an additional series.

1. Open **BubbleChart** and save it as *[your initials]*9-32.

2. In column E, use the FV function to determine the value of an account with the interest rate shown. The original amount is the PV, the amount in the account when the savings program starts. Assume that payments are made at the beginning of the month.

REVIEW

Divide the interest rate by 12 for monthly payments.

3. Create a 3-D bubble chart using cells C6:E10. Place the chart below the data. Choose **Layout 1** and **Style 21**.

4. As the chart title, key **Growth of Your Deposits**. Delete the legend.

5. Edit the horizontal axis title to **Years in Program**. Edit the vertical axis title to **Monthly Savings**.

6. Format the values for both axes appropriately.

7. Size the chart as needed. On the **Chart Tools Format** tab, choose a shape style.

8. Prepare and submit your work.

Exercise 9-33 ◆ Challenge Yourself

Edit chart data. Create and format a stock chart.

A stock chart plots daily stock price information. In the worksheet, the prices must be in this order from left to right: high price, low price, closing price. There are several variations for this chart type with some that include the open price and volume.

1. Open **HighLow** and unhide the **Apr** worksheet. Save the workbook as *[your initials]*9-33.

NOTE

When preparing a stock chart, you should eliminate weekend and other nontrading days.

2. Review the April data and its chart. The close prices are correct. There are, however, other errors in the data. Review the data and edit it as needed.

3. There are errors in the May data. Find and correct them.

4. Create a stock chart for the May data using cells A4:D13. Move the chart to its own sheet. Use **Chart Style 29**. Delete the legend.

5. Format the vertical axis on the chart with a maximum value of 30 and a minimum value of 23.

6. Add a chart title and position it at the left. (Check the April chart.)

7. There are data points at the top and bottom tips of the vertical lines. Select each and format the markers so that they are visible.

8. Prepare and submit your work.

On Your Own

In these exercises you work on your own, as you would in a real-life work environment. Use the skills you've learned to accomplish the task—and be creative.

Exercise 9-34

In a new workbook, key your city, state, and ZIP code in cell A1. In cells A3:A12, enter the dates for the past ten days. Use a local newspaper or an Internet site to determine the high temperature for each of those days and key the values in column B. Create a line chart that plots the daily temperatures with a layout and style of your choice. Place the chart as a separate sheet. Save the workbook as *[your initials]*9-34. Prepare and submit your work.

Exercise 9-35

Build a worksheet with a doughnut chart object to show your weekly expenses. Use at least six expense categories (food, gas, entertainment, books, etc.). Add a chart title and decide whether to show labels or percentages on the segments. Save the workbook as *[your initials]*9-35. Prepare and submit your work.

Exercise 9-36

Create a worksheet that lists first names of six friends in one column and their heights in inches in a second column. Create a column chart sheet with the names on the horizontal axis and heights on the vertical axis. Use a gradient or texture fill for the columns. Make other formatting choices so that your chart is easy to interpret. Hide the worksheet. Save the workbook as *[your initials]*9-36. Prepare and submit your work.

Lesson 10

Inserting Shapes

OBJECTIVES

After completing this lesson, you will be able to:

1. Add and format a callout shape.

2. Create and format text boxes.

3. Insert basic shapes and arrows.

4. Use the Drawing Tools Format tab.

5. Use comments.

6. Insert WordArt.

MCAS OBJECTIVES

In this lesson:
XL07 4.4.3
XL07 5.1.2
XL07 5.3.1

Estimated Time: 1¾ hours

Excel has many design elements that can add visual appeal to your worksheets. A *shape* is a common, recognizable figure, form, or outline. Shapes include rectangles, flowchart symbols, stars, banners, text boxes, lines (with or without arrows), and callouts that can be sized, moved, and styled.

Shapes are placed on a draw layer. The *draw layer* is an invisible, transparent working area that is separate from and on top of worksheet data.

REVIEW

An object is a separate, clickable element in a worksheet. Shapes and charts are objects on the draw layer.

Adding and Formatting a Callout

Shapes, as well as other drawing elements, are available on the Insert tab. A *callout* is descriptive text enclosed in a shape. Callouts typically include a line or arrow that points to data or another object on the worksheet.

Exercise 10-1   ADD A CALLOUT TO A WORKSHEET

Callouts and most other shapes have the following features:

- A *bounding box*, a rectangular outline around the object.

- *Selection handles*, small circles and/or rectangles surrounding the shape's bounding box.

- An *adjustment handle*, a yellow diamond used to change the appearance and design of the shape. Each shape has its own type of adjustments; a few shapes do not have an adjustment handle.

- A *rotation handle*, a green circle that acts like a wand to rotate a shape.

1. Create a new workbook from the **K&KSales** template. The worksheet includes a comment with instructions about keying the date.

REVIEW

Copy the template file to the appropriate folder on your computer. Then click the Microsoft Office Button  and choose **New**. Click **My Templates**.

2. Right-click the **K&KSales** tab and choose **Unhide**. Choose **ComboChart** and click **OK**. The chart is incomplete because there is no data yet.

3. Unhide the **Unit&Dollars** sheet.

4. Add the following data to columns D and F on the **K&KSales** sheet. Columns H and J have formulas that will calculate as you key values.

Figure 10-1

State	Kowabunga	KowOwow
Oregon	2575	2000
Nevada	3550	3000
Washington	5600	4500
California	6500	6700

NOTE

This template has very narrow columns used as separators.

5. Click the **Insert** tab. Notice that the command buttons in the **Illustrations** group are dimmed. This template has sheet protection so that you can edit only certain cells.

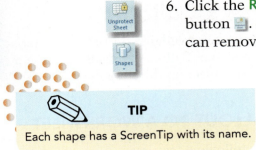

6. Click the **Review** tab. In the **Changes** group, click the Unprotect Sheet button . As long as sheet protection does not use a password, you can remove it.

7. Click the **Insert** tab. In the **Illustrations** group, click the Shapes button . Several categories of shapes are shown in the gallery.

8. In the **Callouts** group, choose **Oval Callout**, first row, third shape. The pointer changes to a thin cross.

Figure 10-2
Choosing a callout

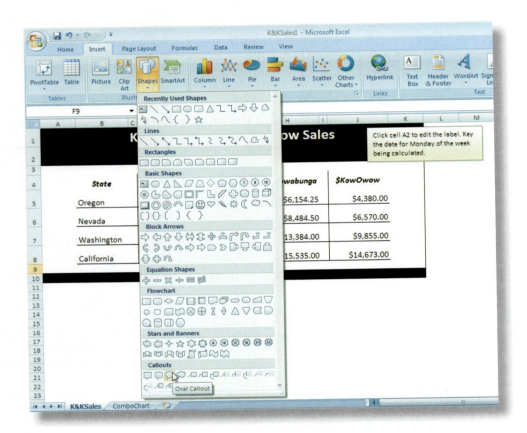

9. Click and drag to draw a rectangular shape starting near cell C12 and extending down to about cell G16. The shape appears with round and square selection handles, one adjustment handle, and a rotation handle. There is a rectangular bounding box, too. The Drawing Tools Format tab is available.

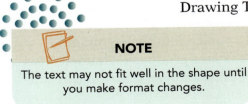

10. Key **Rolling blackouts in Nevada contributed to poor sales.** Since the shape is active, you can simply start keying your text. As you key text, the bounding frame changes to a dashed line.

Figure 10-3
New callout on the
sheet
K&KSales.xltx
K&KSales sheet

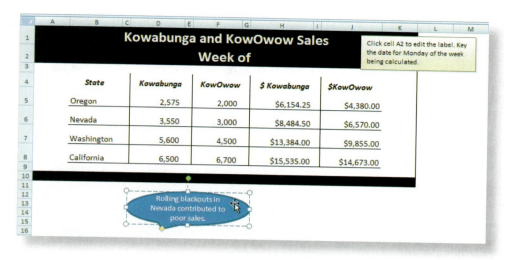

11. Click a cell in row 12. The shape is deselected.

12. Using the four-pointed arrow, click the outline of the callout. It is selected and shows a solid line as its bounding box. The solid line means the entire callout is active and can be edited.

13. Click inside the callout. The text insertion point appears, and the solid line becomes a dashed line. The dashed line boundary means you can work with the text inside the box.

14. Click a cell in row 12. The shape is deselected.

Exercise 10-2   FORMAT AND MOVE A CALLOUT

1. With the four-pointed arrow, click the outline of the callout. The shape displays the solid line boundary. This means edits will affect all text in the shape or the shape itself.

2. Click the **Home** tab. Choose **Cambria** as the font and **10** as the size. All the text in the callout changes.

3. Click inside the callout to display a text insertion point. The boundary displays a dashed line, meaning that your edits will affect only selected text.

4. Double-click **Nevada** to select the word.

Figure 10-4
Changing font of
selected text in a
callout
K&KSales.xltx
K&KSales sheet

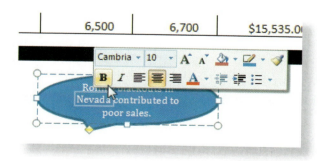

5. Click the Bold button **B** in the Mini toolbar. Only the selected text is changed.

6. Click a cell in row 12.

7. Click the outline of the callout to display the solid line outline.

8. Point at the outline and drag the shape up and toward columns K:M so that the yellow diamond adjustment handle is aligned with the Nevada row and the shape does not obscure any data.

Figure 10-5
Repositioned shape
K&KSales.xltx
K&KSales sheet

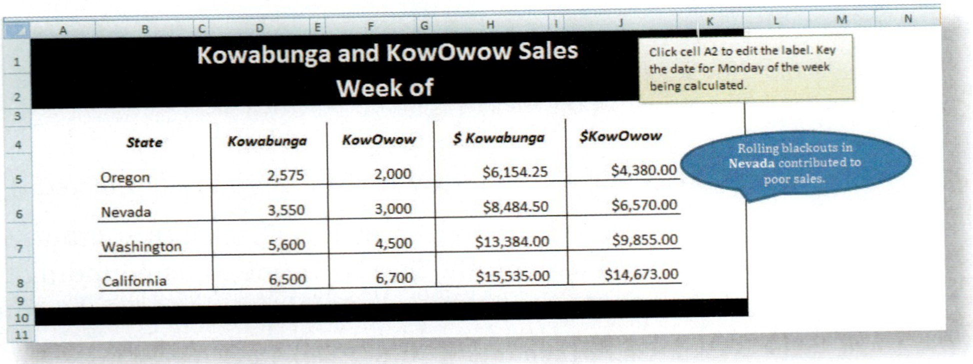

9. Click a cell in the worksheet.

Exercise 10-3   **USE THE FORMAT SHAPE DIALOG BOX**

Although you can make many changes to objects using the command tabs and galleries, you can also use the Format Shape dialog box.
You can open the Format Shape dialog box by:

- Right-clicking the shape and choosing Format Shape from the shortcut menu.

- Selecting the shape so that it displays the solid line boundary and pressing Ctrl + 1.

- Selecting the shape so that it displays the solid line boundary and clicking the Dialog Box Launcher in the Shape Styles group on the Drawing Tools Format tab.

1. Right-click the oval and choose **Format Shape**. The Format Shape dialog box includes several panes for making changes to the shape.

2. In the **Fill** pane, verify that **Solid fill** is selected.

3. Click the arrow for **Color**. Choose **White, Background 1, Darker 35%**.

4. Click **Line Color** and choose **No line**.

5. Choose **3-D Format** to open the pane. A *3-D format* applies a three-dimensional look to an object so that it appears to have a depth as well as a height and width.

6. Click the arrow for **Top** to display the gallery of bevels. A *bevel* is a 3-D effect that resembles the edge of a tabletop.

Figure 10-6
Setting a bevel in
the Format Shape
dialog box
K&KSales.xltx
K&KSales sheet

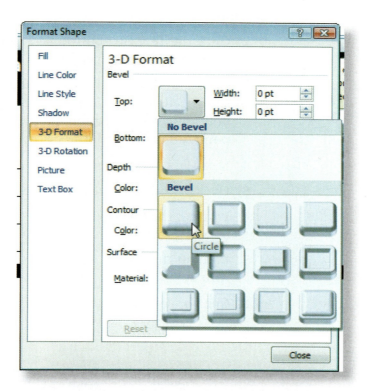

NOTE

A bevel can be displayed as the top part of the object or the bottom. Experiment to see which looks more natural.

7. Choose **Circle**. This is a preset bevel. The other settings in the dialog box enable you to create your own bevel or edit this one.

8. Click **Close**. Click a worksheet cell.

9. Save the workbook as *[your initials]*10-3 in a folder for Lesson 10.

TIP

Be careful when designing special effects on your own so that you do not use too many settings in any one format.

Excel 2007

Using Text Boxes

A *text box* is similar to a callout but does not have connector lines or arrows. You can use a text box to display titles, comments, or notes. It can be formatted with or without borders, fill colors, shadows, or 3-D effects.

Exercise 10-4   ADD A TEXT BOX

1. Click the **Insert** tab.

2. Click the Text Box button. The pointer changes to an upside-down lowercase "T."

3. Click and drag to draw a rectangular shape that spans cells H12:K13. The shape appears with the bounding box, selection handles, a text insertion point, and a dashed-line frame.

4. Key **Klassy Kow Ice Cream, Inc.**

5. Click a worksheet cell. The text box is deselected.

6. Point at the text and click. The dashed-line border appears with the insertion point.

7. Point at the border and click to display a solid line frame.

8. Click a worksheet cell.

NOTE

Whether a Ribbon button includes an icon and text is determined by your screen size and resolution. Your buttons may look slightly different from those in the text.

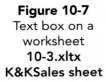

NOTE

If you draw a shape that you do not like, click to select it (it will show the solid bounding line), and press Delete. Then try again.

Figure 10-7
Text box on a worksheet
10-3.xltx
K&KSales sheet

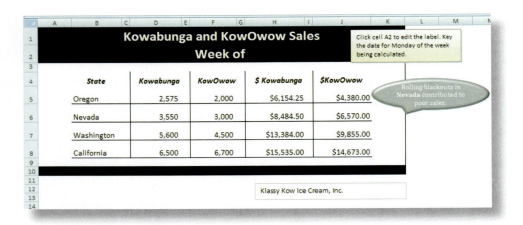

Exercise 10-5   FORMAT AND MOVE A TEXT BOX

1. Point at the text box and click to display a text insertion point.

2. Point at the text and triple-click. This selects all the text.

3. Choose **8-point Cambria** from the Mini toolbar.

4. Click the Italic button I. Click the Align Text Right button ▤.

5. Point at the bottom-left selection handle. Click and drag left until the frame fits closely to the text with the text on a single line.

6. Right-click the text box and choose **Format Shape**.

7. In the **Fill** pane, choose **No fill**.

8. Click **Line Color** and choose **No line**. Click **Close**.

9. Drag the text box with the four-pointed arrow so that it rests within row 10 at cells J10:K10. The black text is not visible on the black border.

10. Triple-click inside the text box to select all the text.

11. In the Mini toolbar, click the arrow with the Font Color button ⎍. Choose **White, Background 1**.

12. Click the text box to display the solid line border.

TIP

You can nudge a selected shape with any arrow key.

Figure 10-8
Completed text box
10-3.xltx
K&KSales sheet

$ Kowabunga	$KowOwow	
$6,154.25	$4,380.00	Rolling blackouts in Nevada contributed to poor sales.
$8,484.50	$6,570.00	
$13,384.00	$9,855.00	
$15,535.00	$14,673.00	
		Klassy Kow Ice Cream, Inc.

13. Press ⬆ or ⬇ to nudge the text box so that it appears in the middle of row 10.

Exercise 10-6   CHOOSE A SHAPE STYLE

1. Click a worksheet cell.

2. Click the **Insert** tab. Click the Text Box button ⎙.

3. Click and drag to draw a text box from cell C20:I22.

4. Key the following paragraph:

   There are two charts for this data. One shows units and one shows units and sales dollars.

5. Point at the text box border and click. Click the **Drawing Tools Format** tab.

6. In the **Shape Styles** group, click the More button ⬛. Choose **Moderate Effect, Dark 1**.

7. Rest the mouse pointer on any selection handle to size the box if the text does not fit. Fit the text box as needed.

8. Click a worksheet cell.

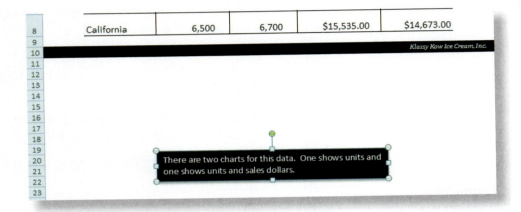

Figure 10-9
Text box with a shape style
10-3.xltx
K&KSales sheet

Inserting Basic Shapes and Arrows

The Shapes gallery includes several categories of common shapes. The Basic Shapes group includes a variety of geometric shapes, a sun, a moon, a smiley face, and more. The Lines group has straight, zig-zag, and wavy lines with and without arrows. There is a separate group for block-style arrows, too. Shapes with an enclosed interior can include text and display effects, fills, and outlines. Adjustment handles depend on the shape and its editability.

Exercise 10-7 ADD A SHAPE AND AN ARROW

1. On the **K&KSales** sheet, click the **Insert** tab.

2. In the **Illustrations** group, click the Shapes button ⬛.

3. In the **Basic Shapes** group, choose **Double Bracket** in the last row, first shape. The pointer changes to a thin cross.

4. Draw a rectangular shape that starts near cell B12 and extends to cell E14. The shape shows a frame, selection handles, an adjustment handle, and a rotation handle.

5. Key **The most recently opened shops are in Oregon.**

6. Triple-click the text and then click the Bold button **B** in the Mini toolbar.

7. Click the shape's outline to display the solid boundary. Then click a cell to better see the shape.

8. Click the **Insert** tab. In the **Illustrations** group, click the Shapes button 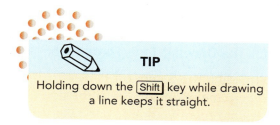. In the **Lines** group, choose **Arrow** (the second shape).

9. Point near cell C5.

10. Hold down [Shift] and drag down to draw a straight line that points to the double-bracketed shape, just below the row 10 border. Release the mouse button first, then the [Shift] key. The line with the arrow has two selection handles, no adjustment handle, and no rotation handle.

11. Click an empty cell. The line is deselected.

TIP

Holding down the [Shift] key while drawing a line keeps it straight.

Exercise 10-8 RESIZE THE NAME BOX

You can resize the Name Box and the formula bar so that you can see longer object names in full. The sizing button resembles a recessed button, between the Insert Function button f_x in the formula bar and the Name Box.

1. Using the four-pointed arrow, select the line with an arrow. The Name Box shows the name of the active shape, but the name may not be completely visible.

2. Point at the sizing button. A two-pointed horizontal arrow appears.

3. Click and drag to the right until you can see the complete shape name.

NOTE

Shapes are named according to their design and numbered in consecutive order. The number is not important.

Figure 10-10
Resizing the Name Box
10-3.xltx
K&KSales sheet

4. Using the four-pointed arrow, select the double-bracketed shape. Look at the Name Box.

5. Click an empty cell.

Exercise 10-9   **USE THE SELECTION AND VISIBILITY PANE**

The Selection and Visibility pane lists objects (shapes, images, graphics, and charts) on a worksheet. You can use the Selection and Visibility pane to select an object, hide or show it, and reset its order. Shapes, objects, and charts are on the invisible drawing layer in a stacking order. This can result in one shape covering another that is beneath it.

NOTE

The numbers for your shapes may be different from the text illustration.

1. Select the line. Click the **Drawing Tools Format** tab.

2. In the **Arrange** group, click the Selection Pane button [Selection Pane]. The pane opens on the right side of the screen. The most recently added shape is at the top of the list and is on the top of the drawing layer. The first shape inserted is at the bottom of the list and at the bottom in the stacking order.

3. In the Selection and Visibility pane, click **Oval Callout *n***. It is selected in the worksheet.

4. In the pane, click **Double Bracket *n***. It is active and selected, and the oval shape is deselected.

TIP

The Name Box is empty when more than one object is selected.

5. Hold down the ⌃Ctrl key and click **Straight Arrow Connector *n*** in the Selection and Visibility pane. Two shapes are selected.

6. Hold down ⌃Ctrl and click **Oval Callout *n***. All three shapes are selected.

Figure 10-11
Selecting multiple shapes in the Selection and Visibility pane
10-3.xltx
K&KSales sheet

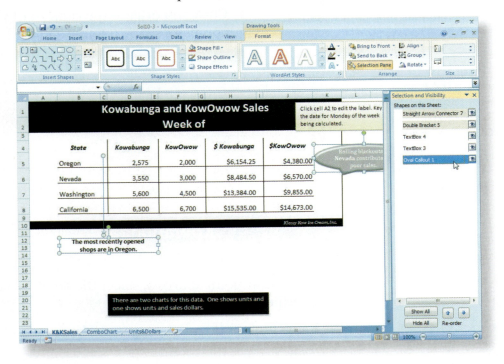

7. Click the Eye button for **Oval Callout** *n*. It is hidden.

8. Hide and then display each of the shapes.

Using the Drawing Tools Format Tab

The Drawing Tools Format tab includes commands that allow you to customize a shape in several ways. You can change it to another shape, rotate it, change colors, and more. The Drawing Tools Format tab is a contextual drawing tool that appears only when a shape is selected.

Exercise 10-10 FORMAT MULTIPLE SHAPES

1. Click a worksheet cell.

2. In the Selection and Visibility pane, click **Straight Arrow Connector** *n*.

3. Hold down Ctrl and click **Double Bracket** *n* in the pane. Both shapes are selected.

4. Click the **Drawing Tools Format** tab.

5. Click the Shape Outline button 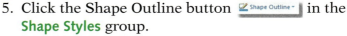 in the **Shape Styles** group.

6. Choose **Black, Text 1**.

7. Click the Shape Outline button 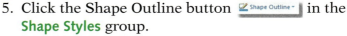 and hover over **Weight**. A list of line thicknesses is displayed.

8. Choose **1½ pt**.

NOTE

You can format multiple shapes from the Ribbon or from the Format Shape dialog box.

Exercise 10-11 COPY AND MOVE OBJECTS

1. Click the **Home** tab. Both shapes should still be selected.

2. Click the Copy button and then click the Paste button. A copy of the grouped shapes is made, on top of the original. You can see the names in the Selection and Visibility pane.

3. Point at the copied shapes to display a four-pointed arrow. Drag the copy to the left of the dollar amount in cell H5 (see Figure 10-12 on the next page).

4. Triple-click the text in the copied bracket shape.

5. Key **Kowabunga flavors have been enhanced.**

Figure 10-12
Copied shapes
10-3.xltx
K&KSales sheet

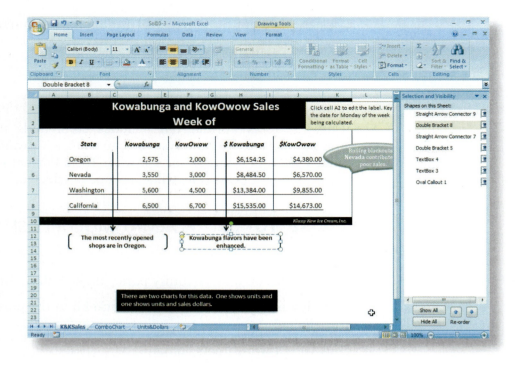

6. Click an empty cell.

Exercise 10-12   SIZE SHAPES

You can size a shape by dragging any of its selection handles. Use a corner handle to size the shape on all sides at once. Use a side handle to change only the width or height. Specific sizes can be set using the Size group on the Drawing Tools Format tab or the Size and Properties dialog box.

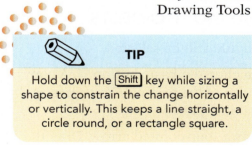

TIP

Hold down the [Shift] key while sizing a shape to constrain the change horizontally or vertically. This keeps a line straight, a circle round, or a rectangle square.

1. Click the connector line for the first bracket shape. It has two selection handles, one at each end. Its name is shaded in the Selection and Visibility pane.

2. Position the pointer on the bottom handle to display a two-pointed arrow.

3. Hold down the [Shift] key and drag the selection handle down to make the line slightly longer, until you see faint red handles around the bracket shape.

4. Release the mouse and then the [Shift] key. Red handles indicate that the objects overlap.

5. Press [Ctrl]+[Z] to undo.

6. Click the first bracket shape to show the solid boundary and eight selection handles. The corner handles are round.

7. Position the pointer on the bottom-right handle to display a two-pointed arrow.

8. Drag the selection handle down and to the right to about cell E15.

9. Click the **Drawing Tools Format** tab. In the **Size** group, note the Shape Height and Shape Width settings for the shape.

10. Click the second bracket shape to show the solid boundary.

11. In the **Size** group, click the **Shape Height** box and key the same height as the first bracket shape. Press Enter.

12. Click the **Shape Width** box and key the same width as the first bracket shape. Press Enter.

13. Click the first line, hold down Shift, and click the second line. Both lines should be selected.

14. Click the **Drawing Tools Format** tab. In the **Size** group, click the Dialog Box Launcher. The Size and Properties dialog box opens.

15. Click in the **Width** box and key **1.85**. Click **Close**. Both lines are the same length.

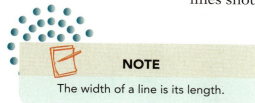

NOTE

The width of a line is its length.

Figure 10-13
Size and Properties dialog box
10-3.xltx
K&KSales sheet

Size and Properties

Size | Properties | Alt Text

Size and rotate

Height: 0"   Width: 1.85"

Rotation: 90°

Scale

Height: Width:

☐ Lock aspect ratio

☐ Relative to original picture size

Crop from

Left: Top:

Right: Bottom:

Original size

Height: Width:

Reset

Close

Exercise 10-13   ALIGN AND NUDGE SHAPES

When you use more than one drawing element, you can arrange the shapes so that they align at their top, left, right, or bottom edges. To align objects, you must select more than one object. With only one object selected, the Align commands are not available. Alignment of shapes uses each object's bounding box and selection handles.

1. Make sure both lines are selected.

2. In the **Arrange** group on the **Drawing Tools Format** tab, click the Align button . Choose **Align Top**. The top selection handles are aligned horizontally.

3. Click one bracket shape. Add the second bracket shape to the selection. Align the bracket shapes at the top.

4. Click an empty cell and then select the first line.

5. Press ← or → to nudge the line as needed away from or closer to the text. Do the same for the second line.

6. Select and nudge each of the bracket shapes as needed.

7. Click an empty cell.

Exercise 10-14   CHANGE A SHAPE

Many shapes, but not all, can be changed to another shape. The connector lines, for example, cannot be changed but the bracket shape can be.

1. Select the second bracket shape so that the solid boundary is visible.

2. Click the **Drawing Tools Format** tab. In the **Insert Shapes** group, click the Edit Shape button ⬚.

3. Choose **Change Shape**. A list of shape categories opens.

4. In the **Basic Shapes** group, find and click **Folded Corner**. The folded corner is the bottom-right one. This shape has one adjustment handle.

5. Click an empty cell.

Figure 10-14
Changing the shape
10-3.xltx
K&KSales sheet

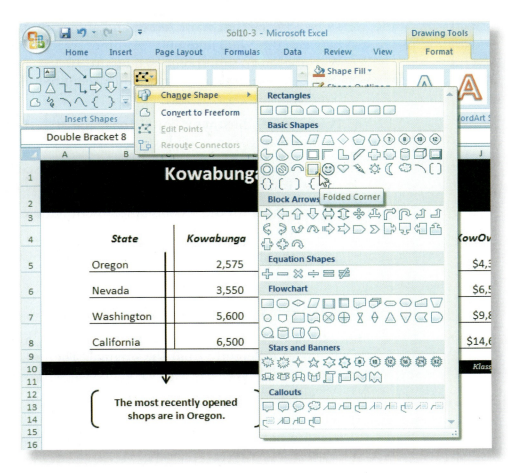

6. Change the first bracket shape to the same folded corner shape, and click an empty cell.

7. Close the Selection and Visibility pane.

Exercise 10-15   USE THE ADJUSTMENT HANDLE

Most shapes have one or more adjustment handles, shown as a yellow diamond. What an adjustment handle does depends on the shape. Some shapes do not have adjustment handles. If they don't, they can only be sized.

1. Click the **ComboChart** tab. Click the chart to select it.

2. Click the **Chart Tools Layout** tab. The **Insert** group has commands for inserting pictures, shapes, and text boxes.

3. In the **Insert** group, click the Shapes button .

4. In the **Block Arrows** group, choose **Left Arrow** in the first row, second shape.

5. Draw a shape that starts left of and above the Nevada column between the 5,000 and 6,000 gridlines, reaching to about the Washington column/point (see Figure 10-15). The shape shows a frame, selection handles, two adjustment handles, and a rotation handle.

6. Point at the adjustment handle near the arrowhead and click. The pointer changes to a solid white arrowhead.

7. Drag the adjustment handle left and right to see how it changes the shape. You cannot move this handle up or down.

8. Experiment with the second adjustment handle. It can only be moved up or down.

9. Adjust the shape to resemble the original arrow.

Exercise 10-16   ROTATE SHAPES

Many shapes have a rotation handle. This allows you to move the shape so that it angles differently from the original. The rotation handle is a small green circle. You can also specify a precise degree of rotation from the Arrange group on the Drawing Tools Format tab.

1. While the arrow is selected, place the mouse pointer over the green rotation handle and click. A circulating arrow surrounds the handle.

Figure 10-15
Ready to rotate
10-3.xltx
ComboChart sheet

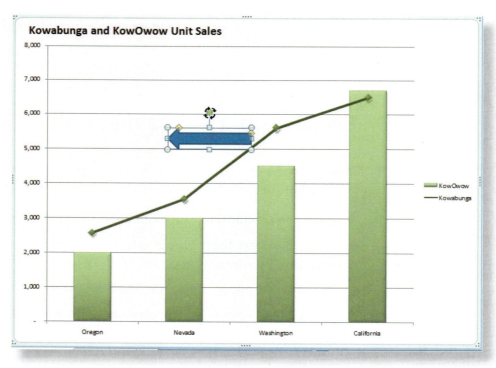

2. While holding down the mouse button, drag the mouse in any direction in a small arc. The shape rotates.

3. Click the Undo button .

4. Repeat Steps 2 and 3 several times so that you get a feel for how the rotation handle moves the shape.

5. With the shape selected and in its original position, click the **Drawing Tools Format** tab. Click the Rotate button ⬛ Rotate ▾.

6. Hover at each option and watch the shape. Live Preview shows the results before you click.

7. Click **Flip Horizontal**. The arrow now points at the Washington data.

Exercise 10-17   STYLE MULTIPLE SHAPES

1. Hold down Ctrl and point at the shape.

2. While holding down Ctrl, drag a copy of the arrow to point at the Nevada point on the line. Release the mouse button first and then Ctrl.

3. Select both arrow shapes.

4. Click the **Drawing Tools Format** tab. In the **Shapes Styles** group, click the More button ⬛ and choose **Moderate Effect, Accent 3**.

5. Click away from the chart.

6. Click the **ComboChart** tab. Hold down Ctrl and click the **Units&Dollars** tab. The sheets are grouped.

7. Right-click either tab and choose **Hide**.

8. Save the workbook as *[your initials]*10-17.

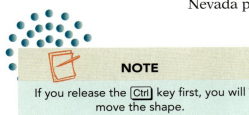

NOTE

If you release the Ctrl key first, you will move the shape.

Using Comments

A *comment* is pop-up explanatory text attached to a cell. In a comment you can inform others what you did or what they should do in the sheet. Comments can be set to display only when you hover over the cell, or they can be displayed at all times.

Cells with comments show a small red triangle in the upper-right corner. The comment appears in a text box when you hover over the cell with the comment.

Exercise 10-18   EDIT A COMMENT

A comment attached to cell J2 is set to show at all times and was repositioned. It hides the red triangle and does not get in the way of any work you might do on the sheet. This is a common practice for templates as a way to include directions to the user.

1. Click the **Review** command tab. There is a **Comments** group on this tab.

2. In *[your initials]*10-17, click cell A2 and press F2. Key **September 1** and press Enter.

3. Point at the comment box to display a four-pointed arrow and click. The comment box has selection handles and the dotted line boundary.

4. Drag the comment box to the right until you see the red triangle indicator in cell J2.

5. Click inside the comment box. The boundary changes to diagonal lines. This means you can edit the text inside the box.

6. Delete **to edit the label** from the comment.

Figure 10-16
Editing a comment
10-17.xltx
K&KSales sheet

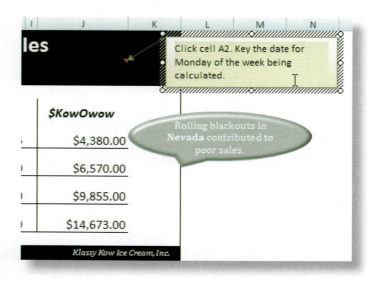

7. Click any cell.

8. Click cell J2. Click the Show All Comments button ![Show All Comments]. The comment is no longer displayed.

9. Hover over cell J2 to display its comment.

10. Click cell J9.

Exercise 10-19 INSERT A COMMENT

1. Right-click cell J9 and choose **Insert Comment**. The comment text box opens and displays the user name for your computer, followed by a colon.

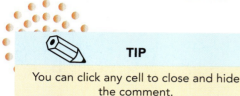

TIP

You can click any cell to close and hide the comment.

2. Key **Units sold are multiplied by average price for the previous month.**

3. Click cell J11 to close the comment text box.

4. Move the mouse pointer over cell J9 to display the comment.

Exercise 10-20 PRINT COMMENTS

1. Right-click cell J2 and choose **Show/Hide Comments**. The comment stays visible.

2. Show the comment for cell J9.

3. Click the Microsoft Office Button. Hover at **Print** and choose **Print Preview**. Comments do not print as a default.

NOTE

You can print comments as they appear on the sheet or at the end of the data on a separate sheet.

4. Close the preview.

5. Click the **Page Layout** tab. In the **Sheet Options** group, click the Dialog Box Launcher. The Page Setup dialog box opens to the **Sheet** tab.

6. In the **Print** group, click the **Comments** arrow. You must use this setting to print comments.

7. Choose **As displayed on sheet**. Click **Print Preview** in the dialog box.

Print

8. Click the Print button in Print Preview and click **OK**. The comments print as they appear on the worksheet.

9. Click cell J2 and click the Show/Hide Comment button  on the **Review** tab.

10. Hide the comment for cell J9.

11. Save the workbook as *[your initials]*10-20.

Exercise 10-21 USE DOCUMENT INSPECTOR

The *Document Inspector* is a feature that checks a document for metadata and personal information. *Metadata* is information that is saved with a document such as your computer name, your user name, the name of the folder, hidden rows/columns/cells, document properties, and more. In some cases, you may want to remove such information from your work before you make it available to others.

1. With *[your initials]*10-20 open, click the Microsoft Office Button and hover at **Prepare**.

2. Choose **Inspect Document**. You may see a message box that asks if you want to save the file; choose **Yes**. The Document Inspector dialog box lists the information that can be found and removed from a workbook.

Figure 10-17
Document Inspector
dialog box
10-20.xltx
K&KSales sheet

Figure 10-17
Document Inspector
dialog box
10-20.xltx
K&KSales sheet

3. Click **Inspect**. This workbook includes comments, document properties, and hidden worksheets. Before removing the data, check the properties.

4. Click **Close**.

5. Click the Microsoft Office Button and hover at **Prepare**.

6. Choose **Properties**. The Document Information Panel opens above the worksheet. There is an author name and a general comment. These settings were part of the template.

Figure 10-18
Document
Information Panel
10-20.xltx
K&KSales sheet

7. Click the Close the Document Information Panel button 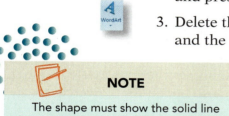.

8. Click the Microsoft Office Button and hover at **Prepare**. Choose **Inspect Document**. Click **Yes** if prompted to save the document.

9. Click **Inspect**. For **Comments and Annotations**, click **Remove All**.

10. Remove the document properties but not the hidden sheets.

11. Click **Close**.

Inserting WordArt

A *WordArt* image is shaped text that may be filled and outlined. A WordArt shape is an object with selection handles, an adjustment handle, and a rotation handle. WordArt is available in all the Office applications.

Exercise 10-22   INSERT WORDART

1. Make a copy of the **K&KSales** sheet.

2. On the copied sheet, click to select one of the folded corner shapes and press Delete.

3. Delete the second text box, each of the two lines, the oval callout, and the text box near row 20.

> **NOTE**
>
> The shape must show the solid line boundary to be deleted. You can delete multiple shapes.

4. Delete the labels in cells A1 and A2.

5. Click the **Insert** tab. Click the WordArt button. The WordArt Gallery displays several variations.

6. Find and click **Fill-White, Drop Shadow**. The shape appears on the sheet with placeholder text.

Figure 10-19
WordArt Gallery

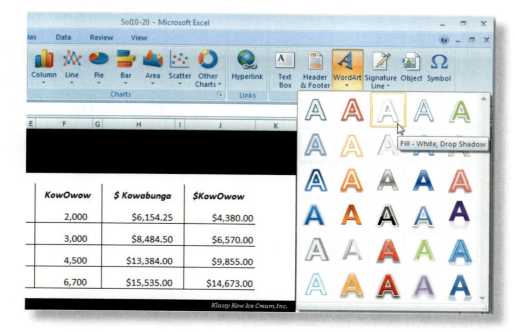

7. With the four-pointed arrow, drag the shape so that it starts near cell A12.

8. Click an empty cell. Then click the WordArt shape. The shape has a dashed line boundary for editing the text and a solid line boundary for changes to the shape itself.

9. Click the WordArt shape several times to see the difference between the boundary appearances.

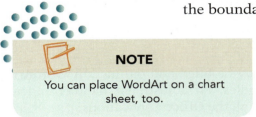

NOTE

You can place WordArt on a chart sheet, too.

10. Display the dashed line boundary and triple-click the placeholder text. Use the Mini toolbar to set 28 points as the font size.

11. Key **Kowabunga and KowOwow Sales**. The text you key replaces the sample text.

Exercise 10-23   EDIT WORDART

1. Select the WordArt shape so that it shows the solid line boundary.

2. Click the **Drawing Tools Format** tab.

3. Click the More button 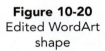 for **WordArt Styles**. A gallery of WordArt styles opens.

4. Hover over a few styles. Live Preview shows the reformatted shape. Some styles use uppercase and some use upper- and lowercase letters.

5. Find and select **Fill-Text 1, Inner Shadow** in the second row.

Figure 10-20
Edited WordArt
shape

6. With the four-pointed arrow, drag the WordArt shape so that it fits in rows 1:2.

7. Click cell A3.

8. Save your workbook as *[your initials]*10-23. Close the workbook.

Using Online Help

The 3-D Format pane enables you to create shapes that have a professional appearance. As you learn more about the options, you can experiment creating your own bevels and other effects.

USE HELP TO LEARN ABOUT 3-D FORMATS

1. In a new workbook, click the Microsoft Office Excel Help button 🔵.

2. Find and review topics about using 3-D format.

3. Close the Help windows.

Lesson 10 Summary

- A shape is a common figure or form. A callout is used to attach an explanation to a cell or other object.

- Shapes are placed on an invisible draw layer, a transparent work area separate from the worksheet data.

- You can change the font within a shape or change its size, shape, rotation angle, and colors.

- Shapes that have a closed interior can have a fill color, as well as an outline or border color. Text within a shape has a color, too. A line shape cannot have fill or text.

- The Format Shape dialog box includes most of the same commands that are on the Drawing Tools Format tab.

- Shape effects include bevels (3-D appearance), shadows, reflections, and more. Not all shapes can use all effects.

- A text box is a rectangle shape for displaying text on the sheet. It can have a fill, a line (border), and special effects.

- Lines, with or without arrows, are shapes.

- The Selection and Visibility pane lists all objects on a worksheet and provides a way to select and reorder the shapes.

- Shapes can be aligned and distributed for a balanced appearance on the sheet. They can also be rotated.

- Most shapes have at least one adjustment handle to redesign the shape into a variation of itself.

- Comments can be used as annotations, notes, or explanations for data on a worksheet.

- Comments are attached to cells and display when the mouse pointer touches a cell with the comment.

- The Document Inspector looks for personal and other information that might not be easily visible in a document.

- You can remove all information found by the Document Inspector before sharing a workbook with other workers.
- Use WordArt to create a design object that is shaped text.
- WordArt is a shape and can be edited and formatted like most shapes.

LESSON 10		Command Summary	
Feature	**Button**	**Task Path**	**Keyboard**
Bevel, add	Shape Effects ▾	Drawing Tools Format, Shape Styles	
Comment, delete	Delete	Review, Comments	
Comment, edit	Edit Comment		Shift + F2
Comment, new	Edit Comment	Review, Comments	Shift + F2
Document Inspector		Microsoft Office, Prepare, Inspect Document	
Shape, change		Drawing Tools Format, Insert Shapes	
Shape, format		Drawing Tools Format, Shape Styles	Ctrl + 1
Shape, insert	Shapes	Insert, Illustrations	
Shape, rotate	Rotate ▾	Drawing Tools Format, Arrange	
Shape, size		Drawing Tools Format, Size, Height/Width	
Shapes, align	Align ▾	Drawing Tools Format, Arrange	
Text box, insert	Text Box	Insert, Text	
WordArt, insert	WordArt	Insert, Text	
WordArt, edit		Drawing Tools Format, WordArt Styles	

Concepts Review

True/False Questions

Each of the following statements is either true or false. Indicate your choice by circling T or F.

T F   1. Any selection handle can be used to size a shape.

T F   2. Callouts can use various shapes to display text.

T F   3. You can change the fill color of a shape from the Ribbon.

T F   4. Metadata and personal information is removed when you save a workbook.

T F   5. The boundary box for a shape displays a dotted line at all times.

T F   6. The adjustment handle is a small green circle.

T F   7. Shadows and bevels are available as special effects for many shapes.

T F   8. A cell with a comment displays a small red triangle.

Short Answer Questions

Write the correct answer in the space provided.

1. What is the small green circle that appears when a shape is selected?

_____

2. What should the pointer look like when you move a shape?

_____

3. What if you cannot see an object's name in the Name Box?

_____

4. What name describes an annotation that appears only when the mouse pointer passes over the cell?

_____

5. What command arranges objects so that the tops are even?

_____

6. Name two categories of Shapes.

_____

7. How can you determine if a cell has a comment without moving the pointer around the sheet?

_____

8. How can you see a list of all shapes and objects on a worksheet?

_____

Critical Thinking

Answer these questions on a separate page. There are no right or wrong answers. Support your answers with examples from your own experience, if possible.

1. What are the differences between comments and callouts? Why and when would you use each?

2. Discuss why and when you should remove metadata and personal information from your work.

Skills Review

Exercise 10-24

Add and format a callout. Create and format a text box.

1. Create a new workbook from the **K&KSales** template. Save the workbook as *[your initials]*10-24.

2. Key the values shown in Figure 10-21.

Figure 10-21

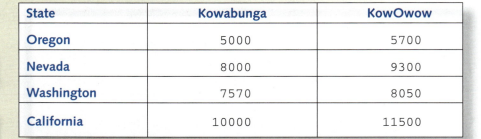

State	Kowabunga	KowOwow
Oregon	5000	5700
Nevada	8000	9300
Washington	7570	8050
California	10000	11500

NOTE

The worksheet protection is set so that you can enter values; you cannot insert shapes until it is removed.

3. Add a callout to a worksheet by following these steps:

   a. Click the **Review** tab. Click the Unprotect Sheet button .

   b. Click the **Insert** tab. In the **Illustrations** group, click the Shapes button.

c. In the **Block Arrows** group, choose **Left Arrow**.

d. Draw a shape starting at cell K8 and extending to about cell N9.

e. Key California benefited from a price promotion.

f. Triple-click the text in the callout. In the Mini toolbar, choose 9-point bold.

g. Click an empty cell.

4. Format a callout by following these steps:

a. Click the shape to display the solid line boundary.

b. Place the pointer on the right-middle handle to display a sizing pointer. Drag the pointer right to fit the text on a single line.

c. Place the pointer on the boundary line to display a four-pointed arrow. Drag the shape so that it points at the vertical middle of row 8.

d. Right-click the shape and choose **Format Shape**.

e. On the **Fill** pane, use **Solid fill**. Click the arrow for **Color**. Choose **Black, Text 1**.

f. Click **Line Color** and choose **No line**.

g. On the **Shadow** pane, click the arrow for **Presets**. From the Outer group, choose **Offset Diagonal Top Right** (first icon, third row).

h. Close the dialog box and click an empty cell.

5. Create a text box by following these steps:

a. Click the **Insert** tab. Click the Text Box button.

b. Draw a box that starts at cell C12 and extends to cell I15.

c. Key Weekly sales are calculated each Saturday evening for the previous week.

d. Triple-click the text and make it bold and centered.

6. Format a text box by following these steps:

a. Click the text box to display the solid line boundary.

b. Click the **Drawing Tools Format** tab. Click the Shape Effects button.

c. In the **Preset** gallery, choose **Preset 2**.

d. Drag a side handle to size the box so that the text displays evenly on two lines. Then drag the shape so that it appears centered below the data.

e. Click an empty cell.

7. Edit cell A2 to show the date for Sunday of this week.

8. Prepare and submit your work.

Exercise 10-25

Use the Drawing Tool Format tab. Insert basic shapes.

1. Open **Contest** and save it as *[your initials]*10-25.

2. In cell C6, use a formula to subtract the guess in column B from the correct amount. Copy the formula through row 19.

NOTE

The wave shape is linked to cell D6 and displays the results of the formula.

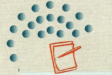

3. Use the MIN function in cell D6 to find the smallest value in column C.

4. Use the Drawing Tools Format tab by following these steps:

   a. Click the wave below row 20 to display the solid boundary.

   b. Click the **Drawing Tools Format** tab.

   c. Click the Shape Fill 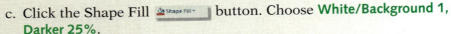 button. Choose **White/Background 1, Darker 25%**.

   d. Click the Shape Outline 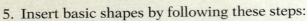 button. Choose **No Outline**.

   e. Click the Shape Effects button. In the **Shadow** gallery, in the **Inner** group, choose **Inside Diagonal Bottom Left** (first icon, third row).

   f. Click the **Home** tab.

   g. Click the Center button. Click the Middle Align button.

   h. Change the font size to 24 points.

   i. Click an empty cell.

5. Insert basic shapes by following these steps:

   a. Click the **Insert** tab. In the **Illustrations** group, click the Shapes button.

   b. In the **Basic Shapes** group, choose **Smiley Face**.

   c. Hold down the Shift key. Click and drag to draw a shape starting at cell D21 and extending the bottom edge of the face to row 26.

   d. Drag the shape so that it appears in the horizontal center of column D.

   e. Select the **Smiley Face** shape to display the solid boundary.

   f. Point at the boundary and hold down the Ctrl key. Drag a copy of the shape to the horizontal center of column A. Release the mouse first and then the Ctrl key.

NOTE

Holding down the Shift key while drawing an elliptical object makes it a circle. Release the mouse button first when finished.

REVIEW

Holding down the Ctrl key when you drag and drop creates a copy of the object.

6. Use the Drawing Tools Format tab by following these steps:

   a. Click the first **Smiley Face**.

   b. Hold down the Ctrl key and click the second face. Hold down the Ctrl key and click the wave. Three shapes are selected.

   c. On the **Drawing Tools Format** tab, click the Align button 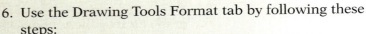. Choose **Align Middle**.

   d. Click the Align button 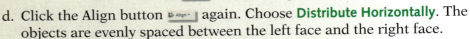 again. Choose **Distribute Horizontally**. The objects are evenly spaced between the left face and the right face.

7. Center the sheet horizontally.

8. Prepare and submit your work.

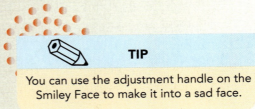

TIP

You can use the adjustment handle on the Smiley Face to make it into a sad face.

Exercise 10-26

Edit and insert comments. Print comments. Use the Document Inspector.

1. Create a new workbook from the **ExpRpt** template and save the workbook as *[your initials]*10-26.

2. Edit a comment by following these steps:

    a. Click cell E1. Click the **Review** tab.

    b. Click the Edit Comment button .

    c. Edit the text to show **Spacebar** instead of **End**.

    d. Click any cell to complete the edit.

3. Insert and format comments by following these steps:

    a. Right-click cell E8 and choose **New Comment**.

    b. Key **Edit cells B3, B8, B13, and B18 to show the date for Monday in the specified week**.

    c. Click the border of the comment box to display a dotted line boundary.

    d. Click the **Home** tab and click the Italic button 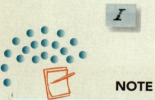.

    e. Right-click cell E1 and choose **Edit Comment**.

    f. Click the border of the comment box to display a dotted line boundary. Click the Italic button.

    g. Insert a comment in cell C30 that shows your first and last name.

> **NOTE**
>
> The comments are set to display at all times.

> **NOTE**
>
> When the dotted line boundary is active, changes affect the shape and all text.

4. Print comments on the worksheet by following these steps:

    a. On the **Review** tab, click the Show All Comments button .

    b. Click the **Page Layout** tab. In the **Sheet Options** group, click the Dialog Box Launcher.

    c. In the **Print** group, click the arrow for **Comments**. Choose **As displayed on sheet**.

    d. Click **Print** in the dialog box and then click **OK**.

5. Print comments on a separate sheet by following these steps:

    a. On the **Review** tab, click the Show All Comments button 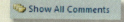. The button is a toggle (on/off).

    b. Click the **Page Layout** tab. In the **Sheet Options** group, click the Dialog Box Launcher.

    c. In the **Print** group, click the arrow for **Comments**. Choose **At end of sheet**. Click **Print** and then click **OK**.

6. Use the Document Inspector by following these steps:

    a. Click the Microsoft Office Button and hover at **Prepare**. Choose **Inspect Document**.

> **NOTE**
>
> Comments need not be visible on screen when you choose to print them on a separate page.

b. Click **Inspect**. For **Comments and Annotations**, click **Remove All**.

c. Remove the document properties.

d. Click **Close**.

7. Prepare and submit your work.

Exercise 10-27

Insert WordArt. Format WordArt.

1. Open **CASales** and save it as *[your initials]*10-27.

2. Delete the contents of cells A1:A2. Insert a row at row 3.

3. Insert WordArt by following these steps:

   a. Click the **Insert** tab. Click the WordArt button .

   b. Find and click **Fill-White, Drop Shadow**.

   c. Triple-click the placeholder text and key **Klassy Kow Ice Cream**. Press
      Enter to start a new line.

   d. Key **Weekly Sales Data**.

4. Format WordArt by following these steps:

   a. Triple-click the first line in the shape and use the Mini toolbar to set
      24 points.

   b. Do the same for the second line.

   c. Select the shape to display a solid line boundary and drag it to
      appear centered in rows 1:4.

   d. In the **WordArt Styles** group, click the arrow next to the Text Fill
      button . Choose **Black, Text 1**.

   e. In the **WordArt Styles** group, click the arrow next to the Text Outline
      button . Choose **No Outline**.

5. Prepare and submit your work.

Lesson Applications

Exercise 10-28

Create and format a shape. Inspect a document.

A text box is a rectangle, but you can use many shapes to display text.

1. Create a new workbook, using the **K&KSales** template. Save the workbook as *[your initials]*10-28. Unprotect the sheet (Review tab).

2. Key the values shown in Figure 10-22.

Figure 10-22

State	Kowabunga	KowOwow
Oregon	15000	16500
Nevada	18000	19200
Washington	17570	18050
California	19000	19500

3. Draw a rounded rectangle shape below the worksheet data that spans from column B to column J. Key **This report is filed each week during the peak selling season for novelty products.**

4. Format the shape box to show the text as bold italic. Use black fill, no outline, and a shadow. Size the shape so that the text is on two lines with equal amounts of text on each. Position the shape to look centered below the data.

5. Remove all comments and properties from the workbook.

6. Prepare and submit your work.

Exercise 10-29

Add and format shapes.

The Stars and Banners category has shapes that can highlight a cell in eye-catching ways.

1. Open **CASales** and save it as *[your initials]*10-29.

2. Select rows 6 through 18 and make them **25.50 (34 pixels)** high.

3. Insert an **Explosion 1** shape from **Stars and Banners** to encircle cell F16. Use no fill and a 1-point black outline.

4. From the **Basic Shapes** category, draw a lightning bolt in cells D1 through F3. Flip the shape so that it points toward the data. Use a gradient fill, no outline, and a shadow.

5. Prepare and submit your work.

NOTE

No fill means you can see the cell contents through the shape. The Line Style pane is in the Format Shape dialog box.

Exercise 10-30

Display cell contents in a shape.

You can link a shape to a cell to display the cell's contents in the shape.

1. Open **Contest**. Save the workbook as *[your initials]*10-30.

2. Delete the wave shape below the data.

3. From the Stars and Banners category, insert a 16-Point Star that spans cells B20 to C28.

4. While the shape is selected, click in the formula bar. Key **=d4** and press Enter. The value from cell D4 appears in the shape.

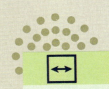

REVIEW

Use the Home tab to apply centering and font choices.

5. Center the contents horizontally and vertically and use 24 point as the font size. Set the page for horizontal centering, too.

6. Format cell D4 to use white as the font color.

7. Edit the text box at the top of the sheet so that it reads . . . **number in the star wins** . . . instead of "in cell D4."

8. Prepare and submit your work.

Exercise 10-31 ◆ Challenge Yourself

Use WordArt. Display cell contents in a shape.

You can link a cell on one worksheet to a shape on another sheet in the same workbook to create a separate display about your data.

REVIEW

Click the Insert Worksheet tab or press Shift + F11 to insert a new worksheet.

1. Open **CASales** and save it as *[your initials]*10-31.

2. Insert a new sheet and name it **BestWeek**.

3. On the new sheet, insert WordArt that says **Best California Sales!** Choose any style, and position the shape so that its bottom edge rests on row 5 and so that it starts in column A.

4. Draw a 16-point star that covers approximately cells B8:F22.

5. On the WeeklySales sheet, key **Best Week** in cell A20. Match its format to cell A19. In cell B20, use the MAX function with the range B19:E19.

6. On the BestWeek sheet, select the star. In the formula bar, key **=** to start a formula. Click the WeeklySales tab and click cell B20. Press Enter.

7. Format the shapes so that they form a cohesive design.

8. Center the sheet horizontally and vertically.

9. Prepare and submit your work.

On Your Own

In these exercises you work on your own, as you would in a real-life work environment. Use the skills you've learned to accomplish the task—and be creative.

Exercise 10-32

Create a workbook using the **K&KSales** template. Fill in values for the two products, and unhide both chart sheets. Delete the title object on each chart and insert WordArt as a title. Save the workbook as *[your initials]*10-32. Prepare and submit your work.

Exercise 10-33

In a new workbook, insert and format seven different shapes. Format each one differently and attractively. Position the shapes so that they overlap in several places. Use the Selection pane to experiment reordering the shapes on the sheet. Save the workbook as *[your initials]*10-33. Prepare and submit your work.

Exercise 10-34

In a new workbook, insert a text box and key your name. Format the shape to have a solid black outline and no fill. Copy the box four times. Next change each text box to a different shape. Use different fills, outlines, and effects for each shape. Experiment with the adjustment handle(s). Save your workbook as *[your initials]*10-34. Prepare and submit your work.

Lesson 11

Using Images and SmartArt Graphics

OBJECTIVES

After completing this lesson, you will be able to:

1. Insert a picture.

2. Add a picture to a header or footer.

3. Create a hierarchy SmartArt shape.

4. Build a cycle SmartArt shape.

5. Use the Research tool.

Estimated Time: 1½ hours

MCAS OBJECTIVES

In this lesson:
XL07 1.2
XL07 2.1.4
XL07 2.3.4
XL07 4.4.1
XL07 4.4.2
XL07 5.3.3
XL07 5.5.4

In a worksheet, you can insert images from a disk, from the Clip Organizer, or from Web galleries. SmartArt Graphics include lists, hierarchy charts (organization charts), matrixes, and other common business diagrams.

The Research tool enables you to insert information from various sources into your worksheet. You can use reference information from your own computer, from a network, or from the Web.

Inserting a Picture

Images can add visual appeal as well as help to explain your work. When you insert an image, Excel treats it as an object, like a shape. You can edit the size, position, and other properties, depending on the type of image.

TIP

For best effect, don't use too many images on a sheet. One or two related images or shapes should work.

Exercise 11-1 INSERT A PICTURE FROM A FILE

To insert a picture from a file, the picture must be in a graphics format that Excel can use. The **KowOwowTrans** file used in this exercise is a *GIF* file (Graphics Interchange Format), a popular graphics format for images on the Web.

1. Open **KowSales**.

2. Click the **Insert** tab. In the **Illustrations** group, click the Insert Picture from File button . The Insert Picture dialog box opens.

3. Navigate to the folder with the **KowOwowTrans** file and click the thumbnail or filename to select it.

4. Click the arrow next to the Views button and choose **Medium Icons**. You can verify that you have chosen the correct image.

Figure 11-1
Inserting a picture
from a file
KowSales.xlsx
K&KSales sheet

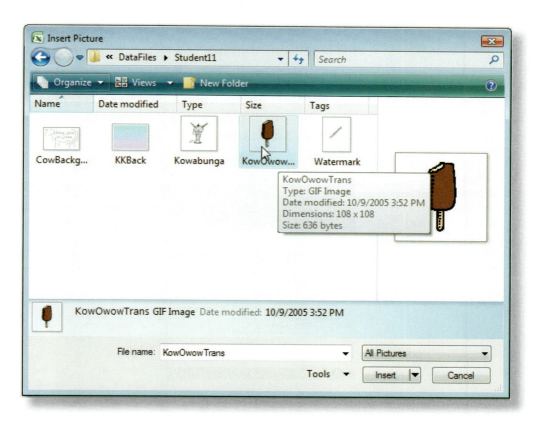

5. Double-click **KowOwowTrans**. The image is inserted at a default size in a default position on the worksheet's drawing layer. Contextual Picture Tools are now available.

6. Point to the bounding box to display a four-pointed arrow. Drag the image below the worksheet data.

REVIEW

Contextual tools appear at the right side of the Ribbon.

Exercise 11-2 CHECK PROPERTIES AND SCALE THE PICTURE

Depending on the type of picture, the Picture Tools Format tab provides various commands. An important command is the one to scale the image. *Scaling* means that you can size the picture by a percentage, larger or smaller.

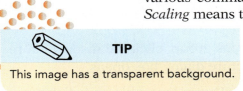

TIP

This image has a transparent background.

1. Click the **Picture Tools Format** tab. In the **Size** group, click the Dialog Box Launcher. The Size and Properties dialog box opens.

2. Click the **Properties** tab. The settings on this tab depend on whether the image is used on a worksheet or a chart sheet.

3. If it's not already selected, click to select **Move but don't size with cells**. This will allow you to size the picture independent of the data.

4. If it's not already selected, click to select **Print object**. You can turn this setting off to print the sheet without the picture.

5. Click the **Size** tab.

6. In the **Scale** group, double-click the percentage value in the **Height** box, key **40**, and press Tab. The **Width** is adjusted automatically because **Lock aspect ratio** is selected.

Figure 11-2
Size and Properties
dialog box
KowSales.xlsx
K&KSales sheet

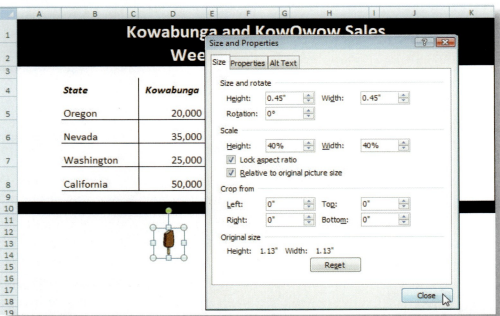

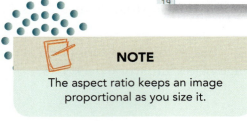

NOTE

The aspect ratio keeps an image proportional as you size it.

7. Click **Close**. The image is 40 percent of its original size.

Exercise 11-3 FORMAT AND COPY AN IMAGE

A picture has many of the same style elements as a shape. You can add 3-D effects, shadows, and more. You may also be able to change the colors for some pictures, based on their original format.

You can copy a picture with regular Copy and Paste commands. And, like shapes, a picture can be dragged using the four-pointed arrow.

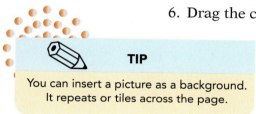

1. Make sure the picture is selected.

2. In the **Picture Styles** group, click the Picture Effects button 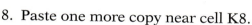.

3. Hover over **Shadow**. In the **Outer** group, choose **Offset Right**.

4. Point at the image to display a four-pointed arrow. Drag the picture to cells A3:A4.

5. Press Ctrl+C and then Ctrl+V. The pasted copy is located in a default location.

6. Drag the copy near cell C6.

7. Press Ctrl+V to paste again. Drag this copy near cell G5.

8. Paste one more copy near cell K8.

9. Click an empty cell to deselect the image.

TIP

You can insert a picture as a background. It repeats or tiles across the page.

Exercise 11-4 INSERT CLIP ART

The Clip Organizer sorts and arranges images from Microsoft and other sources that are on your hard disk. The images are cataloged so that they appear in the Clip Art task pane.

1. Click the **Insert** tab. Click the Clip Art button. The Clip Art task pane opens.

2. In the **Search for** box, key **money**. This searches for images on your computer that have the word "money" in the title or the description.

3. Click **Go**. (If a message box asks if you want to search online, choose **No**.) Clip art images that illustrate money are shown in the task pane. Your images may not be the same as those shown in this text.

4. Double-click the first image (or any available picture). It is inserted on the worksheet.

Figure 11-3
Searching for an
image in the Clip Art
task pane
**KowSales.xlsx
K&KSales sheet**

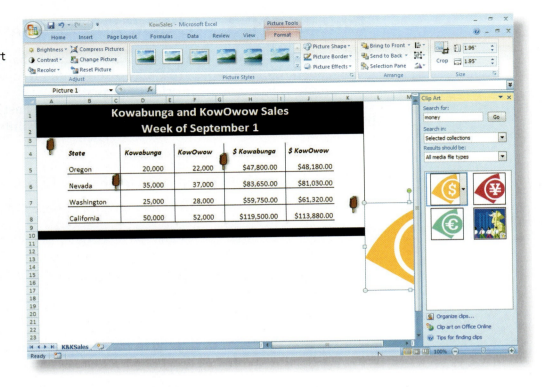

5. Close the Clip Art task pane.

Exercise 11-5   CROP, SIZE, AND STYLE AN IMAGE

Cropping an image allows you to remove part of the picture, working from any of the edges. It takes some guesswork and practice to learn how to crop an image so that it shows what you want to see.

1. Click the **Picture Tools Format** tab.

Crop

2. In the **Size** group, click the Crop button. The insertion point resembles a rectangle with extended edges and includes an arrow.

3. Align the top-left corner of the insertion point shape on the top-left corner handle of the image. The pointer mimics the handle.

4. Drag down and right so that the bounding line just touches the top of the circle design.

5. Align the bottom-left corner of the insertion point on the bottom-left handle of the shape. Drag left so that the bounding line just touches the left of the circle design.

6. Use either corner now to display the original image.

NOTE

If you click away from the image and see regular selection handles, click the Crop button again.

Figure 11-4
Cropped image
KowSales.xlsx
K&KSales sheet

TIP

You can set specific cropping distances in the Size and Properties dialog box. It takes practice and experience to learn the best amounts to use for cropping in this way.

7. Crop the image so that it appears as a dollar sign on a rectangle as shown in Figure 11-4. Click an empty cell to finish cropping.

8. Select the clip art image. Click the **Picture Tools Format** tab.

9. In the **Picture Styles** group, click the More button ⏷. A gallery of preset styles opens.

10. Choose **Bevel Rectangle** in the fourth row for a beveled 3-D effect.

11. Point at the image and drag it to rows 1:2 between columns J:K.

12. Point at the bottom-right handle to display a two-pointed arrow. Drag up to size the shape so that it fits in rows 1:2.

13. In the **Picture Tools** group, click the Recolor button 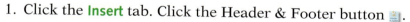. A gallery of preset color variations opens.

14. In the **Light Variations** group, choose **Background color 2 Light**, the first icon.

15. Click an empty cell.

Adding a Picture to a Header/Footer

Exercise 11-6   **INSERT AN IMAGE IN A FOOTER**

You can insert an image from disk into a header or a footer. A company logo is an example of an image that might be used as such.

1. Click the **Insert** tab. Click the Header & Footer button 📄.

2. Click the Go to Footer button 📄. The insertion point is in the center section.

3. Click in the left section. In the **Header and Footer Elements** group, click the Picture button 📄. The Insert Picture dialog box opens.

4. Navigate to the folder with **KowOwowTrans** and click to highlight the filename or icon.

5. Click **Insert**. The code is **&[Picture]**.

6. Click in the center section for the footer. Now you can see the image.

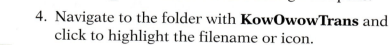

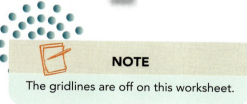

NOTE

The gridlines are off on this worksheet.

Figure 11-5
Inserting a picture in
a footer
KowSales.xlsx
K&KSales sheet

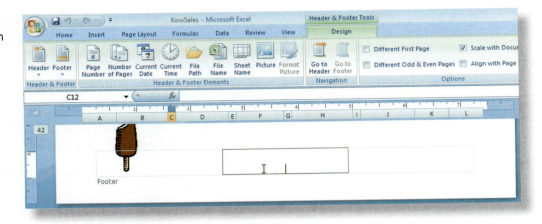

REVIEW

Click the Zoom Out button 🔲 in the
status bar or drag the Zoom slider.

7. Click a cell above the footer area. Set a Zoom size of **40%** and scroll
   to see the page.

Exercise 11-7   SIZE AN IMAGE IN A FOOTER

1. Return to **100%** Zoom size.

2. Scroll to the footer area and click in the left section.

3. In the **Header and Footer Elements** group, click the Format Picture
   button 🖼. The Format Picture dialog box has two tabs for a footer
   image.

4. Click the **Size** tab. In the **Scale** group, double-click the value in the
   Height box, key **65**, and press Tab. Click **OK**.

5. Click after the right square bracket with **&[Picture]**. Press Enter and
   key your first and last name.

6. Click a cell in the worksheet. Press Ctrl + Home.

7. Press Ctrl + P and then Alt + W to open Print Preview. Close Print
   Preview.

Exercise 11-8 CREATE A WATERMARK

A *watermark* is text or an image that appears on top of or behind the data. A watermark is similar to a background image, but it is intended for printed documents. You can simulate a watermark in Excel by inserting the appropriate image in a header or footer.

1. Click the Insert tab. Click the Header & Footer button ▤. The insertion point is in the header center section.

2. In the Header and Footer Elements group, click the Picture button ▤.

3. Navigate to the folder with **Watermark** and click to highlight the filename or icon

4. Click Insert. The &[Picture] code is the same.

5. Click a worksheet cell and set the Zoom size to 60%. This image is text that has been sized and rotated.

6. Click in the center header section.

7. In the Header and Footer Elements group, click the Format Picture button ▤.

8. Click the Picture tab. In the Image control group, set the Brightness to 90%. Click OK.

9. Click a cell in the worksheet. Press Ctrl + Home.

10. Return to normal view and 100% Zoom size.

11. Save the workbook as *[your initials]*11-8 in a Lesson 11 folder.

12. Close the workbook.

Creating a Hierarchy SmartArt Shape

SmartArt is a graphics feature that enables you to quickly display data as a high-quality illustration. These illustrations include bulleted lists, organization charts, cycles, matrixes, pyramids, and more. These graphics include a text pane for ease in keying text. They resize automatically based on how much text you enter. The layouts can be converted to another graphic with little or no extra work. SmartArt graphics are not linked to worksheet data but can be used to clarify and enhance data.

Exercise 11-9 CREATE AND STYLE AN ORGANIZATION CHART

An *organization chart* is an object that displays relationships, usually among workers in a company. Organization charts show hierarchical associations between people. This means there is someone at the top (the superior) with assistants, subordinates, or coworkers.

1. Create a new workbook. Set landscape orientation.

2. Click the **Insert** tab. Click the SmartArt button . The Choose a SmartArt Graphic dialog box shows seven categories of diagrams that can be built as well as an All group. When you click a thumbnail in any category, the pane on the right describes its use.

3. Click **Hierarchy** to open its pane. Click **Organization Chart** (first icon). Read the information at the right and click **OK**. An organization chart with five shapes opens with its Text pane. The SmartArt Tools include a Design and a Format tab.

Figure 11-6
New organization chart

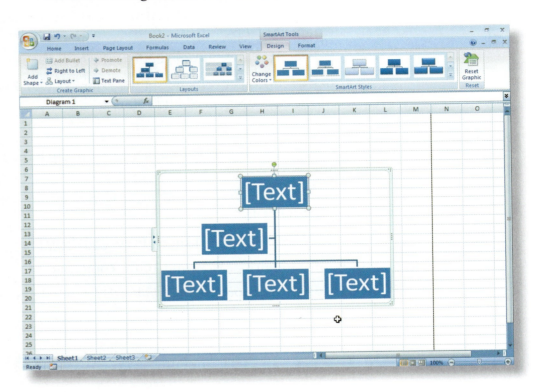

4. Click the **SmartArt Tools Design** tab. In the **SmartArt Styles** group, click the More button. Find and choose **Polished** in the 3-D category.

5. In the **SmartArt Styles** group, click the Change Colors button. In the **Primary Theme Colors** group, choose **Dark 1 Outline**.

6. In the **Create Graphic** group, click the Text Pane button. The Text pane opens or closes. Display the Text pane.

7. Click the **SmartArt Tools Format** tab. Click the Size button.

8. Double-click the value in the **Height** box, key **4**, and press Enter.

9. Set the **Width** to **6**.

> **NOTE**
>
> The Text Pane button toggles the pane on/off. Remember that your screen resolution and size has an effect on how buttons appear.

10. Point at the border of the graphic's frame to display the four-pointed arrow. Drag the shape so that its top-left selection handle is in cell A1. The Text pane moves to the other side.

Exercise 11-10   ADD A SHAPE TO AN ORGANIZATION CHART

Each box in the organization chart is a shape. The top shape is the highest in the hierarchy, and generally there is one top shape. An *assistant shape* represents a helper and is attached to the line that connects the top shape to the rest of the chart. The other three shapes are below the top shape and represent *subordinate* employees.

1. Click the border of the top shape. It shows a solid line boundary, selection handles, and a rotation handle.

2. Click inside the top shape. The text insertion point is visible with a dashed line boundary.

3. Click the shape to display a solid line boundary.

4. Click the **SmartArt Tools Design** tab.

5. In the **Create Graphic** group, click the arrow on the Add Shape button. The menu lists where a shape can be placed.

6. Choose **Add Shape Below**. A fourth shape is added as a subordinate on the bottom row, and the entire graphic is resized.

7. Click the border of the leftmost subordinate shape (bottom row) to display a solid line boundary.

TIP

If you insert a shape in the wrong location, select it and press Delete.

8. Click the arrow on the Add Shape button. Choose **Add Shape Below**. A shape is added as a new subordinate to the subordinate.

Figure 11-7
Adding shapes

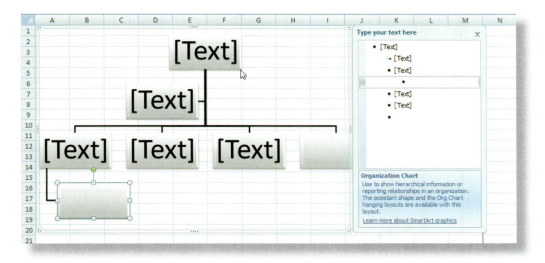

9. Select the top shape to display a solid line boundary.

Exercise 11-11   ADD TEXT TO THE SHAPES

The *Text pane* is a dialog box that is attached to a SmartArt shape. It works like a bulleted or numbered list in Word or PowerPoint. When you're working in the Text pane, pressing Enter inserts a new shape at the current level. Pressing Tab or Shift+Tab demotes or promotes a shape in the graphic. A shape is promoted when it is moved up a level in the hierarchy; it is demoted when it is lowered in the hierarchy. You can also click inside a shape to place a text insertion point for keying data.

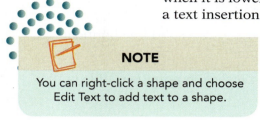

> **NOTE**
>
> You can right-click a shape and choose Edit Text to add text to a shape.

1. Click the **SmartArt Tools Design** tab. If necessary, click the Text Pane button [Text Pane] to display it.

2. Click inside the top shape. The text insertion point appears, and the shape's border displays dashed lines.

3. Key **Conrad Steele** and press Enter. A new line within the shape is available.

4. Key **President and CEO**. Do not press Enter.

5. In the Text pane, click the line below **President and CEO**. This is the entry line for the assistant shape; it is selected with a solid line boundary.

6. Key *[your first and last name]*. Press Enter. A new shape is inserted at the same level.

7. Click the new shape in the graphic and press Delete.

8. In the Text pane, click immediately after the last character in your name and press Shift+Enter. This is a second line in the shape.

9. Key **Executive Assistant** on the second line.

10. In the Text pane, click the next line. This represents the leftmost subordinate shape.

Figure 11-8
Keying text in a shape

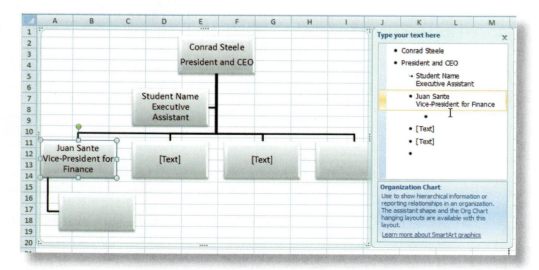

11. Key **Juan Sante** and press Shift + Enter. Key **Vice-President for Finance** as his title.

12. Click inside the second subordinate shape to display a dashed line boundary. Key **Keiko Sumara** and press Shift + Enter.

13. Key **Sales and Marketing** as her second line.

14. For the third subordinate shape, key **Robin McDonald**, and press Shift + Enter. Key **Human Resources**.

15. In the fourth subordinate shape, key **Unknown** on the first line and **Communications** on the second line.

16. Click inside the shape below **Juan Sante** and key *[your instructor's first and last name]*.

17. Click outside the shapes but within the graphic's border. All text boxes are deselected, and you can see the position of the text in the Text pane.

18. Close the Text pane.

19. Place the pointer on the right middle selection handle for the graphic's frame. With a two-pointed sizing arrow, drag the right edge to reach column L.

20. Drag the bottom middle handle to reach row 25.

21. Save the workbook as *[your initials]*11-11.

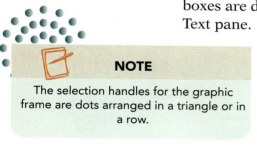

NOTE

If you have extra shapes in your layout, delete them.

NOTE

The selection handles for the graphic frame are dots arranged in a triangle or in a row.

Building a Cycle SmartArt Shape

As part of SmartArt graphics, Excel can build several styles of business diagrams, including List, Cycle, Process, and Relationship diagrams. A *diagram* is an object that illustrates a concept. Diagrams are not linked to worksheet data.

Cycle diagrams illustrate a series of tasks, events, or stages that continue and repeat in a circular manner. Some graphics are called cycles and others are called radials.

Exercise 11-12   CREATE A CYCLE DIAGRAM

1. Click the **Sheet2** worksheet tab.

2. Click the **Insert** tab. Click the SmartArt button.

3. Click **Cycle** in the Choose a SmartArt Graphic dialog box. There are several cycle and radial shapes in this category.

4. Find and click **Block Cycle** in the first row. Read its description and click **OK**. A cycle diagram with five shapes is inserted.

5. In the **Create Graphic** group, click the Text Pane button 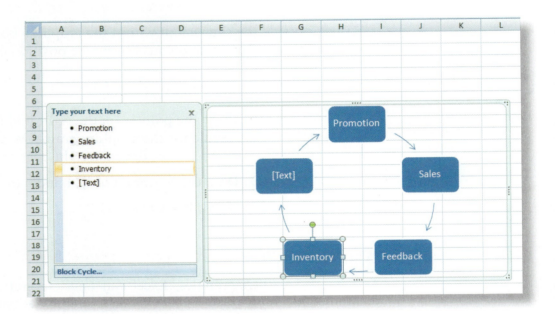 to display the pane.

6. Key **Promotion**. It appears in the top shape and as the first line in the Text pane.

7. Press ↓ to move to the second line in the Text pane and key **Sales**.

8. Press Enter. Another shape is inserted.

9. Press Backspace. The shape is deleted.

10. In the Text pane, click the third line. Key **Feedback**.

11. In the Text pane on the fourth line, key **Inventory**.

Figure 11-9
Cycle diagram
11-11.xlsx
Sheet2 sheet

12. Click a worksheet cell away from the graphic. Only the shape appears.

13. Click a cell near the graphic. The frame and the Text pane open when the graphic is selected.

Exercise 11-13   MOVE TEXT IN THE TEXT PANE

You can make edits in the Text pane as if it were a bulleted Word list. For example, in your cycle shape, "Inventory" should be the top of the cycle. This can be accomplished as a cut-and-paste task.

1. Triple-click **Inventory** in the Text pane. It is selected, and the Mini toolbar opens.

2. Press Ctrl+X. The text and the shape are cut.

3. Click to the left of **Promotion** in the Text pane.

4. Press Enter. A blank line is inserted in the Text pane as well as the new shape.

5. Click the blank line and press Ctrl+V. The cut text is pasted in its new location in the shape and in the Text pane.

6. Click the **SmartArt Tools Design** tab.

7. In the **SmartArt Styles** group, click the More button ⬇. Choose **Polished**.

8. Click the Change Colors button ⬇. Choose **Dark 1 Outline**.

9. Click the empty shape in the graphic and press Delete.

10. Point at the border of the graphic to display the four-pointed arrow. Drag the shape so that its top-left selection handle is in cell A1. The Text pane moves to the other side of the frame.

11. Drag the bottom-right selection handle to reach cell H22.

12. Close the Text pane and click a worksheet cell.

13. Rename the sheet tab as **Cycle**. Save the workbook as *[your initials]***11-13**.

Exercise 11-14   CHOOSE A NEW LAYOUT

Most SmartArt graphics can be changed to another layout. When you choose another layout, the text is remapped to the new shape. In some cases, not all layouts are well-suited to your text.

1. In *[your initials]***11-13**, select the main cycle shape, not an individual box.

2. On the **SmartArt Tools Design** tab in the **Layouts** group, click the More button ⬇.

3. Hover over several thumbnails to see the new layout. Live Preview shows how the graphic will appear.

4. Find and choose **Segmented Cycle**. Close the workbook without saving.

Using the Research Tool

The Research task pane helps you find and insert data from an outside source. Excel has a Research Library that includes a multilanguage thesaurus and dictionary, a translation utility, and an encyclopedia. A *thesaurus* is a reference that lists words that mean the same thing as the word you select.

You can open the Research task pane by:

- Clicking the Research button on the Review tab.

- Clicking a word while holding down the Alt key.

Exercise 11-15 FIND SYNONYMS

A *synonym* is a word that means the same thing as another word. The Research tool can look up labels in cells; it cannot research text that is inside a graphic or shape.

NOTE

If you have different reference books and resources on your computer, expand/collapse each one and check its findings.

NOTE

Click the − sign to collapse a list and the + sign to expand it.

1. Open **Research**. This is a matrix graphic.

2. Hold down Alt and click cell L1. The Research task pane opens with preliminary results for the word "sales." It has searched All Reference Books on your computer. Each resource has an expand or collapse button (+ or −) to indicate whether its list is hidden or shown.

3. Collapse each of the resource items to start.

4. Click the Expand button for **Thesaurus: English (United States)**. There is only one related word, **sale**, so you will not change that label in the diagram.

Figure 11-10
Using the Research task pane
Research.xlsx
Matrix sheet

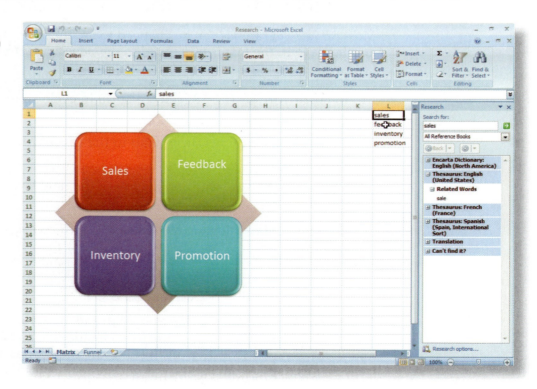

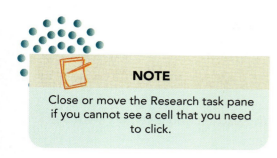

NOTE

Close or move the Research task pane if you cannot see a cell that you need to click.

5. Hold down Alt and click cell L2. The task pane updates to show related words for "feedback."

6. Expand/scroll the **Thesaurus: English (United States)** list. You will replace the word "feedback" in cell L2 with "reaction."

7. Place the mouse pointer on **reaction** in the **criticism (n.)** category.

8. Click the arrow and choose **Insert**. The replacement is made in cell L2, not in the graphic.

Figure 11-11
Choosing a word from the thesaurus
**Research.xlsx
Matrix sheet**

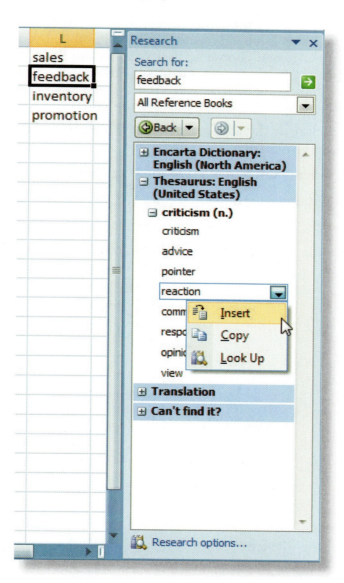

9. Hold down Alt and click cell L3. If necessary, scroll to see the results.

10. Place the mouse pointer on **stock** in the **supply (n.)** category. Click the down arrow and choose **Insert**.

11. Use the Thesaurus to replace **promotion** in cell L4 with **advertising**.

12. Close the Research task pane.

13. Double-click **Promotion** in the matrix diagram and key **Advertising** as its replacement.

14. Replace **Feedback** in the diagram with **Reaction** and **Inventory** with **Stock**.

15. Click a worksheet cell.

Exercise 11-16   TRANSLATE WORDS

As part of the Research tool, Excel can translate words into another language. Although this is a handy feature, you will find that you must be familiar with the language you choose so that you can use the correct grammar, such as the gender of nouns and the tense of verbs.

1. Click the **Funnel** worksheet tab. This is a funnel graphic.

2. Click near the shape to select it. The frame includes a tab at the left with two arrows.

3. Click the tab at the left of the frame. The Text pane opens.

4. Hold down Alt and click cell J1.

5. Click the Expand button 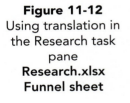 for **Translation** in the Research task pane.

6. In the **To** box, choose **French (France)**.

Figure 11-12
Using translation in the Research task pane
Research.xlsx
Funnel sheet

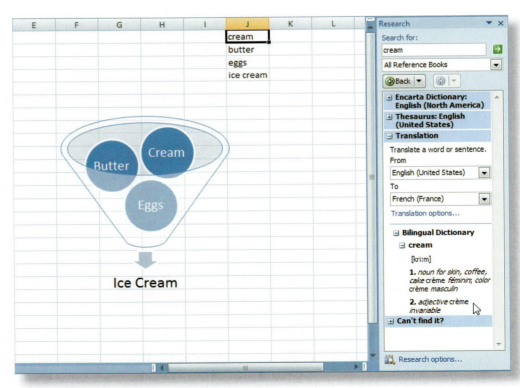

7. Click the Expand button ⊞ for **Bilingual dictionary** if it is not expanded. The translation for "cream" is "crème."

8. Select the shape and double-click **Cream** in the Text pane.

9. Key **La Creme**. You will add the accent on the "e" in the next exercise.

10. Hold down Alt and click cell J2. The Translation group should be expanded, since you just used it. The French word is **beurre**.

11. Select the shape and double-click **Butter** in the Text pane. Key **Le Beurre**.

12. Hold down the Alt key and click cell J3.

13. Double-click **Eggs** in the Text pane and key **Les Oeufs**.

14. Hold down Alt and click cell J4. The dictionary translates both words.

15. In the Text pane, replace **Ice Cream** with **Creme Glace**.

16. Close the Research task pane.

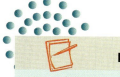

NOTE

Many languages include an article with a noun. In French, the articles are "le," "la," and "les." The translation tool does not include the article, although it does specify masculine or feminine.

Exercise 11-17   USE A SPECIAL SYMBOL

You should add the accent to the "e" in "Crème" so that the words are shown correctly in French. Accented characters are special symbols and can be easily inserted.

1. In the Text pane, click the first line. Then drag to select the first "e" in "Creme."

2. Click the **Insert** tab. In the **Text** group, click the Symbol button Ω. The Symbol dialog box opens.

3. Click the **Font** arrow and key **c** to move to font names that begin with "C." Set the font to **Calibri**.

4. Scroll to find **è**, the accented lowercase "e." This is a *grave* accent.

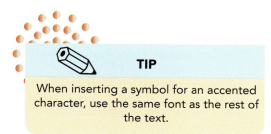

TIP

When inserting a symbol for an accented character, use the same font as the rest of the text.

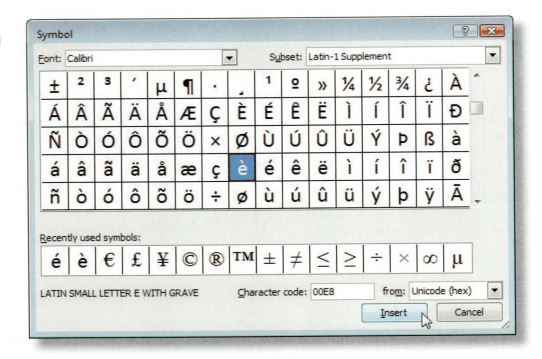

5. Click the character to select it and click **Insert**. Click **Close**. The accented è replaces the original character.

6. Make the same replacement in "Crème Glace."

7. In the Text pane, edit "Glace" to show the correct spelling "Glacée."

8. Close the Text pane. Delete the contents of cells J1:J4.

9. Drag the graphic so that its top-left handle starts in cell A1. Drag the bottom-right handle of the graphic frame to cell J25.

10. On the **SmartArt Tools Design** tab, choose **Polished** from the **SmartArt Styles**. Change the colors to one of the **Colorful** choices.

11. Click a worksheet cell.

Exercise 11-18   SET DOCUMENT PROPERTIES

Excel workbooks have properties. A *property* is a setting or attribute that is stored with the workbook when it is saved. Some properties can be edited, such as the author's name, a subject, or key words. Properties are shown in the Document Information Panel.

1. Click the Microsoft Office Button 🔘.

2. Hover over **Prepare** and choose **Properties**. The Document Information Panel opens at the top of the worksheet.

3. Triple-click in the **Author** box and key *[your first and last name]*.

4. Press `Tab`. Key **SmartArt Graphics** in the **Title** box.

5. Click in the **Comments** box and key the following:
   This workbook will be saved as Excel 97-2003 format for review by all shops.

Figure 11-14
Setting properties
Research.xlsx
Funnel sheet

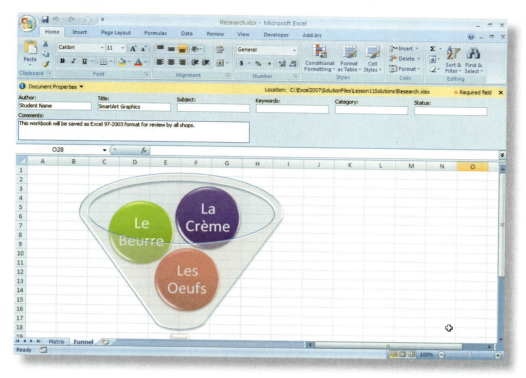

6. Close the Document Information Panel.

7. Save the workbook as *[your initials]*11-18.

8. Press F12. The Save As dialog box shows the current filename.

9. Click the **Save as type** arrow and choose **Excel 97-2003 Workbook**.

10. Edit the filename to *[your initials]*11-18a and click **Save**. The Compatibility Checker alerts you that the SmartArt graphics will not be editable in the earlier versions of Excel.

11. Click **Continue**. Close the workbook.

Using Online Help

Excel has many types of SmartArt graphics. You can use Help to learn about many of the layouts available for use in a workbook.

USE HELP TO LEARN ABOUT SMARTART GRAPHICS

1. In a new workbook, click the Microsoft Office Excel Help button.

2. Find and review topics about images and graphics.

3. Close the Help window when you are finished.

Lesson 11 Summary

- You can place images on a sheet or a chart. Images can be taken from a disk or the Clip Organizer.
- Pictures have properties that depend on how the image was originally created. You can edit some of these properties.
- You can use pictures in headers and footers. Some images, based on their size and color, can be used to mimic a watermark.
- Pictures have most of the same style elements as shapes.
- Cropping an image enables you to hide or mask part of the picture.
- SmartArt graphics include many common business diagrams including Cycle, Target, Radial, Venn, and Pyramid designs.
- SmartArt graphics include organization charts with various levels to illustrate relationships among workers.
- Most SmartArt graphics have a Text pane for easy text entry and editing.
- SmartArt graphics have their own styles and colors. Many can be easily changed into another layout, too.
- SmartArt graphics are not linked to worksheet data.
- You can use the Research task pane to find words that mean the same thing in the same or a different language.
- Document properties include information such as the author name, a title, the subject, key words, and general comments.

LESSON 11		Command Summary	
Feature	**Button**	**Task Path**	**Keyboard**
Clip art		Insert, Illustrations	
Crop picture		Picture Tools Format, Size	
Cycle diagram		Insert, Illustrations	
Document properties		Microsoft Office, Prepare, Properties	
Header/footer picture		Insert, Header & Footer, Header & Elements	
Organization chart		Insert, Illustrations	
Picture/image from file		Insert, Illustrations	
Research		Review, Proofing	Alt+[click]
Symbol, insert		Insert, Text	

Concepts Review

True/False Questions

Each of the following statements is either true or false. Indicate your choice by circling T or F.

T F   1. The font size in a SmartArt graphic adjusts to fit the shape.

T F   2. To crop a picture, you must first rotate it.

T F   3. A thesaurus translates words into another language.

T F   4. Picture Tools are contextual tools for editing a picture inserted from a disk.

T F   5. The text boxes in an organization chart are called *shapes*.

T F   6. Only a few of the SmartArt graphics include a Text pane.

T F   7. Accents for words translated into another language are automatically inserted in the label.

T F   8. In the Research task pane, you can find and use images from the Clip Organizer.

Short Answer Questions

Write the correct answer in the space provided.

1. Name three categories of SmartArt graphics in Excel.

_____

2. How can you display this character: **á**?

_____

3. What type of reference includes words that mean the same thing?

_____

4. What term describes the process of hiding part of a picture?

_____

5. Describe the pointer used to drag a graphic.

_____

6. How can you include your name and a general comment with a workbook?

_____

7. How do you enter text in a shape in a SmartArt graphic?

_____

8. How can you restyle a SmartArt graphic with different colors or shadows?

_____

Critical Thinking

Answer these questions on a separate page. There are no right or wrong answers. Support your answers with examples from your own experience, if possible.

1. The Research task pane allows you to add additional reference sources to those that come with Excel. What types of references might be helpful to business workers? What references might help students?

2. Explore each of the SmartArt categories. Then list a business or school concept that might be appropriately illustrated by each general category.

Skills Review

Exercise 11-19

Insert a picture. Size, color, and copy a picture. Flip and align pictures.

1. Open **KowSales** and save it as *[your initials]*11-19.
2. Insert a picture by following these steps:
   a. Click cell A1.
   b. Click the **Insert** tab. Click the Picture button .
   c. Find and select the **KowOwowTrans** file. Click **Insert**.
   d. With the four-pointed arrow, click and drag the image slightly down and to the right so you can see all the handles.

3. Size, color, and copy a picture by following these steps:

   a. On the **Picture Tools Format** tab, click the Dialog Box Launcher for the **Size** group.

   b. In the **Scale** group, double-click the value in the **Height** box, key **50**, and press ⟨Tab⟩. Click **Close**.

    c. In the **Picture Tools** group, click the Recolor button . Choose one of the **Light Variations**.

   d. Point at the picture and hold down ⟨Ctrl⟩. Drag a copy of the picture to the right of the original.

   e. Hold down ⟨Shift⟩ and click the original image. Both images are selected. Point at either image, hold down ⟨Ctrl⟩, and drag a copy of the pictures to the right of the labels in columns J:K.

   f. Select the first copy (at the left) and use a different **Light Variation** color. Select each of the other copies and choose a different color.

4. Flip and align pictures by following these steps:

   a. Click one of the images on the right. Hold down ⟨Shift⟩ and click the other picture on the right. Both pictures on the right should be selected.

    b. In the **Arrange** group, click the Rotate button . Choose **Flip Horizontal**.

   c. Hold down ⟨Shift⟩ and click the original image and then the first copy so that all four pictures are selected.

    d. In the **Arrange** group, click the Align button . Choose **Align Bottom**.

5. Click cell A12.

6. Click the Microsoft Office Button . Choose **Prepare** and **Inspect Document**. Remove all metadata and personal information.

7. Prepare and submit your work.

Exercise 11-20

Add a picture to a header/footer.

1. Open **KowSales** and save it as *[your initials]***11-20**.

2. Add a picture to a header by following these steps:

   a. Click the **Insert** tab. Click the Header & Footer button 🖺.

   b. Click in the right section. In the **Header and Footer Elements** group, click the Picture button 🖾.

   c. Navigate to the folder with **KowOwowTrans** and click to highlight the filename or thumbnail.

   d. Click **Insert**.

    e. In the **Header and Footer Elements** group, click the Format Picture button 🖾.

REVIEW

Background images do not print.

NOTE

You can use the same filename for the workbook and the Web page because they have different filename extensions.

f. Click the **Size** tab. In the **Scale** group, double-click the value in the **Height** box, key **50**, and click **OK**.

g. Key your name in the left section.

3. Click a cell in the worksheet. Press [Ctrl]+[Home]. Save the workbook.

4. Click the **Page Layout** tab. Click the Background button ⬚. Navigate to the folder with **KKBack**. Insert the file.

5. Change the color of the labels in rows 1:2 to a color that complements the background.

6. Save the workbook as a Web page named *[your initials]*11-20. Change the title for the Web browser to **K & K Sales**.

7. Prepare and submit your work.

Exercise 11-21

Create a hierarchy shape. Add text to an organization chart.

1. Create a new workbook named *[your initials]*11-21. Rename **Sheet1** as **OrgChart**. Set landscape orientation.

2. Create a hierarchy shape by following these steps:

a. On the **Insert** tab, click the SmartArt button ⬚.

b. Click **Hierarchy** and then click **Organization Chart**.

c. On the **SmartArt Tools Design** tab in the **SmartArt Styles** group, click the More button ⬚. Find and choose **Inset**.

d. In the **SmartArt Styles** group, click the Change Colors button ⬚. Choose **Colorful – Accent Colors**.

e. Click the assistant shape, the second icon vertically. Press [Delete].

f. Click the border of the leftmost subordinate shape (bottom row).

g. On the **SmartArt Tools Design** tab in the **Create Graphic** group, click the arrow with the Add Shape button ⬚. Choose **Add Shape Before**.

3. Add text to an organization chart by following these steps:

a. Click the first line in the Text pane.

b. Key **Heinrich Kraus** and press [Shift]+[Enter]. Key **President-Elect**.

c. Click the line below "President-Elect" in the Text pane. Key **Glenn Ladewig**.

d. Click the next line in the Text pane and key **Nassar Eassa**.

NOTE

If you add an unwanted shape, select it and press [Delete].

e. On the next line, key **Ted Artagnan**. On the last line, key **Maria Calcivechia**.

4. Hide the Text pane. Point at the border of the SmartArt shape to display the four-pointed arrow. Drag the shape so that its top-left selection handle is in cell A1. Drag the bottom-right selection handle to reach cell L25.

5. Click a worksheet cell. Insert WordArt using **Fill – Accent 2, Warm Matte Bevel** (fifth row) that displays **Owners Association**. Drag the WordArt shape so that is appears centered over the chart.

6. Center the worksheet horizontally.

7. Prepare and submit your work.

Exercise 11-22

Build a SmartArt diagram. Use the Research tool. Set document properties.

1. Create a new workbook named *[your initials]*11-22. Rename **Sheet1** as **Venn**.

2. Build a SmartArt diagram by following these steps:

   a. Click the **Insert** tab. Click the SmartArt button .

   b. Open the **Relationship** pane. Find and click the **Basic Venn** icon. Click **OK**.

   c. Click the arrow with the Add Shape button. Choose **Add Shape After**.

   d. Click the first line in the Text pane and key **Finance**.

   e. On the second line in the Text pane, key **Marketing**.

   f. On the third line, key **Owners**. On the last line, key **Human Resources**.

   g. Click a cell within the diagram frame.

   h. Close the Text pane. Drag the diagram so that the top-left corner starts in cell A5.

   i. On the **SmartArt Tools Design** tab, click the Change Colors button. Choose **Dark 1 Outline**.

   j. Key **Franchise Integration** in cell A1. Choose a font size and center the label across the diagram.

3. Center the sheet horizontally.

4. Select the diagram so that the frame is visible and no individual shape is selected. Press Ctrl+C. Click cell A24 and press Ctrl+V.

5. Use Research by following these steps:

   a. In cell J23, key **finance**. Key **marketing** in cell J24, **human resources** in cell J25, and **owners** in cell J26.

   b. Hold down Alt and click cell J23. Verify that **All Reference Books** are used.

TIP

You can collapse references that you are not using.

c. Click the Expand button ⊞ for **Thesaurus: English (US)**.

d. Place the mouse pointer on **investment** in the **money (n.)** category. Click the arrow and choose **Insert**.

e. Hold down ⟨Alt⟩ and click cell J24. Insert **promotion** from the **advertising (n.)** category.

f. Look up **human resources** and insert **workforce** in its place.

g. Look up **owners** but do not make a change. Close the Research task pane.

6. Edit a diagram by following these steps:

  a. Select the copied diagram.

  b. On the **SmartArt Tools Design** tab, click the Text Pane button . Drag the Text pane so that you can see the substitute words in column J and the diagram.

  c. Replace **Finance** in the Text pane with **Investment**. Replace **Marketing** with **Promotion**. Replace **Human Resources** with **Workforce**.

  d. Close the Text pane and delete the labels in column J.

7. Set document properties by following these steps:

  a. Click the Microsoft Office Button 🔵.

  b. Choose **Prepare** and then choose **Properties**.

  c. Triple-click in the **Author** box and key *[your first and last name]*.

  d. Press ⟨Tab⟩. Key **SmartArt Venn Diagram** in the **Title** box.

  e. Click in the **Comments** box and key the following:
    This worksheet illustrates two diagrams for the upcoming workshop.

  f. Close the Document Information Panel.

8. Prepare and submit your work.

Lesson Applications

Exercise 11-23

Build a SmartArt list diagram. Insert a picture.

1. Create a new workbook and save it as *[your initials]*11-23.

2. From the SmartArt List pane, create a Vertical Picture Accent List shape.

3. Key Kowabunga on the first line in the Text pane. Key KowOwow on the second line, and Shakes and Malts on the third line. Close the Text pane.

NOTE

Use the Format Shape dialog box to insert clip art.

4. Click the top circle shape to the left of the text. The Insert Picture dialog box opens. Navigate to the appropriate folder and insert **Kowabunga**. Insert **KowOwowTrans** in the second circle shape.

5. Right-click the third circle shape and choose Format Shape. On the Fill pane, choose Picture or texture fill. Click ClipArt. If you have a broadband connection, select Include content from Office Online. Search for an image about "ice cream" and/or "milk." Use a clip that seems appropriate. Click the image and click OK. Click the frame of the main shape to deselect any circles.

TIP

Use a corner handle to resize a shape horizontally and vertically at the same time.

6. On the SmartArt Tools Design tab, choose Polished and Colorful Range – Accent Colors 2 to 3.

7. Click a worksheet cell and insert a WordArt image using a color/style that will complement the SmartArt shape. Key Klassy Kow Ice Cream.

8. Position the WordArt so that it looks centered over the list shape. Size the WordArt for balance. Arrange both shapes so that they will appear centered on a portrait page.

9. Prepare and submit your work.

Exercise 11-24

Use the Research tool.

Use the Research task pane and other resources to change the names of the flavors on a supermarket order sheet from English to Spanish.

REVIEW

Hold down Alt and click the cell to open the Research task pane.

1. Open **SpanishOrderSheet** and save it as *[your initials]*11-24.

2. Look up Vanilla in cell A9 using the Translation tool with Spanish (Spanish-International Sort). Key the Spanish spelling in cell A9.

TIP

To insert a symbol, select the character in the formula bar or the cell and proceed as usual.

3. Repeat these steps to find a Spanish translation for each of the flavors. Use symbols if needed. Close the Research task pane.

4. Choose a different document theme for the order sheet. Then edit the document properties to show the name of the theme in the **Comments** area. Add your name as the **Author** and **Translated Sheet** as the **Title**.

5. Format the appropriate cells in row 3 with a bottom border that uses the second dotted style from the first column of line style choices in the Format Cells dialog box. Make row 3 **7.50 (10 pixels)** high.

6. Use a solid double-line bottom border for row 4 and make it the same height as row 3.

7. Create the same border arrangement for rows 25:26.

8. Prepare and submit your work.

Exercise 11-25

Create a hierarchy diagram.

The Hierarchy SmartArt pane includes charts that show relationships among people. Many of these graphics can be used to show relationships among events, activities, or ideas.

1. Create a new workbook and save it as *[your initials]*11-25.

2. Create a **Table Hierarchy** shape. There should be one top shape. Then add one shape before or after the two shapes on the second row, resulting in three shapes at the second level.

3. Key **Sales** in the top shape or the first line in the Text pane.

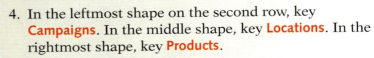
REVIEW

When you press Enter in the Text pane, a new shape at the same level is inserted.

4. In the leftmost shape on the second row, key **Campaigns**. In the middle shape, key **Locations**. In the rightmost shape, key **Products**.

5. Click the first line below **Locations** in the Text pane. Key **Geography**. Click the second line and key **Demographics**. Press Enter and key **Culture**.

6. Click after **Campaigns** in the Text pane. Press Enter and then press Tab. Key these three labels on the level below **Campaigns**.
   Timing
   Success Rate
   Cost

7. In three shapes below **Products**, key these labels:
   Appeal
   Cost Structure
   Portability

8. Choose a style and colors. Position the shape so that it starts at cell A1. Set landscape orientation and size the shape to fill the page.

9. Prepare and submit your work.

Exercise 11-26 ◆ Challenge Yourself

Link a picture of cells.

You can paste a "picture" of cells so that it acts like an image from a disk. A cell picture can be pasted or linked.

NOTE

A linked cell picture has fewer editable attributes than shapes. Use the Format Picture dialog box to add fill and border color.

1. Open **WeeklyData** and save it as *[your initials]*11-26.

2. Insert a sheet and create a WordArt object that says **California Totals**. Position the WordArt so that it starts in cell A1. Name the sheet **Picture**.

3. Copy cells F4:F18 on the **WeeklySales** sheet. Click cell C10 on the **Picture** sheet. Click the arrow with the Paste button. Choose **As Picture** and then **Paste as Picture Link**. The linked cell picture is an object with selection handles.

4. Position the picture so that it is centered below the WordArt. Format the object to have a light fill color that complements your WordArt. Choose an appropriate line color, too.

5. Return to the **WeeklySales** sheet. Delete the weekly values (not totals) for two of the cities.

6. Prepare and submit your work.

On Your Own

In these exercises you work on your own, as you would in a real-life work environment. Use the skills you've learned to accomplish the task—and be creative.

Exercise 11-27

Open **SpanishOrderSheet** and use the Research tool to translate the flavors into another language for which the dictionary is installed on your computer. Save the workbook as *[your initials]*11-27. Prepare and submit your work.

Exercise 11-28

Create a new workbook and save it as *[your initials]*11-28. Create a hierarchy shape that illustrates your ancestors and descendants (if appropriate). Format the shape according to your tastes. Prepare and submit your work.

Exercise 11-29

In a new workbook, create one each of the Matrix and Pyramid SmartArt shapes to illustrate a business or social concept or idea. Create the shape, add text, and style the diagram. Save your workbook as *[your initials]*11-29. Prepare and submit your work.

Unit 3 Applications

Unit Application 3-1

Create and format a combination chart.

Klassy Kow Ice Cream sells ice cream to supermarkets in cases that hold 6, 12, 18, or 24 half-gallon cartons. You have been asked to create a chart that plots the cost per case and the number of cartons per case.

NOTE

The markup is added to the cost to reach the selling price.

1. Open **ICCases** and save it as *[your initials]*u3-1 in a folder for Unit 3.

2. In cell C6, key a formula to determine the cost per case. Copy the formula and use Currency format.

3. In cell D6, key a formula to multiply the per-case cost by 1 plus the markup for the month. Copy the formula and use Currency format.

4. Use empty rows to create an attractive border arrangement for the worksheet. Insert/delete rows if necessary.

5. Use the labels and values in columns A, C, and D to create a clustered column chart on a separate sheet. As the chart title, key **Cost and Selling Price Comparison**. Choose a chart style.

6. Change the chart type for both currency values to a line chart with markers. Show the data labels for all three series.

7. Format the line and its markers and the column so that the chart is attractive and easy to interpret. Position the legend at the left.

8. Edit the document properties to show your name as the author.

9. Prepare and submit your work.

Unit Application 3-2

Insert WordArt. Insert a shape.

The Marketing Department tracks promotions and incentives to determine which are the best sales generators. You have been asked to create a worksheet that shows recent promotions and the resulting increase in sales.

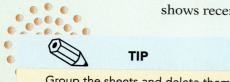

TIP

Group the sheets and delete them at once.

1. Create a new workbook and save it as *[your initials]*u3-2. Delete **Sheet2** and **Sheet3**. Rename **Sheet1** **Promotions**.

2. Key the information in Figure Unit3-1, starting in column B.

Figure Unit 3-1

	B	C
1	Promotions	Sales Increase
2	Guess gumballs	12%
3	Tip calculator	8%
4	10% Off	15%
5	Multiplication table	8%

NOTE

If you keyed the data starting in column A, move it to the right.

3. Make each row **52.50 (70 pixels)** tall.

4. Insert WordArt and key **Klassy Kow Ice Cream**. Rotate the shape 90° left and drag it to column A to fill the same space as the data rows.

5. Insert a rounded corner rectangle shape in columns D:F and key the following:

   These are company-wide averages. Individual shops experience various increases based on location, weather, and other factors.

6. Format the shape and the data with your own choices.

7. Prepare and submit your work.

Unit Application 3-3

Insert a SmartArt shape.

1. Create a new workbook and save it as *[your initials]*u3-3. Delete **Sheet2** and **Sheet3**. Rename **Sheet1 Radial**.

2. Insert a Radial Cycle shape. In the middle object, key **Increased Sales**.

3. Key additional text as follows:

Top shape	**Local promotion on radio and in newspapers.**
Left shape	**State-wide coupon campaign and free decal with purchase.**
Bottom shape	**Regional TV ads with free gift with purchase.**
Last shape	*[Key your own campaign idea for increasing sales.]*

4. Choose a style and colors. Position and size the shape to display well in landscape orientation.

5. Prepare and submit your work.

Unit Application 3-4 ◆ Using the Internet

Build a pie chart.

Search office supply and computer equipment Web sites to build a price list for six items in an office. You might include objects such as a desk, a chair, a bookcase, file cabinet(s), a computer, a monitor, or a printer. For each item, list the name and a price.

Build a pie chart that shows the proportion each item represents of the total cost for all six items. Use a main title for the chart that includes your name. You might need a legend, depending on your other design choices. Place the chart on a separate sheet. Save the workbook as *[your initials]*u3-4. Prepare and submit your work.

unit 4

EXPANDING USES OF WORKBOOK DATA

EXL4.12

Using 3-D References

OBJECTIVES

After completing this lesson, you will be able to:

1. Work with multiple sheets.

2. Create a 3-D reference.

3. Use formulas in a 3-D reference.

4. Use functions in a 3-D reference.

5. Add a digital signature.

MCAS OBJECTIVES

In this lesson:
XL07 1.5
XL07 3.1.2
XL07 5.3.4
XL07 5.3.5

Estimated Time: 1¹/₂ hours

An Excel workbook can have as many worksheets as the computer's memory allows. This enables you to place data on different sheets for ease in tracking and reviewing information. Using a 3-D reference, you can gather information from multiple sheets to calculate grand totals, differences, averages, and more.

Working with Multiple Sheets

There are many applications in which similar data is kept day by day, week by week, month by month on separate sheets in the same workbook. In most instances, the arrangement of the data is identical and only the values are different. At some point, it is quick and easy to gather such data into a summary worksheet.

Exercise 12-1 EDIT A MARKED-AS-FINAL WORKBOOK

When a document has been marked as final by its creator, it is uneditable until that property is reset. You can determine if a workbook has been marked as final by looking in the title bar and in the status bar.

1. Open **ORKowSales**. The title bar shows [Read Only] after the filename.

2. Point at the icon next to Ready in the status bar.

3. Click any cell in an attempt to edit it. You cannot do so.

4. Click the Microsoft Office Button 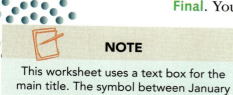. Choose Prepare and Mark as Final. You can now edit the workbook.

5. Make a copy of the Jan-Feb sheet at the end. The new sheet is an exact duplicate of the Jan-Feb sheet.

6. Rename the Jan-Feb tab as Mar-Apr. Without changing the en dash (–), edit "January–February" in the text box to March–April.

7. Make another copy of the original sheet and name it May-June. Edit the text box to correspond.

> **NOTE**
>
> This worksheet uses a text box for the main title. The symbol between January and February is an en dash.

Exercise 12-2 GROUP SHEETS FOR EDITING

1. Click the May-June tab, hold down [Ctrl], and click the Mar-Apr tab.

2. Select cells B5:C9 and press [Delete]. The values are cleared from both sheets.

3. Hold down [Ctrl] and click the Jan-Feb tab. It is added to the group. All three worksheets are selected.

> **REVIEW**
>
> The word [Group] appears in the title bar.

4. Click cell A3 and key Shop to add the label to all three sheets.

5. Click cell D5, key =sum, and press [Tab]. Select cells B5:C5 and press [Enter]. Copy the formula to row 9.

6. Insert a row at row 10.

7. Click cell D10. On the Home tab, click the Sum button Σ ▾ and press [Enter].

8. Insert a row at row 11.

9. In cell C11, key Previous Total. Make it bold and right-aligned.

10. Right-click any sheet tab and choose Ungroup Sheets.

11. Click the Mar-Apr tab and key the values in Figure 12-1.

Figure 12-1

Shop	Chocolate	Vanilla
Eugene	1200	1025
Ashland	1500	1600
Klamath Falls	975	1035
Roseburg	1050	1200
Medford	1800	1560

Excel 2007

12. Click the **May-June** tab and key the values in Figure 12-2.

Figure 12-2

Shop	Chocolate	Vanilla
Eugene	1300	1225
Ashland	1675	1650
Klamath Falls	1975	935
Roseburg	1450	1175
Medford	1645	1800

Creating a 3-D Reference

A *3-D reference* is a formula that refers to a cell or cells in another worksheet in the same workbook. The reference is dynamic, because if the referenced cell is edited, the cell with the 3-D reference reflects the change.

Exercise 12-3   **CREATE A SINGLE-CELL 3-D REFERENCE**

In the **Mar-Apr** worksheet, you will insert a reference to the total for the previous two-month period. The easiest way to create a simple 3-D reference is to point to the desired worksheet tab and cell.

1. Click the **Mar-Apr** tab.

2. Click cell D11 and key **=** to start the formula.

3. Click the **Jan-Feb** tab.

4. Click cell D10 and press ⌐Enter⌐. The reference is inserted in the **Mar-Apr** sheet.

5. Click cell D11 and look at the formula bar. The name of the referenced worksheet is enclosed in single quotation marks and followed by an exclamation point. Quotation marks are inserted when a sheet name includes a value and/or a special character.

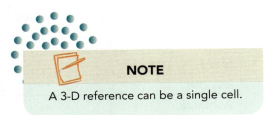

NOTE

A 3-D reference can be a single cell.

Figure 12-3
3-D reference to a cell
ORKowSales.xlsx Mar-Apr sheet

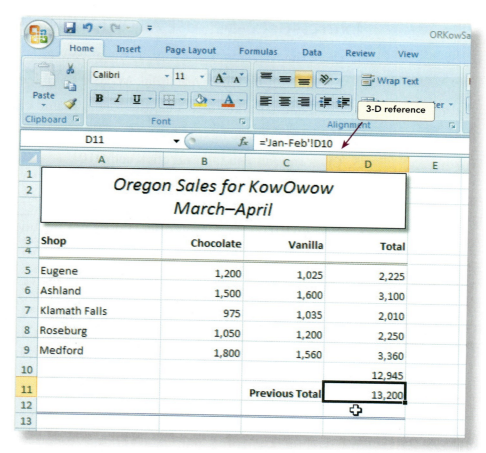

6. Click the **May-June** tab. Click cell D11 and key **=** to start the formula.

7. Click the **Mar-Apr** tab. Click cell D10 and press Ctrl+Enter. Check the formula in the formula bar.

Exercise 12-4   EDIT REFERENCED DATA

If the value in a cell used in a 3-D reference is changed, the cell with the reference is automatically updated.

1. Click the **Mar-Apr** tab. Click cell D11. Notice that the value in cell D11 in the **Mar-Apr** sheet is 13,200.

2. Click the **Jan-Feb** tab. Change the values in cells B5 and C5 to **0**.

3. Click the **Mar-Apr** tab. The new total, **10,700**, is shown in cell D11.

Using a Formula in a 3-D Reference

In addition to a single cell address, you can use a formula in a 3-D reference. A 3-D formula can calculate a total based on data on several sheets. In your workbook, for example, you can use a 3-D reference to determine the first half-year sales by adding the totals from each of the three sheets.

Exercise 12-5   USE ADDITION IN A 3-D REFERENCE

1. Click the **May-Jun** tab. Insert a row at row 12.

2. In cell C12, key **Half-Year Total**. Make it bold and right-aligned.

3. Click cell D12, key **=** to start the formula, and click cell D10.

4. Key **+** to add the next value.

5. Click the **Jan-Feb** tab and click cell D10.

6. Key **+** to add the next value.

7. Click the **Mar-Apr** tab and click cell D10. Press Ctrl + Enter. The reference to cell D10 on the **May-Jun** sheet does not include a worksheet name.

Figure 12-4
3-D reference for a formula
ORKowSales.xlsx
May-June sheet

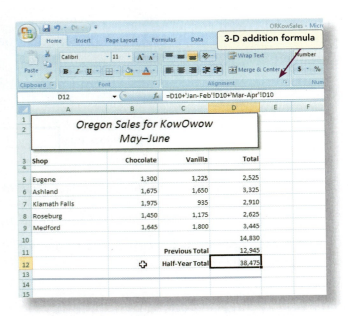

8. Make a copy of the **May-Jun** sheet. Name it **HalfYrTotal** and move it after the **May-Jun** tab.

9. Delete the contents of cells B5:D12.

10. Click cell B5 and key **=** to start a formula.

11. Click the **Jan-Feb** tab and click cell B5. The formula bar shows **='Jan-Feb'!B5**, and a marquee appears around the cell.

12. Key **+** to add the next reference. Click the **Mar-Apr** tab and click cell B5.

13. Key **+** to continue, and add the appropriate reference from the **May-June** sheet.

Figure 12-5
Creating a 3-D formula
ORKowSales.xlsx
May-June sheet

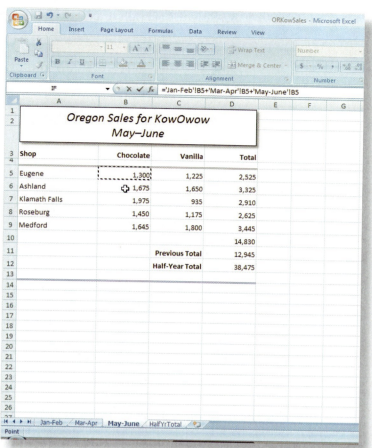

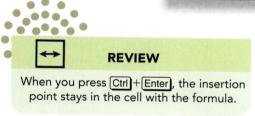
REVIEW

When you press Ctrl+Enter, the insertion point stays in the cell with the formula.

14. Press Ctrl+Enter. The formula is completed, and the result is shown on the **HalfYrTotal** sheet. Look at the formula bar.

15. Copy the formula to cells B6:B9 and then to cells C5:C9.

16. Click cell C5. Excel uses relative references for the cell addresses.

17. Select cells D5:D9 and click the Sum button Σ ▾.

18. Edit the label in the text box to read **First Half** on the second line.

Exercise 12-6   USE MULTIPLICATION IN A 3-D REFERENCE

1. Make a copy of the **Jan-Feb** sheet and move it to be the first sheet on the left. Name the copied worksheet **ProjectedSales**.

2. Edit the text box to show **Projected Second Half** on the second line.

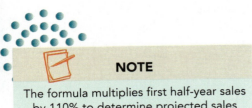

NOTE

The formula multiplies first half-year sales by 110% to determine projected sales that are 10% higher.

3. Select and delete cells B5:C9.

4. Click cell B5 and key **=** to start the formula.

5. Click the **HalfYrTotal** tab and click cell B5.

6. Key ***110%** and press Ctrl+Enter.

7. Copy the formula in cell B5 to cells B6:B9 and then to column C.

Exercise 12-7   COPY AND SCROLL MULTIPLE WORKSHEETS

With several worksheets in your workbook, you may not see all the worksheet tabs at once. The worksheet tab scrolling buttons are at the left edge of the tab names. These buttons allow you to scroll tabs.

The tab scrolling buttons share space with the horizontal scroll bar and are separated from it by the tab split box. You can drag the tab split box to change the number of visible tabs or the size of the horizontal scroll bar.

1. Click the **Jan-Feb** tab. Hold down Shift and click the **HalfYrTotal** tab. Four worksheets are grouped.

2. Right-click any sheet in the group and choose **Move or Copy**. Create copies at the end. Four new worksheets are inserted.

NOTE

Depending on your screen size, you might not be able to drag the tab split bar far enough to see all the tabs.

3. Position the mouse pointer on the tab split box. The pointer is a two-pointed arrow.

4. Click and drag the pointer to the right until you see all the tabs.

Figure 12-6
Dragging the tab split box
ORKowSales.xlsx
Jan-Feb sheet

5. Rename the copied sheets as follows (in the order shown):
   July-Aug
   Sept-Oct
   Nov-Dec
   YrTotal

6. Position the mouse pointer on the tab split box. Drag the pointer to the left so that you see the worksheet tabs up to **HalfYrTotal**.

7. Click each tab scrolling button to see how it moves through the tab names.

8. Right-click any of the tab scrolling buttons. A shortcut menu with a list of the tab names opens.

Figure 12-7
List of worksheet names
ORKowSales.xlsx Jan-Feb sheet

9. Choose **July-Aug**. The sheet is visible and active.

10. Edit the text box to show **July–August**.

11. Click the far-right tab scrolling button. The tab names at the end are visible.

12. Edit the text boxes to **September–October**, **November–December**, and **Year Total**.

13. Double-click the tab split box. The space for tab names adjusts to the default for your screen.

14. Click the **July-Aug** tab. Hold down [Shift] and click the **YrTotal** tab.

15. Delete the contents of cells B5:C9 on these four sheets.

16. Ungroup the sheets. Make sure that none of the text boxes are selected.

Using a Function in a 3-D Reference

In addition to simple arithmetic, you can use functions in a 3-D reference. Although you can key a 3-D formula, you are less likely to make an error by pointing at the references. In addition, when you point, Excel includes the worksheet tab name and the exclamation point so that you don't have to key them.

Exercise 12-8   KEY DATA IN A SELECTED RANGE

By selecting a range before keying the data, you can press Enter to move from one cell to the next in top-to-bottom, left-to-right order. After you complete this exercise, the sheets for July–August, September–October, and November–December will have the same values.

1. Click the **July-Aug** tab. Hold down Shift and click the **Nov-Dec** tab. Three sheets are grouped.

2. Select cells B5:C9.

3. Key the following values in column B and press Enter after each.
   1000
   2000
   1000
   2000
   1000

4. Key these values in column C, pressing Enter after each.
   2000
   1000
   2000
   1000
   2000

5. Click the **YrTotal** tab. The sheets are ungrouped.

6. Click cell B5 and key **=** to start a formula.

7. Click the **HalfYrTotal** tab and click cell B5. Key **+** to add the next reference.

8. Click the **July-Aug** tab and click cell B5. Key **+** to continue.

9. Click the **Sept-Oct** tab, click cell B5, and key **+**. Add the cell for **Nov-Dec** and press Ctrl+Enter.

10. Copy the formula to cells B6:B9 and then to column C.

Exercise 12-9   USE AVERAGE IN A 3-D REFERENCE

1. With the **YrTotal** tab active, click the **Insert Worksheet** tab.

2. Name the new sheet **AverageSales**.

3. Click the **YrTotal** tab and select the text box so that it displays a solid line boundary.

4. Press Ctrl+C, click the **AverageSales** tab, and press Ctrl+V. The text box is copied.

5. Make column A **20.71 (150 pixels)** wide. Makes columns B:D each **13.57 (100 pixels)** wide. Make the text box slightly taller.

6. Edit the second line in the text box to show **Average Monthly Sales**.

7. Copy cells B3:C3 on the **YrTotal** sheet to cells B6:C6 on the **AverageSales** sheet.

8. Copy cells A5:A9 on the **YrTotal** sheet to cells A7:A11 on the **AverageSales** sheet. Right-align these labels.

9. Drag the tab split box to the right so that you can see all the worksheet tab names (or as many as possible).

10. Click cell B7 on the **AverageSales** sheet. Key **=aver** and press Tab to start the function.

11. Click the **Jan-Feb** tab and click cell B5. Its address is inserted in the formula.

12. Key a comma to separate the arguments.

13. Click the **Mar-Apr** tab and click cell B5.

14. Key a comma and click the **May-June** tab.

15. Continue inserting the monthly sheet values up to and including the **Nov-Dec** tab, and press Ctrl + Enter.

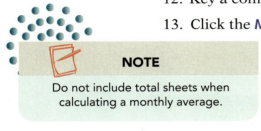

NOTE

Do not include total sheets when calculating a monthly average.

Figure 12-8
Using AVERAGE in a
3-D reference
ORKowSales.xlsx
Nov-Dec sheet

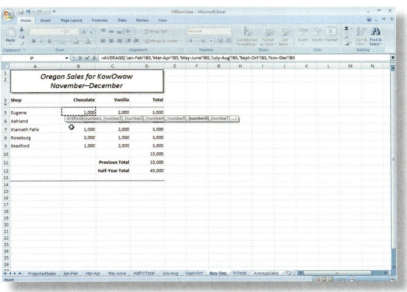

16. View the formula in the formula bar. The result is 917.

17. Copy the formula to cells B8:B11 and then to cells C8:C11.

18. Change the height of rows 6:11 to **22.50 (30 pixels)**.

Exercise 12-10 USE MAX IN A 3-D REFERENCE

1. Make a copy of the **AverageSales** sheet at the end and name it **MaxSales**.

2. Delete the contents of cells B7:C11.

3. Click cell **B7** and click the Insert Function button .

4. Choose **MAX** and click **OK**. Move the Function Arguments dialog box so that you can see the cells you need to click.

5. Click the **Jan-Feb** tab. Click cell **B5**.

6. Click in the **Number2** box in the Function Arguments dialog box.

7. Click the **Mar-Apr** tab. Click cell **B5**.

Figure 12-9
Using the Function Arguments dialog box for a 3-D reference
**ORKowSales.xlsx
Mar-Apr sheet**

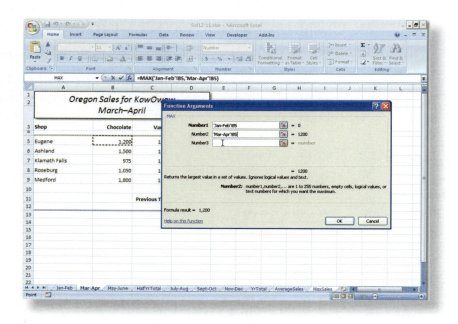

8. Click in the **Number3** box and click the **May-June** tab. Click cell **B5**.

9. In the **Number4** box, select the same cell for **July-Aug**.

10. In the **Number5** box, select the same cell for **Sept-Oct**. In the **Number6** box, select the cell for **Nov-Dec**.

11. Click **OK**.

12. Copy the formula to cells B8:B11 and then to column C.

13. Click the **May-June** tab. In cell B5, key **12000**.

14. Click the **MaxSales** tab and note the new maximum for "Chocolate." Click the **AverageSales** tab and note the higher average for "Chocolate" in Eugene.

Creating a Digital Signature

A *digital signature* is a document property that electronically authenticates the document using computer cryptography. A digital signature is not visible within the document, but it enables you to prohibit others from editing your work. You can add a digital signature to an Excel workbook as a basic security measure for work that you share with others. For high-end safety needs, however, you can purchase signature services from companies that specialize in digital information security.

Exercise 12-11 ADD A DIGITAL SIGNATURE

1. Save the workbook as *[your initials]*12-11 in a folder for Lesson 12.

2. Click the **ProjectedSales** tab, the first sheet in your workbook.

3. Scroll the worksheets to the **MaxSales** tab, the last sheet.

4. Hold down Shift and click the **MaxSales** tab. All worksheets are grouped.

5. Click the Microsoft Office Button  and choose **Prepare**. You cannot create a digital signature for grouped sheets.

6. Click any worksheet cell and ungroup the sheets. Click the **ProjectedSales** tab.

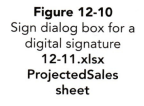

NOTE

The first time you create a digital signature at a computer, you create the Digital ID. You can indicate a name, e-mail address, organization, and location in this ID.

7. Click the Microsoft Office Button. Choose **Prepare** and **Add a Digital Signature**. This first dialog box explains digital signatures.

8. Click **OK**. The Sign dialog box shows the user name as the signing entity. You can also indicate a purpose for signing the document.

9. In the **Purpose for signing this document** box, key **KowOwow Market Analysis**.

Figure 12-10
Sign dialog box for a digital signature
12-11.xlsx
ProjectedSales sheet

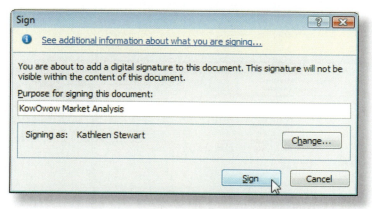

10. Click **Change**. You likely cannot change the signature at your computer.

11. Click **View Certificate**. The Certificate dialog box has three tabs with information about the digital signature. Digital signatures are often managed by a network administrator, so you are unable to edit these settings.

12. Click **OK** and then click **Cancel**. You are back at the Sign dialog box.

13. Click **Sign** and click **OK**. The document is saved and the Signatures pane has opened. There is an icon in the status bar to show that the document is signed.

14. Close the Signatures pane and the workbook.

Exercise 12-12   REMOVE A DIGITAL SIGNATURE

Depending on general computer security and permissions, you can remove a digital signature.

1. Open *[your initials]***12-11**. Look for the icon in the status bar to indicate that this document has a signature. (The Signatures pane may open, too.)

2. Click any cell to key your name. You cannot edit a signed document, because it is read-only.

3. If the Signatures pane is not open, click the Microsoft Office Button . Choose **Prepare** and **View Signatures**.

4. In the Signatures pane, click the user name and then its arrow. Choose **Signature Details**. You can determine from this dialog box that the document has not been edited.

5. Click **Close**. You can remove the signature since you were the one to create it.

6. In the Signatures pane, click the user name and then its arrow. Choose **Remove Signature**. This action cannot be undone.

Figure 12-11
Signatures pane
12-11.xlsx
ProjectedSales
sheet

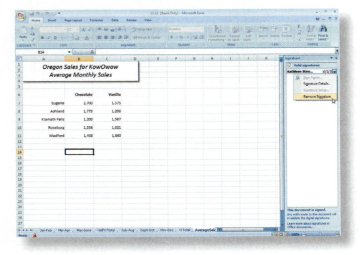

7. Click **Yes** and then click **OK**.

8. Save the workbook using the same name. Close the Signatures pane.

9. Double-click the tab split box. It returns to its default size.

Using Online Help

In addition to a digital signature, you can add a signature line to an Office document. Use Help to learn more about this type of signature.

USE HELP TO LEARN ABOUT SIGNATURES

1. In a new workbook, click the Microsoft Office Excel Help button 🔵.

2. Look up digital signature. Read the information.

3. Close the Help window when you are finished.

Lesson 12 Summary

- All data and formats are copied when you use the Move or Copy dialog box.

- Group worksheets to format them in the same way or to delete or key data on all of them at the same time.

- A 3-D reference is a formula that refers to cells or values in a different worksheet. It can use formulas you key or functions.

- A 3-D reference includes the name of the worksheet followed by an exclamation point. The cell addresses follow.

- The tab scrolling buttons allow you to move through worksheet tabs when you cannot see all of them at once. The buttons share space with the horizontal scroll bar.

- A digital signature is one way to ensure the authenticity of your data.

LESSON 12		Command Summary	
Feature	**Button**	**Task Path**	**Keyboard**
Digital signature	🔲	Microsoft Office, Prepare	

Concepts Review

True/False Questions

Each of the following statements is either true or false. Indicate your choice by circling T or F.

T   F   1. You can apply a 3-D format to a 3-D reference.

T   F   2. Grouped worksheets are permanent.

T   F   3. A 3-D reference may be a single cell.

T   F   4. A function in a 3-D reference uses curly braces instead of parentheses for the arguments.

T   F   5. A 3-D reference can be a formula that refers to cells in another worksheet.

T   F   6. If you cannot see all worksheet tabs, use the horizontal scroll bar to move them into view.

T   F   7. When you edit a cell used in a 3-D reference, you need to update the formula to include the revised data.

T   F   8. A digital signature contributes to data security.

Short Answer Questions

Write the correct answer in the space provided.

1. What is the difference between using Shift and Ctrl to group worksheets?

_____

2. How do you digitally sign a workbook?

_____

3. Describe how a 3-D reference to cell B4 on the Sales worksheet would appear in the formula bar.

_____

4. How can you enter the same data on four sheets at once?

_____

5. Name the buttons that allow you to move worksheet tabs into view.

_____

6. List an advantage of pointing to a 3-D reference rather than keying it.

_____

7. How can you enter data in a range going from top to bottom and then left to right by pressing [Enter]?

_____

8. How do you ungroup sheets?

_____

Critical Thinking

Answer these questions on a separate page. There are no right or wrong answers. Support your answers with examples from your own experience, if possible.

1. Thinking about your school or the company where you work, give an example of a workbook that might use multiple sheets. What would be the purpose of the workbook and how would multiple sheets be used?

2. Why are digital signatures important? Discuss reasons why a business would purchase a third-party service to sign their documents.

Skills Review

Exercise 12-13

Work with multiple worksheets.

1. Open **AdvExp** and save it as *[your initials]*12-13.
2. Set landscape orientation and center the sheet horizontally. Change the document theme to **Oriel** and make other adjustments if needed.
3. Create the same border layout as the one in rows 3:4 for rows 10:11.
4. Work with multiple worksheets by following these steps:
   a. Right-click the **July** tab and choose **Move or Copy**. Choose **(move to end)**. Select **Create a copy** and click **OK**.
   b. Rename **July (2)** as **August**. Edit the label in cell A2.
   c. Copy the **August** sheet, name the copy **September**, and edit the label.
   d. Click the **July** tab. Hold down [Shift] and click the **September** tab.
   e. Select cells D6:D9 and click the Sum button ![Σ·].
   f. Format all values as Currency with no decimals.
   g. Use a light fill for cells A5:D10 to match the border color.
   h. Make rows 6:9 each **22.50 (30 pixels)** tall.
   i. Right-align the labels in row 5.
5. Prepare and submit your work.

REVIEW

The Currency number format is in the Format Cells dialog box.

Exercise 12-14

Work with multiple sheets. Create 3-D references.

1. Open **Charity** and save it as *[your initials]*12-14.

2. Insert a footer.

3. Work with multiple worksheets by following these steps:

TIP

If you insert a footer on the original sheet, it is copied when you copy the sheet.

   a. Make three copies of the **2007** sheet. Name them **2008**, **2009**, and **2010**. Place the sheets in chronological order.

   b. Group the **2008** through **2010** sheets.

   c. Edit the label in cell A2 to remove the year and show only **Contributions**.

   d. Insert a column at column B. Make it the same width as column C.

   e. Delete the values in cells C4:C8.

   f. Insert a row at row 4 and make it **26.25 (35 pixels)** tall.

   g. Select cells B4:C4.

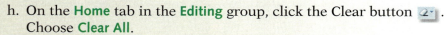

   h. On the **Home** tab in the **Editing** group, click the Clear button. Choose **Clear All**.

   i. Key **Last Year** in cell B4 and **This Year** in cell C4. Make these labels bold and right-aligned.

   j. Ungroup the sheets.

4. Create a 3-D reference by following these steps:

   a. Click the **2008** tab and cell B5.

   b. Key **=** to start a formula. Click the **2007** tab and click cell B4. Press Ctrl+Enter.

   c. Format cell B5 as Currency with no decimals and copy the formula through cell B9.

NOTE

You can prepare the references even though there is no data on the sheets. Key sample data if you want to test your references.

   d. Click the **2009** tab and click cell B5. Key **=**, click the **2008** tab, and click cell C5. Press Ctrl+Enter.

   e. Format cell C5 as Currency with no decimals and copy the formula through cell C9.

   f. Add and format the appropriate reference on the **2010** sheet.

5. Group the **2008** through **2010** sheets and make copies. Display the formulas on the copies.

6. Prepare and submit your work.

Exercise 12-15

Use formulas in 3-D references. Use functions in a 3-D reference.

1. Open **EstAdv** and save it as *[your initials]*12-15. Ungroup the sheets.

2. Use a formula in a 3-D reference by following these steps:

   a. Click the **ThirdQtr** tab and click cell B6.

   b. Key **=** to start the formula.

   c. Click the **July** tab and click cell B6.

   d. Key **+** and click the **August** tab.

   e. Click cell B6, key **+** and click the **September** tab.

   f. Click cell B6 and press Ctrl+Enter.

   g. Copy the formula to cells B7:B9 and then to column C.

   h. Set no fill for the cells that were changed when you copied the formula.

3. Use a function in a 3-D reference by following these steps:

   a. Make a copy of the **Estimated** sheet and place it before this sheet. Name it **Average**.

   b. Click cell B6 on the **Average** sheet.

   c. Click the Insert Function button . Find and choose **AVERAGE**.

   d. Click the **July** tab and click cell B6.

REVIEW

From the Paste Special dialog box, you can choose what is copied.

   e. Click in the **Number2** box. Click the **August** tab and click cell B6.

   f. Click in the **Number3** box. Click the **September** tab and click cell B6. Click **OK**.

   g. Click cell B6 and click the Copy button. Select cells B7:B9 and right-click one of the cells. Choose **Paste Special** and choose **Formulas**. Click **OK**.

   h. Select cells C6:C9 and right-click one of the cells. Choose **Paste Special** and choose **Formulas**. Click **OK**. Press Esc.

NOTE

Multiplying a value by 115% calculates a new value that represents a 15% increase.

4. Create a 3-D reference using a formula by following these steps:

   a. Click the **Estimated** tab and cell B6.

   b. Key **=** and click the **Average** tab.

   c. Click cell B6. Key ***115%** and press Ctrl+Enter.

   d. Copy the formula.

5. Group and copy the **ThirdQtr**, **Average**, and **Estimated** sheets. Rename the copies to include "Formulas" at the end of the tab name.

6. Display the formulas on the appropriate sheets. Prepare these sheets to fit one landscape page.

7. Prepare and submit your work.

Exercise 12-16

Use formulas and functions in 3-D references. Create a digital signature.

1. Open **ProductList**. Save it as *[your initials]*12-16. This workbook has four worksheets, each listing products for a category.

2. Make a copy of the **Beverages** sheet and name it **NewBevPrices**. Place it so that it is the first sheet in the workbook.

3. Use a formula in a 3-D reference by following these steps:

   a. Click cell C4 on the **NewBevPrices** sheet. Key **=** to start a formula.

   b. Click cell C4 on the **Beverages** sheet.

   c. Key ***110%** and press Ctrl+Enter. The new price replaces the previous value.

   d. Copy the formula to cells C5:C13.

TIP

The new price will replace the old one.

4. Apply the **Opulent** document theme. Center the labels in rows 1:2 across the data.

5. Use a single solid bottom border for cells A2:B2. Apply a bottom border to cells A3:B3, but use a dashed style.

6. Create the same border arrangement in rows 13:14, but reverse the location of the dashed and solid lines. Change the height of row 14 to **22.50 (30 pixels)**.

7. Press Shift+F11. Name the new sheet **CategoryAverages**. Place it so that it is the first sheet in the workbook.

8. Click the **Beverages** tab. Copy the label in row 1 to the same row in the **CategoryAverages** sheet. Key **Category Average Price** in cell A2 and match the font.

9. Key these labels in column A starting in row 5.
   Beverages
   Cakes & Pies
   Ice Cream
   Novelties

10. Use a function in a 3-D reference by following these steps:

    a. Click cell B5 and key **=aver** and press Tab.

    b. Click the **Beverages** tab. Select cells C4:C13. Press Ctrl+Enter.

    c. Repeat these steps to show the average price for each of the other categories.

11. Make columns A:B each **18.13 (150 pixels)** wide. Center the labels in rows 1:2 across the data.

12. Use a single solid bottom border for cells A2:B2. Apply a bottom border to cells A3:B3 with a dashed style. Create the same border arrangement in rows 9:10, but reverse the location of the dashed and solid lines.

13. Horizontally center the **CategoryAverages** and **NewBevPrices** sheets. Prepare formula sheets for these two sheets.

14. Save the workbook.

15. Add a digital signature by following these steps:

    a. Save the workbook with the name *[your initials]*12-16 **signed**.

    b. Click the Microsoft Office Button . Choose **Prepare** and **Add a Digital Signature**. Click **OK**.

    c. In the **Purpose for signing this document** box, key **Update Price Lists**.

    d. Click **Sign**. Click **OK**. Close the Signatures pane.

16. Prepare and submit your work.

NOTE

Signing a document hides the data on sheets set for formula display. The signature must be removed to see the data.

Lesson Applications

Exercise 12-17

Work with multiple worksheets. Use a function in a 3-D formula.

This worksheet includes data for three months on one sheet. You will create separate sheets for each month.

1. Open **SandwichSales** and save it as *[your initials]*12-17.

2. Apply the Apex document theme. Center the sheet horizontally.

3. Click cell B10 and note the formula. November sales are projected to be 4% higher than October.

4. Click cell B15. A similar formula applies for December.

5. Make two copies of the sheet and name them November and December. Arrange the sheets in proper month order.

NOTE

December sales are 102% of November sales.

NOTE

If you key the function name immediately after opening the Insert Function dialog box and press Enter, Excel searches for the function.

6. On the November sheet, hide row 3, rows 5:8, and then rows 14:18. On the October and December sheets, hide the appropriate rows.

7. On the December sheet, copy the flavors to cells A22: A25. Key Fourth Quarter Totals in cell A21 and copy the font from cell A14.

8. Click cell B22. Click the Insert Function button and key sum. Press Enter. Click OK. In the Number1 box, select cells B5:E5 on the October sheet. In the Number2 box, select cells B10:E10 on the November sheet. In the Number3 box, select cells B15:E15 on the December sheet. Click OK. Copy the formula to cells B23:B25.

9. Prepare and submit your work.

Exercise 12-18

Use 3-D references. Create a digital signature.

1. Open **Personnel** and save it as *[your initials]*12-18. Rename Sheet1 as Complete. Rename Sheet2 as Birthdays.

2. In cell A1 on the Birthdays sheet, key Employee Birthdays. Make it 18 point.

3. Click cell A2 and key = to start a 3-D reference.

4. Click the Complete tab and cell B3. This reference will display the first name.

5. Key **&** and click cell A3, the last name. Press Ctrl+Enter. The two labels are run together but are missing a space.

6. Press F2 to edit the formula. Click after the ampersand. Key **" "&** (quote, space, quote, ampersand). Press Ctrl+Enter.

7. Copy the formula down to row 14.

8. Click cell B2 on the **Birthdays** sheet and key **=** to start a 3-D reference.

9. Click the **Complete** tab and cell E3. Press Enter. Format the date to show the month spelled out, the date, a comma, and the four-digit year. Copy the formula.

10. Format this sheet using your own design ideas. Save the workbook.

11. Save the workbook again, adding **signed** to the filename, and add a digital signature. The purpose is **Private employee data**.

12. Prepare and submit your work.

NOTE

The ampersand is a concatenation operator. "Concatenate" means to join or run together.

NOTE

To show a space or any character, enclose it in quotation marks. The first ampersand joins the first name to the space; the second ampersand joins the space to the last name.

Exercise 12-19

Work with multiple worksheets. Use a formula in a 3-D reference.

1. Open **ICSandwich** and save it as *[your initials]*12-19.

2. On the **April** sheet, the formula should multiply the March value by 110%. Find and correct the error.

3. The formula on the **May** sheet should multiply the April value by 105%. Find and correct the error.

4. Fix the borders so that the **April** and **May** sheets match the border arrangement on the **March** sheet.

5. Prepare and submit your work.

Exercise 12-20 ◆ Challenge Yourself

Use an IF function in a 3-D reference. Create a digital signature.

The IF statement that you create in this workbook tests whether employees have worked for five or more years.

1. Open **Personnel** and save it as *[your initials]*12-20.

2. Change the year in cells D3, D10, and D13 to the current year.

3. Make a copy of **Sheet1** and name it **Vested**. In cell A1, key **Vested Employees**.

4. Delete columns C, D, E, and then D again. In cell D2, key **Vested?**

5. Key **=now()** in cell D1 and use the same font as the label in cell A1. Format the date to show the month spelled out, the date, a comma, and four digits for the year.

6. Click cell D3 and start an IF function. Click cell D1 and make it an absolute reference.

NOTE

Date arithmetic uses serial numbers; five years is equal to 1825 days.

7. Key **–** to subtract. Click the **Sheet1** tab and cell D3 for the first hire date. Key **>1825** after **D3**. The logical test asks if today minus the hire date is greater than 1,825 days (five years).

8. As the **Value_if_true** entry, key **Yes**. For **Value_if_false**, key **No**.

9. Center the results and copy the formula for the other employees.

REVIEW

If you key the IF function, include quotation marks for text entries. The Function Arguments dialog box provides quotation marks automatically.

10. Format the sheet in an attractive and easy-to-follow layout.

11. Make a copy of the **Vested** sheet and name it **VestedFormulas**. Display the formulas and fit the columns to a single portrait page. Save the workbook.

12. Save the workbook again, adding **signed** to the filename, and add a digital signature. The purpose is **Private employee data**.

13. Prepare and submit your work.

On Your Own

In these exercises you work on your own, as you would in a real-life work environment. Use the skills you've learned to accomplish the task—and be creative.

Exercise 12-21

In a new workbook, key the first and last names of fellow students or coworkers in two columns with a label for each column. On another sheet, use a 3-D reference to show the names in opposite order as the original sheet. Name each sheet with an appropriate name. Save the workbook as *[your initials]*12-21. Prepare and submit your work.

Exercise 12-22

Open **Personnel**. Copy the label in cell A1 to **Sheet2**. In row 2, key **Name** and **Location** as labels in columns A:B. Choose a font and size. Using the & operator, create a 3-D reference in column A that shows the employee's first and last name as a single unit (John Doe). In column B, show the department and location separated by a comma (Marketing, San Francisco). Save the workbook as *[your initials]*12-22. Make a copy of **Sheet2** for formula display. Prepare and submit your work.

Exercise 12-23

Create a new workbook with two worksheets. Using a business problem, personal finance, school grades, or another topic of interest to you, plan labels and values for each sheet that can be used in some way to create 3-D references. Format both sheets attractively. Save your workbook as *[your initials]*12-23. Make a formula sheet. Prepare and submit your work.

Working with tables

OBJECTIVES

After completing this lesson, you will be able to:

1. Prepare a list as a table.

2. Work with the Table Tools Design and Data tabs.

3. Add and filter records in a table.

4. Use COUNTIFS and SUMIFS.

5. Set print areas and print selections.

6. Create a custom view.

Estimated Time: 1½ hours

MCAS OBJECTIVES

In this lesson:
XL07 1.2.2
XL07 1.4
XL07 1.4.3
XL07 1.5.1
XL07 2.4
XL07 2.4.1
XL07 2.4.2
XL07 2.4.3
XL07 3.4.1
XL07 3.7.1
XL07 4.6.1
XL07 4.6.2
XL07 5.5.1

A *table* is a list of information with a row of headers (titles) followed by rows of data. Each row represents a single entity, such as a product, an employee, or an account. Each column shows a piece of information about the entity such as a size, a first name, or a due date. Excel has many table features that enable you to work with the data using database-type commands. For example, you can sort a table to arrange the rows in different orders, or you can filter a table to display only certain rows.

Preparing a List as a Table

A list that can be formatted as a table usually includes a *header row* with descriptive labels. Immediately after the header row are rows of data.

In a list, a row of data is referred to as a *record*. It includes all the categories of data for that row. A *field* is a single category of information; each column is a field. In a telephone list, for example, the column containing the last names is a field. Each column must have a unique *field name*, which is the label in the header row. An individual piece of data in the list is called a *field value*.

When you set up a list for a table, follow these guidelines:

- Key field names or descriptive labels in the first row. This is the header row.

- Do not repeat field names in the header row.

- Start field names with a letter.

- Do not mix data types in the columns. For example, do not mix currency values and text in the same column.

- Keep the list on a worksheet by itself. If you place other information on the worksheet, do not place it below the list.

Figure 13-1
Excel list that can
be formatted as
a table

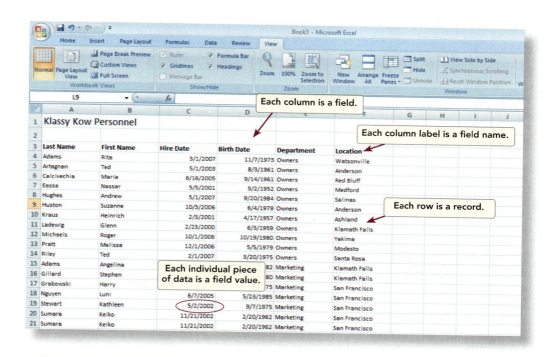

Exercise 13-1 PREPARE A LIST

The **Departments** workbook has four worksheets, each listing employees in a particular department. You can create a new workbook that lists these employees on one sheet.

1. Open **Departments**.

2. Press Ctrl + N. A new workbook opens. It is maximized and on top of the **Departments** workbook.

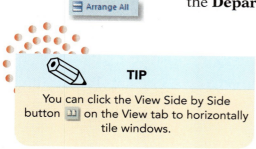

3. Click the **View** tab. Click the Arrange All button . The Arrange Windows dialog box opens.

4. Choose **Horizontal** and click **OK**. Both workbooks are displayed in windows that are the same size. The active workbook has scroll bars and shaded row and column headings for the active cell. (See Figure 13-2 on the next page.)

TIP

You can click the View Side by Side button on the View tab to horizontally tile windows.

Figure 13-2
Tiled windows

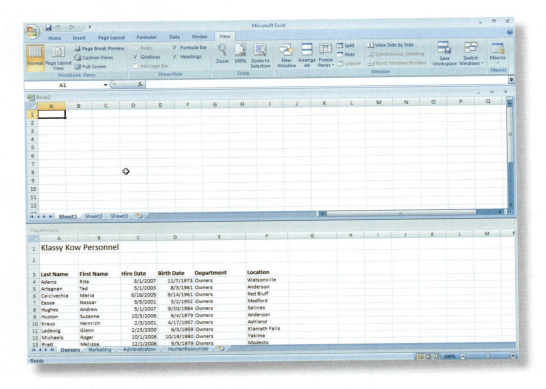

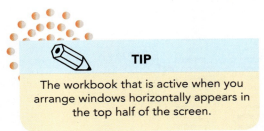

5. Click the **Owners** tab and click cell A1. Press F8 to start Extend Selection mode. Press → to extend the selection to column F.

6. Press Ctrl+↓ two times to extend the selection to row 14.

7. On the **Home** tab, click the Copy button 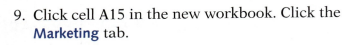.

8. Click cell A1 in the blank workbook and press Enter. Row heights and column widths are not copied.

9. Click cell A15 in the new workbook. Click the **Marketing** tab.

10. Select cells A4:F10 and press Ctrl+C.

11. Press Ctrl+F6 to switch to the new workbook and press Enter.

12. Click cell A22 and maximize the new workbook. The windows are no longer tiled.

13. Press Ctrl+F6. The **Departments** workbook is active.

14. Click the **Administration** tab. Select cells A4:F12 and copy them to cell A22 in your new workbook.

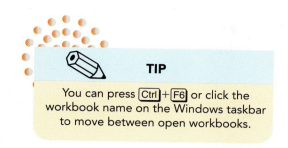

15. Click the next blank cell in column A.

16. Copy cells A4:F9 from the **HumanResources** tab in the **Departments** workbook to your workbook.

17. Close the **Departments** workbook.

18. In your workbook, make columns A:F each **15.71 (115 pixels)** wide.

19. Save the workbook as *[your initials]***13-1** in a folder for Lesson 13.

Exercise 13-2   CREATE A TABLE

The Table Styles gallery offers light, medium, and dark color schemes. After the table is formatted, you can use the Table Tools Design tab to customize your table.

1. Click any name in the **First Name** column.

2. Click the **Home** tab. In the **Styles** group, click the Format as Table button [image]. The gallery of table styles opens.

3. Choose **Table Style Medium 1**. The Format as Table dialog box shows the assumed table cells, A3:F36.

4. Make sure that **My table has headers** is selected.

5. Click **OK**. Filter drop-down lists have been added to the header row, and fill is applied to every other row by the style.

6. Click cell D1. The table is deselected.

7. Click any cell within the table. The **Table Tools Design** tab is context-sensitive. The header row labels are invisible because they are the same color as the fill.

Figure 13-3
Excel Table
13-1.xlsx
Sheet1 sheet

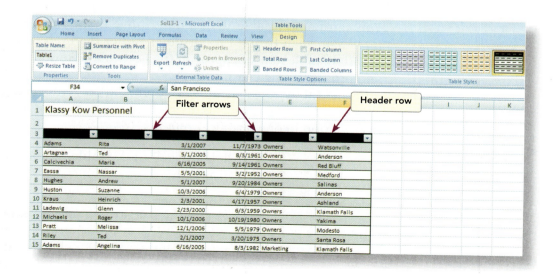

Working with the Table Tools Design and Data Tabs

Exercise 13-3   RESTYLE A TABLE

The Table Style Options and the Table Styles groups provide commands for quickly redesigning your table. You can change the style or show/hide the header and total rows or fill effects.

1. Click anywhere in the table. Click the **Table Tools Design** tab.

2. In the **Table Style Options** group, click to deselect **Header Row**. The first row of labels is toggled off.

3. Click to deselect **Banded Rows**. This removes the fill in alternate rows.

4. Click to select **Banded Columns**. The fill is applied to every other column.

5. Click to select **First Column**. This style shows the data in the first column in bold.

6. Click to deselect both **Banded Columns** and **First Column**.

7. Click to select **Header Row** and **Banded Rows**.

8. Click the More button ⏷ for **Table Styles**. Hover over several different styles to see the live preview.

9. Choose **Table Style Light 15**. Now the header row labels are visible.

Exercise 13-4   NAME A TABLE AND REMOVE DUPLICATES

You can name a table with a descriptive name for easy identification. The table name can be used in formulas rather than referring to cells A3:F36. In addition, table names appear in the Formula AutoComplete list for functions and programming commands.

The Table Tools include a command to remove duplicate rows from a table. A *duplicate row* is identified as a row that has exactly the same information in one or more columns.

NOTE

Tables are named and numbered during a work session. Your table number may be different.

1. Click any cell in the table. Click the **Table Tools Design** tab.

2. In the **Properties** group, click the **Table Name** box. The table has been named **Table1**.

Figure 13-4
Renaming a table
13-1.xlsx
Sheet1 sheet

TIP

You can undo a Remove Duplicates task.

3. Key **Employees** and press Enter. The table is renamed.

4. Review several records to find the duplicate **Sumara** rows. There are also duplicates for Sante and Steele.

5. In the **Tools** group, click the Remove Duplicates button [Remove Duplicates]. The Remove Duplicates dialog box opens. You can specify which columns might contain duplicate data.

6. Click **Unselect All**.

7. Click to select **Last Name** and **First Name**.

Figure 13-5
Remove Duplicates
dialog box
13-1.xlsx
Sheet1 sheet

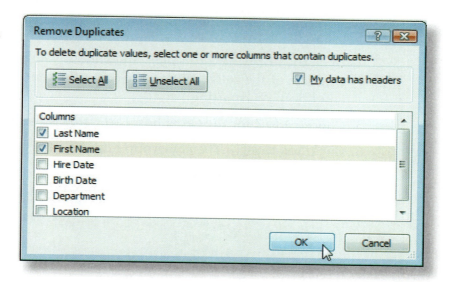

8. Click **OK**. Three duplicate rows have been removed. Click **OK** in the message box.

Exercise 13-5 SORT RECORDS IN A TABLE

Records in a list or table are often entered in no particular order. You can, however, sort them in a specific order to help organize your work.

An *ascending sort* sorts rows in A-to-Z order or lowest value to highest value using the data in one of the columns. A *descending sort* organizes rows in Z-to-A order or highest value to lowest.

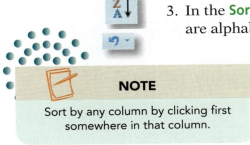

1. Click any cell in the table and click the **Data** command tab.

2. Click anywhere in the **Last Name** column.

3. In the **Sort & Filter** group, click the Sort A to Z button 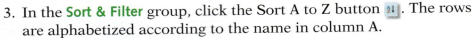. The rows are alphabetized according to the name in column A.

4. Click the Sort Z to A button 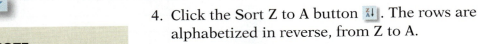. The rows are alphabetized in reverse, from Z to A.

5. Click the arrow next to the Undo button. Undo the two **Sort** actions. The rows are returned to the original order.

> **NOTE**
> Sort by any column by clicking first somewhere in that column.

Exercise 13-6 SORT BY MULTIPLE COLUMNS

Sorting by more than one column sorts within a sort. Review the names to note that some persons have the same last name.

1. Click any cell in the table.

2. On the **Data** tab, click the Sort button . The Sort dialog box opens and enables you to set multiple levels of sorting. Notice that the header row is recognized.

3. Click the arrow next to the **Sort by** box and choose **Last Name**.

4. Click the arrow next to **Values** and choose **Values**. You can sort on the contents of the cells (**Values**), the color, the font, or the icon (from conditional formatting.)

5. Choose **A to Z** for the **Order** box. **Last Name** is the first or primary sort.

6. Click **Add Level**. A **Then by** group opens for the second sort order.

7. Click the arrow for the **Then by** box and choose **First Name**.

8. Choose **Z to A** for the **Order** box. First Name will be the secondary sort.

> **NOTE**
> Sort icons appear next to the Filter arrows in the header row.

Figure 13-6
Sorting by more than
one column
13-1.xlsx
Sheet1 sheet

9. Click **OK**. Notice the order of the rows with "Adams," "Gillard," and "Stewart" as the last names. They are in descending order by first name.

Adding and Filtering Records

A *filter* is a criterion or a specification for data. A filter hides rows that do not meet your criteria. Filters enable you to keep a large list but display only required information. For example, an employee list includes all the workers in a company. To prepare a report about employees in a certain department, you can filter the list to show only those workers.

Exercise 13-7 ADD A RECORD TO A TABLE

A table grows to accommodate a new row if you press Tab when the insertion point is in the last column of the last row. AutoComplete and Pick From Drop-Down List work in tables.

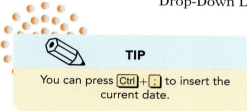

TIP

You can press Ctrl + ; to insert the current date.

1. Click cell F33. This is currently the last row in your table.

2. Press Tab. A new row with appropriate fill is added.

3. Key your first and last name in the appropriate columns. Use today as your hire date and your birth date.

4. Key **m** in the **Department** column and press Enter. AutoComplete works in a table.

5. Key a character to choose any city from column F.

Exercise 13-8 RESIZE A TABLE

There is a *sizing handle* at the bottom-right corner that you can drag to expand or contract a table. You can also specify from the Resize Table dialog box how to size your table.

1. Place the pointer on the sizing handle at the bottom-right corner of cell F34. The pointer changes to a two-pointed arrow.

2. Drag down to expand the table to row 38. The blank rows include the appropriate fill.

3. Place the pointer on the sizing handle and drag to shrink the table to row 30. The data is not deleted; it is just not part of the table.

4. Size the table to include all the rows with data.

5. Click any cell in the table and click the **Table Tools Design** tab.

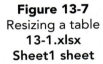 6. In the **Properties** group, click the Resize Table button .

7. In the Resize Table dialog box, edit the range to show **$A$3:g34**.

Figure 13-7
Resizing a table
13-1.xlsx
Sheet1 sheet

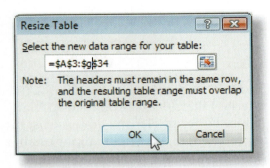

8. Click **OK**. A new column is inserted.

9. Click cell G3 and key **# of Pledges**. Widen the column to show the label.

10. In cell G4, key **1**. Key **2** in cell G5. Key **3** in cell G6. Continue with **4** and **5** in cells G7:G8.

11. Select cells G4:G8 and press Ctrl+C.

12. Click cell G9 and press Ctrl+V. Click cell G14 and press Ctrl+V. Continue until you reach row 33.

13. In the last row, key any whole number between 1 and 5.

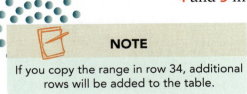

NOTE

If you copy the range in row 34, additional rows will be added to the table.

Exercise 13-9   USE THE FILTER ARROW LISTS

The Filter lists are available from the drop-down arrows next to the header row labels. The options depend on the type of data in the column. What you choose from the list is used to display rows matching your choice and to hide those that don't.

1. Click any cell in the list.

2. Click the **Department** Filter arrow. The list expands to display sort and filter options for text. All labels are selected, so all are shown.

3. Click to deselect **(Select All)**. Then select **Human Resources**.

Figure 13-8
Filtering by
department
13-1.xlsx
Sheet1 sheet

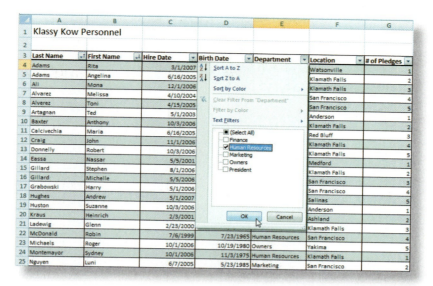

4. Click **OK**. Only the rows that match your filter are displayed. The other rows are hidden. The row headings for visible rows are blue to remind you that the list is filtered. The Filter arrow for **Department** includes an icon to remind you that a filter is applied.

5. Click the **Department** Filter arrow and choose **(Select All)**. Click **OK**.

6. Click the **Location** Filter arrow and deselect **(Select All)**.

TIP

This type of filter is described as an "Or condition" in database terminology because either Klamath Falls or San Francisco meets the criteria.

7. Select **Klamath Falls** and **San Francisco**. Click **OK**. Employees in either of the cities are listed. The status bar shows how many records are displayed.

8. Click the **Department** Filter arrow and choose **Marketing**. Click **OK**. This adds a second filter, which now shows employees in the Marketing department in either city.

9. Click the **Department** Filter arrow and choose **(Select All)**. Click **OK**. Repeat for the **Location** column.

Exercise 13-10   FILTER DATES

1. Click the **Hire Date** Filter arrow. Click to deselect **(Select All)**.

2. Click to select **2006** and click **OK**. All persons who were hired during 2006 are listed.

3. Click the **Hire Date** Filter arrow. Choose **Clear Filter from "Hire Date"** from the list. The filter is removed.

4. Click the **Hire Date** Filter arrow. Choose **Date Filters**. A list of possible ways to filter dates is shown.

5. Choose **All Dates in the Period** and then choose **September**. No employees were hired in September of any year (unless you added yourself in September). (See Figure 13-9 on the next page.)

Excel 2007

Figure 13-9
Choosing a date
filter
13-1.xlsx
Sheet1 sheet

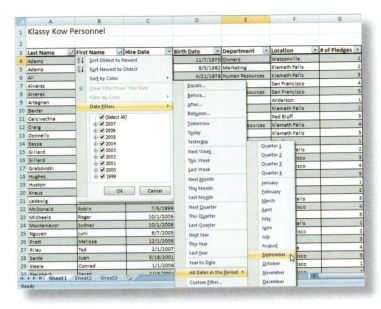

6. Click the **Hire Date** Filter arrow. Choose **Date Filters**.

7. Choose **All Dates in the Period** and then choose **April**. Two employees were hired in April of any year (three if you added yourself in April).

8. Click the **Hire Date** Filter arrow. Choose **Clear Filter from "Hire Date"** from the list.

9. Click the **Hire Date** Filter arrow.

10. Choose **Date Filters** and then choose **Custom Filter**. The Custom AutoFilter dialog box opens.

11. In the first entry box, choose **is after or equal to**.

12. Click in the entry box to the right and key **6/1/2005**. The first filter is that the date be on or after June 1, 2005.

> **NOTE**
>
> "Is after" is equivalent to "greater than" for a date.

13. Click the **And** button.

14. Click the down arrow for the box below the **And/Or** buttons.

15. Choose **is before or equal to**.

Figure 13-10
Building a custom
filter
13-1.xlsx
Sheet1 sheet

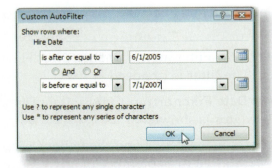

16. Click in the entry box to the right and key **7/1/2007**. The second filter requires that the hire date be on or before July 1, 2007.

17. Click **OK**. These employees were hired between June 1, 2005, and July 1, 2007.

18. Clear the **Hire Date** filter.

Exercise 13-11   SHOW TOTALS IN A TABLE

1. In the **Table Style Options** group, click to select **Total Row**. A total row is added after the last data row. It automatically shows a sum for numerical data.

2. Click cell B35 and then click its arrow.

3. Choose **Count**. This provides a count of the names and shows how many employees are listed.

4. Click cell G35 and choose **Average**. You can set which function is calculated in the total row.

5. In the **Table Style Options** group, click to deselect **Total Row**. The total row is hidden.

Using COUNTIFS and SUMIFS

The COUNTIFS function counts cells based on multiple criteria. This function has two argument groups, the **Criteria_range** and the **Criteria**. However, you can have as many of each as needed. The SUMIFS function works the same way, but it adds values based on the criteria.

Exercise 13-12   CREATE A 3-D FORMULA WITH COUNTIFS

1. Set a 70% view size for **Sheet1**.

2. On **Sheet2**, key the following labels in cells A1:A4:
   Marketing, Klamath Falls
   Finance, Klamath Falls
   Marketing, San Francisco
   Finance, San Francisco

3. Select cells A1:A4 and click the **Data** tab. Click the Sort A to Z button. Widen the column.

4. Click cell B1 and click the Insert Function button .

5. Choose **COUNTIFS** in the **Statistical** category.

6. In the **Criteria_range1** box, click the **Sheet1** tab, and select cells F4:F34. This identifies that the rows in the Location column will be counted. Excel automatically assigns a name to the range based on the header row.

7. Click in the **Criteria1** box. **Sheet2** becomes active again.

8. Key **klamath falls**. The rows will be counted if the city is Klamath Falls.

9. In the **Criteria_range2** box, click the **Sheet1** tab, and select cells E4:E34. This identifies that the rows in the Department column will be counted. (See Figure 13-11 on the next page.)

Figure 13-11
Using COUNTIFS in
a 3-D reference
13-1.xlsx
Sheet1 sheet

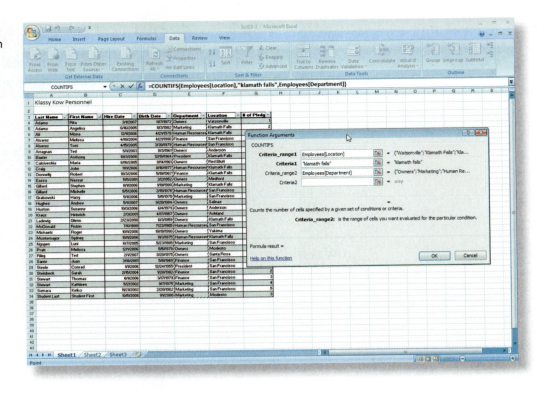

10. Click in the **Criteria2** box.

11. Key **finance**. The rows will be counted if the city is Klamath Falls and if the department is Finance.

12. Click **OK**. There is one employee in the Finance department in Klamath Falls.

13. Click cell B2 and key **=countifs** and press Tab. The Argument ScreenTip shows that **Criteria_range1** is the first argument.

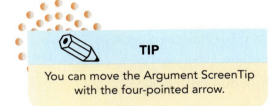

TIP

You can move the Argument ScreenTip with the four-pointed arrow.

14. Click the **Sheet1** tab, and select cells F4:F34.

15. Key a comma to separate the arguments. **Criteria1** is the next argument.

16. Key **"san francisco"** and key a comma. You must key the quotation marks when you key arguments.

17. For the **Criteria_range2** argument, select cells E4:E34 on **Sheet1**.

18. Key a comma, key **"finance"** for the **Criteria2** argument, and press Enter. There are four employees.

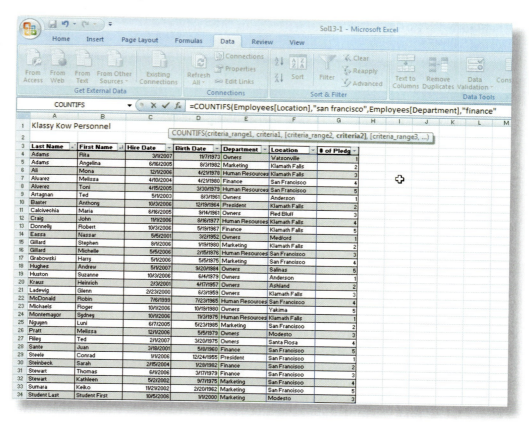

19. Use **COUNTIFS** for the other scenarios indicated on **Sheet2**.

20. Save the workbook as *[your initials]***13-12**.

Exercise 13-13   USE SUMIFS

1. On **Sheet2** in *[your initials]***13-12**, key the following department names in cells A7:A10:

   # of Pledges, Marketing, Klamath Falls
   # of Pledges, Marketing, San Francisco
   # of Pledges, Finance, Klamath Falls
   # of Pledges, Finance, San Francisco

2. Click cell **D7** and click the Insert Function button f_x.

3. Choose **SUMIFS** in the **Math & Trig** category.

4. In the **Sum_range** box, click the **Sheet1** tab, and select cells G4:G34. This identifies that rows in the # of Pledges column will be summed.

5. Click in the **Criteria_range1** box, click the **Sheet1** tab, and select cells F4:F34. This identifies that the first criteria will be the location.

6. Click in the **Criteria1** box. Key **klamath falls**. The rows will be summed if the city is Klamath Falls.

7. In the **Criteria_range2** box, click the **Sheet1** tab, and select cells E4:E34. (See Figure 13-13 on the next page.)

Figure 13-13
Using SUMIFS in a
3-D reference
13-12.xlsx
Sheet1 sheet

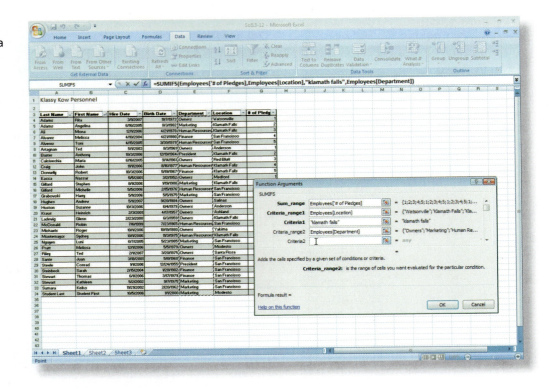

8. Click in the **Criteria2** box. Key **marketing**. The rows will be summed if the city is Klamath Falls and if the department is Marketing.

9. Click **OK**. There are four pledges for the Marketing department in Klamath Falls.

10. Click cell D8 and key **=sumifs**. Press Tab.

11. Click the **Sheet1** tab and select cells G4:G34 for the **Sum_range** argument.

12. Key a comma and select cells F4:F34 for the **Criteria_range1** argument.

13. Key a comma and key **"san francisco",** for the **Criteria1** argument. The comma introduces the **Criteria_range2** argument.

14. Select cells E4:E34 and key a comma.

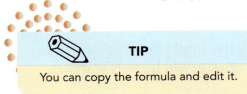

TIP

You can copy the formula and edit it.

15. Key **"marketing"** as the **Criteria2** argument and press Enter. There are 15 pledges.

16. Use SUMIFS in cells D9:D10 on **Sheet2**.

17. Save the workbook as *[your initials]*13-13.

Exercise 13-14 USE THE TEXT FUNCTION

The TEXT function displays a value as text in the number format that you specify. The value is then considered text and is not used in calculations. There are a variety of instances when this is helpful. Displaying dates is one of them.

1. On **Sheet1** in *[your initials]***13-13** in cell G1, key **=today()** and press Enter. Make it 16-point to match the label in cell A1.

2. Format the cell to show the date with the month spelled out, the date, a comma, and four digits for the year. The date is too wide to be displayed.

Figure 13-14
Date is too wide
13-13.xlsx
Sheet1 sheet

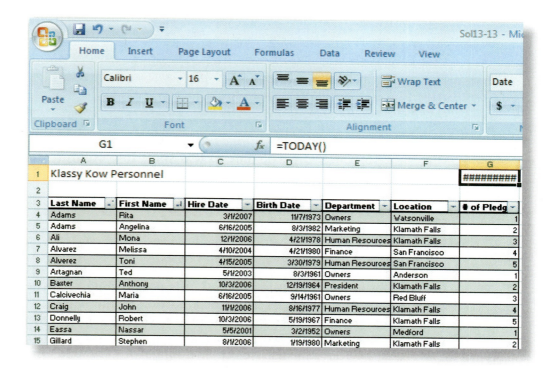

3. Set column G to **15.71 (115 pixels)** to match the other columns.

4. Delete the contents of cell G1.

5. Click the Insert Function button 𝑓ₓ.

6. Choose **TEXT** in the **Text** category.

7. In the **Value** box, key **today()** to use the current date.

8. Click in the **Format_text** box. In this box, you key format codes to display the date as you want it to appear.

9. Key **mmmm** to show the month spelled out.

10. Press Spacebar for a space after the month.

11. Key **d** to show the date without a leading zero.

12. Key a comma to appear after the date.

13. Press ⌐Spacebar⌐ for a space after the comma.

14. Key **yyyy** to show four digits for the year.

Figure 13-15
Using the TEXT
function
13-13.xlsx
Sheet1 sheet

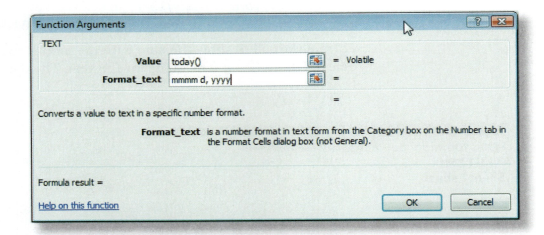

15. Click **OK**. The date as text spills into column H.

16. Right-align the date. It spills into column F.

17. Save the workbook as *[your initials]***13-14**.

Setting Print Areas

A *print area* is the range of cells to be printed. The default print area is the entire worksheet. To print a portion of the worksheet, you can select cells and define them as the print area. If you set your own print area, it can be saved with the workbook.

You can also select any range of cells and print them by using the Selection choice in the Print what area of the Print dialog box. When you use this method, the selection is not saved with the workbook.

Exercise 13-15   SET AND CLEAR A PRINT AREA

1. On **Sheet1** in *[your initials]***13-14**, click the arrow in the Name Box. The table name is listed.

2. Choose **Employees**. The table is selected.

3. Click the **Page Layout** tab. Click the Print Area button ⬚. Choose **Set Print Area**. The range is outlined by a dashed outline.

4. Click a cell outside the table to see the outline better.

5. Press Ctrl+P and press Alt+W to open Print Preview. As you can see, only the selected print area will be printed. In portrait orientation, it requires two pages.

6. Print the area and close Print Preview.

7. On the **Page Layout** tab, click the Print Area button 📄. Choose **Clear Print Area**. The print selection is removed.

Exercise 13-16 PRINT NONCONTIGUOUS SELECTIONS

If you select ranges that are not next to each other, Excel prints each one on a separate page. To print such selections on the same page, you can copy and paste a link for each range to another area of the worksheet or to another worksheet. A *link* is a 3-D reference.

1. Click the **Sheet2** tab in *[your initials]***13-14**.

2. Select cells A1:B1. This is data about Klamath Falls.

3. Hold down Ctrl and select cells A3:B3, additional data about Klamath Falls.

4. Hold down Ctrl and select cells A7:D7, more data about Klamath Falls.

5. Hold down Ctrl and select cells A9:D9. These are four noncontiguous ranges.

Figure 13-16
Selecting noncontiguous ranges for printing 13-14.xlsx Sheet2 sheet

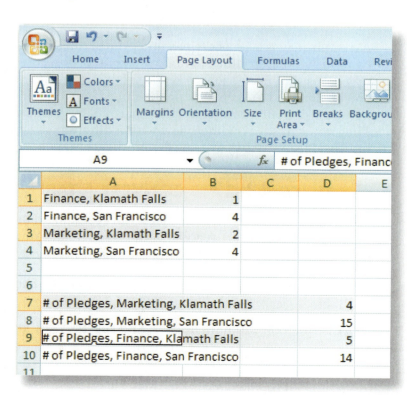

Excel 2007

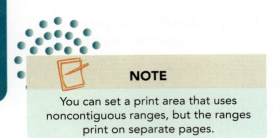

NOTE

You can set a print area that uses noncontiguous ranges, but the ranges print on separate pages.

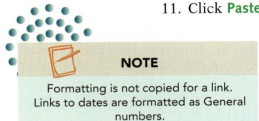

NOTE

Formatting is not copied for a link. Links to dates are formatted as General numbers.

6. Press Ctrl+P. Click the button for **Selection** in the **Print what** group.

7. Click **Preview**. Each selection will be printed on its own page.

8. Press PageDown and PageUp to view the print selections. Close the preview.

9. Select cells A1:B1 and click the Copy button.

10. Click the **Sheet3** tab and right-click cell A1. Choose **Paste Special**.

11. Click **Paste Link**. The range is copied to cell A1 with a 3-D reference.

12. On **Sheet2**, select cells A3:B3 and click the Copy button.

13. Click the **Sheet3** tab and right-click cell A2. Choose **Paste Special**. Click **Paste Link**.

14. Paste a link for cells A7:D7 and then for cells A9:D9 on **Sheet3**.

15. Delete cells B3:C4. Select and drag cells D3:D4 to cells B3:B4. Adjust column widths. You can now print this sheet to show noncontiguous ranges so that they appear as one.

16. Print the sheet. Save the workbook as *[your initials]*13-16.

Creating Custom Views

A *custom view* is a set of display and print settings for a workbook. It includes column widths, gridlines, window size and position, the active sheet, and more. You can use a view to keep certain arrangements of your data so that you do not need to keep making the same changes. For example, you can save one view of your workbook with a particular sheet on top and no gridlines. Then you can save another view with a different sheet active or some sheets hidden. Custom views are saved with the workbook.

Exercise 13-17   CONVERT A TABLE TO A RANGE

You cannot create custom views if a workbook has a table. You can, however, convert the table into regular columns of data. You can select rows and columns in a table using the same commands as for a workbook.

1. While *[your initials]*13-16 is open, click the **Sheet1** tab. This is the table.

2. Insert a column at column A and set the View size to **100%**. This will make it easier to select the table.

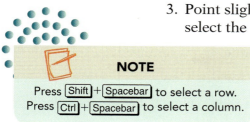

3. Point slightly above any header label to display a black arrow. Click to select the column. The first click selects all the data, not the header.

4. With the black arrow, click again. The second click includes the header.

5. Point at the first name in any row to display the black arrow and click. The row is selected.

6. Point at the top-left corner of the table border to display a black arrow that points down and right. Click to select the entire table.

7. Click the **Table Tools Design** tab. In the **Tools** group, click the Convert to Range button [Convert to Range].

8. The message asks if you want to convert the table. Choose **Yes**. The border and fill are maintained, but the table features and commands are removed.

9. Click cell A1. Save the workbook as *[your initials]*13-17.

Exercise 13-18   CREATE CUSTOM VIEWS

1. While *[your initials]*13-17 is open, click the **Sheet1** tab.

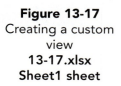

2. Click the **View** tab. Click the Custom Views button [Custom Views]. The Custom Views dialog box shows that there are currently no views for your workbook.

3. Click **Add**. The Add View dialog box opens.

4. Key **Original** as the name for this view.

5. Make sure that **Print settings** and **Hidden rows, columns and filter settings** are selected.

6. Click **OK**.

Figure 13-17
Creating a custom view
13-17.xlsx
Sheet1 sheet

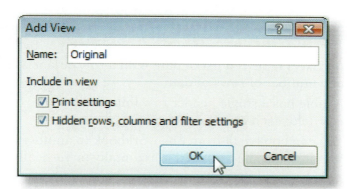

7. Delete column A on **Sheet1**.

8. On the **View** tab, click to deselect **Gridlines**.

9. Hide **Sheet2** and **Sheet3**.

10. On the **View** tab, click the Custom Views button 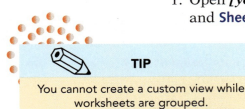. The dialog box shows your first view name.

11. Click **Add**. Key **NoGrid** as the name for this view.

12. Make sure **Print settings** and **Hidden rows, columns and filter settings** are selected. Click **OK**.

13. Save the workbook as *[your initials]***13-18** and close it.

Exercise 13-19   DISPLAY VIEWS

1. Open *[your initials]***13-18**. It opens in the **NoGrid** view with **Sheet2** and **Sheet3** hidden.

2. On the **View** tab, click the Custom Views button.

> **TIP**
>
> You cannot create a custom view while worksheets are grouped.

3. Choose **Original** and click **Show**.

4. Close the workbook without saving.

Using Online Help

Filters are like queries in a database. They allow you to display only those rows that meet your conditions.

USE HELP TO LEARN ABOUT FILTERS

1. In a new workbook, press F1.

2. Look up filters. Read the information.

3. Close the Help window.

Lesson 13 Summary

- An Excel table is a list of data with a row of labels as titles, followed by any number of rows of data.

- A table has a single header row followed by rows of data. Each column is a field; each row is a record.

- You can copy data from one workbook to another in tiled windows. Windows can be arranged horizontally or vertically.

- A table is created from the Styles group on the Home tab. The table styles include light, medium, and dark color schemes.

- Table style options include a header row, banded rows or columns, a total row, and emphasized first and last columns.

- A table is automatically named, but you can assign a more descriptive name from the Properties group.
- The Remove Duplicates command automatically searches for and deletes data rows that are duplicates based on the fields that you specify.
- You can sort a table by single or multiple columns.
- A filter displays certain rows from a table. The Filter arrow lists are quick ways to choose which records should be shown.
- COUNTIFS and SUMIFS are functions that count and sum ranges based on multiple criteria.
- The TEXT function displays a value (or date) as text using the format keyed in the second argument. The value is then not used in calculations and can be formatted with text attributes.
- You can set a print area that is different from the entire worksheet. A print area can be saved for future use.
- A print selection is not saved. If you choose more than one selection, each one prints on a separate page.
- A custom view is a set of display and print choices for a workbook. You can save several views with a workbook.

LESSON 13	Command Summary		
Feature	**Button**	**Task Path**	**Keyboard**
Arrange windows	Arrange All	View, Window	
Convert table to range	Convert to Range	Table Tools Design, Tools	
Custom view	Custom Views	View, Workbook Views	
Paste link		Home, Clipboard	
Print area, clear		Page Layout, Page Setup	
Print area, set		Page Layout, Page Setup	
Remove duplicates	Remove Duplicates	Table Tools Design, Tools	
Sort, A to Z		Data, Sort & Filter	
Sort, multiple	Sort	Data, Sort & Filter	
Sort, Z to A		Data, Sort & Filter	
Table, create		Home, Styles	Ctrl + L
Table, name		Table Tools Design, Properties	
Table, redesign		Table Tools Design, Table Style Options	
Table, resize	Resize Table	Table Tools Design, Properties	
Table, style		Table Tools Design, Table Styles	

Concepts Review

True/False Questions

Each of the following statements is either true or false. Indicate your choice by circling T or F.

T F   1. You can arrange two workbooks to be side by side vertically or horizontally.

T F   2. To determine the average of a range that is subject to multiple criteria, use AVERAGEIFS.

T F   3. Filter lists can be set to show only specific rows.

T F   4. The total row for a table can only calculate totals for numerical columns.

T F   5. Print areas can be saved with the workbook.

T F   6. An ascending sort arranges rows in alphabetical order.

T F   7. If you want to use more than one condition and an operator such as "greater than," use a Custom Filter.

T F   8. The TEXT function converts a label into a value using the format codes that you key.

Short Answer Questions

Write the correct answer in the space provided.

1. What name describes workbook properties such as hidden sheets, gridlines, and column widths that have been saved for repeated displaying when needed?

   _____

2. How could you set a table to show fill on every other row?

   _____

3. What format codes display a month so that it is spelled out?

   _____

4. What does a filter do?

   _____

5. What type of sort would arrange rows so that the largest number is first?

_____

6. What are the arguments for the COUNTIFS function?

_____

7. What is the default print area for a worksheet?

_____

8. Describe one way to print only cells A5:D10.

_____

Critical Thinking

Answer these questions on a separate page. There are no right or wrong answers. Support your answers with examples from your own experience, if possible.

1. In your school or the company where you work, what uses can you think of for sorting and filtering data?

2. What do you see as advantages of formatting a list as a table? Why might you not want to do so? Give some specifics to illustrate your point.

Skills Review

Exercise 13-20

Prepare a list as a table. Work with the Table Tools and the Data tabs.

1. Open **Products** and save it as *[your initials]*13-20.
2. Prepare a list as a table by following these steps:
   a. Insert a column at column A and make it **3.57 (30 pixels)** wide.
   b. Click any product name in column B and click the **Home** tab.
   c. Click the Format as Table button .
   d. Choose **Table Style Light 10**.
   e. In the Format as Table dialog box, click cell B3 and drag to select cells B3:D38.
   f. Click to select **My table has headers**. Click **OK**.

TIP

Use a View size that allows you to work easily.

3. Work with the Table Tools and the Data tabs by following these steps:

   a. Click anywhere in the table.

   b. Click the **Table Tools Design** tab.

   c. In the **Table Style Options** group, click to select **Banded Columns**. Banding in this style refers to borders.

   d. Click the **Data** tab. Click anywhere in the Price column.

    e. Click the Sort A to Z button.

4. Center the labels in rows 1:2 over the table. Set the font color to match the table style.

5. Make a copy of the sheet and move it to the end.

6. Work with the Table Tools and the Data tabs by following these steps:

   a. Click anywhere in the table on the copied sheet.

   b. Click the **Table Tools Design** tab.

    c. In the **Table Styles** group, click the More button. Choose **Table Style Medium 2**.

   d. In the **Table Style Options** group, click to deselect **Banded Columns**. Deselect **Banded Rows**.

   e. Click the **Data** tab. Click anywhere in the Price column.

    f. Click the Sort Z to A button.

7. Set the font color for rows 1:2 to match the table.

8. Prepare and submit your work.

Exercise 13-21

Prepare a list as a table. Add records to a table. Filter records.

1. Open **Products** and save it as *[your initials]*13-21.

2. Prepare a list as a table by following these steps:

   a. Insert a column at column A and make it **3.57 (30 pixels)** wide.

   b. Click any product name in column B and click the **Home** tab.

   c. Click the Format as Table button.

   d. Choose **Table Style Dark 1**.

   e. In the Format as Table dialog box, edit the range to show cells **=$B$3:$D$38**.

   f. Click to select **My table has headers**. Click **OK**.

3. Add records to a table by following these steps:

   a. Hover over the bottom-right sizing handle in cell D38.

   b. With the two-pointed arrow, drag to expand the table to row 40.

   c. Starting in cell B39, key the following records:

   | Italian soda | Regular | 4.59 |
   | Gelato | Regular | 3.69 |

4. Filter a table by following these steps:

    a. Click any cell in the list. Click the **Table Tools Design** tab.

    b. Click the **Price** Filter arrow. Click to deselect **(Select All)**.

    c. Click to select **$1.59**, **$1.79**, **$1.89**, and **$1.99**. Click **OK**.

    d. Name the worksheet tab **Filter1**. Copy the sheet and name the copy **Filter2**.

    e. On the **Filter2** sheet, click the **Price** Filter arrow and choose **Number Filters**. Then choose **Custom Filter**.

    f. In the first entry box, choose **is greater than or equal to**.

    g. Click in the entry box to the right and key **2**.

    h. Click the **And** button.

    i. Click the down arrow for the box below the **And/Or** buttons. Choose **is less than or equal to**.

    j. Click in the entry box to the right and key **20**. Click **OK**.

5. Prepare and submit your work.

Exercise 13-22

Use COUNTIFS.

1. Open **DevWeek** and save it as *[your initials]*13-22.

2. In cells C38:C42, key the following:

    Group A, Tuesday
    Group B, Tuesday
    Group C, Tuesday
    Group D, Tuesday
    Group E, Tuesday

3. Use COUNTIFS by following these steps:

    a. Click cell E38 and click the Insert Function button .

    b. Choose **COUNTIFS** in the **Statistical** category.

    c. In the **Criteria_range1** box, select cells F4:F36.

    d. Click in the **Criteria1** box. Key **a**.

    e. Click in the **Criteria_range2** box and select cells G4:G36.

    f. Click in the **Criteria2** box and key **tuesday**. Click **OK**.

    g. Copy the formula to cells E39:E42. Then edit each copy to show the correct group.

4. Select cells C38:E42 and apply a double outline border and single dashed lines for the bottom of each row. Increase the indents for both columns of data to move the labels and values away from the borders.

5. Make a copy of the sheet and hide rows 3:36. Display the formulas and fit the data to a portrait page.

6. Prepare and submit your work.

Exercise 13-23

Set a print area. Create custom views.

1. Open **RetireAcct** and save it as *[your initials]*13-23.
2. Set landscape orientation.
3. Set a print area by following these steps:
   a. Select cells H3:M18.
   b. Click the **Page Layout** tab.
   c. Click the Print Area button . Choose **Set Print Area**.
   d. Adjust column widths and print the area.
4. Create custom views by following these steps:
   a. Click the **View** tab. Click the Custom Views button .
   b. Click **Add**. Key **Original** as the name.
   c. Select both **Print settings** and **Hidden rows, columns and filter settings**.
   d. Click **OK**.
   e. Hide columns H:S.
   f. Click the **View** tab. Click the Custom Views button 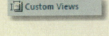. Click **Add**. Key **2007**. Select both **Print settings** and **Hidden rows, columns and filter settings**. Click **OK**.
   g. Unhide the hidden columns. Then hide columns B:G and N:S.
   h. Click the **View** tab. Click the Custom Views button 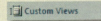. Click **Add**. Key **2006**. Click **OK**.
   i. Create a view for the 2005 data.
5. Show the original view. Prepare and submit your work.

Lesson Applications

Exercise 13-24

Create and style a table. Filter records.

1. Open **WeeklyCount** and save it as *[your initials]*13-24.

2. Use landscape orientation and set the left, right, top, and bottom margins to 0.5 inches. If you plan to use a header/footer, change those margins to .35 inches.

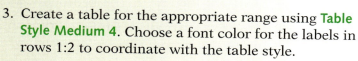

TIP

You can change the orientation and the margins from the Page Setup dialog box.

3. Create a table for the appropriate range using **Table Style Medium 4**. Choose a font color for the labels in rows 1:2 to coordinate with the table style.

4. Show the total row with a sum for all the numerical columns. Fit the worksheet to a single page.

5. Make three copies of the sheet.

6. On the **Week1 (2)** sheet, filter the data to show those rows in which the Saturday count is greater than or equal to 150. While the records are filtered, apply the same filter to Sunday.

7. On the **Week1 (3)** sheet, filter the data to show only the Nevada rows. Sort by city.

8. On the **Week1 (4)** sheet, sort by city. Hide the days except for Friday, Saturday, and Sunday. Then filter the rows to show only cities in which sales on each of those three days reached or exceeded 150.

9. Prepare and submit your work.

Exercise 13-25

Use COUNTIFS and AVERAGEIFS.

1. Open **Properties** and save it as *[your initials]*13-25.

2. Click the **Summary** sheet. In column B, use a 3-D reference with COUNTIFS to calculate how many homes meet the two criteria specified in column A.

3. In column C, use a 3-D reference with AVERAGEIFS to calculate an average recent sales price for the specified home category. Format the results as Currency with no decimals.

4. Make a formula sheet for the **Summary** sheet and fit it to one landscape page.

5. Prepare and submit your work.

Exercise 13-26

Filter data. Create a custom view.

1. Open **Properties** and save it as *[your initials]*13-26.

2. Delete the **Summary** sheet.

> **REVIEW**
>
> You cannot create custom views for workbooks with tables.

3. Convert the table to a regular data range. Then create a custom view named **All**.

4. Hide all the rows except those for homes with five bedrooms. Then create a view named **5 Bedrooms**.

5. Create views named **4 Bedrooms**, **3 Bedrooms**, **2 Bedrooms**, and **1 Bedroom**.

6. Show the **4 Bedrooms** view.

7. Prepare and submit your work.

Exercise 13-27 ◆ Challenge Yourself

Remove duplicates. Use the TEXT function. Use COUNTIFS.

The TEXT function can be used to show the day of the week instead of a date. You can format the day to be abbreviated or spelled out (Mon or Monday).

> **NOTE**
>
> A list need not be formatted as a table to use Remove Duplicates.

> **TIP**
>
> Select the cells for the Replace task.

> **NOTE**
>
> Look up formatting codes for dates in Help.

1. Open **FreeDays** and save it as *[your initials]*13-27.

2. Click a cell within the data and click the **Data** tab. Remove any duplicates in which the first and last name are the same.

3. Change the label in cell D3 to **This Year**. Then replace the years with the current year. Start with a Find what string of **195?** and replace it with **200***n*, with *n* being this year. Repeat for each decade.

4. Insert a column at column E. In cell E3, key **Day**.

5. In column E, use the TEXT function to convert the date in column D. In the **format_text** argument, key codes that show only the day of the week, spelled out.

6. Left-align the days in columns E and F. Increase the indent for the results in column E so that there is more space between the days and the dates in column D.

7. In cell B38, key **Day Off and Birthday the Same**. In cells B39:B43, key the five weekdays, spelled out.

8. In cells C38:C43, use COUNTIFS to count how many employees have their usual day off on the same weekday as their birthdays.

9. Make a formula copy of the sheet fit to one landscape page.

10. Prepare and save your work.

On Your Own

In these exercises you work on your own, as you would in a real-life work environment. Use the skills you've learned to accomplish the task—and be creative.

Exercise 13-28

In a new workbook, use two columns to key the first and last names of 25 fellow students, coworkers, or relatives and friends. In the third column, key the person's hair color. Include a label for each column. Format the data as a table and name it **HairColor**. Sort the rows alphabetically by last name. Make as many copies of the sheet as you have hair colors in your list. On each sheet, show one hair color group. Save the workbook as *[your initials]*13-28. Prepare and submit your work.

Exercise 13-29

Open **WeeklyCount**. Create custom views to show each state separately. Save your workbook as *[your initials]*13-29. Prepare and submit your work.

Exercise 13-30

In a new workbook, create a list of 15 retail stores or restaurants in your city. In separate columns, list a phone number, the year they started in business, and an average hourly wage for someone who works at the establishment (guess/estimate if necessary). Format the data as a table. Sort the rows by year started in business, with the oldest establishment listed first. Show an average hourly wage in the total row. Save your workbook as *[your initials]*13-30. Prepare and submit your work.

Using Named Ranges and Structured References

OBJECTIVES

After completing this lesson, you will be able to:

1. Use named ranges.

2. Name a constant.

3. Document range names.

4. Work with structured references.

5. Use lookup functions.

Estimated Time: 1½ hours

MCAS OBJECTIVES

In this lesson:
XL07 1.3.1
XL07 3.1.1
XL07 3.1.3
XL07 3.1.4
XL07 3.3
XL07 3.5.1
XL07 5.5

A *defined name* is a range name that you create and assign. Range names can be used in formulas and to move around the workbook. There are several reasons for using range names:

- Range names are easier to remember than cell addresses.

- You are less likely to make an error selecting a range name than by keying a cell address.

- Named ranges appear in Formula AutoComplete lists.

- You can use range names for navigation.

- Range names make formulas easier to understand.

Using Named Ranges

When naming ranges, you should follow these basic rules:

- Begin range names with a letter.

- Do not use single-letter range names, such as "n."

- Do not use range names that resemble cell addresses, such as "A5."

- Keep range names relatively short.

- Use uppercase letters, an underscore, or a period to separate words (FirstQuarter, First_Quarter, or First.Quarter). Do not use spaces.

- Do not use special characters such as hyphens (-) or symbols ($, %, &, #).

TIP

Use short, recognizable range names.

Excel has reserved, hidden range names that you should not use. These special names include Print_Area, Print_Titles, Consolidate_Area, and Sheet_Title. If you name a range on your worksheet with one of these names, you override Excel's use of the names.

TABLE 14-1 Examples of Acceptable and Unacceptable Range Names

Acceptable Names	Unacceptable Names
Week1	Week 1
Week_1	Week-1
Week.1	Week:1
WeekNo1	Week#1
Wk1	W1 or W

Exercise 14-1   **USE RANGES FOR NAVIGATION**

You can use the Name Box or the Go To command to quickly move to named ranges in a worksheet.

1. Open **JuneExp**.

2. Click the down arrow in the Name Box. The range names in the workbook are listed.

Figure 14-1
Range names in the workbook
JuneExp.xlsx
Expenses sheet

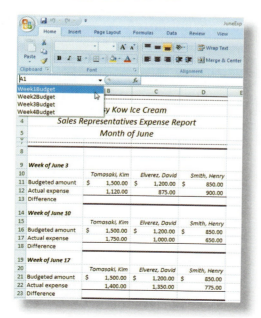

REVIEW

Another keyboard shortcut for the Go To command is F5.

3. Choose **Week1Budget**. The range is highlighted on the worksheet.

4. Right-click the **AutoCalculate** area in the status bar and click to select **Sum**. The sum of the first week's budget amounts is shown.

5. Press Ctrl+G. The Go To dialog box shows defined range names and recently used cell addresses.

6. Double-click **Week2Budget**. The range is highlighted.

Exercise 14-2   NAME A DEFINED RANGE

There are several ways to create a named range. After selecting the cells on the worksheet, you can:

• Click the Name Box, key the range name, and press Enter.

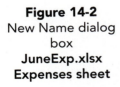

• Click the Define Name button on the Formulas tab. Key the range name and click **OK**.

• Click the Name Manager button on the Formulas tab. Click **New**, key the range name, and click **OK**.

1. Select the range B12:D12. Click the Name Box (not its arrow).

2. Key **ActualWk1** and press Enter.

3. Select the range B17:D17. Click the Name Box, key **ActualWk2**, and press Enter.

4. Click the **Formulas** tab.

5. Select cells B22:D22. In the **Defined Names** group, click the Define Name button. The New Name dialog box opens with a suggested name from column A.

Figure 14-2
New Name dialog box
JuneExp.xlsx
Expenses sheet

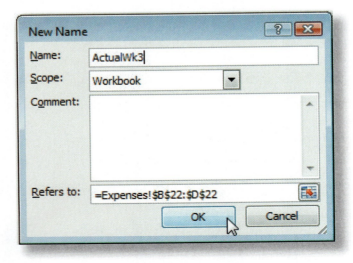

6. Key **ActualWk3** and click **OK**.

7. Select cells B27:D27. In the **Defined Names** group, click the Name Manager button ⬚. The Name Manager dialog box lists the existing defined names in the workbook.

Figure 14-3
JuneExp.xlsx
Expenses sheet
Name Manager
dialog box

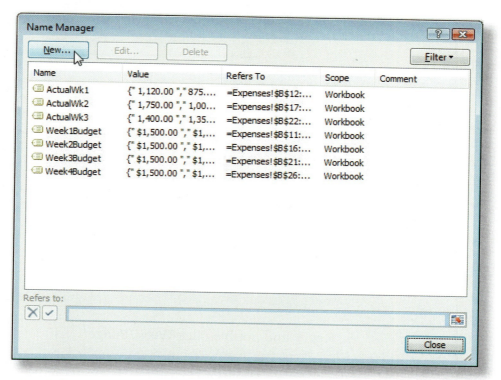

8. Click **New**. The New Name dialog box opens with the suggested name.

9. Key **ActualWk4** and press Enter. Close the Name Manager dialog box.

10. Click the arrow in the Name Box and choose one of your new ranges.

11. Press F5 and choose a range from the Go To dialog box.

12. Press Ctrl + Home.

Exercise 14-3 USE NAMED RANGES IN A FORMULA

When you use a range name in a formula, the formula is easy to understand at first glance. For example, a formula such as **=sum(FirstQtrSales)** conveys its purpose more quickly than **=sum(B12:F12)**.

As you build a formula, you can key a *display trigger* to see defined range names in a Formula AutoComplete list. This saves time and increases your accuracy. You can also use the Paste Names dialog box to add named ranges to a formula.

1. On the **Expenses** sheet, select cell B30.

2. Key **=sum** to start the SUM function and press Tab. The ScreenTip indicates that the first argument is **number1**.

Excel 2007

REVIEW

In the SUM function, arguments are separated by commas.

3. Key **w** to display defined names and functions that begin with **W**. The ranges are at the top of the list with an icon that is different from the functions.

4. Double-click **Week1Budget** and key a comma. The ScreenTip shows that **number2** is the next argument.

Figure 14-4
Using range names in Formula AutoComplete
JuneExp.xlsx
Expenses sheet

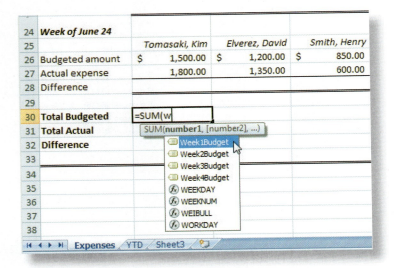

5. Key **w** and double-click **Week2Budget**.

6. Key a comma, key **w**, and double-click **Week3Budget**.

7. Repeat these steps to include **Week4Budget** and press Enter. The sum is $14,200.

8. In cell B31, key **=sum(** and press F3. The Paste Name dialog box lists the existing range names.

9. Click **ActualWk1** and click **OK**.

10. Key a comma and press F3. Double-click **ActualWk2**.

11. Add the remaining range names to the formula. Press Enter when finished. The result is $13,570.

12. Select cell B30 and look at the formula in the formula bar.

13. Calculate the difference in cell B32.

Exercise 14-4   INSERT DATA WITHIN A NAMED RANGE

Named ranges can be more robust than simple cell references. This means that they are updated more easily when you make changes within your data. For example, if you insert a row/column within a defined name range, it is included in any formulas that reference the range.

1. On the **Expenses** sheet, insert a column at column C.

2. In cell C10, key your last name, a comma, and your first name.

3. Key **2000** in cell C11 and **1500** in cell C12.

4. Copy these three cells so that your data is shown for all four weeks. The totals in rows 30:32 are updated as you work.

5. Click the arrow in the Name Box and choose **ActualWk1**. Notice that your data is now included in the named range.

Exercise 14-5 CREATE RANGE NAMES AUTOMATICALLY

Depending on how a worksheet is arranged, you can assign range names automatically. If columns and rows have labels and the data is consistent, you can quickly name several ranges with one command.

1. On the **YTD** sheet, select the range A3:D9.

2. Click the **Formulas** tab. Click the Create from Selection button . The Create Names from Selection dialog box shows that the top row and left column will be used to define range names.

Figure 14-5
Creating range names automatically
JuneExp.xlsx
YTD sheet

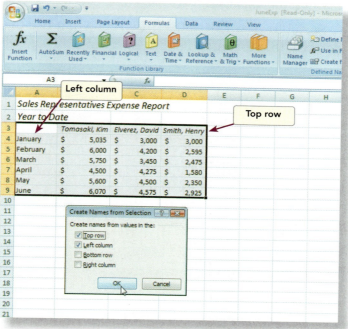

3. Click **OK**. Range names have been created for each of the months and each of the salespersons.

4. Click the arrow in the Name Box. Choose **January**.

5. Click the down arrow in the Name Box and choose any salesperson's name.

NOTE

Range names are sorted alphabetically in the Name Box list.

Exercise 14-6   DELETE RANGE NAMES

You can delete one or more range names using the Name Manager dialog box. If you delete a range name that is used in a formula, Excel displays the error #NAME? in the cell.

1. On the **YTD** sheet, click the **Formulas** tab.

2. Click the Name Manager button 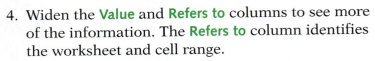. The named ranges on both sheets are listed in the dialog box.

3. Drag the bottom-right corner of the dialog box to expand it.

4. Widen the **Value** and **Refers to** columns to see more of the information. The **Refers to** column identifies the worksheet and cell range.

5. Select all the defined names on the **YTD** sheet. Do not select any on the **Expenses** sheet.

6. Click **Delete** and click **OK**. None of these names were used in a formula, and no error messages appear.

7. Select **ActualWk1** in the dialog box list. Click **Delete** and then click **OK**. Close the dialog box.

8. Click the **Expenses** tab.

9. Scroll to view rows 30:32. Two cells that use the **ActualWk1** named range in a formula display an error.

Figure 14-6
Error after deleting a range name
JuneExp.xlsx
Expenses sheet

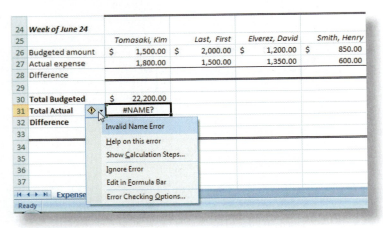

10. Hover over the Error Checking button and click its arrow. The name is no longer recognized.

11. Press Esc to remove the shortcut menu.

Exercise 14-7   SUPPRESS ERRORS FOR PRINTING

If you were to print this sheet now, the errors print as displayed. You can suppress Excel error value messages from printing. This lets you review the data without your attention being drawn to errors that will be corrected later.

1. Save the workbook as *[your initials]*14-7 in a folder for Lesson 14.

2. Press Ctrl+P to open the Print dialog box.

3. Press Alt+W to open Print Preview. The errors are displayed.

4. Click the Page Setup button.

5. Click the **Sheet** tab. In the **Print** group, click the arrow next to the **Cell errors as** box, and choose **blank**.

6. Click **OK**. The errors will not print.

7. Close Print Preview. The error messages are still visible in the sheet.

Exercise 14-8   SETTING THE SCOPE FOR A NAMED RANGE

The *scope* for a defined name is its location applicability. By default, range names are assigned to the workbook. If you use a range name on **Sheet1**, you cannot use the same name on a different sheet in the same workbook. You can, however, set a scope for a new range name so that it is assigned to a particular sheet. Then you can use the same range name scoped to a different sheet.

1. Click the **YTD** tab.

2. Click the Name Box arrow. These are the named ranges on the **Expenses** sheet.

> **NOTE**
>
> If you create names from a selection, you will not be able to change the scope.

3. Choose **Week1Budget**. The pointer returns to the **Expenses** sheet, because that is where the range is located.

4. Click the **YTD** tab. Click the **Formulas** tab and select cells B4:D4.

5. Click the Define Name button 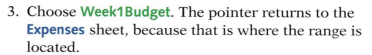. The New Name dialog box shows the selected range with a suggested name that uses the label in the column to the left.

6. Click the **Scope** arrow. The sheets in the workbook are listed as well as the workbook itself.

7. Choose **YTD**. This name will only be used on this sheet.

8. Click in the **Comment** box. Defined name comments appear with the range name in Formula AutoComplete.

9. Key **These are sales for three salespersons**. Click **OK**. (See Figure 14-7 on the next page.)

Excel 2007

Figure 14-7
Changing the scope
for a name
14-7.xlsx
YTD sheet

10. Click the Name Box arrow. These are the named ranges on both sheets.

11. Choose **Week1Budget**. The pointer returns to the **Expenses** sheet.

12. Click the Name Box arrow. The **January** name does not appear in the list because it is scoped to the **YTD** sheet.

Exercise 14-9   MODIFY DEFINED NAMES

You can change a range name or redefine the range to which it refers. Formulas are updated to show the new name or include the new data.

TIP

The Name Manager dialog box includes a Filter button with preset filters for displaying defined names in the list.

1. On the **Expenses** sheet, click the Name Manager button.

2. Select **Week1Budget** in the list. Click **Edit**. The Edit Name dialog box is the same as the New Name dialog box, but the scope cannot be changed.

3. In the **Name** box, edit the name to **Week1**. Click **OK** and close the Name Manager dialog box.

4. Click cell B30. The formula has been updated to show the new range name.

5. Click the **YTD** tab, and click the Name Manager button.

6. Choose **January** in the list of names and click **Edit**. The **Refers to** entry shows the cell range.

7. Edit the range to **$B$9:$D$9** and click **OK**. Click **Close**.

8. Click the Name Box arrow and choose **January**. The June values are highlighted.

9. Click the Name Manager button. Choose **January** and click **Edit**. Change the **Name** to **June** and click **OK**. Click **Close**.

Naming a Constant

If you multiply all expenses by 110% to project next year's budget, 110% is a constant. A *constant* is a value that does not change. Constants can be named and used in formulas like named ranges. This can make it easier to understand the purpose of the constant in a formula.

Exercise 14-10 NAME A CONSTANT

You use the New Name dialog box to name a constant. Named constants appear in the Formula AutoComplete lists only when they are scoped to the workbook.

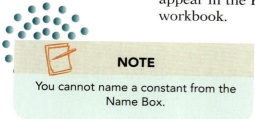

> **NOTE**
> You cannot name a constant from the Name Box.

1. Click the **YTD** tab.

2. Press Ctrl+F3. This is the keyboard shortcut to open the Name Manager dialog box.

3. Click **New**. In the **Name** box, key **Increase**.

4. In the **Comment** box, key **This is a projected dollar increase**.

5. In the **Refers to** text box, delete existing data and key **=1000**.

Figure 14-8
Naming a constant
14-7.xlsx
YTD sheet

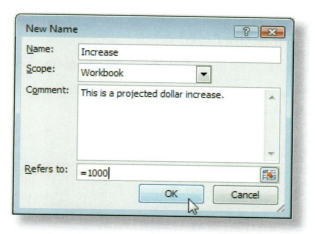

6. Click **OK**. Click **Close**.

7. Click the arrow in the Name Box. Named constants do not appear in this list.

8. Press Esc to close the list.

Exercise 14-11 USE A CONSTANT IN A FORMULA

1. Copy the range A3:D9 to cells A11:D17.

2. Delete the contents of cells B12:D17.

3. Click cell B12. Key **=** and click cell B4.

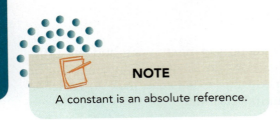

NOTE

A constant is an absolute reference.

4. Key **+inc** to display the Formula AutoComplete list.

5. Double-click **Increase** in the list and press `Enter`. The constant value (1000) is added to the value in cell B4.

6. Copy the formula in cell B12 to the range B13:B17 and then to columns C and D. All the formulas use the constant range name.

Documenting Range Names

The Paste List command in the Paste Name dialog box creates a table of the workbook's range names. You can create this list on a separate worksheet and use it as documentation for your workbook.

Exercise 14-12   CREATE A RANGE NAME LIST

1. Rename **Sheet3** as **Documentation**.

2. In cell A1, key **Expense Report Range Names**.

3. In cell A2, press `Ctrl`+`;` and press `Enter`. The current date is inserted.

4. In cell A3, key **Name**. In cell B3, key **Range**.

5. Select cell A4 and click the Use in Formula button . The range names are listed.

6. Choose **Paste Names**. The Paste Name dialog box opens.

7. Click **Paste List**. The range names and cell references are pasted in two columns starting in cell A4.

Figure 14-9
A pasted range name list
14-7.xlsx
Documentation sheet

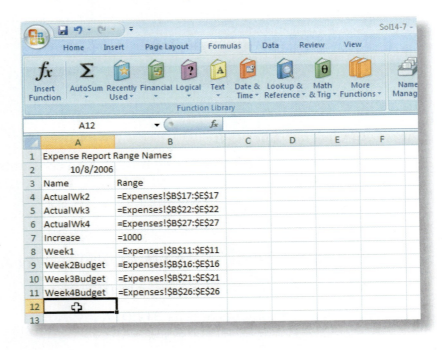

8. Adjust column widths as needed. Apply **All Borders** to the range names starting at row 3.

9. Save the workbook as *[your initials]*14-12.

10. Close the workbook.

Working with Structured References

When you create an Excel table, the columns are automatically assigned a name based on the header row. Although this seems like a range name, it is known as a *structured reference*. A *structured reference* is a name used to refer to an identifiable range within an Excel table. Structured references include the columns with names based on the header row. Other structured references for a table are #All, #Data, #Headers, #This Row, and #Total Row. Theses names appear in Formula AutoComplete, but they do not appear in the Paste Names list.

Exercise 14-13   REVIEW STRUCTURED REFERENCES

1. Open **Shipments**.

2. Click the **Formulas** tab and the Name Manager button. There are no named ranges in this workbook.

3. Click **Close** and select cells A3:J21.

4. Click the **Home** tab. Click the Format as Table button. Choose **Table Style Light 1**. Click **OK**.

5. Click the **Formulas** tab and the Name Manager button. The table is automatically named as a range. Close the dialog box.

6. Click the **Table Tools Design** tab. Click the **Table Name** box and key **Shipments**. Press Enter.

7. In the **Table Style Options** group, click to select **Total Row**.

8. Click cell J22. The Total Row uses the SUBTOTAL function. Its arguments include a number that indicates what function is being used.

9. Click the Insert Function button. The Function Arguments dialog box shows the two arguments. **[Due]** is the structured reference to that column in the table.

Figure 14-10
Structured reference
to a table column
Shipments.xlsx
OutOfState sheet

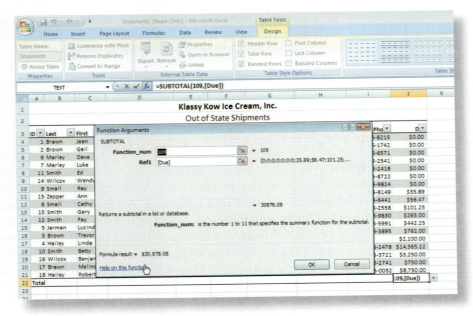

10. Click **Help on this function**. The Help window opens to the SUBTOTAL function. Here you can see that **Function_num 109** sums the values and ignores any hidden values.

11. Close the Help window. Click **Cancel** in the Function Arguments dialog box.

12. Click cell B22 and choose **Count** as the function.

13. Look in the formula bar to see the structured reference to **[Last]**.

14. Click the **Formulas** tab and the Name Manager button. Structured references do not appear in the list.

15. Close the dialog box.

Exercise 14-14 USE STRUCTURED REFERENCES IN FORMULAS

1. Click cell D24.

2. Key **=coun** and double-click **COUNTIF**. The first argument is the range. You want to count the values in the Due column in the Shipments table.

3. Key **s** to display the Formula AutoComplete list.

4. Double-click **Shipments**, the table name. Next you need the column name.

5. Key **[** to trigger the display of the structured references.

6. Double-click **Due** and key **]** to complete the reference.

7. Key a comma to move to the **criteria** argument.

REVIEW

The COUNTIF function has two arguments, the range and the criteria.

8. Key **">0"** to count records that have a balance due. The quotation marks are necessary because you are keying the formula and there is an operator with the value.

9. Press Enter. Excel provides the closing parentheses. There are 11 customers who owe money.

10. Click cell D25.

11. Key **=aver** and double-click **AVERAGEIF**. The first argument is the range.

12. Key **s** and double-click **Shipments**.

13. Key **[** to trigger the display of the structured references.

14. Double-click **Due** and key **]** to complete the reference.

15. Key a comma to move to the **criteria** argument.

16. Key **">0"** to average amounts that are greater than 0.

17. Press Enter. The average amount due is $2,807.10. Format your results.

18. Save the workbook as **[your initials]14-14**. Close the workbook.

Using Lookup Functions

The Lookup & Reference category of functions obtains data or displays information from the current worksheet or other workbooks.

Lookup functions display information from a table by scanning the columns or rows to look up, or find, data. The *lookup table* is a definable range of labels and/or values, often on a separate sheet. The VLOOKUP function scans the table's columns to find data that match a value, a vertical lookup. HLOOKUP works the same way but scans rows to find the data, a horizontal lookup.

Exercise 14-15   USE VLOOKUP

The workbook for this exercise has three worksheets. The first worksheet lists account names, the second worksheet lists discount percentages allowed by account name, and the third worksheet shows payment methods based on the discounts.

The vertical lookup table is located on the **Discounts** worksheet. VLOOKUP uses the label in column A to find the appropriate discount in column B. The rows in a vertical lookup table should be sorted by column A for the function to work properly.

It is a good practice to name a lookup table so that you can refer to it easily in the VLOOKUP function.

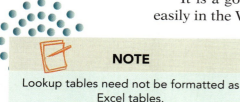

NOTE

Lookup tables need not be formatted as Excel tables.

1. Open **AcctPay**.

2. Click the **Discounts** tab. This sheet contains the lookup table that will be used in the VLOOKUP function. The table lists the discount allowed by each vendor.

TIP

Precede range names for lookup tables with a "T" so you can easily recognize that they are lookup "t"ables.

NOTE

Remember that the appearance of some buttons depends on the screen size and resolution.

NOTE

In the Range_lookup text box, key FALSE if you want Excel to find only exact matches to the lookup value. If you key TRUE or leave it empty, Excel finds the closest match. To find the closest match, the data must be sorted by the first column.

3. On the **Discounts** worksheet, select the range A2:B10.

4. Click the Name Box. Key **TDiscounts** and press Enter. You'll use this range name to refer to this table in the VLOOKUP function.

5. Click cell A2. Click the **Data** tab.

6. Click the Sort A to Z button ↕. The lookup table should be sorted in ascending order by its first column.

7. Click the **Accounts** tab and select cell C4. The VLOOKUP function here will look up the discount rate for the company name in column B.

8. Click the **Formulas** tab. Click the Lookup & Reference button 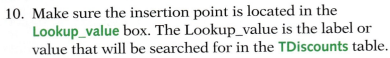.

9. Choose **VLOOKUP**. The Function Arguments dialog box opens.

10. Make sure the insertion point is located in the **Lookup_value** box. The Lookup_value is the label or value that will be searched for in the **TDiscounts** table.

11. Click cell B4. Excel will look for this company name in the **TDiscounts** table.

12. Click in the **Table_array** box. The Table_array is the range name (or address) of the table with the discounts.

13. Press F3. Double-click **TDiscounts**, the range name for your lookup table.

14. Click in the **Col_index_num** box. The Col_index_num identifies which column in the TDiscounts table contains the discounts.

15. Key **2**. Column B is the second column. In Lookup functions, you cannot key the column letter but must identify it by counting columns from the left.

16. Leave the **Range_lookup** box empty. This tells Excel to look for the closest match to your lookup value, the company name. This is an optional argument for Lookup functions.

Figure 14-11
Using VLOOKUP
AcctPay.xlsx
Accounts sheet

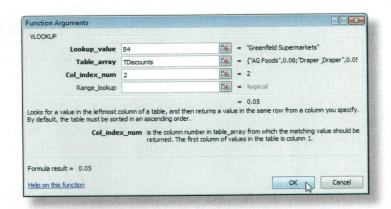

17. Click **OK**. The discount from Greenfield Supermarkets is .05 (decimal equivalent of 5%).

18. Click the **Discounts** tab. Verify that Greenfield Supermarkets gives a 5% discount.

19. On the **Accounts** sheet, copy the formula to the range C5:C20. **#N/A** appears in the blank rows, an error message to indicate that there is missing data.

20. Format cells C4:C20 as Percent with two decimals.

21. In cell A13, key **1259**. In cell B13, key **ov** and press ⌜Enter⌟ to accept the AutoComplete suggestion. The formula looks up the company name in the **TDiscounts** table and displays the appropriate discount.

Exercise 14-16   TRANSPOSE DATA WHILE COPYING

When you copy a range of cells, you can paste it in a transposed layout. It is one way to change the orientation of a vertical table to horizontal and vice versa.

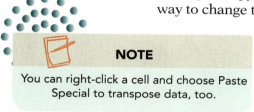

NOTE

You can right-click a cell and choose Paste Special to transpose data, too.

1. Click the **PayMethod** tab. This is a vertical layout that you will convert to horizontal.

2. Select cells B10:C14. This data uses two columns and five rows. To transpose it, you need two rows and five columns.

3. Click the Copy button 📋.

4. Click cell A2.

5. Click the arrow with the Paste button 📋 and choose **Transpose**.

Figure 14-12
Transposed copied data
AcctPay.xlsx
PayMethod sheet

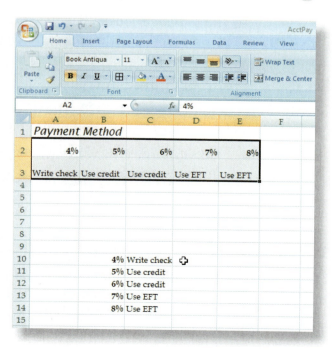

6. Press Esc.

7. Delete the contents of cells B10:C14.

Exercise 14-17 USE HLOOKUP

The HLOOKUP function is similar to VLOOKUP, but the lookup table is arranged in rows. The **PayMethod** sheet now has a horizontal lookup table.

1. Select cells A2:E3. Click the Name Box, key **TPayMethod**, and press Enter.

2. On the **Accounts** sheet, select cell D4. You'll use the HLOOKUP function to match the discount rate in cell C4 to a value in the TPayMethod table and display the related payment method.

3. Click the Insert Function button 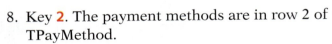. In the **Lookup & Reference** category, choose **HLOOKUP** and click **OK**.

4. In the **Lookup_value** box, click cell C4. The Lookup_value is the label or value to be checked, the discount rate in this case.

5. Click in the **Table_array** box. This is where Excel will look up the value shown in cell C4.

6. Key **tpaymethod**.

7. Click in the **Row_index_num** box. The Row_index_num identifies which row in the TPayMethod lookup table contains the payment method.

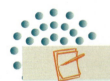

> **NOTE**
>
> The methods are in the second row of the named table but the third row of the worksheet.

8. Key **2**. The payment methods are in row 2 of TPayMethod.

9. In the **Range_lookup** box, key **false**. This tells Excel to only find exact matches for the discounts in column C.

10. Click **OK**. A 5% discount is paid by credit.

11. Copy the formula to the range D5:D20. The discounts that do not have exact matches in the TPayMethod table show #N/A.

12. Click the **PayMethod** tab. Notice there is no 4.5% rate here.

13. Click the **Accounts** tab. Invoice 1252 does not show a method because it has a 4.5% discount rate.

Exercise 14-18 EDIT AN HLOOKUP FUNCTION

If you leave the Range_lookup box empty, Excel will look for approximate matches. When no exact match is found, Excel displays the largest value that is less than the lookup value. Invoice #1252 has a 4.5% discount, but that value is not in the lookup table.

1. Click cell D4 and click the Insert Function button 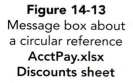. The Function Arguments dialog box shows your current arguments.

2. Delete **FALSE** from the **Range_lookup** box. Click **OK**.

3. Copy the formula to the range D5:D20. Look at Invoice #1252. Because the Range_lookup box was left empty, Excel uses the largest value in the lookup table (4%, Write check) that is less than 4.5%.

4. Widen column D. Notice the method for Greenfield Supermarkets.

5. Click the **Discounts** tab and change the Greenfield discount to **3%**.

6. Return to the **Accounts** worksheet. The HLOOKUP function now shows #N/A for that company, because there is no value in the lookup table that is less than 3%.

Exercise 14-19   CREATE AND REMOVE A CIRCULAR REFERENCE

A *circular reference* is a cell address in a formula that refers to the formula's location. Formulas with circular references display a zero or are blank.

1. Click the **Discounts** tab and select cell C2.

2. Click the Insert Function button 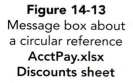. Choose the **Logical** category, choose **IF**, and click **OK**.

3. Click cell C2 to set the **Logical_test** argument. Notice that this is the same cell in which you are building the function. This will be a circular reference.

4. Key **<=4%** after **C2** to determine if the discount is less than or equal to 4%.

5. Click in the **Value_if_true** box and key **Less than 4%**.

6. Click in the **Value_if_false** box and key **Greater than 4%**.

7. Click **OK**. The circular reference message box opens.

Figure 14-13
Message box about a circular reference
AcctPay.xlsx
Discounts sheet

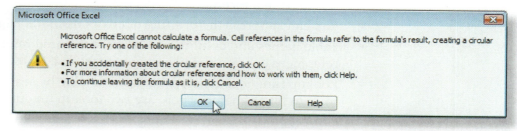

8. Click **OK** in the message box. Excel opens a Help screen.

9. Read the information and close the Help screen. The status bar shows the location of the error.

10. Change the reference from C2 to **b2** in the formula bar and press Enter.

11. Copy the formula to cells C3:C10. Widen the column.

12. Select cells C2:C10. On the **Home** tab, click the Increase Indent button. The labels are indented 1 space from the left edge of the cell.

13. Save the workbook as *[your initials]***14-19**. Close the workbook.

Using Online Help

Structured references are designed to make it easier to work with Excel tables. They are especially useful because table data ranges often change, and the cell references for these references adjust automatically.

USE HELP TO LEARN MORE ABOUT STRUCTURED REFERENCES

1. Look for Help topics about structured references.

2. Read the information. Close the windows.

Lesson 14 Summary

- Range names must begin with a letter, cannot use spaces or special characters, and should be short and descriptive.
- Use range names rather than cell addresses for navigation and in formulas. In a formula, key the first character of a range name to see it listed in Formula AutoComplete.
- Range names can be deleted, changed, or redefined.
- Range names can be scoped to the workbook or to a particular sheet.
- You can paste a table of range names and cell references on the worksheet for documentation.
- A constant is a value that does not change. A constant can be named and used in a formula.
- You can suppress the printing of errors from the Page Setup dialog box.
- Table names and column names are structured references. The references can be used like range names in a formula.
- Lookup functions display data from a table by scanning the columns or rows to find a match. There are two lookup functions, VLOOKUP and HLOOKUP.

- Select the option to transpose data while pasting it to arrange the data in a column or a row.
- A circular reference is a cell address in a formula that refers to itself. Excel cannot calculate a circular reference.

LESSON 14		Command Summary	
Feature	**Button**	**Task Path**	**Keyboard**
Constant, create	Name Manager	Formulas, Defined Names	
Delete range	Name Manager	Formulas, Defined Names	Ctrl + F3
Name range	Define Name ▾	Formulas, Defined Names	
Name range from selection	Create from Selection	Formulas, Defined Names	
Paste names	Use in Formula ▾	Formulas, Defined Names	F3
Scope, set	Define Name ▾	Formulas, Defined Names	
Transpose data	Paste	Home, Clipboard	

Concepts Review

True/False Questions

Each of the following statements is either true or false. Indicate your choice by circling T or F.

T F   1. A range name can include the wildcard characters * (asterisk) and ? (question mark).

T F   2. Structured references refer to values in another workbook.

T F   3. A constant is a value that does not change.

T F   4. The scope for a range name can be set by columns and rows.

T F   5. You can print a worksheet with or without formula errors such as #NAME? or #N/A.

T F   6. When you delete a range name, Excel substitutes cell addresses in formulas.

T F   7. Lookup functions belong to the Database category.

T F   8. A circular reference repeats a formula across the range.

Short Answer Questions

Write the correct answer in the space provided.

1. Where can you see a drop-down list of existing range names without opening a dialog box?

_____

2. What triggers the display of table names in Formula AutoComplete?

_____

3. Which range name is acceptable: 1stQtr, FirstQtr, Qtr 1?

_____

4. What term describes a value that does not change?

_____

5. Describe what the **VLOOKUP** function does.

_____

6. What term describes a formula that refers to its own location?

_____

7. After copying data, how can you arrange row data into a column?

_____

8. What key triggers the display of table column names in Formula AutoComplete?

_____

Critical Thinking

Answer these questions on a separate page. There are no right or wrong answers. Support your answers with examples from your own experience, if possible.

1. What types of information might be constant for your school or the company where you work? How could these constants be used in formulas?

2. In your school or the company where you work, what lookup tables might be created? How would these lookup tables be used in a workbook?

Skills Review

Exercise 14-20

Define and delete named ranges. Modify defined names. Use ranges in a formula.

1. Open **Bev&Cone**. Save it as *[your initials]*14-20.
2. Define and delete a range by following these steps:
   a. Click cell A4 and press F8. Press → two times. Press Ctrl+↓.
   b. Click the Name Box and key **Products**. Press Enter.
   c. Name cells D4:D17 as **BevPrices**.
   d. Name cells D18:D24 as **ConePrices**.
   e. Click cell B4. Click the **Formulas** tab. Click the Name Manager button .
   f. Click **Filter** and choose **Names with Errors**.
   g. Select both references and click **Delete**. Click **OK**.
   h. Click **Filter** and choose **Clear Filter**.
   i. Select the **Database** reference and click **Delete**. Click **OK**.

> **TIP**
> The cells in a named range need not be contiguous.

3. Modify defined names by following these steps:

   a. In the Name Manager dialog box, select the **ConesSundaes** reference. Click **Edit**.

   b. Edit the name to just **Cones** and click **OK**.

   c. Edit the **Shakes** reference to name it **ShakesMalts**.

   d. Close the Name Manager dialog box.

4. Use a range name in a formula by following these steps:

   a. Select cell C27 and click the Insert Function button. Choose **MAX** in the **Statistical** category.

   b. With the insertion point in the **Number1** box, press F3 and choose **BevPrices**. Click **OK**. Click **OK** again.

   c. In cell C28, key **=min** and press Tab.

   d. Key **b** and double-click **BevPrices** in the Formula AutoComplete list.

   e. Press Enter.

   f. In cell B27, key **Maximum beverage price** and right-align it.

   g. In cell B28, key **Minimum beverage price**.

   h. Find the average price in cell C29 and key the label in cell B29.

   i. Calculate the same data for cones in cells C30:C32. Add similar labels in column B.

   j. Format the results as Currency with two decimals.

5. Prepare and submit your work.

Exercise 14-21

Name and edit a constant. Use a constant in a formula. Document range names.

1. Open **PriceIncreases**. Save it as *[your initials]*14-21.

2. Name a constant by following these steps:

   a. Click the **Formulas** tab. Click the Name Manager button.

   b. Click **New**. In the **Name** box, key **IncA**.

   c. Place the insertion point in the **Refers to** box, delete the existing information, and key **=110%**.

   d. Click **OK**.

   e. Click **New**. In the **Name** box, key **IncB**. In the **Refers to** box, key **=115%**. Click **OK**.

   f. Create one more constant named **IncC** for **=120%**. Close the Name Manager dialog box.

3. Use constant names in a formula by following these steps:

   a. In cell E5, key **=d5*** and press F3. Choose **IncA** and click **OK**.

   b. In cell F5, key **=d5*in** and double-click **IncB**.

   c. In cell G5, multiply cell D5 by the constant **IncC**.

   d. Copy the formulas to the remainder of the products and use the Paste Options to copy the formulas but not the formatting.

4. Document range names by following these steps:

   a. Insert a worksheet and name it **Documentation**.

   b. Click the **Formulas** tab.

   c. Click the Use in Formula button  and choose **Paste Names**. Click **Paste List**.

   d. Adjust column widths.

5. Edit a constant by following these steps:

   a. Click the **Products** worksheet tab. Click the Name Manager button.

   b. Select the **IncA** reference and click **Edit**.

   c. In the **Refers to** box, delete the existing information, and key **=106%**. Click **OK**.

   d. Select the **IncB** reference and click **Edit**. Change the percentage to **=108%**. Click **OK**.

   e. Change the third constant to **110%**. Close the Name Manager dialog box.

6. On the **Documentation** sheet, click cell A15. Paste the names again.

7. Prepare a formula copy of the **Products** sheet. Set it to fit to a single landscape page.

8. Prepare and submit your work.

REVIEW

Use the Scale to Fit group on the Page Layout tab to fit a sheet to one page.

Exercise 14-22

Name a table range. Work with structured references.

1. Open **PriceGroups**. Save it as *[your initials]*14-22.

2. Name a table range by following these steps:

   a. Click a cell in the table on the left and click the **Table Tools Design** tab.

   b. Click the **Table Name** box.

   c. Key **Products** and press [Enter].

3. Work with structured references by following these steps:

   a. Select cell G4 and key **=coun**.

   b. Double-click **COUNTIF** in Formula AutoComplete.

   c. Key **pr** and double-click the table name.

   d. Key **[** to trigger the list of columns in the table.

   e. Double-click **Price** and key **]** to close the reference.

NOTE

Table names display with an icon different from functions in Formula AutoComplete.

f. Key a comma to move to the **criteria** argument.

g. Key **<=1** and press ⟨Enter⟩. There is an error in the formula.

h. Click OK in the message box.

i. Key quotes around **"<=1"** and press ⟨Enter⟩.

4. Work with structured references by following these steps:

a. Select cell G5 and click the Insert Function button ⟨fx⟩.

b. Find and double-click **COUNTIF** in the Statistical category.

c. In the **Range** box, key **products[price]**, the table and field names.

d. Click in the **Criteria** box and key **<=5**. Click **OK**.

e. Complete the remaining two formulas for column G.

5. Make a copy of the sheet and hide columns A:E. Display the formulas.

6. Prepare and submit your work.

Exercise 14-23

Use lookup functions. Document range names.

1. Open **TastersPay**. Save the workbook as *[your initials]*14-23.

2. Use VLOOKUP by following these steps:

a. Click the **LookupTables** tab.

b. Select cells A2:B5 and click the Name Box.

c. Key **TBonus** and press ⟨Enter⟩.

d. Click in column A and click the **Data** tab. Click the Sort A to Z button ⟨↓⟩.

e. Select cell D4 on the **Tasters** worksheet. Click the Insert Function button ⟨fx⟩. Choose the **Lookup & Reference** category, choose **VLOOKUP**, and click **OK**.

NOTE

Data in a vertical lookup table must be sorted by the first column in ascending order. The ScreenTip for the Sort A to Z button shows Sort Smallest to Largest for a column of values.

f. With the insertion point in the **Lookup_value** box, click cell C4. The function will look for this pay rate in the **TBonus** table to determine the bonus.

g. Click in the **Table_array** box. Press ⟨F3⟩ and double-click **TBonus**.

h. In the **Col_index_num** box, key **2**.

i. In the **Range_lookup** box, key **false**. Click **OK**.

j. Copy the formula but not the formatting. Format the range as Currency with no decimals.

3. Use HLOOKUP by following these steps:

a. On the **LookupTables** sheet, name cells A11:D12 as **TGroup**.

NOTE

The bonus amount is in the second column of the lookup table.

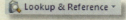

b. Click cell E4 on the **Tasters** worksheet. Click the **Formulas** tab. Click the Lookup & Reference button ⟨Lookup & Reference ▾⟩. Choose **HLOOKUP**.

   c. Place the insertion point in the **Lookup_value** box and click cell C4.

   d. Place the insertion point in the **Table_array** box. Press [F3] and double-click **TGroup**.

   e. In the **Row_index_num** box, key **2** and click **OK**. #N/A appears for the first result.

   f. Copy the formula without formatting to row 13. All of the results show an error message.

   g. Click the **LookupTables** tab. Right-click the row 12 heading and cut the row. Then insert the cut cells at row 11.

   h. Return to the **Tasters** sheet. The formula still results in error messages.

   i. Click the arrow in the Name Box and choose **TGroup**. The range definition was altered when you cut the cells.

   j. Click the **Formulas** tab and the Name Manager button . Select the **TGroup** reference and correct its range.

   k. Return to the **Tasters** sheet and center the results in column E.

4. Document range names by following these steps:

   a. Click the **LookupTables** tab. Key **Range Names** in cell G1 using 14-point Perpetua.

   b. Click cell G2.

   c. Press [F3] and choose **Paste List**.

5. Make a copy of the **Tasters** sheet and display the formulas fit to one landscape page.

6. Prepare and submit your work.

Lesson Applications

Exercise 14-24

Use named ranges. Use lookup functions.

1. Open **CustAccts** and save it as *[your initials]*14-24.

2. In cell B26 in the **Accounts** worksheet, use **=now()** with a custom format to show the date with three characters for the month, two digits for the date, no comma, and four digits for the year.

3. Select cells E4:E25 and define the range as **Amount**. Name cells F4:F25 as **Late**.

4. In cell G4, key a formula using these two range names to add the late fee and the amount. Copy the formula without formatting to cells G5: G25.

5. In the **CustTable** worksheet, name the lookup table **TCust**.

6. Use a VLOOKUP function in cell C6 in the **Accounts** worksheet to display the company name based on the customer number in column A. Since column A is incomplete, the result is an error message. Copy the formula.

7. Key the information shown in Figure 14-14, starting in cell B6. Press [Tab] for the company name.

Figure 14-14

Customer No.	Company Name	Invoice Date	Amount	Late Fee
1018		=today()	$500	$25
1020		=today()+ 1	$1000	$55
1019		=today()+ 2	$1400	$75
1014		=today()+ 3	$2500	$85

NOTE

Increasing the indent for a number removes the right alignment and indents from the left.

8. Increase the indent four times for the customer numbers. Fix the formatting in column G.

9. Set a print area to exclude the rows with **#N/A**.

10. Make a formula copy for the **Accounts** sheet fit to one landscape page.

11. Prepare and submit your work.

Exercise 14-25

Work with range names. Document range names.

1. Open **PriceRange** and save it as *[your initials]*14-25.

2. Create a documentation sheet with a list of the range names.

3. Review all the formulas to find errors. Correct the errors and format the results.

4. Edit the document properties to show your name as the author and an appropriate title for the workbook.

5. Prepare a formula sheet that hides columns A:E.

6. Prepare and submit your work.

Exercise 14-26

Use named ranges. Use VLOOKUP.

1. Open **Journal** and save it as *[your initials]*14-26.

2. In the **Table** sheet, name the lookup table **TAccounts**. Notice that there are two columns that can be searched, columns B and C (2 and 3).

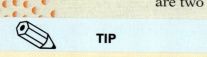

TIP

Do not include the column labels when naming a lookup table range.

3. In cell C5 in the **Journal** sheet, use a VLOOKUP formula for the account number (in cell A4) that displays the related description. In cell D5, use a VLOOKUP formula that matches the account number and shows the category.

4. Copy the formulas to row 24 and note that the results are not correct. Check Account #201 on the **Table** sheet to see what the description should be.

TIP

When you leave the Range_lookup argument empty in a lookup function, you must sort the data in ascending order by the first column/row.

5. Sort the **TAccounts** table by the first column in ascending order. Then check your formulas again.

6. Key the information shown in Figure 14-15, starting in cell B8. Press [Tab] for the Description and Category columns.

Figure 14-15

Account #	Description	Category	Amount
101			5000
202			1200
101			8000
103			12000
202			4300
303			1000

7. Increase the indent three times for the account numbers. Hide the rows that display #N/A. Center the sheet horizontally.

8. Make a copy of the sheet for formulas and fit it to a landscape page.

9. Prepare and submit your work.

Exercise 14-27 ◆ Challenge Yourself

Work with structured references.

Structured references include names for the entire table, all the data, a row, the columns, the header row, and the total row. They are automatically used in some calculations, and you can key or paste them in others.

1. Open **DropCard** and save it as *[your initials]*14-27. Name **Sheet1** as **Cards1**.

2. In cell O3, key **City Total**. It is consumed into the table.

3. In cell O4, key **=sum(** and drag to select cells C4:N4. Excel uses the structured references in the formula. Press Enter. The formula is automatically filled down the column. The AutoCorrect Options button provides an option to undo this task. Do not do so.

4. Click the **Table Tools Design** tab and rename the table as **Cards**. Check any formula in column O.

5. On **Sheet2**, key **Total** in cell B1 and **Average** in cell C1. Key **January** in cell A2 and fill the remaining 11 months in column A.

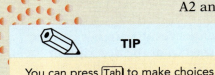

TIP

You can press Tab to make choices in a Formula AutoComplete list instead of double-clicking the item.

6. Click cell B2 and key **=sum(** and key **c** to display a Formula AutoComplete list. Double-click the table name **Cards** and key **[** to trigger a list of references in the table. Double-click **Jan**, key **]**, and press Enter.

7. Complete the formulas for this sheet.

8. Make a copy of **Sheet2** and display the formulas.

9. Make a copy of **Cards1** and name it **Cards2**. Rename the table on this sheet as **Cards2**.

10. In cell A37 on **Cards2**, key **Grand Total**. In cell B37, key **=sum** and press Tab. Key **c** and double-click **Cards2**. Key **[** to trigger the reference list. Scroll to the bottom of this list and click once at **#Data**. This reference includes all cells in the table but not the header row. Press Tab, key the closing **]**, and press Enter. The result is 113,210 and this is incorrect.

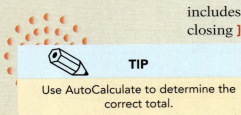

TIP

Use AutoCalculate to determine the correct total.

11. The formula is acceptable, but there is something in the table that skews the number. Do whatever is necessary in the table so that your formula will show the correct total (56,603).

12. Prepare and submit your work.

On Your Own

In these exercises you work on your own, as you would in a real-life work environment. Use the skills you've learned to accomplish the task—and be creative.

Exercise 14-28

Create a worksheet that lists 12 months (January-December) in column A. In columns B:F, identify five expense categories for your personal finances. Create range names for each month and for each expense. Create formulas in a totals row and column using the range names. Save the workbook as *[your initials]*14-28. Prepare a formula sheet and a documentation sheet with range names. Prepare and submit your work.

Exercise 14-29

Open **DropCard** and convert the table to a range. Then create range names for each month and each city. Prepare a documentation sheet. Save the workbook as *[your initials]*14-29. Prepare and submit your work.

Exercise 14-30

In a new workbook, create a lookup table that lists the names of five colors. In the second column, key a "prize" for each color. For example, **Blue** might be **$100 Gift Certificate**. On another sheet, key the names of 10 persons (real or fictitious); in a second column, key the name of one of the colors. In a third column, use a lookup function to determine the prize for each person. Make your own design decisions. Save the workbook as *[your initials]*14-30. Prepare and submit your work.

Unit 4 Applications

Unit Application 4-1

Use a nested IF formula in a 3-D reference. Use COUNTIF. Add a digital signature.

Employees receive a salary increase based on performance ratings. You have some work to do on the worksheet to calculate the increase and the new salary.

1. Open **SalaryInc** and save it as *[your initials]*u4-1 in a Unit 4 folder. This workbook is marked as final.

2. Insert a worksheet named **Increases** after the **SalaryProjections** sheet.

3. Move the data in cells D19:E22 on the **SalaryProjections** sheet to cell A1 on the **Increases** sheet.

4. Use an IF function in cell E6 on the **SalaryProjections** sheet. The first **Logical_test** is that cell **D6=2**, the first rating possibility. If this is true, multiply the value in cell C6 by the appropriate cell (with an absolute reference) on the **Increases** tab.

NOTE

If the employee's rating is 2, his/her salary is multiplied by 4%. If the rating is not 2, determine if it is 3. If the rating is neither 2 nor 3, it is 4 and the salary is multiplied by 6%.

5. If cell D6 is not equal to 2, nest an IF function. This **Logical_test** is that cell **D6=3** for the next performance rating. The **Value_if_true** entry should multiply cell C6 by the appropriate percentage. If cell D6 is not 3, multiply cell C6 by the final percentage.

6. Format the results as Currency with no decimals and copy the formula.

7. Use a formula in column F to add the increase to the current salary. Copy the formula and format the results appropriately.

NOTE

A mirror image uses the same border styles and row heights in reverse positions.

8. In cell D19, key **Over $60,000**. Use COUNTIF in cell F19 to count those salaries that are equal to or greater than $60,000. Format the result appropriately.

9. Create a mirror image of the borders in rows 3:4 in rows 20:21.

10. Make a formula sheet and hide the columns with no formulas.

11. Create a digital signature for the workbook with this purpose: **Confidential salary information**.

12. Prepare and submit your work.

Unit Application 4-2

Create, sort, and filter a table. Use Lookup functions. Update file properties.

1. Open **VacDays** and save it as *[your initials]*u4-2.

2. Create a table using **Table Style Light 1** on the **2007** sheet. Name the table **Vacation** and sort alphabetically by last name and ascending by date.

3. Insert two columns before column C. Key **Level** as the label in C3 and **Days** in cell D3.

4. Name the ranges on the **LevelDays** sheet as lookup tables. In the **Level** column on the **2007** sheet, look up the level for the employee. In the **Days** column, look up the number of vacation days allowed.

5. Make two copies of the **2007** sheet. Name one **FirstHalf** and the other **SecondHalf**. On the appropriate sheet, filter the table to list employees who took (or plan to take) vacation during the specified time period.

6. Group the **FirstHalf** and **SecondHalf** sheets. Choose a row that will work for both sheets to display the total number of vacation days used. Key **Number of Days** in one column, and make it bold and right-aligned. Ungroup the sheets. In the column to the right of the label, key the number of vacation days used after using AutoCalculate to determine the value. Complete each sheet separately.

7. Edit the document properties to show your name as the author and **Vacation Record** as the title.

8. Prepare and submit your work.

Unit Application 4-3

Name ranges. Use SUMIFS.

1. Open **TimeExpenseLog** and save it as *[your initials]*u4-3.

2. Name cells B5:B28 as **Reps**. Name the state cells as **Loc**. Then assign the range names **Times** and **Costs** for columns D and E.

3. Use SUMIFS in the **Total Time and Costs** section below the main data. Format the data appropriately.

4. Copy the sheet and hide rows 1:28. Display the formulas. Remove horizontal centering and set landscape orientation.

5. On **Sheet2**, paste the range names. Name the sheet **Documentation**.

6. Prepare and submit your work.

Unit Application 4-4 ◆ Using the Internet

Create, name, sort, and filter a table.

Look for a Web site that lists some type of data (music, movies, daily temperatures, addresses, restaurants). Copy all or a large section of the data into a worksheet. Arrange and format the data as a table. Name the table and then experiment with sorting and filtering. Save the workbook as *[your initials]*u4-4. Prepare and submit your work.

unit 5

AUDITING, ANALYZING, AND CONSOLIDATING DATA

Using Auditing tools

OBJECTIVES

After completing this lesson, you will be able to:

1. Evaluate a formula.
2. Set a data validation list.
3. Trace precedents, dependents, and error messages.
4. Find and correct errors.
5. Troubleshoot errors.
6. Use the Watch Window.
7. Use IFERROR.

MCAS OBJECTIVES

In this lesson:
XL07 1.2.1
XL07 1.4.1
XL07 1.4.3
XL07 3.1.1
XL07 3.6.1
XL07 5.3.5

Estimated Time: 1 hour

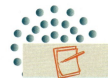

Auditing is the practice of examining cells and formulas for accuracy, similar to proofreading an essay. It is good business practice to audit your work and correct errors before printing or e-mailing.

NOTE

"Auditing" applies to many types of financial records and documents.

Excel contains several tools and features that help you audit your worksheets. Many errors show a message in the cell and are easy to spot. Some errors, however, require diligence and an eye for details.

Evaluating a Formula

Excel performs background error checking each time you open a workbook and while you are working. It looks for patterns, expected ranges, consistencies, and other issues. Cells with a potential problem display the tiny green triangle in the upper-left corner. Some formula errors also display

NOTE

You can enable or disable background error checking on the Formulas pane in the Excel Options dialog box.

an error value message in the cell. Table 15-1 describes error value messages.

The Formulas pane in the Excel Options dialog box lists the types of errors for which Excel can look. These include formulas that refer to empty cells, inconsistent formulas, and formulas that display an error value message.

TABLE 15-1 Excel Error Value Messages

Error Value in Cell	Description
#DIV/0	The formula (or macro) divides by zero. This message might also appear when the formula divides by an empty cell.
#N/A	The formula uses a value that is not available.
#NAME?	The formula uses unrecognized text, such as a range name that does not exist.
#NULL!	The formula refers to an intersection of cell ranges that do not intersect.
#NUM!	The formula uses an invalid numeric value, such as a negative number when a positive number is needed.
#REF!	The formula uses a cell reference that is not valid.
#VALUE!	The formula uses the wrong type of argument or operand.

Exercise 15-1   EVALUATE A FORMULA

If a cell displays an error value message, you can review the formula, step by step, to determine where the mistake is located. When you evaluate a formula, Excel shows each part of the formula and its results. This can help you determine where the problem is or where it starts.

1. Open **ConsolidatedPies**. There are a number of errors in this sheet, shown by green triangles and the error value messages.

 2. Click cell B19 and hover over its Error Checking button 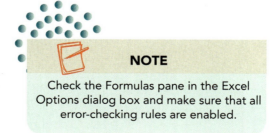. The ScreenTip indicates that the problem is the wrong data type.

NOTE

Check the Formulas pane in the Excel Options dialog box and make sure that all error-checking rules are enabled.

Figure 15-1
ScreenTip about the
error
ConsolidatedPies.xlsx
PieSales sheet

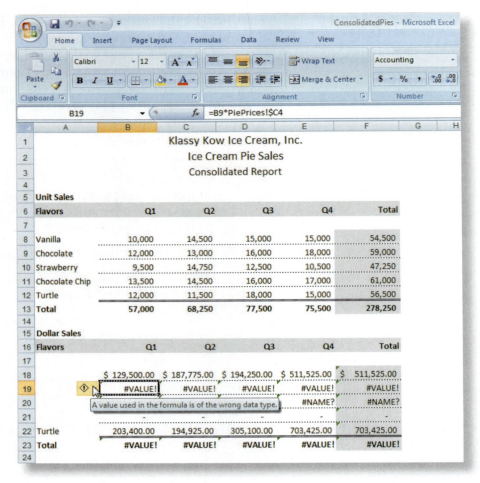

3. Click the arrow next to the Error Checking button ⬦. The first list item shows that this is an **Error In Value**. The other items are error-checking options for this type of error. **Show Calculation Steps** is an option for errors that display an error value message.

4. Choose **Show Calculation Steps**. The Evaluate Formula dialog box opens and shows the first cell reference and its initial evaluation. The formula in cell B19 multiplies cell B9 (12000) by a hyphen (-), shown in quotation marks. Quotation marks identify text, so this formula is multiplying 12000 by text.

Figure 15-2
Evaluate Formula
dialog box
ConsolidatedPies.xlsx
PieSales sheet

5. Click **Evaluate**. The result of this formula is an error value message, #VALUE!.

6. Click **Restart**. The formula is shown with its cell references this time, B9*PiePrices!$C4. The underline indicates that B9 will be the first part of the formula checked.

7. Click **Step In**. The first step in the formula calculates that cell B9 = 12000. That's correct.

8. Click **Step Out**. The next element, PiePrices!$C4, will be evaluated.

9. Click **Step In**. The **PiePrices** sheet is displayed. Cell C4 contains a hyphen that Excel has identified as a constant. This is the source of the error.

> **NOTE**
>
> The Evaluate Formula dialog box does not correct the formula. It checks each part to help you determine what is wrong.

10. Click **Step Out** and then click **Close**.

11. Click the arrow with the Error Checking button. Choose **Help on this error**. A related Help window opens.

12. Click **Show All**. Read the explanations and close the Help window. You will correct the error later.

Setting a Data Validation List

Data validation is a process in which Excel checks a value or label to make sure it matches conditions that have been set. For example, you can set data validation for a range of cells so that the values must be between 5 and 15. If you key 16 in a cell in that range, you will see an error message. In a data validation list, you specify values or labels that are acceptable. Those items are then available in a drop-down list for the cell.

When you set data validation, you can include a message that explains what should be done to correct the error. You can also set whether to prohibit the entry or allow it with a warning.

Exercise 15-2   CREATE A DATA VALIDATION LIST

1. Select cells A8:A11. Click the Name Box and key **Flavors** and press Enter. You will use this range name to create a list used to validate data entry in rows 18:22. You are deliberately not including cell A12.

2. While cells A8:A11 are selected, click the **Data** tab.

3. In the **Data Tools** group, click the Data Validation button . The Data Validation dialog box opens.

4. Click the **Settings** tab. Click the arrow for the **Allow** text box.

5. Choose **List**. This criterion specifies that only labels from a particular list can be keyed or selected.

6. Verify that both **Ignore blank** and **In-cell dropdown** are selected. With a List setting and these options, you will be able to choose from the list with a drop-down list. A blank cell is acceptable and not considered invalid.

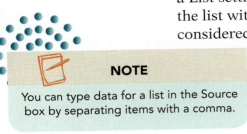

NOTE

You can type data for a list in the Source box by separating items with a comma.

7. Click in the **Source** box. You can paste a range name or select the range of labels in the worksheet.

8. Press F3 and double-click **Flavors**.

Figure 15-3
Data validation settings
ConsolidatedPies.xlsx
PieSales sheet

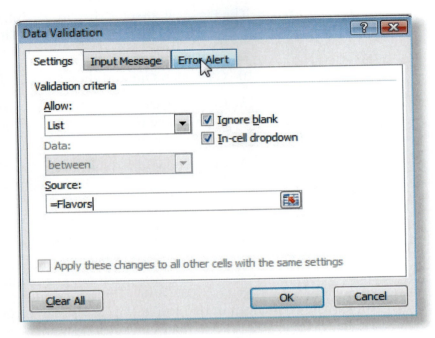

Exercise 15-3   SET AN ERROR MESSAGE FOR DATA VALIDATION

Excel can display an error message if an entry violates your settings. You can determine what the message says. You can also use an input message, which appears on screen as soon as the cell is clicked.

1. Click the **Error Alert** tab.

2. Click to select **Show error alert after invalid data is entered**.

3. Click the arrow next to the **Style** box. There are three types of error alerts for message boxes.

4. Choose **Warning**. A warning style displays an exclamation point in a yellow triangle. It will show a screen message but will allow the entry to be made.

5. In the **Title** box, key **Pie Flavors** and press [Tab] to move to the next box.

6. In the **Error message** box, key **These are the pie flavors used to develop this worksheet.**

Figure 15-4
Data validation error
alert
ConsolidatedPies.xlsx
PieSales sheet

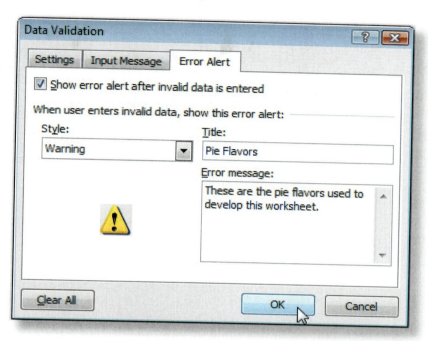

7. Click **OK**. The data validation settings and the error alert are applied to the range A8:A11.

Exercise 15-4   USE AND COPY DATA VALIDATION SETTINGS

1. Click cell A8 and click the **Home** tab. Click the Copy button.

2. Select cells A18:A22 and click the arrow below the Paste button.

3. Choose **Paste Special**. Choose **Validation** and click **OK**.

4. Press [Esc]. Now both flavor groups include the data validation.

5. Click cell A18 and its arrow. Choose **Vanilla** from the list.

6. Click cell A19 and its arrow. Choose **Chocolate**.

7. Choose the flavors for cells A20:A21 in the same arrangement as cells A10:A11. Note that Turtle was not included in your validation list.

8. Press [Ctrl]+[Home].

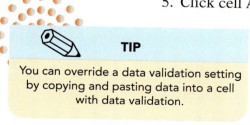

TIP

You can override a data validation setting by copying and pasting data into a cell with data validation.

Exercise 15-5   CIRCLE INVALID DATA

Invalid data represents a label or value that does not match the data validation list. As long as you have used a Warning or an Information style box, these types of entries are allowed.

1. Click the **Data** tab.

2. In the **Data Tools** group, click the arrow with the Data Validation button ⊞ Data Validation ▾ .

3. Choose **Circle Invalid Data**. Red circles appear around the Turtle flavor that you did not include in your data validation settings.

4. Click the arrow next to the Data Validation button ⊞ Data Validation ▾ . Choose **Clear Validation Circles** button. The flavor is acceptable even though it is not in the list.

Tracing Precedents, Dependents, and Error Messages

In addition to evaluating a formula in steps and setting data validation, you can use other auditing tools. Some of these tools trace the relationships between a formula and its related cells. The Formula Auditing group on the Formulas tab has tools to show the flow of a formula and how one formula relates to another.

TABLE 15-2 Formula Auditing Group

Name	Button	Description
Trace Precedents	⊱ Trace Precedents	Traces the source of a formula's result.
Trace Dependents	⊰ Trace Dependents	Traces the cells dependent on a cell's contents or results.
Remove Arrows	⊱ Remove Arrows ▾	Removes all precedent, dependent, and trace error arrows.
Show Formulas	🔣 Show Formulas	Displays all formulas instead of results.
Error Checking	◈ Error Checking ▾	Provides options to open an error-checking dialog box for correcting the error or to trace an error value message.
Evaluate Formula	⊘ Evaluate Formula	Shows each part of the formula with its results in steps.
Watch Window	Watch Window	Displays or hides the Watch Window for viewing a formula's results.

Exercise 15-6   TRACE PRECEDENTS

A *precedent* is a cell that "precedes" and contributes to the formula's results. It provides data for the formula. A precedent cell that contains an error will generate an error in the formula.

Trace Precedents

1. Click the **Formulas** tab. Select cell B19.

2. In the **Formula Auditing** group, click the Trace Precedents button . A blue dot and line connect the formula to one cell providing data, cell B9. A black dashed line points to a worksheet icon to indicate that the formula depends on a cell on another worksheet (PiePrices!C4). Something is wrong in one or both of those cells. Although the lines pass through several cells, the cell with the dot and the icon are the precedents.

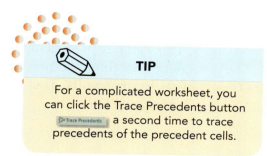

TIP

For a complicated worksheet, you can click the Trace Precedents button Trace Precedents a second time to trace precedents of the precedent cells.

Figure 15-5
Precedents traced in the worksheet **ConsolidatedPies.xlsx PieSales sheet**

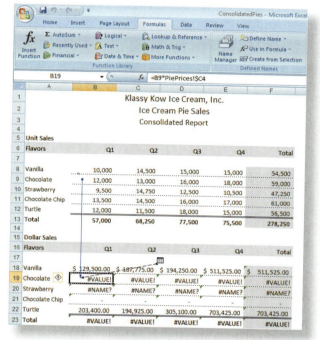

Remove Arrows

3. Click the arrow next to the Remove Arrows button .

4. Choose **Remove Precedent Arrows**. The arrows are removed.

Error Checking

5. Click the arrow next to the Error Checking button in the **Formula Auditing** group.

6. Choose **Trace Error**. The same precedents are shown.

7. Click the Remove Arrows button .

Exercise 15-7   TRACE DEPENDENTS AND ERROR MESSAGES

A *dependent* is a cell that "depends" or relies on another cell. You can use this feature to see what formulas are affected by a specific cell.

Trace Dependents

1. Click the Trace Dependents button . Red lines and arrows point to cells that depend on the value in cell B19 (cells E19 and B23).

2. Click the arrow next to the Remove Arrows button . Choose **Remove Dependent Arrows**.

3. Click cell F19.

4. Click the Trace Precedents button . This cell has precedent (blue) and dependent (red) arrows. The precedent dots (blue) show that something in columns I, M, or Q contributes to the results. The dependent dots (red) show that cell F19 depends on cell E19. This does not indicate where the error starts.

5. Click the Remove Arrows button .

6. Click the arrow next to the Error Checking button in the **Formula Auditing** group.

7. Choose **Trace Error**. The error is traced to cell B19, which depends on cell B9 and the other worksheet.

8. Click the Remove Arrows button .

Finding and Correcting Errors

In addition to the formula auditing tools, you can use the Go To Special dialog box to find cells with errors, cells that are blank, cells with constants, and other data types. Some of these options can help you find various types of problems in your worksheet. Table 15-3 summarizes the options available in the Go To Special dialog box.

TABLE 15-3 Go To Special Selections

Option	Description
Comments	Selects all cells that contain comments.
Constants	Selects all cells with values and/or labels that do not change.
Formulas	Selects all cells with formulas. You can choose to find cells that result in numbers, text, logicals (Yes or No, True or False), or error values.
Blanks	Selects all cells that are empty.
Current region	Selects all cells up to the first blank cell.
Current array	Selects all cells in the array.
Objects	Selects all objects, such as shapes and images.
Row differences	Selects all cells in the current row with contents different from the active cell.
Column differences	Selects all cells in the current column with contents different from the active cell.
Precedents	Selects all cells that support the active cell.
Dependents	Selects all cells that depend on the active cell.
Last cell	Selects the last cell with data on the worksheet.
Visible cells only	Selects only cells that can be seen and excludes hidden cells and cells in hidden rows or columns.
Conditional formats	Selects all cells that have a conditional format applied.
Data validation	Selects cells that have data validation settings applied.

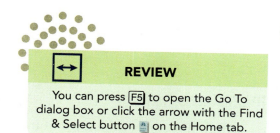

REVIEW

You can press F5 to open the Go To dialog box or click the arrow with the Find & Select button on the Home tab.

Exercise 15-8   USE GO TO SPECIAL

1. Press Ctrl+Home.

2. Press Ctrl+G. The Go To dialog box opens and lists range names.

3. Click **Special** in the Go To dialog box. The Go To Special dialog box opens.

4. Select **Formulas**. This option will highlight all cells with formulas. The results of the formulas can be values, text, logical TRUE or FALSE entries, or error value messages.

5. Make sure each of these is selected: **Numbers**, **Text**, **Logicals**, and **Errors**.

6. Click **OK**. All cells with formulas are selected.

7. Press Ctrl+Home. Press Ctrl+G. Click **Special**.

8. Select **Formulas**. Deselect **Numbers**, **Text**, and **Logicals**. Select only **Errors**.

Figure 15-6
Selecting cells with errors
ConsolidatedPies.xlsx
PieSales sheet

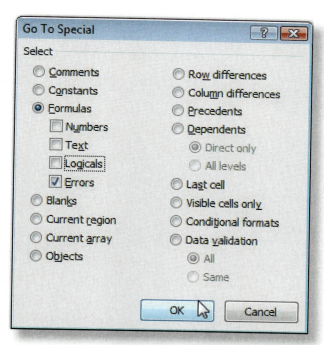

9. Click **OK**. All cells with error value messages are selected.

10. Press Ctrl+Home and then press Ctrl+G. Click **Special**.

11. Choose **Blanks**. Click **OK**. Empty cells within the area that was or is used by the worksheet are highlighted.

12. Click cell B23. Press Ctrl+G and click **Special**.

13. Choose **Precedents** and **All levels**. Click **OK**. Several cells are highlighted.

14. Press Ctrl + Home.

Exercise 15-9 USE MULTIPLE WINDOWS

Although Excel can help you find errors, it does not correct them for you. You must manually correct errors. When you have more than one sheet involved, you can open a window for each sheet and tile the windows. Multiple windows show the same workbook.

1. Click the **PiePrices** worksheet tab. Click cell C4. The Chocolate pie has no price.

2. Look at the formula bar. The cell is not empty, because it has a hyphen. A simple typing error like this can affect more than you expect.

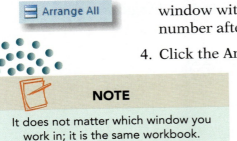

3. Click the **View** tab. Click the New Window button . A second window with the same worksheet opens. The title bar includes a number after the workbook name to indicate which copy is visible.

4. Click the Arrange All button. Choose **Vertical** and click **OK**.

NOTE

It does not matter which window you work in; it is the same workbook.

5. In the window on the left, click the **PieSales** sheet. Scroll the window so that you can see rows 18:23.

6. In the window on the right, show the **PiePrices** sheet.

Figure 15-7
Using multiple windows
ConsolidatedPies.xlsx
PieSales sheet

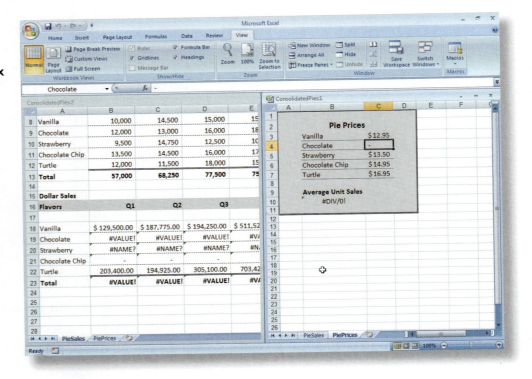

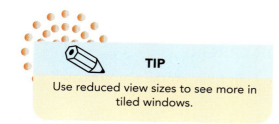

7. In cell C4 on the **PiePrices** sheet, key **12.95** and press Enter. Errors in row 19 in the **PieSales** sheet are corrected, because they depended on cell C4.

8. Click cell B20 in the **PieSales** sheet. Click the **Formulas** tab.

9. Click the arrow next to the Error Checking button 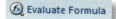 in the **Formula Auditing** group.

10. Choose **Trace Error**. The error is traced to cell B10.

11. Click the Remove Arrows button ⟨Remove Arrows ▾⟩.

12. Click the Evaluate Formula button ⟨Evaluate Formula⟩. The Evaluate Formula dialog box shows that the formula multiplies cell B10 by Strawberry. The contents of cell B10 will be evaluated first.

13. Click **Evaluate**. The value for cell B10 is 9500. That's correct. **Strawberry** is underlined for evaluation next.

14. Click **Evaluate**. Excel shows the #NAME? error.

15. Click **Evaluate**. The formula tries to compute but returns #NAME?. Strawberry is a range name used in this formula.

16. Click **Close**.

17. Click the arrow in the Name Box. There is no range name for Strawberry.

18. Choose **Chocolate**. The range names are scoped to the workbook, so cell C4 in the window on the right is active. The range identifies a price in the **PiePrices** sheet.

19. Click cell C5 in the **PiePrices** sheet and press Ctrl+F3. The Name Manager dialog box opens.

20. Click **New**. The name Strawberry is shown in the **Name** box, because Excel accepts the label in the adjacent cell B5.

21. Click **OK**. Click **Close**. More errors are corrected.

22. Widen the columns to show all the data.

23. Maximize either window and close it. The workbook is still open.

Troubleshooting Errors

Not all errors are apparent or found by Excel. For example, two columns of data might contain exactly the same values for different time periods. Excel would not see this as an error, but you'd probably be suspicious if you spotted it.

Excel also might flag some cells with errors when, in fact, the formulas are correct. You'll want to examine all cells that Excel marks with green triangles. Sometimes you can tell Excel to ignore the errors.

Exercise 15-10 LOOK FOR ERRORS

This exercise assumes that all error-checking rules on the Formulas tab in the Excel Options dialog box are selected.

1. Hover over the Error Checking button for cell F18 on the **PieSales** sheet and click its arrow. This formula refers to empty cells.

2. Press (Esc). Look at the formula bar. The formula refers to cells that have no data in columns I, M, and Q.

3. Check the errors for cells F19 and F20. These errors are the same type.

4. Note the values in columns E and F for these rows. Column F should be a total of all four quarters.

5. Select cell F18. Click the **Formulas** tab.

6. Click the arrow next to the Error Checking button in the **Formula Auditing** group. Choose **Trace Error**. An information box opens. You can use this button only for errors that display an error value message such as #NAME?.

7. Click **OK** to close the information box.

8. Click the Trace Precedents button . The formula in cell F18 refers to empty cells to the right.

Figure 15-8
Formula referring to empty cells
ConsolidatedPies.xlsx
PieSales sheet

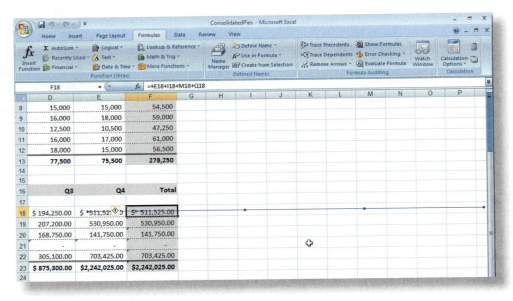

9. Click the Remove Arrows button .

10. Click cell E18. There is no error triangle, but the value is substantially larger than the three previous quarters. The formula is a sum of the three previous columns, but it should multiply unit sales by the pie price (E8*PieSales!$C3).

11. Click the Show Formulas button . Notice that cell E19 has a similar incorrect formula.

12. Click the Show Formulas button ⬚ Show Formulas.

Exercise 15-11   CORRECT ERRORS

1. Delete the contents of cells E18:E19 and F18:F22.

2. In cell F18, key = and select cell F8. Key * and click the **PiePrices** tab.

3. Click cell C3, the vanilla price. Notice that the range name is inserted in the formula bar. Press Enter.

4. In cell F19, key = and click cell F9. Key ***c** to display the Formula AutoComplete list.

5. Double-click **Chocolate** and press Enter.

6. In cells F20:F22, complete the formulas for the other flavors.

> **NOTE**
>
> Since range names are absolute, you cannot copy the formula in column F.

7. Copy the formula in cell D18 to cell E18. Do the same for cells D19:E19.

8. Click cell B21 and key = to start a new formula. Click cell B11, key *, and click the **PiePrices** tab. Click cell C6 and press Enter.

9. Copy the formula to cells C21:E21.

10. Click the Show Formulas button . Scroll to see the formulas in columns E:F and rows 22:23.

11. Hide the formulas.

12. Select cell E22 and enter a formula that computes the correct total.

13. Select cell E23. The formula should sum cells E18:E22, not the values in row 23.

14. Correct the formula.

15. Click cell F23. It refers to empty cells.

16. Press Delete.

17. Click the top of the AutoSum button Σ AutoSum ▾ (not its arrow) in the **Function Library** group.

18. Press Enter to accept the assumed range.

Using the Watch Window

The *Watch Window* is a pane that displays a formula and its results. You can add formula cells to the window and watch the results as you edit precedent or dependent cells. This is helpful for large worksheets or

3-D references in which you cannot see dependent, precedent, and formula cells all at once.

Exercise 15-12   USE THE WATCH WINDOW

You will change the pie prices and watch how the formulas on the **PieSales** sheet are recalculated.

1. Click the **PiePrices** tab. Click the **Formulas** tab.

2. Click the Watch Window button 🔲. The Watch Window pane opens.

3. Click **Add Watch**. The Add Watch dialog box opens so that you can select cells to be watched.

4. Click the **PieSales** tab. Select the range B18:E22.

Figure 15-9
Preparing the Watch Window
ConsolidatedPies.xlsx
PieSales sheet

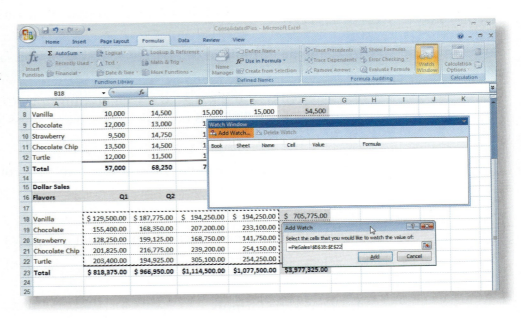

5. Click **Add**. Information about each cell and its formula is shown in the pane.

6. In the Watch Window, click the Task Pane Options button 🔽 in the title bar.

7. Choose **Size**. The bottom-right corner displays a two-pointed arrow.

8. Drag the sizing handle down to display all the rows in the pane, and press Enter.

Figure 15-10
Resized Watch
Window
ConsolidatedPies.xlsx
PiePrices sheet

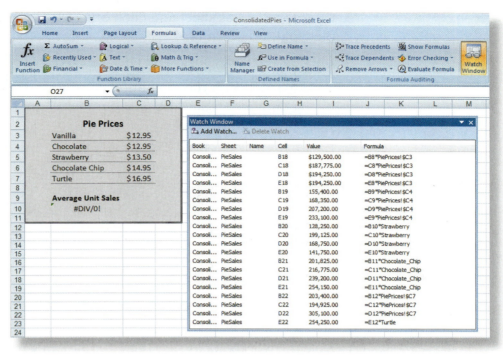

9. Click cell C3 in the worksheet. Key the following values in cells C3:C7, watching the Watch Window pane as you do.

16.95
17.50
18.95
18.95
20.50

Exercise 15-13 DELETE A WATCH

Cell references remain in the Watch Window pane until you delete them.

1. Click the first row in the Watch Window pane.

2. Hold down [Shift] and click the last row. All the rows are selected.

3. Click **Delete Watch**. All references are removed.

4. In the Formula Auditing group, click the Watch Window button.

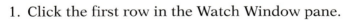

NOTE

You can also click the Close button ⊠ in the Watch Window pane.

Exercise 15-14 CORRECT DIVISION BY ZERO

There is a cell on the **PiePrices** sheet that displays the error value #DIV/0 to indicate that the formula is dividing by zero.

1. Click cell B10. Hover over the Error Checking Options button ◇ to see the ScreenTip for the error.

2. Click the **PieSales** sheet and click cell F13. This is the total number of pies sold. It is correct.

3. Click the **PiePrices** sheet and click cell B10.

4. Press F2. Cell F13, the total number of units, should be divided by the number of quarters. The number of quarters is a constant value.

5. Delete the zero and key **4**. Press Enter.

6. Format cell B10 to show no decimals. Remember that Excel rounds the value when you choose no decimals.

Exercise 15-15   MARK A WORKBOOK AS FINAL

When you mark a workbook as final, it is saved and set as read-only. *Read-only* is a document property that prohibits editing and saving the file with the same name. You can remove the read-only property or make edits and save the file with another name.

1. Save the workbook as *[your initials]***15-15** in a folder for Lesson 15.

2. Click the Microsoft Office Button and choose **Prepare**.

3. Choose **Mark As Final**. The message box tells you that the file will be saved. The same name will be used.

4. Click **OK**. An explanatory message box confirms what has happened.

5. Click **OK**. There is an icon in the status bar, and the title bar shows **[Read-Only]**.

6. Close the workbook.

Using IFERROR

Excel error value messages are general and appear as the results for certain types of formula errors. You can use the IFERROR function to specify your own error message. IFERROR is in the Logical category, and it has two arguments. The first argument is Value, or the formula that might return an error message. The second argument is Value_if_error for the text that you want to appear in the cell.

Exercise 15-16   USE IFERROR

1. Open **ConsolidatedPies**. The original file has error value messages.

2. Click cell B19. This formula multiplies by a value on the **PiePrices** sheet. When an error results, that is a likely place to look for a problem.

3. Press Delete.

4. On the **Formulas** tab, click the Insert Function button .

5. In the **Search for a function** box, key **iferror** and press Enter. Click **OK**.

6. In the **Value** box, click cell B9 and key * to start the formula.

7. Click the **PiePrices** sheet and cell C4. The range name **Chocolate** is substituted in the dialog box.

8. Click in the **Value_if_error** box. Key **Check cell/value on the PiePrices sheet.** This text will appear in the cell instead of #VALUE!.

Figure 15-11
Using IFERROR
**ConsolidatedPies.xlsx
PieSales sheet**

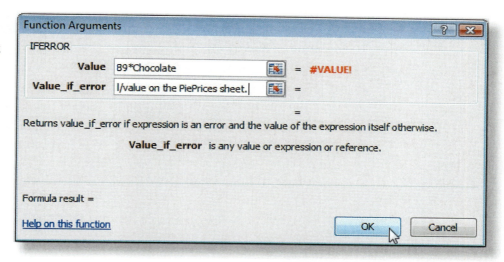

9. Click **OK**. Your own error message appears in the cell. Widen the column.

10. Save the workbook as *[your initials]*15-16 and close it.

Using Online Help

There are many ways to validate data as it is being entered into a worksheet. You can include screen messages both before any data is entered and after invalid entries are made.

USE HELP TO LEARN ABOUT VALIDATING DATA

1. Look for topics about data validation.

2. Read the information. Close the windows.

Lesson 15 Summary

- Auditing is the practice of examining cells and formulas for accuracy. Excel provides several tools to help you audit your worksheet for accuracy.

- Excel performs background error checking. Possible errors are noted with a tiny green triangle. Some cells display an error value message.

- When a cell displays an error value message, you can review each element in the formula step by step.

- One way to help eliminate some types of errors is by setting data validation. This command specifies what data is permissible in a range of cells.

- The Formula Auditing group on the Formulas tab includes commands for tracing and evaluating formula errors.

- A precedent contributes or provides data to a formula's result.

- A dependent is a cell that relies on another cell for its value.

- You can use the Go To Special dialog box to select cells with errors, blanks, and other types of data.

- Although Excel can help you locate errors, you must manually correct them.

- The Watch Window displays formula cells and related information in a separate window.

- The IFERROR function enables you to create your own error messages.

LESSON 15		Command Summary	
Feature	**Button**	**Task Path**	**Keyboard**
Circle invalid data	Data Validation	Data, Data Tools	
Data validation	Data Validation	Data, Data Tools	
Evaluate formula	Evaluate Formula	Formulas, Formula Auditing	
Multiple windows	New Window	View, Window	
Remove arrows	Remove Arrows	Formulas, Formula Auditing	
Trace dependents	Trace Dependents	Formulas, Formula Auditing	
Trace error	Error Checking	Formulas, Formula Auditing, Error Checking	
Trace precedents	Trace Precedents	Formulas, Formula Auditing	
Watch window	Watch Window	Formulas, Formula Auditing	

Concepts Review

True/False Questions

Each of the following statements is either true or false. Indicate your choice by circling T or F.

T F   1. Excel finds and corrects most formula errors.

T F   2. Precedent arrows point to cells used in the formula.

T F   3. You can press Ctrl+G to find specific types of cells.

T F   4. Data validation verifies the accuracy of values and formula results.

T F   5. The Evaluate Formula dialog box shows each argument in a formula and its cell reference.

T F   6. The Watch Window displays the current time, date, and number of edits.

T F   7. Data validation settings can be copied from one range to another.

T F   8. #NAME? is an error value message.

Short Answer Questions

Write the correct answer in the space provided.

1. If a cell provides data for a formula, what type of cell is it?

_____

2. How can you set your own error messages?

_____

3. A cell that relies on other cells for data is called what?

_____

4. How can you monitor a formula if the worksheet is large and you cannot see the formula cell?

_____

5. What does the error value #DIV/0 mean?

_____

6. Name two categories of cells that can be selected by using the Go To Special dialog box.

_____

7. What is the term for examining a worksheet's cells and formulas for accuracy?

_____

8. Describe what a data validation list can do.

_____

Critical Thinking

Answer these questions on a separate page. There are no right or wrong answers. Support your answers with examples from your own experience, if possible.

1. Explore the Data Validation dialog box. What other circumstances might be candidates for using this feature?

2. The Go To Special dialog box is helpful when auditing a workbook. Discuss instances when you might use selection options in this dialog box that you did not try in this lesson.

Skills Review

Exercise 15-17

Trace precedents and dependents. Evaluate a formula. Set a data validation list.

1. Open **UnitAndDollarSales**. This workbook has a circular reference, so a message box opens.

2. Click **OK** in the message box. Close the Help window. The circular cell reference is noted in the status bar.

3. Trace precedents and dependents by following these steps:

   a. Select cell F9. This is the circular reference.

   b. Click the **Formulas** tab.

   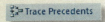
   c. Click the Trace Precedents button .

   d. Click cell F10 and click the Trace Precedents button .

   e. Click an empty cell in column G. In addition to the blue lines and dots, the border marks the dependent cells. You can now see that cell F9 is included in its own formula.

   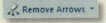
   f. Click the Remove Arrows button .

   g. Copy the formula from cell F8 to cell F9.

4. Evaluate a formula by following these steps:

   a. Select cell E18.

   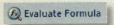
   b. Click the Evaluate Formula button 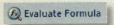 . The formula multiplies cell E8 by **French_Vanilla**.

    c. Click **Step In**. The first step evaluates cell E8 as 15,000.

    d. Click **Step Out**. **French_Vanilla** is underlined.

    e. Click **Evaluate**. The error message #NAME? signifies that there is a problem with this range name.

    f. Click **Close**.

    g. Click the Name Manager button. There are no named ranges in the workbook. Click **Close**.

    h. Click cell D18. The formulas in this row should multiply the units from row 8 by the prices in rows 27:31. This cell did not use a range name, so there is no error.

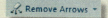

    i. Select cells C27:D31. Click the Create from Selection button. Click **OK** to use the left column as range names. Several errors are corrected.

5. Trace precedents and dependents by following these steps:

    a. Click cell B20.

    b. Click the Trace Precedents button. Cell B10 is marked.

    c. Click the Trace Dependents button. This error affects cells in rows 20 and 23.

    d. Click the Trace Dependents button again. The error traces to cell F23.

    e. Click the Remove Arrows button. There is no Strawberry range in this workbook.

    f. Press F2 and double-click **Strawberry**. Press F3 and double-click **Caramel_Pecan**. Press Enter.

    g. Copy the formula in cell B20 to cells C20:D20.

    h. Fix the range name error in cell D21.

6. Set a data validation list by following these steps:

    a. Select cells A18:A22. These cells will have the data validation settings.

    b. Click the **Data** tab. Click the Data Validation button.

    c. Click the **Settings** tab. Click the arrow with the **Allow** box. Choose **List**.

    d. Click to select **Ignore blank** and **In-cell dropdown**.

    e. Click in the **Source** box. Select cells A8:A12.

    f. Click the **Error Alert** tab. Click to select **Show error alert after invalid data is entered**.

    g. Click the arrow next to the **Style** box. Choose **Information**. In the **Title** box, key **Flavors** and press Tab.

    h. In the **Error message** box, key **Use correct pie name and spelling**. Click **OK**.

    i. Click the arrow next to the Data Validation button. Choose **Circle Invalid Data**.

    j. Click cell A19, key **Strawberry**, and press Enter. This flavor is not in the data validation list.

    k. Click **OK** in the information box.

NOTE

The Circle Invalid Data command identifies cells in which the contents do not match what is set in the Data Validation dialog box.

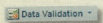

l. Choose the flavors to match the list in cell A8:A12.

m. Click the arrow next to the Data Validation button . Choose **Clear Validation Circles**.

7. Save the workbook as *[your initials]*15-17.

8. Prepare and submit your work.

Exercise 15-18

Find and correct errors. Troubleshoot errors.

1. Open **2QtrReport** and save it as *[your initials]*15-18.

2. Find and correct errors by following these steps:

   a. Select cell C9. Click the arrow with its Error Checking button. This is an inconsistent formula.

   b. Look at the formula bar. The addition formula is correct.

   c. Click cell B9. This cell uses the SUM function, so cell C9 is not really an error.

   d. Select cell C9. Click the arrow with its Error Checking button. Choose **Copy Formula From Left**. The error triangle is removed.

   e. Click cell E9. Click the arrow with its Error Checking button. This is an invalid name. In this case, it's the function name.

   f. Choose **Edit in Formula Bar**. Change **total** to **sum** and press Enter.

   g. Click cell B14. This formula multiplies cell B5 by a price on the **Prices** sheet.

   h. Click the **Prices** sheet. The sugar cone price is in cell B2.

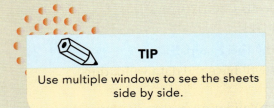

   i. On the **Units&Dollars** sheet in cell B14, correct the formula to show cell B2. Copy the formula to row 17.

   j. Click cell D14. This formula uses the wrong price. Check the **Prices** sheet and edit the formula as needed.

   k. Check and correct the prices for shakes and malts.

3. Troubleshoot errors by following these steps:

   a. Select cell C14. This formula originally referred to a cell that was moved or deleted.

   b Look at the formula bar. There is an addition symbol (+) after the equal sign, but it has no effect on the formula and is not necessary.

   c. Click the arrow with the Error Checking button and choose **Help on this error**.

   d. Read the Help information and close the window.

   e. In cell C14, key **=** and click cell C5. Key ***** and click the **Prices** sheet. Click cell B3 and press Enter.

   f. Copy the formula to row 17.

> **TIP**
>
> Use multiple windows to see the sheets side by side.

> **REVIEW**
>
> The keyboard shortcut to show formulas is Ctrl + ~.

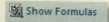 Show Formulas

g. Click the Show Formulas button  . Review the formulas carefully for inconsistencies.

h. Click cell F9. This formula uses the wrong range.

i. Press F2 and edit the formula to show **f5:f8**. Press Enter.

j. Click the Show Formulas button .

4. Format all dollar values with a floating dollar sign and two decimals.

5. Make a copy of the **Units&Dollars** sheet and show the formulas. Fit the sheet to a portrait page.

6. Mark the workbook as final.

7. Prepare and submit your work.

Exercise 15-19

Use the Watch Window.

1. Open **SalinasSales** and save it as *[your initials]***15-19**.

2. Click cell C13. The formula calculates total revenue from the sale of the products listed in column C. The prices are on the **Prices** sheet.

3. Click the **Prices** sheet. You will change the prices and watch the revenue numbers on the **4thQtr** sheet.

4. Use the Watch Window by following these steps:

 Watch Window

a. On the **Formulas** tab, click the Watch Window button .

b. Click **Add Watch**.

c. Click the **4thQtr** sheet tab. Select cells C13:F13 and click **Add**.

d. Click the Task Pane Options button ▼ and choose **Size**. Size the window so that you can easily watch the changes.

e. Change the prices as shown in Figure 15-12.

Figure 15-12

Product	Price
Cake	19.99
Pies	17.99
Kowabunga	3.09
KowOwow	2.99
Sodas	2.35
Sundaes	3.25
Cones	2.79
Malts	2.79
Shakes	2.79

    f. Click the first watch row in the Watch Window.

    g. Hold down ⎡Shift⎤ and click the last row in the Watch Window.

    h. Click **Delete Watch**.

    i. Close the Watch Window.

5. Add a digital signature to your workbook with a purpose that specifies confidentiality of the values.

6. Prepare and submit your work.

Exercise 15-20

Use IFERROR.

1. Open **PieReport** and save it as *[your initials]*15-20.

2. Use IFERROR by following these steps:

    a. Click cell B16 and note the formula. You will use the same formula with the error.

    b. Press ⎡Delete⎤.

    c. Click the **Formulas** tab. Click the Insert Function button.

    d. In the **Logical** category, choose **IFERROR**.

    e. In the **Value** box, click cell B7. Key * and click the **PiePrices** sheet. Click cell C4.

    f. In the **Value_if_error** box, key **Check PiePrices sheet**.

    g. Click **OK**.

    h. Copy the formula to cells C16:E16.

NOTE

The reference to cell B7 is relative. The reference to the chocolate pie price is absolute.

3. Widen the columns to show the complete message.

4. Fit the sheet to one landscape page.

5. Prepare and submit your work.

Lesson Applications

Exercise 15-21

Trace precedents and dependents. Find and correct errors. Troubleshoot errors.

1. Open **2QtrSales** and save it as *[your initials]*15-21.

2. In each sheet, find and correct the error(s).

3. On the Nevada sheet, circle invalid data and correct the errors.

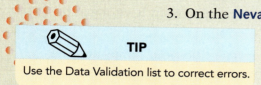

TIP

Use the Data Validation list to correct errors.

4. Group the worksheets and format the values as Number with commas and no decimals. Right-align the labels in cells B3:E3.

5. Prepare and submit your work.

Exercise 15-22

Troubleshoot and correct errors.

Klassy Kow Ice Cream makes sales projections based on a year's sales and a percentage increase. Before you can complete projections for the next two years, you need to correct errors in the formulas.

1. Open **2YrProjected** and save it as *[your initials]*15-22.

2. Key the following values in cells C5:C8:

C4:	14000000
C5:	10000000
C6:	13500000
C7:	10500000

3. Cut cells A11:A15 and insert them at cell F4, shifting the cells to the right. Fix the borders and row heights.

4. Determine what is wrong in column D. A percentage increase divides the difference by the previous year's total.

5. In column E, multiply this year's sales by 1 plus the percentages in column D. Then multiply this result by 108%, an additional sales goal for the year.

6. Format the values in column F to be the same as those in column D.

7. The formula in column G should project an increase using the percentages in column F.

8. Format dollar amounts with floating dollar signs and no decimals. Recenter the labels in rows 1:2 across the data.

9. Make a copy of the sheet to display formulas fit to a landscape page.

10. Prepare and save your work.

Exercise 15-23

Troubleshoot errors.

The Balance workbook needs to be audited. It is planned to be a template and does not contain any values. You can still trace errors and see error value messages.

1. Open **Balance** and save it as *[your initials]*15-23.

2. Cells with formulas display a hyphen or an error value message. Use whatever tools seem appropriate to determine what is wrong and correct the errors.

3. Set file properties to show an appropriate title, your name, and the company name in the Comment box.

4. Save your workbook.

5. Key the values in Figure 15-13 to test your workbook.

Figure 15-13

Current assets	
Cash and securities	1500
Accounts receivable	1750
Inventories	550
Other	235
Total current assets	
Fixed assets	
Property, plant, and equipment	2500
(Less depreciation)	250
Net fixed assets	
Other assets	
Total assets	
Liabilities and Owner's Equity	
Current liabilities	
Debt due for repayment	1250
Accounts payable	1000
Other current liabilities	335
Total current liabilities	
Long-term debt	1000
Other long-term liabilities	
Total long-term liabilities	
Owners' Equity	2700
Total liabilities and owners' equity	

6. Save the workbook with test values as *[your initials]*15-23a.

7. Prepare and submit your work.

Exercise 15-24 ◆ Challenge Yourself

Troubleshoot errors and correct errors. Create a data validation list.

> **TIP**
>
> You need not key a space after the commas in the Source box.

> **NOTE**
>
> The TEXT function allows the date to be right-aligned and spill into the adjacent left cell.

There are several errors on the Oregon sales worksheet for sundaes. In addition, you have been asked to print the comments on the worksheet.

1. Open **SundaeSalesOR** and save it as *[your initials]*15-24.

2. Select cells B4:B18. In the Data Validation dialog box, create a list by keying city names in the **Source** box. Separate the cities by a comma. The cities are Ashland, Eugene, Klamath Falls, Medford, and Roseburg. Choose the cities in that order for cells B4:B8 and then for the other sizes.

3. Evaluate the formula in cell I6 and correct it. Check the other formulas and correct them.

4. Find the error in cell I1 and correct it. Then move the formula to cell J1.

5. Use Go to Special to select cells with comments. Then click the **Review** tab and show the comments.

6. Prepare a formula sheet and hide the comments.

7. Prepare and submit your work.

On Your Own

In these exercises you work on your own, as you would in a real-life work environment. Use the skills you've learned to accomplish the task—and be creative.

Exercise 15-25

Create a list of 15 song titles and artists in separate columns. For the third column, use a data validation list that displays the music category, creating your own categories. You can place the validation list on a separate sheet or key it directly in the **Source** box. Make formatting and layout decisions. Save your workbook as *[your initials]*15-25. Prepare and submit your work.

Exercise 15-26

Create a list of labels and values to track information about your cell phone minutes. Possible columns might be day of the week, time of call, length of call, incoming/outgoing, etc. Include some data that can use formulas. Create range names for the data and use the range names in formulas. Plant deliberate errors in your work so that you see error triangles and error value messages. Save your workbook as *[your initials]*15-26. Prepare and submit your work.

Exercise 15-27

Open **Balance** and nest each formula within IFERROR with an error message of **Calculation incorrect**. Save the workbook as *[your initials]*15-27. Prepare and submit your work.

Using What-IF Analysis

OBJECTIVES

MCAS OBJECTIVES

In this lesson:
XL07 2.1
XL07 3.1.1
XL07 3.1.3
XL07 4.1.1
XL07 4.2.1
XL07 4.3.1
XL07 4.3.2
XL07 4.3.3
XL07 5.3.2
XL07 5.3.3
XL07 5.4.2

After completing this lesson, you will be able to:

1. Create a scenario.

2. Set highlight cells rules.

3. Manage scenarios.

4. Forecast with a trendline.

5. Use Goal Seek.

6. Use Solver.

Estimated Time: 1¹/₂ hours

What-if analysis is a procedure in which you vary values to predict future results. For example, you can analyze what company revenues would be if you charge $12 for ice cream cakes or if you raise the price to $14.

Excel has several analytical tools for forecasting values and results. You can create scenarios that let you save and review possibilities. You can work out mathematical problems by using Solver or Goal Seek. You can even add trendlines to charts.

Creating a Scenario

A *scenario* is a set of values saved with the workbook. You can save several scenarios and then view different solutions for your worksheet. Scenarios allow you to perform what-if analysis by entering new values for certain cells to see what happens.

Exercise 16-1   ENABLE AND RUN A MACRO

A *macro* is a Visual Basic routine included in a workbook. A workbook that has a macro must be saved as a *macro-enabled workbook* with an **xlsm** filename extension. Because macros are typical hiding places for computer viruses, you can choose settings in the Trust Center that protect against your opening an infected macro file.

1. Click the Microsoft Office Button and choose **Excel Options**.

2. Click **Trust Center** to open the pane. The first two groups enable you to view privacy information and to search online for more information.

3. Click **Trust Center Settings**. Click **Macro Settings**.

4. Click to select **Disable all macros with notification** if it is not selected. This is the default setting. With this choice, you will see an opening message box if a workbook contains a macro.

Figure 16-1
Macro Settings pane

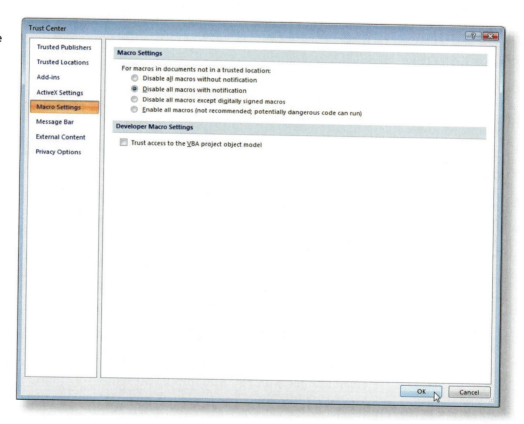

5. Click **OK** to close the Trust Center. Click **OK** to close the Excel Options dialog box.

6. Open **ConsolidatedReport**. The security message panel above the formula bar tells you that the macros have been disabled. Macros must be enabled to be used.

7. Click **Options**. Choose **Enable this content** and click **OK**. You will now be able to run the macro.

Figure 16-2
Microsoft Office
Security Options
dialog box
**Consolidated
Report.xlsm
Sheet1 sheet**

NOTE

This workbook is set at a 75% view size.

8. Click the **View** tab. Click the Macros button. The Macro dialog box shows that there is one macro in this workbook named **CompanyName**.

9. Click **Run**. This macro inserts the company name in cell A1.

Exercise 16-2   CREATE A SCENARIO

In a scenario, you normally refer to ranges of cells. These include cells that can change and cells that show results. If you name these ranges, managing scenarios is easy.

1. Select cells D22:D26. Click the **Name Box** and key **Prices**. Press Enter.

2. Name cells F14:F18 as **DollarSales**.

3. Name cell F19 as **TotalSales**.

4. Click the **Data** tab. In the **Data Tools** group, click the What-If Analysis button .

5. Choose **Scenario Manager**. The Scenario Manager dialog box opens. There are now no scenarios in your workbook.

6. Click **Add**. The Add Scenario dialog box opens.

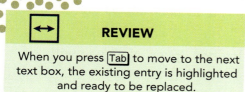

7. In the **Scenario name** box, key **Current Prices**. Press Tab.

8. In the **Changing cells** box, press F3. The Paste Name dialog box opens with the named ranges.

9. Choose **Prices** and click **OK**. The Add Scenario dialog box is still open.

10. Press Tab. In the **Comment** box, key **This scenario shows sales at current prices.**

11. Notice the Protection options. Protection settings work only if the worksheet is protected. When **Prevent changes** is selected, the values in a scenario are locked and cannot be edited. You can also hide a scenario if the workbook is protected.

Figure 16-3
Adding a scenario
Consolidated Report.xlsm Sheet1 sheet

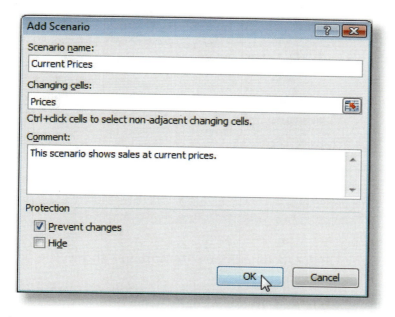

12. Click **OK**. The Scenario Values dialog box shows each of the cells from the Prices range with its current value. Do not change any values.

13. Click **OK**. The Scenario Manager dialog box lists the scenario you just created.

Exercise 16-3   ADD SCENARIOS TO THE WORKSHEET

You will now add two more scenarios with different prices for each of the pies.

1. With the Scenario Manager dialog box open, click **Add**.

2. In the **Scenario name** box, key **Reduced Prices**.

3. Press [Tab]. Excel shows the last range you used for **Changing cells**, the Prices range, cells D22:D26. A marquee appears around the range in the worksheet. Your new scenario will be for this same range of cells.

4. Press [Tab]. In the **Comment** box, key **This scenario shows sales at reduced prices.**

5. Click **OK**. The Scenario Values dialog box opens. Now you will change each price.

6. Key the values shown, pressing [Tab] to move from one text box to the next. If you press [Enter] before you have completed the changes, click **Edit** and then click **OK** to return to the Scenario Values dialog box.

Vanilla	19.95
Chocolate	20.95
Strawberry	21.5
Chocolate_Chip	23.5
Turtle	25

Figure 16-4
Changing scenario values
Consolidated Report.xlsm Sheet1 sheet

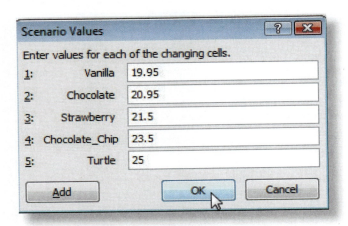

7. Click **OK**. The Scenario Manager shows the names of both scenarios.

8. Click **Add**. In the **Scenario name** box, key **Increased Prices.**

9. Press [Tab] two times. In the **Comment** box, key **This scenario shows sales at higher prices.**

10. Click **OK**. Original prices are shown. Key each new price as shown.

Vanilla	24.95
Chocolate	25.95
Strawberry	24.95
Chocolate_Chip	26
Turtle	28

11. Click **OK**. The Scenario Manager shows all three scenario names.

12. Click **Close**. The **CurrentPrices** scenario is displayed in the worksheet.

13. Click a blank cell in the worksheet.

Setting Highlight Cells Rules

Highlight cells rules are conditional formatting applied when the cell or range meets specified conditions set with comparison or relational operators. For example, you might set conditional formatting for cells with values greater than a certain value to be shown in a different color.

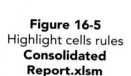

Exercise 16-4   SET A HIGHLIGHT CELLS RULE

1. Click the arrow with the **Name Box** and choose **DollarSales**.

2. Click the **Home** tab. Click the Conditional Formatting button .

3. Hover over **Highlight Cells Rules**. A list of basic rules opens.

Figure 16-5
Highlight cells rules
**Consolidated
Report.xlsm
Sheet1 sheet**

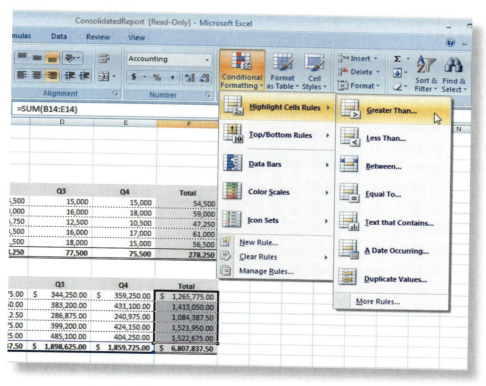

4. Choose **Greater Than**. A Greater Than dialog box opens.

5. Key **1500000** and press [Tab].

6. Click the arrow and choose **Red Text**. Click **OK**.

7. Click an empty cell to better see the formatting. It is applied to the DollarSales range.

Exercise 16-5 CREATE A NEW FORMATTING RULE

This particular rule uses "greater than," which is not the same as "greater than or equal to." You can use "greater than or equal to" by choosing a different option for the Highlight Cells Rules list. With the More Rules option, you can also choose any format from the Format Cells dialog box.

1. Click the **Name Box** arrow and choose **DollarSales**.

2. Click the Conditional Formatting button [icon].

3. Hover over **Highlight Cells Rules** and choose **More Rules**. The New Formatting Rule dialog box opens.

4. In the **Edit the Rule Description** group, click the arrow with **Cell Value**. In addition to checking the value, you can format based on other properties.

5. Choose **Cell Value**.

6. Click the arrow with **greater than** and choose **greater than or equal to**.

7. Click in the rightmost text box and key **1500000**. Your condition states that if the cell value is equal to or greater than 1,500,000, conditional formatting will be applied. Next, you'll define the formatting.

8. Click **Format**. The Format Cells dialog box opens.

9. Click the **Font** tab. Choose **Bold** in the **Font style** list. Click the arrow for **Color** and choose **Accent 6**.

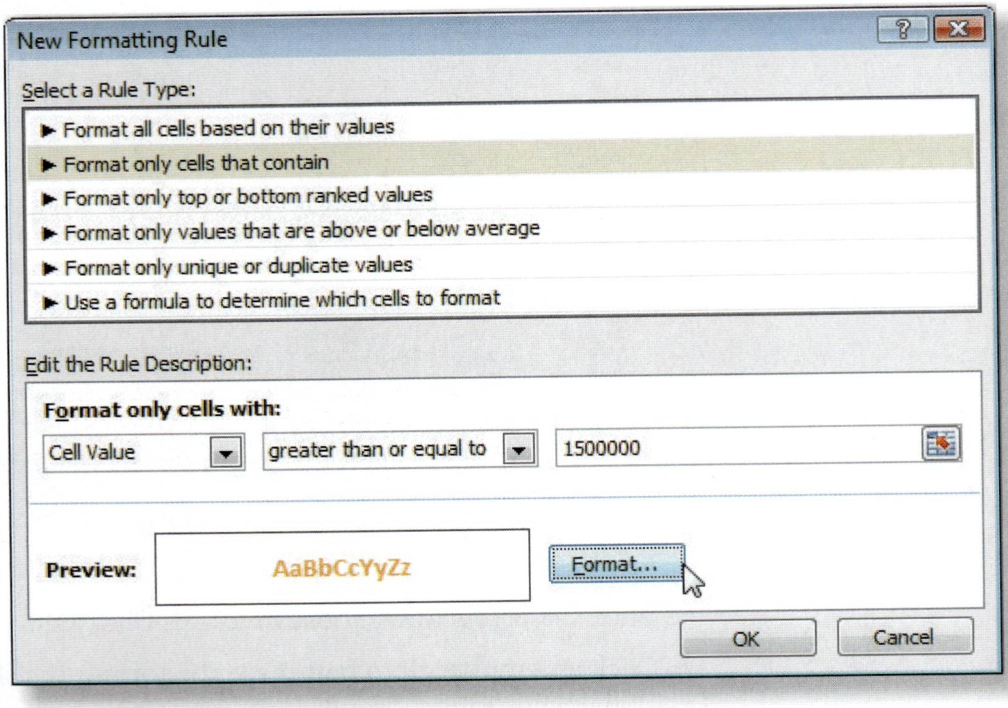

Figure 16-6
New Formatting Rule
dialog box
**Consolidated
Report.xlsm
Sheet1 sheet**

10. Click OK. The preview area shows your conditional formatting.

11. Click OK. Click any cell to deselect the range.

Exercise 16-6 SET TWO HIGHLIGHT CELLS RULES

1. Select cells B6:E10. Click the Conditional Formatting button.

2. Hover over **Highlight Cells Rules** and choose **Greater Than**.

3. Key **18000** and press Tab.

4. Choose **Light Red Fill with Red Text**. Click OK. No cells are greater than 18,000. You can set the value at 17,999 for this rule to work as expected.

5. Click the Conditional Formatting button. Choose **Manage Rules**. The Conditional Formatting Rules Manager dialog box shows rules for the current selection.

6. Click **Edit Rule**. Change the value to **=17999** and click OK.

7. Click OK again and then click an empty cell.

8. Select cells B6:E10 and click the Conditional Formatting button.

9. Hover over **Highlight Cells Rules** and choose **More Rules**.

10. In the **Edit the Rule Description** group, choose **Cell Value**.

11. Choose **greater than or equal to**.

12. In the rightmost box, key **16000**.

13. Click **Format**. Click the **Font** tab. Choose **Bold Italic** in the **Font style** list. Click OK.

14. Click OK again and click an empty cell. Cells D10 and E7 meet both conditions and have bold italic red text with red fill.

Managing Scenarios

Scenarios are saved with the workbook. You can edit them, show them, or print a summary report for them. While the workbook is open, you can display each scenario one at a time to assess results and make a decision.

Exercise 16-7 SHOW SCENARIOS

You can watch the changes in the relevant cells as you switch from one scenario to another.

1. Click the **Data** tab. In the **Data Tools** group, click the What-If Analysis button.

2. Choose **Scenario Manager**.

3. Position the Scenario Manager dialog box so that you can see the pie prices and the total dollar sales.

4. Select **Reduced Prices** in the **Scenarios** list.

5. Click **Show**. The worksheet shows reduced pie prices and the resulting total dollar sales. No total dollar amounts are shown in the Accent 6 color now.

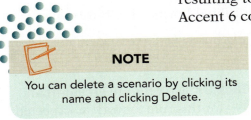

NOTE

You can delete a scenario by clicking its name and clicking Delete.

6. Double-click **Increased Prices** in the **Scenarios** list. The worksheet now shows higher pie prices with new dollar results, three in Accent 6.

7. Double-click **Current Prices**. The worksheet shows current prices and dollar results.

Exercise 16-8   EDIT A SCENARIO

1. With the Scenario Manager dialog box open, choose **Increased Prices** in the **Scenarios** list.

2. Click **Edit**. The Edit Scenario dialog box is the same as the Add Scenario dialog box.

3. Press ⎄Tab to reach the **Comment** box. Each time you edit a scenario, Excel adds a line to the comment with the user's name and the current date.

4. Edit the comment to show **Modified by <your name> on <current date>**.

NOTE

The values in the Scenario Values dialog box are formatted as General numbers.

5. Click **OK**. The Scenario Values dialog box opens.

6. Change the **Chocolate_Chip** price to **28.95**. Click **OK**. The **Current Prices** scenario is still displayed.

7. Double-click **Increased Prices** in the **Scenarios** list.

Exercise 16-9   PRINT A SCENARIO SUMMARY REPORT

A *scenario summary report* is a formatted description for each scenario in the worksheet. It shows the cells that change and the results in an outline format on a separate worksheet.

1. With the Scenario Manager dialog box open, click **Summary**. The Scenario Summary dialog box opens.

2. Make sure the **Report type** is **Scenario summary**.

3. In the **Result cells** box, select the range F14:F19 on the worksheet.

Figure 16-7
Scenario Summary
dialog box
**Consolidated
Report.xlsm
Sheet1 sheet**

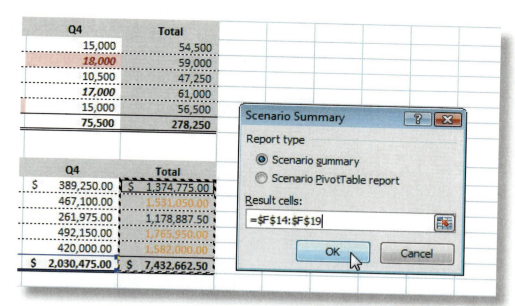

NOTE

If you had named cells F14:F18 individually, you would see those range names instead of cell addresses in the report.

4. Click **OK**. A new worksheet appears, summarizing the scenarios.

5. Click the plus symbol (+) to the left of row 3. Row 4 is unhidden to show the scenario descriptions.

6. Click the minus symbol (−) to the left of row 5. The **Changing Cells** section (rows 6:10) is hidden.

7. Click the plus symbol (+) to the left of row 5 to display the **Changing Cells** section again.

Figure 16-8
Scenario summary
report
**Consolidated
Report.xlsm
Scenario Summary
sheet**

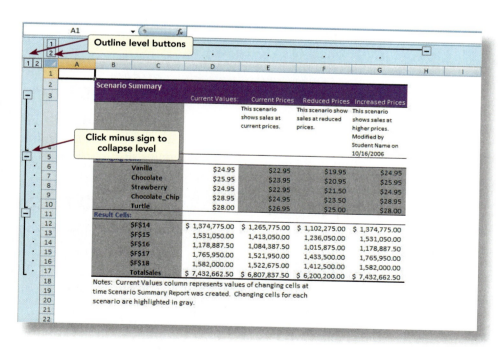

Exercise 16-10   SAVE A MACRO-FREE WORKBOOK

This workbook has a macro. When you resave it, you can keep it as a macro-enabled workbook or you can save it as a macro-free workbook.

1. Press F12 and name the workbook as *[your initials]*16-10 in a folder for Lesson 16.

2. Click the **Save as type** arrow and choose **Excel Workbook**.

3. Click **Save**. An information box alerts you about the macro. Macros are stored in Visual Basic (VB) modules.

Figure 16-9
Saving a macro-free workbook
Consolidated Report.xlsm

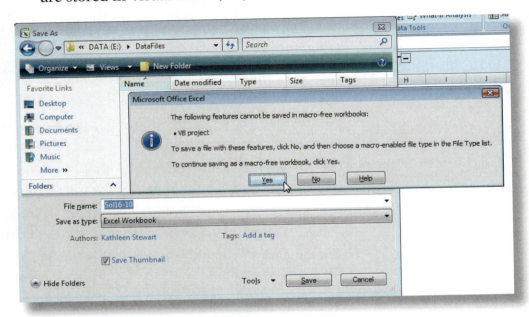

4. Click **Yes**.

Forecasting with a Trendline

A common way to analyze and predict business data is to forecast future results based on past performance. A *trendline* is a line in a chart that points out and predicts general tendencies or directions in the values.

Exercise 16-11   CREATE AND FORMAT A CHART

You'll first create a column chart showing chocolate chip pie sales.

1. Click the **Sheet1** tab.

2. Click the **Data** tab. Click the What-If Analysis button. Choose **Scenario Manager**.

3. Show the **Current Prices** scenario. Click **Close**.

4. Select the range B9:E9, quarterly unit totals for the chocolate chip pie.

5. Press F11. A column chart on its own sheet is created.

6. Click the **Chart Tools Layout** tab. Click the Chart Title button and choose **Above Chart**. Edit the chart title object to **Projected Sales of Chocolate Chip Pies**.

7. Select and delete the legend.

8. Click the **Chart Tools Design** tab and choose **Style 25**.

Exercise 16-12   ADD A TRENDLINE TO A CHART

1. Click the **Chart Tools Layout** tab.

2. Click the Trendline button. There are four types of trendlines listed.

3. Choose **Linear Trendline**. A linear trendline is a straight line and is well-suited to data that increases or decreases at a steady rate.

Figure 16-10
Adding a linear trendline to a chart
16-10.xlsx
Chart1 sheet

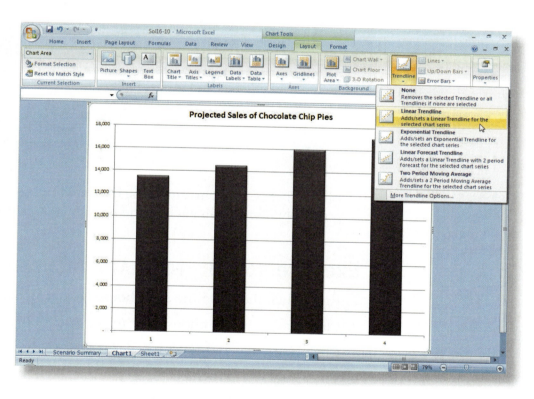

4. Right-click the trendline and choose **Format Trendline**.

5. Click **Trendline Options**. There are actually six types of trendlines that can be used.

6. In the **Forecast** group, in the **Forward** box, key **4** to project sales for the next four quarters. (See Figure 16-11 on the next page.)

Figure 16-11
Forecasting four
future periods
16-10.xlsx
Chart1 sheet

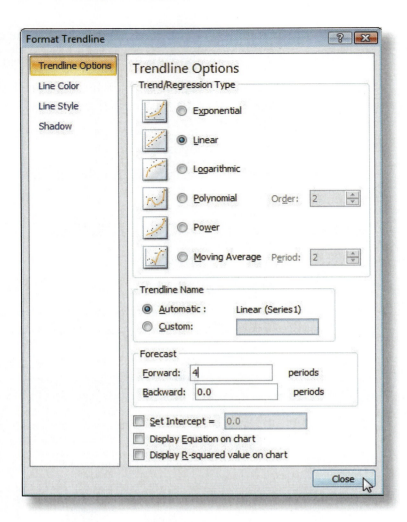

7. Click **Close**. Given current sales, the trendline shows that sales will gradually increase in each of the next four quarters.

Exercise 16-13   FORMAT A TRENDLINE

1. Right-click the trendline and choose **Format Trendline**.

2. Click **Line Style** and choose **2 pt** in the **Width** box.

3. Click **Line Color** and choose **Red, Accent 2** as the **Color**.

4. Click **Trendline Options**.

5. In the **Trendline Name** group, choose **Custom**.

6. Key **Next Four Quarters** in the **Custom** box. Click **Close**.

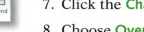

7. Click the **Chart Tools Layout** tab and click the Legend button .

8. Choose **Overlay Legend at Right**.

Figure 16-12
Formatted trendline
16-10.xlsx
Chart1 sheet

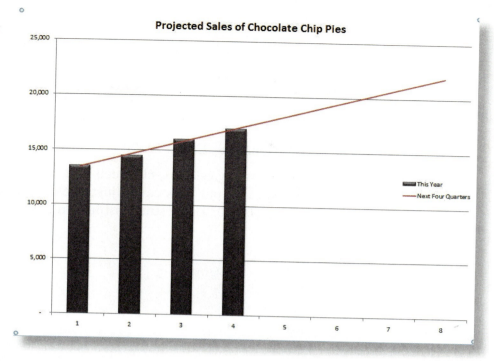

Projected Sales of Chocolate Chip Pies

9. Click the **Chart Tools Design** tab. Click the Select Data button.

10. Choose **Series1** and click **Edit**. Change the series name to **This Year**.
    Click **OK** twice.

11. Click the blue background. Click the **Sheet1** tab.

12. In the range C9:E9, key these values.

    12000   **10000**   **18000**

13. Click the **Chart1** tab. Even with lower sales in two quarters, the trend
    is for higher sales.

14. Save the workbook as *[your initials]*16-13.

Using Goal Seek

Goal Seek allows you to "backsolve" a cell value to reach a desired outcome.
Backsolving might be considered what-if analysis in reverse. That is, you
know the results of a formula and you adjust values or arguments in the
formula to reach those results. For example, suppose you want to reach a
particular total dollar sales for pies. You can backsolve to determine how
many pies you would have to sell or what price to set.

Exercise 16-14   **USE GOAL SEEK TO DETERMINE
                       A PRICE**

Suppose you want to sell $1,750,000 worth of vanilla pies. You can use Goal
Seek to determine a pie price to reach that level of sales.

1. Rename **Sheet1** as **PieSales** and select cell F14.

2. Click the **Data** tab. Click the What-If Analysis button ⊞ What-If Analysis ▾. Choose **Scenario Manager**. Show the **Current Prices** scenario. Click **Close**.

3. Click the What-If Analysis button ⊞ What-If Analysis ▾. Choose **Goal Seek**. The Goal Seek dialog box opens. The **Set cell** box shows the active cell. This cell has the formula that should result in $1,750,000.

4. In the **To value** box, key **1750000**.

5. In the **By changing cell** box, click cell D22 in the worksheet, the price of a vanilla pie. Goal Seek can adjust one cell at a time to reach your goal of $1,750,000. The results assume unit sales are the same.

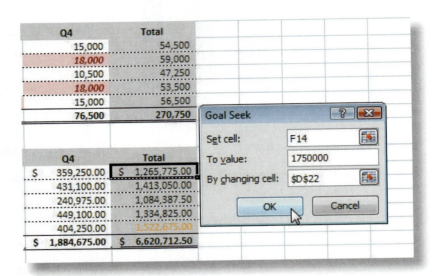

Figure 16-13
Using Goal Seek to set a price
16-13.xlsx
PieSales sheet

6. Click **OK**. The Goal Seek Status dialog box shows that a solution was found. It is shown in cell D22. You would have to increase the price to $35.21 to reach sales of $1,750,000.

Figure 16-14
Goal Seek status after a solution is found
16-13.xlsx
PieSales sheet

7. Click **Cancel**. Nothing is changed in the worksheet.

Exercise 16-15   USE GOAL SEEK TO DETERMINE UNITS SOLD

1. Click the What-If Analysis button [What-If Analysis ▾]. Choose **Goal Seek**. The **Set cell** entry shows the active cell.

2. In the **To value** box, key **1750000**.

3. Click in the **By changing cell** box.

4. Click cell F6 in the worksheet, the current total number of vanilla pies sold. This cell has a SUM formula.

5. Click **OK**. Excel displays an error message, because Goal Seek cannot change the value in a cell that has a formula. It can change only a cell that has a value.

6. Click **OK** in the error message box.

7. Select cells B6:E6 and click **OK**. The message box informs you that the reference must be to a single cell.

8. Click **OK** in the error message box.

9. Select cell E6 and click **OK**. A solution is found.

10. Click **Cancel**. Nothing is changed in the worksheet.

> **NOTE**
>
> Goal Seek can change one adjustable cell with a value. It cannot be used for more than one cell at a time.

Using Solver

Solver is an Excel add-in. An *add-in* is a feature or command that supplies some type of enhanced capability. Excel has several add-ins, some of which are installed separately from the main program.

    Solver backsolves the value for a cell with a formula. It is useful for backsolving problems more complex than those handled by Goal Seek.

    Solver has the following components:

- A *target cell* with a formula that you want to result in a particular value.

- *Adjustable cells* that relate directly or indirectly to the target cell and that Solver changes to produce the desired result.

- Limitations, or *constraints,* placed on the target cell, adjustable cells, or other cells directly or indirectly related to the target cell.

Exercise 16-16   USE SOLVER TO DETERMINE UNITS SOLD

A *parameter* is the data or information that Solver needs to determine a solution. It is similar to an argument in a function.

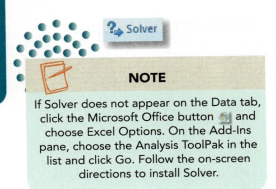

NOTE

If Solver does not appear on the Data tab, click the Microsoft Office button and choose Excel Options. On the Add-Ins pane, choose the Analysis ToolPak in the list and click Go. Follow the on-screen directions to install Solver.

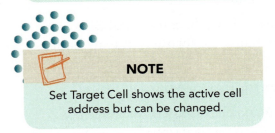

NOTE

Set Target Cell shows the active cell address but can be changed.

1. Select cell F14. Click the **Data** tab. In the **Analysis** group, click the Solver button ?➔ Solver. The Solver Parameters dialog box opens.

2. In the **Set Target Cell** box, verify that **$F$14** is shown.

3. In the **Equal To** group, choose **Value of**.

4. Key **1500000** in the **Value of** box. This tells Solver that you want the formula in cell F14 to compute to 1,500,000.

5. Click in the **By Changing Cells** box. Position the dialog box so that you can see row 6.

6. Select cells B6:E6 in the worksheet, quarterly unit sales for vanilla pies. These values affect the formula results in cell F14.

Figure 16-15
Solver Parameters
dialog box
16-13.xlsx
PieSales sheet

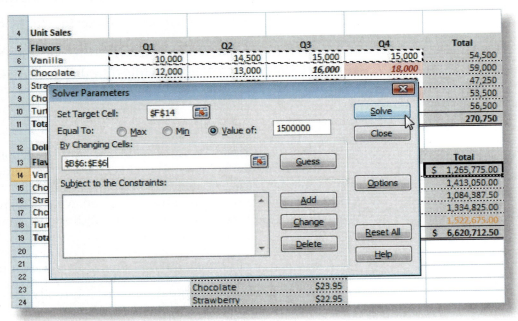

7. Click **Solve**. The solution runs across cells B6:E6. The Solver Results dialog box allows you to keep the solution or return to the original values. You can also save the solution as a scenario.

8. Click **Save Scenario**. In the **Scenario Name** box, key **Solver 1**.

9. Click **OK**. The Solver Results dialog box is open.

10. Choose **Restore Original Values** and click **OK**. The worksheet is not changed.

Exercise 16-17 ADD SOLVER CONSTRAINTS

1. With cell F14 still selected, click the Solver button 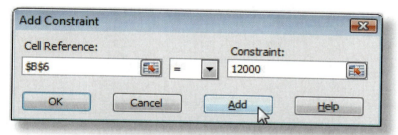 . Excel remembers your most recent parameters.

2. In the **Equal To** group, verify that **Value of** is set to **1500000**.

3. Verify that the **By Changing Cells** box shows **$B$6:$E$6**.

4. Click in the **Subject to the Constraints** box and click **Add**. The Add Constraint dialog box opens.

5. With the insertion point in the **Cell Reference** text box, select cell B6 in the worksheet.

6. Click the arrow for the middle (operator) box and choose **=**.

7. In the **Constraint** box, key **12000**. This sets a requirement that the value in cell B6 (vanilla pie sales for the first quarter) be 12,000.

Figure 16-16
Adding a constraint
16-13.xlsx
PieSales sheet

8. Click **Add**. The Add Constraint dialog box opens for another constraint.

9. With the insertion point in the **Cell Reference** box, select cell D6.

10. Click the arrow for the operator box and choose **=**.

11. In the **Constraint** box, key **16000**. This requirement is that the value in cell D6 (third quarter sales) be 16,000.

12. Click **OK**. The Solver Parameters dialog box lists both constraints.

Figure 16-17
Multiple constraints
16-13.xlsx
PieSales sheet

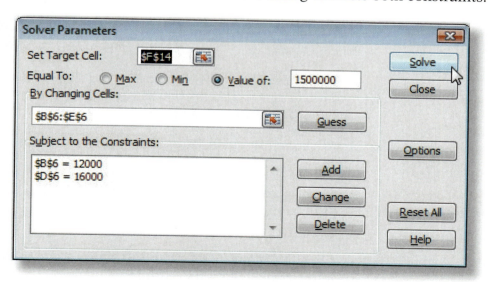

13. Click **Solve**. The sales for the first and third quarter are set at the constraint values, and the second and fourth quarter are adjusted accordingly.

14. Click **Save Scenario**. Key **Solver 2** and click **OK**.

15. Choose **Restore Original Values** and click **OK**. The worksheet returns to its original values.

Exercise 16-18   EDIT A SCENARIO REPORT

Because you saved your Solver solutions as scenarios, you can create a scenario summary report to show those two possibilities.

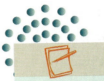

NOTE

It does not matter which scenario name is highlighted when you create a summary report.

1. Click the What-If Analysis button 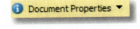. Choose **Scenario Manager**. Your solver solutions are included in the Scenario Manager dialog box.

2. Choose **Summary**. Make sure **Scenario summary** is selected. Move the dialog box if row 14 is obscured.

3. Specify the **Result cells** by selecting cells B14:F14 in the worksheet. Click **OK**.

4. Hide columns D:G (Current Values through Increased Prices).

5. Click the plus symbol (+) to the left of row 3.

6. Hide rows 6:10. Widen columns H:I so that the comment fits on two lines.

7. Make row 4 **37.50 (50 pixels)** tall. Increase the indent once for cells H3:H20 and cells I3:I20.

8. Add a single right vertical border to cells I2:I20 and a single left vertical border to cells B2:B20.

Exercise 16-19   SAVE A DOCUMENT WITH A THUMBNAIL PREVIEW

The document properties include a setting that creates a thumbnail preview of your worksheet. This preview is visible in the Open dialog box to help you confirm which file is being opened.

1. Click the Microsoft Office Button 🗔 and choose **Prepare**.

2. Choose **Properties**. The Document Information Panel opens.

3. Click the Properties Views and Options button ⓘ Document Properties ▾ and choose **Advanced Properties**. The Properties dialog box for your workbook opens.

4. Click the **Summary** tab. This tab shows some of the same information in the panel with a few additional choices.

Figure 16-18
Saving a thumbnail
as a property
16-13.xlsx
PieSales sheet

Sol16-13 Properties

| General | Summary | Statistics | Contents | Custom |

Title:

Subject:

Author: Student Name

Manager:

Company: School or Company

Category:

Keywords:

Comments:

Hyperlink base:

Template:

☑ Save Thumbnails for All Excel Documents

OK   Cancel

5. Key your name as the author and your school/business as the company.

NOTE

Select the filename in an Open dialog box or Explorer window to see the thumbnail.

6. Click to select **Save Thumbnails for All Excel Documents**. Click **OK**.

7. Close the Document Information Panel.

8. Save the workbook as *[your initials]***16-19**. Close the workbook.

Using Online Help

Solver, Goal Seek, and scenarios can be used to find solutions to fairly sophisticated business problems. Learn more about what-if analysis in general.

ASK A QUESTION ABOUT WHAT-IF ANALYSIS

1. Look for Help topics about what-if analysis, projecting values, data tables, and Solver.

2. Read the information and close the windows.

Lesson 16 Summary

- What-if analysis tests values in a worksheet to predict future results.
- A scenario is a saved set of values for specific cells, saved with a name in the workbook.
- You can add multiple scenarios to a workbook.
- Scenarios can be edited, displayed, or deleted when necessary.
- A scenario summary report is an outline about each scenario in the worksheet.
- Highlight cells rules are conditional formatting for cells to display a chosen format when a requirement is met.
- Highlight cells rules use comparison and relational operators. Two rules can be true at the same time.
- Business forecasting can be accomplished with a trendline added to a chart. A trendline illustrates and predicts general tendencies of values.
- In backsolving, you specify the desired results of a formula and adjust values to reach those results.
- Goal Seek adjusts a single cell value to reach a desired outcome in a formula.
- Solver is a what-if analysis tool. Its parameters are a target cell, adjustable cells, and constraints or limitations on the target or adjustable cells.
- Document properties include an optional thumbnail preview that is visible in the Open dialog box.

LESSON 16	Command Summary		
Feature	**Button**	**Task Path**	**Keyboard**
Goal seek	What-If Analysis	Data, Data Tools	
Highlight cells rules	Conditional Formatting	Home, Styles	
Scenario, create	What-If Analysis	Data, Data Tools	
Scenario, edit	What-If Analysis	Data, Data Tools	
Solver	Solver	Data, Analysis	
Thumbnail preview		Microsoft Office, Prepare, Properties	
Trendline, add	Trendline	Chart Tools Layout, Analysis	

Concepts Review

True/False Questions

Each of the following statements is either true or false. Indicate your choice by circling T or F.

T   F   1. Highlight cells rules specify the results of a formula.

T   F   2. A scenario summary report is created on its own sheet.

T   F   3. Goal Seek uses parameters to set restrictions on each cell.

T   F   4. A trendline highlights the most common data points in a series.

T   F   5. You can use named ranges or cell addresses to build a scenario.

T   F   6. What-if analysis allows you to use an IF statement in more than one formula.

T   F   7. Only one setting for highlight cells rules formatting can be visible.

T   F   8. In Solver, you can have more than one adjustable cell.

Short Answer Questions

Write the correct answer in the space provided.

1. What does Solver call a limitation or restriction on a cell?

    _____

2. What button includes Goal Seek, Scenario Manager, and Data Tables?

    _____

3. How can you display values that are lower than the target so that they are easily spotted on a worksheet?

    _____

4. What term describes the data that Solver needs to determine a solution?

    _____

5. Where can you access all document properties?

    _____

6. In a scenario summary report, what do the expand and collapse buttons do?

    _____

7. What term might be described as what-if analysis in reverse?

_____

8. How can you prepare a chart to show projected future sales?

_____

Critical Thinking

Answer these questions on a separate page. There are no right or wrong answers. Support your answers with examples from your own experience, if possible.

1. In your schoolwork or in your job, how could you use scenarios?

2. Think of what-if analysis problems that you face as an employee or a student. How could you use the tools covered in this lesson, such as trendlines, Goal Seek, and Solver?

Skills Review

Exercise 16-20

Create scenarios. Set highlight cells rules. Manage scenarios.

1. Run a macro by following these steps:
    a. Click the Microsoft Office Button 🔘 and choose **Excel Options**.
    b. Click **Trust Center**. Click **Trust Center Settings**. Click **Macro Settings**.
    c. Click to select **Disable all macros with notification** if it is not selected.
    d. Click **OK** to close the Trust Center. Click **OK** to close the Excel Options dialog box.
    e. Open **Shakes&Malts**.
    f. Click **Options** in the security warning message panel.
    g. Choose **Enable this content** and click **OK**.
    h. Click the **View** tab. Click the Macros button 📷.
    i. Choose **CompanyName** and click **Run**.
2. Save a macro-free workbook by following these steps:
    a. Press F12 and name the workbook *[your initials]*16-20.
    b. Click the **Save as type** arrow and choose **Excel Workbook**.
    c. Click **Save**. Click **Yes**.

3. Create a scenario by following these steps:

a. Select cells B3:D4. Click the **Formulas** tab. Click the Create from Selection button . Use the top row for range names. Click **OK**.

b. Name cell B5 as **OctDollars**. Name cell C5 as **NovDollars** and cell D5 as **DecDollars**.

NOTE

This worksheet includes a named constant for the price.

c. Click the **Data** tab. Click the What-If Analysis button . Choose **Scenario Manager**.

d. Click **Add**.

e. In the **Scenario name** box, key **Modest Sales**. Press `Tab`.

f. In the **Changing cells** box, select cells B4:D4 in the worksheet. Press `Tab`.

g. In the **Comment** box, key **Assumes modest sales**. Click **OK**.

h. Do not change any values. Click **OK**.

TIP

While the default comment is selected, key the new one to replace it.

i. Click **Add**. Key **Best Sales** in the **Scenario name** box. Press `Tab`. Do not change the **Changing cells** box.

j. Press `Tab`. For the **Comment**, key **Assumes high sales**. Click **OK**.

k. Key the following values for each of the changing cells:

Oct	18000
Nov	20000
Dec	19000

l. Click **OK**. Click **Add**.

m. Key **Worst Sales** as the scenario name. For the **Comment**, key **Assumes low sales**. Click **OK**.

n. Key the following values:

Oct	9000
Nov	10000
Dec	9500

o. Click **OK**. Click **Close**.

4. Set highlight cells rules by following these steps:

a. Select cell E5 and click the **Home** tab.

b. Click the Conditional Formatting button and hover over **Highlight Cells Rules**.

c. Choose **More Rules**.

d. Choose **Cell Value**.

e. Choose **greater than or equal to**.

f. Click in the rightmost text box and key **80000**.

g. Click **Format**. On the **Font** tab, choose **Bold Italic**. For **Color**, choose **Purple, Accent 4**.

h. Click **OK** twice.

i. Select cells B5:D5. Click the Conditional Formatting button and hover over **Highlight Cells Rules**.

j. Choose **Between**.

k. In the first text box, key **25000**. In the second one, key **26500**.

l. Choose **Custom Format** in the **With** box. On the **Font** tab, choose **Bold Italic**.

m. On the **Fill** tab, choose a light shade of the same Accent 4 color.

n. Click **OK** twice.

5. Manage scenarios by following these steps:

a. Click the **Data** tab. Click the What-If Analysis button 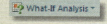.

b. Choose **Scenario Manager**.

c. Choose **Modest Sales** in the **Scenarios** list. Click **Edit**.

d. Change the value for October to **15000**. Click **Show**.

e. In the Scenario Manager dialog box, click **Summary**.

f. Choose **Scenario summary**.

g. In the **Result cells** box, select the range B4:D5.

h. Click **OK**.

6. Prepare and submit your work.

Exercise 16-21

Create and manage scenarios.

1. Open **Malts&Shakes** and click **Options** in the security message panel. Choose **Enable this content** and click **OK**. Click the **View** tab and the Macros button . Choose **CompanyName** and click **Run**.

2. Save a macro-free workbook by following these steps:

a. Press F12 and name the workbook *[your initials]*16-21.

b. Click the **Save as type** arrow and choose **Excel Workbook**.

c. Click **Save**. Click **Yes**.

3. Edit a scenario by following these steps:

a. Click the **Data** tab.

b. Click the What-If Analysis button 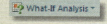. Choose **Scenario Manager**.

c. Click **Modest Sales** in the **Scenarios** list. Click **Edit**.

d. As a revised **Comment**, key **Assumes average sales**. Click **OK**.

e. Key the following new values for each of the changing cells:

Oct	10500
Nov	13500
Dec	10000

f. Click **OK** and show the **Modest Sales** scenario. Close the dialog box.

4. Press Ctrl+G and choose **Special**. Choose **Conditional formats** and click **OK**. On the **Home** tab, click the Conditional Formatting button and choose **Manage Rules**. Edit the rule to use a light color from the document theme colors.

5. Click the **Formulas** tab. Edit the constant **Price** to be **3.29**.

6. Name cell B5 as **OctDollars** and cell E5 as **TotalDollars**.

7. Create a scenario summary report by following these steps:

   a. Click the **Data** tab. Click the What-If Analysis button . Choose **Scenario Manager**.

   b. Click **Summary**. Make sure that **Scenario summary** is selected.

   c. For **Result cells**, select cells B5:E5. Click **OK**.

   d. Show the scenario comments.

8. Prepare and submit your work.

Exercise 16-22

Forecast with a trendline.

1. Open **Sodas** and save it as *[your initials]*16-22.

2. Show the **Best Sales** scenario.

3. Create a column chart sheet for cells B3:D4. Add a chart title above the chart that displays **Ice Cream Sodas**. Choose a chart style.

4. Forecast with a trendline by following these steps:

   a. Click the **Chart Tools Layout** tab.

   b. Click the Trendline button .

   c. Choose **More Trendline Options**.

   d. Choose **Logarithmic** in the **Trend/Regression Type** group.

   e. In the **Trendline Name** group, choose **Custom**.

   f. Key **Next Six Months** in the **Custom** box.

   g. In the **Forecast Forward** box, key **6**.

   h. Click **Close**.

NOTE

A logarithmic line is a curved line and is suited to values that increase/decrease quickly and then level out.

5. Format a trendline by following these steps:

   a. Right-click the trendline and choose **Format Trendline**.

   b. Use a 2-pt **Width** and a color that contrasts with your chart style. Click **Close**.

   c. Click the **Chart Tools Design** tab. Click the Select Data button . Name the first series as **Unit Sales**.

6. Prepare and submit your work.

Exercise 16-23

Use Goal Seek. Use Solver. Manage scenarios.

1. Open **XmasCakes** and save it as *[your initials]*16-23.
2. Use Goal Seek by following these steps:

    a. In the **CreditUnion** worksheet, select cell B9. The formula uses the PMT function to determine the monthly car payment.

    b. Click the **Data** tab. Click the What-If Analysis button 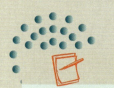 .

    c. Choose **Goal Seek**. In the **To value** box, key **350**. This is the desired car payment.

    d. Select cell B6 for the **By changing cell** box. This is the amount that would have to be borrowed.

    e. Click **OK** to find a solution. Click **OK** to keep the solution.

    f. Select cell F9. The formula uses the FV function to determine what the savings account will be worth in four years.

    g. Click the What-If Analysis button 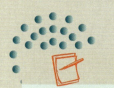 . Choose **Goal Seek**.

    h. In the **To value** box, key **7000**, the amount you would like to have in four years.

    i. Use cell F8 for the **By changing cell** box. This is the interest rate.

    j. Click **OK**. Excel tries but cannot find a solution.

    k. Click **Cancel**.

    l. Click the What-If Analysis button 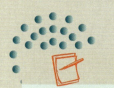 . Choose **Goal Seek**. Set up the same problem by changing the monthly deposit.

    m. Click **OK** to keep the solution.

3. Click the **DecoratingSchedule** tab. Select cell D4. The formula in cells D4:D8 multiplies hours worked per week by the number of cakes decorated in an hour. This determines how many cakes a decorator can complete in a week.

4. Select cell F4. The formula in the range F4:F8 multiplies the worker's hourly wage by hours worked.

5. Select cells B9:F9 and click the AutoSum button on the **Home** tab.

6. Use Solver by following these steps:

    a. Select cell D9. This is the target cell, because you want to make a certain number of cakes.

    b. Click the **Data** tab. Click the Solver button  .

    c. Key **750** in the **Value of** box, the number of cakes that must be completed this week.

    d. In the **By Changing Cells** box, select cells B4:B8. You will vary how much each person works to get the most cakes made.

NOTE

Goal Seek sets the borrowed amount to a negative number, because the PMT function assumes the lender's (the credit union's) perspective.

TIP

Goal Seek cannot always find a solution.

e. Click **Solve**.

f. Click **Save Scenario**. Key **Any Hours** in the **Scenario Name** box. Click **OK**.

g. Choose **Restore Original Values**. Click **OK**.

TIP

Key spaces between words in scenario names so that the summary report includes spaces in the names.

7. Add constraints to a Solver problem by following these steps:

a. Click the Solver button .

b. Click **Add** in the **Subject to the Constraints** group.

c. In the **Cell Reference** box, click cell B4.

d. Click the arrow for the middle (operator) box and choose **=**.

e. In the **Constraint** box, key **30**. This means that Carl can work only 30 hours.

f. Click **Add**. In the **Cell Reference** box, select cell B7.

g. Choose **=** as the operator. In the **Constraint** box, key **30**. Click **OK**.

h. Click **Solve**.

i. Click **Save Scenario**. Key **Restricted Hours** and click **OK**.

j. Choose **Restore Original Values**. Click **OK**.

8. Create a scenario summary report with cell D9 for the **Result cells**.

9. Prepare and submit your work.

Lesson Applications

Exercise 16-24

Set highlight cells rules.

1. Open **Daily** and save it as *[your initials]*16-24.

2. Fill in the labels that are missing in column A.

3. Format cells A3:H19 as a table with a header row using Table Style Light 9.

NOTE

The Format Entire Row option is only available in a table for a selected column.

4. Point at the Sat column label to display a black arrow and click to select the column. Then create a highlight cells rule using Between. For values between 15,000 and 16,500, format the entire row with fill color similar to the one used in the table style.

5. Format cells B4:H19 with a highlight cells rule that shows values greater than 25,000 with green fill and dark green text.

6. Prepare and submit your work.

Exercise 16-25

Create and manage scenarios. Use Goal Seek.

1. Open **GrowthRate** and save it as *[your initials]*16-25.

2. In cell D14, calculate first-quarter KowOwow sales for next year using the information about the Sales Forecast Formula on the worksheet. Copy the formula without formatting to complete this section of the sheet.

TIP

Use Paste Special to copy values or formulas without formatting. Use the Format Cells dialog box to solve alignment problems.

NOTE

The Scenario Values dialog box shows 1.5% in its decimal equivalent of 0.015. The dialog box does not show the percent sign.

3. Format all values to show no decimal positions. Use Accounting Number Format with no decimals for the values in row 14.

4. In cell H14, use SUM with a range that does not include values from last year. Copy the formula. Show a dollar sign with the value in row 14.

5. Show a total in cell H17 with matching formatting.

6. Add a scenario named 1.5% Growth with the changing cell as cell H4. Include your name in the comment.

7. Use Goal Seek to find a Quarterly Growth Rate that will result in $4,000,000 in sales (cell H17). Save the Goal Seek solution as a scenario named New Growth and include your name in the comment.

8. Create a scenario summary report for cells D14:G16.

9. Prepare a formula copy of the **SalesForecast** worksheet, hiding columns A:C.

10. Prepare and submit your work.

Exercise 16-26

Use Solver. Create and manage scenarios.

1. Open **EasterCake** and save it as *[your initials]*16-26.

TIP

Select the ranges and then use the Create from Selection button .

TIP

A profit margin is the percentage or dollars earned on each cake. Profits start to decline after 200 cakes are made.

NOTE

If the shop makes 50 additional cakes, they make no more money if the multiplier is 2%.

2. Create range names for cells B4:C6, B8:C9, B11:C13.

3. In cell C11, build a formula to calculate profit at the shop's capacity of 200 cakes. Multiply **Maximum_Cakes** *****Price** *****Profit_Margin**.

4. In cell C12, build a formula to calculate profit for 50 cakes over the capacity of 200. The formula is explained in the shape on the sheet.

5. In cell C13, build a formula that sums profits from shop capacity and from overcapacity.

6. Use Solver to determine how many extra cakes should be made to maximize total profit at the current price and with the 2% multiplier. The target cell is the total profit; set it to find the maximum. The changing cell is the number of extra cakes.

7. Save the Solver solution as a scenario named **2% Multiplier** and restore the original values.

8. On the worksheet, change the multiplier to **1%** and run Solver again. Save the solution as a scenario named **1% Multiplier**.

9. Edit the sheet to use a **3%** multiplier, run Solver, and save the solution as a scenario named **3% Multiplier**.

10. Create a scenario summary report with cell C13 as a result cell.

11. Make a formula copy of the **EasterCakes** sheet and delete the shape. Make necessary adjustments. Fit the sheet to one page.

Exercise 16-27 ◆ Challenge Yourself

Use Solver.

You've been asked to determine minimum labor cost for a holiday weekend. The weekend consists of 100 hours, and the shop has four employees. Some employees are limited in the number of hours they can work, but the total hours worked must be 100 hours.

1. In a new workbook, key **Klassy Kow Ice Cream Shops** as a main label. As a second label, key **Holiday Weekend**.

2. In row 3, key **# of Hours** in column B. In column C, key **Hourly Rate**. In column D, key **Weekend Pay**.

3. In row 4 in column A, key **Employee 1**. Fill up to and including **Employee 4**. In the row below **Employee 4**, key **Total**.

4. Key hourly rates for each employee.

Employee 1	**$9.25**
Employee 2	**$10.50**
Employee 3	**$9.75**
Employee 4	**$8.50**

5. In column D, use a formula to determine the weekend pay for each employee.

6. In column B, key **25** hours for each employee so that the total is 100. Show a sum for columns B and D for the hours and weekend pay.

7. Use Solver to find the lowest total weekend pay, changing the number of hours for each employee with the following constraints.

   - Employee 1 hours   **<=25**
   - Employee 2 hours   **=30**
   - Employee 3 hours   **>=30**
   - Employee 4 hours   **<=25**
   - Total number of hours   **=100**

8. Keep the Solver solution.

9. Format the worksheet with an attractive design.

10. Save the workbook as *[your initials]*16-27. Prepare and submit your work.

On Your Own

In these exercises you work on your own, as you would in a real-life work environment. Use the skills you've learned to accomplish the task—and be creative.

Exercise 16-28

In a new workbook, key labels, values, and formulas for a sports activity with which you are familiar. Use players or team names, scores, and other statistics. Save your first set of values as a scenario. Add best-case and worst-case scenarios for your players/teams. Create a scenario summary report. Save the workbook as *[your initials]*16-28. Prepare and submit your work.

Exercise 16-29

Create a workbook that lists dates from today to 15 days from now in one column. In the second column, show the day of the week (Monday, Tuesday). In the third column, key a value to represent the number of hits to a Web site. Experiment using highlight cells rules that you have not used in this lesson. Add labels and other formatting effects to prepare a professional worksheet.

Exercise 16-30

In a new workbook, key the names and prices of five items that you would like to buy. Sum the values. Then use Solver to set the sum to a new total that is lower than the current sum by changing the price of each of the items. If Solver cannot find a solution or finds an unacceptable one, try adding constraints. Solve for reasonable prices. Save the workbook as *[your initials]*16-30. Prepare and submit your work.

Consolidating and Linking Workbooks

OBJECTIVES

After completing this lesson, you will be able to:

1. Create a static data consolidation.

2. Create a dynamic data consolidation.

3. Consolidate data by category.

4. Link workbooks.

5. Examine and edit links.

MCAS OBJECTIVES

In this lesson:
XL07 1.3.1
XL07 1.5.1
XL07 3.1.2
XL07 3.8
XL07 5.3.2

Estimated Time: 1¹/₂ hours

Consolidation is a process in which data from multiple worksheets or workbooks is combined and summarized. For example, if each shop submits sales data in a separate workbook, the main office can consolidate individual workbooks to create a single summary report.

Worksheets and workbooks can be consolidated when:

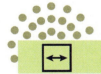

REVIEW

A 3-D reference is a formula that refers to another worksheet in the same workbook.

- Common data appears in the same position on each worksheet. This is known as consolidating *by position*.

- Worksheets have the same row or column labels. This can be referred to as consolidating *by category*.

Linking is a process in which formulas refer to cells in another workbook. Linking is similar to using a 3-D reference within a workbook.

Creating a Static Data Consolidation

A *static consolidation* summarizes values and enters a result. The result does not recalculate if a value used in consolidating is changed. You might use a static consolidation when you are preparing a report and know that all supporting data is final.

The Consolidate command can use one of several functions to summarize values, including SUM, AVERAGE, COUNT, and others.

Exercise 17-1 PREPARE A WORKSHEET FOR CONSOLIDATION

The sheet used for consolidation is usually empty of values. It often includes the same or similar labels as those used in the source sheets.

1. Open **4QtrSandwiches**.

2. Make a copy of the **December** sheet at the end. Name it **4thQtr**.

3. Edit cell A4 to show **Fourth Quarter**.

4. On the **4thQtr** sheet, delete the contents of cells B6:E9. This sheet is ready for consolidating data.

Exercise 17-2 CREATE A STATIC CONSOLIDATION

1. Make sure cells B6:E9 are selected on the **4thQtr** worksheet.

2. Click the **Data** tab. In the **Data Tools** group, click the Consolidate button 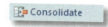. The Consolidate dialog box opens.

3. In the **Function** box, check that **Sum** is the function to be used.

4. Click in the **Reference** box.

5. Click the **October** tab. The reference shows the name of the worksheet with an exclamation point.

6. Select cells B6:E9. The cell addresses are added to the entry with absolute references.

7. Click **Add**. The range appears under **All references**. You can add another reference for the consolidation.

8. Click the **November** tab. The same range is selected in the **November** sheet, and the **Reference** box shows the sheet name and cell addresses.

9. Click **Add**. The second reference appears under **All references**.

10. Click the **December** tab. Because everything is in the same position on these worksheets, your work in consolidating the data is minimal (See Figure 17-1 on the next page.)

REVIEW

Check the ScreenTip for a button if your button appears different from the text figures. Button appearance depends on your screen size and resolution.

REVIEW

The Consolidate dialog box collapses when you select a range on the worksheet.

Figure 17-1
Using the
Consolidate dialog
box
4thQtrSandwiches.xlsx
December sheet

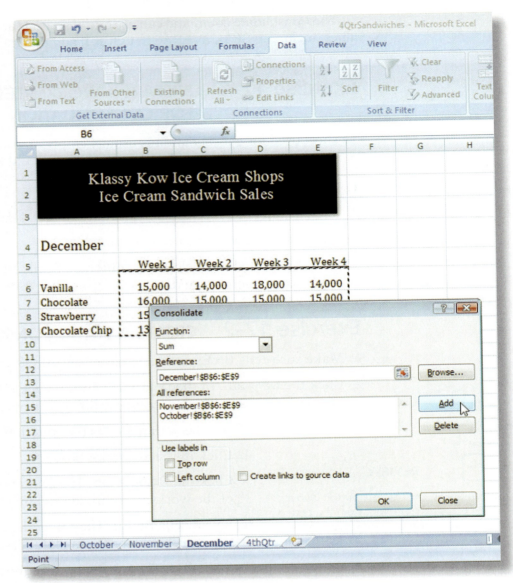

11. Click **Add**. The **All references** box lists the three ranges that will be summed on the **4thQtr** worksheet.

12. Click **OK**. The **4thQtr** sheet shows the sum of the values from the monthly worksheets.

Exercise 17-3 EDIT UNDERLYING DATA

If you change a value in one of the monthly worksheets, the consolidated sheet does not recalculate.

1. Select cell B6 on the **4thQtr** worksheet.

2. Look at the formula bar. It holds a value (46200), not a formula.

3. Click the **October** tab. Select cell B6 and key **0**.

4. Click the **4thQtr** tab. The value is not updated.

5. Delete the contents of cells B6:E9 in the **4thQtr** worksheet.

Creating a Dynamic Data Consolidation

A *dynamic consolidation* creates a formula that refers to the other worksheets. The formula is recalculated if you make a change in any of the supporting worksheets.

Dynamic consolidation is appropriate when values in the supporting worksheets might be changed after you consolidate, and you always want your workbook to reflect the most current information.

Exercise 17-4   CREATE A DYNAMIC CONSOLIDATION

Excel saves the references used in the most recent Consolidate command. To edit or change the consolidation, you might not need to re-enter the references if you have not closed Excel.

When you choose the option to link to the source data in the Consolidate dialog box, Excel creates an outline with 3-D references. An *outline* is a summary worksheet that can display or hide details.

REVIEW

A scenario summary report is an outline.

1. Select cells B6:E9 on the **4thQtr** worksheet.

2. Click the **Data** tab. Click the Consolidate button 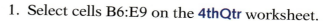 . The references to the other worksheets are still shown. (If they are not, repeat steps 3–11 in Exercise 17-2.)

3. Click to select **Create links to source data**. This option creates a dynamic consolidation.

4. Click **OK**. Outline symbols appear at the left. The numbers to the left of the column A header indicate how many levels of detail are in the outline. The plus and minus symbols (Expand and Collapse buttons) are used to display and hide levels of detail. This outline has two levels of detail.

5. Click the plus (+) symbol for row 9. Immediately above row 9 are the monthly values for vanilla (row 6) from the other worksheets (See Figure 17-2 on the next page.)

Figure 17-2
Displaying detail in
an outline
4thQtrSandwiches.xlsx
4thQtr sheet

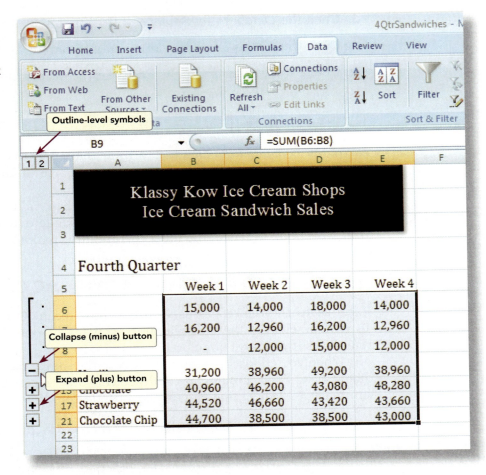

6. Click the minus (−) symbol for row 9. Individual values are hidden.

7. Click the plus (+) symbol for row 21. Monthly values for chocolate chip are displayed.

8. Select cell B18. Notice in the formula bar that it is a 3-D formula.

9. Click the minus (−) symbol for row 21 to hide the details.

10. Select cell B9 and note its value (31200).

11. Click the **October** tab. In cell B6, key **10000**.

12. Click the **4thQtr** tab. The new result in cell B9 includes the value you just keyed.

13. Click the plus (+) symbol for row 9. The October value is in cell B8.

14. Collapse row 9.

Exercise 17-5   DISPLAY FORMULAS IN AN OUTLINE

The level symbols are at the top of the outline column. They display 1 and 2 because this outline has two levels. Level 1 shows totals; Level 2 shows details.

1. Click the Level 2 outline symbol. The entire worksheet expands.

2. Press [Ctrl]+[`] to display the formulas. You can see the name of each sheet used in a formula.

Figure 17-3
Displaying formulas in an outline
4thQtrSandwiches.xlsx
4thQtr sheet

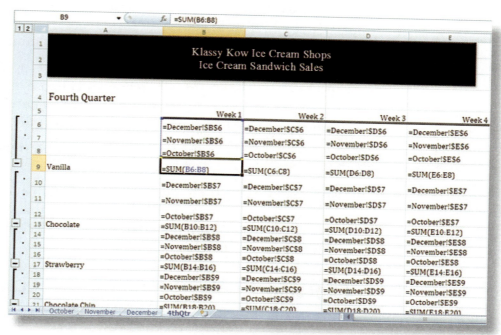

3. AutoFit the columns and set landscape orientation.

4. Save the workbook as *[your initials]*17-5 in a folder for Lesson 17.

5. Click the Level 1 symbol. The details are hidden.

6. Press [Ctrl]+[`] to hide the formulas.

7. Click anywhere in row 13. In the **Outline** group on the **Data** tab, click the Show Detail button . This is the same as clicking the Expand button next to the row heading.

8. Click the Hide Detail button .

9. Save the workbook and close it.

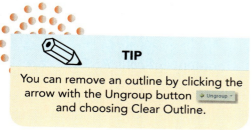

TIP

You can remove an outline by clicking the arrow with the Ungroup button [Ungroup ▾] and choosing Clear Outline.

Consolidating Data by Category

In the previous exercises, you consolidated by position. All source data was arranged in identical order and location. You can also consolidate data by category. In this case, worksheets have the same row and column labels, but the data is organized differently.

Exercise 17-6   SET UP DATA TO BE CONSOLIDATED

1. Open **4QtrSandwiches**.

2. Copy the **December** sheet at the end. Name the copy **Averages**. Edit cell A4 to show **Averages**.

3. In the **October** worksheet, right-click the column E heading and choose **Cut**.

4. Right-click the column B heading and choose **Insert Cut Cells**. The week order on this worksheet is now different from the order on the other worksheets. Select any cell to deselect the column.

5. In the **November** worksheet, right-click the row 8 heading. Choose **Cut**.

6. Right-click the row 7 heading and choose **Insert Cut Cells**. The flavor order on this worksheet is different from the other worksheets. Select any cell.

> **REVIEW**
>
> If you do a regular cut and paste, Excel replaces existing data with the cut cells.

Exercise 17-7   USE AVERAGE TO CONSOLIDATE BY CATEGORY

When you consolidate data by category, you must include labels in the consolidation ranges. The consolidation worksheet should not show any labels as you start the consolidation.

1. In the **Averages** worksheet, delete the contents of cells A5:E9. Leave the range selected on the worksheet.

2. Click the **Data** tab. In the **Data Tools** group, click the Consolidate button  .

3. Click the arrow for the **Function** box and choose **Average**.

4. Click in the **Reference** box.

5. Click the **October** tab and select cells A5:E9. This range includes labels for the rows and the columns.

6. Click **Add** in the Consolidate dialog box. The range appears under **All references**.

7. Click the **November** tab. The same range is assumed.

8. Click **Add**.

9. Click the **December** tab and click **Add**.

10. In the **Use labels in** group, click to select **Top row** and **Left column**.

Figure 17-4
Consolidating by
category
4thQtrSandwiches.xlsx
Averages sheet

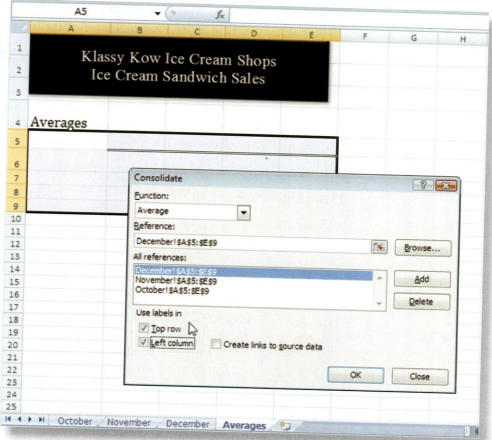

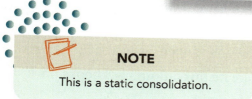

NOTE

This is a static consolidation.

11. Click **OK**. The **Averages** worksheet averages the values from the monthly sheets. The Vanilla average for Week 1 is 15,400.

Exercise 17-8 CONSOLIDATE DATA BY USING MAX

1. Select any cell in the **Averages** worksheet to deselect the range.

2. Copy the **Averages** sheet at the end, and rename it **Maximums**. Edit cell A4 to show **Maximums**.

3. On the **Maximums** sheet, delete the contents of cells A5:E9. Leave the range selected.

4. Click the Consolidate button [Consolidate]. Click the arrow for the **Function** box and choose **Max**. You'll use the same references as before. The options in the **Use labels in** group are also still selected.

5. Click to select **Create links to source data**. This will create a dynamic consolidation with 3-D references.

6. Click **OK**. The **Maximums** sheet calculates the highest value from the three monthly worksheets. The Vanilla maximum for Week 1 is 16,200. There are two outline levels, one to show the weekly numbers (details) and one to show the maximum. Notice that the sheet now extends to column F.

7. Select any cell to deselect the range. Click the Level 2 symbol. The outline expands to show all the references. Column B is inserted in a dynamic consolidation by category to identify the workbook.

8. Press Ctrl + -. Widen columns as needed.

9. Set landscape orientation.

10. Save the workbook as *[your initials]*17-8. Close the workbook.

Linking Workbooks

Linking combines data from multiple workbooks into a summary workbook. When any workbook is changed, the summary workbook recalculates its formulas.

> **NOTE**
>
> Linking workbooks is designed for environments in which files are always accessible.

Linked workbooks depend on one another. The *dependent workbook* is the file that obtains data from other workbooks. Dependent workbooks use *external reference formulas*, formulas that refer to cells in another workbook. The *source workbook* is the file with data used by a dependent workbook in an external reference formula.

You can create an external reference formula in several ways. You can:

- Point to the cell(s) if the source workbook is open.

- Use the Consolidate command and create links. Both workbooks must be open.

- Key the formula with the workbook, sheet, and cell references. This can be tedious and requires that you type accurately, but the source workbook need not be open.

Exercise 17-9   LINK WORKBOOKS BY POINTING

When you point to an external reference, Excel supplies the proper syntax. The syntax for an external reference is:

='[WorkbookName]WorksheetName'!CellAddress

> **NOTE**
>
> When you point to an external reference, Excel uses an absolute reference. You can change it if you want to copy the formula.

1. Open **YogurtOR**. This will be the source workbook.

2. Save the workbook as *[your initials]*17-9OR. Leave it open.

3. Open **YogurtNV**. This will be the dependent workbook.

4. Save the workbook as *[your initials]*17-9NV.

5. Click the **View** tab. In the **Window** group, click the Arrange All button 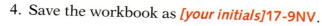 .

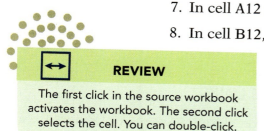

6. Choose **Vertical** and click **OK**. The active window is tiled on the left.

7. In cell A12 in *[your initials]*17-9NV, key **Vanilla**.

8. In cell B12, key **=** to start a formula.

9. Click cell B6 in the Nevada workbook and key **+** to add.

10. Double-click cell B6 in *[your initials]*17-9OR, the Oregon workbook. An external reference is entered with the name of the workbook and an absolute reference for the cell.

REVIEW

The first click in the source workbook activates the workbook. The second click selects the cell. You can double-click.

Figure 17-5
Creating an external reference
17-9OR.xlsx and
17-9NV.xlsx

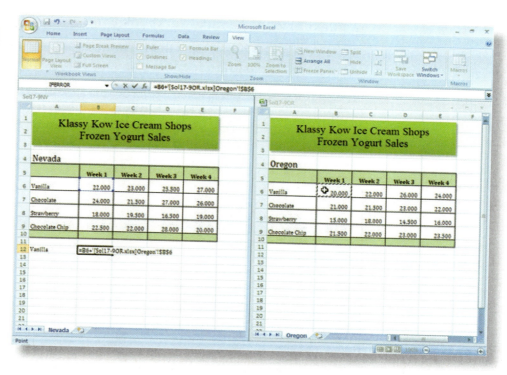

11. Press [Enter]. The formula in cell B12 in the Nevada workbook adds the Vanilla values for Week 1 from both workbooks.

12. Select cell B12 in the Nevada workbook.

13. Edit the formula to remove the absolute reference. Delete only the dollar signs ($).

14. Copy the formula to the range B13:B15. These are the totals for the other flavors for Week 1.

15. In the Nevada workbook, copy and paste cells A7:A9 to cells A13:A15.

Examining and Editing Links

While a source workbook is open, the external reference in the dependent workbook does not show a path. A *path* is an identifier preceding a filename that includes the name of the drive and the series of folders specifying the file location. If you close the source workbook, the dependent workbook shows the full filename and path.

When you open a workbook with linked formulas, Excel recalculates the external reference formulas.

Exercise 17-10   EXAMINE LINKS

You can see the path of a link when you close the source workbook. Excel alerts you to the existence of links when you open a dependent workbook.

1. Close the Oregon workbook, the source workbook.

2. Maximize the Nevada workbook, *[your initials]***17-9NV**.

3. Select cell B12 and view the formula in the formula bar. It now includes the path to identify the source workbook.

4. Click the **Data** tab. In the **Connections** group, click the Edit Links button 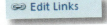. The Edit Links dialog box lists information about source files for this workbook. **Update** is set to **Automatic**.

Figure 17-6
Edit Links dialog box
17-9NV.xlsx
Nevada sheet

5. Click **Close** without making any changes. Make a note of the Vanilla total in cell B12.

6. Save and close the Nevada workbook, *[your initials]***17-9NV**.

7. Open the Oregon workbook, *[your initials]***17-9OR**, the source workbook.

8. Change the Vanilla value for Week 1 to **0**. Save and close the workbook.

9. Open *[your initials]***17-9NV**, the dependent workbook. The security message panel tells you that automatic update is disabled. Check cell B12.

Figure 17-7
Security message bar
17-9NV.xlsx
Nevada sheet

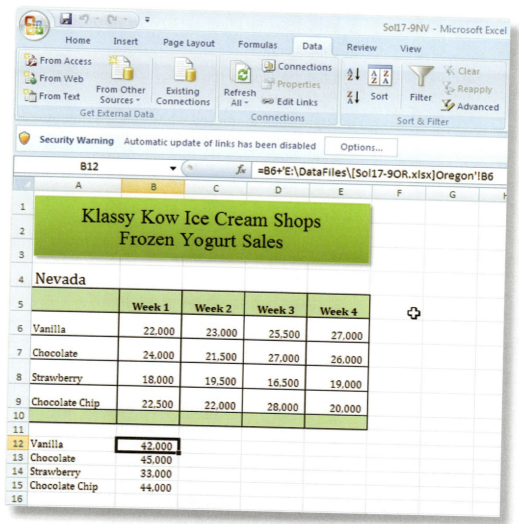

10. Click **Options**. This Microsoft Office Security Options dialog box is similar to the macro security dialog box.

11. Choose **Enable this content** and click **OK**. The worksheet shows the new Vanilla total (cell B12) based on the change you made in the Oregon workbook.

12. Save and close the Nevada workbook.

Exercise 17-11   MOVE A SOURCE WORKBOOK

If you move the source workbook to another location, Excel will not be able to find it when you open the dependent workbook.

1. Open the Oregon workbook, *[your initials]***17-9OR**, the source workbook.

2. Change the Vanilla value in cell B6 to **50000**. Save and close the workbook.

3. Press Ctrl + O. Right-click *[your initials]***17-9OR**.

4. Choose **Cut**.

5. Click **Desktop** in the **Navigation** pane (on the left side of the Open dialog box).

6. Right-click in unused white space in the middle and choose **Paste**. This moves the workbook from your folder to the Desktop for your computer. Leave the dialog box open.

Exercise 17-12   EDIT LINKS

As you open the dependent workbook, you can edit the link to show the new location of the source workbook.

1. In the navigation line, navigate to your Lesson 17 folder. The Oregon workbook is no longer in this location.

2. Open *[your initials]***17-9NV**, the dependent workbook. The same security message panel opens.

3. Click **Options**. Choose **Enable this content** and click **OK**. Excel displays a message that the links cannot be updated, because the workbook is not in the folder where it was when you created the link.

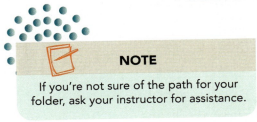

NOTE

If you're not sure of the path for your folder, ask your instructor for assistance.

Figure 17-8
Message that links cannot be updated
17-9NV.xlsx
Nevada sheet

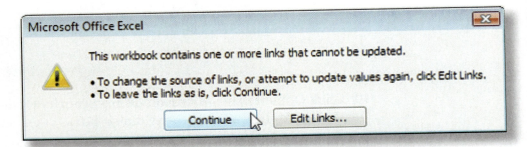

Microsoft Office Excel

This workbook contains one or more links that cannot be updated.

- To change the source of links, or attempt to update values again, click Edit Links.
- To leave the links as is, click Continue.

Continue   Edit Links...

4. Click **Continue**. The formula has not been updated to show a new total in cell B12.

5. Click the **Data** tab. Click the Edit Links button . There is only one link in this workbook.

6. Click **Change Source**. The Change Source dialog box opens so that you can set a new location for the source workbook.

7. Click **Desktop** in the **Navigation** pane.

8. Click *[your initials]***17-9OR** and click **OK**. The Edit Links dialog box shows the new location, and the formula has been updated to show the new results.

9. Click **Close**. The formula shows the recalculated Vanilla total (72,000).

10. Save the file.

Exercise 17-13   BREAK LINKS

If you no longer need external references in a workbook, you can delete the contents of those cells. As long as you delete the contents of all cells with links, the external reference is removed. You can also keep the results in the dependent workbook but break the link to the source workbook.

1. In *[your initials]***17-9NV**, select the range with links, B12:B15.

2. Click the **Data** tab. Click the Edit Links button .

3. Click **Break Link**. Excel displays a message warning you that when you break a link, the linked formulas are converted to values.

4. Click **Break Links**. Click **Close**.

5. Click cell B12. The formula bar shows the value from the linked formula, but the formula is now removed.

Exercise 17-14   RESTRICT PERMISSION TO A WORKBOOK

Information Rights Management (IRM) is an Office 2007 feature that allows the administrator of a computer to create access settings for a document. This means you can determine who may read, edit, copy, or print a document. Restrictions are set and saved with the document and are effective no matter where the document is. Permission is specified with an e-mail address.

1. Save your workbook as *[your initials]*17-14.

2. Click the Microsoft Office Button and choose **Prepare**.

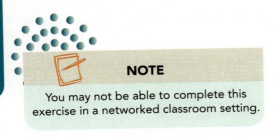

3. Choose **Restrict Permission** and then **Restricted Access**. The Permission dialog box opens.

4. Click to select **Restrict permission to this workbook**. **Read** permission allows someone to review the document with no changes.

Figure 17-9
Permission dialog box
17-14.xlsx
Nevada sheet

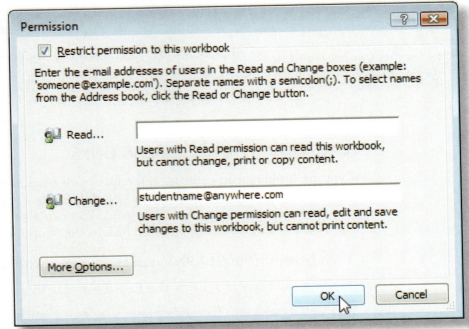

5. Click in the **Change** box. Key *your e-mail address*. Click **OK**. The security panel shows a message.

6. Save and close the workbook.

7. Open *[your initials]* **17-14**. The security message panel is open, and there is an icon on the status bar to remind you that this document has restricted access.

Figure 17-10
Security panel for restricted permission
17-14.xlsx
Nevada sheet

8. Click **Change Permission**. If you are the administrator of this computer, you can remove the restriction.

9. Click to deselect **Restrict permission to this workbook**. Click **OK**.

10. Save and close the workbook.

11. Press Ctrl+O. Click **Desktop** in the **Navigation** pane. Right-click *[your initials]***17-9OR** and choose **Cut**.

12. Navigate to your Lesson 17 folder.

13. Right-click in unused white space and choose **Paste**. This moves the workbook back to your folder.

14. Close the Open dialog box.

Using Online Help

If you use data from multiple worksheets on a regular basis, there are numerous ways in which linking might be helpful. Use Microsoft Excel Help to get ideas about how you might use linking in other ways.

USE HELP TO LEARN ABOUT LINKING WORKBOOKS

1. Look for topics about linking workbooks. Review subtopics of interest to you.

2. Read the information and close the windows.

Lesson 17 Summary

- In data consolidation, information from several worksheets or workbooks is summarized.

- You can consolidate by position when values are in the same location on each worksheet.

- In a consolidation by category, the supporting worksheets have the same row and column labels, but the data is organized differently.

- The results of a static consolidation are not updated if the supporting data changes.

- Dynamic consolidations create links using 3-D cell references to the supporting worksheets. The results appear in an outline, in which you can hide or display details.

- In a dynamic consolidation, changes made in the supporting worksheets are reflected in the consolidated worksheet.

- Linking occurs when formulas refer to cells in another workbook.

- Formulas that refer to cells in another workbook are called external reference formulas. Linked workbooks are either dependent or source workbooks.

- When you create an external reference by pointing, Excel uses proper formula syntax for the source workbook.
- After workbooks have been linked, you can review and update the links. A path is the identifier preceding a filename that indicates the drive and folder location of the file.
- Excel alerts you to the existence of links when you open a dependent workbook.
- If you move a source workbook, you need to edit the link in the dependent workbook so that Excel can re-establish the link.
- External references can be deleted from the dependent workbook. You can also break links but keep results in the dependent workbook.
- With Information Rights Management, an administrator can determine who is allowed to read, edit, print, or copy a document.

LESSON 14		Command Summary	
Feature	**Button**	**Task Path**	**Keyboard**
Consolidate data	Consolidate	Data, Data Tools	
Links, edit	Edit Links	Data, Connections	
Restrict permission		Microsoft Office, Prepare, Restrict Permission	

Concepts Review

True/False Questions

Each of the following statements is either true or false. Indicate your choice by circling T or F.

T   F   1. Static and dynamic consolidations initially show the same results.

T   F   2. Linking refers to formulas that depend on cells in another workbook.

T   F   3. Permissions can be used for linking workbooks.

T   F   4. Data to be consolidated must be in the same location on each worksheet.

T   F   5. A dependent workbook has external reference formulas.

T   F   6. An external reference shows the complete path if the source workbook is closed.

T   F   7. After you establish a link in a workbook, you cannot move the source workbook from its folder.

T   F   8. Restricted permission may prohibit you from printing a document.

Short Answer Questions

Write the correct answer in the space provided.

1. What type of data consolidation updates the summary worksheet each time a source worksheet is changed?

_____

2. Name three functions that can be used for data consolidation.

_____

3. On what command tab is the Consolidate button shown?

_____

4. How can you convert a linked formula to its value?

_____

5. What is IRM?

_____

6. How do you hide details in an outline?

_____

7. When you consolidate by category, what do you include when selecting the range in the supporting worksheet?

_____

8. How can you determine if you have permission to change a workbook?

_____

Critical Thinking

Answer these questions on a separate page. There are no right or wrong answers. Support your answers with examples from your own experience, if possible.

1. If you are creating a year-end report of your course grades, would you use static or dynamic consolidation? Explain your decision.

2. Why might Information Rights Management be important at your school or where you work?

Skills Review

Exercise 17-15

Create a static data consolidation. Create a dynamic consolidation.

1. Open **WorkersComp** and save it as *[your initials]*17-15.
2. Copy the **4thQtr** sheet to the end and name the copy **Static**. Delete the contents of cells B7:D12.
3. Create a static data consolidation by following these steps:
   a. Select cells B7:D12 in the **Static** worksheet.
   b. Click the **Data** tab. Click the Consolidate button 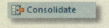.
   c. In the **Function** box, choose **Sum**.
   d. In the **Reference** box, click the **1stQtr** tab and select cells B7:D12. Click **Add**.
   e. Click the **2ndQtr** tab and click **Add**.
   f. Repeat these steps for the **3rdQtr** and **4thQtr** worksheets.
   g. When all four references are shown in the **All references** box, click **OK**.
4. Select cells E7:E12 and click the AutoSum button .

NOTE

The consolidated columns are summed to determine each city's yearly total.

5. Edit the labels in cells B6:D6 as follows:

   1st Month   **2nd Month**   **3rd Month**

6. Key **Total** in cell E6.

7. Format the new column to match the existing work. Re-center the labels in rows 2:4 across the data.

8. Edit the document properties to show your name as the author and your school/company name. Add a thumbnail preview.

9. Make a copy of the **4thQtr** sheet at the end and name it **Dynamic**.

10. Create a dynamic consolidation by following these steps:

    a. In the **Dynamic** worksheet, delete the contents of cells B7:D12.

    b. Click the **Data** tab. Click the Consolidate button .

    c. In the **Function** box, choose **Sum**.

    d. In the **Reference** box, click the **1stQtr** tab and select cells B7:D12. Click **Add**.

    e. Repeat these steps for the other quarters.

    f. Click to select **Create links to source data**. Click **OK**.

    g. Expand the Carson City row.

11. Edit the labels in cells B6:D6 as follows:

    1st Month   **2nd Month**   **3rd Month**

12. Make a copy of the **Dynamic** sheet and display the formulas. Fit the columns and set the orientation to landscape.

13. Group and hide the first through fourth quarter sheets.

14. Prepare and submit your work.

Exercise 17-16

Consolidate data by category.

1. Open **2QtrSandwiches** and save it as *[your initials]*17-16.

2. Click each tab and note the arrangement of data in each sheet.

3. Copy the **June** sheet to the end and name the new sheet **Minimums**. Delete the contents of cells A5:E9.

4. Consolidate by category by following these steps:

   a. Select cells A5:E9 on the **Minimums** sheet.

   b. Click the **Data** tab. Click the Consolidate button .

   c. In the **Function** box, choose **Min**. In the **Reference** box, click the **April** worksheet tab and select cells A5:E9.

   d. Click **Add**.

   e. Repeat these steps for the **May** and **June** worksheets.

   f. In the **Use labels in** group, click to select **Top row** and **Left column**.

   g. Click to select **Create links to source data**. Click **OK**.

5. Edit cell A4 to show **Minimum Sales**.

6. Copy the **Minimums** sheet to the end. Show outline detail by clicking the Level 2 outline symbol.

7. Display formulas on this copied sheet and AutoFit the columns. Use landscape orientation.

8. Group and hide the monthly sheets.

9. Prepare and submit your work.

Exercise 17-17

Link workbooks. Examine and edit links.

1. Open **YogurtCA** and delete the contents of cells B6:E9 and cell A4. Rename the sheet **Consolidated**.

2. Save the workbook as *[your initials]*17-17.

3. Link workbooks by following these steps:

   a. Press Ctrl+O. Navigate to the folder with the files for this lesson.

   b. Select the files **YogurtCA**, **YogurtNV**, **YogurtOR**, and **YogurtWA**.

   c. Click **Open**. All four workbooks are opened as well as your workbook.

   d. Click the **View** tab. Click the Arrange All button . Tile the windows vertically.

   e. Click in each window and scroll it so that you can see cell B6.

   f. Select cell B6 in your workbook and key **=** to start a formula.

   g. Double-click cell B6 in **YogurtCA** and key **+** to continue.

   h. Double-click cell B6 in **YogurtNV** and key **+**.

   i. Add cell B6 from **YogurtOR** and **YogurtWA** to the formula. Press Enter when finished.

4. Edit and copy an external reference by following these steps:

   a. Maximize your workbook window and select cell B6.

   b. Press F2.

   c. Edit the formula to remove the absolute references and make them relative. Press Enter when finished.

   d. Copy the formula in cell B6 for the rest of the totals.

5. Close all the files, saving yours.

NOTE

By starting with one of the source workbooks, you maintain the same format.

Arrange All

TIP

If filenames are not contiguous, select the first one and then hold down Ctrl while selecting each of the others.

REVIEW

If you key a plus sign (+) at the end of the formula, Excel will suggest a correction.

REVIEW

To make the reference relative, click anywhere within $B$6 and press F4 to cycle through the options.

6. Examine and edit links by following these steps:

   a. Open *[your initials]*17-17. Note the total for Vanilla in Week 1.

   b. Click the **Data** tab and the Edit Links button .

   c. Select **YogurtNV** in the list and click **Open Source**.

   d. Change the Vanilla value for Week 1 in the **YogurtNV** sheet to **0**. Close the workbook without saving.

   e. Click the **Data** tab and the Edit Links button .

   f. Click **Break Link**. Click **Break Links**. Click **Close**.

7. Save the workbook with this change as *[your initials]*17-17a.

8. Prepare and submit your work.

Exercise 17-18

Examine and edit links.

1. Open **Locations** and **States**. Ignore the security message panel. Save the **Locations** workbook as *[your initials]*17-18a. Save the **States** workbook as *[your initials]*17-18b.

> **↔ REVIEW**
>
> The active file is tiled on the left in a vertical arrangement and on the top in a horizontal layout.

2. Click the **View** tab. Click the Arrange All button . Tile the windows vertically.

3. Examine and edit links by following these steps:

   a. Click cell D8 in *[your initials]*7-18a.

   b. Press Delete .

   c. Key **=** and double-click cell B5 in *[your initials]*17-18b. Press Enter .

   d. Click cell D11 in *[your initials]*17-18a. Key **=** and double-click cell B53 in *[your initials]*17-18b. Press Enter .

   e. Click cell D12 in *[your initials]*17-18a. Key **=** and double-click cell B25 in *[your initials]*17-18b. Press Enter .

   f. Click cell D14 in *[your initials]*17-18a. Key **=** and double-click the abbreviation for Iowa in *[your initials]*17-18b. Press Enter .

   g. Correct errors in cells D21 and D24 in *[your initials]*17-18a.

4. Close *[your initials]*17-18b. Save *[your initials]*17-18a.

5. Restrict permissions for a workbook by following these steps:

   a. Click the Microsoft Office Button and choose **Prepare**.

   b. Choose **Restrict Permissions** and **Restricted Access**.

   c. Click to select **Restrict permission to this workbook**.

   d. Click in the **Change** box and key *your e-mail address*.

   e. Click **OK**.

   f. Save and close the workbook.

6. Prepare and submit your work.

Lesson Applications

Exercise 17-19

Create a static consolidation.

1. Open **Expenses** and save it as *[your initials]*17-19.

2. Copy the **June** sheet to the end and name it **Totals**.

3. In the **Totals** worksheet, delete column B. Make the three remaining columns each **16.43 (120 pixels)** wide.

4. Delete the contents of cells B4:C11. Then consolidate the appropriate data from the **May** and **June** sheets using SUM without links to the source data.

5. Create a conditional format for cells C4:C11 in **Totals**. Choose **More Rules** from the Highlight Cells Rules list. Choose **Use a formula to determine which cells to format**. In the **Edit the Rule Description** box, key **=c4>=b4**. Click **Format** and choose **Red, Accent 2** as the font color.

6. Set all values to use a floating dollar sign.

7. Add a comment in cell B13 and key **These are consolidated results**. Show the comment.

8. Edit the document properties to show **Budget Results** as the title, your name as the author, and your school/company.

9. Prepare and submit your work.

Exercise 17-20

Create a dynamic consolidation.

1. Open **CupUse** and save it as *[your initials]*17-20. Delete the unused sheets.

2. Copy **Sheet1** and edit it to show values for last year. Name the sheets.

Figure 17-11

Last Year	Qtr 1	Qtr 2	Qtr 3	Qtr 4
Small	45000	51000	55000	43000
Medium	60000	60500	69000	60500
Large	53000	52000	59000	50000

3. Group the sheets and click the Select All button . Set the font size to 12 point; set the main title to 16 point. Right-align the labels in cells B3:E3. Use commas with no decimals for all values. Use additional formatting to design your worksheets.

NOTE

Subtract last year from this year to calculate the difference.

4. Create a consolidated worksheet that averages the values with links to the source data. Name the sheet. Display all details in the outline.

5. Copy either of the source sheets and name it **Difference**. Use a 3-D formula to compute the difference between this year and last year.

6. Prepare and submit your work.

Exercise 17-21

Examine and edit links.

1. Open **NewPriceList** and save it as *[your initials]***17-21b**.

2. Open **ShopOrder** and save it as *[your initials]***17-21a**. Check the links for this workbook to determine if it is correct for your current work session.

3. Compare the prices in *[your initials]***17-21a** to the price list and edit the formulas as needed.

4. Review the formulas in column D to see if they are correct. The formula in cell D16 should sum all the rows and multiply by 104.5% to include the sales tax.

5. Key a test quantity for each item if you prefer.

6. Delete test quantities and copy the sheet to display the formulas. Hide columns A and B.

7. Prepare and submit your work.

Exercise 17-22 ◆ Challenge Yourself

Link workbooks.

1. Open **Locations** and **States**. The security message panel should close when both workbooks are open.

2. Save the **Locations** workbook as *[your initials]***17-22a**. Delete the contents of cells D4:D27.

3. Save the **States** workbook as *[your initials]***17-22b**. Name the data range as **Abbrevs**.

4. Use a VLOOKUP function in cell D4 in *[your initials]***17-22a** to look up the state abbreviation. Copy the formula and center the results.

5. Make a formula sheet and hide columns A:B.

6. Prepare and submit your work.

On Your Own

In these exercises you work on your own, as you would in a real-life work environment. Use the skills you've learned to accomplish the task—and be creative.

Exercise 17-23

Create a new workbook with four sheets, named **Week1** through **Week4** to track the number of phone calls received and sent. Group the sheets to key the days of the week (spelled out) in column A, starting in row 3. Key labels in row 2 for **Sent** and **Received**. Key an appropriate main label. Key values for the number of calls made and received for each day each week. Format your sheets attractively. Create a consolidated worksheet for monthly totals. Save the workbook as *[your initials]*17-23. Prepare and submit your work.

Exercise 17-24

Open **YogurtCA** and **YogurtNV**. Arrange the windows vertically. From the **View** tab, create a workspace named *[your initials]*17-24. Close both workbooks and open the workspace. These are copies of the original files in the layout that you saved as a workspace. Copy the **California** sheet and name the copy **Consolidated**. On the **Consolidated** sheet, show combined sales for both states in a static consolidation. Save **YogurtCA** as *[your initials]*17-24. Workspaces and workbooks have different filename extensions. Close **YogurtNV** without saving. Prepare and submit your work.

Exercise 17-25

In a new workbook, list 10 area codes with the city and state, using three columns. Save this workbook as *[your initials]*17-25a and leave it open. In another workbook (dependent file), key names, cities, and states for 15 people using the same cities that you used in your source workbook. In a fourth column, use VLOOKUP to show their area codes. Add labels and format this sheet in a professional layout. Save the dependent workbook as *[your initials]*17-25b. Prepare and submit your work.

Unit 5 Applications

Unit Application 5-1

Set data validation. Find and correct errors.

1. Open **ProjCakeSales** and save it as *[your initials]*u5-1.

> **TIP**
>
> To use a range for data validation that is on a different sheet, the range must be named.

2. Note the defined range name used on **Sheet2**. Use **List** data validation for cells B8:E8 on the **ThisYear** sheet and complete the labels. Center the labels.

3. Merge and center cells B7:E7.

4. Use whatever method you prefer to find and correct errors.

5. Copy cells A3:F14 to the range A15:F26. Edit the label in row 15 to show **Next Year Projected Sales**.

6. Create formulas to project next year's sales, assuming an 8% increase over this year's sales.

7. Set the document properties to show your name as the author and a thumbnail preview.

8. Make a copy of the sheet to display formulas. Hide column A and AutoFit the others.

9. Prepare and submit your work.

Unit Application 5-2

Link workbooks.

1. Open **NoveltyLastYr** and **NoveltyThisYr**.

2. Create a new workbook while these files are open. Save it as *[your initials]*u5-2.

3. Copy cells A1:A2 from either of the completed sheets to your workbook. Change cell A2 to **Sales Manager Bonuses**. Key the labels shown in Figure U5-1 on the next page, starting in cell A3.

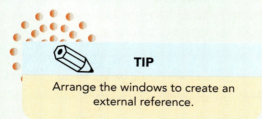

> **TIP**
>
> Arrange the windows to create an external reference.

Figure U5-1

	A	B	C	D	E
3	Manager	Goal	Actual	Difference	Bonus
4	Holly Maplethorpe (CA)				
5	John Frisbee (NV)				
6	Adrian Needlehoffen (OR)				
7	Jamica Martin (WA)				

4. In the Goal column, multiply last year's total dollar sales for each manager and state (in the **NoveltyLastYr** workbook) by 110%.

5. In the Actual column, link to the total dollar sales for each manager for this year.

6. In the Difference column, subtract the Goal amount from the Actual amount.

NOTE

You can close the source workbooks after completing the external references.

7. Use an IF expression in the Bonus column. If the difference is greater than $15,000, the manager receives $5,000. Otherwise, show **No Bonus** in the column.

8. Design and format your worksheet. Rename the worksheet **Bonuses**. Delete the other worksheets.

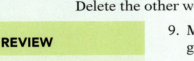

REVIEW

Use the Page Layout tab to print gridlines and headings.

9. Make a copy of the sheet for formula display with gridlines and headings.

10. Prepare and submit your work.

Unit Application 5-3

Predict quarterly sales for next year. Use Goal Seek. Create scenarios.

1. Open **ForecastNextYear**.

2. Enable and run the macro. Save the file as a macro-free workbook **[your initials]u5-3**.

REVIEW

Click the Macros button on the View tab to run a macro.

3. Create range names from the selection for cells A4:B7. Name cell H8 Total.

4. In cells B4, B5, and B7, create formulas that calculate the growth rate as a percentage of Nevada's rate. California's growth rate is 80% of Nevada's; Oregon's growth rate is 60%; and Washington's is 65% of Nevada's rate. (*Hint:* Multiply Nevada's rate by the state's percentage.) These cells should be formatted as percents with two decimals.

5. In columns D:G, estimate sales on the basis of the previous quarter's sales and the growth rate for the state. The quarter formula multiplies the previous quarter by the growth rate plus 100%.

6. Total the first through fourth quarters for next year in column H. Then total columns D through H in row 8.

7. Format dollar values to show commas and no decimals. Add a dollar sign to the values in rows 4 and 8. Design and format the sheet attractively to highlight its purpose. Rename the sheet Forecast. Delete unused worksheets.

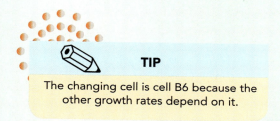

TIP

The changing cell is cell B6 because the other growth rates depend on it.

8. Create a scenario named Current Estimate using cell B6 as the changing cell.

9. Use Goal Seek to find the growth rates necessary to achieve $400 million in total sales. Save the results as a scenario named $400M.

10. Create a scenario summary report using B4:B7,H8 as Result cells. On the summary sheet, change the title in cell B2 to Klassy Kow Ice Cream, Inc., Quarterly Growth Rates. Collapse row 5 and hide the Notes rows. Change cell D3 to Target Values.

11. Prepare and submit your work.

Unit Application 5-4 ◆ Using the Internet

Set data validation. Set conditional formatting.

From an auction or retail Web site, compile a list of 15 DVD movie titles. Include the title, a category, the headline actor, and the company that produced and/or released the film. Limit your category options to four, using genres such as comedy, action, drama, etc.

Create a worksheet that lists the categories and companies in separate columns. Name each list as a range and name this sheet **Validation**.

On another sheet in the same workbook, key the DVD titles and the headline actor names in separate columns. For the category and company columns, select the appropriate cells and set validation to use the ranges on the other sheet. Complete these two columns using the drop-down lists. Apply conditional formatting to show one of the categories (your choice) in a different font color.

Include main and column labels and format the sheet attractively. Save the workbook as *[your initials]*u5-4. Prepare and submit your work.

unit 6

EXPLORING DATA AND TABLE FEATURES

EXL6.18

Using External Data Sources

OBJECTIVES

After completing this lesson, you will be able to:

1. Use text sources.

2. Manage imported data.

3. Use Web sources.

4. Use database sources.

5. Export Excel data.

MCAS OBJECTIVES

In this lesson:
XL07 1.2
XL07 1.2.2
XL07 1.3.1
XL07 1.4.3
XL07 1.5
XL07 2.1.1
XL07 2.3.2
XL07 2.3.4
XL07 2.3.5
XL07 2.4
XL07 3.7.1
XL07 3.7.2
XL07 5.4.2

Estimated Time: 1¹/₂ hours

In the business world, data moves back and forth among employees, departments, customers, and software programs. *Importing* data means that information from an outside source or program is brought into Excel. *Exporting* occurs when Excel data is sent to another program.

Using Text Sources

You can import data from a Microsoft Word document to an Excel worksheet. After the data is imported, you can format the data in Excel as usual.

A *text file* is unformatted or raw data. Text files make it possible for almost all programs to share data.

There are several methods for importing Word or text data into an Excel worksheet. Three of them are:

- Copying and pasting text using the Clipboard

- Dragging and dropping text from Word to Excel

- Opening a text file in Excel

Exercise 18-1 COPY AND PASTE FROM WORD

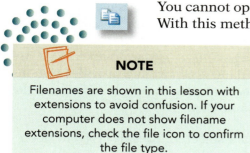

You cannot open a Word document in Excel, but you can use Copy and Paste. With this method, the imported data includes Word formatting.

1. Create a new workbook.

2. Start Word and open **Employees.docx**, a Word table.

3. Press Ctrl+A to select the table.

4. Click the Copy button 📋 on the **Home** tab. The table is copied to the Windows Clipboard.

5. Click the Microsoft Excel button on the taskbar to return to your workbook.

6. With cell A1 selected, click the Paste button 📋. The table is copied with most of its formatting, and the data is selected.

Figure 18-1
Word table pasted into Excel
Book1.xlsx
Sheet1 sheet

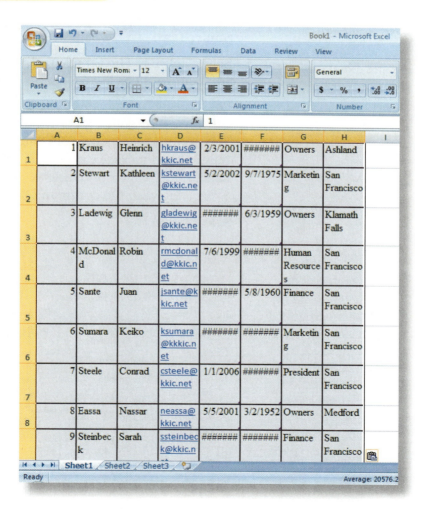

Exercise 18-2   REVIEW DATA AND SMART TAGS

When you copy data from one program to another, it usually needs to be formatted to better fit its new purpose and application. In this case, the columns are not wide enough.

Imported data may display Smart Tags. *Smart Tags* are markers that are attached to certain recognized types of data. A Smart Tag provides options for common tasks associated with that type of data. A purple triangle in the lower-right corner of a cell indicates a Smart Tag.

NOTE

If the data is not selected, click cell A1 and press F8. Then press Ctrl+End.

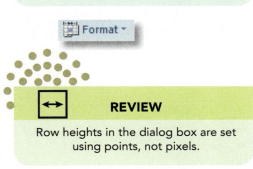

Format ▼

REVIEW

Row heights in the dialog box are set using points, not pixels.

ⓘ

NOTE

Smart Tag markers do not print.

1. With the pasted data selected, press Ctrl+1 to open the Format Cells dialog box.

2. Click the **Border** tab. In the **Presets** group, click **None**. Click **OK**. All borders are removed.

3. With the pasted data selected, click the Format button Format ▼ in the **Cells** group. Choose **Row Height**. Key **16** and click **OK**.

4. Adjust column widths to fit the data, and deselect the cells. The cells in columns E and F contain Smart Tags.

5. Select cell E1. The Smart Tag Actions button ⓘ is adjacent to the selected cell.

6. Position the pointer over the Smart Tag Actions button ⓘ and click its down arrow. The Smart Tag Actions menu opens. Because this is a date, date-related tasks are available, such as showing a calendar in Microsoft Outlook. You can remove a Smart Tag with the command **Remove this Smart Tag**.

7. Select cell A1.

Figure 18-2
Smart Tag for a date
Book1.xlsx
Sheet1 sheet

D	E	F	G
hkraus@kkic.net	2/3/2001	4/17/1957	Owners
kstewart@kkic.net	5/2/ ⓘ ▼	9/7/1975	Marketing
gladewig@kkic.net	2/23/	Date: 2/3/2001	
rmcdonald@kkic.net	7/6/	Sho̲w my Calendar	es
jsante@kkic.net	3/18/		
ksumara@kkic.net	11/21/	R̲emove this Smart Tag	
csteele@kkic.net	1/1/	St̲op Recognizing "2/3/2001" ▶	
neassa@kkic.net	5/5/	S̲mart Tag Options...	
ssteinbeck@kkic.net	2/15/2004	1/28/1982	Finance
tartagnan@kkic.net	5/1/2003	8/3/1961	Owners
mcalcivechia@kkic.net	6/16/2005	9/14/1961	Owners
talverez@kkic.net	4/15/2005	3/30/1979	Human Resources
lnguyen@kkic.net	6/7/2005	5/23/1985	Marketing

Exercise 18-3   CREATE A CUSTOM FORMAT

You can create your own display features for any data, a *custom format*. You create custom formats with formatting codes. In this exercise, you'll create a custom format to show the # symbol with the employee ID numbers in column A.

To display a character as part of the formatting, the character must be enclosed in quotation marks. Text, symbols, or numbers enclosed in quotes in a format specification are known as *literals*.

1. Select cells A1:A13 and press ⌃Ctrl+1.

2. Click the **Number** tab. In the **Category** list, choose **Custom**.

3. In the **Type** box, delete **General** and key **"#"00**. The # symbol inside the quotation marks is a literal. It will appear in front of every number to which this formatting is applied. Notice how Excel shows in the **Sample** box what the custom format will look like for the first number in your selected range. The 00 code means that the value will show as many digits as required with no decimals and a leading zero for single digits.

Figure 18-3
Creating a custom format
Book1.xlsx
Sheet1 sheet

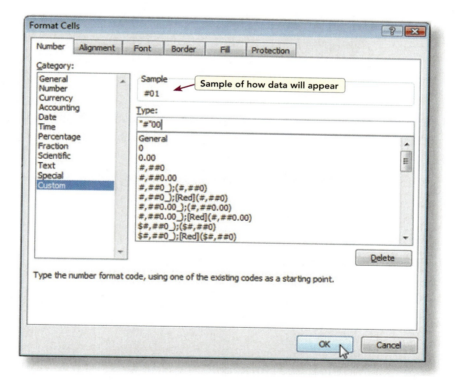

4. Click **OK**. The employee numbers are all prefixed with the # symbol.

5. Select cell A1 to deselect the range.

Exercise 18-4   DRAG AND DROP A WORD DOCUMENT

You can select and drag Word text to a worksheet. You must be able to see the text to be copied and the destination sheet.

1. Click the Restore Down button on the Excel title bar.

2. Click the Word window and click its Restore Down button. Both windows should be visible.

3. Size and position the windows so that you can see cell A1 on **Sheet2** in the Excel workbook and any part of the Word table.

4. Click in the Word table and press Ctrl+A to select the entire table.

5. Point anywhere in the text to display a solid white arrow.

6. Hold down Ctrl and drag the Word table to cell A1 in the Excel window. Release the mouse button first and then release Ctrl.

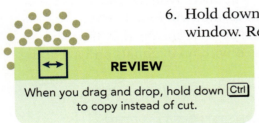

REVIEW

When you drag and drop, hold down Ctrl to copy instead of cut.

7. Adjust the row heights and column widths.

8. Close the Word document without saving, but leave Word running.

Exercise 18-5   USE COPY AND PASTE SPECIAL

You can use Paste Special to copy a text file into Excel. This method of importing text data is useful when you need only portions of a text file. You can use this method with any program that reads text files.

1. In Word, press Ctrl+O.

2. Find and open **StuffedAnimalsCatalog.docx**.

3. Press Ctrl+A and click the Copy button.

4. Return to **Sheet3** in your workbook.

5. Right-click cell A1 and choose **Paste Special**. In the **As** list, choose **Text** to paste unformatted text from the Word document.

6. Select **Paste** if it is not already selected, and then click **OK**.

7. Adjust column widths.

8. Save the workbook as *[your initials]*18-5 in a folder for Lesson 18. Close the workbook.

9. Close the file in Word without saving. Exit Word.

10. Return to Excel with no workbook open.

Exercise 18-6 GET A TEXT FILE

You can get or open a text file in Excel. The Text Import Wizard starts automatically to help you. A *wizard* is a series of dialog boxes that guides you through completing a task.

Text is usually separated into columns by tabs, commas, spaces, or a similar character. The character that separates pieces of data in a text file is a *delimiter*. Text files have a **.txt** filename extension.

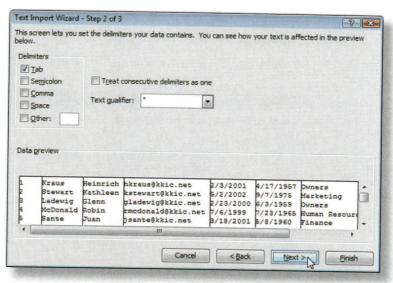

From Text

1. Press Ctrl+N. Click the **Data** tab.

2. In the **Get External Data** group, click the From Text button From Text. The Import Text File dialog box lists files that have **prn**, **txt**, or **csv** as filename extensions.

3. Double-click **Employees.txt**. The Text Import Wizard opens. The wizard has determined that the file is delimited and will start the importing with the first row. There is a preview of the data, too.

4. Click **Next**. The Text Import Wizard – Step 2 of 3 page shows that the delimiter is a tab. This means that data in the text file is separated into columns by tabs. If there are multiple consecutive delimiters, they can be treated as one.

Figure 18-4
Text Import Wizard
Book2.xlsx
Sheet1 sheet

5. Click **Next**. The Text Import Wizard – Step 3 of 3 page allows you to set the format for each column. Everything defaults to the General format.

6. Click **Finish**. The Import Data dialog box asks where you want to place the data and assumes cell A1 of the current sheet.

7. Click **OK**.

8. Widen the columns if needed.

9. Close the workbook without saving.

Managing Imported Data

As you import a text file, you can choose options in the Text Import wizard that may help you arrange the imported data. After it is imported, you can also use data tasks to convert text into columns and vice versa.

Exercise 18-7   SET IMPORT OPTIONS

1. Press Ctrl+N. Click the **Data** tab.

2. In the **Get External Data** group, click the From Text button 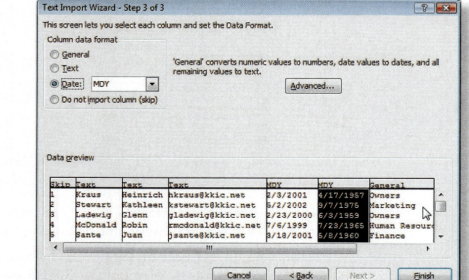.

3. Double-click **Employees.txt**. The first Text Import Wizard page needs no changes.

4. Click **Next**. The tab as a delimiter is correct. Review the preview of the data.

5. Click **Next**. You can choose to not import a column and set a more specific format for others.

6. Click in the first column in the preview area. Click to select **Do not import column (skip)**.

7. Click in the second column (last name) and click to select **Text** as the **Column data format**.

8. Select **Text** for the first name and the e-mail address.

9. Select **Date** as the column format for the two date columns.

Figure 18-5
Setting import
options
Book3.xlsx
Sheet1 sheet

10. Set the last two columns as **Text**.

11. Click **Finish**. Click **OK**.

> ## Exercise 18-8   CREATE THEME FONTS AND COLORS
>
> You can set your own preferences for a document and then save those settings as a theme. Text that is imported into a new workbook uses the Office document theme and the Cambria and Calibri fonts. To save your own document theme, set the fonts, colors, and effects first. Then save the layout as your theme.

1. Click the **Home** tab. Click any cell in the data.

2. View the **Font** name and click its arrow. The Headings font is Cambria and the Body font is Calibri.

3. Insert a row at row 1. Key **Imported from Human Resources**. Make it 18-point Cambria. Your workbook uses the Office theme and both theme fonts.

4. Click the **Page Layout** tab. In the **Themes** group, click the Fonts button . Choose **Create New Theme Fonts**.

5. Click the **Heading font** arrow and key **t**. Choose **Times New Roman**.

6. Click the **Body font** arrow and key **a**. Choose **Arial**.

Figure 18-6
Creating new theme
fonts
**Book3.xlsx
Sheet1 sheet**

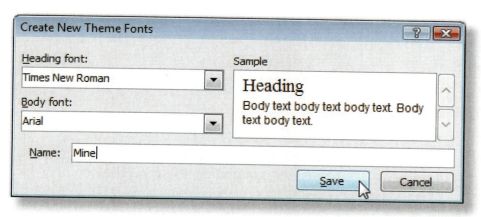

7. In the **Name** box, key **Mine**. Click **Save**. The fonts in your document are updated immediately.

8. In the **Themes** group, click the Colors button . Choose **Create New Theme Colors**. The Create New Theme Colors dialog box shows the colors for the Office theme. Dark 1 and Light 1 are black and white.

9. Click the arrow for **Text/Background Dark 2** and choose **Black, Background 1, Lighter 50%**.

10. Click the arrow for **Text/Background Light 2** and choose **White, Text 2**.

11. Click the arrow for **Accent 1** and choose **More Colors**. The Color Picker is a color spectrum. You can drag the crosshairs to choose a hue; then you can drag the slider at the right to select a shade of that color.

Figure 18-7
Creating new theme
colors
Book3.xlsx
Sheet1 sheet

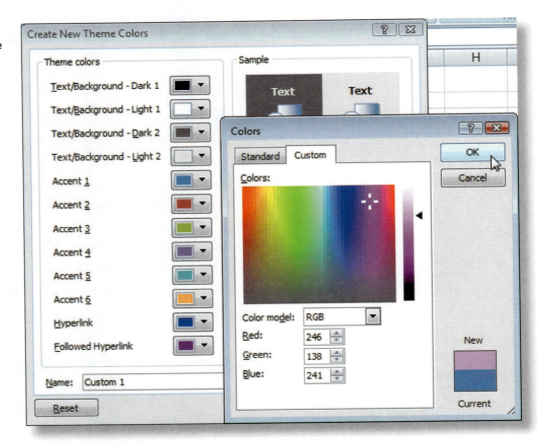

12. Build any color you prefer for **Accent 1** and click **OK**.

13. Choose or build your own colors for the remaining accent colors. You need not change the Hyperlink colors.

14. In the Name box, key **Mine**. Click **Save**.

Exercise 18-9   SAVE A DOCUMENT THEME

Your new fonts and colors are available in this document. If you save these settings as a theme, you can apply it like any of the other document themes.

1. Click the **Home** tab. Click the arrow with the Font Color button . This is your color set.

2. Press Esc.

3. Click the arrow for the **Font** box. Check the theme fonts at the top of the list.

4. Press Esc.

5. Click the **Page Layout** tab. Click the Themes button .

6. Choose **Save Current Theme**. The Save Current Theme dialog box shows the default folder for themes. Themes have a **thmx** extension.

7. In the **File name** box, key **Mine**.

8. Click **Save**.

9. Click the Themes button. Your theme is listed in the **Custom** group.

10. Press Esc.

Exercise 18-10   REMOVE DUPLICATE DATA

If data is arranged in a tabular format, you can use the Remove Duplicates command. The data does not have to be formatted as a table.

1. Click the **Data** tab.

2. In the **Data Tools** group, click the Remove Duplicates button.

3. Click **Unselect All**. Then click to select **Column A** and **Column B**.

4. Click **OK**. Two duplicate rows have been deleted.

5. Click **OK** in the message box.

6. Save the workbook as *[your initials]*18-10. Close it.

Exercise 18-11   CONVERT TEXT TO COLUMNS

Some text is better managed if the words are in separate columns. First and last names can be sorted by both names if two columns are used. Cities and states are another example of data that might be better manipulated if in two columns rather than one. As long as the data is separated by an identifiable character, Excel can separate such text into more than one column.

NOTE

If you do not see the From Text button ![From Text], click the Get External Data button first.

1. Press Ctrl+N. Click the **Data** tab.

2. Click the From Text button ![From Text]. Double-click **OneName.txt**.

3. Click **Next**. The delimiter is a tab. Notice that the employee's name is in a single column. It's also all uppercase.

4. Click **Next**. Use **General** for all the fields and do not skip any.

5. Click **Finish**. Click **OK**.

6. Select cells C1:C13. These are the cells that need to be converted to columns.

7. In the **Data Tools** group, click the Text to Columns button. The Convert Text to Columns wizard is similar to the Import Text wizard. The data in column C is delimited by a space.

8. Click **Next**. Click to select **Space** as the delimiter. Deselect **Tab** if necessary.

9. Click **Next**. A **General** format is acceptable.

10. Click **Finish**. You will replace the current columns C and D with two new columns.

11. Click **OK**. AutoFit the columns.

Exercise 18-12   USE PROPER AND SUBSTITUTE

The PROPER and SUBSTITUTE functions belong to the Text category. You can use PROPER to convert uppercase characters to proper case. *Proper case* capitalizes the first character and sets the remaining characters lowercase. The PROPER function has one argument, Text. Usually that argument is a cell reference for the label to be changed.

The SUBSTITUTE function replaces characters in a text string with new characters, similar to the Replace command. With SUBSTITUTE, however, you can specify which occurrence of the character is to be replaced.

1. Click cell C15 and click the Insert Function button.

2. Choose the **Text** category and **PROPER**. In the **Text** argument box, click cell C1 and press `Enter`. The name is converted to proper case in cell C15. You could edit each name in cells C1:D13 and nest the name within the PROPER function.

NOTE

If you nest a label within the PROPER function by keying the arguments, you must include the label in quotation marks.

3. Delete the contents of cell C15.

4. Select the column headings for columns E:F. Right-click either one and choose **Insert**. Two columns are inserted.

5. Click cell E1. Click the Insert Function button. Choose the **Text** category and **PROPER**. In the **Text** argument box, click cell C1 and press `Enter`.

6. Copy the formula to row 13 and then to column F.

7. Insert a column at column C.

8. Click cell C1. Click the Insert Function button f_x. Choose the **Text** category and **SUBSTITUTE**. In the **Text** argument box, click cell B1. This is the text string in which the substitution will take place.

9. Click in the **Old_text** box and key **-** as the character that will be replaced.

10. Click in the **New_text** box. Notice that the hyphen is enclosed in quotation marks; it is a literal. Leave this box empty to substitute nothing.

11. Click in the **Instance_num**. Key **1** to substitute nothing for the first occurrence of the hyphen.

Figure 18-8
Using SUBSTITUTE
to remove a hyphen
Book4.xlsx
Sheet1

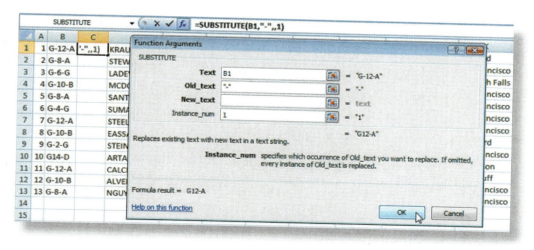

12. Click **OK**. The text string shows the code without the hyphen at the first occurrence.

13. Copy the formula to row 13.

14. Hide column B. Then hide columns D:E. AutoFit columns as needed.

15. Click the **Page Layout** tab. Click the Themes button. Choose **Mine**. Your theme fonts are applied.

Using Web Sources

HTML, Hypertext Markup Language, is commonly used on Web pages. Most data stored in HTML format can be imported into Excel. You can:

- Drag a selected Web page table into Excel.

- Use the Web Query command to get information from a Web page.

Excel 2007

Exercise 18-13   COPY FROM THE WEB BY DRAGGING

You can import HTML data to a worksheet by dragging selected data from the browser window to the Excel window. In this exercise, you'll use an existing HTML file and don't need to connect to the Internet.

1. Rename **Sheet1** as **Text**. Rename **Sheet2** as **Web**.

2. Press Ctrl+O. Click the arrow next to **All Excel Files** and select **All Web Pages**.

3. Select **ThirdQtr.htm**, but do not open it yet.

4. Click the arrow with **Open** and choose **Open in Browser**. (If a security warning box opens, click **Yes**.) A new window opens, showing the HTML file in your Web browser.

5. Size and position the windows so that you can see the top half of the data in the browser window and cell A1 in the **Web** sheet.

6. Point just before the beginning of the subtitle, "Product Sales by State."

7. Select up to and including "15,600," the last value for the first "Washington" row.

8. Point at the highlighted data in the browser window to display a white arrow, and drag the selected data to cell A1 in the Excel window.

Figure 18-9
Dragging data from
the Web to Excel
Book4.xlsx
Web sheet

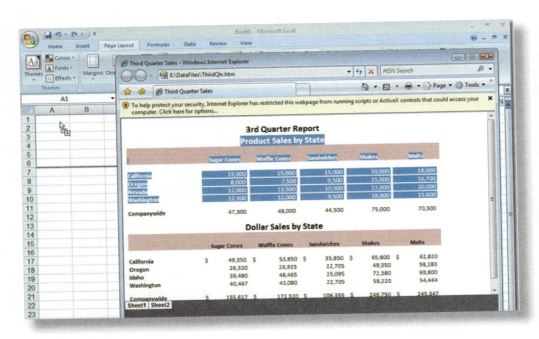

9. Adjust the column widths. Close the browser window.

Exercise 18-14 CREATE A WEB QUERY

A *Web query* is a request for data from a Web page. The Web query command allows you to choose and import tables or preformatted data from a Web page into Excel.

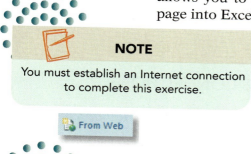

NOTE

You must establish an Internet connection to complete this exercise.

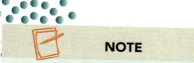

NOTE

If you do not see table markers, click the Show Icons button 🔳.

NOTE

Web sites are updated on a regular basis, so your screen may not match the illustrations in this text.

1. Establish an Internet connection if necessary while Excel is running.

2. Name **Sheet3** as **WebQuery** and select cell A1.

3. Click the **Data** tab. In the **Get External Data** group, click the From Web button 🔳 From Web . If a security information message opens, click **Yes**. The New Web Query dialog box opens.

4. In the New Web Query **Address** text box, delete any addresses and key http://www.moneycentral.msn.com.

5. Press [Enter] or click **Go**. Importable tables are marked with small black arrows in yellow rectangles. Your Internet connection speed affects how quickly you will see the arrows.

6. Locate the DOW, NASDAQ, and S&P indexes on the page.

7. Hover over any small yellow arrow. The table it represents is outlined with a thick border.

Figure 18-10
Creating a Web query
Book4.xlsx
WebQuery sheet

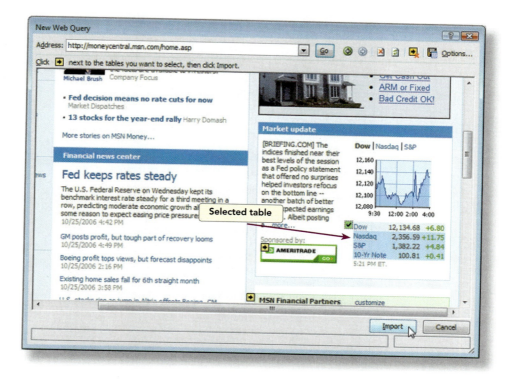

8. Click the arrow to select the DOW, NASDAQ, and S&P stock indexes. The arrow changes to a check mark in a green rectangle.

9. Click **Import**. Choose **Existing worksheet**. The target cell is A1.

10. Click **OK**. You will see a temporary message that Excel is getting the data.

Exercise 18-15   MANAGE CONNECTIONS

This workbook now has a data connection. A *connection* in a workbook is a setting that identifies the source of the data.

1. Click the **Data** tab. In the **Connections** group, click the Properties button . The External Data Range Properties dialog box opens. The range has a default name.

2. In the **Name** box, key **StockQuotes**. The **Refresh control** group determines how often the worksheet will check the Web site to update the data. Note the remaining options and close the dialog box.

Figure 18-11
Naming an external
data range
Book4.xlsx
WebQuery sheet

External Data Range Properties

Name: StockQuotes

Query definition
☑ Save query definition
☐ Save password

Refresh control
☑ Enable background refresh
☐ Refresh every 60 ⬍ minutes
☐ Refresh data when opening the file
　☐ Remove external data from worksheet before closing

Data formatting and layout
☑ Include field names 　☐ Preserve column sort/filter/layout
☐ Include row numbers 　☑ Preserve cell formatting
☑ Adjust column width

If the number of rows in the data range changes upon refresh:
◉ Insert cells for new data, delete unused cells
◯ Insert entire rows for new data, clear unused cells
◯ Overwrite existing cells with new data, clear unused cells

☐ Fill down formulas in columns adjacent to data

OK   Cancel

8. Click the arrow to select the DOW, NASDAQ, and S&P stock indexes. The arrow changes to a check mark in a green rectangle.

9. Click **Import**. Choose **Existing worksheet**. The target cell is A1.

10. Click **OK**. You will see a temporary message that Excel is getting the data.

Exercise 18-15   MANAGE CONNECTIONS

This workbook now has a data connection. A *connection* in a workbook is a setting that identifies the source of the data.

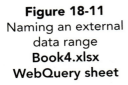

1. Click the **Data** tab. In the **Connections** group, click the Properties button . The External Data Range Properties dialog box opens. The range has a default name.

2. In the **Name** box, key **StockQuotes**. The **Refresh control** group determines how often the worksheet will check the Web site to update the data. Note the remaining options and close the dialog box.

Figure 18-11
Naming an external data range
Book4.xlsx
WebQuery sheet

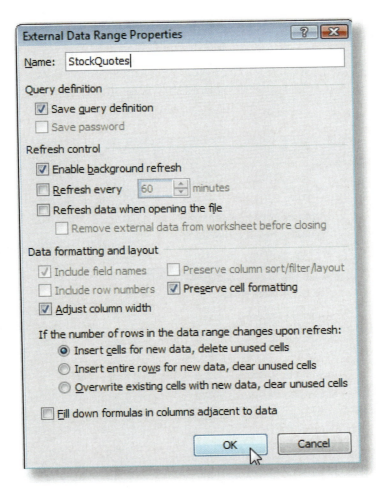

Microsoft Query runs a query on an Access database or one of several other data sources. A *query* is a command that specifies and extracts records from a database table or list.

Exercise 18-16   IMPORT AN ACCESS TABLE

1. With *[your initials]*18-15 open, press Shift + F11.

2. Name the sheet **Database**.

Figure 18-12
Workbook

shows **Access Databases** as the file type.

4. Navigate to the folder with files for this lesson. Choose **Carolina. accdb**. The Select Table dialog box opens. It lists tables and queries in the database.

5. Find and click **tblCustomers**. Click **OK**. In the Import Data dialog box, you can choose how the data is formatted in Excel.

Figure 18-13
Importing an Access table
18-15.xlsx
Database sheet

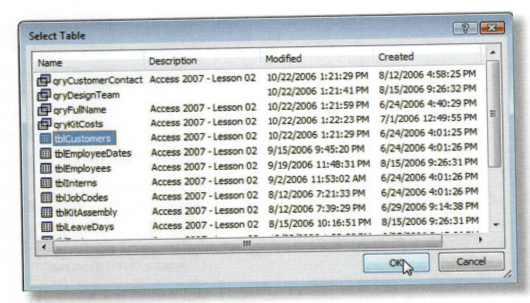

6. Choose **Table** and click **OK** to import the data starting at cell A1. The data is formatted as an Excel table and probably uses one of your theme colors.

7. Choose a different table style.

Exercise 18-17   USE MICROSOFT QUERY

With MS Query, you have more options for methods of importing data. You can choose fields from the database table and filter the records as well.

1. Insert a new sheet and name it **MSQuery**.

2. Click the **Data** tab. In the **Get External Data** group, click the From Other Sources button . The menu lists several sources for outside data.

3. Choose **From Microsoft Query**. The Choose Data Source dialog box lists database formats on the **Databases** tab.

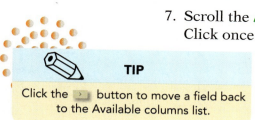

> **TIP**
> An OLAP (Online Analytical Processing) file is a type of database.

4. Choose **MS Access Database** and click **OK**. The Select Database dialog box opens along with a message box that displays **Connecting to data source**.

5. Navigate to your folder and choose **Carolina.accdb**.

6. Click **OK**. The Query Wizard – Choose Columns page opens. This wizard lists the names of queries and tables in the database.

7. Scroll the **Available tables and columns** list and locate **tblCustomers**. Click once to select it.

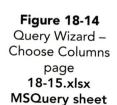

> **TIP**
> Click the ⟩ button to move a field back to the Available columns list.

8. Click the plus (+) symbol next to **tblCustomers**. The individual fields or columns in the table are listed.

9. Double-click **CompanyName**. It moves to the **Columns in your query** list.

10. Double-click each of these field names:
    ContactName
    BillingAddress
    City
    State
    PostalCode

Figure 18-14
Query Wizard – Choose Columns page
18-15.xlsx
MSQuery sheet

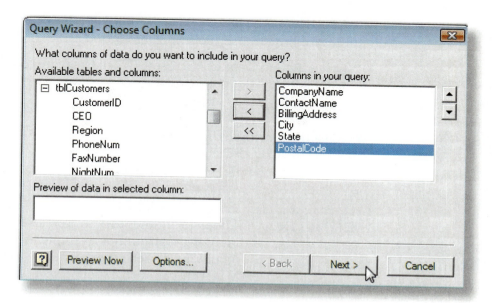

11. Click **Next**. The Query Wizard – Filter Data page opens.

12. Double-click **State**. The label is inserted in the **Only include rows where:** section.

13. Click the arrow below **State** and choose **equals**.

14. Click the arrow for the box on the right and choose **NC**. This filter will import only records in which the state is North Carolina.

Figure 18-15
Query Wizard – Filter
Data page
18-15.xlsx
MSQuery sheet

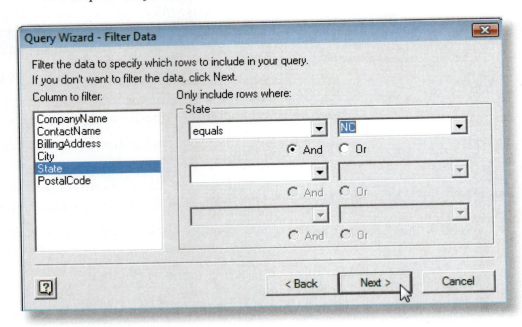

15. Click **Next**. The Query Wizard – Sort Order page opens.

16. Click the **Sort by** arrow and choose **CompanyName**. Choose **Ascending** if it is not already selected.

17. Click **Next**. The Query Wizard – Finish page opens. You can now choose how to use the imported data.

18. Select **Return Data to Microsoft Office Excel** and click **Finish**. The Import Data dialog box opens.

19. Click **OK**. The Access table is now an Excel table.

20. Save the workbook as *[your initials]***18-17**.

Exporting Excel Data

Excel makes it easy to save a workbook in formats used by other programs. When you save a workbook in another format, you are "exporting" the data to a different program. For example, when you save an Excel workbook as a Web page, you are "exporting" the data to HTML. You can also export Excel data to several types of text files as well as XML.

TIP

You cannot save an Excel worksheet in Access format. Access can, however, import text files.

Exercise 18-18   COPY DATA TO WORD

You cannot save a workbook as a Word file with the **.docx** extension. However, you can use the Clipboard to copy and paste a worksheet into Word. The result is a Word table.

1. On the **MSQuery** worksheet, click cell A1.

2. Press [F8] to start Extend mode. Press [Ctrl]+[End].

3. Click the Copy button .

4. Start Word. (If Word is already running, open a new document.)

5. In the Word window, click the Paste button . The Excel data is pasted as a Word table.

6. Close the Word document without saving and close Word.

7. Return to your workbook and press [Esc] to cancel the marquee.

Exercise 18-19   SAVE A WORKBOOK AS A TEXT FILE

Saving a workbook in a text file format lets you export Excel data to programs that cannot otherwise read Excel files. A text file format saves a single sheet.

1. Select all the data in the **MSQuery** worksheet.

2. Click the Microsoft Office Button and choose **Save As**.

> **TIP**
>
> If you purchase a mailing list from a commercial source, it is probably in text format.

3. In the Save As dialog box, click the arrow for the **Save as type** box. Find and choose **Text (Tab delimited)**. This will create a text file with tabs to separate the columns/fields.

4. In the **File name** box, key *[your initials]***18-19**.

5. Click **Save**. An information message tells you that the selected file type (text format) cannot save multiple worksheets. It can save only the current worksheet.

6. Click **OK**. Another message box informs you that there might be some formatting and other features that do not convert to the text format.

7. Click **Yes**. The selected data has been exported to a text format. To see how the exported data appears in a program that reads text files, you can use Notepad.

> **NOTE**
>
> Saving a worksheet as a text file changes the worksheet's tab name to the filename of the text file.

8. From the Windows taskbar, click **Start**. From the **All Programs** menu, choose **Accessories** and then choose **Notepad**.

9. From the Notepad **File** menu, choose **Open**.

10. Navigate to and select *[your initials]*18-19.txt. Click **Open**. The raw text file opens in the Notepad window. Notice that font and table style information are not exported.

11. Close the file and Notepad.

12. In your workbook, change the worksheet's tab name to **MSQuery**. Select cell A1.

13. Save *[your initials]*18-19 as an Excel workbook and close it.

Exercise 18-20   DELETE A DOCUMENT THEME

You can delete any themes that you created. Workbooks that used the theme do retain the formatting. When you delete a theme, you should also delete the settings for fonts, colors, and effects for the theme.

1. Open a new workbook.

2. Click the **Page Layout** tab. Click the Themes button.

3. Right-click **Mine** in the **Custom** group. Choose **Delete**.

4. Click **Yes**.

5. Click the Fonts button. Right-click **Mine** at the top of the list. Choose **Delete**. Click **Yes**.

6. Click the Colors button. Right-click **Mine** at the top of the list. Choose **Delete**. Click **Yes**.

Using Online Help

Exchanging data across the Web is growing in importance for many workers. Use Help to learn about the XML format.

USE HELP TO EXPLORE EXCHANGING DATA

1. Look for Help topics about XML.

2. Read the information. Close the windows.

Lesson 18 Summary

- You can import Word data into a worksheet by performing a copy and paste or by dragging and dropping.

- Imported data might display Smart Tags, which are markers attached to certain recognized data types.

- A custom format is a display specification created with Excel's formatting codes.

- A literal is a symbol, character, or value that is part of the format. It is enclosed in quotation marks within the format code.
- When a text file is opened in Excel, the Text Import Wizard opens with options for how to import the file.
- A wizard is a series of dialog boxes that guide you through completing a task.
- Text files contain unformatted, raw text. List-type data is separated into columns by a delimiter character, usually a space, tab, or comma.
- You can apply any document theme to imported data.
- To create your own theme, define the fonts, colors, and effects for the document. Then save the theme with a new name.
- Text can be converted to arrange delimited data into multiple columns.
- You can select and drag data from the Web into an Excel worksheet.
- A Web query is a request to get table or preformatted data from a Web page.
- External data is managed by commands in the Connections group on the Data tab. These commands include naming the connection and refreshing the data.
- Microsoft Query is a program that performs queries on database files. A query is a command that extracts records from a list.
- You can save Excel data as a text file or copy or drag it to a Word document.

LESSON 18		Command Summary	
Feature	**Button**	**Task Path**	**Keyboard**
Connection, name	Connections	Data, Connections	
Connection, refresh		Data, Connections	
Import Access data	From Access	Data, Get External Data	
Microsoft Query		Data, Get External Data	
Open text file	From Text	Data, Get External Data	Ctrl + O
Remove duplicates		Data, Data Tools	
Save text file		Microsoft Office, Save As	F12
Text to columns		Data, Data Tools	
Theme colors, create	Colors ▾	Page Layout, Themes, Create New Theme Colors	
Theme fonts, create	A Fonts ▾	Page Layout, Themes, Create New Theme Fonts	
Theme, save		Page Layout, Themes, Save Current Theme	
Web query	From Web	Data, Get External Data	

Concepts Review

True/False Questions

Each of the following statements is either true or false. Indicate your choice by circling T or F.

T   F   1. Importing data is similar to auditing a workbook.

T   F   2. After data has been imported, it can be formatted like any worksheet data.

T   F   3. In a custom format, enclose text or values that are part of the format in curly braces.

T   F   4. A drag and drop is a copy if you press and hold Shift.

T   F   5. Save a document theme before setting its fonts and colors.

T   F   6. Text files use a delimiter to separate columns.

T   F   7. You can refresh all workbook connections at the same time.

T   F   8. A Web query and Microsoft Query work the same way.

Short Answer Questions

Write the correct answer in the space provided.

1. What two categories of fonts can you save for a theme?

2. How can you identify a Smart Tag?

3. What program enables you to get data from an Access file as well as other databases?

4. What is a delimiter?

5. What does the PROPER function do?

6. Name two programs that allow you to open, view, and edit a plain text file.

7. How can you determine which data is importable through a Web query?

_____

8. What group on the Data tab includes commands to manage external data references?

_____

Critical Thinking

Answer these questions on a separate page. There are no right or wrong answers. Support your answers with examples from your own experience, if possible.

1. Describe types of data or tables that your school or your company might import into Excel from the Web. Describe why it would be helpful to have and analyze the data in Excel.

2. When you import Web data, it can be static or dynamic. Dynamic data refreshes when it is changed at the original file or site. Give examples of data that might need to be refreshed daily. Give examples of data that might need to be imported once.

Skills Review

Exercise 18-21

Use text data sources. Manage imported data.

1. Use a text data source by following these steps:
   a. In Word, open **StuffedAnimalsCatalog.docx**.
   b. Set the Zoom percentage to **50%**.
   c. Point in the left margin area to the left of **Stuffed**. With the white right-pointing arrow, select all the data by dragging.

   d. Click the Copy button .
   e. Close the Word document without saving, but leave Word open.
   f. In cell A1 in a new workbook, click the Paste button.

2. Manage imported data by following these steps:
   a. Set left alignment for cells A1:A2.
   b. Widen column B to fit all names in column B on a single line in the cell. Do the same for the labels in row 4.
   c. Set a row height of **18.00 (24 pixels)** for the data rows.
   d. Remove the borders.

e. Key **=today()** in cell A3. Format the date to show the month spelled out, no day, and four digits for the year. Left-align the date.

f. Center the labels in rows 1:3 across the data. Center the sheet.

3. Rename the sheet **Catalog**. Save your workbook as *[your initials]*18-21.

4. Prepare and submit your work.

Exercise 18-22

Use text data sources. Manage imported data. Convert text to columns.

1. Use a text data source by following these steps:

   a. Save a new workbook as *[your initials]***18-22**.

   b. Click the **Data** tab. Click the From Text button .

   c. Navigate to find **CorporateCustomerList.txt** and double-click the name. The file is delimited with commas.

   d. Click **Next**. Click to select **Comma**. Click to deselect other delimiters.

   e. Click **Next**. Scroll to click in the **TaxStatus** column and then click to select **Do not import column (skip)**.

   f. Click in the **TaxID** column and click to select **Do not import column (skip)**.

   g. Click **Finish**. Click **OK**.

NOTE

Imported data is not always clean, but you can usually make a few changes to fix it.

2. Manage imported data by following these steps:

   a. Select cells E4:F4. These two cells are in the wrong columns.

   b. Drag the range to cells F4:G4 and click **OK** to replace the contents.

   c. Do the same for cells E12:F12.

   d. Click cell D4. This data should be in column E.

   e. Drag the data to cell E4.

   f. Do the same for cell D12.

   g. Click cell C4. The name and address are in one cell.

   h. Click in the formula bar and drag to select the address.

   i. Press Ctrl+X to cut the data. Click cell D4, press F2, and press Ctrl+V to paste.

   j. Repeat these steps for cell D12.

NOTE

Two new columns make room for the converted text.

3. Convert text to columns by following these steps:

   a. Select the column headings for columns F:G. Right-click either heading and choose **Insert**.

   b. Select cells E1:E12.

   c. Click the **Data** tab. Click the Text to Columns button . This data is delimited.

   d. Click **Next**. Click to select **Space**. Click to deselect other delimiters.

   e. Click **Finish**.

4. Manage imported data by following these steps:

   a. Select cells G2:G12 and press `Ctrl`+`1`. Click the **Number** tab.

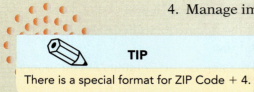

TIP

There is a special format for ZIP Code + 4.

   b. Choose **Custom**. In the **Type** box, key **00000-0000** to show the ZIP Code + 4. Click **OK**.

   c. Select cells H2:H12 and press `Ctrl`+`1`. Click the **Number** tab.

   d. Choose **Special**. In the **Type** list, choose **Phone Number**. Click **OK**.

   e. Format the fax numbers the same way.

5. Fit the columns and use landscape orientation. Fit the sheet to a single page.

6. Prepare and submit your work.

Exercise 18-23

Use Web sources. Import database records. Manage imported data.

1. Use Web sources by following these steps:

   a. Create a new workbook and save it as *[your initials]*18-23.

   b. Press `Ctrl`+`O`. Find and select **PromoOverstock.htm** but do not open it.

   c. Click the arrow next to **Open** and select **Open in Browser**. (If you see a security message, click **Yes**.)

   d. Size and position the windows so that you can see the data in the browser and cell A1 in the worksheet.

   e. Select all the data in the browser by dragging. Point at the highlighted data and drag it to cell A1 in the worksheet.

   f. Close the browser.

2. Manage imported data by following these steps:

   a. Widen the columns.

   b. Rename the sheet **Overstock**.

   c. Click the **Page Layout** tab. Click the Fonts button and choose **Create New Theme Fonts**.

   d. Choose **Tahoma** as the Heading font. Use **Tahoma** for the Body font. Key **MyTheme** as the name and click **Save**.

   e. Click the Themes button . Choose **Save Current Theme**. Key **MyTheme** as the name and click **Save**.

3. Import database records by following these steps:

   a. Rename **Sheet2** as **NewPromo**.

   b. Click the **Data** tab.

   c. Click the From Other Sources button . Choose **From Microsoft Query**.

   d. Choose **MS Access Database** and click **OK**.

e. In the **Database Name** list, select **Carolina.accdb** and click **OK**.

f. In the **Available tables and columns** list, locate **tblStuffedAnimals**, and select it so that it is highlighted in blue.

g. Click the ⟩ button. Six fields are listed in the **Columns in your query** list.

h. Click **Picture** in the list and click the ⟨ button. This field will not be imported.

i. Click **Next**. In the Query Wizard – Filter Data page, double-click **ProductGroup**. In the operator box, choose **equals** and then choose **C** in the box to its right. Choose **Or** between the filter rows.

j. In the second filter row, choose **equals** as the operator and choose **D** as the criteria. Click **Next**.

k. Sort ascending by **ProductName**. Click **Next**.

l. Select **Return Data to Microsoft Office Excel** and click **Finish**.

m. Select **Existing worksheet** if it is not already selected. Click **OK**.

> **REVIEW**
>
> The filter chooses records that belong to either the C or D category, in other words, both groups.

4. Manage imported data by following these steps:

a. Make all rows **18.75 (25 pixels)** tall.

b. Show the Total row with an average.

c. Format the prices to show a dollar sign and two decimals.

5. Prepare and submit your work.

6. Delete a document theme by following these steps:

a. Click the **Page Layout** tab.

b. Click the Themes button. Right-click **MyTheme** in the **Custom** group. Choose **Delete**. Click **Yes**.

c. Click the Fonts button. Right-click **MyTheme** at the top of the list. Choose **Delete**. Click **Yes**.

Exercise 18-24

Export data to Word.

1. Open **ShopOrder** in Excel and ignore warnings about the links.

2. Export data to Word by following these steps:

a. Select cells A1:D16.

b. Click the Copy button.

c. Start Word if necessary.

d. In a new Word document, click the Paste button.

e. Widen the price column.

f. Press Ctrl+End and key *[your first and last name]*.

3. Save the Word document as *[your initials]*18-24 in your folder.

4. Prepare and submit your work. Close the Excel workbook without saving.

Lesson Applications

Exercise 18-25

Use Web data sources. Use text sources.

1. Open the HTML file **Week1Promo** in your browser. Copy all the data to cell A1 in a new workbook. Close the browser.

2. Open **StuffedAnimalsCatalog** in Word. Copy all the data to Sheet2 in your workbook. Format this sheet so that it is easy for you to find information. You can close Word.

3. On Sheet1, use 3-D references to display the appropriate cost and quantity for the items listed.

TIP

You can copy the reference in column C to column D and adjust the formatting.

4. Rename Sheet1 as Week1. Format this sheet attractively. Center it horizontally.

5. Save the workbook as *[your initials]*18-25.

6. Make a copy of the Week1 sheet and display the formulas.

7. Prepare and submit your work.

Exercise 18-26

Import database records. Export Excel data as a text file.

1. In a new workbook, use Microsoft Query to create a query for the Access database **Carolina.accdb**. Use tblVendors and these columns: VendorID, VendorName, ContactName, and PhoneNum. Expand tblVendors and double-click each field name to place it in the query list. Import the records with no filtering or sorting.

2. Insert a row at row 1 and key Carolina Stuffed Animals Kit Suppliers. Choose a font size. Edit the labels in the header row to show spaces between the words and spell out "Number."

NOTE

You can apply the format first and then force right alignment for the phone numbers.

3. Select the first phone number and press F2. Then press Enter. This forces right alignment of the value. Repeat this for each phone number. Then format all phone numbers to use a Special Number format with the area code in parentheses.

4. Design your table in a professional layout. Name this sheet Vendors.

5. On Sheet2, create a query for the same database using the ProductID and ProductName fields from tblStuffedAnimals. Sort by Product ID in ascending order.

6. Edit and format this table to match or complement the Vendors table. Include a main label. Name the sheet appropriately.

7. Save the workbook as *[your initials]*18-26.

8. Save the Vendors sheet as a tab-delimited text file named *[your initials]*18-26.txt.

9. Open *[your initials]*18-26.txt in Notepad, and key your name on a line by itself at the top. Save and close the text file.

10. Prepare and submit your work.

Exercise 18-27

Use text sources. Manage imported data.

1. In a new workbook, get the text file **Employees.txt**. It is tab-delimited. Do not import date columns.

2. Start Word and open **NewHires**. Copy all the data to cell B16.

3. Format this data to match what's already on the sheet. Number these employees and assign a department and city to each of them.

4. Close the Word document and Word.

5. Insert two rows at the top for a main label and column labels. Determine your own labels and formatting for the sheet Remove duplicates.

6. Save the data as an Excel workbook named *[your initials]*18-27.

7. Prepare and submit your work.

Exercise 18-28 ◆ Challenge Yourself

Use text data sources. Manage imported data.

1. In a new workbook, get the text file **StateAbbreviations.txt**. Import it with the correct delimiter.

2. Delete the contents of cells A61:E68.

3. Edit the entries that are not converted properly.

4. Use PROPER to show the state name in proper case; the abbreviation should be all caps.

5. Insert a main label that reads U.S. Post Office State Abbreviations. Repeat the label as a print title.

6. Complete the formatting for the sheet.

7. Save the Excel workbook as *[your initials]*18-28.

8. Prepare and submit your work.

On Your Own

In these exercises you work on your own, as you would in a real-life work environment. Use the skills you've learned to accomplish the task—and be creative.

Exercise 18-29

Use a weather Web site to find a 7- or 10-day forecast for your city (or the closest city to it). Import the data into a worksheet. The data may include text and graphics. Decide how to format the data. Include labels that clearly identify the information. Save the workbook as *[your initials]*18-29. Prepare and submit your work.

Exercise 18-30

In a new workbook, create an list of 15 or more friends and family members, including yourself. Include name, address, city, state, ZIP, and phone numbers. Don't worry about formatting. Save the workbook as *[your initials]*18-30. Export the data to Word. Set landscape orientation in Word and save the Word document as *[your initials]*18-30. Prepare and submit your work.

Exercise 18-31

Create a Web query for a Web site that has importable tables. Look for something of interest to you on a Web site with which you are familiar (try your school or company site). When the data is in Excel, arrange and format it. Save the workbook as *[your initials]*18-31. Prepare and submit your work.

Lesson 19

Exploring List Ranges

OBJECTIVES

After completing this lesson, you will be able to:

1. Sort and filter a list range.

2. Create advanced filters.

3. Use subtotals.

4. Use database functions.

5. Create and edit outlines.

Estimated Time: 2 hours

MCAS OBJECTIVES

In this lesson:
XL07 3.3.1
XL07 4.5.1
XL07 4.5.2
XL07 4.6
XL07 4.6.2
XL07 4.6.3
XL07 4.6.4

In Excel, a *list range* can be defined as a series of worksheet rows that contain related information. A list can be formatted as a table but need not be. By naming a list as a range, you can use specialized list commands.

When data is organized and named as a list range, you can:

- Add data to the list.

- Sort the rows.

- Apply filters.

- Use functions in the Database category.

- Show subtotals and outlines.

- Create a summary known as a PivotTable.

Sorting and Filtering a List Range

A list range includes a *header row* with descriptive labels. Immediately after the header row are rows of data. A data row is a *record*. It includes all the categories of information for that row. A *field* is a single category of information; each column is a field. Each column must have a unique *field name*, which is the label in the header row. An individual piece of data in the list is called a *field value*.

Follow the same guidelines when preparing data for a list range as you would for preparing a table.

A *filter* creates a subset of data from a list range by displaying only records that meet specified conditions. Records that do not meet the conditions are temporarily hidden. The Filter arrow lists provide sorting options for ascending and descending orders, sorting and filtering by color, and using special number or text filters.

Exercise 19-1   NAME AND FORMAT A LIST RANGE

1. Open **OutOfState.**

2. Select cells A3:J21. This data can be named as a list range.

3. Click the **Name Box** and key **Shipments**.

4. Press Enter.

5. Select cells G4:G21. Click the Conditional Formatting button .

6. Choose **Highlight Cells Rules** and **Text That Contains**.

7. Set a rule to show cells that contain **ct** with green fill and green text.

8. While the cells are still selected, click the Conditional Formatting button . Choose **Highlight Cells Rules** and **Text That Contains**.

9. Set a rule to show cells that contain **ny** with red fill and red text.

10. Select cells F19:F21. Change the font color to **Red, Accent 2**.

Exercise 19-2   SORT BY CONDITIONAL FORMATTING

1. Click the **Name Box** arrow and choose **Shipments**. The list range is selected.

2. Click the **Data** tab.

3. In the **Sort & Filter** group, click the Filter button . Filter arrows are displayed in the header row for each column.

4. Click the Filter arrow for the State/Province column. The options include ascending or descending sorts as well as color sorting and filtering.

5. Choose **Sort by Color**. This column has both font and cell colors applied and both options are listed.

6. Choose **Sort by Cell Color** and then the light green. The Connecticut cells are sorted at the top in their existing order. Since the cells with green fill also have green text, you could choose to sort by the cell or font color.

Figure 19-1
Filter options for State/Province column
OutOfState.xlsx
OutOfState sheet

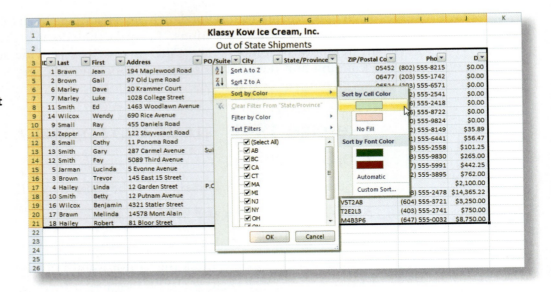

7. Press ⌨Ctrl+⌨Z. The sort is undone.

8. Click the Filter arrow for the City column. Choose **Sort by Color**. This data only has a font color.

9. In the **Sort by Font Color** list, choose the accent color. The Canadian city rows are sorted to the top in the same order.

10. Press ⌨Ctrl+⌨Z.

11. Click the Filter arrow for the State/Province column and choose **Sort by Color**.

12. Choose **Custom Sort**. You can use the colors in an order that you specify.

13. In the **Sort** dialog box, click the **Sort by** arrow and choose **State/Province**.

14. In the **Sort On** box, choose **Cell Color**.

15. In the **Order** box, choose the red color and **On Top**.

TIP

You can edit data while the rows are sorted or filtered.

16. Click **Add Level**. Click the **Then by** arrow and choose **State/Province**.

17. In the **Sort On** box, choose **Cell Color**. In the **Order** box, choose the green color and **On Top**.

Figure 19-2
Multi-level color sort
OutOfState.xlsx
OutOfState sheet

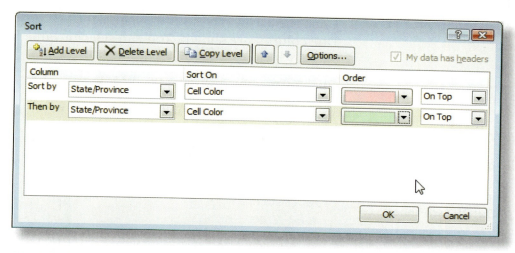

18. Click **OK**. The red-filled cells are first.

19. Press Ctrl + Z.

Exercise 19-3   FILTER BY CELL ATTRIBUTES

A *cell attribute* is any property or format setting. Conditional formatting is an attribute. You can filter rows by color and font attributes even if there is no conditional formatting applied.

1. Click the Filter arrow for the City column. Choose **Filter by Color**.

2. In the **Filter by Font Color** list, choose **Automatic**. Automatic is the default black color; the city names that were in the accent color are hidden.

3. Click the Filter arrow for the City column. Choose **Clear Filter from "City."**

Exercise 19-4   CREATE CUSTOM FILTERS

In a custom filter, you can use comparison operators, such as greater than (>) or less than (<). You can use "And" and "Or" operators to create multiple conditions. These operators allow you to:

- Display the results of a single criterion, such as >500.

- Display either of two items in a column. For example, you can show rows with either "Smith" *or* "Jacobs" as last name.

- Display records that fall within a range, such as values between 500 *and* 1000 (>=500 and <=1000).

1. Click the Filter arrow for the Due field. Choose **Number Filters**. A list of operators opens.

2. Choose **Between**. The Custom AutoFilter dialog box shows the two operators, and the **And** button is chosen.

3. Click the arrow next to the upper-right text box. The values in the Due column are shown. You can select a value from this list, or you can key a value.

4. Click in the box and key **100**.

5. Key **300** in the lower-right text box.

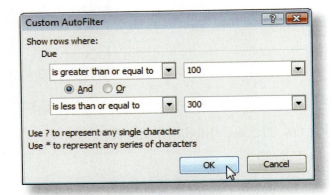

6. Click **OK**. Only two records meet this criteria.

7. Click the Filter arrow for the Due column. Choose **Clear Filter from "Due."**

8. Click the Filter arrow for the Last field and choose **Text Filters**. A list of text operators opens.

9. Choose **Equals**. The Custom AutoFilter dialog box shows one operator.

10. Click the arrow next to the upper-right text box and choose **Smith**.

11. Choose **Or**.

12. Click the arrow for the lower-left operator box and choose **equals**. Click the arrow next to the lower-right text box and choose **Small**. This filter will show customers whose name is either Smith or Small.

Figure 19-4
An "Or" custom
AutoFilter
OutOfState.xlsx
OutOfState sheet

Custom AutoFilter

Show rows where:
Last

| equals | ▼ | Smith | ▼ |

○ And ● Or

| equals | ▼ | Small | ▼ |

Use ? to represent any single character
Use * to represent any series of characters

OK   Cancel

13. Click **OK**. The filtered list shows records for Smith and Small.

14. Remove the filter.

Creating Advanced Filters

You can accomplish fairly complex filtering using the Filter arrows. If you have an unusual requirement, however, you can create an advanced filter. It is more flexible but does require a bit more work on your part. In an advanced filter, you can:

- Use more complex criteria.

- Use computations in the criteria.

- Extract or copy the filtered results to another location.

When you use an advanced filter, you set up a criteria range and can set an output range. The output range allows you to show the filter results apart from the original list.

Exercise 19-5   SET THE CRITERIA RANGE

A *criteria range* is an area on a worksheet that sets the conditions that filtered data must meet. The criteria range must be at least two rows. The first row must contain some or all of the field (column) names used in the header row. In the rows below a field name, you key conditions or filters for the field.

When creating a criteria range, follow these guidelines:

TIP

It is good practice to place criteria on a separate worksheet. If you add or delete rows or columns from the list, the criteria range is not affected.

- If you key criteria for more than one column (field) in the same row, you have created a filter in which the conditions are connected by an "And."

- If you key criteria for more than one column in different rows, you have created a filter in which the conditions are connected by an "Or."

1. Insert a new worksheet to the right of the **OutOfState** worksheet. Name it **Criteria**.

TIP

Copying field names from the list to the criteria range ensures that field names are identical.

2. Copy cells A3:J3 from the **OutOfState** worksheet to row 2 in the **Criteria** worksheet.

3. On the **Criteria** sheet, select cells A2:J3.

4. Click the **Name Box** and key **Criteria**. Press [Enter]. Your criteria range specifies two rows.

Exercise 19-6   FILTER DATA IN PLACE

When you filter in place, the results of the filter are displayed in the existing list, similar to using the Filter arrows.

1. In cell D3 on the **Criteria** worksheet, key ***road***, and press Enter. This is the filter condition. The wildcard character (*) will find rows in which the word "road" appears anywhere in the cell.

Figure 19-5
Completed criteria range
OutOfState.xlsx
Criteria sheet

2. Display the **OutOfState** worksheet and click anywhere in the list.

3. Click the **Data** tab. In the **Sort & Filter** group, click the Advanced button . The Advanced Filter dialog box opens with the **List range** and **Criteria range** already specified. When you use the name "Criteria" for the criteria range, Excel automatically uses it in an advanced filter.

Figure 19-6
Creating an advanced filter
OutOfState.xlsx
OutOfState sheet

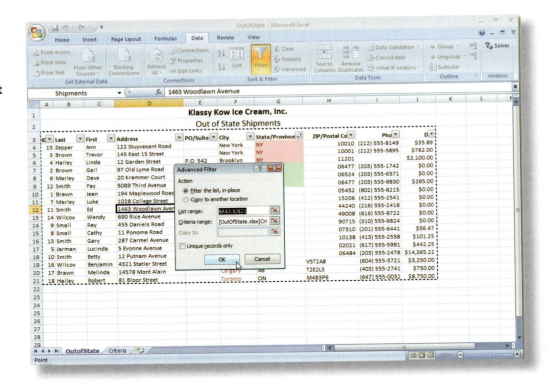

4. Choose **Filter the list, in-place** if it is not already selected.

5. Click **OK**. The list is filtered to show addresses that include the word **Road**. The Filter arrows have been removed.

6. In the **Sort & Filter** group, click the Clear button .

Exercise 19-7   CREATE AN OUTPUT RANGE

You can copy the results of an advanced filter to another location in the worksheet, known as the *output range*. Unlike a filter in place, the rows in the original list are not filtered. The output range must be on the same sheet as the list range.

1. On the **OutOfState** sheet, copy cells A3:J3 to cells M3:V3 on the same sheet.

2. Select cells M3:V3.

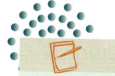

NOTE

Normally you would not want to place an output range below the list. This area should be reserved for expanding the list.

3. Click the **Name Box**, key **Output**, and press ⏎Enter⏎. You only need to specify a header row for an output range. Filtered results will use as many rows as needed below the output header row.

4. Click cell M3 to deselect the range.

Exercise 19-8   FILTER DATA TO AN OUTPUT RANGE

Although your output range includes all the fields of your list, you can create output ranges that contain only selected fields, and the fields can be in any order.

1. Return to the **Criteria** worksheet. The criteria range still includes ***road*** in the Address field.

2. Key **ct** in cell G3. This is an "And" filter because both the Address and the State/Province criteria are on the same row.

Figure 19-7
Criteria range for an advanced "And" filter
OutOfState.xlsx
Criteria sheet

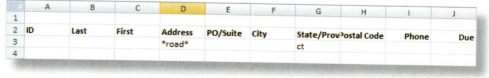

	A	B	C	D	E	F	G	H	I	J
1										
2	ID	Last	First	Address	PO/Suite	City	State/Prov	Postal Code	Phone	Due
3				*road*			ct			
4										

3. Return to the **OutOfState** worksheet. Click the **Name Box** arrow and choose **Shipments**.

4. On the **Data** tab, click the Advanced button 🔽 Advanced . The **List range** and **Criteria range** are assumed.

5. Choose **Copy to another location**. The **Copy to** box becomes available.

6. In the **Copy to** box, key **output**.

7. Click **OK**. Scroll to cell M3 to see your output. Only one row meets the criteria. Widen columns if necessary.

8. Display the **Criteria** worksheet.

9. Delete the existing criteria in cells D3 and G3.

10. In cell D3, key ***ave*** to find customers whose address includes the word "Avenue." You need to key only as much of the word as necessary to distinguish it.

Excel 2007

11. In cell G4, key **ct** to find customers in Connecticut. This is an "Or" filter because the criteria are on separate rows.

12. Click the **Formulas** tab and the Name Manager button. You need to redefine the criteria range to include another row.

13. Choose **Criteria** and click **Edit**. Edit the range in the **Refers to** text box to include row 4. (The address should read: **=Criteria!$A$2:$J$4**.)

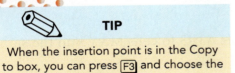

> **TIP**
>
> When the insertion point is in the Copy to box, you can press F3 and choose the output range name.

14. Return to the **OutOfState** worksheet. The list range should still be selected.

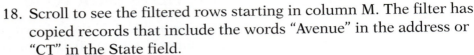

15. On the **Data** tab, click the Advanced button. The **List range** and **Criteria range** are assumed.

16. Select **Copy to another location**. Notice that Excel uses your last output range in the **Copy to** box.

17. If the **Copy to** text box does not show **$M$3:$V$3**, key **output**. Click **OK**. The new output replaces any existing data.

18. Scroll to see the filtered rows starting in column M. The filter has copied records that include the words "Avenue" in the address or "CT" in the State field.

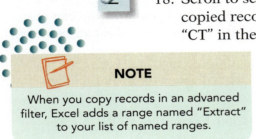

> **NOTE**
>
> When you copy records in an advanced filter, Excel adds a range named "Extract" to your list of named ranges.

19. Select the entire output range (M3:V11). On the **Home** tab, click the Clear button in the **Editing** group. Choose **Clear All**.

20. Save the workbook as *[your initials]***19-8**.

Using Subtotals

In a named range list, you can use the Subtotals command to insert subtotals based on groups of data. When you use this command, Excel creates formulas that calculate values for certain rows in a list. The formulas use statistical functions, such as SUM, AVERAGE, and COUNT.

Excel presents subtotal results in an outline. An *outline* groups worksheet rows into detail and summary rows.

Exercise 19-9 USE SUBTOTAL

The Subtotal command groups the rows and then calculates a subtotal. To use subtotals effectively, you should sort the rows by the column that is used for grouping. To show a subtotal of amount due by state/province, you should sort by state/province.

1. In *[your initials]***19-8**, click a cell in the State/Province column.

2. Click the **Data** tab. Click the Sort A to Z button.

Subtotal

3. In the **Outline** group, click the Subtotal button . A message box informs you that the header row is not apparent. Since the data is not formatted as a table, Excel also sees the labels in rows 1:2.

4. Click **Cancel**.

5. Click the **Name Box** arrow and choose **Shipments**.

6. Click the Subtotal button. The Subtotal dialog box opens. If you select the list range, the header row is assumed.

7. Click the arrow for **At each change in** and select **State/Province**. Every time the state or province changes, Excel will calculate a subtotal.

Figure 19-8
Subtotal dialog box
19-8.xlsx
OutOfState sheet

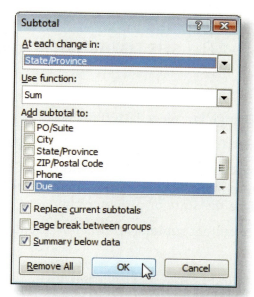

8. Click the arrow for **Use function**. You can use any of these functions to calculate a subtotal.

9. Select **Sum**. Excel will sum the rows for each state or province.

10. In the **Add subtotal to** box, click to select **Due**. Click to deselect any other column names that are selected.

11. Click **OK**. The list is grouped by state/province with a sum of the amount due for each state or province. The outline has three levels and is expanded.

Figure 19-9
Subtotals in the worksheet
19-8.xlsx
OutOfState sheet

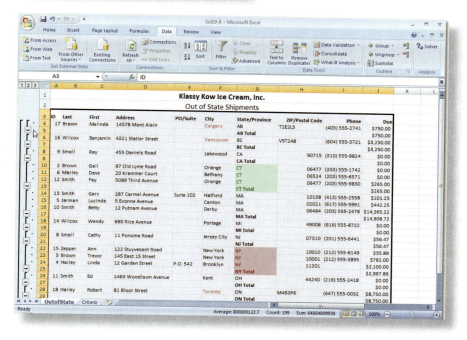

12. Click the minus symbol (−) for row 5. Details for Alberta are hidden, and only the Alberta sum is shown.

13. Hide the details for several states/provinces.

14. Click the Level 3 outline symbol. The third level displays all the rows.

15. Click the Level 2 outline symbol. The second level shows only the sums.

16. Click the Level 1 outline symbol. The first level is a grand total.

17. Click the Level 3 symbol. The outline is expanded.

Exercise 19-10   SUBTOTAL WITH AVERAGE

1. Click the Subtotal button [Subtotal] .

2. For **At each change in**, select **State/Province**.

3. Click the arrow for **Use function**. Choose **Average**.

4. In the **Add subtotal to** box, click to select **Due**. Click to deselect any other column names. This subtotal will calculate averages in the Due field every time the state or province changes.

5. Select **Replace current subtotals** if it is not already selected.

6. Click **OK**.

7. Click the Subtotal button [Subtotal] . Click **Remove All**. All subtotals are removed.

Using Database Functions

Database functions perform statistical calculations only for rows that match your criteria. This allows you to control which rows are used in the calculation.

Database functions use the following syntax: *FunctionName (ListName, Field,Criteria)*. The first argument, *ListName*, refers to the list range on the worksheet. You can enter it as a cell range or a range name.

The second argument, *Field,* is the field or column used in the calculation. You can key the field name in quotation marks or key the field's column number in the list. The first column in the list (starting at the left) is 1, the second column is 2, and so on.

The third argument, *Criteria,* is a range that contains the condition(s) for the records to be included in the calculation. You can enter it by cell address or range name.

TABLE 19-1 Database Functions

Function	Result
DAVERAGE	Averages the values in a field
DCOUNT	Counts the cells with numbers in a field
DCOUNTA	Counts the nonblank cells in a field
DMAX	Displays the largest value in the field
DMIN	Displays the smallest value in the field
DSUM	Adds the values in the field
DGET	Extracts or displays a single record that matches the criteria

Exercise 19-11   USE DMIN

You can use DMIN to find the smallest amount due in the list. A regular MIN function would find 0 as the smallest amount. With DMIN, you can specify that the amount be greater than zero.

1. Press Shift + F11 and name the sheet **Statistics**. Move it to the right of the **OutOfState** worksheet.

2. In cell A1, key **Statistics for Out-of-State Shipments**.

3. In cell A2, key **Minimum Amount Due**. Make both cells 16 point and widen the column to fit the label in cell A2.

4. Copy cells A3:J3 from the **OutOfState** worksheet to cells A15:J15 in the **Statistics** worksheet. This part of the sheet will be a criteria range.

5. In cell J16, key **>0**. With this criterion, the amount due must be greater than 0 for the record to be used in the formula.

6. Select cell B2 and click the Insert Function button .

7. In the **Or select a category** box, choose **Database**. In the **Select a function** list, choose **DMIN** and click **OK**. The Function Arguments dialog box opens.

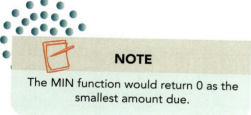

NOTE

The MIN function would return 0 as the smallest amount due.

8. With the insertion point in the **Database** box, press F3. Double-click **Shipments**, the name of your list.

9. In the **Field** box, key **"due"** including the quotation marks. This is the name of the field in your list that is to be used in the DMIN formula. (See Figure 19-10 on the next page.)

Figure 19-10
The DMIN function
and its arguments
19-8.xlsx
Statistics sheet

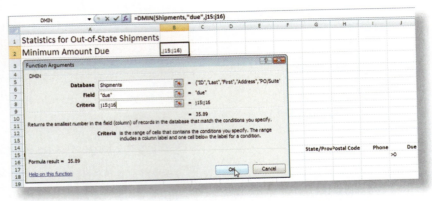

10. In the **Criteria** box, key **j15:j16**, the range that holds your criteria. Click **OK**. The result is the smallest amount due in the list.

Exercise 19-12   USE DCOUNT

With the DCOUNT database function, you can count the number of records in the list with Due amounts greater than 0.

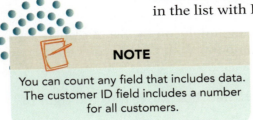

NOTE

You can count any field that includes data. The customer ID field includes a number for all customers.

1. In cell A3, key **Number of Customers Who Owe**. Match the font size and widen the column.

2. Select cell B3 and click the Insert Function button *fx*.

3. Choose the **Database** category and **DCOUNT**. Click **OK**.

4. In the **Database** box, press F3. Double-click **Shipments**.

5. In the **Field** box, key **1** for the first column in the list. You can key either the field name in quotes, or the column number, with the leftmost column in the list numbered as 1.

NOTE

The COUNT function would count all customer IDs.

6. In the **Criteria** box, key **j15:j16**. Click **OK**. The result is the number of records with a Due amount greater than 0.

7. Save the workbook as *[your initials]*19-12. Close the workbook.

Creating and Editing Outlines

An outline groups and summarizes data. It can show all details, selected details, or only summary data. Excel creates outlines automatically when you use the Subtotal and Consolidate commands or when you create a scenario summary.

You can create your own outline by preparing a list with subtotals and grand totals. The formulas for the subtotals and grand totals must be in a consistent location in the list.

An outline can be arranged by row or by column. In a row outline, formula rows are either above or below the related data. In a column outline, formula columns are either to the left or the right of related columns.

When working with outlines, keep these points in mind.

- A worksheet can have only one outline.

- An outline can include all the data on a worksheet or a selected range of data.

- An outline can have up to eight levels.

Exercise 19-13 USE THE SUBTOTAL FUNCTION

In addition to automatic subtotals, there is a SUBTOTAL function. You can use it for sums, as well as averages, counts, standard deviations, and more.

1. Open **DropCard**. This worksheet has been prepared for row and column outline use. It has a total row available below each state group and a subtotal column for each quarter.

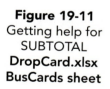

TIP

In most row outlines, the summary row is below the data. In most column outlines, the summary column is to the right of the data.

2. Click cell E5. Click the Insert Function button *fx*. In the **Search for a function** box, key **subtotal** and press Enter. The SUBTOTAL function is found.

3. Click **OK**. The Function Arguments dialog box shows that SUBTOTAL has two arguments, **Function_num** and **Ref1**. The function number is a number that you key ranging from 1 to 11 or 101 to 111.

4. Click **Help on this function**. The help window identifies the functions that you can use for a subtotal. For a sum, you use **9**.

Figure 19-11
Getting help for SUBTOTAL
DropCard.xlsx
BusCards sheet

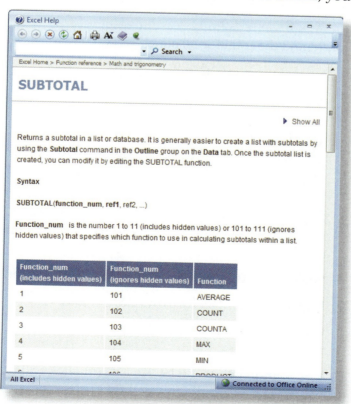

5. Close the Help window.

6. Key **9** in the **Function_num** box.

7. Click in the **Ref1** box. This is the range to be subtotaled.

8. Select cells B5:D5. Click **OK**. The subtotal is 275.

9. Copy the formula to cells E6:E18.

10. Select cells E5:E18. Hold down Ctrl and drag a copy of the range to cells I5:I18. This copies the formula with a relative reference.

TIP

Use a reduced Zoom size to work efficiently.

11. Copy the range to cells M5:M18 and Q5:Q18.

12. Click cell E21.

13. Key **=subt** and press Tab.

14. Double-click **9 – SUM** in the Formula AutoComplete list.

15. Key a comma (**,**) to separate the arguments.

16. Select cells B21:D21 and press Enter.

17. Copy the formula for the cities in Oregon and then for the other quarters.

18. Complete the SUBTOTAL function for Nevada and Washington.

Exercise 19-14   ADD GRAND TOTALS

The grand totals include one for each city by year, one for each state by month, and the total for all states.

1. Click cell R5. Click the **Home** tab.

2. Click the AutoSum button ∑ ▾. Cells E5, I5, M5, and Q5 are recognized as subtotals and automatically selected for the SUM function.

3. Press Enter. The total is 1105.

4. Copy the formula to cells R6:R18.

5. Copy this formula to cells R21:R25, cells R28:R33, and cells R36:R42. Click any copied cell to verify the same formula with a relative cell reference.

6. Select cells B19:R19. Click the AutoSum button ∑ ▾.

7. Repeat these steps for rows 26, 34, and 43.

8. Click cell B44. The formula should add each of the monthly state totals.

9. Key **=** and click cell B19. Key **+** and click cell B26. Key **+** and click cell B34. Key **+** and click cell B43. Press Enter. The total is 4395.

10. Copy the formula to cells C44:R44.

Exercise 19-15 CREATE AN AUTO OUTLINE

With a list prepared and formulas in a consistent location, Excel can create an Auto Outline. Using your existing formulas, it will create the appropriate style and number of levels.

1. Click cell A5. You can click any cell in the list to create the outline.

2. Click the **Data** tab. In the **Outline** group, click the arrow on the Group button.

3. Choose **Auto Outline**. Excel creates a combination row-and-column outline. There are three row levels and three column levels.

Figure 19-12
Auto outline
DropCard.xlsx
BusCards sheet

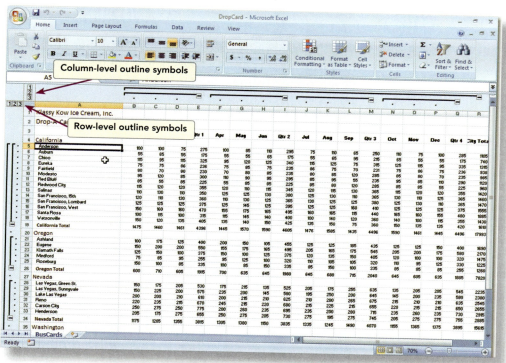

4. Click the Level 1 column symbol. Only the city totals are displayed.

5. Click the Level 2 column symbol. The quarters and city totals are shown, but not the individual months.

6. Click the Level 3 column symbol. All the column details are displayed.

7. Click the Level 1 row symbol. The monthly grand total is displayed with the California label for row 4.

8. Click the Level 2 row symbol. The state totals are displayed, but not the cities.

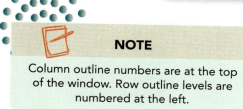

NOTE

Column outline numbers are at the top of the window. Row outline levels are numbered at the left.

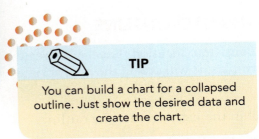

TIP

You can build a chart for a collapsed outline. Just show the desired data and create the chart.

9. While the second level is shown, you can expand an individual state.

10. Click the + (Expand) symbol for row 19, California. The California group is expanded, and all the cities are shown.

11. Collapse the California data.

12. Click the Level 3 row symbol. The outline is expanded.

13. Save the workbook as *[your initials]*19-15. Close the workbook.

Exercise 19-16   CREATE A ROW OUTLINE MANUALLY

You can manually create outline groupings in a list without formulas. You first must insert empty rows below each group. Excel uses the empty rows to develop the outline.

1. Open **OutOfState**.

2. Name cells A3:J21 as **Shipments**.

3. Click the **Data** tab and click the Sort button . Click to select **My data has headers**. Sort by state/province in ascending order.

4. Insert a blank row at row 5. This separates Alberta from British Columbia.

5. Insert a blank row at row 7 to separate the British Columbia records.

6. Insert a blank row at row 9 for the California records.

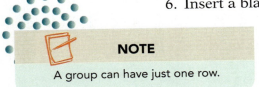

NOTE

A group can have just one row.

7. Insert blank rows where needed to separate the remaining states/provinces.

8. Click the row 4 heading to select the row for Alberta.

9. Click the **Data** tab. In the **Outline** group, click the arrow on the Group button .

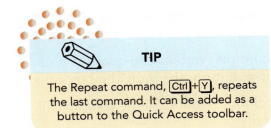

TIP

The Repeat command, Ctrl+Y, repeats the last command. It can be added as a button to the Quick Access toolbar.

10. Choose **Group**.

11. Select the row 6 heading, the British Columbia record.

12. Press Ctrl+Y to repeat the **Group** command.

13. Select row 8, the California record. Press Ctrl+Y.

14. Select rows 10 through 12, the Connecticut records. Press Ctrl+Y.

15. Select and group the rows for the remaining states/provinces.

Exercise 19-17　EXPAND AND HIDE DETAILS

After you've manually set up an outline, you can display only those portions of your list that are needed.

1. Click the Level 1 outline symbol. Because there are currently no totals, nothing is shown.

2. Click the Level 2 outline symbol. The outline is expanded. You can hide individual groupings by clicking the outline symbols.

3. Click the minus symbol (−) for the CA record. The record is hidden.

4. Collapse each state so that only the Canadian provinces are displayed (AB, BC, ON).

5. Hide the blank rows.

6. Save the workbook as *[your initials]*19-17.

7. Close the workbook.

Using Online Help

Outlines and lists are well suited to data that is often summarized in some way. Explore more about how outlines might be helpful in your work.

USE HELP TO LEARN ABOUT OUTLINES

1. Look for Help topics about outlines.

2. Read the information. Close the windows.

Lesson　19　Summary

- A list range is a series of rows and columns that contain related information, similar to a database. A list is similar to a table but does not use the table format.

- List ranges have a header row, followed by rows of data, known as records. Each column is a field. Field names in the header row should be unique.

- Name a list range to include the header row and all the data rows.

- You can sort data in a list range. Use the Sort dialog box to sort by more than one column.

- A filter creates a subset of data from a list range, using specified conditions.

- Filters can be applied to a list range. The Filter arrows display in the header row like a table.

- Filters can use conditional formatting settings as well as cell and font colors.

- Use a custom filter to create specialized criteria, including comparison operators, such as greater than (>) or less than (<). You can use "And" and "Or" operators for multiple conditions.

- Advanced filters use a criteria range, a worksheet area specifying conditions for filtered data.

- In an advanced filter, you can show the results in another location on the worksheet.

- The Subtotal command automatically inserts subtotal calculations based on groups of data. The results are presented in an Excel outline.

- The Database functions are a category of functions for list ranges. They perform calculations on a field based on conditions that you set.

- Outlines can be created automatically for list ranges if they include properly organized data and formulas.

LESSON 19		Command Summary	
Feature	**Button**	**Task Path**	**Keyboard**
Advanced filter	Advanced	Data, Sort & Filter	
Auto outline	Group	Data, Outline	
Filter	Filter	Data, Sort & Filter	Ctrl + Shift + L
Outline, create	Group	Data, Outline	
Repeat			Ctrl + Y
Subtotal	Subtotal	Data, Outline	

Concepts Review

True/False Questions

Each of the following statements is either true or false. Indicate your choice by circling T or F.

T F   1. Any worksheet can be used as a list range.

T F   2. The first row in a list is the header row.

T F   3. Outline commands are available on the Data tab.

T F   4. An advanced filter uses a criteria range and an output range.

T F   5. A list range prepared for subtotals should be sorted by the column used for grouping.

T F   6. The SUBTOTAL function can use SUM, AVERAGE, or others to calculate a value.

T F   7. Outline levels are unlimited.

T F   8. Database functions use the same arguments as statistical functions.

Short Answer Questions

Write the correct answer in the space provided.

1. A list range is similar to what Excel feature?

_____

2. Name two database functions.

_____

3. In addition to ascending and descending, in what other ways can a list be sorted?

_____

4. What creates a subset of data from a list based on specific conditions?

_____

5. Name two functions that you can use with the Subtotal command.

_____

6. When criteria are keyed on the same row in a criteria range, how is the criteria and/or filter described?

_____

7. What term is used to describe conditional formatting and other cell formats?

_____

8. How can you set "Or" criteria in an advanced filter?

_____

Critical Thinking

Answer these questions on a separate page. There are no right or wrong answers. Support your answers with examples from your own experience, if possible.

1. Suppose that your company maintains its sales order information in a list. The columns are order date, customer ID, ship date, shipping method, sales representative, total amount, and discount. Describe what types of reports you could prepare using filters.

2. Describe the difference between the statistical function AVERAGE and the database function DAVERAGE.

Skills Review

Exercise 19-18

Sort and filter a list range.

1. Open **DayCount1** and save it as *[your initials]***19-18**.
2. Sort a list range by following these steps:

   a. Select cells A3:I35 and name the range **Daily**.
   b. Click the **Data** tab. Click the Sort button 📊.
   c. Make sure there is a check mark for **My data has headers**.
   d. Sort by state in A to Z order.
   e. Add a level to sort by city, also in A to Z order.
   f. Click **OK**.
3. Filter a list range by following these steps:
   a. Select the list range.
   b. On the **Data** tab, click the Filter button 🔽.
   c. Click the Filter arrow for the Monday column.
   d. Choose **Filter by Color** and choose the red X.
   e. Hide columns D:I.
4. Center the labels in rows 1:2 across the list. Center the sheet horizontally. Adjust row heights and column widths as needed.
5. Mark the workbook as final.
6. Prepare and submit your work.

Exercise 19-19

Filter a list range. Create an advanced filter.

1. Open **DayCount2** and save it as *[your initials]*19-19. Make a copy of the **CustCount** sheet.

2. Filter a list range by following these steps:
   a. Select cells A3:I35 on the **CustCount** sheet and name the range **Monday**.
   b. With the range selected, click the **Data** tab. Click the Filter button .
   c. Click the Filter arrow for Monday.
   d. Choose **Number Filters** and **Between**.
   e. Build a custom filter to find values between 100 and 150.
   f. Click **OK**.

> **NOTE**
> The Between operator creates an "And" condition.

3. Create an advanced filter by following these steps:
   a. Insert a new worksheet, name it **Criteria**, and position it to the right of the **CustCount (2)** worksheet.
   b. Key **Criteria Sheet** in cell A1 in the **Criteria** sheet and make it 14 point.
   c. Copy cells A3:I3 from the **CustCount (2)** sheet to cell A2:I2 in the **Criteria** sheet.
   d. On the **Criteria** sheet, name cells A2:I3 as **Criteria**. Key **nv** in cell B3.
   e. Select cells A3:I35 on the **CustCount (2)** sheet and name the range **Daily**.
   f. On the **CustCount (2)** sheet, copy cells A3:I3 to cells K3:S3. Name cells K3:S3 as **Output**.
   g. Select the **Daily** range.
   h. On the **Data** tab, click the Advanced button . Choose **Copy to another location**. In the **Copy to** box, press F3 and double-click **Output**. Click **OK**.

4. Adjust the output range for visibility. Hide all columns up to the output range.

5. Prepare and submit your work.

Exercise 19-20

Use subtotals in a list. Use database functions.

1. Open **DayCount2** and save it as *[your initials]*19-20a.

2. Name the list **Database**. On the **Data** tab, click the Sort button . Select **My data has headers**. Sort by state and then city in A to Z order.

3. Create subtotals by following these steps:
   a. Select the list.
   b. Click the **Data** tab and click the Subtotal button.
   c. Click the arrow for **At each change in** and choose State.
   d. Click the arrow for the **Use function** box and choose **Sum** if it is not already displayed.

e. In the **Add subtotal to** list, click to select each of the seven days. Click **OK**.

f. Click the Level 2 outline symbol to display only state totals. Hide column A and fit the other columns.

4. Prepare and submit your work.

5. Open **Properties** and save it as *[your initials]*19-20b.

6. Use database functions by following these steps:

a. Name cells A3:I27 as **Database**.

b. Insert a worksheet and name it **Summary**.

c. In cell A1, key **Homes Less Than 15 Years Old**. Make it 14 point.

d. In cell A3, key **Highest Price**. In cell A4, key **Lowest Price**. In cell A5, key **Number of Homes**. Make all three labels 12-point Cambria and adjust the width of column A appropriately.

NOTE

The criteria finds homes that are 15 or fewer years old.

e. Copy cells A3:I3 on the **Properties** sheet to cells K3:S3 in the same sheet.

f. Key **<=15** in cell P4.

g. Select cell B3 on the **Summary** sheet, and click the Insert Function button *fx*.

h. For the **Or select a category** box, choose **Database**. In the **Select a function** list, choose **DMAX**. Click **OK**.

i. In the **Database** box, press F3, and double-click **Database**. In the **Field** box, key **"last sale price"** with quotation marks. In the **Criteria** box, click the **Properties** tab and select cells P3:P4. Click **OK**.

NOTE

When you select criteria from another worksheet, Excel includes an identifier with the worksheet name and an exclamation point.

j. Select cell B4 and click the Insert Function button *fx*. Choose the **Database** category and **DMIN**. Click **OK**.

k. In the **Database** box, press F3, and double-click **Database**. In the **Field** box, key **"last sale price"** with quotation marks. In the **Criteria** box, click the **Properties** tab and select cells P3:P4. Click **OK**.

TIP

You can copy the function and adjust the references.

l. In cell B5, create a DCOUNT database function.

7. Format cells B3:B4 as Currency with no decimals. Use the same font as the labels in column A.

8. Prepare a formula sheet for the **Summary** sheet.

9. Prepare and submit your work.

Exercise 19-21

Create and edit an outline.

1. Open **Properties** and save it as *[your initials]*19-21.

2. Select and name the list **Database**. Sort the list in descending order by last sale price.

3. Create an outline by following these steps:

   a. Right-click the row 8 heading and insert a row. In cell A8, key **Over $400,000**. Make it bold.

   b. Insert a blank row at row 15. In cell A15, key **$300,000 to $399,999**. Make it bold.

   c. Insert a row at row 20. In cell A20, key **$200,000 to $299,999**. Make it bold.

   d. In cell A31, key **Less than $200,000**. Make it bold.

   e. Select the row headings for rows 4:7.

   f. Click the **Data** tab. In the **Outline** group, click the arrow on the Group button ⊞ Group ▾ .

   g. Choose **Group**.

   h. Select rows 9 through 14 and press Ctrl + Y .

   i. Create groups for the remaining price ranges.

4. Edit an outline by following these steps:

   a. Click cell B8. Use the COUNT function to count the cells in the range B4:B7. Make the results bold.

   b. Do the same for the other price ranges.

   c. Select the list and use 10-point Cambria.

   d. Click the Level 1 outline symbol.

   e. Hide row 3.

   f. Make any other necessary changes.

5. Prepare and submit your work.

Lesson Applications

Exercise 19-22

Filter a list range.

1. Open **AccPay** and save it as *[your initials]*19-22.

2. Name cells A4:F21 as **Accounts**.

3. Starting in cell A12, add the records shown in Figure 19-13, replacing "xx" with the current year.

NOTE

Check the formulas in columns C and F.

Figure 19-13

Account	Date Rec'd	Due Date	Amount	Late Fee
Western Cable	1/3/xx		975	
Continental Power and Gas	2/4/xx		2456	Yes
USA Telephone	3/8/xx		932.37	
Visa/MasterCard	4/10/xx		1832.77	Yes
US Express	5/15/xx		2458	Yes
Avalon Financial Services	7/10/xx		350	Yes
Federal Shipping	9/7/xx		1200	

NOTE

You need not key commas when values are preformatted. You must, however, key decimal points when a significant value follows the decimal point.

4. Fix formatting inconsistencies.

5. Select the list range. Turn on filtering and show only records that do not have a late fee. Hide unused rows in the list range.

6. Prepare and submit your work.

Exercise 19-23

Use database functions. Create subtotals.

1. Open **Properties** and save it as *[your initials]*19-23.

2. Name the list range **Database** and sort by number of bedrooms in ascending order.

3. Insert a new worksheet and name it **Report**. In cell A1 on the **Report** sheet, key **Summary for 4-Bedroom Homes**. Make the labels 16-point Cambria.

4. Set 12-point Cambria for cells A2:B6. Starting in cell A2, key the following labels in the range A2:A6:

Lowest Price

Highest Price

Largest Lot

Oldest Home

Newest Home

5. Create a criteria range that starts in cell A14 in the **Report** sheet, with the condition that properties have four bedrooms.

REVIEW

Copy labels for the criteria range to ensure consistency and accuracy.

6. On the **Report** sheet, use database functions to show the price of the lowest-priced four-bedroom home, the price of the most expensive home, the largest lot for four-bedroom homes, the age of the oldest home, and the age of the newest four-bedroom home.

7. Format money values as Currency with no decimal places.

TIP

The criteria are the same for these calculations, but the field changes. Remember to type the field name in quotation marks and spell it exactly as it is in the list.

8. Make a copy of the **Properties** sheet and name it **Subtotals**. Sort by number of bedrooms in ascending order, with a secondary sort by number of baths in ascending order.

9. Create subtotals for the Bedrooms field using the COUNT function.

10. Edit the summary label from **1 Count** to **1 Bedroom Total**. Do this for all the labels.

11. Collapse all details except for four-bedroom homes.

12. Prepare and submit your work.

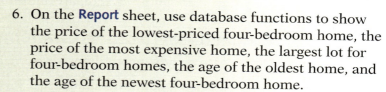

REVIEW

Use the Sort dialog box to sort by multiple fields.

Exercise 19-24

Sort a list range. Create outline groups. Use subtotals in a list range.

1. Open **UpdatedEmp** and save it as *[your initials]*19-24. Name **Sheet1** as **Employees**. Select cell A16.

2. Open **AddEmp.doc** in Word. Copy the entire table to cell A16 in your worksheet. Close Word.

TIP

Use the Format Painter to quickly copy formats from one cell to a range of cells.

3. Format the imported data to match the existing rows, including the row height and vertical cell alignment.

4. Select and name the range. Then sort by department in ascending order. Insert a blank row after each department group.

5. Outline and group each department and the president. In the blank row for the Finance group, key **Total** in column E. Make it bold and right-aligned. Key or copy the same label in the blank row for each of the departments (except the president).

6. Use the SUBTOTAL function in column F to count the number of employees in each department. Make the results bold.

REVIEW

Use Help to build a SUBTOTAL function to count labels.

7. Increase the indent once for the department names and reset the **Total** labels if necessary. Adjust other column widths so it is easier to read the data. Center the page horizontally.

8. Prepare and submit your work.

Exercise 19-25 ◆ Challenge Yourself

Create an advanced filter.

1. Open **UpdatedEmp** and save it as *[your initials]*19-25. Name **Sheet1** as **Employees**.

2. In Word, open **NewEmp**. Copy only the two data rows (no labels) to cell A16 in your workbook. Fix the copied data to match the existing data, and assign each employee to one of the existing departments.

REVIEW

Subtract the date hired from today and divide by 365.25, and use parentheses to order the formula.

3. Name the list as a range and sort by Last Name in ascending order.

4. In cell G2, key **Years Employed**. Format the label to match the other labels.

5. In column G, use a formula to determine years employed as of today. Format the results to show one decimal and increase the indent four times.

REVIEW

Use the Name Manager to add a column to a named range.

6. Redefine the list range name to include column G. Re-center the main label over the data.

7. Create an output range starting in cell I2 that shows only the First Name and Last Name fields.

NOTE

To use "and" logic in a filter, show the field twice in the criteria range and enter the conditions on the same row.

8. Create a criteria range to find employees who have been employed between 5 and 10 years. Show the **Years Employed** field twice in the criteria range to use "and" logic. Run this advanced filter and show the results in the output range.

9. Key **5-10 Years** as a label in cell I1 and format it.

10. Set landscape orientation. Fit the sheet to a single page.

11. Prepare and submit your work.

On Your Own

In these exercises you work on your own, as you would in a real-life work environment. Use the skills you've learned to accomplish the task—and be creative.

Exercise 19-26

Create a list with at least 24 rows of data that will be grouped and outlined about television shows or movies. Decide on the fields' names, but use several fields that can be subtotaled in some way (name, star, time, length, day, year, network, studio, etc). Decide how to sort and then group your data. Create the groups manually or use formulas to create an AutoOutline. Show relevant subtotals where possible. Format the data attractively. Save the workbook as *[your initials]*19-26. Prepare and submit your work.

Exercise 19-27

Find a Web site that has a list or catalog that you can copy into a worksheet. Copy the data and arrange it as a list. Add a header row if necessary. Name the list range. Apply data bars, color scales, or icon sets in some way to your list. Then create a filter that uses your conditional formatting in a logical way. Save the workbook as *[your initials]*19-27. Prepare and submit your work.

Exercise 19-28

Create a list of 20 or more automobile/SUV/truck names. Include fields for the model name, manufacturer, style, engine size/type, suggested price, and a couple of other features. Build your list so that you will be able to use three database functions on another sheet to show pertinent statistics about your vehicle list. Format both sheets attractively. Save the workbook as *[your initials]*19-28. Prepare and submit your work.

Using Data tables and PivotTables

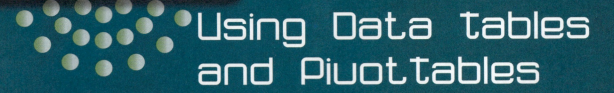

OBJECTIVES

MCAS OBJECTIVES

In this lesson:
XL07 1.3
XL07 1.3.1
XL07 2.3
XL07 2.3.3
XL07 3.1.1
XL07 3.2
XL07 4.1.2
XL07 4.3
XL07 4.5
XL07 4.5.2

After completing this lesson, you will be able to:

1. Build a one-variable data table.

2. Build a two-variable data table.

3. Analyze data in a PivotTable.

4. Create a PivotTable.

5. Use multiple calculations.

6. Create a PivotChart.

Estimated Time: 2 hours

A *data table* is a range of cells that calculates the results of changing values in one or more formulas. A data table enables you to display multiple versions of a problem at once. Excel has two types of data tables, a one-variable data table and a two-variable data table.

A *PivotTable* is an interactive summary report that combines and compares data from a list. The term "pivot" comes from the ability to rotate or move things around in the table.

Building a One-Variable Data Table

A one-variable data table shows the results of a formula in which one argument is changed. You might use a one-variable data table to calculate net profit from cake sales as the price is changed. The price is the variable, and a data table will show the results of a profit formula based on different prices.

Exercise 20-1 PREPARE FORMULAS AND INPUT VALUES

A one-variable data table can have more than one formula.

1. Open **MacCake**.

2. In cell C6, use a formula to determine the profit per cake by subtracting the ingredient and labor costs from the price.

3. In cell C9, use a formula to determine sales by multiplying the number sold by the price.

4. In cell C10, add the ingredient and labor costs and then multiply the result by the number of cakes sold.

5. In cell C11, use a formula to determine net profit by subtracting total costs from total sales. You will refer to the price and the formulas in cells C9:C11 in your data table.

6. In cell F4, key = and click cell C9. Press Enter. It is better to refer to the formula rather than rekeying it.

7. In cell G4, key = and click cell C10. Press Enter. By referring to the cell with the formula, you can be sure that the data table will update if changes are made to the original information.

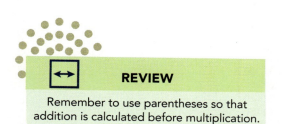

NOTE

At a price of $20.50, there is no profit; this is the break-even point.

REVIEW

Remember to use parentheses so that addition is calculated before multiplication.

Figure 20-1
Building data table formulas
MacCake.xlsx
Sheet1 sheet

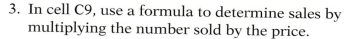

	A	B	C	D	E	F	G	H
		SUBTOTAL	▾	× ✓ fx	=C10			
1		Profit Calculator for						
2		Macadamia Ice Cream Cake						
3		Purchase price	$20.50					
4		Cost of ingredients	$7.75			$10,250.00	=C10	
5		Cost of labor	$12.75					
6		Profit per cake	$0.00					
7								
8		Number of cakes sold	500					
9		Total dollar sales	$10,250.00					
10		Total costs	$10,250.00					
11		Net profit	$0.00					
12								

8. In cell H4, key = and click cell C11. Press Enter.

REVIEW

To create a series, key the starting value in the first cell of the series, key the next value in the second cell, select the two cells, and drag the Fill handle across the range to fill.

9. In cell E5, key **$20.50** as the first input value.

10. In cell E6, key **$21.50** as the second input value. These two values have an increment of one.

11. Select cell E5:E6 and fill down the column to **$30.50** in cell E15. Cells E5:E15 are column input values. They will be substituted for cell C3 in the formulas.

Figure 20-2
Adding input values for data table
MacCake.xlsx
Sheet1 sheet

	E5		f_x	20.5				
	A	B	C	D	E	F	G	H	I
1		Profit Calculator for						
2		Macadamia Ice Cream Cake						
3		Purchase price	$20.50					
4		Cost of ingredients	$7.75			$10,250.00	$10,250.00	$0.00
5		Cost of labor	$12.75		$20.50			
6		Profit per cake	$0.00		$21.50			
7					$22.50			
8		Number of cakes sold	500		$23.50			
9		Total dollar sales	$10,250.00		$24.50			
10		Total costs	$10,250.00		$25.50			
11		Net profit	$0.00		$26.50			
12					$27.50			
13					$28.50			
14					$29.50			
15					$30.50			
16								
17								

Exercise 20-2 CREATE A DATA TABLE

In a one-variable data table, *input values* can be in a column or a row. When the input values are in a column, the formulas must start one column to the right of the first value and one row above. Additional formulas must be in the same row.

NOTE

When the input values are in a row, the first formula is one column to the left of the first value and one row below. Additional formulas must be in the same column.

The Data Table command substitutes the values in column E into the formula for the cell that you specify. The *data table range* includes the formulas and all the input values. This will be the location of the results.

1. Select cells E4:H15. This is the data table range. Excel will calculate each formula in row 4 using the price in column E.

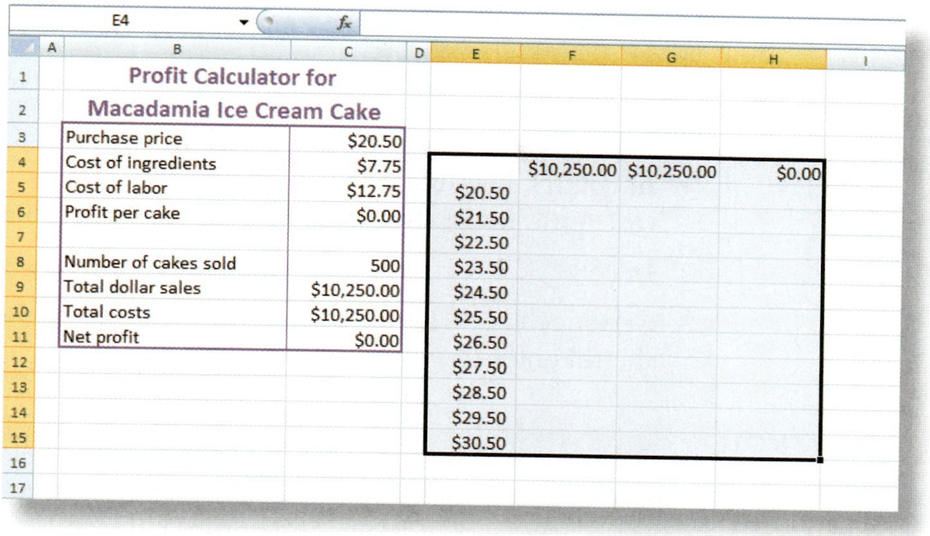

Figure 20-3
Selecting the data
table range
MacCake.xlsx
Sheet1 sheet

2. Click the **Data** tab. Click the What-If Analysis button ![What-If Analysis] .

3. Choose **Data Table**. In the Data Table dialog box, you specify the cell address that should be changed in each of your formulas. Your table has adjustable prices in a column, so you'll use the **Column input cell** box.

4. In the **Column input cell** box, key **c3**. This is the cell address (the price) used directly or indirectly in your formulas. Its value will be replaced by the values in column E.

5. Click **OK**. The range F5:H15 displays the results of each formula in row 4 for each input value in column E.

NOTE

Use Currency in the Format dialog box to show a floating dollar sign.

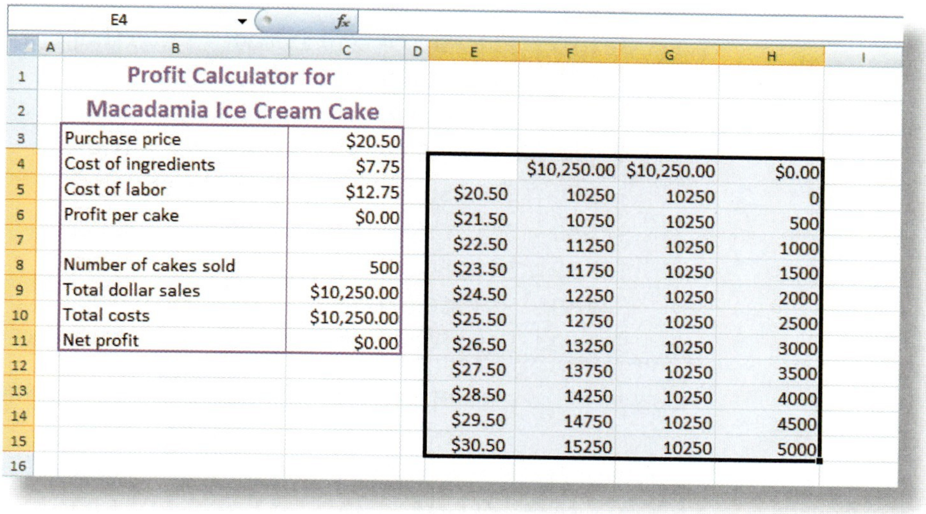

Figure 20-4
Results of the Data
Table command
MacCake.xlsx
Sheet1 sheet

6. Format the results as Currency with two decimals.

Exercise 20-3 FORMAT THE DATA TABLE

You can format the data table and add labels that clearly identify its contents and purpose.

1. In cell F3, key **Total Sales**. In cell G3, key **Total Costs**. In cell H3, key **Net Profit**. Make these labels bold and centered.

2. In cell E3, key **=c3** to show the current price.

3. Select cells E3:H3 and set the font color to **White, Background 1** and the fill color to **Purple, Accent 4**.

> **NOTE**
>
> When setting borders, choose the color, the line style, and then the border.

4. Select cells E3:H15 and press Ctrl + 1. Set a medium thick **Purple, Accent 4 Outline** border. Do not close the dialog box.

5. Change the border color to **Black, Text 1**. Then add a thin middle vertical border. Click **OK**.

6. In cell E1, key **Costs and Profit for**. In cell E2, key **$20.50-$30.50 Price Range**.

7. Copy the format from the labels in cell B1 and then center cells E1:E2 across the appropriate range.

Figure 20-5
Formatting the data table
MacCake.xlsx
Sheet1 sheet

	Costs and Profits for $20.50–$30.50 Price Range			
$20.50	Total Sales	Total Costs	Net Profit	
	$10,250.00	$10,250.00	$0.00	
$20.50	$10,250.00	$10,250.00	$0.00	
$21.50	$10,750.00	$10,250.00	$500.00	
$22.50	$11,250.00	$10,250.00	$1,000.00	
$23.50	$11,750.00	$10,250.00	$1,500.00	
$24.50	$12,250.00	$10,250.00	$2,000.00	
$25.50	$12,750.00	$10,250.00	$2,500.00	
$26.50	$13,250.00	$10,250.00	$3,000.00	
$27.50	$13,750.00	$10,250.00	$3,500.00	
$28.50	$14,250.00	$10,250.00	$4,000.00	
$29.50	$14,750.00	$10,250.00	$4,500.00	
$30.50	$15,250.00	$10,250.00	$5,000.00	

Exercise 20-4 INSERT AN EN DASH AND A POINTER

To show a range of numbers or dates, you should use the *en dash*. It is a typographical symbol, slightly longer than a hyphen, used to mark ranges of labels and/or values.

A *pointer* is a conditional format that highlights a cell in your data table. You can highlight the price in the table that matches the price in the setup information.

1. Click cell E2 and press F2 to edit the contents.

2. Click to the left of the hyphen and delete it.

3. Click the **Insert** tab.

4. In the **Text** group, click the Symbol button Ω. Click the **Special Characters** tab.

5. Choose **En dash** and click **Insert**. Close the dialog box.

Figure 20-6
Inserting an en dash
MacCake.xlsx
Sheet1 sheet

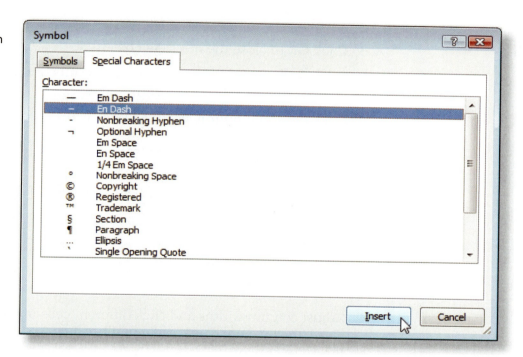

6. Select cells E5:E15. Click the **Home** tab.

7. Click the Conditional Formatting button. Choose **Highlight Cells Rules** and then **Equal To**.

8. In the Equal To dialog box, click cell C3.

9. Click the arrow for the format options and choose **Custom Format**.

10. Build a format to show the accent fill and white text if the cell value is equal to cell C3. Click **OK** to return to the sheet.

11. In cell C3, key **25.5** and press Enter. The formulas recalculate and the pointer moves.

Exercise 20-5   DELETE, EDIT, AND COPY A DATA TABLE

Excel uses the TABLE function in a data table. It is an array formula, identified by curly braces in the formula bar. An *array formula* performs multiple calculations that display a single result or multiple results. You cannot delete individual cells in an array formula. You can change the input values or other arguments in the formula, and the table is recalculated. If you copy a data table, you copy the results, not the formula.

1. Select cell F6. In the formula bar, notice that the TABLE function is enclosed in curly braces. These braces mark an array formula.

2. Press Delete. A message box indicates that you cannot change part of a table.

3. Click **OK** to close the message box.

4. Select cells F5:H15. Press Delete. The results of the data table are deleted. You can delete the entire table.

5. Click the Undo button ↺ . The table is restored.

6. In cell E6, key **21** and press Enter. Part of the table is recalculated.

7. Click the Undo button ↺ .

8. Select any cell in the table with a result. Press Ctrl+G.

9. Click **Special**. Choose **Current array** and click **OK**. The data table is highlighted.

10. Click the Copy button ⧉ .

11. Display **Sheet2** and click the Paste button ⧉ .

12. Adjust column widths and click different cells in the table to check the formula bar. The data table values are copied; the formulas are not.

13. Return to **Sheet1**. Press Esc to cancel the marquee and click cell A1.

Building a Two-Variable Data Table

A two-variable table uses two sets of input values but only one formula. You can create a two-variable data table to calculate profits based on different prices and numbers sold.

In a two-variable data table, one set of input values must be in a column, the other in a row. The single formula is placed in the cell above the column values and to the left of the row values.

Exercise 20-6   SET UP INPUT VALUES AND THE FORMULA

1. Select cells E5:E15 and click the Copy button .

2. Select cells F18:P18 and right-click any cell in the range. Choose **Paste Special**.

⟷ REVIEW

To transpose a range, select the same number of cells as the copied range.

3. Choose **Values** in the **Paste** group. Click to select **Transpose** in the **Operation** group. Click **OK**. Press Esc to remove the marquee.

4. Format these values as Currency with two decimals.

5. Key **200** in cell E19 and **225** in cell E20.

6. Select cells E19:E20 and fill a series to **500** in cell E31.

7. In cell E18, key **=c11** to refer to the net profit formula.

Figure 20-7
Two-variable data table
MacCake.xlsx
Sheet1 sheet

	C	D	E	F	G	H	I	J	K	L	M	N	O	P
	E18		▼	fx	=C11									
10	$10,250.00		$25.50	$12,750.00	$10,250.00	$2,500.00								
11	$2,500.00		$26.50	$13,250.00	$10,250.00	$3,000.00								
12			$27.50	$13,750.00	$10,250.00	$3,500.00								
13			$28.50	$14,250.00	$10,250.00	$4,000.00								
14			$29.50	$14,750.00	$10,250.00	$4,500.00								
15			$30.50	$15,250.00	$10,250.00	$5,000.00								
16														
17														
18			$2,500.00	$20.50	$21.50	$22.50	$23.50	$24.50	$25.50	$26.50	$27.50	$28.50	$29.50	$30.50
19			200											
20			225											
21			250											
22			275											
23			300											
24			325											
25			350											
26			375											
27			400											
28			425											
29			450											
30			475											
31			500											
32														

Exercise 20-7   CREATE AND FORMAT THE DATA TABLE

1. Select cells E18:P31. The data table range includes the formula, the input row, the input column, and all the cells for the results.

2. Click the **Data** tab. Click the What-If Analysis button .

📝 NOTE

You can prepare more than one data table on a worksheet. A data table must be on the same sheet as the formulas.

3. Choose **Data Table**. Your table has quantities in a column and prices in a row.

4. In the **Row input cell** box, key **c3**. This is the cell address (the price) used indirectly in your formula. Its value will be replaced by the values in row 18.

5. In the **Column input cell** box, key **c8**. This cell represents the number sold, also used indirectly in the formula. Its value will be replaced by the values in column E in the table.

6. Click **OK**. The data table is calculated.

7. Format the profit values as Currency with two decimal places.

8. Select cells E18:P31. Build the same border layout as you did in the one-variable data table.

9. In cell E17, key **Units**. In cell F17, key **Prices**. Set both labels to use **Purple, Accent 4** as the font color, bold, and 16 point.

10. Select cells F17:P17 and click the Merge and Center button .

11. Select cells F18:P18. Click the Conditional Formatting button. Choose **Highlight Cells Rules** and **Equal To**. Build a format to show the accent fill and white text if the cell value is equal to cell C3.

12. Select cells E19:E31. Set the same conditional formatting if the cell value is the same as cell C8.

13. Select cells F19:P31. Set the same conditional formatting if the cell value is the same as cell E18.

NOTE

Some profit levels can be reached in more than one way.

Figure 20-8
Formatting the two-variable data table
MacCake.xlsx
Sheet1 sheet

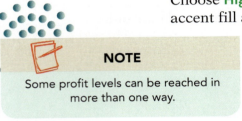

Units						Prices						
$2,500.00	$20.50	$21.50	$22.50	$23.50	$24.50	$25.50	$26.50	$27.50	$28.50	$29.50	$30.50	
200	$0.00	$200.00	$400.00	$600.00	$800.00	$1,000.00	$1,200.00	$1,400.00	$1,600.00	$1,800.00	$2,000.00	
225	$0.00	$225.00	$450.00	$675.00	$900.00	$1,125.00	$1,350.00	$1,575.00	$1,800.00	$2,025.00	$2,250.00	
250	$0.00	$250.00	$500.00	$750.00	$1,000.00	$1,250.00	$1,500.00	$1,750.00	$2,000.00	$2,250.00	$2,500.00	
275	$0.00	$275.00	$550.00	$825.00	$1,100.00	$1,375.00	$1,650.00	$1,925.00	$2,200.00	$2,475.00	$2,750.00	
300	$0.00	$300.00	$600.00	$900.00	$1,200.00	$1,500.00	$1,800.00	$2,100.00	$2,400.00	$2,700.00	$3,000.00	
325	$0.00	$325.00	$650.00	$975.00	$1,300.00	$1,625.00	$1,950.00	$2,275.00	$2,600.00	$2,925.00	$3,250.00	
350	$0.00	$350.00	$700.00	$1,050.00	$1,400.00	$1,750.00	$2,100.00	$2,450.00	$2,800.00	$3,150.00	$3,500.00	
375	$0.00	$375.00	$750.00	$1,125.00	$1,500.00	$1,875.00	$2,250.00	$2,625.00	$3,000.00	$3,375.00	$3,750.00	
400	$0.00	$400.00	$800.00	$1,200.00	$1,600.00	$2,000.00	$2,400.00	$2,800.00	$3,200.00	$3,600.00	$4,000.00	
425	$0.00	$425.00	$850.00	$1,275.00	$1,700.00	$2,125.00	$2,550.00	$2,975.00	$3,400.00	$3,825.00	$4,250.00	
450	$0.00	$450.00	$900.00	$1,350.00	$1,800.00	$2,250.00	$2,700.00	$3,150.00	$3,600.00	$4,050.00	$4,500.00	
475	$0.00	$475.00	$950.00	$1,425.00	$1,900.00	$2,375.00	$2,850.00	$3,325.00	$3,800.00	$4,275.00	$4,750.00	
500	$0.00	$500.00	$1,000.00	$1,500.00	$2,000.00	$2,500.00	$3,000.00	$3,500.00	$4,000.00	$4,500.00	$5,000.00	

TIP

A thin bottom border for each row can enhance readability of a large table.

14. In cell C3, key **22.5** and press Enter. All formulas recalculate and all pointers move.

15. Save the workbook as *[your initials]*20-7 in a folder for Lesson 20.

16. Close the workbook.

Analyzing Data in a PivotTable

A *PivotTable* is a summary report. It is a report in which you can sort, filter, and calculate large amounts of data. PivotTables are interactive, because you can quickly rearrange rows and columns to vary what is displayed and how it is summarized. The process of rearranging your data is known as "pivoting" the data.

TABLE 20-1 PivotTable Areas

Area	Description
Column Label	Area that shows labels for the values above the values.
Values	Fields from the list that are summarized. They are usually numeric.
Row Label	Area that shows labels for the values to the left of the values.
Report Filter	Fields by which the PivotTable is filtered.

Exercise 20-8   VIEW DATA IN A PIVOTTABLE

Most PivotTables are created on a separate worksheet in a workbook. In this exercise, you'll learn about PivotTables by examining an existing one. The data for a PivotTable must be a list or a table; it can also be an external list or database reference.

1. Open **SalinasSodas**. The **List** sheet tracks the date, the size, and the flavor sold for ice cream sodas in the Salinas shop.

2. Click the **Name Box** arrow and select **Database**. This is the range name assigned to the list.

3. Click the **PivotTable** tab. The PivotTable uses the list to show flavors and sizes for each date with related subtotals and a grand total.

4. Click anywhere within the PivotTable. The PivotTable Field List pane opens. PivotTable Tools include an Options tab and a Design tab.

Figure 20-9
PivotTable for
soda list
SalinasSodas.xlsx
PivotTable sheet

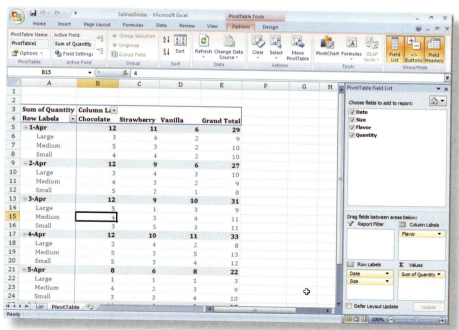

Exercise 20-9   PIVOT FIELDS IN THE PIVOTTABLE FIELD LIST PANE

To change the way the information is displayed in the PivotTable, you rearrange the fields in the PivotTable Field List pane. It takes some practice to know where in the pane a field should be placed. But, if you don't like the results, you can simply place them again in a different area.

You can place multiple fields as column or row labels. The order of the fields in the pane determines how the PivotTable is organized. Notice that Flavor is a column label.

1. In the **Choose fields to add to report** area, click to deselect **Flavor**. The field is deleted from the PivotTable, and only the Size field is displayed.

Figure 20-10
Field removed from a PivotTable
SalinasSodas.xlsx
PivotTable sheet

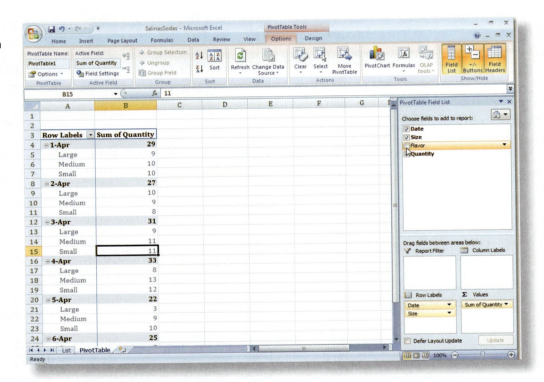

2. In the **Choose fields to add to report** area, click to deselect **Size**. Size was a row label. Now only the Date field is summarized, essentially showing a grand total per day.

3. In the **Choose fields to add to report** area, click to deselect **Date**. Now there are no details and one total for the shop.

4. In the **Choose fields to add to report** area, click to select **Date**. The default area for a value field is the Row Label area. The dates are now displayed as rows in the table.

5. In the **Choose fields to add to report** area, click to select **Size**. The Size field is also a row label. Numerical fields are automatically summed.

6. In the **Choose fields to add to report** area, click to select **Flavor**. It is placed as a row label and summed.

7. In the **Row Labels** area of the PivotTable Field List pane, click the arrow with **Flavor**. You can move the field within the area or move it to another area.

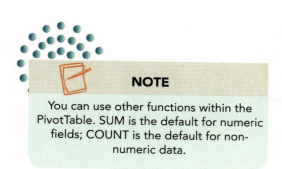

NOTE

You can use other functions within the PivotTable. SUM is the default for numeric fields; COUNT is the default for non-numeric data.

Figure 20-11
Moving a field to another area
SalinasSodas.xlsx
PivotTable sheet

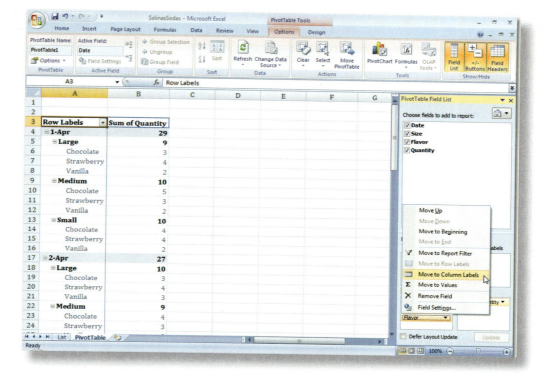

8. Choose **Move to Column Labels**. The table shows flavors as column fields now.

9. In the PivotTable, click the **Column Labels** arrow. You can sort and filter the labels and choose which are displayed.

10. Click to deselect **Strawberry**. Click **OK**. That flavor is no longer shown in the table.

11. Click the **Column Labels** arrow. Click to select **Strawberry**. Click **OK**.

12. Click the **Row Labels** arrow. There are two row labels, so there is a **Select field** box.

13. Click the arrow for the **Select field** box and choose **Size**.

14. Click to deselect **Large**. Click **OK**. That size is not displayed.

15. Display the large size again.

16. In the **Row Labels** area of the PivotTable Field List pane, click the arrow with **Size**. Choose **Move Up**. The size field is now the major label and the date is secondary.

17. Delete the **PivotTable** worksheet.

Creating a PivotTable

To create a PivotTable from a list range, you use the PivotTable button on the Insert tab. If your data is formatted as an Excel table, there is a Summarize with Pivot button on the Table Tools Design tab.

Exercise 20-10   CREATE A PIVOTTABLE

1. With **SalinasSodas** open, click any cell in the list range.

2. Click the **Insert** tab.

3. In the **Tables** group, click the PivotTable button. The Create PivotTable dialog box opens. Your list range is assumed as the **Table/Range** setting, and the new report will be placed on a new worksheet.

4. Click **OK**. A blank PivotTable layout and the PivotTable Field List pane are open on a new sheet.

Figure 20-12
Empty PivotTable layout
SalinasSodas.xlsx
Sheet1 sheet

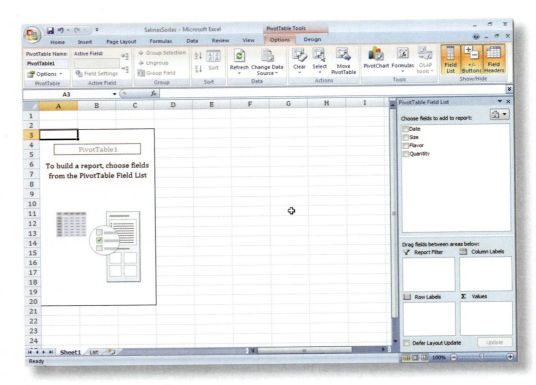

5. In the **Choose fields to add to report** area, click each field name to select it. The Quantity field is placed in the Values area and the others are set as Row Labels.

6. Point at **Size** in the **Row Labels** area. With the four-pointed arrow, drag **Size** to the **Column Labels** area. The dates and flavors remain as row labels.

7. Set the Zoom size to **75%** so that you can see the entire PivotTable.

Exercise 20-11 USE PIVOTTABLE TOOLS OPTIONS

PivotTables are formatted with a table style similar to those available for an Excel table. There is a PivotTable Styles gallery with several options.

1. Click anywhere in the PivotTable. Click the **PivotTable Tools Design** tab.

2. In the **PivotTable Styles** group, click the More button .

3. Choose **Pivot Style Light 9**. This style includes a vertical border for the row labels.

4. In the **PivotTable Style Options** group, click to deselect **Column Headers**. This removes the emphasis from the column headers, not the headers.

5. In the **PivotTable Style Options** group, click to deselect **Row Headers**. The row headers are the dates.

6. Click to select **Column Headers** and **Row Headers**.

7. Click the **PivotTable Tools Options** tab. The Show/Hide group at the right toggles off the Field List pane, the expand/collapse buttons, and the field headers.

8. Click the Field Headers button . The two field captions are removed from the table.

9. Click the Expand/Collapse button . The +/− symbols with the dates are hidden.

10. Click both buttons again to show the elements in the PivotTable.

Exercise 20-12 EDIT FIELD SETTINGS

1. Click cell A3. This is a value field calculating a **Sum**.

2. On the **PivotTable Tools Options** tab in the **Active Field** group, click the Field Settings button . The Value Field Settings dialog box opens.

3. In the **Custom Name** box, key **Quantity Sold**. Click **OK**. (See Figure 20-13 on the next page.)

Figure 20-13
Changing field
settings
SalinasSodas.xlsx
Sheet1 sheet

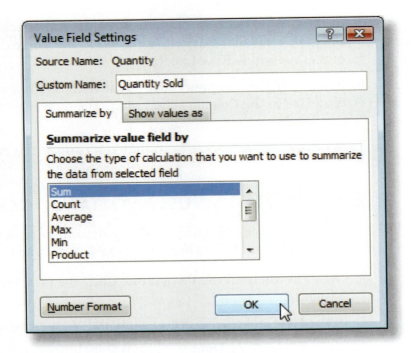

NOTE

You can change fonts in a PivotTable from the Home tab or the Mini toolbar.

4. Make cell A3 16-point Cambria. Widen the column.

5. On the **PivotTable Tools Options** tab, turn off **Field Headers**.

6. Click cell A5, the first date. Click the collapse button (-). The flavors are hidden for that date.

7. Right-click cell A6. Choose **Expand/Collapse** and then choose **Collapse Entire Field**. The date is the field and all are collapsed.

8. Right-click any date in column A. Choose **Expand/Collapse** and then choose **Expand Entire Field**. The flavors are shown in column A.

 9. While any date is selected, click the Field Settings button in the **Active Field** group on the **PivotTable Tools Options** tab.

10. Click the **Layout & Print** tab. The items are currently displayed in an outline form with labels in the same column. The date and flavor fields are in column A; the flavor field is indented to distinguish it.

11. Click to deselect **Display labels from the next field in the same column (compact form)**.

12. Click to deselect **Display subtotals at the top of each group**.

Figure 20-14
Layout & Print tab
in Field Settings
dialog box
**SalinasSodas.xlsx
Sheet1 sheet**

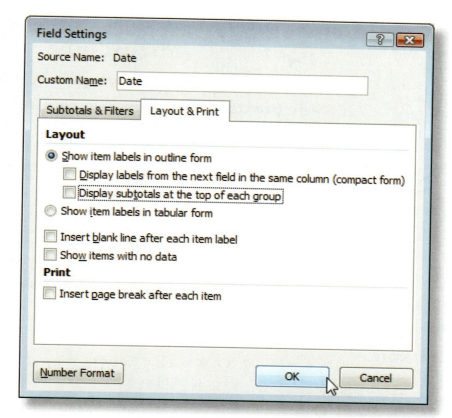

13. Click **OK**. The flavors are now in column B and subtotals are at the bottom of each group.

14. Click the Field Settings button in the **Active Field** group. Click the **Layout & Print** tab.

15. Click to select **Display labels from the next field in the same column (compact form)**. Click **OK**. The table occupies less space in this compact form.

16. Click cell A5 and click the Sort Newest to Oldest button. The dates are arranged with the most current date first.

17. Click in the **PivotTable Name** box in the **PivotTable** group. Key **FlavorSummary**. Press Enter. The table name is a property that appears in Formula AutoComplete and other structured reference lists.

18. Rename the sheet **PivotTable1**. Save the workbook as *[your initials]*20-12.

Using Multiple Calculations

In addition to counting and summing data, you can perform other statistical operations, such as AVERAGE, MIN, and MAX. You can also create calculated fields and formulas in a PivotTable.

Excel 2007

Exercise 20-13   USE MULTIPLE FIELDS AND FUNCTIONS

1. In *[your initials]*20-12, insert a new worksheet and name it **PivotTable2**.

2. Click the **Insert** tab. In the **Tables** group, click the PivotTable button. Since the insertion point is in a new sheet, no list range is assumed as the **Table/Range** setting.

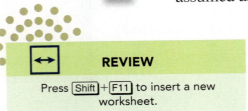

REVIEW

Press Shift + F11 to insert a new worksheet.

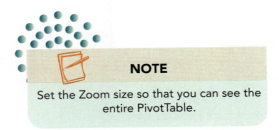

NOTE

Set the Zoom size so that you can see the entire PivotTable.

3. Click in the **Table/Range** box and press F3. Double-click **Database**.

4. Verify that **Existing worksheet** is selected. Click **OK**. A blank PivotTable layout and the PivotTable Field List pane are open.

5. In the **Choose fields to add to report** area, click to select **Flavor**. It is the first field added to the **Row Labels** area.

6. Click to select **Size** as the second item in the **Row Labels** area.

7. Click to select **Quantity**. It is placed as the **Values** field. The quantities are summed without regard to the dates.

8. Click **Sum of Quantity** in cell B1. Click the Field Settings button. Change the **Custom Name** to **Quantity by Flavor**. Click **OK**. Widen the column if necessary.

9. Point at **Quantity** in the **Choose fields to add to report** area. Drag the field name to the **Values** area again. There are now two value items, both showing the same sum. A column label (cell B1) has been added now that there are two columns of values.

Figure 20-15
Using two values
20-12.xlsx
PivotTable2 sheet

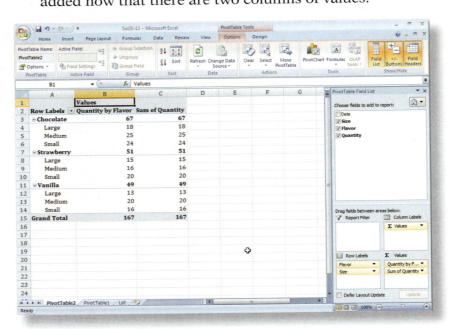

10. Select **Sum of Quantity** in cell C2. Click the Field Settings button .

11. Choose **Average** in the **Summarize value field by** list. Change the **Custom Name** to **Average Sold**. Click **Number Format**. Format the field as **Number** with no decimals. Click **OK** twice.

12. Click cell B2 and key **Flavor Totals**. This changes the field name.

13. Click the **PivotTable Tools Design** tab. In the **PivotTable Styles** group, click the More button [▾]. Choose **Pivot Style Light 22**.

Exercise 20-14   ADD A CALCULATED FIELD

You can add calculated fields to a PivotTable using the existing fields in the report. In your current PivotTable, for example, you can calculate a supplies cost for each soda flavor if the container costs 10 cents.

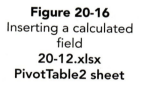

1. Select any cell in column C. Click the **PivotTable Tools Options** tab.

2. In the **Tools** group, click the Formulas button [ ] .

3. Choose **Calculated Field**. The Insert Calculated Field dialog box opens.

4. In the **Name** box, key **Cost**.

5. In the **Formula** box, delete the zero and the space after the = sign.

6. Double-click **Quantity** in the **Fields** list. It is inserted in the formula.

7. Key ***.1** after **Quantity** in the **Formula** box. The formula multiplies the quantity by ten cents ($0.10).

Figure 20-16
Inserting a calculated field
20-12.xlsx
PivotTable2 sheet

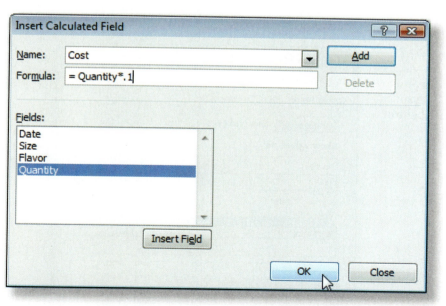

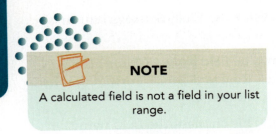

NOTE

A calculated field is not a field in your list range.

8. Click **OK**. The calculated field, **Sum of Cost**, is inserted as a new values item and it is summed.

9. Select cell D2 and click the Field Settings button 🔲 Field Settings. Change the **Custom Name** to **Container Cost**. Click **Number Format**. Use Currency with two decimal places. Click **OK**.

Exercise 20-15 SET HOW VALUES ARE SHOWN

Values can be shown as percentages instead of the actual numbers. This is a field setting and can be changed for each field as needed. One option shows a percentage of the total that each item represents. This PivotTable displays a total at the bottom for each column.

1. Click anywhere in the PivotTable. Click the **PivotTable Tools Options** tab.

🔲 Options ▾

2. Click the Options button 🔲 Options ▾ in the **PivotTable** group. The PivotTable Options dialog box includes many settings that are available in other dialog boxes.

3. Click the **Totals & Filters** tab. Click to deselect **Show grand totals for columns**. Click **OK**. The grand totals are hidden.

4. Point at **Cost** in the **Choose fields to add to report** group and drag it to the **Values** area. It is named **Sum of Cost**. This is your calculated field.

5. Right-click cell E2 and choose **Value Field Settings**.

6. Change **Custom Name** to **% of Container Cost**.

7. Click the **Show values as** tab. The values are currently shown in a normal fashion.

8. Click the arrow for **Show values as** and choose **% of column**.

Figure 20-17
Setting how values are shown
20-12.xlsx
PivotTable2 sheet

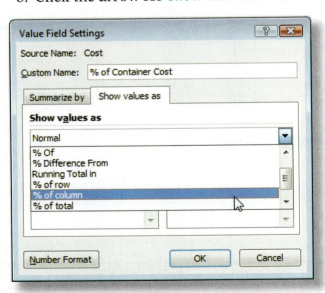

9. Click **OK**. Using large chocolate sodas as an example, the cost of the containers ($1.80) is 10.78% of the total cost of containers.

10. Click in the **PivotTable Name** box in the **PivotTable** group. Key **ContainerSummary**. Press [Enter].

Exercise 20-16   REFRESH DATA

A PivotTable is associated with the list, but it may not be automatically updated if you make changes to the original data.

1. Click the **List** tab. Select cells D4:D12, the quantities for April 1. Drag them to column F.

2. Click the **PivotTable2** tab. The values have not changed.

3. Click the **PivotTable Tools Options** tab. Click the Refresh button in the **Data** group. The values are updated.

4. Click the **List** tab. Move the cells back to column D.

5. Click the **PivotTable2** tab.

6. Click the Refresh button 🔄.

7. Click the Options button 🔘 Options ▾ in the **PivotTable** group.

8. Click the **Data** tab. There is an option here that refreshes the data each time the workbook is opened. Click **Cancel**.

9. Click cell A15. The PivotTable Field List pane is hidden.

10. Save the file as *[your initials]*20-16.

Creating a PivotChart

A PivotChart is associated with a PivotTable in the same workbook. You can create a PivotChart for an existing PivotTable, or you can create a PivotChart as you create a new PivotTable.

When you create a PivotChart for an existing PivotTable, the chart layout follows the table layout. Category fields in the chart (the x-axis in a column chart) are the rows in the table. The series (the values being plotted) are the columns in the table. After a PivotChart is created, you can edit it much like a regular chart.

Exercise 20-17   CREATE A PIVOTCHART FOR AN EXISTING PIVOTTABLE

1. Display the **PivotTable1** worksheet. Click anywhere in the PivotTable.

2. In the **Choose fields to add to report** area, click to deselect **Flavor**. Only sizes are summed in the table.

3. Click the **PivotTable Tools Options** tab.

4. Click the PivotChart button in the **Tools** group.

5. Choose **Clustered Column** and click **OK**. The PivotChart is placed as an object in the sheet. The PivotChart Tools include a Design and a Layout tab.

6. On the **Design** tab, click the Move Chart button. Choose **New sheet** and click **OK**. There is a PivotChart Filter pane and the PivotTable Field List pane.

Figure 20-18
Building a PivotChart
20-16.xlsx
Chart1 sheet

7. In the **Choose fields to add to report** area, click to select **Flavor**. It is added to the **Axis Fields** area. The chart shows sizes for each flavor on each day.

8. Drag **Flavor** in the **Axis Fields** area to the **Legend Fields** area. This makes for a busy chart.

9. Drag **Flavor** back to the **Axis Fields** area.

10. In the PivotChart Filter pane, click the arrow for **Flavor**. You can filter which flavors are shown in the chart.

11. Click to deselect **Strawberry** and **Vanilla**. Click **OK**.

Figure 20-19
Filtered data in the
PivotChart
**20-16.xlsx
Chart1 sheet**

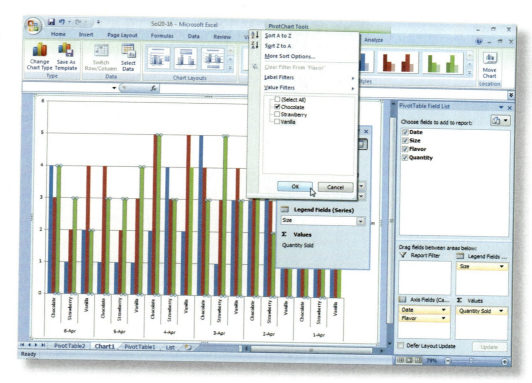

12. Close the PivotChart Filter pane. Close the PivotTable Field List pane.

13. Click the **PivotChart Tools Design** tab and choose **Style 42**.

14. Click the **PivotChart Tools Layout** tab. Use a centered, overlay title that reads **Chocolate Sodas by Size**. Position the title at the top left of the plot area.

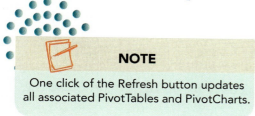

NOTE

One click of the Refresh button updates all associated PivotTables and PivotCharts.

15. Rename the sheet **PivotChart1**.

16. Click the **PivotTable1** worksheet tab. The table was updated as the chart was.

17. Click the **List** tab. Drag cells D4:D21 to column F. These are April 1 data.

18. Click the **PivotChart1** worksheet tab. Click the **PivotChart Tools Analyze** tab. Click the Refresh button. The chart and all PivotTables are updated. April 1 is missing.

19. Click the **PivotTable1** worksheet tab. April 1 does not show data.

20. Click the **List** tab. Move the cells back to column D.

21. Click the **PivotTable1** tab. Click the Refresh button.

22. Save the workbook as **[your initials]20-17**.

Exercise 20-18   CREATE A PIVOTCHART FROM THE LIST

If you create a PivotChart directly from the list, Excel creates an associated PivotTable for the chart.

1. Display the **List** sheet and click any cell in the list.

2. Click the **Insert** tab. Click the arrow on the PivotTable button 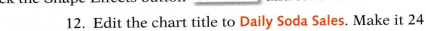.

3. Choose **PivotChart**. Verify that the correct range is selected and that a new worksheet will be used.

4. Click **OK**. A blank chart and its associated table, also blank, are inserted.

5. In the **Choose fields to add to report** area, click to select **Date**. It is placed in the **Axis Fields** area and as **Row Labels**.

6. Click to select **Quantity**. It is a **Values** field. Columns in the chart represent quantity without regard to flavor or size.

7. On the **PivotChart Tools Design** tab, click the Move Chart button 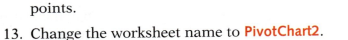. Choose **New sheet** and click **OK**.

8. Close the PivotChart Filter pane. Close the PivotTable Field List pane. Delete the legend.

9. Right-click any column and choose **Format Data Series**. On the **Fill** pane, click to select **Vary colors by point**. Click **Close**.

10. Click the **PivotChart Tools Format** tab. In the **Current Selection** group, click the arrow with the **Chart Elements** box and choose **Series "Total."**

11. Click the Shape Effects button ⌨ Shape Effects ▾ and set a Circle Bevel.

12. Edit the chart title to **Daily Soda Sales**. Make it 24 points.

13. Change the worksheet name to **PivotChart2**.

14. Save the workbook as *[your initials]*20-18. Close the workbook.

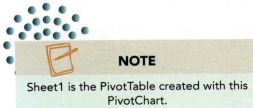

NOTE

Sheet1 is the PivotTable created with this PivotChart.

Using Online Help

PivotTables are a powerful tool with many variations. Use Help to learn more about general features of PivotTables and when you might use them.

USE HELP TO LEARN MORE ABOUT PIVOTTABLES

1. Look for Help topics about PivotTables.

2. Read the information. Close the windows.

Lesson 20 Summary

- A data table is a range of cells that displays the results of different values in one or more formulas. The data table range includes the formula(s) and input values.

- In a one-variable data table, input values are substituted for a single variable in the formula(s). Input values usually increase or decrease incrementally.

- A one-variable data table can calculate multiple formulas that refer to the same input cell.

- Data tables use an array formula. Input values in the table can be edited, but a result cell cannot be edited because it is part of the table array.

- A two-variable data table uses two sets of input values, one in a column and one in a row. It has its own layout rules.

- A PivotTable is an interactive table that allows row and column headings to be rearranged to show different layouts of the data.

- Fields used in a PivotTable can be added, removed, and rearranged.

- PivotTables can perform a number of statistical calculations, such as SUM and AVERAGE.

- Calculated fields and formulas can also be used to summarize fields in a PivotTable.

- A PivotChart displays the data from an associated PivotTable. The chart layout follows the table layout.

LESSON 20		Command Summary	
Feature	**Button**	**Task Path**	**Keyboard**
Calculated field	Formulas	PivotTable Tools, Options, Tools	
Data table	What-If Analysis	Data, Data Tools	
En dash	Symbol	Insert, Text	
Field headers	Field Headers	PivotTable Tools, Options, Show/Hide	
Field settings	Field Settings	PivotTable Tools, Options, Active Field	
PivotChart	PivotChart	PivotTable Tools, Options, Tools	
PivotTable	PivotTable	Insert, Tables	
Refresh PivotTable	Refresh	PivotTable Tools, Options, Data	
Show values as	Options	PivotTable Tools, Options, PivotTable	

Concepts Review

True/False Questions

Each of the following statements is either true or false. Indicate your choice by circling T or F.

T F   1. A data table and a PivotTable use the same data.

T F   2. A two-variable data table can calculate more than one formula.

T F   3. PivotTables summarize information from a list or database.

T F   4. You can delete any number of results from a data table.

T F   5. Each PivotTable in a workbook must have a separate list as its data source.

T F   6. In a one-variable data table, the input values can be in a row or a column.

T F   7. Multiple rows in a PivotTable are known as upper and lower rows.

T F   8. To delete a field from a PivotTable, click it and press Delete .

Short Answer Questions

Write the correct answer in the space provided.

1. On what command tab do the Table and PivotTable commands appear?

_____

2. What is an array formula?

_____

3. How can you display an en dash in a label?

_____

4. Describe how the input values must be arranged for a two-variable data table.

_____

5. Name the three areas generally used to prepare a PivotTable.

_____

6. How can you show a field twice in a PivotTable?

_____

7. How could you change the font for a field in a PivotTable?

_____

8. To use your own formula in a PivotTable, what button would you click?

_____

Critical Thinking

Answer these questions on a separate page. There are no right or wrong answers. Support your answers with examples from your own experience, if possible.

1. A PivotTable is a simple, yet sophisticated tool. What are pros and cons of allowing others to edit your PivotTable?

2. Identify and describe a situation in your personal life in which a one- or two-variable data table might be helpful. Use "dummy" data and develop your ideas in a worksheet.

Skills Review

Exercise 20-19

Create a one-variable data table. Create a two-variable data table.

1. Open **SummerCake** and save it as _[your initials]_20-19.

2. Select cells B4:C6, B8:C9, and B11:C13. Click the **Formulas** tab. Click the Create from Selection button . Use the left column to name these ranges.

3. Complete the formulas in cells C11:C13 as specified on the **Documentation** sheet.

REVIEW

Press F3 to display the Paste Name list as you build formulas.

4. Create a one-variable data table by following these steps:

   a. In cell B17, key **$15.95**. Key **$16.95** in cell B18. Fill down to $25.95 in cell B27.

   b. In cell C16, key a reference to the total profit cell.

   c. Select the range B16:C27.

REVIEW

The data table substitutes the values in column B for cell C5 in the formulas.

   d. Click the **Data** tab. Click the What-If Analysis button 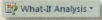 and choose **Data Table**.

   e. Key **c5** in the **Column input cell** box. Click **OK**.

   f. Format the results to match the prices.

5. Create data pointers by following these steps:

   a. Select cells C17:C27. Click the **Home** tab.

   b. Click the Conditional Formatting button . Build a condition to show solid black fill and white font if the cell value is the same as cell C13.

   c. Select cells B17:B27.

   d. Click the Conditional Formatting button. Apply the same format if the cell value is the same as cell C5.

   e. In cell B16, key **Prices** and make it bold and right-aligned.

   f. Add an outline border to the table with a vertical border between the columns.

6. Create a two-variable data table by following these steps:

   a. Copy the range B17:B27 to cells E17:E27.

   b. Key **1%** in cell F16. Key **2%** in cell G16. Fill to 5% in cell J16.

   c. Key **=c13** in cell E16.

   d. Select the range E16:J27.

   e. Click the **Data** tab. Click the What-If Analysis button  and choose **Data Table**.

   f. Key **c9** in the **Row input cell** box.

   g. Key **c5** in the **Column input cell** box. Click **OK**.

   h. Select cells E17:E27. Verify that the conditional formatting was copied.

   i. Select cells F16:J16. Show black fill and white font if the cell value equals the value in cell C9.

   j. Select cells F17:J27. Apply the same conditional formatting if the cell value equals the value in cell C13.

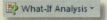

REVIEW

The data table substitutes the values in the column and the percents in the row for cells C5 and C9 in the formulas.

7. Format all dollar amounts as Currency (floating dollar sign) with no decimals. Fix the borders. Fit the worksheet to a single page.

8. Key a new price and multiplier (within the ranges shown).

9. Prepare and submit your work.

Exercise 20-20

Analyze data in a PivotTable. Create a PivotTable.

1. Open **EmpPivot** and save it as *[your initials]*20-20. Display the **PivotTable** sheet.

2. Analyze data in a PivotTable by following these steps:

   a. Click cell B4. Click the **PivotTable Tools Options** tab.

   b. In the **Active Field** group, click the Field Settings button .

   c. Change the **Custom Name** to **Female Employees**. Click **OK**.

d. Click cell C4 and repeat the steps to change the name to **Male Employees**.

e. Click cell A4. Click the Options button 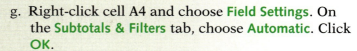 in the **PivotTable** group.

f. Click the **Display** tab. Click to deselect **Display field captions and filter drop-downs**. Click **OK**.

g. Right-click cell A4 and choose **Field Settings**. On the **Subtotals & Filters** tab, choose **Automatic**. Click **OK**.

h. Click the **PivotTable Tools Design** tab. Use **Pivot Style Medium 15**.

i. Click in the **PivotTable Name** box in the **PivotTable** group. Key **PTSummary** and press **Enter**.

3. Insert page breaks at cells A20, A28, and A35.

4. Set rows 1:3 as print titles. Horizontally center the sheet.

5. Create a PivotTable by following these steps:

a. Click the **EmpCounts** tab. Click in the list.

b. Click the **Insert** tab. Click the PivotTable button.

c. Verify that the range is A3:F35 and that a new worksheet will be used.

d. Click **OK**.

e. In the **Choose fields to add to report** group, click to select **State**.

f. Click to select **City**.

g. Click to select **Students**. It is placed as a **Values** field.

h. Click cell B3. Click the Field Settings button. Change the **Custom Name** to **Employees Who Are Students**.

i. Click cell A4. Click the **PivotTable Tools Options** tab. Click the Field Headers button to turn off field captions.

j. Click the Field Settings button. On the **Layout & Print** tab, click to deselect **Display subtotals at the top of each group**. Click **OK**.

k. Use **Pivot Style Medium 15**.

l. Click in the **PivotTable Name** box in the **PivotTable** group. Key **StudentCount** and press **Enter**.

6. Copy the label in cell A1 on the **PivotTable** sheet to this sheet. Center the sheet horizontally.

7. Prepare and submit your work.

Exercise 20-21

Use multiple calculations.

1. Open **EmpPivot** and save it as *[your initials]*20-21. Display the **PivotTable** sheet.

REVIEW

A page break inserts above the active cell. To repeat the command, press **Ctrl**+**Y**.

TIP

Check your work in Print Preview or in Page Layout View in a reduced zoom size.

2. Use a calculated field by following these steps:

   a. Click **Sum of Males** in cell C4.

   b. Click the arrow for **Sum of Males** in the **Values** area of the **PivotTable Field List** pane. Choose **Remove Field**.

   c. In the **Choose fields to add to report** area, click to select **Number of Employees**.

   d. Select cell B4. Click the Field Settings button . Change the name to **# of Females**.

   e. Change **Sum of Number of Employees** in cell C4 to **# of Employees**.

   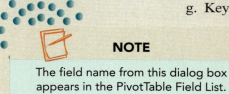

   f. Select any cell in column C. Click the Formulas button. Choose **Calculated Field**.

   g. Key **Percent Female** in the **Name** box.

   h. In the **Formula** box, delete the zero and the space after the = sign. Double-click **Females** in the **Fields** list. Key **/** for division. Double-click **Number of Employees**. Click **OK**.

> **NOTE**
>
> The field name from this dialog box appears in the PivotTable Field List.

   i. Select cell D4 and change the name to **% Female**. In the Value Field Settings dialog box, format the values as Percentage with 2 decimal places.

3. Use multiple calculations by following these steps:

   a. Select any cell in column C.

   b. Click the Formulas button. Choose **Calculated Field**. Key **Growth Rate** as the name.

> **NOTE**
>
> The decimal equivalent of 120% is 1.2.

   c. In the **Formula** box, delete the zero and the space after the =. Double-click **Number of Employees** in the **Fields** list. Key ***1.2** after **Number of Employees** in the formula box. Click **OK**.

   d. Select cell E4 and change the name to **20% Growth**. In the Value Field Settings dialog box, format the values as Number with 0 decimal places.

4. Set how values are shown by following these steps:

   a. In the **Choose fields to add to report** area, click to select **Students**.

   b. Select cell F4 and click the Field Settings button . Change the **Custom Name** to **Student % of Total**.

   c. Click **Show values as**. Click the arrow for **Show values as** and choose **% of total**. Click **OK**.

   d. Click cell B6. Click the Options button. Click the **Display** tab. Click to deselect **Display field captions and filter drop-downs**. Click **OK**.

   e. On the **PivotTable Tools Options** tab, name the table **PTData**.

5. Edit the label in cell A1 to **Miscellaneous Part-Time Employee Data**.

6. Use **Pivot Style Light 22**. Fit the data to one portrait page.

7. Prepare and submit your work.

Exercise 20-22

Create a PivotChart.

1. Open **CorpAccts** and save it as *[your initials]*20-22.

2. Create a PivotChart by following these steps:

   a. Click anywhere in the date column and sort the records in A to Z order.

   b. Click the **Insert** tab. Click the arrow on the PivotTable button. Choose **PivotChart**.

   c. Verify that the correct range and a new worksheet will be used. Click **OK**.

   d. In the **Choose fields to add to report** area, click to select **Date**.

   e. Click to select **Invoice Amount**. Both fields are added to the **Axis Fields** area.

   f. Point at **Invoice Amount** in the **Axis Fields** area. With the four-pointed arrow, drag it to the **Values** area.

   g. Right-click cell B1 and choose **Value Field Settings**. Change **Custom Name** to **Invoice Total**. Change the **Summarize value field by** to **Sum**. Click **OK**.

3. Format a PivotChart by following these steps:

   a. Click to select the chart and move it to its own sheet.

   b. Close the PivotChart panes.

   c. On the **PivotChart Tools Design** tab, choose **Style 41**.

   d. Right-click a value on the vertical axis and format it to show Currency with no decimals.

NOTE

The PivotTable for the chart is Sheet1.

   e. Delete the legend.

   f. Edit the chart title to **Invoice Total by Day**. Make it 24 points.

4. Change the worksheet name to **InvoiceChart**.

5. Prepare and submit your work.

Lesson Applications

Exercise 20-23

Create one- and two-variable data tables.

1. Open **AdjGrowth** and save it as *[your initials]*20-23.

2. In cell B20, key a reference to the total dollar sales formula for next year. Make it bold.

3. In cell A21, key **1.00%**. In cell A22, key **1.25%**. Fill a range down to **2.00%** in cell A25. Format the percentages as bold. These percentages are possible overall growth rates.

4. Create a data table here that shows sales if the overall growth rate is changed to the percents shown in column A. Format the results.

5. Add conditional formatting in column A to show the percent differently when it matches the percent shown on the worksheet. Do the same for the values in column B.

6. In cell E20, key **1.00%**. In cell F20, key **1.25%**. Fill a range across to **2.00%** in column I. Format the percentages as bold.

7. In cell D21, key **1**. In cell D22, key **1.15**. Fill a range down to **1.9** in row 27. Format these values as a number with two decimals and bold.

8. In cell D20, key a reference to the total dollar sales forecast for KowOwows for next year.

9. Create a data table that shows KowOwow sales if the overall growth rate and the adjusted growth factor are varied. Format the results and add appropriate conditional formatting. Make all columns the same width with attention to the data and the data table.

10. Format both data tables in an attractive manner. Adjust the margins so that the sheet fits on a single page.

11. Prepare and submit your work.

Exercise 20-24

Analyze a PivotTable. Create a PivotChart.

1. Open **NoveltiesQtr2** and save it as *[your initials]*20-24. Display the **PivotTable** worksheet.

REVIEW

If you edit the list, refresh the data in the PivotTable.

2. Analyze the list and the PivotTable. Find and correct the error in the PivotTable to remove the blank column and row.

3. Remove the **Sum of Total** field and replace it with the **April** field.

4. Change the name **Sum of April** to **Total April Sales**. Format the values to show a comma and no decimal places.

5. Filter the data to show only Washington values.

6. Hide the field captions and do not show any row totals. Name the table with a relevant name.

7. Set outline and vertical borders for the data. Set column widths.

8. Create a Clustered Cylinder PivotChart for the data.

9. Choose a style for the chart. Edit the title to show **Washington April Sales**. Choose a font size. Make other formatting decisions to enhance your chart.

10. Prepare and submit your work.

Exercise 20-25

Create a two-variable data table.

1. In a new workbook, key **5%** in cell C5 and **10%** in cell D5. Fill this range to **25%** in cell G5.

2. In cell B6, key **$5.00**. In cell B7, key **$10.00**. Fill this range to $100.00 in cell B25.

3. Key the following information at the top of the sheet.

	A	B
1	Tip Calculator	
2	Sale Amount	$100
3	Tip Percentage	15%
4	Tip	

4. In cell B4, key a formula that multiplies the amount by the percentage to determine the dollar amount of the tip.

5. Key a reference to the formula in cell B5 and build the data table.

6. Format your information in a professional, easy-to-understand style.

7. Save the workbook as *[your initials]*20-25.

8. Prepare and submit your work.

Exercise 20-26 ◆ Challenge Yourself

Create a PivotTable with multiple fields.

1. Open **ConsolidatedSandwiches** and save it as *[your initials]*20-26.

2. Create a static data consolidation on the **4thQuarter** sheet, summing the values.

3. Build a PivotTable for the **4thQuarter** sheet. Show only the flavors as a Row Label.

4. Create a calculated field named **ProjWk1** that multiplies the Week 1 value by **1.5** to calculate a 150% increase. Do the same for each of the weeks.

5. Edit the names for the calculated fields to show **Projected Wk 1** and so on.

6. Add a main label for the PivotTable. Choose a style or design your own layout. Name the PivotTable.

7. Prepare and submit your work.

On Your Own

In these exercises you work on your own, as you would in a real-life business environment. Use the skills you've learned to accomplish the task—and be creative.

Exercise 20-27

Key basic labels for an unpaid credit card balance amount, an interest rate, and a monthly finance charge (formula cell). You can use a straightforward determination of a finance charge by multiplying the balance due by the rate divided by 12. After you key the basic data and formula, build a two-variable data table that calculates finance charges using several interest rates and balances due from $100 to $1,000 in $50 increments. Format the sheet attractively. Save the workbook as *[your initials]*20-27. Prepare and submit your work.

Exercise 20-28

Create a list of high and low temperatures for the past 30 days in your city. Use an Internet site or develop your own data based on your research and knowledge. Create a PivotTable for your list on a separate sheet to show high temperatures and the number of days that reached that temperature. Format the PivotTable attractively. Create a second PivotTable that shows the low temperatures. Save the workbook as *[your initials]*20-28. Prepare and submit your work.

Exercise 20-29

In a new workbook, key **Add This Number** in cell A1. Key **To This Number** in cell A2. In cell A3, key **To Reach This Sum**. Key sample values and the appropriate formula (cell B3) in column B. Next build an addition table to show the results for addition for values from 1–25. Format the sheet and the table so that it is easy to find the answer. Fit it to one landscape page. Save the workbook as *[your initials]*20-29. Prepare and submit your work.

Unit 6 Applications

Unit Application 6-1

Import a text file. Create an advanced filter. Use subtotals.

REVIEW

Change the Files of type setting to open a text file. When you open a text file, the Text Import Wizard starts.

1. Open **Animals.txt**, a delimited text file, in Excel, but do not import the field that follows the price field. (The first item is Dog001.) After importing, fix obvious errors.

2. Insert rows and the following labels.

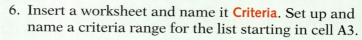

	A	B	C	D	E	F
1	Stuffed Animal Promotion					
2	Current Value of Inventory					
3	Catalog No.	Name	Group	Price	Quantity	Value

3. In column F, use a formula to calculate the dollar value of the inventory.

4. Name the list range. Sort it by value in descending order.

5. Make your own format decisions. Horizontally center the sheet.

REVIEW

Copy the labels from the list for the criteria and output ranges.

6. Insert a worksheet and name it **Criteria**. Set up and name a criteria range for the list starting in cell A3.

7. In the **Animals** sheet, create and name an output range starting in cell I3.

8. Create an advanced filter to find records in which the **Value** is greater than $3,000 and the **Group** is D. Show the results in the output range. Cut and paste the results with labels to cell A10 in the **Criteria** worksheet.

REVIEW

Use the Sort dialog box for a multiple sort.

9. Copy the **Animals** sheet and name the copy **Subtotals**. Sort the **Subtotals** sheet by group in ascending order and by value in descending order. Use subtotals to show the inventory value of each group. Format the sheet to be attractive and easy to read.

10. Save the workbook as *[your initials]***u6-1** in a Unit 6 folder.

11. Prepare and submit your work.

Unit Application 6-2

Query an Access database. Create a PivotTable.

1. In cell A1 in a new workbook, create a Microsoft Query for the MS Access file **Carolina.accdb**. Use all columns from **tblStuffedAnimals** except **Picture**. Do not use a filter, but sort by product name in ascending order. Name the sheet **Animals**.

NOTE

Excel automatically names the imported data "Table_ Query_from_MS_Access_ Database." You can replace it with a shorter name if you prefer.

TIP

There is a button on the Table Tools Design tab that creates a PivotTable.

2. Use **Table Style Medium 1**. Insert spaces in the labels in the header row. Center the data.

3. Create a PivotTable for the table in a new worksheet. Use **ProductGroup** as a row label and **ProductID** and **Price** as value fields. Show an average for the **Price** and count the **ProductID**. Format the price data as Currency. Change the names to appropriate labels for the data.

4. In cell A1, key **Average Price per Group**. Make it 16 point. Choose a style for the PivotTable. Do not show the field headers (captions). Center the data.

5. Rename the sheet as **PivotTable**. Delete the unused sheets.

6. Save the workbook as *[your initials]*u6-2.

7. Prepare and submit your work.

Unit Application 6-3

Create two-variable data tables.

TIP

You can apply additional formatting to a PivotTable from the Home tab.

TIP

Group the sheets for some formatting, but you cannot apply conditional formatting to grouped sheets.

1. Open **MathTables** and save it as *[your initials]*u6-3.

2. In cells F3:F5 on each sheet, key sample values and the formula. Use a value from the top row and a value from the column.

3. Build two-variable data tables on each sheet. Decide how many decimal positions to show, if any.

4. Add borders and conditional formatting pointers to the tables. Center the sheets. Make the formula cell invisible in the data table.

5. Make a formula copy of each sheet.

6. Prepare and submit your work.

Unit Application 6-4 ◆ Using the Internet

Import data from the Web.

Find the current online class schedule of your community college or any university. Use a Web query or other method to import at least 25 rows of the schedule into a new workbook.

In the worksheet, clean up the list to show basic information about the schedule (you decide). If credit hours are not imported, add a column and key credit hour values. Create a constant for the tuition rate per credit hour. Then show total tuition per course in another column.

Format your schedule attractively. Save the workbook as *[your initials]*u6-4. Prepare and submit your work.

unit 7

EXPLORING MACROS, TEMPLATES, AND WORKGROUPS

Working with Macros

OBJECTIVES

After completing this lesson, you will be able to:

1. Run and view a macro.

2. Edit and print a macro.

3. Record a macro.

4. Assign a macro to a button.

5. Create a macro workbook.

MCAS OBJECTIVES

In this lesson:
XL07 1.3
XL07 1.4
XL07 4.4.3
XL07 5.1
XL07 5.4.2

Estimated Time: 1½ hours

A *macro* is a sequence of commands and/or keystrokes that automate a task. A macro can perform data entry, formatting, command execution, and dialog box selections. For example, you can create a macro that keys your company name in a specific font and size. Then you run the macro whenever you need to enter the company name in a worksheet.

Excel macros are recorded in the Visual Basic for Applications programming language (VBA), but you don't need to know that language to create and use macros.

Running and Viewing a Macro

Macros are stored in macro-enabled workbooks. These workbooks have an **xlsm** filename extension to distinguish them from macro-free workbooks. A workbook with a macro must be open for its macro(s) to be used. Macros are "run" or executed from the View tab or the Developer tab. The Developer tab is not shown in the Ribbon as a default.

Macros are common places for hackers to hide viruses and similar destructive programs. Because of this possibility, the Trust Center enables you to choose how a macro-enabled workbook is recognized and opened.

Exercise 21-1   RUN A MACRO

1. Click the Microsoft Office Button and choose **Excel Options**.

2. Click **Trust Center** to open the pane. Click **Trust Center Settings**. Click **Macro Settings**.

3. Click to select **Disable all macros with notification** if it is not selected. With this setting, you will see the security message panel if a workbook contains a macro.

4. Click **OK** to close the Trust Center. Click **OK** to close the Excel Options dialog box.

5. Open **ORSales**. This workbook contains macros, and the security message panel notes that. Note that the insertion point is in cell B5.

6. Click **Options**. Choose **Enable this content**. Click **OK**.

7. Click the **View** tab. Click the Macros button. The Macro dialog box opens. This workbook has one macro named CompanyName. It is selected and its name is entered in the Macro name box.

Figure 21-1
Macro dialog box
ORSales.xlsm
January sheet

8. Click **Run**. The dialog box closes, and the macro moves the insertion point to cell A1, inserts two labels, and formats them.

Exercise 21-2 OPEN THE VISUAL BASIC EDITOR

You use the *Visual Basic Editor* to view, edit, or create a macro. The Visual Basic Editor is made up of several windows. The code that makes up the macro is displayed in the *Code window*. *Code* consists of programming lines written in the Visual Basic language. Some lines are preceded by an apostrophe and shown in green. These are comments and explanations.

The macro in this workbook is a *subroutine macro*, which is a command sequence that can be run from the worksheet or from another macro. Subroutine macros start with the word *Sub* followed by the macro name and a set of parentheses. Subroutine macros end with *End Sub*.

1. Click the **View** tab. Click the Macros button.

2. Choose **Edit**. The Visual Basic Editor starts. The Code window is the large window on the right in Figure 21-2. The smaller windows on the left are the Project Explorer and the Properties window. Look in the Project Explorer window for the **Modules** folder. Macros are stored in modules in the workbook. This macro is in **Module1**.

NOTE

If you do not see the Project Explorer window, choose **View, Project Explorer**. If the Properties window is not displayed, choose **View, Properties Window**. If you do not see the macro code, choose **View, Code**.

Figure 21-2
Visual Basic Editor
ORSales.xlsm
January sheet

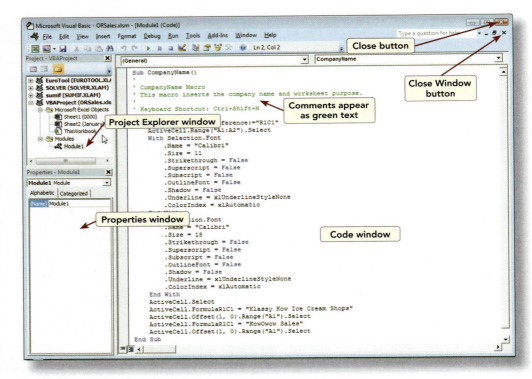

3. Look in the Code window. The macro begins with **Sub** followed by the macro name, **CompanyName**, and a set of parentheses (). The next six lines are green and begin with an apostrophe. These are comment lines that describe the macro and show the shortcut, and they include blank lines for ease in reading the code.

4. Look for the comment indicating the keyboard shortcut. It is Ctrl + Shift + N.

5. Scroll to the bottom of the macro. Look for **End Sub**. This marks the end of the macro.

6. Click the Close button in the Visual Basic title bar. The Visual Basic Editor closes, and your worksheet appears.

NOTE

The Close Window button x closes the macro but leaves the Visual Basic Editor open.

Editing and Printing a Macro

Even if you have no knowledge of Visual Basic programming, you will probably be able to determine how to make simple edits to text within macros and to formatting parameters in macros.

For example, the code .Name="Calibri" formats a cell to use that font. To change the font to Cambria, you simply type "Cambria" in place of "Calibri" in that line in the macro. When editing a macro, you must be careful not to change spaces and punctuation, because those elements are part of the code.

Exercise 21-3 EDIT A MACRO

While you are editing code in the Visual Basic Editor, a line might display in red. This signifies an error in the code. If you cannot determine what the error is, press Ctrl + Z to undo and try again.

TIP

The line .Size=11 in the macro shows the default font size.

1. Press Alt + F11, the keyboard shortcut to open the Visual Basic Editor.

2. In the Code window, locate the line **.Size=18**. This line sets the font size for text that follows.

3. Change **18** to **22**. The next time you run this macro, the labels will use a larger font size.

4. Locate the line that includes the text **"Klassy Kow Ice Cream Shops"** near the end of the macro.

NOTE

Text that should be displayed when the macro is run is enclosed in quotation marks.

5. Position the insertion point after the word **Shops**, inside the quotation marks.

6. Key a comma, press Spacebar, and key **Inc.** inside the quotation marks. The label will include "Inc." the next time the macro is run.

7. Locate the line that includes **"KowOwow Sales."**

NOTE

Changes to your macro code are saved in the Visual Basic Editor. However, you must save the workbook containing the macro to permanently save the changes.

8. Delete **KowOwow** and key **Kowabunga**. The label will display "Kowabunga Sales" the next time the macro is run. (See Figure 21-3 on the next page.)

Figure 21-3
Editing a macro
ORSales.xlsm
January sheet

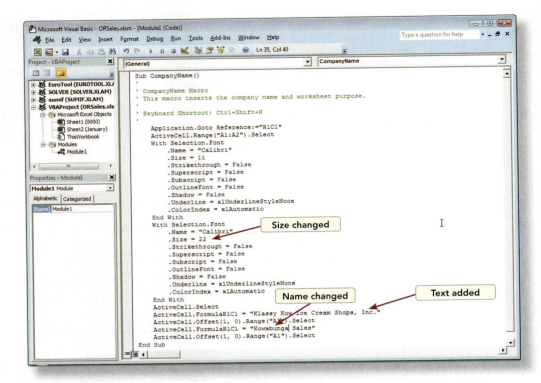

9. Click the Close button on the Visual Basic title bar.

Exercise 21-4   USE A MACRO KEYBOARD SHORTCUT

If a macro is recorded with a keyboard shortcut, you can use keystrokes to run the macro. To test your edited macro, you should reset the worksheet to the way it was when you first opened it.

1. Select cells A1:A2. Click the **Home** tab.

2. In the **Editing** group, click the Clear button 🖉▾. Choose **Clear All**. This deletes the contents and the formatting.

3. Select cell B5. This is the location of the insertion point when you opened the workbook.

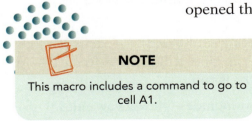

NOTE

This macro includes a command to go to cell A1.

4. Press Ctrl+Shift+N. The macro inserts the labels in the new font size with "Inc." added as well as "Kowabunga."

5. Select cells A1:A2. Click the Clear button 🖉▾. Choose **Clear All**.

6. Select cell B5. The worksheet is reset.

7. Press Alt+F11.

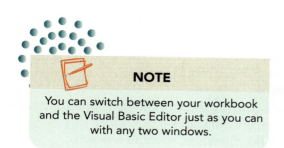

NOTE

You can switch between your workbook and the Visual Basic Editor just as you can with any two windows.

8. In the Code window, locate the second line with **.Name="Calibri"**.

9. Change **Calibri** to **Cambria**.

10. Change the line **.Size=22** back to a size of 18.

11. Click the workbook name on the Windows taskbar.

12. Press Ctrl + Shift + N.

Exercise 21-5 ADD A COMMENT AND PRINT A MACRO

1. Click **Microsoft Visual Basic** on the Windows taskbar.

2. Scroll to the top of the Code window. Position the insertion point to the right of the first apostrophe under **Sub CompanyName()**.

3. Press Spacebar and key *[your first and last name]*. Press ↓. Your name is shown in green, indicating that it has been added as a comment.

4. Choose **File**, **Print**. The Print – VBAProject dialog box opens.

5. In the **Range** group, choose **Current Module** if it is not already selected.

6. In the **Print What** group, choose **Code** if it is not already selected.

Figure 21-4
Printing a macro
ORSales.xlsm
January sheet

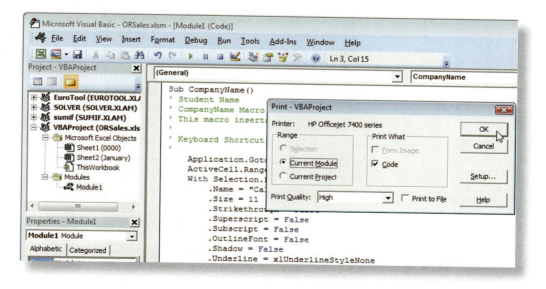

7. Click **OK**. The macro is printed.

8. Switch to your workbook.

Recording a Macro

To record a macro, you name it and then perform each step and command as if you were actually doing the task yourself. Excel converts all your keystrokes and selections into Visual Basic code.

Macros are stored in workbooks. As long as the workbook with a macro is open, you can use that macro in any open workbook.

Follow these guidelines to help you decide where to store a macro:

- Special-purpose macros that will be used with only one workbook should be stored in that workbook. Templates might have special-purpose macros.

- General-purpose macros used on a regular basis can be stored in a workbook that contains only macros. Anytime this workbook is open, any other open workbook can use its macros.

- General-purpose macros that should be available at all times can be stored in the Personal Macro Workbook. Excel creates a Personal Macro Workbook, named **Personal.xlsb**, in the XLStart folder if you choose this option while creating a macro. The Personal Macro Workbook opens as a hidden workbook each time you start Excel.

> **NOTE**
>
> Explore Help topics about the Personal Macro Workbook if you have your own computer at work or home.

Exercise 21-6   RECORD A MACRO WITH ABSOLUTE REFERENCES

Macro names must begin with a letter and cannot contain spaces or special characters. If you use a keyboard shortcut, you should enter an uppercase letter in the Record Macro dialog box so that you do not override existing Windows or Excel shortcuts. For example, if you enter "s" in the Record Macro dialog box as the shortcut key, you override the Save command shortcut, Ctrl + S.

A macro can be recorded with relative or absolute references. When Relative Reference is on, the macro carries out its actions relative to the active cell when the macro is run. It does not record specific cell addresses but records positioning commands. If Relative Reference is off when you record a macro, cell addresses are recorded as part of the macro. Pointer movement is not recorded.

> **NOTE**
>
> All macro keyboard shortcuts include Ctrl. When you use an uppercase letter in the Record Macro dialog box, the shortcut is Ctrl + Shift + any letter of the alphabet.

1. Clear all from cells A1:A2. Click cell B5.

2. Click the **View** tab. Click the arrow on the Macros button .

3. Check that **Use Relative References** is not selected; it should be off for this exercise. (The button appears outlined if it is on/selected.)

4. Click the arrow on the Macros button . Choose **Record Macro**. The Record Macro dialog box opens.

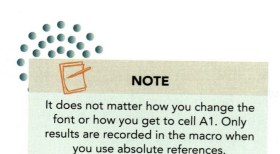

NOTE

It does not matter how you change the font or how you get to cell A1. Only results are recorded in the macro when you use absolute references.

5. In the **Macro name** box, key **CompanyInfo**.

6. Position the insertion point in the **Shortcut key** box. Press [Shift] and key **k**. The complete shortcut is shown.

7. Make sure that **Store macro in** shows **This Workbook**.

8. In the **Description** box, delete any existing information and key **Displays company name and date.**

Figure 21-5
Record Macro
dialog box
ORSales.xlsm
January sheet

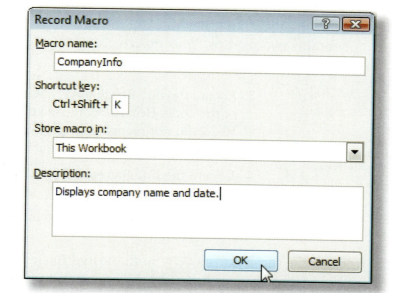

9. Click **OK**. The Stop Recording button ▫ appears at the left of the status bar (next to the mode indicator). You will click this button to stop recording.

Figure 21-6
Stop Recording
button in status bar
ORSales.xlsm
January sheet

20	
21	
22	
23	
24	

◄◄ ◄ ► ►◄ **January**
Ready ▫

10. Press [↑] four times and [←] once to position the insertion point in cell A1. The cell address A1 is recorded.

11. Format the cell for 18-point Cambria. The font setting is recorded in the macro.

12. Key **Klassy Kow Oregon Shops** and press [Enter]. The insertion point is in cell A2.

13. Format the cell for 14-point Cambria.

14. Type **=today()** and press [Enter]. The insertion point is in cell A3.

15. Press [↑] to reposition the pointer in cell A2. Press [Ctrl]+[1].

16. Click the Number tab and choose **Custom** in the list. Enter format codes to display the date as the month spelled out and four digits for the year (no day). Close the dialog box.

17. Click the Stop Recording button 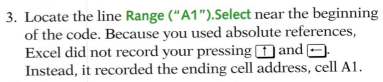 on the status bar. Your macro is complete.

18. Clear all from cells A1:A2 and click cell B12.

19. Press [Ctrl]+[Shift]+[K]. The macro carries out its actions in cells A1:A2, because the cell addresses were absolute. It did not matter where the insertion point was located when you executed the macro.

Exercise 21-7   DELETE A MACRO

1. Click the **View** tab. Click the Macros button 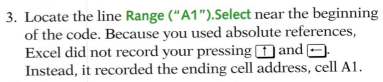. The workbook now contains two macros. Your macro, **CompanyInfo**, is selected.

2. Click **Edit**. The Visual Basic Editor starts.

> **NOTE**
>
> It is possible that your macro is in Module2. Open that module from the Project Explorer window if necessary.

3. Locate the line **Range ("A1").Select** near the beginning of the code. Because you used absolute references, Excel did not record your pressing [↑] and [←]. Instead, it recorded the ending cell address, cell A1.

4. Locate the line **Range("A2").Select** in the middle of the code.

5. Locate the third reference to cell A2 near the end of the macro, where you formatted the date.

6. Click the Close button [X] on the Visual Basic Editor title bar.

7. Clear all from cells A1:A2. Select cell B5.

8. Press [Alt]+[F8]. This is the keyboard shortcut to open the Macro dialog box.

9. Click to select **CompanyInfo** and click **Delete**.

10. Choose **Yes** to delete your macro.

Exercise 21-8   USE RELATIVE REFERENCES IN A MACRO

If Relative Reference is on as you record a macro, the macro records each pointer movement command. Then you need to note where the insertion point is located when you run the macro.

> **NOTE**
>
> Make sure the insertion point is in cell B5.

1. Click the **View** tab. Click the arrow on the Macros button 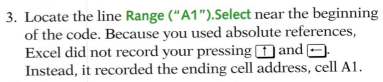.

2. Click to select **Use Relative References**; it should be on. (The button appears outlined.)

3. Click the Record Macro button 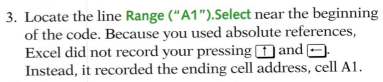 on the status bar. The Record Macro dialog box opens. This button toggles between Record Macro and Stop Recording.

4. In the **Macro name** box, key **CompanyInfo**.

5. Position the insertion point in the **Shortcut key** box. Press [Shift] and key **k**.

6. Make sure the **Store macro in** option is **This Workbook**.

7. In the **Description** box, key **Displays company name and date.**

8. Click **OK**. The Record Macro dialog box closes.

9. Press ⬆ four times. Press ⬅. These pointer movement commands are recorded in the macro.

10. Format the cell as 18-point Cambria.

11. Key **Klassy Kow Oregon Shops** and press ⟨Enter⟩.

12. Format cell A2 as 14-point Cambria, key **=today()** and press ⟨Ctrl⟩+⟨Enter⟩.

> **NOTE**
>
> ⟨Ctrl⟩+⟨Enter⟩ keeps the insertion point in the active cell.

13. Format the date to show the month spelled out and four digits for the year.

14. Click the Stop Recording button  on the status bar.

15. Clear cells A1:A2.

16. Select cell C15 and press ⟨Ctrl⟩+⟨Shift⟩+⟨K⟩. The macro carries out its tasks relative to cell C15. The labels are inserted four rows up and one column to the left.

17. Clear all from cells B11:B12 and select cell B5.

18. Press ⟨Ctrl⟩+⟨Shift⟩+⟨K⟩. The macro works properly.

Exercise 21-9 REVIEW MACRO CODE

1. Press ⟨Alt⟩+⟨F11⟩.

2. In the Project window, find the **Modules** folder and expand it. You can determine if the macros are in one module or in separate modules.

3. If the Code window does not show the **CompanyInfo** macro, double-click **Module2** in the Project window.

4. In the Code window, locate the line **ActiveCell. Offset(4, -1).Range("A1").Select**. This code is a command to go up four rows (–4) and to the left one column (–1) ending in cell A1. When you use relative references, Excel records these positioning commands.

> **NOTE**
>
> A module can contain multiple macros. Macros within the same module are separated by a horizontal line.

5. Position the insertion point to the right of the first apostrophe under **Sub CompanyInfo().**

6. Press ⟨Spacebar⟩ and key *[your first and last name]*. Press ⬇.

7. Click the Close button  on the Visual Basic Editor title bar to close the editor.

8. Clear all from cells A1:A2.

9. Save the file as *[your initials]*21-9 in a new folder for Lesson 21.

Assigning a Macro to a Button

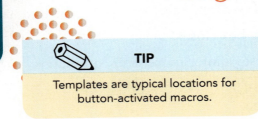

You can assign a macro to a *button* so that the macro runs when you click the button on the worksheet. A button is a *form control*, an object on the sheet that lets the user direct tasks or activities. You can use various types of buttons and other objects to run macros, display information, make choices, or perform a specific action.

Exercise 21-10 DISPLAY THE DEVELOPER TAB

The Button tool is on the Developer tab. This is a command tab with specialized tasks; it is not shown by default in the Ribbon. In addition to controls, it includes the Code group for working with macros.

1. Click the Microsoft Office Button and choose **Excel Options**.

2. On the **Popular** pane, click to select **Show Developer tab in the Ribbon**. Click **OK**.

3. Click the **Developer** tab.

Exercise 21-11 DRAW A BUTTON

Buttons are objects, like shapes. When you edit a button, it displays diagonal lines or a dotted pattern around its edges. The diagonal lines mean you can edit the text. The dotted pattern allows you to edit other button properties.

1. In the **Controls** group, click the Insert button .

2. Position the pointer over the first icon in the Form Controls category. The ScreenTip indicates that this is the Button tool 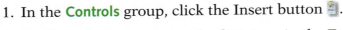.

Figure 21-7
Inserting a button form control
21-9.xlsm
January sheet

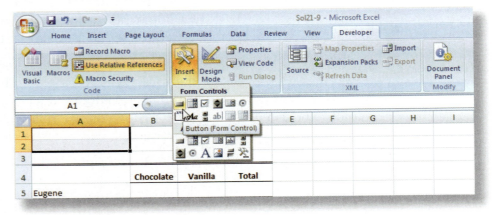

3. Click the Button tool. The pointer turns into a thin crosshair.

4. Draw a shape from cell E1 to F2. The Assign Macro dialog box opens with the names of macros in your workbook.

Figure 21-8
Assign Macro
dialog box
21-9.xlsm
January sheet

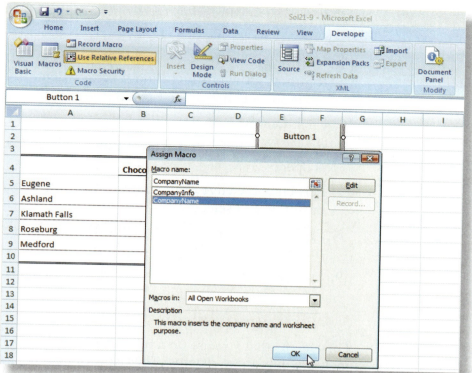

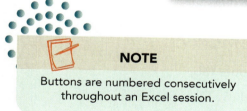

NOTE

Buttons are numbered consecutively throughout an Excel session.

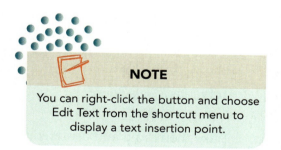

NOTE

You can right-click the button and choose Edit Text from the shortcut menu to display a text insertion point.

5. Select **CompanyName** and click **OK**. The button shows default text, "Button1."

6. Right-click the border of the button and choose **Format Control**. The Format Control dialog box opens, and the button shows a dotted pattern boundary.

7. On the **Font** tab, choose 10-point Calibri bold. Click **OK**. The button text changes to bold.

8. Click inside the button to display a text insertion point. The boundary changes to diagonal lines.

9. Delete the default text and key **Display Name**.

10. Point at a selection handle and size the button to better fit the text.

11. Click cell C12. The button is deselected.

Exercise 21-12   DELETE A BUTTON

When you point at a button, the pointer changes to a pointing finger. You must right-click a button to change its properties, because left-clicking a button runs the macro.

1. Click the button control. The macro runs and places the labels in cells A1:A2. The **CompanyName** macro used absolute references, so the insertion point can be anywhere when you click the button.

2. Press Ctrl+P. Press Alt+W to open print preview. Notice that button controls do not print by default.

3. Close the preview.

4. Right-click the button. Choose **Format Control**. Click the **Properties** tab. You can choose **Print object** if you want to print the button.

5. Click **Cancel**.

6. Right-click the button. The button is selected, and the shortcut menu is open.

7. Left-click the edge of the button. The shortcut menu closes, but the button is still selected.

8. Press Delete. The button is removed, but the macro is still stored in the workbook.

9. Save the workbook as *[your initials]*21-12. Close the workbook.

Creating a Macro Workbook

For macros that you use on a regular basis, you can create a workbook that includes only these macros. Then you can open this workbook every time you use Excel, and the macros are available for any of your work.

Exercise 21-13   RECORD MACROS

1. In a new workbook, click the **Developer** tab.

2. In the Code group, click the Use Relative References button so that it is not active; it should be off.

3. Click the Record Macro button .

4. Name this macro **Weeks**. In the **Shortcut key** box, press Shift and key **w**.

5. Make sure the **Store macro in** box shows **This Workbook**.

6. In the **Description** box, key **Displays Weeks 1-4**. Click **OK**.

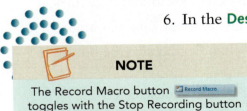

NOTE

The Record Macro button toggles with the Stop Recording button on the Developer tab.

7. Press Ctrl+G, key **b3**, and press Enter. These keystrokes position the insertion point in cell B3.

8. Select cells B3:E3 and make them bold and centered.

9. Key **Week 1** in cell B3.

10. Fill the labels to **Week 4** in cell E3.

11. Click the **Developer** tab. Click the Stop Recording button .

12. Clear all from cells B3:E3.

13. In the **Code** group, verify that relative references are off; use absolute references in the next macro, too.

14. Click the Record Macro button . Name the macro **SalesLabel** and store it in this workbook with a shortcut of Ctrl+Shift+S.

15. In the **Description** box, key **Displays main labels**. Click **OK**.

16. Select cells A1:A2 and set 16-point Cambria.

17. Key **Klassy Kow Ice Cream, Inc.** in cell A1 and press Enter.

18. Key **Monthly Sales for** and press Spacebar. Press Enter.

19. Click the **Developer** tab. Click the Stop Recording button Stop Recording.

20. Clear all from cells A1:A2.

Exercise 21-14   SAVE, HIDE, AND USE A MACRO WORKBOOK

Your workbook appears empty, but it does include two macros. You can hide the workbook and still use its macros. When you save a workbook with macros, you must save it as a macro-enabled workbook. It will have a file extension of **xlsm**.

1. Click the Save button 📄 on the Quick Access toolbar.

2. Navigate to your folder.

3. In the **Save as type** box, choose **Excel Macro-Enabled Workbook**.

4. In the **File name** box, key *[your initials]*21-14. Click **Save**.

5. Click the **View** tab. In the **Window** group, click the Hide button Hide. The macro workbook is open but hidden.

6. Create a new workbook.

7. In cell A1, press Ctrl+Shift+S to run the **SalesLabel** macro.

8. Press Ctrl+Shift+W to run the **Weeks** macro.

9. Close the new workbook without saving. Your macro workbook is still open and hidden.

10. On the **View** tab, click the Unhide button Unhide.

11. Choose *[your initials]*21-14 and click **OK**.

12. Save and close the workbook.

13. Click the Microsoft Office Button 🔘 and choose **Excel Options**.

14. On the **Popular** tab, click to deselect **Show Developer tab in the Ribbon**. Click **OK**.

Using Online Help

Macros are a valuable tool for automating routine data entry and tasks. There are several ways to run macros in addition to what you have tried in the lesson.

USE HELP TO LEARN MORE ABOUT RUNNING MACROS

1. Search for topics related to running macros.
2. Print Help windows if you think you can use them.
3. Close the Help windows.

Lesson 21 Summary

- A macro is a sequence of commands and keystrokes, converted to Visual Basic for Applications (VBA) code as you record them.
- In the Trust Center, you can set how a workbook with macros opens to avoid potential insecure files.
- You must enable macro content to run macros.
- You can run a macro from the View tab, from the Developer tab, with a keyboard shortcut, or from a button.
- Use the Visual Basic Editor to review and edit macro code.
- Press Alt+F11 to open the Visual Basic Editor. You print macro code from the Visual Basic Editor.
- Subroutine macros start with the word "Sub" followed by the macro name. Subroutine macros end with "End Sub."
- Macros are stored in workbooks. Delete a macro if you no longer need it.
- Macro names must begin with a letter and cannot use spaces or special characters. Keyboard shortcuts should include Shift so that you do not override Excel's own shortcuts.
- You can record macros with relative or absolute cell references.
- Use the Button tool on the Developer tab to create a button control. You can assign a macro to a button.
- A macro workbook can include only macros and be hidden so that macros are available at all times.

LESSON 21		Command Summary	
Feature	**Button**	**Task Path**	**Keyboard**
Button control		Developer, Controls, Insert	
Macro, delete		Developer, Code or View, Macros	Alt+F8
Macro, edit		Developer, Code or View, Macros	Alt+F11
Macro, record	Record Macro	Developer, Code	
Macro, run		View, Macros	Alt+F8
Macro, stop recording	Stop Recording	Developer, Code	
Use relative references	Use Relative References	Developer, Code or View, Macros	

Concepts Review

True/False Questions

Each of the following statements is either true or false. Indicate your choice by circling T or F.

T F   1. Macros are stored in workbooks.

T F   2. When you record a macro, your keystrokes and selections are saved and converted into Visual Basic for Applications code.

T F   3. An acceptable name for a macro is **&MyName**.

T F   4. To run a macro, click the Developer tab and choose Insert Macro.

T F   5. Existing macros can be edited on the worksheet and resaved.

T F   6. You must set an option in the Trust Center for each macro you write.

T F   7. A macro workbook must be open for its macros to be used.

T F   8. You must know Visual Basic to record a macro.

Short Answer Questions

Write the correct answer in the space provided.

1. What button should you click when you have finished creating your macro?

   _____

2. What does the acronym "VBA" represent?

   _____

3. How can you determine if a line in a macro is explanatory or simply a comment?

   _____

4. What pane in the Excel Options dialog box includes settings that control security warnings?

   _____

5. What Ribbon command tab includes form controls and other programming tasks?

   _____

6. Name two types of cell references you can use in macros.

   _____

7. What is the keyboard shortcut to open the Visual Basic Editor?

_____

8. What would happen if you used Ctrl + P as a shortcut to run a macro?

_____

Critical Thinking

Answer these questions on a separate page. There are no right or wrong answers. Support your answers with examples from your own experience, if possible.

1. What advantages might there be to studying Visual Basic as a programming language?

2. What types of macros might be helpful to you in completing your class work?

Skills Review

Exercise 21-15

Run a macro. Edit a macro. Print a macro.

NOTE

Check the Trust Center to verify that you will be notified if a workbook contains macros.

NOTE

Because you are resaving a macro-enabled workbook, you need not specify that file type in the Save As dialog box.

NOTE

If the code is not visible, expand the **Modules** folder in the Project Explorer window and double-click **Module1**. This module has two macros.

1. Open **AprilExp**. Click **Options** in the security message panel and choose **Enable this content**. Click **OK**.

2. Save the workbook as _[your initials]_**21-15**.

3. Run a macro by following these steps:
   a. Select cell C8.
   b. Click the **View** tab. In the **Macros** group, click the Macros button 📊.
   c. Choose **Salesmen** and click **Run**.
   d. Select cells C8:E8. Click the **Home** tab. Click the Clear button 2▾. Choose **Clear All**.

4. Edit a macro by following these steps:
   a. Press Alt + F11. Note the keyboard shortcut for the **Salesmen** macro subroutine.
   b. Find the line that includes the text **"Your name here."**
   c. Delete **Your name here** and key your first and last name. Be sure to leave the quotation marks.
   d. Locate the line **"Your Instructor"** and key your instructor's name between the quotation marks.
   e. Locate the line **"Your Friend"** and key the name of a friend between the quotation marks.

f. Find the line **Selection.Font.Italic = True** and key **Bold** in place of **Italic**.

g. At the top of the Code window, position the insertion point after the first apostrophe under **Sub Salesmen()**.

h. Press Spacebar once and key *[your first and last name]*.

5. Print a macro by following these steps:

a. Choose **File** and **Print**. In the **Range** group, choose **Current Module**.

b. In the **Print what** group, choose **Code**. Click **OK**.

 c. Click the Close button on the Visual Basic Editor title bar.

6. Run a macro by following these steps:

a. Select cell C8. Press Ctrl + Shift + S.

b. Widen columns to show each name.

c. Run the macro in cells C13, C18, and C23.

7. Fit the sheet to one portrait page.

8. Prepare and submit your work.

Exercise 21-16

Record a macro. Run a macro. Print a macro.

1. Open **SalinasHoliday**. This workbook is macro-enabled, but it does not currently have any macros.

2. Save the workbook as *[your initials]*21-16.

3. Record a macro by following these steps:

a. Click the **View** tab. Click the Macros button . Click to select **Use Relative References**; it should be on/active.

b. Click cell A7. The macro will run from this cell.

c. On the status bar, click the Record Macro button .

d. Name the macro **ApplyRowShading**. In the **Shortcut key** box, hold down Shift and key **s**.

e. Make sure that the **Store macro in** choice is **This Workbook**.

f. In the **Description** box, key **Applies shading to the current row**. Click **OK**.

g. Hold down Ctrl + Shift and press → to select all cells with data in the row.

h. Click the **Home** tab. Click the arrow for the Fill Color button . Choose **White, Background 1, Darker 25%**.

i. Press Home. Then press ↓ two times to position the insertion point in cell A9.

j. On the status bar, click the Stop Recording button .

4. Run a macro by following these steps:

   a. Press Ctrl+Shift+S to apply the shading to the cells in row 9.

   b. Run the macro in the odd-numbered rows with data.

5. Print a macro by following these steps:

   a. Press Alt+F11. If the **ApplyRowShading** macro does not appear in the Code window, expand the **Modules** folder in the Project window, and then double-click **Module1**.

   b. Position the insertion point after the first apostrophe under **Sub ApplyRowShading()**. Press Spacebar and key *[your name]*.

   c. Choose **File**, **Print**. Choose **Current Module** and **Code**. Click **OK**.

   d. Close the Visual Basic Editor.

6. Prepare and submit your work.

Exercise 21-17

Assign a macro to a button. Run a macro.

1. Open **AprilExp**. Click **Options** and choose **Enable this content**. Click **OK**.

2. Save the workbook as *[your initials]*21-17.

3. Assign a macro to a button by following these steps:

   a. Click the Microsoft Office Button and choose **Excel Options**.

   b. On the **Popular** pane, click to select **Show Developer tab in the Ribbon**. Click **OK**.

   c. On the **Developer** tab in the **Controls** group, click the Insert button.

   d. Click the Button tool. Draw a button that almost fills column E in rows 7:8.

   e. Select **BudgetAmounts** in the Assign Macro dialog box and click **OK**.

   f. Click inside the button, delete the existing text, and key **Insert Budget $**.

   g. Right-click an edge of the button and choose **Format Control**.

   > **NOTE**
   >
   > If you see only a Font tab in the Format Control dialog box, close the dialog box and select the button again to show the dotted pattern outline.

   h. On the **Font** tab, choose 9-point bold.

   i. Click the **Properties** tab and select **Print object**.

   j. Click the **Size** tab. In the **Size and rotate** group, set the **Height** to **.4**. Click **OK**.

4. Run a macro by following these steps:

   a. Select cell C9 and click the button.

   b. Run the macro in cells C14, C19, and C24.

5. Prepare and submit your work.

Exercise 21-18

Record a macro. Create a macro workbook.

1. Create a new workbook.

2. Record a macro by following these steps:

   a. If the Developer tab is not displayed, complete steps 3a-b in Exercise 21-17.

   b. Click the **Developer** tab.

   c. In the **Code** group, click the Use Relative References button  if it is not already active; it should be on.

   d. In the **Code** group, click the Record Macro button ⬚ Record Macro . In the **Macro name** box, key **PayrollA**.

   e. In the **Shortcut key** box, press Shift and key **a**. Verify that the **Store macro in** option is **This Workbook**. In the **Description** box, key **Insert main payroll labels**. Click **OK**.

   f. Click the **Home** tab. Set the font to 16-point Cambria and key **Weekly Payroll Data** in cell A1.

   g. In cell A2, set the font to 14-point Cambria and key **Week of** and press Spacebar.

   h. Widen the column to accommodate the longest label.

   i. Click the Stop Recording button ⬚ Stop Recording .

   j. Select cells A1:A2. On the **Home** tab, click the Clear button 2▾. Choose **Clear All**.

   k. Reset the width of column A to the same width as the other columns.

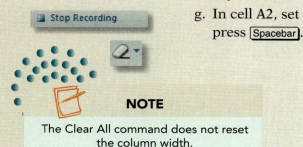

NOTE

The Clear All command does not reset the column width.

3. Record a macro by following these steps:

   a. Click the **Developer** tab. In the **Code** group, check that relative references will be used.

   b. In the **Code** group, click the Record Macro button ⬚ Record Macro . Name this macro **PayrollB**.

   c. In the **Shortcut key** box, press Shift and key **b**. Verify that the **Store macro in** option is **This Workbook**. In the **Description** box, key **Insert employee names**. Click **OK**.

   d. Select cells A3:C10 and set them to 12-point Cambria.

e. Starting in cell A3, key these names in column A:

Ahmed Javii
Elvira Chavez
Burton Odaliso
Jerry Greenstreet
Songquan Jung
Pedro Ramirez
Francois Duval
Rosa Barone

f. Click the Stop Recording button .

g. Select cells A3:C10 and clear all.

4. Create a macro workbook by following these steps:

a. Click the Save button 🖫 on the Quick Access toolbar. Navigate to your folder.

b. In the **Save as type** box, choose **Excel Macro-Enabled Workbook**.

c. In the **File name** box, key *[your initials]***21-18**. Click **Save**.

d. Click the **View** tab. In the **Window** group, click the Hide button .

e. Create a new workbook.

f. In cell A1, press Ctrl+Shift+A to run the **PayrollA** macro.

g. Press Ctrl+Shift+B to run the **PayrollB** macro.

h. Save the workbook macro-free as *[your initials]***21-18a**. Close it.

i. On the **View** tab, click the Unhide button . Choose *[your initials]***21-18** and click **OK**.

j. Save and close the workbook.

5. Prepare and submit your work.

Lesson Applications

Exercise 21-19

Record a macro. Assign a macro to a button. Print a macro.

In this exercise, you create an order form that includes a command button to open a price list workbook.

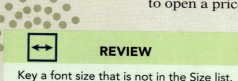

REVIEW

Key a font size that is not in the Size list.

1. Open a new workbook and save it as a macro-enabled workbook named *[your initials]*21-19.

2. Format cells A1:A2 as 21-point Calibri. Key **Klassy Kow Ice Cream** in cell A1 and **Online Order** in cell A2.

3. In cells A3:C3, key the following labels, starting in cell A3:

   Product   **Quantity**   **Price**

4. Make the labels in row 3 bold and centered. Set the width for all three columns to **20.71 (150 pixels)**. Set the height for row 3 to **26.25 (35 pixels)**. Center the labels in rows 1:2 across the data.

5. Delete **Sheet2** and **Sheet3** and rename **Sheet1** as **OrderForm**.

6. Select cell A4 and save the workbook.

TIP

A macro does not need a keyboard shortcut if you plan to run it from a button.

7. Record a macro named **OpenPrices**. Do not use a shortcut. Store the macro in **This Workbook**. For the **Description**, key **Opens the price list**.

8. When the macro begins recording, open the file **ProductList** and switch back to your workbook. Then stop recording.

9. Close **ProductList**.

10. Draw a button that covers cells D1:E2 and assign the **OpenPrices** macro to it. Edit the text on the button to show **Price List** and format it as bold. Format the button control so that it will print.

11. Print the macro with your name as a comment after the macro name.

12. Prepare and submit your work.

Exercise 21-20

Record a macro. Run a macro.

In this exercise, you create a macro that automates making a copy of a worksheet.

1. Open **CASodas** and save it as a macro-enabled workbook named *[your initials]*21-20.

2. Record a new macro named **CopySheet** with a shortcut. The description is **Copies worksheet**.

3. When recording begins, copy the worksheet to the end. Then stop recording.

4. Run the macro for a total of four worksheets. Rename the copied sheets **Oregon**, **Nevada**, and **Washington**.

5. Group the **Oregon**, **Nevada**, and **Washington** worksheets and delete the contents of cells B4:D12.

6. Add the **California** worksheet to the group and select cell B4. Add a footer to all sheets.

7. Print the macro with your name as a comment after the macro name.

8. Prepare and submit your work.

REVIEW

Use the Page Setup dialog box from the Page Layout tab to add the same footer to grouped sheets.

Exercise 21-21

Edit a macro.

In the phone order form, there are macros with errors. Find the errors and fix them.

1. Open **StartForm** and save it as *[your initials]*21-21.

2. Run the macros. Determine what is wrong and edit each macro to correct its errors.

3. Clear all from the worksheet and run the macros again.

4. Print the macros with your name as a comment.

5. Prepare and submit your work.

Exercise 21-22 ◆ Challenge Yourself

Record, test, edit, and print a macro.

In a macro, Excel records the results of commands with current settings in the worksheet. For example, if you record a macro while the sheet is set for portrait orientation, that setting is included in the macro code.

1. Save a macro-enabled workbook as *[your initials]*21-22.

NOTE

Use the Page Setup dialog box or Page Layout view to create or delete a header on a blank worksheet.

2. Record a macro with a keyboard shortcut and a description that inserts your standard header.

TIP

On your own computer at work or home, store a header macro in the Personal Macro Workbook so that it is always available.

3. Delete the header that was created as you recorded the macro.

4. Key some sample data on the sheet and run your macro. If it does not work, delete it and try again.

5. Print the macro with your name as a comment.

6. Prepare and submit your work.

On Your Own

In these exercises you work on your own, as you would in a real-life work environment. Use the skills you've learned to accomplish the task—and be creative.

Exercise 21-23

In a new workbook, create a macro that you would find helpful in your school work or at your job. Use a description for the macro that illustrates the purpose well. Use Help to review how to run a macro from a hot spot and draw objects to try this. Save the macro-enabled workbook as *[your initials]*21-23. Test and edit your macro. Add your name as a comment in the macro. Prepare and submit your work.

Exercise 21-24

Use the Internet to find information about macros or Visual Basic routines that are available from expert users or from Microsoft or its partners. In a new workbook, describe what macros you found, where and how macros can be purchased, what tasks they perform, and how much they cost. Save the workbook as *[your initials]*21-24. Prepare and submit your work.

Exercise 21-25

In a new workbook, create a macro that performs some task that you would like to try. Store it in the Personal Macro Workbook. After you have recorded, tested, and edited your macro, close the workbook without saving. Then open a new workbook and run the macro. In this new workbook, unhide the **personal.xlsb** workbook. This file, **personal.xlsb**, has been saved in a folder named XLSTART on your computer. It opens as a hidden file each time you start Excel so that your macro is always available. Unhide it and delete the macro that you recorded. Then save and close the workbook.

Lesson 22

Using templates

OBJECTIVES

MCAS OBJECTIVES

In this lesson:
XL07 1.2.1
XL07 1.4
XL07 1.4.2
XL07 1.5
XL07 5.1
XL07 5.1.2
XL07 5.2.1
XL07 5.3.3
XL07 5.4
XL07 5.4.2

After completing this lesson, you will be able to:

1. Use an installed template.
2. Add worksheet protection.
3. Use an online template.
4. Create a user template.
5. Use workbook protection.

Estimated Time: 1½ hours

NOTE

A template helps to eliminate repetitive work.

A template is a model workbook, designed to be used as the basis for new, but similar, workbooks. A weekly sales report with summary calculations and charts need not be started from scratch each week. You can design a template with all the labels and formulas and then create a workbook each week based on that template. You only need to key in the appropriate values for the week and e-mail or print.

Using an Installed Template

NOTE

Excel has a default workbook template with three blank worksheets that is used each time you create a new workbook.

Excel has sample custom templates that are included with a standard software installation. A *custom template* is a workbook template that may include values, formulas, labels, images, fill, borders, and even macros.

When you create a workbook based on a template, it has the same name as the template, followed by a number.

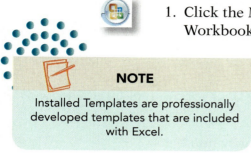

Exercise 22-1 CREATE A WORKBOOK BASED ON AN INSTALLED TEMPLATE

1. Click the Microsoft Office Button . Choose **New**. The New Workbook dialog box opens.

> **NOTE**
>
> Installed Templates are professionally developed templates that are included with Excel.

2. Click **Installed Templates** in the **Templates** pane. The Installed Templates pane lists the names of several templates.

3. Double-click **Expense Report**. A new workbook opens in Page Layout View. It is a copy of the template.

Figure 22-1
Choosing an installed template

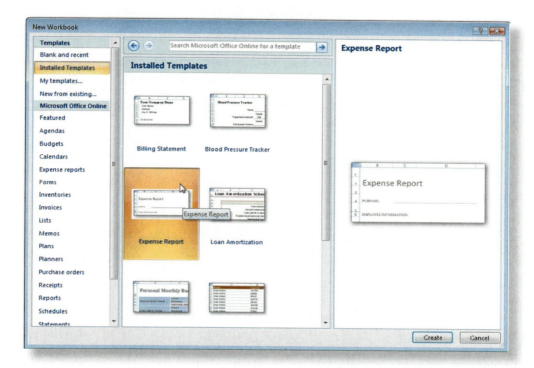

4. Zoom out to **80%** magnification. This worksheet uses a variety of design principles. The gridlines are off, the main data section is a table, and fill and borders are used to emphasize sections.

Exercise 22-2 EDIT AND SAVE A WORKBOOK BASED ON A TEMPLATE

This template opens with the insertion point in cell C4, the cell where the purpose is keyed.

1. Key **Annual Convention** and press Tab three times.

2. Key **12345** as the statement number.

3. Click cell L4. Key the date for the first day this month in **mm/dd/yy** format. Press Enter.

4. Key the date for the last day of this month in **mm/dd/yy** format. Press Enter.

5. Click cell C7.

6. Key *[your first and last name]*.

7. Click cell G7. Key **Sales Manager** as your position. Press Tab three times.

8. Key **888-44-8888** as the social security number.

9. In cell C8, key **Marketing** as the department.

10. Click in the Employee ID box. Key **87654**.

11. Click cell B11. This is the first data row below the header in the table.

12. Press Ctrl+; and press Tab.

NOTE

The keyboard shortcut to enter the current date is Ctrl+;.

13. Key **111** as the **Account** and press Tab.

14. Key **Travel to client** as the **Description**.

15. Press Tab to reach the **Fuel** column and key **10**. Key **8.50** for **Meals**.

16. Click cell L11 and press Tab. A new row is inserted.

17. Press F12. The Save As dialog box opens.

18. Save the workbook as *[your initials]*22-2 in a Lesson 22 folder.

19. Click the **View** tab and hide the workbook.

Adding Worksheet Protection

Designing a template can be a lot of work. You can make sure that others do not accidentally delete formulas, change colors, edit labels, or make other revisions by protecting cells from being changed. You can lock shapes and images so that they cannot be moved or resized. The Locked property is in the Format Cells dialog box. This property works with the Protect commands on the Review tab to allow you to prohibit changes to your work.

Exercise 22-3   EDIT AN INSTALLED TEMPLATE

You can open an installed template and save it as a new template using a different name. This allows you to preserve the original and create your own template. When you *open* a template, the original opens, not a copy. You must locate where templates are stored on your computer to open them for editing.

Many templates are saved with some type of *protection*. Protection locks cell contents to prevent editing.

1. Press Ctrl + O.

2. Navigate to the folder where **ExpenseReport** (and the other installed templates) is stored.

3. Double-click **ExpenseReport**. The original template file is opened.

4. Set an 80% zoom size.

5. Click in the center section of the header and key **Klassy Kow Ice Cream, Inc**.

6. Select cells B13:L17. With the four-pointed arrow, drag the range to rows 26:30.

7. Click the table-sizing handle. Drag down to size the table to reach row 25.

8. Click anywhere in the table. Click the **Table Tools Design** tab. Choose **Table Style Medium 25**.

9. Change **Department** to **Store** in cell B8.

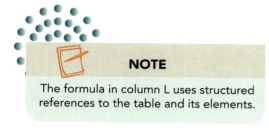

NOTE

The formula in column L uses structured references to the table and its elements.

REVIEW

The table-sizing handle is at the bottom-right corner.

Figure 22-2
Edited Expense Report sheet
ExpenseReport.xltx
Expense Report sheet

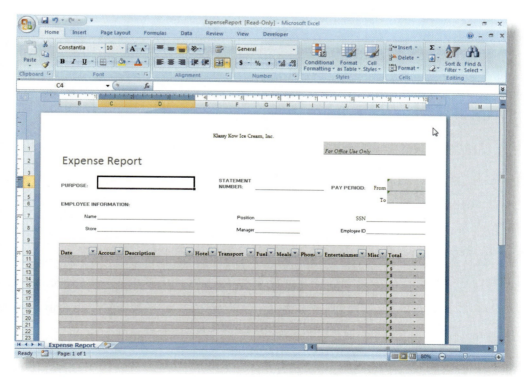

Exercise 22-4   CHANGE THE LOCKED PROPERTY

Cells and shapes, like workbooks, have properties. One of those properties is whether or not the cell or shape is *locked*. When a cell is locked, it cannot be changed if the worksheet is protected.

By default, all cells are locked. However, the Locked property has no effect until the worksheet is protected.

1. Click cell C4. This is a cell that the user will edit; it should not be locked.

2. Press Ctrl+1. Click the **Protection** tab. The Locked property is selected. If worksheet protection were activated, you would not be able to key a purpose in this cell.

3. Click to deselect **Locked**. Now this cell will be editable because it will be unlocked.

4. Read the message on the Protection tab. Click **OK**.

Figure 22-3
Changing the Locked property
ExpenseReport.xlsx
Expense Report sheet

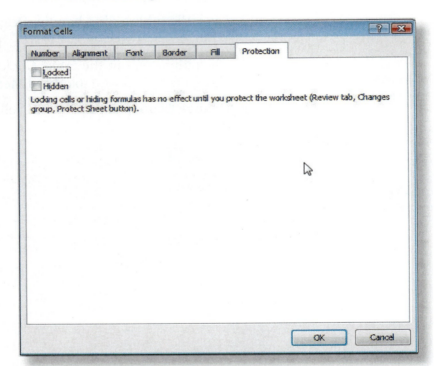

5. Click cell G4. Hold down Ctrl and click each of the following cells: L4, L5, C7, C8, G7, G8, K7, K8. All of these cells should be unlocked.

6. Right-click any one of the selected cells and choose **Format Cells**. Click the **Protection** tab.

7. Click to deselect **Locked**. Click **OK**.

8. Select cells B11:K24. These are table cells in which data can be keyed.

9. Press ⌈Ctrl⌉+⌈1⌉. Click the **Protection** tab. Click to deselect **Locked**. Click **OK**.

10. Unlock cells C28, C30, G28, G30, and L27.

Exercise 22-5   PROTECT THE WORKSHEET

If a worksheet is protected, locked cells and shapes cannot be changed. Templates are a logical location for locking and protecting cells.

1. Click cell C4.

2. Click the **Review** tab. In the **Changes** group, click the Protect Sheet button. You can choose to allow some type of changes after the sheet is protected.

3. Click to select **Select locked cells**, **Select unlocked cells**, **Format columns**, and **Format rows**. This means that a user can click to select any cell. They will also be able to change column width and row height.

Figure 22-4
Protect Sheet
dialog box
ExpenseReport.xlsx
**Expense Report
sheet**

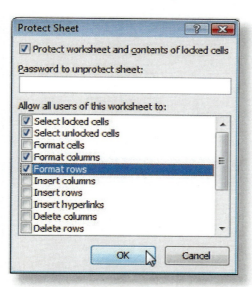

4. Click **OK**.

5. Click cell B4. You did not unlock this cell.

6. Press ⌈Delete⌉. You cannot delete the contents, because it should be locked and protected.

7. Click **OK** in the message box.

8. Click the first date cell and key today's date. Press ⌈Tab⌉. This cell was unlocked, so your entry is allowed.

9. Delete the date. Click cell C4.

Exercise 22-6   UPDATE PROPERTIES

All workbooks have properties. The thumbnail or preview image of a workbook is displayed in the Open and Templates dialog boxes when the file is selected.

1. Click the Microsoft Office Button . Choose **Prepare** and then **Properties**. The Document Information Panel opens.

Excel 2007

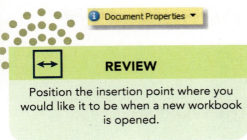

REVIEW

Position the insertion point where you would like it to be when a new workbook is opened.

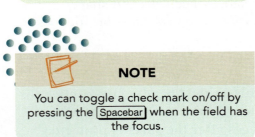

NOTE

You can toggle a check mark on/off by pressing the [Spacebar] when the field has the focus.

2. Click the Property Views and Options button
   ⓘ Document Properties ▾ . Choose **Advanced Properties**. The
   Properties dialog box has five tabs. The options in
   the General tab are settings that are automatically
   maintained.

3. Click the **Summary** tab. You can enter most of the
   metadata about your document from this tab.

4. For the **Title**, key **Salesmen's Expense Report**. As the
   subject, key **Reimbursement**.

5. Change the author to *[your first and last name]*.

6. Change the company to *[your school or company
   name]*.

7. Click to select **Save Thumbnails for All Excel
   Documents**. Click **OK**.

Figure 22-5
Updated properties
**ExpenseReport.xlsx
Expense Report
sheet**

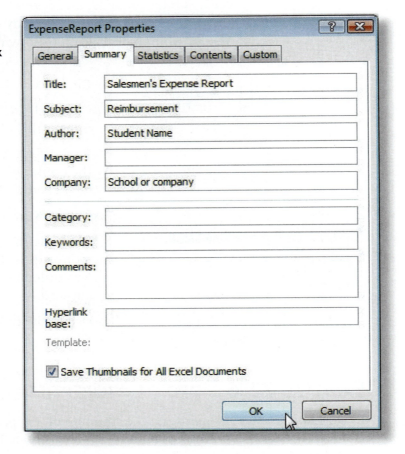

8. Close the Document Information Panel.

9. Adjust column widths if any data is wrapped or truncated.

10. Click cell C4.

Exercise 22-7   SAVE A TEMPLATE

To preserve the original template, you should save this revised version with a different name. You should save your own templates in the Templates folder for your computer. Templates are easiest to use when they appear in the My Templates tab of the New dialog box. You can store templates anywhere, but only certain folders are listed in this dialog box.

1. Press F12.

2. Note the folder location. This is the folder where the Installed Templates are stored.

3. Navigate to the folder for your templates.

4. Key *[your initials]*22-7 as the new **File name**. Excel will add the **xltx** extension to identify this as a template.

5. Note the **Save as type**. It should be **Excel Template**, since you started with a template.

TIP

To find where general templates are stored, save a workbook as an Excel Template and note the folder location in the Save As dialog box.

Figure 22-6
Saving a workbook as a template
Sol22-7.xltx
Expense Report sheet

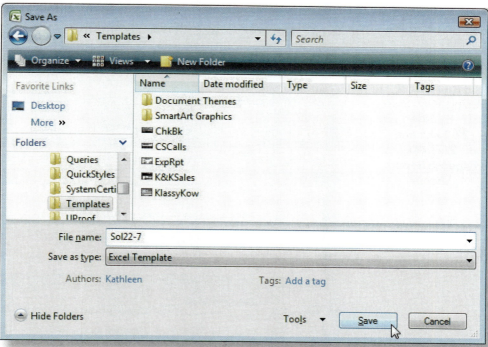

NOTE

If you do not see your template, check with your instructor or lab manager for additional help.

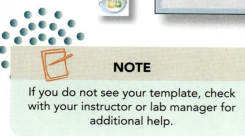

6. Click **Save**. Close the template.

7. Click the Microsoft Office Button and choose **New**.

8. Click **My templates**. Templates that you create are displayed in this dialog box.

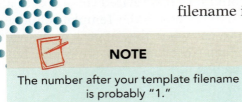

Excel 2007

9. Click once to select your template and see its preview image.

10. Click **OK**. A copy of the template opens as a new workbook. The filename includes a number after the template name.

NOTE

The number after your template filename is probably "1."

11. Press [F12]. Save this as an Excel workbook in your Lesson 22 folder named *[your initials]*22-7. You can use the same name as the template because the files have different filename extensions.

Exercise 22-8   USE VIEW SIDE BY SIDE

You can now compare the original template to your revised version. You may have forgotten that you hid the workbook that you created from the original template.

1. Click the **View** tab. Click the Unhide button . The names of hidden workbooks are listed.

2. Click to select *[your initials]*22-2 and click **OK**.

3. In the **Window** group, click the View Side by Side button. The two workbooks are tiled horizontally.

Figure 22-7
Using View Side by Side
22-2.xlsx and 22-7.xlsx Expense Report sheets

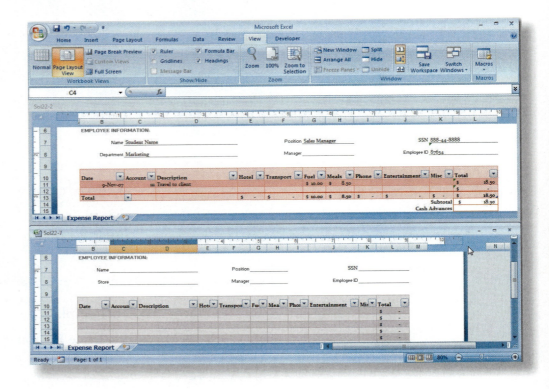

4. Click the Synchronous Scrolling button so that it shows an outline. *Synchronous scrolling* means that the windows will move in tandem.

5. Press ⬇ until you see both windows scroll vertically.

6. Click the View Side by Side button ▥ . The workbooks are reset to full-screen.

7. Save and close both workbooks.

Exercise 22-9   DELETE A TEMPLATE

You should delete your template from the classroom computer.

1. Open the New Workbook dialog box. Click **My templates**.

2. Right-click your template and choose **Delete**.

3. Choose **Yes**.

4. Click **Cancel** twice to return to a blank Excel screen.

Using an Online Template

Microsoft Office Online maintains a *Template Gallery* that is a collection of templates for Word, Excel, PowerPoint, and Access. You can preview templates, find ones that you like, edit them, and save them to your computer.

Exercise 22-10   DOWNLOAD AN ONLINE TEMPLATE

The New Workbook dialog box lists categories of online templates to help you find one that fits your purpose. Some of the templates have been developed by Microsoft Corporation, and some have been created by expert users.

1. Click the Microsoft Office Button 🔘 . Choose **New**.

2. View the categories in the **Microsoft Office Online** list.

3. Click **Budgets**. There are buttons to show/hide those templates that are created by users other than Microsoft Corporation.

4. Click **Personal budget**. There is a thumbnail at the right with its size and a rating. (See Figure 22-8 on the next page.)

NOTE

Microsoft Office Online is updated regularly, so you may see templates different from those shown in this text. Use your skills to find the template or a similar one.

Figure 22-8
Online template gallery

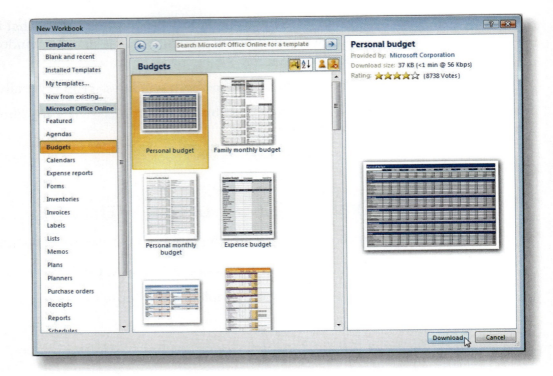

5. Click **Download**. A message box alerts you that your copy of Microsoft Office must be valid.

6. Click **Continue**. The template opens as a new workbook. When the title bar shows [Compatibility Mode] after the filename, the workbook is currently in Excel 97-2003 format.

7. Press F12. Save this as an Excel Workbook named *[your initials]*22-10.

8. Close the workbook and reopen it. Now it is not running in compatibility mode and you can use all Excel 2007 features and commands.

Exercise 22-11 EDIT AND SAVE A TEMPLATE

When you download a template from Microsoft Office Online, you have a regular workbook that you can edit. You can then save this workbook as a template so that you have your own template.

   A footer in the template means that any new workbook based on that template includes the footer.

1. Click the **Insert** tab. Click the Header & Footer button. Click **Custom Footer**.

2. In the **Left section** box, key *[your first and last name]*.

3. In the **Center section** box, add the filename and the sheet name.

4. In the **Right section**, key **Page** and press Spacebar.

5. Click the Insert Page Number button . Press [Spacebar], key **of**, and press [Spacebar]. Click the Insert Number of Pages button . Click **OK** twice.

6. Press [Ctrl]+[P] and then [Alt]+[W] to open Print Preview. This is a two-page worksheet.

7. Press [PageDown]. Close the preview.

8. Click the **Home** tab. Click the Find & Select button . Choose **Replace**.

9. Key **0** (zero) in the **Find what** box. Do not key anything in the **Replace with** box. This will replace all the zeros with blank/empty cells.

10. Click **Find Next**. Click **Replace**. One replacement is made.

11. Click **Replace All**. Click **OK** in the message box.

12. Click **Close**. Some cells that show a zero do not contain a zero.

13. Click cell C5. This is a reference to cell B5 so that wages are repeated from month to month.

14. Click cell C11. This, too, is a reference to the previous month so that the mortgage/rent payment need not be rekeyed every month.

15. Click cell B8. Of course, formula cells were not replaced.

16. Right-click cell C5 and choose **Insert Comment**.

17. Delete the user name and key the following:

    Wages are assumed to be the same from month to month. If a new amount is entered for any given month, it is then assumed for the next month.

18. Click an edge of the comment and size it so that the text fits on four lines and is only as tall as necessary. Drag it up to the right of the label in cell A1.

Figure 22-9
Adding a comment
22-10.xlsx
Personal budget
sheet

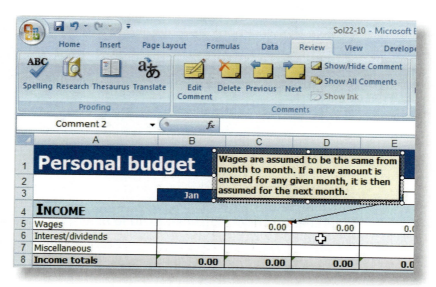

Excel 2007

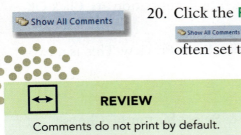

Show All Comments

REVIEW

Comments do not print by default.

19. Click an empty cell. The comment is hidden.

20. Click the **Review** tab. Click the Show All Comments button
    so that it is active or on. Comments in a template are
    often set to be shown.

21. Click the Microsoft Office Button . Choose
    Prepare and then **Properties**.

22. Click the Property Views and Options button
    . Choose **Advanced Properties**. Click the
    Summary tab.

23. For the **Title**, key **Personal Budget**. As the subject, key **Month-to-month
    tracking**. Change the author to *[your first and last name]*. Change the
    company to *[your school or company name]*.

24. Click to select **Save Thumbnails for All Excel Documents**. Click **OK**.
    Close the Document Information Panel.

25. Press F12. In the **File name** box, key *[your initials]*22-11.

26. Click the **Save as type** arrow. Choose **Excel Template**. The folder
    changes to the template location for your computer. Note the name
    and location of this folder.

27. Click **Save**. Close the template.

Exercise 22-12   USE AND DELETE A TEMPLATE

1. Open the New Workbook dialog box. Click **My templates**.

2. Double-click *[your initials]*22-11. A new workbook opens with the
   template name followed by a number.

3. Fill in your own sample data with wages for January and some
   expenses.

4. Save the workbook as *[your initials]*22-12. Close the workbook.

5. Open the New Workbook dialog box. Click **My templates**.

6. Right-click your template and choose **Delete**.

7. Choose **Yes**. Click **Cancel**.

Creating a User Template

A *user template* is one that you create and use for your day-to-day tasks.
Most templates include everything except the data that changes each time
the template is used. This can include labels, formatting, range names, and
formulas.

Exercise 22-13 BUILD A TEMPLATE

1. In a new workbook, click the Select All button to the left of and above the column A and row 1 headings. This selects all cells on the worksheet.

2. Set the font to 12-point Calibri. Format cells B2:B3 as 18 point.

3. Key **Klassy Kow Ice Cream Shops** in cell B2. In cell B3, key **Advertising Expenses for** and press [Spacebar].

4. In cell C6, key **Week 1**. Make it bold and centered. Fill to **Week 4** in cell F6.

5. Key **Shop** in cell B6 and **Total** in cell G6. Match the formats to the other labels.

6. Open **Shops** in Word. Select and copy all the data to cells B7:B38. Close Word.

7. Set the font to Calibri for the shop cities. Make column B **22.14 (160 pixels)** wide.

8. Make columns A and H **2.14 (20 pixels)** wide. Make rows 1 and 5 **22.50 (30 pixels)** tall.

9. Select cells B2:G3 and center the labels across the data.

10. Select cells A1:H39 and add a thick solid outline border.

11. Add a solid thinner bottom border to cells A4:H4.

12. Add a dotted middle and bottom horizontal border to cells A7:G38.

13. Add solid thin left and middle vertical borders to cells C7:G38.

Exercise 22-14 ADD A FORMULA AND HIDE ZEROS

You can hide zero values so that a formula with nothing to calculate shows an empty cell, rather than a hyphen or a zero.

1. Select cell G7. This cell will show a sum of the four weeks.

2. Click the AutoSum button . Because there are no values above or to the left of the cell, AutoSum does not suggest a range.

3. Select cells C7:F7 and press [Enter]. A zero results.

4. Copy the formula through row 38.

5. Click the Microsoft Office Button . Choose **Excel Options**. Click **Advanced**.

6. In the **Display options for this worksheet** group, click to deselect **Show a zero in cells that have zero value**.

7. Click **OK**. Zero values are hidden on the sheet. (See Figure 22-10 on the next page.)

8. Select cell G7 to deselect the range.

Excel 2007

Figure 22-10
Template labels,
formulas, and
formatting
BookN.xlsx
Sheet1 sheet

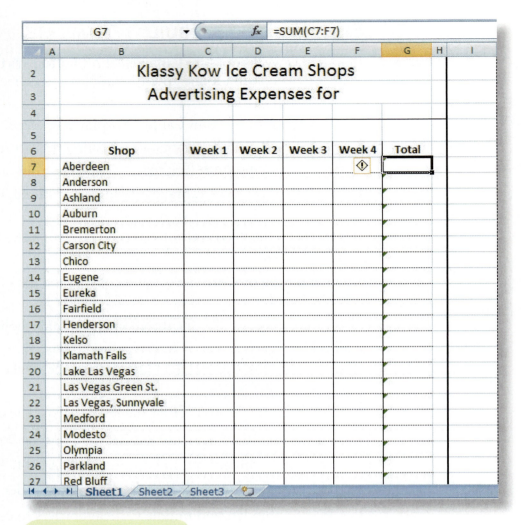

Exercise 22-15   ADD DATA VALIDATION

1. Select cells C7:F38. These are cells in which advertising amounts will be keyed.

2. Click the **Data** tab. Click the Data Validation button .

3. Click the **Settings** tab. Click the arrow with the **Allow** box. Choose **Whole number**. Decimals or fractions will not be allowed.

4. Click the arrow next to the **Data** box. Choose **greater than or equal to**.

5. In the **Minimum** box, key **25**. This sets a minimum expense of $25.

6. Click the **Error Alert** tab. Click the arrow for the **Style** box. Choose **Warning**. This style displays an exclamation point in a yellow triangle. It will show a message but allow the entry.

7. In the **Title** box, key **Minimum Advertising Required** and press Tab.

8. In the **Error message** box, key **Each shop must spend a minimum of $25 per week on local advertising**.

9. Click **OK**.

Exercise 22-16 USE A VALIDATION INPUT MESSAGE

You can have Excel display a data validation message as soon as the pointer enters a cell with the validation settings. This type of message guides the user's input before any entry is made.

1. Select cells C7:F7. You will show an input message only in the first row of expenses.

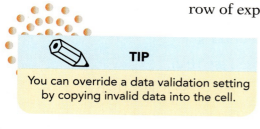

TIP

You can override a data validation setting by copying invalid data into the cell.

2. Click the Data Validation button 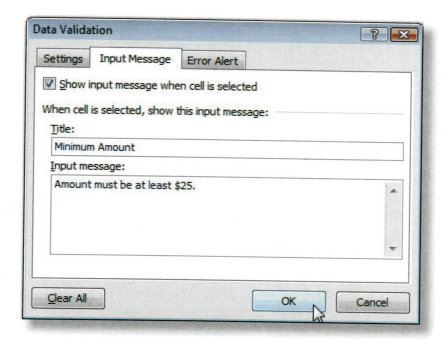. Click the **Input Message** tab.

3. In the **Title** box, key **Minimum Amount**.

4. In the **Input message** box, key **Amount must be at least $25.**

Figure 22-11
Input message
**BookN.xlsx
Sheet1 sheet**

5. Click **OK**. The input message is displayed because the range is selected.

6. Click cell C7.

7. Key **35** and press ⌷Tab⌷. This entry meets the data validation setting, because it is greater than 25.

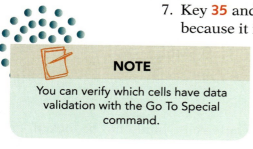

NOTE

You can verify which cells have data validation with the Go To Special command.

8. Key **20** and press ⌷Tab⌷. This amount violates the data validation setting, but your error alert choices allow you to continue.

9. Click **Yes**. The value is entered into the cell.

Exercise 22-17   ADD CONDITIONAL FORMATTING AND A COMMENT

Because your data validation warning will allow an entry less than $25, you can apply conditional formatting to highlight cells that violate your data validation settings.

1. Select cells C7:F38. Click the **Home** tab.

2. Click the Conditional Formatting button .

3. Choose **Highlight Cells Rules**. Choose **Less Than**.

4. Build a condition to show red text if the value is less than 25.

5. Click any cell to deselect the range. The value in cell D7 is shown in red because it is less than 25.

6. Delete the contents of cells C7:D7.

7. Right-click cell B3. Choose **Insert Comment**.

8. Delete the user name and key **Click cell B3 and press F2 to edit. Key the month and press Enter.**

9. On the **Review** tab, show all comments. Size the comment box to be as small as possible to show the text.

10. Select cells C7:G38. Format them as Currency with no decimals.

11. Center the sheet horizontally.

12. Click the Microsoft Office Button . Choose **Prepare** and **Properties**.

13. Click the Property Views and Options button . Choose **Advanced Properties**.

14. Click the **Summary** tab. Set the title to **Monthly Advertising Expenses**. Key your name as the author.

15. Key the following in the **Comments** box:

   This sheet is prepared at the end of each month to track advertising expenses paid by each shop.

16. Click to select **Save Thumbnails for All Excel Documents**. Click **OK**.

17. Close the Document Information Panel.

Exercise 22-18   PROTECT THE SHEET WITH A PASSWORD

1. Click cells C7:F38.

2. Hold down `Ctrl` and click cell B3. These cells should not be locked.

3. Press `Ctrl`+`1`. Click the **Protection** tab.

4. Click to deselect **Locked**. Click **OK**.

5. Click cell B3.

6. Click the **Review** tab. In the **Changes** group, click the Protect Sheet button 🗎.

7. Click to select **Select locked cells**, **Select unlocked cells**, **Format columns**, and **Format rows**.

Figure 22-12
Using a password to
protect a sheet
BookN.xlsx
Sheet1 sheet

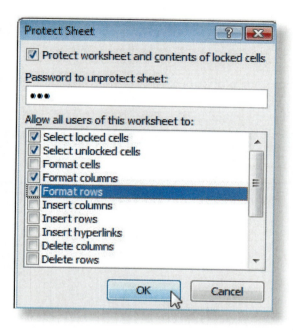

8. In the **Password to unprotect sheet** box, key **123**. Passwords are optional.

9. Click **OK**. The Confirm Password dialog box opens. You must rekey your password to make sure you keyed it correctly the first time.

10. Key **123** to confirm your password. Click **OK**.

11. Rename **Sheet1** as **AdvExpense**. Delete **Sheet2** and **Sheet3**.

Exercise 22-19   CREATE A TEMPLATES FOLDER

The My Templates tab in the New dialog box shows templates that are in C:\Users*UserName*\AppData\Roaming\Microsoft\Templates. *UserName* is the name for your computer. If you create a folder within this folder, its name appears in the New dialog box as a separate tab.

1. Press F12.

2. Change **Save as type** to **Excel Template**. The default Templates folder is opened.

3. Click the New Folder button. You will create a folder within the Templates folder.

4. Key **NewTemplates** and press Enter. The new folder is opened.

5. In the **File name** box, key *[your initials]*22-19.

6. Click **Save**. The workbook is saved as a template.

7. Close the workbook.

Exercise 22-20 CREATE A WORKBOOK FROM A TEMPLATE

1. Open the New Workbook dialog box. Click **My templates**. Your folder appears as a tab.

Figure 22-13
NewTemplates tab in dialog box

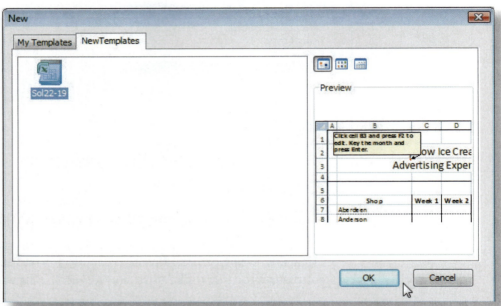

2. Click the **NewTemplates** tab.

3. Double-click the file *[your initials]*22-19. A copy of the template opens named as the template with a number.

4. Add the current month to the label in cell B3.

5. Key the information shown here. Watch for data validation messages.

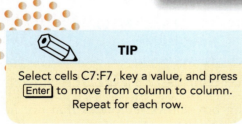

TIP

Select cells C7:F7, key a value, and press Enter to move from column to column. Repeat for each row.

Shop	Week 1	Week 2	Week 3	Week 4
Aberdeen	27	32	35	28
Anderson	25	20	24	32
Ashland	45	55	50	34
Auburn	50	35	37	48
Bremerton	29	18	30	25

6. Save your work as an Excel workbook named *[your initials]*22-20 in your Lesson 22 folder.

7. Close the workbook.

Exercise 22-21   REMOVE PROTECTION AND THE PASSWORD

1. Press Ctrl + O.

2. Navigate to the folder where templates are stored and then to your templates folder.

3. Select the file *[your initials]*22-19 and click **Open**. This is the original template, not a copy.

4. Click the **Home** tab. When a worksheet is protected, many of the command buttons are dimmed and unavailable.

5. Click the **Review** tab. In the **Changes** group, click the Unprotect Sheet button. The Unprotect Sheet dialog box prompts for the password.

6. In the **Password** box, key **123**. Click **OK**.

NOTE

Make sure you complete the last step of this exercise. Template files remain on the computer until they are deleted.

7. Delete the formula in cell G7. Protection for this worksheet is off, so you can make any change.

8. Close the template without resaving.

9. Open the New Workbook dialog box. Click **My templates**. Click the **NewTemplates** tab. Delete the file *[your initials]*22-19 and then click **Cancel**.

Using Workbook Protection

You can apply both worksheet and workbook protection to a workbook. Workbook protection prevents worksheet windows from being sized and moved. You can also prevent adding, deleting, renaming, moving, or hiding worksheets.

Exercise 22-22   CREATE A WORKBOOK TEMPLATE

A workbook template has multiple predesigned sheets. You create and save a workbook template the same way you create an individual worksheet template.

1. Create a new workbook with four worksheets. Name the worksheets **California**, **Oregon**, **Nevada**, and **Washington**.

2. Group all four worksheets. Click the Select All button. Set the font to Cambria 12 point. Format cells B2:B3 as 18 point.

3. In cell B2, key **Monthly Sales Data for** and press ⌴Spacebar. In cell B3, key **Sugar and Waffle Cones**.

4. In cell C6, key **Week 1**. Make it bold and centered. Fill to **Week 4** in cell F6.

5. Key **Shop** in cell B6 and **Total** in cell G6. Match the format.

6. Make column B **22.14 (160 pixels)** wide. Make columns A and H **2.14 (20 pixels)** wide.

7. Center the labels in rows 2:3 across the data.

8. Select cells A1:H21 and add a thick solid outline border. Design your own remaining borders and/or fill for sheets.

9. Select cell G7. Click the AutoSum button ∑ ▾. Select cells C7:F7 and press ⌷Enter⌷. Copy the formula through row 20.

10. Hide the zeros. Format cells C7:G20 as Currency with no decimals.

11. Center the sheets horizontally. Ungroup the worksheets.

12. In the **California** worksheet, edit the label in cell B2 to show **Monthly Sales Data for California**.

13. Repeat the previous step for each of the other worksheets with the appropriate state.

Exercise 22-23   ADD SHEET AND WORKBOOK PROTECTION

1. Group the sheets. Select cells C7:F20. Add cell B2 to the selection.

2. Press ⌷Ctrl⌷+⌷1⌷. Click the **Protection** tab. Click to deselect **Locked**. Click **OK**.

3. Click cell C7. Ungroup the sheets.

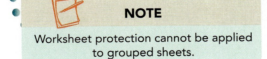

> **NOTE**
>
> Worksheet protection cannot be applied to grouped sheets.

4. Click the **Review** tab. Click the Protect Sheet button 🗐. Click to select **Select locked cells**, **Select unlocked cells**, **Format columns**, and **Format rows**. Click **OK**.

5. Repeat step 4 for the remaining sheets.

6. Click the **California** tab.

7. On the **Review** tab, click the Protect Workbook button 🗐.

> **NOTE**
>
> The Repeat command, ⌷Ctrl⌷+⌷Y⌷, does not work for Protect Sheet.

8. Choose **Protect Structure and Windows**. The Protect Structure and Windows dialog box opens. The **Structure** option refers to deleting, moving, hiding, inserting, or renaming worksheets. The **Windows** option applies to resizing, moving, or closing windows.

9. Select both **Structure** and **Windows**. Do not use a password.

Figure 22-14
Protecting structure
and windows
Book2.xlsx
California sheet

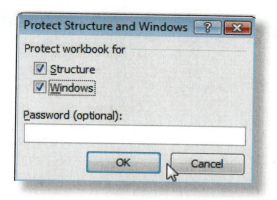

10. Click **OK**.

11. Click the Save button. In the **File name** text box, key *[your initials]*22-23.

12. For **Save as type**, choose **Excel Template**.

REVIEW

When you choose **Excel Template**, the folder updates to the default Templates folder for your computer.

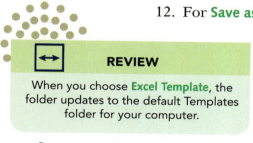

NOTE

There is no Close Window button ✕ for a Windows-protected workbook.

13. Double-click the **NewTemplates** folder and click **Save**.

14. Click the Microsoft Office Button. Choose **Close**.

15. Open the New Workbook dialog box. Click **My templates**. Click the **NewTemplates** tab. Choose *[your initials]*22-23 and click **OK**.

16. Click the **Insert Worksheet** tab. You cannot insert or delete worksheets in a protected workbook.

17. Try to maximize the window. There are no sizing buttons. Workbook protection prevents you from resizing the window.

18. Click the Microsoft Office Button. Choose **Close**.

Exercise 22-24 DELETE A FOLDER AND FILES

1. Press [Ctrl]+[O]. If you have just completed the previous exercise, the **NewTemplates** folder may be open.

2. Click the « button in the Address bar and choose **Templates**.

3. Right-click the **NewTemplates** folder. Choose **Delete**. (See Figure 22-15 on the next page.)

4. Click **Yes**. The folders and its contents are deleted.

Figure 22-15
Deleting a templates
folder and contents

5. Click **Cancel** to close the Open dialog box.

Using Online Help

Templates can increase your productivity when used properly. Look for more information about templates in Help, including tips about changing defaults.

USE HELP TO LEARN ABOUT TEMPLATES

1. Look up templates using Help.

2. Expand any definitions to learn about the default worksheet and workbook templates.

3. Close the Help windows.

Lesson 22 Summary

- Excel includes installed templates that can be opened, edited, and resaved.
- When you create a workbook from a template, the new workbook is named with the template name and a number. Use the Save As command to save the workbook with an appropriate filename.
- You can open any template to edit it. You can resave it with the same name if you prefer.
- The Locked property is a setting that controls whether or not a cell or object can be edited. This property works with the Protect Sheet command.
- When you use worksheet protection, the user cannot edit or change cells or objects unless they have been unlocked.
- Microsoft Office Online is a Web site with professionally designed templates for each product in the Office suite including Excel.
- To create your own template, key and format labels, values, and formulas in a worksheet.
- You can suppress the display of zeros when there are no values for a formula to calculate.
- Many templates include data validation and conditional formatting.
- A workbook template has multiple predesigned worksheets.
- Workbook protection prevents the user from resizing or moving the windows and from adding, deleting, or changing the worksheets.
- You can assign a password to a protected worksheet as well as to a protected workbook.
- If you create a folder in the default Templates folder, it appears as a separate tab in the New dialog box.

LESSON 22		Command Summary	
Feature	**Button**	**Task Path**	**Keyboard**
Hide zeros		Microsoft Office, Excel Options, Advanced	
Lock/unlock cell		Home, Cells, Format, Format Cells	Ctrl + 1
Protect sheet		Review, Changes	
Protect workbook		Review, Changes, Protect Workbook, Protect Structure and Windows	
Template, open		Microsoft Office, Open	Ctrl + O
Template, save		Microsoft Office, Save As	F12
Template, use		Microsoft Office, New	
Unprotect sheet		Review, Changes	
View side by side		View, Window	

Concepts Review

True/False Questions

Each of the following statements is either true or false. Indicate your choice by circling T or F.

T F   1. A protected worksheet may have cells that cannot be edited.

T F   2. Templates can include values, labels, comments, and formatting.

T F   3. Passwords can be assigned with worksheet protection.

T F   4. A workbook created from a template is named **Untitled**.

T F   5. Workbook properties include the author, the company, and the Locked setting.

T F   6. The name of a hidden workbook does not appear in the Open dialog box.

T F   7. All templates are listed as Installed Templates in the New Workbook dialog box.

T F   8. A template can have multiple worksheets.

Short Answer Questions

Write the correct answer in the space provided.

1. What option should you click in the New Workbook dialog box to use a template that you created and saved yesterday?

   _____

2. How can you edit a workbook that is protected?

   _____

3. Name two command tasks that enhance a template's usefulness.

   _____

4. How can you show blank cells instead of zeros on a worksheet?

   _____

5. What cell property works with sheet protection?

   _____

6. What choice would you make in the New Workbook dialog box to browse the Web for templates?

   _____

7. How can you create a new template from an existing one?

_____

8. How can you display a workbook that is hidden?

_____

Critical Thinking

Answer these questions on a separate page. There are no right or wrong answers. Support your answers with examples from your own experience, if possible.

1. In your school or the company where you work, what documents might be candidates for templates?

2. How can worksheet protection add to your productivity?

Skills Review

Exercise 22-25

Use and edit an installed template. Add worksheet protection.

1. Use an installed template by following these steps:
   a. Click the Microsoft Office Button and choose **New**.
   b. Click **Installed Templates**. Double-click **Personal Monthly Budget**.
   c. Save the workbook as an **Excel Workbook** named *[your initials]*22-25 in your lesson folder. This workbook has several tables and uses an icon set in several of them. Sample data is included.
   d. Look at each of the tables. Click several cells to note which cells have sample data and which have formulas.

2. Edit an installed template by following these steps:
   a. Set a 70% view size.
   b. Click cell E4. You would enter a value for your income in this cell.
   c. Select cells E4:E5 and press Delete. The sample data is deleted.
   d. Select and delete the following cells: E7:E8, C12:D15, H12:I12, and C25:D25.

NOTE

The sheet uses separator columns and rows to distinguish the tables.

NOTE

When you protect a sheet with a table, you cannot resize the table.

3. Add worksheet protection by following these steps:

    a. Select cells E4:E5. Hold down [Ctrl] and add cells E7:E8 to the selection.

    b. Press [Ctrl]+[1]. Click the **Protection** tab. Click to deselect **Locked**. Click **OK**.

    c. Select cells C12:D21. Press [Ctrl]+[1]. Click the **Protection** tab. Click to deselect **Locked**. Click **OK**.

    d. Unlock the appropriate cells in each of the remaining tables.

    e. Click the **Review** tab. Click the Protect Sheet button.

    i. Click to select **Select locked cells**, **Select unlocked cells**, **Format columns**, and **Format rows**. Click **OK**.

4. Update properties by following these steps:

    a. Click the Microsoft Office Button and choose **Prepare**.

    b. Choose **Properties**. Click the Property Views and Options button [Document Properties ▼] and choose **Advanced Properties**.

    c. Click the **Summary** tab.

    d. Key **Personal Budget** as the title. Key **Income and expenses** as the subject.

    e. Key *[your first and last name]* as the author.

    f. Verify that a thumbnail will be included.

    g. Click **OK**. Close the Document Information Panel.

5. Key some sample data to test your work and save the file as *[your initials]22-25a*.

6. Prepare and submit your work.

NOTE

The tables require that you enter a projected amount as well as the actual amount.

Exercise 22-26

Use an online template.

1. Use an online template by following these steps:

    a. Click the Microsoft Office Button. Choose **New**.

    b. Click in the Search Microsoft Office Online box.

    c. Key **packing slip** and press [Enter].

    d. Click the first thumbnail for **Packing slip**.

    e. Click **Download**. Click **Continue** in the message box about the validity of your copy of Office.

2. Build a new template from an online template by following these steps:

    a. Replace **Your Company Name** with **Klassy Kow Ice Cream, Inc.** Turn off **Merge and Center** and left-align the label.

    b. Delete **Your company slogan**.

    c. Click cell F7 in the **Ship to** section. Key **=** and then click cell D5. Press Enter.

    d. In cell F8, key a reference to cell D6. Create a reference for the phone number data.

    e. Click cell F11. Key **=** and click cell F5. Press Enter.

    f. Copy the reference to cell F15.

    g. Delete cells D10:D12. This is sample data from the template.

3. Update properties by following these steps:

    a. Click the Microsoft Office Button 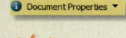 and choose **Prepare**.

    b. Choose **Properties**. Click the Property Views and Options button

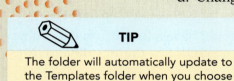 . Click the **Summary** tab.

    c. Change the author to *[your first and last name]*.

    d. Change the company to **Klassy Kow Ice Cream, Inc.**

    e. In the **Comments** box, key **This packing slip is included with all shipments from the Klamath Falls distribution facility.**

✏ TIP

The folder will automatically update to the Templates folder when you choose the file type.

---

    f. Save the workbook with a thumbnail image. Click **OK**.

    g. Close the Document Information Panel.

    h. Click cell D5.

4. Press F12 and save the workbook as a template named *[your initials]*22-26 in the Templates folder. Close the template.

5. Create a new workbook based on your template. Key the address information in cells D5:D8.

    5000 West Monroe Street
    Indianapolis, IN 45678
    111-555-3455
    111-555-3456

6. In cells F5:F6, key the name and company.

    Bruce Bailey
    All Flavors

7. In cells D10:D12, key the order information.

    =today()
    KK70403
    P70403

8. Key the following product information.

Product	Description	Unit Type	Order Quantity	Ship Quantity
KK103	24 pack, French Vanilla	1/2 gal	3	3
KK234	12 pack, Raspberry Swirl	1/2 gal	3	3

9. Save the workbook as *[your initials]*22-26 in your lesson folder.

10. Delete a template by following these steps:

    a. Open the New Workbook dialog box.

    b. Click **My templates**.

    c. Right-click *[your initials]*22-26 and delete it.

11. Prepare and submit your work.

Exercise 22-27

Create a user template.

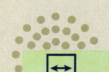
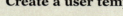
REVIEW

Subtract the starting time from the ending time and multiply the result by 24.

1. Open **PTTimeSheet**.

2. Create a table for cells B6:F29 using **Medium Style 3**.

3. The hours column should have a formula to determine the number of hours worked. Key dummy data to test your formula.

4. Add data validation by following these steps:

    a. Select the cells that will show the start and end times.

    b. Click the **Data** tab. Click the Data Validation button 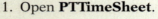. Click the **Settings** tab.

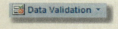

    c. For the **Allow** box, choose **Time**. In the **Data** box, choose **between**. In the **Start time** box, key **10 AM**. For the **End time**, key **11 PM**.

    d. Click the **Error Alert** tab. Use an **Information** style. For the **Title**, key **Standard Hours**.

    e. In the **Error message** box, key **Normal available part-time hours are between 10 am and 11 pm**. Click **OK**.

5. Apply conditional formatting by following these steps:

    a. Select the cells that will show hours worked per employee.

    b. Click the **Home** tab. Click the Conditional Formatting button .

    c. Create a format that shows the cell contents as bold italic if the value is greater than 8.

6. Select the cell where the insertion point should be when the template is used to create a workbook.

7. Save the worksheet as a template by following these steps:

   a. Press F12. For the **Save as type** box, choose **Excel Template**.

   b. In the **File name** box, key *[your initials]22-27*.

   c. Click **Save**. Close the template.

8. Use a template by following these steps:

   a. Click the Microsoft Office Button  and choose **New**. Click **My templates**.

   b. Double-click *[your initials]22-27*.

   c. Starting in the appropriate cell, key the following data for the Bremerton shop.

Name	Date	Start Time	End Time
[your name]	*[today]*	10:30 am	4:30 pm
Keiko Yang	*[yesterday]*	11 am	8:30 pm
Janice Green	*[tomorrow]*	9 am	4:30 pm

   d. Save the Excel Workbook as *[your initials]22-27* in your folder.

9. Delete a template by following these steps:

   a. Open the New Workbook dialog box.

   b. Click **My templates**. Delete *[your initials]22-27*.

10. Prepare and submit your work.

REVIEW

Excel switches to the Templates folder for your computer when you choose Excel Template as the file type.

NOTE

Template files remain on the computer until they are deleted.

Exercise 22-28

Use worksheet and workbook protection.

1. Open **ORKowO**.

2. Create a workbook template by following these steps:

   a. On the Page Layout tab, set the **Width** and **Height** settings to **1 page**.

   b. Design an attractive layout for the sheet using borders, fill, and anything else you would like to try.

   c. Use a formula for column G to sum the other columns.

   d. Make three copies of the **FirstQtr** sheet and name them for the other three quarters. Use a different color scheme for each quarter. Change the tab color on each sheet to match its color scheme.

   e. Edit cell B3 to show the correct quarter on each sheet.

   f. In the properties, show your name as the author and your school or company name. Show a thumbnail.

3. Set worksheet and workbook protection by following these steps:

   a. Group the sheets and select the cells that will require data entry.

   b. Press Ctrl+1. Click the **Protection** tab. Click to deselect **Locked**. Click **OK**.

c. Ungroup the sheets.

d. Click the **FirstQtr** tab. Click the **Review** tab. Click the Protect Sheet button . Do not use a password.

e. Select **Select locked cells**, **Select unlocked cells**, **Format columns**, and **Format rows**. Click **OK**.

f. Use the same sheet protection for each sheet.

g. Click the **Review** tab. Click the Protect Workbook button 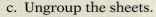. Choose **Protect Structure and Windows**.

h. Click to select **Structure** and deselect **Windows**. Do not use a password. Click **OK**.

4. Save a workbook template by following these steps:

a. Press F12. In the **File name** box, key *[your initials]*22-28.

b. For the **Save as type** option, choose **Excel Template**.

c. Make sure the location is the regular Templates folder. Click **Save**.

5. Prepare and submit your work.

6. Delete the template from the computer if requested by your instructor.

Lesson Applications

Exercise 22-29

Edit and use a template. Add worksheet protection.

1. Open the **KlassyBirth** template to be edited.

2. Delete both images and make row 4 the same height as row 2. Use fill in row 29 to match row 5. Match the row height, too.

3. Use an AND function in column E that tests if the customer is between the age range specified.

4. Use an OR function in column F that tests if the customer is either female or younger than 5. Assume that column D will show M or F to indicate male or female.

5. Create an IF function in column G that shows "Yes" if the customer is male. If not, it should show nothing.

6. Add a comment in cell A3 that explains what is calculated in the formulas using one or two sentences. Size the comment to cover most of cell A3.

TIP

If the Save As dialog box does not show the Templates folder, choose Excel Workbook as the file type and then choose Excel Template again.

7. Unlock cells that will be used for data entry. Position the insertion point and protect the sheet without a password.

8. Save the template as *[your initials]*22-29 and close it.

9. Create a workbook from your template and key sample data for five customers. If anything does not work properly, edit the template and try again.

10. Save the workbook with sample data as *[your initials]*22-29.

11. Prepare and submit your work.

12. Delete the template *[your initials]*22-29 from your templates folder if requested.

Exercise 22-30

Use an online template. Add worksheet protection.

1. In the New Workbook dialog box, find and download the **Asset depreciation schedule** template in the **Schedules** category.

2. In cell F2, key **=now()** and format it to show the month spelled out, the date, a comma, and four digits for the year.

3. On the original sheet, click the cells and review the formulas.

4. Center the column labels. Change the color scheme to black/gray/white, using black fill where there is a dark color, light gray where there is a light color, black borders where needed, and text as appropriate.

5. Check that cells F3:F5 are unlocked. Protect the sheet. Click cell F3.

6. Save this workbook as a template named *[your initials]*22-30 in the Templates folder. Close the template.

7. Create a workbook from your template for an asset that initially cost $10,000 and that has a salvage value of $1,000 and a useful life of ten years.

8. Make a copy of the worksheet. Edit the data on the copied sheet to determine depreciation for an asset that cost $76,000 and will have a useful life of eight years. It is expected to be worth $15,000.

9. Save the workbook as *[your initials]*22-30. Prepare and submit your work.

Exercise 22-31

Use an installed template.

1. Create a new workbook from the **Loan Amortization** template in the Installed Templates category.

2. Save the Excel workbook as *[your initials]*22-31.

3. Fill in data for a mortgage loan of $200,000 for 20 years at 5.375%. The loan will start on the first day of next month. Assume that there will be no extra payments.

4. Add a footer with your name at the left and the filename in the center. In the right section, key **Page** and press Spacebar. Then use the buttons to create an entry that will show **Page *n* of *N*:** pages.

5. Use Print Preview or Page Layout View to check the worksheet. Adjust the bottom margin to separate the footer from the data.

6. Prepare and submit your work.

Exercise 22-32 ◆ Challenge Yourself

Edit a user template.

1. Open the **FTTimeSheet** template for editing.

2. Save the template as a template named *[your initials]*22-32.

3. This template has several errors. Find and correct all errors and resave the template.

4. Create a workbook from your template and key sample data to test your work. Save the workbook as *[your initials]*22-32.

5. Prepare a formula sheet.

6. Prepare and submit your work.

On Your Own

In these exercises you work on your own, as you would in a real-life work environment. Use the skills you've learned to accomplish the task—and be creative.

Exercise 22-33

Open **CancerPledge**. This sheet is to be designed as a template. The formulas in row 30 are not correct, and you need additional formulas on the sheet. Use some type of conditional formatting for the **Difference** column. Make decisions about what other features to use in the template and how to reformat it. Save it as a template named *[your initials]*22-33. Use sample data to test your work. Prepare and submit your work.

Exercise 22-34

Download a Microsoft Office Online template that covers something of interest to you or something with which you are familiar. Review/key sample data, if any, and check the formulas. Make your own design or layout changes to the template. Save the workbook as a template named *[your initials]*22-34. Prepare and submit your work.

Exercise 22-35

Create a workbook template for tracking your grades in three courses, each course on a separate sheet. Assume the same grading scales and categories. For example, each sheet can list **Exams**, **Assignments**, **Participation**, **Essays**, **Homework**, etc. Determine if you have uses for data validation and/or conditional formatting. Insert a relevant comment on the first sheet. Add worksheet and workbook protection. Save the template as *[your initials]*22-35. Prepare and submit your work.

Lesson 23

Using Workgroup Features

OBJECTIVES

After completing this lesson, you will be able to:

1. Create a shared workbook.

2. Track changes.

3. Print a change history sheet.

4. Compare and merge workbooks.

5. Accept or reject changes.

MCAS OBJECTIVES

In this lesson:
XL07 5.1
XL07 5.1.1
XL07 5.1.2
XL07 5.2.2

Estimated Time: 1¹/₂ hours

A *shared workbook* is one that several users can access at the same time. A shared workbook is usually stored on a network drive and available to any member of a workgroup. A *workgroup* is a set of workers who use the workbook.

This lesson simulates a three-person workgroup. The group members are:

• User 1, Keiko Sumara, Sales and Marketing Manager

• User 2, Kim Tamasaki, Contract Sales Representative

• User 3, Juan Sante, Vice President

Your instructor may assign you to a specific role or ask that you rotate roles. As you complete the lesson, complete the steps for your role but note what your coworkers are doing.

Creating a Shared Workbook

A shared workbook is generally kept in a single location on a network drive with all users able to access it at the same time. A shared workbook can also be copied so that each user keeps his or her own copy while working. At some point, the copies are combined.

In a shared workbook, you cannot do the following:

- Delete worksheets.

- Insert or delete cell ranges. You can insert or delete rows or columns.

- Merge cells.

- Add or edit charts, images, shapes, or hyperlinks.

- Use conditional formatting.

- Use data validation.

- Use worksheet protection.

- Create or change passwords.

- Insert subtotals.

- Create an Excel table.

- Create or edit macros. You can create a macro in an unshared, open workbook and use the macro in a shared workbook.

- Create or modify scenarios, outlines, PivotTables, and data tables.

Exercise 23-1　CREATE A SHARED WORKBOOK

User 1 will create a workbook that will be shared with User 2 and User 3.

> **NOTE**
>
> If you are unable to use a network in class, you can copy and share the workbook by e-mail or portable media. If you are working alone, you can change the user name each time you act as a different user.

> **NOTE**
>
> Make a note of the default User name so that you can return to it later.

1. **USER 1, Keiko Sumara:** Click the Microsoft Office Button 🔘 and choose **Excel Options**. Click **Popular**. Change the **User name** to **Sumara**. Click **OK**.

   USER 2, Kim Tamasaki: Click the Microsoft Office Button 🔘 and choose **Excel Options**. Click **Popular**. Change the **User name** to **Tamasaki**. Click **OK**.

   USER 3, Juan Sante: Click the Microsoft Office Button 🔘 and choose **Excel Options**. Click **Popular**. Change the **User name** to **Sante**. Click **OK**.

2. **USER 1:** Open **RepQuotas**. Save the workbook as *[your initials]*23-1Sumara in a Lesson 23 folder for your workgroup.

3. **USER 1:** Click the **Review** tab. Click the Share Workbook button 🔲. The Share Workbook dialog box opens.

4. **USER 1:** On the **Editing** tab, select **Allow changes by more than one user at the same time**. The user name for your computer appears in the **Who has this workbook open now** list. (See Figure 23-1 on the next page.)

Figure 23-1
Editing tab in the
Share Workbook
dialog box
**RepQuotas.xlsx
Quotas sheet**

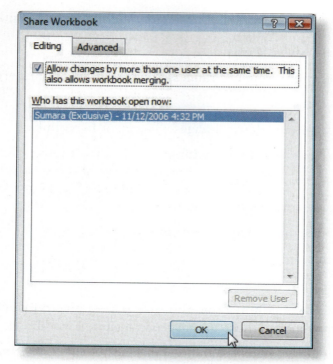

5. **USER 1:** Click **OK**. A dialog box notes that the workbook will be saved.

6. **USER 1:** Click **OK**. The filename shows **[Shared]** in the title bar.

7. **USER 2:** Open *[your initials]***23-1Sumara** in the folder for your group. Save the workbook as *[your initials]***23-1Tamasaki** in the same folder.

8. **USER 3:** Open *[your initials]***23-1Sumara** in the folder for your group. Save the workbook as *[your initials]***23-1Sante** in the same folder.

Tracking Changes

In a shared workbook, Excel can track changes to the data. It creates a list of changes known as the *change history*. The Advanced tab in the Share Workbook dialog box includes settings for how changes are tracked in a shared workbook.

The change history options on the Advanced tab of the Share Workbook dialog box are as follows:

• The Track Changes group activates the change history. When you share a workbook, this setting is automatically enabled. You can turn this setting off or set the number of days for which changes are followed.

• The Update Changes group specifies how often you see changes from other users. If you select **When file is saved**, you see updates from other users when you save your own copy of the workbook. If you select **Automatically every** and set a time interval, you see others' changes at the specified interval. This setting assumes that workers are sharing one copy of the workbook on a network.

- The Conflicting Changes Between Users group specifies how you handle conflicting changes when you save the shared workbook. If you select **Ask me which changes win**, you see a dialog box when a conflict occurs and can decide what to do. If you select **The changes being saved win**, Excel keeps only your changes when you save the workbook.

NOTE

Excel does not track format changes.

- The Include in Personal View group specifies personal printing and filtering options for the shared workbook. These should be selected when each user wants to save individual print and filter options.

Exercise 23-2   SET CHANGE HISTORY OPTIONS

1. **ALL USERS:** Click the **Review** tab. Click the Share Workbook button . Click the **Advanced** tab.

2. Click the down arrow next to the **Keep change history for** box until the number of days is **20**.

3. Select **When file is saved** in the **Update changes** group if it is not already selected.

4. Select **Ask me which changes win** in the **Conflicting changes between users** group if it is not already selected.

5. Make sure both **Print settings** and **Filter settings** are selected.

Figure 23-2
Advanced tab in the Share Workbook dialog box
23-1.xlsx
Quotas sheet

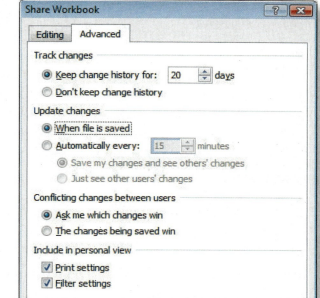

6. Click **OK**. The change history options are set.

Excel 2007

Exercise 23-3 ACTIVATE CHANGE HIGHLIGHTING

You can have changes to cell contents highlighted in a shared workbook.

1. **ALL USERS:** On the **Review** tab, click the Track Changes button

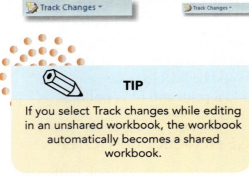

2. Choose **Highlight Changes**. The Highlight Changes dialog box opens. The **Track changes while editing** option is already selected because User 1 designated this as a shared workbook.

3. Make sure **When** is selected.

4. Click the arrow for the **When** box and choose **Not yet reviewed**. This setting enables you to accept or reject changes made by others that you have not yet seen.

5. Make sure that the **Who** box shows **Everyone**. Your option here is to select **Who** and specify certain users.

6. Make sure **Where** is not selected. This sets a specific range of cells for tracking changes. Otherwise, the entire worksheet is tracked.

7. Make sure **Highlight changes on screen** is selected.

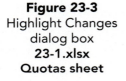

TIP

If you select Track changes while editing in an unshared workbook, the workbook automatically becomes a shared workbook.

Figure 23-3
Highlight Changes dialog box
23-1.xlsx
Quotas sheet

Highlight Changes	?	✕

☑ Track changes while editing. This also shares your workbook.

Highlight which changes

☑ When: Not yet reviewed ▼

☐ Who: Everyone ▼

☐ Where:

☑ Highlight changes on screen
☐ List changes on a new sheet

[OK]   [Cancel]

8. Click **OK**. The dialog box tells you that no changes were found. Click **OK**.

Exercise 23-4 TRACK AND HIGHLIGHT CHANGES

When the tracking feature is in effect, a colored border appears around any cell that is changed with a small revision triangle in the upper-left corner of the cell. The row and column headings also change color, showing you where changes have been made. The colors used depend on your workstation settings, and you will see different colors for the other users when all the work is combined. When you place the mouse pointer on the cell, a comment box appears describing who made the change and when.

1. **USER 1, Sumara:** Change cell C7 to **200000**.

2. **USER 1:** Change cell C12 to **215000**.

3. **USER 1:** Position the mouse pointer on cell C7 and then on cell C12 to see the comment boxes for your changes.

4. **USER 2, Tamasaki:** Change cell D25 to **175000**.

5. **USER 2:** Change cell D4 to **Annual Estimate**.

6. **USER 2:** Position the mouse pointer on cell D25 and then on cell D4 to see the comment boxes for your changes.

7. **USER 3, Sante:** Change cell D24 to **300000**.

8. **USER 3:** Change cell C15 to **160000**.

9. **USER 3:** Position the mouse pointer on cell D24 and then on cell C15 to see the comment boxes for your changes.

Exercise 23-5 ADD COMMENTS IN A SHARED WORKBOOK

Comments are added automatically when you make a change to a shared workbook. Adding your own comments is a good way to exchange ideas and suggestions in a shared workbook.

1. **USER 1, Sumara:** Click cell D9.

2. **USER 1:** Click the New Comment button on the **Review** tab. Key **Please verify this number; it seems low.**

Figure 23-4
New comment added
23-1.xlsx
Quotas sheet

	A	B	C	D	E	F	G	H
1								
2		Klassy Kow Ice Cream, Inc.						
3		Sales Quotas for Contract Sales Representatives						
4		Contractor	Company Quota	Rep's Estimate				
5		Abramson, Michael	$250,000	$200,000				
6		Atkinson, Kathleen	$300,000	$240,000				
7		Benson, Jerry	$200,000	$175,000				
8		Baanu, Nicole	$300,000	$275,000	Sumara:			
9		Conley, Stephen	$200,000	$21,000	Please verify this			
10		Cruz, Ensenada	$145,000	$155,000	number; it seems low.			
11		Diko, Akiko	$300,000	$290,000				
12		Dominguez, Vittorio	$215,000	$90,000				
13		Fitzgerald, Glenn	$100,000	$140,000				
14		Gable, Barbara	$160,000	$80,000				
15		Gutierrez, Luis	$120,000	$135,000				
16		Hanson, Kerri	$110,000	$85,000				
17		Jackson, Larry	$90,000	$120,000				

3. Click another cell to hide the comment.

4. **USER 2, Tamasaki:** Click cell C26.

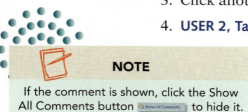

NOTE

If the comment is shown, click the Show All Comments button Show All Comments to hide it.

5. **USER 2:** Click the New Comment button 📝. Key **This value is below last year's.**

6. Click another cell to hide the comment.

7. **USER 3, Sante:** Click cell C18.

8. **USER 3:** Click the New Comment button 📝. Key **We might need to adjust this number higher.**

9. Click another cell to hide the comment.

10. **ALL USERS:** Save your workbook using the same name.

Printing a Change History Sheet

In addition to viewing changes on screen, you can print a history of these changes. This sheet, named **History**, details each change that was made. The **History** sheet is a generated worksheet, similar to a scenario summary report.

Exercise 23-6 DISPLAY AND PRINT A HISTORY WORKSHEET

1. **ALL USERS:** Click the **Review** tab. Click the Track Changes button ![Track Changes]. Choose **Highlight Changes**.

2. **ALL USERS:** Make sure **When** is selected and set it to **All**. For the **Who** box, select **Everyone**.

3. **ALL USERS:** Click to select **List changes on a new sheet** and click **OK**. The **History** sheet is added to the workbook. The **History** sheet has Filter arrows so that you can choose which changes to view.

Figure 23-5
A History sheet
23-1.xlsx
History sheet

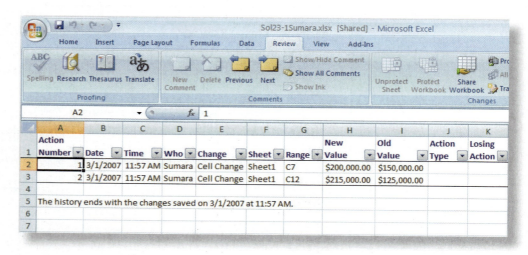

4. **ALL USERS:** Add a header to the **History** sheet and print it.

5. **USER 1, Sumara:** Save your workbook with the same name and leave it open.

6. **USER 2, Tamasaki:** Save your workbook with the same name and close it.

7. **USER 3, Sante:** Save your workbook with the same name and close it.

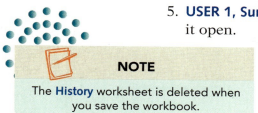

NOTE

The **History** worksheet is deleted when you save the workbook.

Comparing and Merging Workbooks

After each workgroup member has saved his or her own copy of a shared workbook, the individual members' workbooks can be compared and merged into one file. For workbooks to be compared and merged, the following requirements must be met:

• The original workbook must have been shared before copies were made.

• The original workbook must have the change history option turned on.

• Each copy of the workbook must have been made from the original, have a different filename, and have no passwords.

• The merging must occur before the expiration of the change history days.

Exercise 23-7   **DISPLAY THE COMPARE AND MERGE BUTTON**

The Compare and Merge Workbooks command is not shown in the Ribbon. You can, however, add it to the Quick Access toolbar.

1. **ALL USERS:** Click the Customize Quick Access Toolbar button . A list of commonly used commands opens.

2. Choose **More Commands**. The Excel Options dialog box opens to the **Customize** pane.

3. Click the **Choose commands from** arrow and choose **Commands Not in the Ribbon**. The commands are listed alphabetically.

4. Scroll to find and click **Compare and Merge Workbooks**.

5. Click **Add**. It appears in the toolbar list at the right. (See Figure 23-6 on the next page.)

Figure 23-6
Adding a task to the
Quick Access toolbar
23-1.xlsx
Quotas sheet

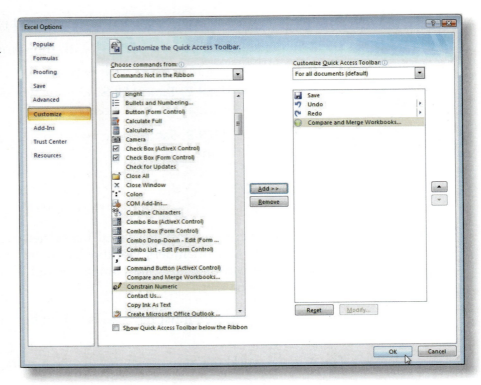

6. Click **OK**. The button appears to the right of the others in the Quick
   Access toolbar.

Exercise 23-8   COMPARE AND MERGE WORKBOOKS

The main copy of the shared workbook is *[your initials]***23-1Sumara**. User 1,
Sumara, should begin this exercise, starting with *[your initials]***23-1Sumara**
open.

1. **USER 1**: Click the Compare and Merge Workbooks button ⬤. The
   Select Files to Merge Into Current Workbook dialog box opens.
   Locate your workgroup folder.

2. **USER 1**: Choose *[your initials]***23-1Tamasaki** and click **OK**. Cells D4
   and D25 show changes. These are the cells that Tamasaki changed,
   and they are outlined in color.

3. **USER 1**: Click the Compare and Merge Workbooks button ⬤.
   Double-click *[your initials]***23-1Sante**. The cells with changes made
   by Sante (C15 and D24) are outlined in a different color.

4. **USER 1**: Save the merged workbook as *[your initials]***23-8Sumara** in
   your workgroup folder.

5. **USER 2, Tamasaki**: Open *[your initials]***23-8Sumara**. Save the
   workbook as *[your initials]***23-8Tamasaki** in your workgroup folder.

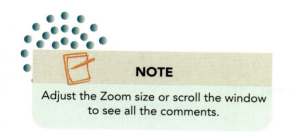

NOTE

Adjust the Zoom size or scroll the window to see all the comments.

6. **USER 3, Sante**: Open *[your initials]*23-8Sumara. Save the workbook as *[your initials]*23-8Sante in your workgroup folder.

7. **ALL USERS**: Click the Show All Comments button Show All Comments. These are the comments that were keyed.

Accepting or Rejecting Changes

After workbooks are merged, you can review the changes and decide whether to accept or reject them. You can review them one at a time or all at once.

Exercise 23-9   ACCEPT OR REJECT CHANGES

All users complete this exercise through step 8 in their own workbook.

1. Click the **Review** tab. Click the Track Changes button Track Changes ▾. Choose **Accept or Reject Changes**. The Select Changes to Accept or Reject dialog box opens.

2. Verify that **When** is selected and that **Not yet reviewed** appears in the box.

3. Click **OK**. The Accept or Reject Changes dialog box opens, and a marquee appears around the first change in cell C7. The dialog box shows who made the change and what it was.

Figure 23-7
Accepting or rejecting changes
23-8.xlsx
Quotas sheet

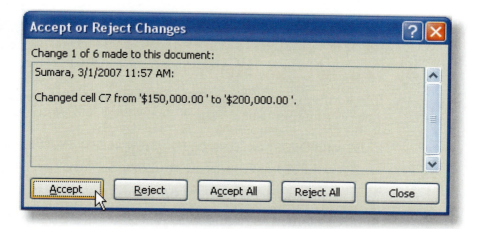

4. Click **Accept**. The next change highlighted is in cell C12.

5. Click **Accept** for the change in cell C12.

6. Click **Accept** for the change in cell D25.

7. Click **Reject** to reject the change to cell D4. The label reverts to the original.

8. Reject the changes in cells D24 and C15.

9. **USER 1**: Save the workbook as *[your initials]*23-9Sumara in the workgroup folder.

10. **USER 2**: Save the workbook as *[your initials]*23-9Tamasaki in the workgroup folder.

11. **USER 3**: Save the workbook as *[your initials]*23-9Sante in the workgroup folder.

12. **ALL USERS**: Add a header or footer to show your name. Set comments to print at the end of the sheet on a separate page.

13. Save and close the workbook.

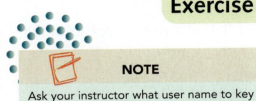

Exercise 23-10   RESET THE USER NAME AND QUICK ACCESS TOOLBAR

NOTE

Ask your instructor what user name to key for the classroom computer.

1. Click the Microsoft Office Button 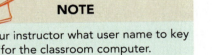 and choose **Excel Options**. Click **Popular**. Change the **User name** to the default name for your computer.

2. Click **Customize** to open the pane.

3. Click **Compare and Merge Workbooks** in the list on the right.

4. Click **Remove**. Click **OK**.

Using Online Help

In addition to sharing a workbook across a local network, you can use Excel Services to publish and share a workbook across the Web.

USE MICROSOFT EXCEL HELP TO LEARN ABOUT EXCEL SERVICES

1. Look for help topics about Excel Services.

2. Read and print relevant information.

3. Close the Help windows.

Lesson 23 Summary

- A shared workbook is used by more than one person at a time. Users who share workbooks are a workgroup.
- A shared workbook is typically found in a networked environment. Shared workbooks have some limitations.
- A workbook must be saved before it can be shared.
- Excel keeps track of changes in a shared workbook. It creates a list of changes known as the change history.
- In a shared workbook, you can highlight changes on the screen while editing.
- Comments are added automatically when you make a change to a shared workbook. You also can add your own comments.
- If each user has a separate copy of a shared workbook, the workbooks can be compared and merged.
- After workbooks are merged, you can review the changes and either accept or reject the changes.

LESSON 23		Command Summary	
Feature	**Button**	**Task Path**	**Keyboard**
Accept/reject changes	Track Changes	Review, Changes	
Add button to toolbar		More Commands	
Change history options	Share Workbook	Review, Changes	
Highlight changes	Track Changes	Review, Changes	
History sheet	Track Changes	Review, Changes	
Merge workbooks		Quick Access Toolbar	
Share workbook	Share Workbook	Review, Changes	
User name		Microsoft Office, Excel Options, Popular	

Concepts Review

True/False Questions

Each of the following statements is either true or false. Indicate your choice by circling T or F.

T   F   1. A workgroup is a set of workbooks used by three workers.

T   F   2. You can insert and delete worksheets in a shared workbook.

T   F   3. The list of edits made to a shared workbook is its change history.

T   F   4. You can set changes to be highlighted on screen or printed on a separate worksheet.

T   F   5. Comments are added to edited cells in a shared workbook.

T   F   6. A consolidated workbook assembles a single sheet from all copies of a shared workbook.

T   F   7. User changes are color-coded in a shared workbook.

T   F   8. A cell with a change displays a small triangle in the upper-right corner.

Short Answer Questions

Write the correct answer in the space provided.

1. How do you change the computer's user name?

_____

2. What command button allows you to print a change history sheet?

_____

3. What is required for three users to work on the same workbook at the same time?

_____

4. What can users do if they want to save their own edits to a shared workbook?

_____

5. Name three tasks that are prohibited in a shared workbook.

_____

6. What command combines user copies of a workbook into one file?

_____

7. As you review changes in a merged workbook, what can you do about those changes?

_____

8. What is a workgroup?

_____

Critical Thinking

Answer these questions on a separate page. There are no right or wrong answers. Support your answers with examples from your own experience, if possible.

1. If you have a job, what other department do you work with on a regular basis? At your school, what departments or divisions might work together? Explain how work might be shared between workers and departments.

2. You can share a workbook so that all users are working on it at the same time. Users can also make their own copies, work separately, and merge work later. When might it be better to make separate copies for each user rather than work with one file?

Skills Review

Exercise 23-11

Create a shared workbook.

NOTE

The Skills Review exercises assume the same workgroup as the lesson. The workbook you create in this lesson is used in Exercises 23-12 through 23-14.

1. **USER 1, Sumara:** Click the Microsoft Office Button and choose **Excel Options**. Click **Popular**. Change the **User name** to **Sumara**. Click **OK**.

2. **USER 2, Tamasaki:** Click the Microsoft Office Button and choose **Excel Options**. Click **Popular**. Change the **User name** to **Tamasaki**. Click **OK**.

3. **USER 3, Sante:** Click the Microsoft Office Button and choose **Excel Options**. Click **Popular**. Change the **User name** to **Sante**. Click **OK**.

4. **USER 1**: Create a shared workbook by following these steps:

   a. Open **VendorList**.

   b. Save the workbook as *[your initials]*23-11Sumara in a workgroup folder.

   c. Delete **Sheet2** and **Sheet3**.

   d. Click the **Review** tab. Click the Share Workbook button .

   e. Select **Allow changes by more than one user at the same time**. Click **OK** twice.

   f. **USER 2**: Open *[your initials]*23-11**Sumara** and save the workbook as *[your initials]*23-11**Tamasaki** in the workgroup folder.

   g. **USER 3**: Open *[your initials]*23-11**Sumara** and save the workbook as *[your initials]*23-11**Sante** in the workgroup folder.

5. **ALL USERS**: Set change history options by following these steps:

   a. Click the **Review** tab. Click the Share Workbook button. Click the **Advanced** tab.

   b. Click the arrow for **Keep change history for** and set days to **10**.

   c. Select **When file is saved** in the **Update changes** group.

   d. Select **Ask me which changes win** in the **Conflicting changes between users** group.

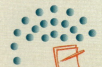

   e. Make sure both **Print settings** and **Filter settings** are selected.

   f. Click **OK**.

   g. On the **Review** tab, click the Track Changes button .

   h. Choose **Highlight Changes**. Make sure **When** is selected.

   i. Click the arrow for **When** and choose **Not yet reviewed**.

   j. Make sure **Highlight changes on screen** is selected.

   k. Click **OK** twice.

6. **ALL USERS**: Prepare and submit your work.

Exercise 23-12

Track changes.

1. **USER 1**: Open *[your initials]*23-11**Sumara** from Exercise 23-11.

2. **USER 2**: Open *[your initials]*23-11**Tamasaki** from Exercise 23-11.

3. **USER 3**: Open *[your initials]*23-11**Sante** from Exercise 23-11.

4. **ALL USERS**: Track changes by following these steps:

   a. On the **Review** tab, click the Track Changes button.

   b. Choose **Highlight Changes**. Make sure **When** is selected.

NOTE

You will see revision comments as you key changes. The phone column is formatted to show hyphens.

c. For the **When** option, choose **Not yet reviewed**.

d. Make sure **Highlight changes on screen** is selected. Click **OK** twice.

e. **USER 1**: Insert a row at row 21. Starting in cell A21, add a vendor/supplier by keying the following data:

| 1016 | Gerrard's | 18 Field Lane | Eureka, CA | 7075553300 |

f. **USER 2**: Insert two rows at row 21. Starting in cell A22, add a vendor/supplier by keying the following data:

| 1017 | RS, Inc. | 22 Antoine Road | Las Vegas, NV | 7025550090 |

g. **USER 3**: Insert three rows at row 21. Starting in cell A23, add a vendor/supplier by keying the following data:

| 1018 | Tri-City | 1A Ginger Way | Klamath Falls, OR | 5415550002 |

h. **USER 1**: Change the last four digits of the phone number in cell E6 to **7003**.

i. **USER 2**: Change the last four digits of the phone number in cell E6 to **0003**.

j. **USER 3**: Change the last four digits of the phone number in cell E6 to **1003**.

5. **USER 1**: Save the workbook as *[your initials]*23-12Sumara in the workgroup folder.

6. **USER 2**: Save the workbook as *[your initials]*23-12Tamasaki in the workgroup folder.

7. **USER 3**: Save the workbook as *[your initials]*23-12Sante in the workgroup folder.

8. **ALL USERS**: Prepare and submit your work.

Exercise 23-13

Print a change history worksheet.

NOTE

If you are starting a new work session, reset the user name for your computer.

1. **USER 1**: Open *[your initials]*23-12Sumara from Exercise 23-12.

2. **USER 2**: Open *[your initials]*23-12Tamasaki from Exercise 23-12.

3. **USER 3**: Open *[your initials]*23-12Sante from Exercise 23-12.

4. **ALL USERS**: On the **Review** tab, click the Track Changes button 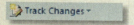. Choose **Highlight Changes**. For the **When** option, choose **Not yet reviewed**. Make sure **Highlight changes on screen** is selected. Click **OK** twice.

5. Insert comments by following these steps:

   a. **USER 1**: Select cell B6 and click the New Comment button . Key **Company will change name within 90 days**. Click another cell.

   b. **USER 2**: Select cell B11 and click the New Comment button . Key **New president on board next month**. Click another cell.

   c. **USER 3**: Select cell E10 and click the New Comment button . Key **Area code to be split within three months**. Click another cell.

6. **USER 1**: Save the workbook as *[your initials]*23-13Sumara in the workgroup folder.

7. **USER 2**: Save the workbook as *[your initials]*23-13Tamasaki in the workgroup folder.

8. **USER 3**: Save the workbook as *[your initials]*23-13Sante in the workgroup folder.

9. **ALL USERS**: Create a change history worksheet by following these steps:

   a. Click the **Review** tab.

   b. Click the Track Changes button . Choose **Highlight Changes**.

   c. Click to select **List changes on a new sheet**. Click **OK**.

10. **ALL USERS**: Add a header or footer to the **History** sheet and print it.

11. **ALL USERS**: Prepare and submit your work.

NOTE

Restore the default user name for your computer if you are not continuing to the next exercise.

Exercise 23-14

Compare and merge workbooks. Accept or reject changes.

1. **ALL USERS**: Display the Compare and Merge Workbooks button by following these steps:

   a. Click the Customize Quick Access Toolbar button . Choose **More Commands**.

   b. Click the **Choose commands from** arrow and choose **Commands Not in the Ribbon**.

   c. Scroll to find and click **Compare and Merge Workbooks**.

   d. Click **Add**. Click **OK**.

2. **USER 1**: Compare and merge workbooks by following these steps:

   a. Open *[your initials]*23-13Sumara.

   b. **USER 1**: Click the Compare and Merge Workbooks button 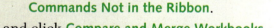.

   c. **USER 1**: Choose *[your initials]*23-13Tamasaki and click **OK**.

   d. **USER 1**: Repeat these steps to merge *[your initials]*23-13Sante.

   e. Save the merged workbook as *[your initials]*23-14Sumara in the workgroup folder.

NOTE

Set or verify the user name for your computer.

3. **USER 2**: Open *[your initials]*23-14**Sumara**. Save the workbook as *[your initials]*23-14**Tamasaki** in the workgroup folder.

4. **USER 3**: Open *[your initials]*23-14**Sumara**. Save the workbook as *[your initials]*23-14**Sante** in the workgroup folder.

5. **ALL USERS**: Accept or reject changes by following these steps:

  a. Click the **Review** tab. Click the Track Changes button .

  b. Choose **Accept or Reject Changes**.

  c. Choose **When** and **Not yet reviewed**. Click **OK**.

  d. Click **Accept** to accept the change for cell A21.

  e. Click **Accept** for each change in row 21.

  f. Choose the original value for cell E6 and click **Accept**.

  g. Accept all the changes for rows 22 and 23.

> **TIP**
>
> You can click Accept All to accept all changes from the current change on.

6. **ALL USERS**: Prepare and submit your work.

7. **ALL USERS**: Hide the Compare and Merge Workbooks button by following these steps:

  a. Click the Customize Quick Access Toolbar button. Choose **More Commands**.

  b. Click **Compare and Merge Workbooks** in the list on the right.

  c. Click **Remove**. Click **OK**.

> **NOTE**
>
> Restore the default user name for your computer if you are not continuing to the next exercise.

Lesson Applications

Exercise 23-15

Create a shared workbook. Track changes. Print a change history.

You have been asked to share the fourth-quarter workbook so that shop managers can make their projections for the first quarter next year.

REVIEW

Expand/collapse the formula bar to work with multi-line labels.

1. Open **ProjShakeMalt**. Save it as *[your initials]*23-15.

2. Share the workbook and set the change history to **25** days.

3. Turn on tracking so that changes that have not been reviewed are shown on screen.

4. Edit the label in cell A2 to show **First Quarter**. Change the worksheet tab name to **1stQtr**.

5. Change the months to **Jan**, **Feb**, and **Mar**.

6. Change the unit values as follows:

   Jan: 12000   **Feb: 15000**   **Mar: 18000**

7. Change the value of the constant **Price** to **$2.39**.

NOTE

You must save changes before creating a change history worksheet.

8. Save the workbook and create a change history worksheet. Print the history sheet.

9. Prepare and submit your work.

Exercise 23-16

Track changes.

The price list workbook is used by all shop owners, so it needs comments that clarify what each owner should do to complete and update the list.

1. Open **AllProducts**. Save it as *[your initials]*23-16.

2. Turn on Track Changes and delete the comment in cell C1.

3. Add this comment to cell C3: **Edit these prices to your shop's current prices**. Show the comment.

4. Size and position comment boxes so that none overlap or obscure text.

5. Calculate values in column D according to the information in the comment in cell D3.

6. Prepare and submit your work.

Exercise 23-17

Compare and merge workbooks. Accept or reject changes.

The third-quarter sales report is being updated by staff members. When all are finished, you will merge these workbooks and accept or reject changes.

1. Open **ThirdQtr**. Save it as *[your initials]*23-17.

2. Share the workbook and set the change history to 20 days.

3. Edit cell B5 to **20000**, cell C6 to **12500**, and cell D24 to **2.49**. Save the workbook as *[your initials]*23-17a.

4. Edit cell D7 to **14000**, cell D22 to **2.49**, and cell E5 to **19000**. Save the workbook as *[your initials]*23-17b. Close the workbook.

5. Open *[your initials]*23-17. Merge *[your initials]*23-17a and *[your initials]*23-17b, in this order.

6. Accept the change in B5; reject the change in cell C6; accept the changes in cells D24, D7, D22, and E5.

7. Save the merged workbook as *[your initials]*23-17.

8. Prepare and submit your work.

Exercise 23-18 ◆ Challenge Yourself

Create a shared workbook. Track changes. Compare and merge workbooks. Accept or reject changes.

Keiko Sumara wants to develop five new ice cream flavors for next summer and to project sales of 1-, 2-, and 3-scoop waffle cones. She has asked for help from Kim Tamasaki and Juan Sante. These are the three people in your workgroup.

NOTE

Set the user name for your computer before starting work.

- User 1, Keiko Sumara, Sales and Marketing Manager
- User 2, Kim Tamasaki, Contract Sales Representative
- User 3, Juan Sante, Vice President

1. **USER 1**: Create a worksheet with main labels and column titles for 1-, 2-, and 3-scoop waffle cones. Key five ice cream flavor names in a column, using your imagination to develop flavor names. Key values to estimate how many of each size you would expect to sell in a week. Format the worksheet in a professional manner.

2. **USER 1**: Save the workbook as *[your initials]*23-18Sumara in a workgroup folder. Share the workbook.

3. **USERS 2 and 3**: Open the shared workbook and save it as *[your initials]*23-18Tamasaki and as *[your initials]*23-18Sante. Track changes. Change three flavor names to your own ideas and adjust several values. Save and close your workbook.

4. **USER 1**: Open your workbook and compare and merge the other two. Save the merged workbook as *[your initials]*23-18SumaraMerged.

5. **USERS 2 and 3**: Open the merged workbook and save it as *[your initials]*23-18TamasakiMerged and as *[your initials]*23-18SanteMerged.

6. **ALL USERS:** Review the changes. Accept names you prefer and values that seem reasonable. Prepare and submit your work.

7. **ALL USERS:** Restore the default user name for your computer.

On Your Own

In these exercises you work on your own, as you would in a real-life work environment. Use the skills you've learned to accomplish the task—and be creative.

Exercise 23-19

Create a workgroup and develop a worksheet to list 15 music/song titles and artists. Share the workbook. Name it **Shared23-19** and save it in a group folder. Provide a copy of the workbook to each person in the group. Change several titles and artists in your copy of the workbook and save it as *[your initials]*23-19. Have one member of the group merge the original workbook. Then make copies of the merged workbook. Each member can then accept or reject changes. Save the final workbook as *[your initials]*23-19Merged in the group folder. Compare all results. Prepare and submit your work.

Exercise 23-20

Look up information in Help about collaboration. Then determine what you can try with a classmate or coworker so that you can both work live on the same document. Use any workbook from this lesson or develop your own. Have each person make changes and decide how to handle them. Save one copy of the final workbook named *[your initials]*23-20. Prepare and submit your work.

Exercise 23-21

Open any file from the lesson and save it as *[your initials]*23-21. Track changes and add a comment. Make some type of change to the workbook. Use the Send command to e-mail the workbook to your instructor or to your own e-mail account.

Unit 7 Applications

Unit Application 7-1

Create a template. Record a macro. Protect a template.

Corporate headquarters analyzes the number of health insurance claims by city. They tally the claims by month and display the data in a chart. You have been asked to create a template for this work.

REVIEW

Use Create from Selection to name multiple ranges.

TIP

You cannot easily copy formulas with range names. Key the cell range in the formula for easier copying.

1. Open **ClaimsByCity**.

2. Open **Shops** in Word and copy all the data starting in cell B5.

3. Add labels for a total for each city and a total for each month.

4. Create range names for each city's values and for each month's values.

5. Use columns/rows as separators for borders and design your sheet so that it is easily read. Set it to fit centered on a landscape page.

6. Enter formulas for the totals. Hide the zeros. Format all values as Commas with no decimals.

7. Rename Sheet1 as ClaimsData. Delete Sheet2 and Sheet3.

8. Create a 3-D column chart on its own sheet that will display totals by month. Determine a title and delete the legend.

9. Record a macro that inserts your name and your school/company in cells M42 and M43. Delete these labels after the macro is completed.

10. Unlock cells in which data will be entered.

11. Protect the sheet without a password and with column and row formatting capability. Save *[your initials]*u7-1 as a macro-enabled template in the Templates folder for your computer. Close the template.

REVIEW

Template files remain on the computer until they are deleted. Always leave Excel in its default settings for the next class or student.

12. Create a workbook based on the template and key sample information for a couple of cities. Run the macro. Check the chart, too. Edit the template if necessary, resave it, and try again if things do not work properly.

13. Save *[your initials]*u7-1 as a macro-enabled workbook in a folder for Unit 7.

14. Delete the template from the Templates folder.

15. Prepare and submit your work.

Unit Application 7-2

Create a template. Protect a sheet.

A balance sheet is a financial statement that shows a company's assets, its liabilities, and its owners' (or shareholders') equity. From a completed worksheet, you can create a template.

1. Open **BalanceSheet**.

2. Fix the alignment problem in column E. Delete values but not formulas.

3. Select all cells on the sheet and apply Red, Accent 2 fill. Then set white fill for cells B2:F30.

NOTE

Because you are not using the template to create a new workbook, you can save this template in your Unit 7 folder.

4. Set cells B2:F30 as the print area.

5. Insert a comment for the cell in which the user should edit the month. Set the comment to be shown.

6. Unlock cells for data entry. Protect the sheet to allow selection of cells and formatting of columns without a password.

7. Save the workbook as a template named *[your initials]u7-2*.

8. Prepare and submit your work. Delete the template from your computer if necessary.

Unit Application 7-3

Record a macro.

The company contributes to employees' retirement funds, keeping a yearly total by state. You can record macros to streamline creation of each year's report.

1. Open **401K** and save it as a macro-enabled workbook named *[your initials]u7-3*.

2. Record a macro named **CopySheet** without relative references. Copy the worksheet by using the tab shortcut menu so that the sheet for the new year precedes the current sheet. On the copied sheet, delete contribution amounts but not formulas. Click cell B5 and stop recording.

3. Delete the copy created while recording. Add your name as a comment in the macro.

4. Run the macro and name the new sheet **2008**. Edit the label in cell A3.

5. Key a 3-D reference in cell B5 to multiply the value from the previous year by 104.5%. Copy the formula as needed.

6. Edit the properties to show a title, your name, and **Klassy Kow Ice Cream, Inc.** as the company. Use a thumbnail.

7. Prepare and submit your work.

Unit Application 7-4 ◆ Using the Internet

Share a workbook. Compare and merge workbooks. Accept and reject changes.

Work with two classmates to form a workgroup. Your task is to find five items each (a total of 15 items) that could be used in a fund-raising contest. These might be prizes such as a new car, a trip to Japan, a large-screen TV, and smaller items. Find items, descriptions, and prices, and list the Web site for each item.

USER 1: Create a workbook for your group. The worksheet should show your five items, Web addresses, descriptions, and prices. Include a main title and labels as needed. Format the sheet attractively. Share the workbook.

USERS 2 and 3: Make a copy of the shared workbook and save it. Edit the data to show your five items and save the workbook.

ALL USERS: With a copy of each workbook, compare and merge the workbooks. Track changes and keep five items you would use in a contest. Prepare and submit your work.

APPENDIX

Microsoft Objective/Domain		Covered in Lesson Exercise	
Creating and Manipulating Data			
1.1	Insert data by using AutoFill	See Below	
1.1.1	Fill a series	3.12	
		3.13	
1.1.2	Copy a series	3.14	
		3.15	
1.2	Ensure data integrity	3.1	4.6
		3.2	5.1
		3.3	11.15
		3.4	11.16
		3.5	18.6
		3.6	18.7
		3.7	
		4.5	
1.2.1	Restrict data using data validation	15.2	15.5
		15.3	22.15
		15.4	22.16
1.2.2	Remove duplicate rows from spreadsheets	13.4	
		18.10	
1.3	Modify cell contents and formats	1.9	20.1
		1.10	20.6
		1.11	20.11
		1.12	20.12
		2.1	21.1
		2.9	
1.3.1	Cut, copy, and paste data and cell contents	4.7	17.6
		4.8	18.1
		4.9	18.5
		4.10	18.14
		6.16	18.18
		14.16	20.5
1.4	Change Worksheet Views	13.18	21.2
		13.19	21.9
		16.7	21.10
		16.8	22.14
		16.9	
1.4.1	Change views within a single window	1.1	1.8
		1.2	4.15
		1.3	15.12
		1.4	15.13
		1.5	

Microsoft Objective/Domain		Covered in Lesson Exercise	
1.4.2	Split windows	4.15	
		22.8	
1.4.3	Open and arrange new windows	1.7	18.4
		13.1	18.13
		15.9	
1.5	Manage worksheets	12.2	18.15
		12.7	22.3
1.5.1	Copy worksheets	4.2	
		5.18	
		17.1	
1.5.2	Reposition worksheets within workbooks	6.13	
1.5.3	Rename worksheets	2.13	
1.5.4	Hide and unhide worksheets	8.9	
1.5.5	Insert and delete worksheets	4.2	
		6.12	
Formatting Data and Content			
2.1	Format worksheets	16.18	
2.1.1	Use themes to format worksheets	2.2	
		18.8	
		18.9	
		18.20	
2.1.2	Show and hide gridlines and headers	3.21	
2.1.3	Add color to worksheet tabs	2.13	
2.1.4	Format worksheet backgrounds	5.18	
		11.8	
2.2	Insert and modify rows and columns	See Below	
2.2.1	Insert and delete cells, rows, and columns	4.3	4.11
		4.4	4.12
			4.13
2.2.2	Format rows and columns	2.5	
		2.6	
2.2.3	Hide and unhide rows and columns	4.14	
2.2.4	Modify row height and column width	2.7	
		2.8	
2.3	Format cells and cell content	3.10	
		3.11	
		20.3	
2.3.1	Apply number formats	2.10	6.15
		2.11	6.18
		5.7	7.19

Microsoft Objective/Domain		Covered in Lesson Exercise			
2.3.2	Create custom cell formats	4.26 6.17	6.20 18.3		
2.3.3	Apply and modify cell styles	3.18 4.24 4.25 7.6	7.7 7.8 7.9 20.15		
2.3.4	Format text in cells	2.3 2.4 2.12 4.16 4.17 4.18	4.19 4.21 5.10 11.17 18.2		
2.3.5 (3.7.2)	Convert text to columns	18.11			
2.3.6	Merge and split cells	4.20			
2.3.7	Add and remove cell borders	4.22 4.23	8.5		
2.3.8	Insert, modify, and remove hyperlinks	8.13			
2.4	Format data as a table	13.2 13.17	18.16 18.17		
2.4.1	Apply Quick Styles to tables	3.16 3.17	13.3 13.8		
2.4.2	Add rows to a table	13.11			
2.4.3	Insert and delete rows and columns in tables	13.7			
Creating and Modifying Formulas					
3.1	Reference data in formulas	3.8 3.9 5.2 5.3 5.4	5.5 5.6 5.8 5.9 20.16		
3.1.1	Create formulas that use absolute and relative cell references	2.15 2.16 2.17 5.11 5.12 5.14 7.16 7.17 7.18 7.20	7.21 8.1 8.2 8.3 8.4 8.6 8.7 14.19 15.1 15.6	15.7 15.10 15.11 15.14 16.14 16.15 16.16 16.17 20.2 20.7	8.10 8.11
3.1.2	Create formulas that reference data from other worksheets or workbooks	12.3 12.4 12.5 12.6	12.9 12.10 17.2 17.3	17.4 17.7 17.9–17.13	

Microsoft Objective/Domain		Covered in Lesson Exercise		
3.1.3	Manage named ranges	14.1 14.2 14.4 14.5	14.8 14.9 14.10	14.11 14.12 16.1 16.3
3.1.4	Use named ranges in formulas	14.3		
3.2	Summarize data using a formula	6.3 6.8 6.9 6.14	6.19 20.13 20.14	
3.2.1	Use SUM, COUNT, COUNTA, AVERAGE, MIN, and MAX	2.18 2.19	6.1 6.2 6.5 6.7	
3.3	Summarize data using subtotals	14.13 14.14		
3.3.1	Create and modify list ranges	19.1 19.11 19.12		
3.4	Conditionally summarize data using a formula	See Below		
3.4.1	Using SUMIF, SUMIFS, COUNTIF, COUNTIFS, AVERAGEIF, AVERAGEIFS	6.4 6.6	13.12 13.13	
3.5	Look up data using a formula	See Below		
3.5.1	Using VLOOKUP, HLOOKUP	14.15 14.17 14.18		
3.6	Use conditional logic in a formula	See Below		
3.6.1	Using IF, AND, OR, NOT, IFERROR	7.1 7.2 7.3	7.4 7.5 15.16	
3.7	Format or modify text using formulas	See Below		
3.7.1	Format text by using formulas: PROPER, UPPER, LOWER, SUBSTITUTE	13.14 18.12		
3.7.2 (2.3.5)	Convert text to columns	18.11		
3.8	Display and print formulas	5.18		
Presenting Data Visually				
4.1	Create and format charts	9.1 9.2 9.20	9.21 9.22	
4.1.1	Select appropriate data sources for charts	9.10 9.11	16.11	

Microsoft Objective/Domain		Covered in Lesson Exercise		
4.1.2	Select appropriate chart types to represent data sources	9.14 9.24 16.12 20.17 20.18		
4.1.3	Format charts using Quick Styles	9.3 9.4 9.6		
4.2	Modify charts	9.13		
4.2.1	Add and remove chart elements	9.5 9.7 9.8 9.9 9.15	9.16 9.17 9.18 9.19 16.13	
4.2.2	Move and size charts	9.12		
4.2.3	Change chart types	9.23 9.25		
4.3	Apply conditional formatting	20.4		
4.3.1	Manage conditional formats by using the Conditional Formatting Rule Manager	4.28 6.11 16.5		
4.3.2	Allow more than one rule to be true	16.6		
4.3.3	Apply the following conditional formats: highlight, top and bottom rules, data bars, color scales, and icon sets	4.27 5.13 6.10	8.12 16.4	
4.4	Insert and modify illustrations	See Below		
4.4.1	Insert and modify pictures from files	11.1 through 11.5 11.7		
4.4.2	Insert and modify SmartArt graphics	11.9 through 11.14		
4.4.3	Insert and modify shapes	10.1 through 10.17 10.22 10.23 21.11	21.12	
4.5	Outline data	20.8 20.9		
4.5.1	Group and ungroup data	19.15	19.16	19.17
4.5.2	Subtotal data	19.9 19.10 19.13	19.14 20.10	
4.6	Sort and filter data	19.5 through 19.8		
4.6.1	Sort data by using single or multiple criteria	13.5	13.6	

Microsoft Objective/Domain		Covered in Lesson Exercise		
4.6.2	Filter data by using AutoFilter	13.9 13.10	13.11 19.4	
4.6.3	Filter and sort data by using conditional formatting	19.2		
4.6.4	Filter and sort data by using cell attributes	19.3		
Collaborating and Securing Data				
5.1	Manage changes to workbooks	21.3 through 21.8 21.13 22.1 22.9	22.10 22.12 22.24	23.10
5.1.1	Insert, display, modify, and resolve tracked changes	23.2 23.3 23.4	23.6 23.9	
5.1.2	Insert, display, modify, and delete comments	10.18 10.19 10.20	22.17 23.5	
5.2	Protect and share workbooks	See Below		
5.2.1	Protect workbooks and worksheets	22.4 22.5 22.18 22.23		
5.2.2	Enable workbooks to be changed by multiple users	23.1 23.7 23.8		
5.3	Prepare workbooks for distribution	See Below		
5.3.1	Remove private and other inappropriate data from workbooks	10.21		
5.3.2	Restrict permissions to a workbook	16.1 17.14		
5.3.3	Add keywords and other information to workbook properties	11.18 16.19 22.6		
5.3.4	Add digital signatures	12.11 12.12		
5.3.5	Mark workbooks as final	12.1 15.15		
5.4	Save workbooks	1.6 1.13	2.14 22.19	
5.4.1	Save workbooks for use in a previous version of Excel	8.14		

Microsoft Objective/Domain		Covered in Lesson Exercise	
5.4.2	Using the correct format, save a workbook as a template, a Web page, a macro-enabled document, or another appropriate format	1.16 5.20 16.10 18.19 21.14	22.2 22.11 22.13 22.22
5.5	Set print options for printing data, worksheets, and workbooks	1.14 1.15 6.21	7.12 7.13 14.7
5.5.1	Define the area of a worksheet to be printed	3.19 13.15	13.16
5.5.2	Insert and move a page break	7.10 7.11 7.15	
5.5.3	Set margins	3.22	
5.5.4	Add and modify headers and footers	3.20 7.14	8.8 11.6
5.5.5	Change the orientation of a worksheet	5.16	
5.5.6	Scale worksheet content to fit a printed page	5.17	

Glossary

3-D format Style that applies a three-dimensional look to a shape. (10)

3-D reference A cell address in a formula that refers to cells in another worksheet. (12)

Absolute reference A cell address that does not change when copied in a formula. (5)

Active cell The cell that is ready for data outlined with a thick border. (1)

Add-in Excel function, feature, or command that makes the workbook easier to use. It is installed separately from the main program. (16)

Adjustable cells Cells that can be changed in a Solver solution. (16)

Adjustment handle Yellow diamond handle on a shape used to change the appearance and design of the shape. (10)

Annuity A series of equal payments made at regular intervals for a set period of time. (7)

Argument Values or cell ranges between parentheses in a function; they are what a function needs to complete its calculation. (6)

Arithmetic mean An average of values calculated by adding the values and then dividing the total by the number of values. (6)

Arithmetic operators Math symbols for calculations (+, −, /, and *). (2)

Array A collection of cells or values that is used as a group in formulas or functions. (14)

Array formula A formula that carries out multiple calculations showing one or more results. (20)

Ascending sort Order in which data are arranged from lowest to highest value or A to Z. (13)

Assistant shape Shape that represents a helper. (11)

Auditing Practice of examining cells and formulas for accuracy. (15)

AutoCalculate Feature that displays sums, averages, counts, maximums, or minimums in the status bar for selected cells. (2)

AutoComplete Feature that displays a suggested label after the first character is keyed in a cell in the column. (4)

AutoCorrect Excel feature that corrects common spelling errors as you type. (3)

AutoFill Feature that copies or extends data from a cell or range to adjacent cells.

AutoFit Sizes a column to fit its longest entry or sizes a row to the font. (2)

Axis Horizontal or vertical line that encloses chart data. (9)

Axis title Optional label for the axis. (9)

Background An image that displays on screen for the worksheet. (5)

Backsolve What-if analysis in reverse. It involves knowing the results and then determining the formula arguments. (16)

Bevel 3-D effect for shapes that resembles the edge of a tabletop. (10)

Border Outline above, below, or around a cell or range of cells. (4)

Bounding box Imaginary rectangular box or outline for shapes. (10)

Button Control or object on a worksheet that runs tasks or activities. (21)

Callout Descriptive text enclosed in a shape with a pointer or arrow connector. (10)

Cell Intersection of a column and row in a worksheet with an address or reference, such as cell B5. (1)

Cell address Column letter and row number that identifies a location in the worksheet. (1)

Cell alignment Feature that describes and sets how the contents of a cell are positioned within the cell. (4)

Cell attribute Cell property or format setting. (19)

Cell reference The cell address or location in the worksheet. (1)

Change history List of changes made to cells in a shared workbook that can be printed. (23)

Character space Average width of a character in a font. (2)

Character string Sequence of letters, numbers, or other symbols. (3)

Chart Visual display of worksheet data. (9)

Chart area Background of a chart. (9)

Chart object Chart that appears on the same sheet as the worksheet data. (9)

Chart title Optional title or name for the chart. (9)

Circular reference A cell address in a formula that refers to itself. (14)

Code Lines written in a programming language. (21)

Color scale Solid cell fill of varying shades based on values within a range. (4)

Code window Part of the Visual Basic Editor that displays the macro programming commands. (21)

Column Vertical group of cells in a worksheet identified by alphabetic letter. (1)

Combination chart Chart with series that used different chart types. (9)

Comment A pop-up cell attachment with descriptive or explanatory text. (10)

Consolidate by category Consolidation in which data in multiple worksheets or workbooks are located in different locations. (17)

Consolidate by position   Consolidation in which data in multiple worksheets or workbooks are located in the same locations. (17)

Consolidation   Procedure in which data from more than one worksheet or workbook are combined and summarized. (17)

Constant   A value used in formulas that does not change. (14)

Constraint   A restriction or requirement for a cell value when using Solver. (16)

Cost   The original price of an item or asset. (7)

Criteria range   An area on a worksheet that holds conditions for a filter. (19)

Crop   Remove parts of an image from view. (11)

CSV   Filename extension for comma-separated values format, a simple text file. (8)

Custom template   A workbook model with sample values, labels, formulas, and images. (22)

Custom view   Display and print settings that can be saved with a workbook. (13)

Data bar   Bar-shaped fill in a cell based on values within a range. (4)

Data label   Optional title for each value in a chart. (9)

Data marker   Object that displays individual values, such as a bar or column. (9)

Data point   One value from the data series. (9)

Data series   Collection of related values in the worksheet. (9)

Data table   A cell range that displays results from changing values in a formula. One or two of the formula arguments can be changed. (20)

Data table range   A cell range that includes the data table formula(s) and all input values. (20)

Data validation   Process in which cell entries are checked and matched to specified conditions. (15)

Defined name   User-created name for a range of cells. (14)

Dependent   A cell that relies on another cell for its value. (15)

Dependent workbook   A workbook that has linked formulas (external references) that refer to another workbook. (17)

Depreciation   Decline in the financial value of a business asset. (7)

Descending sort   Order in which data are arranged from highest to lowest value or Z to A. (13)

Diagram   Object that illustrates an idea or concept. (11)

Digital signature   Document property that certifies and authenticates the data. (12)

Display trigger   Character keyed while Formula AutoComplete is open to show a list of choices. (14)

Document Inspector   Feature that lists metadata and other personal information in a workbook file so that such data can be removed. (10)

Document theme   Built-in set of fonts, colors, and effects used in a workbook. (2)

Drag-and-drop pointer   Four-pointed arrow that appears when the pointer rests on the edge of a cell. It is used to copy or cut a cell or range by dragging. (4)

Draw layer   Invisible, transparent working surface, separate from and on top of the worksheet, that holds drawing objects and images. (10)

Dynamic consolidation   A data consolidation that results in a formula. (17)

Electronic spreadsheet software   Computer software that produces reports with calculations, list management, or charts. (1)

Embedded chart   Chart object; a chart that appears on the same sheet as the data. (9)

En dash   Typographical symbol slightly longer than a hyphen used to separate ranges of values or labels. (20)

End Sub   Code that ends a subroutine macro. (21)

Exploded pie chart   Pie chart in which one or more slice(s) is detached from the rest of the pie. (9)

Exponentiation   Math operation that raises a number to a power. (2)

Extension   Four characters preceded by a period, added to a filename. (2)

External reference formula   Formulas that refer to cells in another workbook. (17)

Field   A single category or column of data in a list. (13) (19)

Field name   The column label in the header (first) row of a table or list. (13) (19)

Field value   An individual piece of data in a cell, list, or table. (13) (19)

Filename   Document name or identifier. (2)

Fill   Background pattern or color for a cell or range of cells. (4)

Fill handle   Small rectangle at the lower-right corner of a cell or range used for extending a series or copying data. (3)

Filter   Criteria that set a specification for which data will be shown, creating a subset of records from a list. (13) (19)

Financial function   Formula that performs a common business calculation involving money. (7)

Folder   Storage location for work files on a disk. (1)

Footer   Data that print at the bottom of each page in a worksheet. (3)

Formula   Equation that performs a calculation on values in a worksheet. (2)

Formula AutoComplete   Feature that displays a list of functions and range names that match the spelling of what is keyed. (6)

Function   Built-in mathematical formula for common mathematical, statistical, financial, or other calculation. (2) (6)

Function Arguments   Dialog box that displays help and entry areas for completing a function. (6)

FV Financial function argument that specifies the value of the cash at the end of the time period. (7)

GIF file Graphics Interchange Format, a format for images used on a Web site. (11)

Goal Seek Command that backsolves or adjusts the value in a cell to reach a desired outcome. (16)

Gradient Blend of colors used to fill charts and other objects. (9)

Gridline Horizontal or vertical line in the chart plot area to mark values. (9)

Header Data that print at the top of each page in a worksheet. (3)

Header row First row in a table with descriptive labels for each column. (3) (13) (19)

Highlight cells rules Conditional formatting that sets conditions using relational or comparison operators. (16)

HMTL Hypertext Markup Language, a widely used format for Web pages. (5)

Home Cell A1

Horizontal (category) axis What is shown in a chart, created from row or column headings. (9)

Hyperlink A clickable text or object that, when clicked, displays another file, another program, or an Internet site/address. (8)

Icon set Set of three, four, or five icons displayed in a cell based on values within a range. (4)

Information Rights Management Office 2007 feature that enables a user to set permissions about who can edit, save, print, or copy a document. (17)

Input values Numbers keyed in either a row or column for a data table. (20)

Integer A whole number or a number with no decimal or fractional parts. (8)

Interval Number of steps between values or labels in a series. (3)

Invalid data Label or value that does not match data validation settings. (15)

KeyTip Keyboard shortcut that appears on screen when Alt is pressed.

Label An entry in a cell that begins with a letter. (2)

Landscape Print orientation that prints a horizontal page that is wider than it is tall. (5)

Leading zero A zero shown as the first digit in a value. (4)

Legend Chart object that explains the colors, textures, or symbols used in the chart. (9)

Life Number of periods over which an asset is depreciated. (7)

Line break Location in a label where text is split to a second line, made by pressing Alt + Enter. (5)

Link A 3-D reference to a cell. (13)

Linking Procedure in which formulas in a worksheet refer to cells in another workbook. (17)

List range A series of rows with related data organized in columns. (19)

Live Preview Feature that displays design changes before they are applied. (2)

Locked Cell, shape, or object property that makes the cell/shape unavailable for editing. (22)

Logical function Formula that determines whether or not something is true. (7)

Lookup table Range of values and/or labels named and used for Lookup functions. (14)

Macro A sequence of commands and keystrokes that performs a task, saved as a Visual Basic routine in a workbook. (16) (21)

Macro-enabled workbook An Excel workbook with a macro and an .xlsm extension. (16)

Mail-enabled The ability to e-mail a file without closing the application. (8)

Math hierarchy Mathematical rules that determine which part of a formula is calculated first. (5)

Metadata Information that is included and saved with a document, such as the computer name, the user named, revision dates, etc. (10)

Microsoft Office button Button next to the Quick Access toolbar that opens the File menu. (1)

Mixed reference A cell address that adjusts either the row or the column when the formula is copied. (5)

Name Box Text box in the formula bar that shows the current cell address. (1)

Nested function A function inside another function. The second or third functions are used as arguments in the first function. (8)

Nper Financial function argument that specifies the total number of payments or time periods. (7)

Numeric keypad Set of number and symbol keys at the right of the keyboard. (4)

Object Separate, clickable element or part of a worksheet. (3)

Office Clipboard Temporary memory area that can hold up to 24 copied elements across Office products. (4)

Order of operation/precedence Mathematical rules that determine which part of a formula is calculated first. (5)

Organization chart Object that illustrates hierarchical relationships, usually among company workers. (11)

Outline A summary worksheet that can show or hide details. Worksheet data that are grouped into detail and summary rows. (17)

Output range An area on a worksheet that holds the results of an advanced filter. (19)

Page break Code shown as a solid or dashed line to signal where the printer will start a new page. (7)

Page orientation Print setting that determines landscape or portrait layout. (5)

Parameter The data or information needed by Solver to determine a solution. (16)

Path   File identifier that includes the drive and series of folders to locate a file. (17)

Period   The time for which depreciation is calculated. (7)

Pick From Drop-Down List   Feature that displays a list of all labels already in a column. (4)

PivotChart   A chart that is associated with a PivotTable. (20)

PivotTable   Interactive summary report built from data in a list. (20)

Pixel   A single screen dot. (2)

Plot area   Rectangular bounding area for the category and value axes. (9)

Point   1/72 of an inch, used to measure fonts. (2)

Pointer   Conditional formatting that highlights a cell in a data table based on its matching one of the formula results/cells. (20)

Portrait   Print orientation that prints a page that is taller than it is wide. (5)

Precedent   A cell that contributes or provides data to a formula's results. (15)

Print area   The range of cells to be printed. (13)

Property   Setting or attribute that is stored with the workbook. (11)

Protection   Worksheet/workbook setting that prohibits edits to locked cells, shapes, and objects. (22)

PV   Financial function argument that specifies the current cash value of the money transaction. (7)

Quick Access toolbar   Customizable toolbar with buttons for frequently used commands. (1)

Range   A group of cells that forms a rectangle. (2)

Range address   Upper-left and lower-right cell addresses separated by a colon. (2)

Rate   Financial function argument that specifies the interest rate for the time period. (7)

Read-only   Document property that prohibits editing and saving with the same filename. (15)

Record   One row of data in a table or list. (13) (19)

Relative reference   A cell address that adjusts to the row or column where a copied formula is located. (5)

Replacement string   Sequence of characters that is exchanged for existing data in the Replace command. (3).

Ribbon   A set of command tabs with buttons, galleries, and controls. (1)

Rotation handle   Green oval handle (circle) on a shape used to rotate the shape using the mouse. (10)

Rounding   To make a value larger or smaller depending on a specified digit to the left or right of the decimal point. (8)

Row   Horizontal group of cells identified by a number in a worksheet. (1)

Salvage   The value of an asset after it has been depreciated. (7)

Scale   Size an image by a percentage so that it is proportional. (11)

Scenario   A saved set of values for a worksheet. (16)

Scenario summary report   A formatted report in outline style that lists changing and results cells for each scenario in a worksheet. (16)

Scope   The location for which a defined range name is applicable. (14)

Secondary axis   Separate set of values for a data series. (9)

Selection handles   Small black rectangles, circles, or dots that surround and indicate a selected or active object. (9)

Selection handles   Eight circles or rectangles surrounding the bounding box of shape. (10)

Selection pointer   White cross-shaped pointer used to select cells. Solid black arrow to select rows/columns. (2)

Serial number   Number system assigned to dates, counting from January 1, 1900, as 1.

Series   List of labels, numbers, dates, or times that follows a pattern. (3)

Shading   Background color or pattern for a cell or range of cells. (4)

Shape   Common, recognized figure, form, or outline. (10)

Shared workbook   Workbook that can be used by several people at the same time. (23)

Sizing handle   Marker at bottom-right corner of a table used to expand or contract a table. (13)

SmartArt   Graphic shapes that include lists, processes, hierarchies, cycles, matrices, and pyramids. (11)

Solver   An Excel add-in that backsolves the value for a cell with a formula. (16)

Source workbook   A workbook that contains cells used in an external reference in a dependent workbook. (17)

Static consolidation   A data consolidation that results in a value. (17)

Stop   A color in a gradient that refers to its position on the gradient's color scale. (9)

Structured reference   Name used to identify a range in an Excel table. (14)

Style   Set of formatting specifications for labels and/or values. (7)

Sub   Code that begins a subroutine macro. (21)

Subordinate shape   Shape that represents an employee. (11)

Subroutine macro   Command sequence that can be run from a workbook or from within another macro. (21)

Super ScreenTip   A box on screen with the name and purpose of a button when you hover over a button or control. (1)

Synchronous scrolling   Feature that allows multiple windows to move in the same direction by the same number of rows/columns. (22)

Synonym   A word that means the same thing. (11)

Syntax   Structure or necessary parts and the order of those parts for a function. It is an equal sign (=), the function name, and the arguments in parentheses. (6)

Table   Data arrangement in rows with a single header row. A list of information with a row of headers followed by rows of data. (3) (13)

Target cell   Formula cell parameter for a Solver solution. (16)

Template   Model or sample workbook that can include labels, values, formulas, themes, styles, alignment settings, and borders. It is saved with an .xltx extension. (5)

Template Gallery   Collection of Office Online templates for downloading. (22)

Text box   Drawing object with no connector lines for displaying text. (10)

Text pane   Dialog box attached to a SmartArt shape used for entering text in an outline style. (11)

Texture   Grainy or non-smooth appearance used to fill charts and other objects. (9)

Thesaurus   Reference book that lists words with the same meaning. (11)

Tick mark   Line or marker on an axis to display values. (9)

Trendline   A line added to a chart that points out and forecasts future directions and trends in values. (16)

Type   Financial function argument that specifies whether the payment/deposit is made at the beginning or end of the period. (7)

User template   A template created by a worker with values, formulas, labels, images, and more for daily use. (22)

Value   An entry in a cell that begins with a number or an arithmetic symbol. (2)

Vertical (value) axis   Horizontal or vertical range of values from the worksheet.

Visual Basic Editor   Window used to view, edit, or create a macro. (21)

Visualization   Format elements that display bars, colors, or icons with values for quick comparison. (4)

Volatile   Function characteristic that causes it to depend on the system in which the workbook is opened. (6)

Watch Window   A pane that shows formulas and results while a worksheet is being edited. (15)

Watermark   Text or image that appears behind printed data, similar to a background image. (11)

What-if analysis   Business practice of varying values in a worksheet to forecast and predict future results. (16)

Whole number   Value without a fraction or decimal. (5)

Wildcard   Character that represents one or more letters or numbers. (3)

Windows Clipboard   Temporary memory area that holds cut or copied data. (4)

WordArt   Application that inserts shaped and colored text as an object. (10)

Workbook   Excel file that holds worksheets with data. A workbook has an .xlsx filename extension. (1)

Workgroup   People who share work. (23)

Worksheet   Individual page or sheet in a workbook, shown by a tab at the bottom of the screen. (1)

XLS   Filename extension for files saved in previous Excel versions. (8)

XPS   XML Paper Specification file format for saving formatted files. (1)

Zoom size   Setting that controls how much of the worksheet appears at once on the screen. (1)

Index